BOOKS BY *Paul Weiss*

Beyond All Appearances (1974)
Cinematics (1975)
First Considerations (1977)
The God We Seek (1964)
History: Written and Lived (1962)
The Making of Men (1967)
Man's Freedom (1950)
Modes of Being (1958)
Nature and Man (1947)
Nine Basic Arts (1961)
Our Public Life (1959)
Philosophy in Process, Vol. 1: 1955–1960 (1966)
Philosophy in Process, Vol. 2: 1960–1964 (1966)
Philosophy in Process, Vol. 3: 1964 (1968)
Philosophy in Process, Vol. 4: 1964–1965 (1969)
Philosophy in Process, Vol. 5: 1965–1968 (1971)
Philosophy in Process, Vol. 6: 1968–1971 (1975)
Philosophy in Process, Vol. 7: 1975–1976 (1978)
Reality (1938)
Religion and Art (1963)
Right and Wrong: A Philosophical Dialogue Between Father and Son, with *Jonathan Weiss*
 (1967)
Sport: A Philosophic Inquiry (1969)
The World of Art (1961)

PRINCIPAL CONTRIBUTIONS BY *Paul Weiss*

American Philosophers at Work, edited by Sidney Hook (1956)
American Philosophy Today and Tomorrow, edited by H. M. Kallen and Sidney Hook
 (1935)
The Concept of Order, edited by Paul Kuntz (1968)
Contemporary American Philosophy, edited by John E. Smith (1970)
Design and Aesthetics of Wood, edited by Eric A. Anderson and George F. Earl (1972)
Determinism and Freedom, edited by Sidney Hook (1958)
The Dimensions of Job, edited by Nahum N. Glatzer (1969)
Dimensions of Mind: A Symposium, edited by Sidney Hook (1960)
Evolution in Perspective, edited by G. Schuster and G. Thorson (1971)
The Future of Metaphysics, edited by Robert Wood (1970)
Human Values and Economic Policy: Proceedings, edited by Sidney Hook (1967)
Law and Philosophy, edited by Sidney Hook (1964)
Mid-Twentieth Century American Philosophy, edited by Peter A. Bertocci (1974)
Moments of Personal Discovery, edited by R. M. MacIver (1952)

Moral Principles in Action, edited by R. Anshen (1952)
Perspectives on Peirce, edited by R. Bernstein (1965)
Philosophical Essays for A. N. Whitehead, edited by O. Lee (1936)
Philosophical Interrogations, edited by S. and B. Rome (1964)
Philosophy and History, edited by Sidney Hook (1963)
The Relevance of Whitehead, edited by I. Leclerc (1961)
Science, Philosophy, and Religion: Proceedings (1941–)
Studies in the Philosophy of Charles Sanders Peirce, edited by C. P. Wiener and F. H. Young (1952)

EDITED WORKS BY *Paul Weiss*

Collected Papers of Charles Sanders Peirce (six volumes), editor, with *Charles Hartshorne* (1931–35)

PHILOSOPHY

By PAUL WEISS

IN PROCESS

VOLUME 7

April 13, 1975–June 21, 1976

Southern Illinois University Press
Carbondale and Edwardsville

Feffer & Simons, Inc.
London and Amsterdam

LIBRARY OF CONGRESS CATALOGING IN PUBLICATION DATA (REVISED)

WEISS, PAUL, 1901–
PHILOSOPHY IN PROCESS.

CONTENTS:—V. 1. 1955–1960.—V. 2. 1960–1964.—V. 3
MARCH–NOVEMBER 1964.—V. 4. November 26, 1964–September 2, 1965.—
V. 5. September 3, 1965–August 27, 1968.—v. 6. August 28, 1968–May 22,
1971.—V. 7. April 13, 1975—June 21, 1976.
    1.   PHILOSOPHY—COLLECTED WORKS.   I.   TITLE.
B945.W396P5   191   63–14293
ISBN 0–8093–0821–5 (V. 7)

To *Charles Hendel*

PREFACE

THE SIX PRECEDING VOLUMES of this series have not been widely reviewed—a fate, I understand, suffered by most multi-volume works. Still, when the individual volumes were reviewed, they were dealt with very favorably, and sometimes at considerable length. Perhaps one day the entire set will be examined as a single whole. I hope so. Together, the volumes cover over twenty years of rather persistent writing, running to some five thousand pages. It is perhaps appropriate to call a halt now. In any case, increased printing and publishing costs have made it impossible to continue their publication. Indeed, it was thought desirable to terminate the series with Volume 6; only later was it found possible to make provision for the present volume, as the last. Consequently, I have not written anything more in the present vein since the last entry, and do not plan to do so.

As I look back over the seven volumes, I find that they contain much material worth considering, preserving, utilizing, and expanding. A few thinkers have already found new, important explorations there; others have found discussions which were more extensive and better formulated than in my other works. At some later time, I myself intend to go through all the volumes carefully, hoping that they will provide me with new clues, openings, and perspectives. If it seems strange for an author to talk in this way, it is perhaps because one has put to a side the fact that the writing of the volumes has been spread out over more than twenty years. That is quite a period for one with a poor memory, who has been, and still is caught up in a number of other systematic inquiries.

As will soon be evident, this volume contains more explicit autobiographical material than all the others combined. Since my primary concerns are exhibited in the philosophic discussions, these, despite their impersonal formulations, could be said to be autobiographical also. It would not be incorrect to say, too, that the explicit autobiographical portions have some philosophic import. The two, therefore, should not be entirely separated. But then it becomes less evident just what they together reveal about the author or the scheme of things. The fact does not, I believe, affect the value of the different entries, or the possible use of any apart from the rest.

P.W.

Washington, D.C.
January 1977

PHILOSOPHY IN PROCESS

1975

April 13

I have just returned from a visit to Southern Illinois University where I gave an address on "The Art and Science of Man" in connection with the dedication of Faner Hall. The talk was very well received; I spoke with as much control, clarity, and effectiveness as I have ever done.

I was shown through the library, and had a visit with Dr. Duckett who is in charge of the archives. I had already arranged to have all my manuscripts and my files, together with whatever books, photographs, paintings, and recordings that Jonathan will consent to have released, to be given to the library, as part of its archives on American philosophy. The archives already include the *Nachlass* of Dewey, Tufts, Paul Carus, and Pepper. The work at the library is careful and intelligent; I am glad to have my things part of its enterprise. Mr. Duckett, a surprisingly shy and diffident man, has the archives under intelligent, firm, and imaginative control; due to him the library will be a center for research on American philosophy, and eventually on a number of other topics which are to spin off on their own, but which initially are brought together here because of their connection with American philosophy. We discussed a number of names, and I think Duckett will soon be writing to Charles Hartshorne, Mortimer Adler, F.S.C. Northrop, and a number of others, at my suggestion. I don't know whether or not he will take up my idea that he see what could be done to become the repository for the Metaphysical Society of America, as well as for the intellectual history of American Catholicism.

Vernon Sternberg acted as my host, though I do not think he was officially in charge. I was given a tour of the building which houses his press. It is remarkably well structured, for light, efficiency, and cooperative work among the various editors, production managers, stock clerks, mailing machines, and the like. But I was most struck with the fine spirit of the employees; they seemed to be efficient and joyous. A number of them had purchased copies of my books (the more recent ones for the most part) or had received them as gifts from the press, and had me autograph them.

Vernon Sternberg reminds me somewhat of my dean, Jude Dougherty. Both are very conservative, politically and moralistically; they are strong traditionalists. But both also are receptive to ideas to an unusual degree. The combination makes for strength and openness. Were they only conservative, they would be far behind the times; were they only open, they would lack direction and critical determination. The combination enables them to be adventurous and yet cautious, imaginative and yet careful, surefooted and wise. I have been fortunate in being able to work with both of them.

I saw the sheets which indicated how my books are going. I have seen an account that the average book published by a university press sells about 1,300 copies in five years, and that a sale of 5,000 in one year is very good. I am pleased to see that about half my books have done better than that—*Our Public Life* the worst. As of December 1974, the *Sport* book has sold over 7,500 (hardback and paper together), *The World of Art* almost that many, *Nine Basic Arts* almost 5,500, the *Modes of Being* a little over 4,200, *Nature and Man* 3,500, *The God We Seek* 2,500, and *Man's Freedom* almost 2,000. Some of these have of course been in existence for more than ten years, and some of them, for example, *Nature and Man,* and *Man's Freedom,* had already been published by others and had had some sales. What is most interesting to me is that *Philosophy in Process* has been slowly but steadily selling. It is not yet up to that 1,300 five year average of university press books, in part because of its stiff price. The volumes have sold 908, 677, 675, 543, 501 (Volumes 1 to 5). I was delighted, therefore, when Vernon suggested that I continue with the series and begin to write volume 7. I think it may prove a way for me to break through the block in writing from which I now seem to be suffering.

I have been wanting to start "You, I, and the Others" for the last month or so. I have glanced through the 400-odd pages of quickly typed observations which I made last summer, but I have not yet been able to see my way clear into the writing of the book. I have not yet grasped the theme, the focus, the structure of it. Writing in *Philosophy in Process* may enable me to do this. The last entry in volume 6 is May 22, 1971. There is, therefore, a four-year gap between the end of that volume and the beginning of this. In that interval I saw Volume 6 (and I think) Volume 5 through the press. I also completed the manuscripts and then saw both *Beyond All Appearances* and *Cinematics* through the press.

Though I wrote what immediately follows on the 8th of this month, I think it not inappropriate for me to include it here. It was intended as the beginning of the manuscript, "You, I, and the Others," or at least as an outline, on the basis of which I could begin work on such a book. If it had served as such an outline, more likely than not I would have destroyed it after it had served its purposes. But now it will be preserved. Since a number of people have said that they prefer Philosophy in Process to my other writings, they may welcome these tentative investigations, though, strictly speaking, my intent was not to have my observations on the nature of the self and the other be a part of this work.

One more preliminary remark: there are passages in the previous volumes of *Philosophy in Process* which are clearer, better written, and at least as well argued as those in my other works. Sometimes, apparently, I can write straight off, better and clearer and just as well-argued philosophy as I can after many, many revisions. The rule is not absolute: I am confident that most of my other books are better sustained and better reasoned, by and large. But I have seen passages of considerable length that have been quoted from the *Philosophy in Process* volumes, which I can neither correct nor improve upon.

1] To be conscious of the self is to be self-conscious.

2] To be self-conscious is to attend to the self from the position of another.

3] From the position of another I (and that of any other man), I am a 'you'.

4] From the position of another, I confront myself as a 'me'.

5] In confronting the me I penetrate beyond it.

6] Beyond the me is the I.

7] When I am self-conscious I penetrate to the I via me.

8] The reaching to another position and the penetration beyond the me is the work of a conscious, active I.

9] The I that is arrived at via the me is an attenuation of the conscious, active I.

10] To be self-conscious is to be aware of a part of myself, approached via me from the position of another.

11] Self-consciousness does not presuppose that another is conscious of me, for there may not be a living being at the assumed position.

12] The assumption of the position of another from which I am approached via a me is the constituting of an authoritative we.

13] If there is no other man at the assumed position, an authoritative we is projective.

14] If there is another man at the assumed position but he is not penetrating beyond my me, the authoritative we is representative.

15] If another is conscious of me when I am, my self-consciousness duplicates the route from his position to me, with some penetration beyond that position and my me.

16] Another is conscious of me as a you.

17] To know that I am known as a you is to be self-conscious of myself as the object of another's consciousness.

18] I become aware that there is another I when I penetrate beyond his you.

19] If there is another I making it possible for me to be self-conscious, we become constitutents of a we.

20] Us is a we opposing and opposed by what is not a constituent of the we.

21] A collective us is in opposition to the I's that sustain a we.

22] An allied us is in opposition to what is not part of our we.

23] A community is an allied us standing in opposition to nature and the members of other communities.

24] Mankind is an allied us standing in opposition to nature.

25] A community is a portion of mankind in opposition to other portions.

26] To be aware of an opponent is to be aware of that which frustrates penetration or control.

27] To be frustrated is to be subject to a condition governing oneself and something else.

28] A withdrawal from a frustration makes possible the identification of oneself with a common condition.

29] The identification with a common condition is the constituting of a contrastive we or us.

30] In a contrastive we or us, we penetrate beyond another's you toward his I.

31] The penetration of another meets greater and greater resistance.

32] What is known of another is of him as penetrated but resistant.

33] I become aware of another's individuality by experiencing his resistance as issuing from an unreached source.

34] I become aware that another has rights by experiencing his resistance as active, in the form of an insistence.

35] I become aware that another has a mind by experiencing his resistance as constituting a we and an us.

36] I become aware that another has an identity by experiencing his resistance as persistent.

37] I become aware of another as having worth by experiencing his resistance as a constituent of a resistant we and us.

38] What I encounter of another is always qualified by the you through which it is reached.

39] My experiencing of another is not identical with his experiencing.

40] I participate in another's pains, pleasures, emotions, and intentions sympathetically; he participates in them constitutively.

41] To be aware of another is to distinguish an I and a you within a we and an us.

While I am continuing the writing of this volume, I will continue to try to write "You, I, and the Others" and, eventually, to begin the book on the American Constitution which I have had in the back of my mind since I began to give a course on the topic in the law school. I will also continue to paint and draw, on and off. I am now having a show at the art school of the Catholic University, which was asked for by John Winthrow, one of the instructors there. The show is well presented but, so far as I know, nothing was bought, though the works are much better than those that I had in my show in New Haven, when I sold at least a half dozen.

April 14

There are a number of angles from which one can approach actualities:

1] They can be dealt with all together, apart from any connection with the finalities. They are then merely nuances, distinguishable but not distinct intensive regions within a single field. Were one to assume that this was a primordial state, one would have to credit the finalities with the power which enables the actualities to become distinct and, as distinct, to be related to one another under the dominance of the finalities. There never was a time, though, when actualities, severally or together, were not affected by and subject to the finalities. The envisagement of the actualities as mere tones in a single all-encompassing field is, therefore, to be viewed as the outcome of an abstraction. The abstraction is the result of our reading into the domain of actualities one or the other of the different finalities, to yield five distinct nuanced fields:

A substantial field has nuanced items in affiliative connections to constitute a single aesthetic totality; a field of being has the actualities merely separable, with an intensity greater than the connective tissue between them; an intelligible field has the nuances function as terms for a rational structure, 'a logical space'; an existential field has the nuances at a distance from one another, and even as extended, but without allowing them to be occupants, since, somewhat like the contents of a Kantian form of intuition, they are just fillings in extensions; and a unitary field of value in which the actualities function as exemplars or epitomizations of the very totality in which they are delimited portions.

But now it seems that, instead of abstracting from the finalities, I have in fact not only assumed them but have treated the actualities as already being subject to them, though without allowing the actualities any distinctiveness or reality of their own. This is true but only as a consequence of the attempt to understand the nature of the fields in which different actualities are inseparable components. There is nothing else but the finalities in terms of which a field can be characterized. But it is not true that the actualities are being envisaged as though they are being subjected to the finalities; the actualities are not yet acknowledged to have any distinct status, so that they could be said to be subject to the finalities. Instead, what we have is the acknowledgement of five different kinds of fields within which one can delimit actualities as inseparable nuances interconnected with one another in one of five different ways.

Are each of the five fields envisageable from the position of each of the five finalities? It seems so. But then not only do we, for example, have a substantial aesthetic field, but we face it as that which is itself a primary ground, a reality, an intelligible unit, an extended domain, and a value. The approach to actualities as merely in a field thus turns out to be the outcome of an acceptance of the position of some finality, the envisagement of five distinct fields from that position, and the identification of actualities as inseparable nuanced intensive delimitations within those fields.

2] Each actuality is an irreducible unit. It stands away from all else with a center of its own, where it has maximum density and intensity. It is the possessor of all its expressions, the convergent point of every part, the explanation of all that it exhibits itself to be, the origin of action, and an irreducible value, giving value to all else. These characterizations, though, depend on our having made a distinction between what the actuality is in itself, and what it has made manifest or to what it has been related. If that fact be abstracted from, an actuality, despite its dense intensity, is indeterminate, lacking any features. It will then not be distinguishable from any other. More, since the absolutely indeterminate is identical with nothing, the actuality as in itself will be indistinguishable from nothing at all.

An actuality in itself can not be understood apart either from what it is related to as a base, or from what in fact is providing it with determinations, or from itself as already determined by something else. In every case, its status of an in-itself is enjoyed only together with and in contradistinction from some other status which is equally basic.

One can imagine the first case to require nothing but finalities, each self-differentiated; there would then be no need to make any reference to actualities except as possible independent occupants of differentiated positions within the finalities. The finalities would then be understood to be as they in fact are when they have been affected by the various actualities and are thus in the state of being able to express themselves in a multiplicity of actual places. But when, in the present case, attention is focussed on an actuality in itself, one is dealing with what opposes, interplays with, and is presupposed by the finalities. Consequently, one is forced to go beyond the statement that actualities in themselves are abstractions.

Actualities in their severalty are independent of one another, and are independent of all the finalities. If they are to be said to be indeterminate in themselves, and yet to be distinguished from one another and from nothingness, their indeterminateness will have to

be one with something distinctive, even unique in every case. Is this
not the resistance-insistence of the actuality? Each actuality in itself
is impenetrable at the same time that it originates an insistence
which is met with counter-insistencies originating with the different finalities. Its resistance-insistence is not tolerable of predicates,
characterizations, and therefore of determinations; nevertheless, it
is distinct from all others in the way it functions. It is indeterminate
in contradistinction with the determinations it will receive from
other entities, but this does not preclude it from being distinct from
all others. It will not be 'numerically distinct', which is to say distinct
despite the fact that it shares predicates with others, but distinct as
an agent, a source of power or energy, as that with which others
interplay. Numerically distinct items are public entities, marked off
from one another as units regardless of the predicates they sustain,
but actualities in themselves are not together with one another and
therefore are not distinguishable numerically or in other public
ways. Instead, actualities in themselves distinguish themselves by
insisting on themselves.

We can not know how actualities in themselves distinguish
themselves except by taking a position outside them and seeing
how they interplay with what is then available to them. As in
themselves they are centers from which resistant-insistencies issue
and then interplay with counter-insistencies issuing from the
finalities. Since, as in themselves, the actualities are at the boundary
line at which the insistencies of finalities come to an end, the
actualities can be said to provide distinct barriers beyond which the
finalities cannot reach and therefore which they cannot determine.

Leibniz had a brilliant solution to this kind of problem. He took
all the monads to have the very same content, but to differ one from
the other in the degree of clarity of that content—God having every
distinguishable item distinct, and the lowest of dumb things having
none of them distinct. Such an account allows one to say that all
things in themselves are alike in one way and unalike in another,
and to explain the latter without having recourse to anything but
the manner in which the components of the content are able to
function. His view, though, seems to require that every possible
degree of distinction be realized. He thereby makes the universe
into a plenum of monads, differing in the degree to which they
distinguish their components, not as constituents (since that would
make the monads be composites) but as the objects of internal

'perceptions'. His view would also require that men be arranged in a hierarchy and not be on a footing; in any case, each man would necessarily have some items confused which others do not.

The Leibnizian answer can be adapted to the present problem of understanding actualities in themselves, by taking each actuality to insist on itself with equal force but to express that insistence in a plurality of expressions which are interconnected in distinctive ways. One still leaves over the question as to why there should be distinctive ways, and what those ways are like, and why it is that a number of entities seem to share in the kind of expressions they produce, so as to constitute classes of men, animals, vegetables, and so forth.

One must avoid the extremes of supposing that an actuality in itself is unique, and therefore merely taking for granted the answer to the question as to what makes an individual be an individual, and of supposing that all actualities in themselves are exactly alike and therefore denying that there is a plurality of them. Once again, a reference to the finalities is needed.

Actualities in themselves are in relation to each of the finalities as merely different oppositional irreducibles. They are interrelated via the finalities and, as so interrelated, are terminal points for the finalities. But where, in the first case, the finalities were taken to be self-differentiated, with the actualities as the mere limits of the self-differentiation and enjoying no status of their own, in the present the actualities are terminal points able to oppose the finalities. The opposition, however, can be taken to be the correlative of the finalities as having withdrawn from their own expressions. The terminal points of the expressions of the finalities will be the actualities in themselves just so far as the finalities maintain themselves in opposition to what they have made possible. The finalities will not be the source of the actualities in themselves but they will provide a position in terms of which one will be able to understand the actualities in themselves as merely different from one another.

Each actuality in itself, on this account, will have five dimensions, for it will be in opposition to each of the five finalities. It will also be different from the other actualities in themselves in five distinct ways, the nature of the difference being expressed in the nature of the withdrawn finality which continues to function as their link.

3] Actualities are part of a cosmos, where they are subject to the various finalities. As cosmic entities they are all subject to the same laws, are in the same space, and in the same time, and so on. But actualities differ in grade: there are men and there are protons. Are the laws, space, and so forth applicable primarily to the ultimate particles of physics, with men and other complex entities to be understood as merely clusters of those particles, or do the laws, and so forth apply directly to the composites as well as to the ultimate particles? On the one hand, it seems as if we can account for men's cosmic roles solely by attending to the particles within their confines, and therefore taking 'men' to be merely shorthand ways of dealing with clusters of those particles; on the other, it seems as if men themselves are to be taken as irreducibles, since it is also true that it is as single units that they fall from heights, move about, are subject to cosmic conditionings, and act. There does not seem to be an incompatibility between the two views. It is apparently true that men in the cosmos are functions of their contained parts and also true that they are units subject to cosmic conditions. A unit, undivided man falls at the same time and at the same rate as the particles within him do.

Men are subject to specialized forms of cosmic laws at the same time that they are subject to the very forms of the laws which affect the ultimate particles. Men interact with men at the same time that they interact with what is not human. And what is true of laws is true of space and time, of affiliations, and so forth.

As cosmic entities, men are essentially public; they are bodies, complex and unitary at the same time that they are regions where a plurality of other entities of various grades also function cosmically. The fact does not compromise the acknowledgment of distinctive activities on the part of men, which do not illustrate or specify cosmic laws. Those activities are to be accounted for by attending to man's privacy, his distinctive objectives, his intentions, and the like.

4] I have argued in *Beyond All Appearances* that all actualities are qualified by the finalities, and that they differ in grade depending on the number of finalities they are able to internalize, thereby becoming instances of those finalities and able to oppose them. In addition, I have held that the actualities interplay with intruding finalities and thereby acquire determinations at the same time that they express themselves; and that with expressions of the finalities they constitute appearances. There is no need to repeat here what was said in that work.

5] What was not made clear enough, and what is not yet clear enough in "First Considerations" is the account of the uniqueness of actualities. I have already remarked that no general theory of individuality will account for individuals since it will apply indifferently to a plurality of entities, and that no references to individualized things will explain individuality without begging the question. But if account is taken of the difference between difference and uniqueness, and of the power of an actuality in relation to its own expressions, an explanation of individuality can be given.

An actuality is not simply different from others if by that one means it is without any features at all. Such a difference would also seem to require that all discriminable portions of it stand away as different from one another. Each actuality, apart from all finalities, is intrinsically irreducible, real, with a nature, distension, and incomparable value. It is as such that it is different from other actualities.

Difference is not uniqueness. Not only may it be the product of a self-differentiation of a larger whole, whereas uniqueness is singular in source as well as outcome, but only uniqueness is thoroughgoingly ontological, accounting for even while it presupposes difference, whereas difference may never reach further than to allow one to isolate something. A unique being is a self-individuated one; it possesses, internalizes, converges, and centers what is different, intrusive, and determining, to produce what thereafter will be expressed with uniqueness. Uniqueness is difference intensified and given ontological force; it pulls into a single indivisible whatever diversity any difference might have. It gives body to realities, distensions, and so forth, by adding degrees of intensity to them.

A unique being is a self-individuating one, a self-solidifying, self-centering one, able thereafter to act as an unduplicable expressive substance. Why was such an act of self-individuation engaged in? What engaged in it?

Self-individuation is needed in order to preserve difference, to allow an actuality to stand away from the finalities and therefore to allow the finalities to stand away from it. If it be said that the finalities engage in an act of self-differentiation, it should also be said that actualities engage in an act of self-individuation. One can also maintain that the finalities require that actualities engage in self-individuation in order that the finalities be able to make their own self-differentiation end in genuine differences; and one can equally well maintain that actualities require the finalities to engage in self-differentiation in order that the actualities be able to make their self-maintenance end in uniqueness. Each requires the other to function in a distinctive way in order for it (and therefore the other) to be able to be fully expressive. We always have both actualities and finalities each functioning on its own, insistent on itself, maintaining itself, but faced with the intrusive presence of the other. Each requires that the other maintain itself against it in order that it be able to maintain itself against that other. Each is the presupposition of the other's functioning. To account for uniqueness is therefore one with accounting for self-differentiation; it is also to take advantage of the fact that each actuality is initially (that is, relative to uniqueness) different from every other, a difference within which it is distended, and so forth.

April 15

Taking the position of each finality in turn, the finalities and actualities can be found together in five distinct ways:

1] *Diffusely*: Here the finalities are fields in which actualities are unseparated nuances or intensities. The different finalities provide different ways in which the diffuseness occurs, and therefore different ways in which the nuances are interconnected. But to speak of an interconnection of nuances is not yet to allow the supposition that actualities are granted any other status but that of being locatable, demarcatable, delimited continuants within the finalities. Nor must it be supposed that the actualities have been absorbed in the finalities, for it is equally true that the finalities are being expressed, and this requires independent actualities.

2] *Separately*: Here the finalities and the actualities stand apart from one another, each with its own integrity and nature, unaffected by the other. The one is finite and contingent; the other, unlimited and necessary. The separation can be envisaged in any one of five ways—a separation in indifference, of equal irreducibles, of rational correlatives, of independent functioning insistencies, and of different bases of value. The last allows one to take either the actualities or the finalities to provide a measure of the value of the other. If the actualities are the measure, the finalities are seen to lack diversity, usability, pertinence, availability, familiarity, and the like; if finalities provide the measure, the actualities

will be seen to lack stability, self-sufficiency, permanence, and the ability to control and connect limited abilities.

3] *Rationally*: Here the actualities and the finalities provide an explanation and sources of names for one another. Neither can be understood in and of itself, but only with reference to what is not itself. If we try to understand an actuality in terms of other actualities we still will have not understood all the actualities together; similarly, if we understand one finality in terms of the others, we will not yet have understood the finalities together. But if we start with the finalities we can understand the actualities as so many specializations, epitomizations of all of them; if, instead, we start with the actualities we can take the finalities to be so many different absolutizations of them all. The two kinds of explanation belong together. If we have only one we have to presuppose either actualities or finalities as explanations not explained.

4] *Dynamically*: Actualities and finalities interplay with one another. Not only are their insistent expressions interlocked to constitute appearances in a context, but they affect one another. Each of the actualities is also affected by others, and each of the finalities is affected by the other finalities. Each actuality is subject to conditioning and control by all the finalities and is so far adjectival to it; each finality is subject to a reciprocal intrusion by the actualities and is so far not pure, not simple, but diversified, a simulacrum of the diffuse condition indicated under the first heading. There is, however, a difference between the diffuse presence of a finality in which the actualities are so many nuances, and the finalities as qualified by the actualities. In the latter case the actualities continue to have an integrity of their own and to express themselves over time, whereas in the case of nuanced finalities we have only demarcatable actualities.

5] *Adaptively*: Here the actualities internalize qualifications which they acquire because of the finalities, and the finalities accommodate the qualifications to which the actualities subject them. There are different grades of actualities depending on just how many different kinds of qualifications they are able to internalize. All internalize the qualifications due to Substance, but only man internalizes the qualifications of all the finalities. These internalizations are to be distinguished from the internal presence of the actualities and finalities in one another. The latter was already dealt with under the fourth heading, for these different types of reality in their dynamic intrusion do not stop at the surface of one another but reach somewhat below. The qualifications are not mere adjuncts; they make a difference to the qualified. But they always remain continuations of their sources, and subject that on which they impinge to the control of those sources. When the qualifications are internalized they are taken over by the entities on which the qualifications have been imposed. The adaptations are of five distinct kinds in the case of the actualities because of their difference in kind; in the case of the finalities the adaptations differ in kind because of the manners in which the different finalities function with respect to the same totality of actualities.

The above account is relativistic in the sense that each heading is the product of the assumption of the position of one of the finalities; it is absolutistic in that under each heading the relationships of the actualities and the finalities, in all five ways, are prescribed. How could it be known there is more than one position? How could the different positions be compared? There must be a single position from which one can look at all the finalities. But if there is a single position, will we not have to give up our metaphysical pluralism and end with a single absolute, and perhaps even with a monism?

In *Modes of Being* I made a detailed criticism of the different primary answers that one might give to the problem of the one and the many and, therefore, to the problem of how the finalities could be together. I think the criticism still stands. But the solution I gave to the problem requires modification, or at least addition. One modification was provided in the course of the response I made to critics in connection with the celebration of my seventieth birthday. I there distinguished between the kind of unity which was characteristic of the actualities together and the kind that was characteristic of the finalities together. But it still was not clear just how the finalities were together, and what the One for them might be.

If we consider the finalities by themselves, apart from the actualities, as was done in *Modes of Being* and in the *Response,* no other answers I think are possible. But the discussion of the last days shows that we ought not to consider either actualities or finalities apart from one another. Once this is recognized we can go on to remark that just as each finality provides a One for all the actualities, so each actuality provides a One for all the finalities.

Actualities come and go; they are finite and limited; not all of them are able to envisage the finalities, and those which are able—men—may not in fact do so. Still, each provides a One for the finalities, not consciously or deliberately, but ontologically. There are then as many Ones for the finalities as there are actualities. The fact that they come to be and pass away does not stand in the way of there always being a One for all the finalities; there are always actualities present. There can not be a universe without actualities and finalities and, therefore, without a One for the other in the guise of a Many.

Is the One imposed on, prescriptive, or is it present with, descriptive? Or, following the lead of the *Modes of Being,* are there five different ways in which a One is related to a Many, or five different kinds of Ones for the five distinguishable many finalities? If the answer is affirmative, are we not back to a plurality of Ones, which themselves must be somehow united?

When actualities internalize the qualifications that they obtain from the finalities, they make themselves be individuals. Individuality is the outcome of the internalization of the qualifications, an intensification and solidification of them. This unity is distinct from those marked out by the '.', ',', ')' and '. · .', referred to in the *Modes of Being;* it is a withdrawn unification and an aboriginal source, an act of negativing the independence of that which is impinging on it as well as that which it is expressing. This does not mean that Unity or value is a finality prior to the others or superior to them in any way, but only that individuality is the most basic and pervasive way of referring to what actualities of any grade are.

An individual is a self-centered convergence of what qualifies it. Does this not make it a One which stands away from the finalities and does not in fact function as a One for them? It does stand away, and that gives the One a status and a reality equal to the Many with which it is to be contrasted. But the standing away also allows it to function with reference to the Many, and thereby become a One for and of it, as well as to provide a structure for it and be dynamically in interplay with it.

If this is correct, it seems as if I was wiser than I knew when I concentrated on various kinds of unity in dealing with the modes of Being. All the finalities stand in contrast with individual actualities; these contrast with the finalities as a Many. I could not discover this so long as I remained confined to the realm of the finalities. The One which each individual actuality provides is a source of the various Ones which are involved with the finalities as constituting a contrasting Many.

By a roundabout way, and with quite different consequences, I here touch on something like a Neoplatonic view. But there is a signal difference—the One which is not yet involved with the Many is not prior to them; it is a consequence of an activity which presupposes the action of the finalities on the entity, and thus can be said to presuppose a Many and the various Ones which enable that Many to be. A precondition for the different Ones is a source; the other Ones are preconditions for this only as mediated by the finalities they unify. An individual, therefore, can be viewed as standing away from the various Ones and the Many finalities; it enjoys its status apart from the finalities at the same time that it depends on the activities of those finalities and provides them with a One that enables those finalities to be together.

If the finalities make a Many only because of the presence of distinct Ones, and if these Ones have their source in an individual which itself is a product of the utilization of qualifications by the finalities together, do we not presuppose an individual One in order to account for that One? Not exactly. The process of individuation presupposes qualifications by the finalities. Once individuality has been attained an individual becomes a source of various Ones. Before the individuality is achieved, the Ones are in the process of achieving independence from the Many on which they operate; after individuality has been achieved they are empowered to act on the finalities. Before there is an individual, the finalities are together because the actualities are present, though not yet individuated.

This way of speaking runs the danger of giving a temporal order to what is not temporally ordered at all. There is not a time when we have just the finalities united in various ways and then later a time when the actualities which provide those ways are self-individuated. From the very start every actuality is an individual substance. The explanation offered is an analytic one, endeavoring to distinguish the various components and conditions for individuation, and accounting for the grounding of the various Ones which, apart from individuality, function with respect to the Many finalities.

The present account differs from that in *Modes of Being,* in considering the four Ones there distinguished as being provided by actualities, and in attending to still another One which, though it obtains content and occasion from the activities of the finalities, contrasts with that Many, and in that sense testifies to the irreducible ultimacy of both the actualities and the finalities. Unlike the Neoplatonists, Spinozists, and Hegelians, it does not take the primal One to be prior to the various finalities, to be in effect a super-finality, but rather takes it to be limited and to be capable of coming to be and passing away. Despite its primacy, there is no permanence to any particular as a One.

Because men are the outcome of the internalization of qualifications from all the finalities, each is able to enrich his individual One, a One of all those finalities, with content derived from these finalities. The peculiarity of the One that each actuality provides is that it is an individual and nothing more. The individuality which is man has within it (not as parts, but as constituting a single One, with the individual substance as a base or ground) qualifications of all the finalities. One can say, therefore, that the One which a man provides is the five finalities individuated. Since the individuality of man is inseparable from his being, intelligibility, existence, and value, it would also be correct to say that a man is a One standing in contrast with all the finalities, as a conjoint instance of all of them, were it not for the fact that a conjunction requires a reference to a One in addition to the items conjoined. We must, therefore, take the individuality of man to be a product, which not only intensively unifies the qualifications that Substance introduces, but which lays hold of and possesses the qualifications of the other finalities at the same time, and in such a way as to make them an integral part of that individuality. Individuality is prior to the reality, nature, existence, and value of a man in the sense that these are possessed by him, made integral to himself in the course of an act of self-individuation. Though the qualification produced by Substance is not prior to the other qualifications, the role of individuality has precedence over the others.

It was said earlier that internalization reflects the operation of Unity or Value, rather than that of Substance. This points up the fact that it is necessary to differentiate the process of internalization from its product—or more completely, the product, the various qualifications, the structure, the activity, and the directionality of self-individuation, from one another.

*   *   *

Kafka left word that his works were to be destroyed on his death; Whitehead left similar instructions. It is fortunate for all of us that Kafka's instructions were not followed; it is unfortunate that Whitehead's were. Both, I think, misconstrued their status and responsibilities. Once a man has ventured into public, or even placed himself in a position where he is to become, or wants to become a public individual, he no longer has a strong claim on what he has written, published or unpublished, private material or public. He does not know just what parts of his writings will prove important or unimportant, what will throw light on what he had already done, what will help others see what he perhaps never saw. Having once accepted the role of a contributor of something for public consumption, he is obligated, I think, to provide every possible clue he can to what he meant and to its value. That means that he must leave the material, finished and unfinished, polished or not, personal or semipersonal, for those who follow after to judge. If it is thought to be useless or corruptive, it will be up to those others to determine what is to be done with it. No man can properly judge what will be of value and what will seem to be trivial by those who approach the material from another perspective, at another time, with other values.

There are things in my papers which I would prefer not to have written and which I would be ashamed to acknowledge today; but I think it is not for me to judge myself or to determine what it is with which I will be judged, if judged I am. My defects and failures, my vices and blind spots are not voided by my destroying evidences of them. There is no question but that I have them and that, taken by and large, I am not much better, if better at all, than most men, and not much worse, if worse at all, than they. But just how I differ is what may be of interest; what bearing this may have on what I have written is something I can not determine and which I do not have any right to determine, once I have allowed myself to offer contributions for public consumption.

Does this mean that I ought now to save every scrap of paper, keep a careful record of what I daily do, write down every vagrant thought? Were I a Goethe or a Molière, a Rembrandt or a Keats, perhaps. Not believing I am, but not denying that what I have written has proved of interest to some and may prove to be of interest to others later, I take the intermediate stand of saving letters written to me, holding in reserve manuscripts of books whose viability, sense, value, and finality is not clear to me, and destroying the working notes I make as I go along—the last, not purposively to hide anything from anyone but because I treat them as scaffolding to be torn down when the edifice is well under way. Scaffolding which I leave behind for uncompleted or even projected buildings are for others to use as they see fit, and not for me to destroy, for if there is no building, the scaffolding nevertheless may point the way for others to make a building, even better than one I might have envisaged or produced.

April 16

Every actuality is a One *of* all the finalities because it is qualified by them all; as a localized presence of those qualifications it functions as a One which is dependent on them. But each actuality is also, at least, a substantial individual. As such it is a One *for*. But them either a substantial individual, despite the fact that it has internalized only the qualification due to Substance, somehow becomes a One for all the finalities, or it is a One for Substance—which as a unity is in no need of a One for it. The escape from this difficulty depends on the recognition of the fact that a substantial, individual actuality possesses itself as qualified by all the finalities. It becomes a One for all of them by virtue of a forward thrust of itself as an individual substance.

What is true of all actualities is of course true of men. But a man, in addition, functions as a One for the finalities from within and at his center; it is at that center that the qualifications which are due to the finalities are unified, under the aegis of his substantial individuality. He is, consequently, a One for all the finalities in a double way. He makes the One of them, in the form of the qualifications which he receives, become a One for them as mediators for himself as centered; and he, as a center which is the outcome of the solidification and intensification of a convergent possession of the qualifications he receives from all the finalities, functions as a One for all these finalities. This 'One for' is himself as at once substantial, real, intelligible, distended, and unitary; the last four, though, are dependent on the substantial as that which identifies itself with them.

When there were no men, there was no centered reality able to be a One for all the finalities. Nevertheless, the finalities were a Many and therefore did presuppose a One. Were it possible for the finalities to be without any bearing on actualities, a One for the finalities would have to be understood along the lines laid down in the *Modes of Being*. But if, as I now think is the case, the finalities are always involved with actualities, and if every actuality is an individual which has internalized the qualification it has received from Substance, then there always is a One for the finalities, at least in the form of an actuality whose substantial individuality is mediated by the qualifications received from all the finalities.

A man, it should therefore be said, makes a 'One of', which is himself in himself, be a 'One for' by insistently thrusting outward; he also provides a 'One for' by using the qualifications he has from all the finalities as mediators of the fivefold 'One for' that he constitutes through his insistent thrust. What is the difference between these two kinds of Ones? The 'One for' which makes use of qualifications is like the 'One for' which is provided by subhuman realities, except that the possessive insistent center of a man is much richer than that characteristic of a thing. The 'One for' which is at the center of a man and which makes use of the qualifications as mediators, directly pertains to the finalities, at the same time that it is mediated by the 'One for' which it thrusts toward the finalities in the shape of a unified set of qualifications of them. The latter is a 'One for' the finalities as cosmological, as making a difference to the actualities; the former is a 'One for' the finalities as they stand by themselves, each distinctive and independent, but still together with the rest.

Must we then say that were there no men, there would be no set of finalities apart, by themselves? As was indicated the other day, there are a number of ways in which finalities and actualities are together, at the same time that both are by themselves. To be by itself each must have the other be by itself. A withdrawal from an involvement by one requires the independent status of the other. No particular thing could stand wholly away from the finalities, but all things together constitute a domain which stands away from the finalities, though only as somehow already diffusely present and therefore integral with the finalities, or as subject to some expression of the finalities. The first of these alteratives ignores the question as to whether or not finalities and actualities stand apart. The second alternative, though it allows for a distinction between the finalities in themselves and the finalities as expressed at their most attenuated, does not make provision for the actualities in themselves, apart from and independent of the finalities.

Though it is the finalities in a cosmological guise which produce qualifications, it does not follow that the qualifications when made into mediators of a 'One for' the finalities is a One for those finalities as cosmological. The intrusion of the substantial individuality of a thing on the qualifications it suffers gives those qualifications a standing which reverses that which they had as mere qualifications, since it makes them one and insistent for the finalities as standing apart from them. Though the qualifications are due to the finalities, when functioning as mediators for an individual substance those qualifications have the status of a 'One for' finalities which stand apart from them. They would not have that status, to be sure, were there no cosmos in which the finalities impinged on the actualities. But this is only to say that there is an analytic precedence of cosmology to ontology when we attend to mediators which are converted into 'Ones for'. A precedence of ontology over cosmology occurs when we attend to the fact that all 'Ones for' owe their presence to a thrust outward from the center of actualities. The difference here between men and other actualities lies solely in the fact that the thrust outward by men is by enriched substantial individuals, while the thrust outward by what is not human is by bare substantial individuals, or by such individuals as only partially enriched.

To account for individuals is to begin from qualifications and is, therefore, to give precedence to cosmology. This is a precedence which, as was just indicated, is analytic of the situation; it does not entail any temporal priority. If we do not seek to explain individuals but, instead, seek to show how what is subhuman can provide a 'One for' finalities, we must begin with actualities as ontological entities. At every moment, though, we have both the actualities and the finalities separate and together. As separate they are related as 'Ones for' a Many; as together, they make up a cosmos as well as a diffused field, an intelligible whole, and a valuational unity.

A man's ontological status with respect to the finalities has now been dealt with in abstraction from him as having a self with its various roles of mind, reason, psyche, sensibility, and spirit—to use the terms (though not the order) stated in *Beyond All Appearances*. These different phases of the self, and the self itself, are the outcome of an account of man which not only deals with man in terms of the concepts of the One and the Many but attends to the nature of the One that he constitutes when he internalizes the qualifications to which he is subject. In that internalization he not only solidifies and intensifies the qualifications, and not only achieves the status of a 'One of' which can become a 'One for' the finalities, but goes on to diversify that One in the form of instances of those finalities. He is, therefore, able to give each of the finalities a distinctive role in his internal economy, in addition to giving them all the status of constituents of a single One, himself.

It is perhaps misleading to speak of a man in himself as at a center. This might tempt one to suppose that somehow there is a hard core within him which is not involved with anything else. It would be better to say that the One, which is a man, has various degrees of internality, and that over that range of degrees it is possible to distinguish the different roles of psyche, mind, and so on. The One which encompasses all of these is the self. The self is a One when contrasted with the finalities together; it is diverse when, while still remaining apart from the finalities, some role is emphasized as an instance standing in opposition to a distinguished finality.

*   *   *

I have been told that a number of people have been demanding of Paul Schilpp, the editor of the Library of Living Philosophers, that I be included in the series. He has, so far, resisted, apparently on two grounds: He is said to resent the fact that I have refused to contribute to previous works in the series, and that I have written unfavorable reviews of some of them. Even if it were true, which it is not, that the reviews I wrote were mean, vicious, immoral, unkind, I think that would not be a relevant consideration, any more than the fact that I have not contributed to his series. I did not contribute because when he approached me in connection with the first of the volumes (on Dewey), he commanded that I write on the relation of Dewey and Peirce, without asking me whether or not I was interested in doing this. To my knowledge he never asked me to contribute again. In any case, I was not interested in writing the type of critique which he needed. There are some who are excellent at such studies; I think I am not. At any rate, I was busy doing other types of things.

The only relevant consideration I think is whether or not I merit being in the series; whether or not I am on a footing with the others who have been made the object of these detailed and for the most part excellent examinations. I would like being included, but I will not do anything to assure such inclusion. I was asked by a mutual friend, who is most anxious not to have his role known, to placate Schilpp in some way; he said it would remove the only barrier in his decision to include me. Whether or not my inclusion depends on such action, it is certainly not something in which I wish to engage.

Perhaps the matter is of little import, for I am now sending out copies of "First Considerations" to a dozen or so philosophers, asking them to make critical comments on parts or the whole of the work. If all goes well I intend to put the comments, with my replies, in the appendix of the published book. Only two philosophers— Hilary Putnam and Roderick Chisholm—have said that they would not engage in the enterprise.

I tried, as best I could, to ask philosophers of the most diverse stripes to let me have their comments. But I did not write to mere logicians or to philosophers of science. Perhaps if I had written them, and others who had strong positivistic or empirical leanings I would have received further rejections or would not have had the benefit of a reply. I would like to have the reaction of such men, but I do not know them well enough to feel justified in writing to them. As it is, Milton Fisk and Richard Rorty are writing critiques; they are very able men who, so far as I can see, are without much sympathy for what I have said, the approaches I take, or even of the enterprise in which I engage. I hope that their criticisms will be sufficiently basic and wide-ranging as to make unnecessary comments of similar bent from others. Honest, strong thinkers, even if initially unsympathetic with what I am doing, should be able to expose what is fundamentally amiss, demand clarifications and explanations, and exhibit hesitations and doubts which will not differ widely from those that are rooted in positions which are radically opposed to my own. Any competent philosopher should be able to see the limitations and flaws of positions quite close to his own—even of positions which overlap his. Those who start from positions rather alien to mine might sharpen issues in ways the others will not, but they will not necessarily point up difficulties that the others would not see or mention.

Over the years I have found that the criticisms that I have made of my own works and of special points within them, and the difficulties I have underscored and tried subsequently to deal with, have been sharper and more difficult to handle than those which have been made in reviews or by my students. It is conceivable that I have been insufficiently acute in my grasp of what is being said by others, but I do not think so.

I have faced critics on two signal occasions. In *Philosophical Interrogations* they made a number of incisive points, no one of which, though, seemed to me to be difficult to answer. In the 100A issue of the *Review of Metaphysics,* the symposiasts who spoke at the celebration in honor of my seventieth birthday, did pose some basic difficulties, which I acknowledged in my *Response.* I do not think, though, that they affected the roots of what I have been maintaining, though some of them—particularly Lieb's comments about my views of time—point up important areas which I have not entered or mastered as well as I should.

Hartshorne in his *Creative Synthesis and Philosophic Method* offers seven criteria in terms of which a metaphysican should be evaluated. He says there that I have a high degree of originality, comprehensiveness and balance, and readability, but that there is some lack of clarity, coherence, and integration, and an inability to defend my views against strong forms of competing doctrines. He says nothing about his number 5, the ability to grasp diverse possible or historical perspectives on problems. His are not criticisms as much as assessments or evaluations. Granted their justice, it is not clear how much value is to be given to each point. Is originality more or less important than clarity? Is coherence more important than comprehensiveness? Can a great philosopher be strong in only one of these—say originality, and weak in the others? Kant, surely, is deficient in clarity, coherence, and integration, comprehensiveness and balance, the ability to grasp diverse perspectives, and readability. This would leave him strong only in originality and the ability to defend his views. Evidently, other criteria are needed, and weights have to be assigned to the different factors if one is to be able to use Hartshorne's list with consistency and effectiveness.

No matter whether or not the assessments Hartshorne makes of me are correct—and I find it very difficult to decide how just his assessments are and how much weight I am to give to each—they do not provide criticisms of arguments and positions to which I can attend and to which perhaps I should yield, or which should lead me to modify the positions I have developed. In the course of that work Hartshorne does criticize me, but the criticisms are broad-gauged and somewhat vague. He says that I am too rhetorical, too dualistic, and that my reference to Existence seems to be verbal only. But I argued for the reality of Existence from many different sides—from the fact of contemporaneity, from the continuation of the extension of an actuality with the extension beyond it, and from the presence of actualities in causal changes. The charge of dualism, though, has some merit. I do distinguish actualities and finalities quite sharply; I do distinguish inside and outside, man and nature, and (what I think Hartshorne is focussing on) the four modes of being (in *Modes of Being,* the work he has in mind) as though they were two pairs of entities. But if by 'dualism' one means two irreducibles having no bearing on one another, and for which there is no mediator, I surely am not a dualist. I have long maintained that each item has a bearing on every other; most recently I have been urging that every entity thrusts itself forward, and that at any point where it might be said to stop and, therefore, have content with which it must grapple, it also moves beyond. More, I have been urging that wherever anything may be taken to stop, it is also being lured beyond.

All that we know is environed by mystery, not in the sense that it merely fringes what we have to the fore, but as conditioning it, affecting it, limiting and enticing it. The mystery may take the shape of an unknown, faced in terror, or it may take the shape of a domain of ignorance encompassing but also directing what it is that we have articulately mastered.

A dualist has a pair of items each in itself; but whatever is in itself, I would contend, and have tried to show in different ways and on different occasions, is also involved with other entities. To be in itself is but one phase or role, one status enjoyed together with, conditioned by and conditioning others in which the entity is involved with what else there be. A dualist has a Many without a One; or he has a One and also a Many. But I have persistently maintained that there is no One without a Many, nor a Many without a One, and that the two have to be for one another, even though they do and must enjoy the status of being what they are.

April 17

'Come here.'
'Me?'
'Yes, you.'

The 'me' and the 'you' are not identical, but they do overlap. The 'you' might merely mark out someone from a number. But even if it serves to direct one to another and to penetrate toward what he is in himself, it is not altogether separable from the designating individual. The 'me', instead, is acknowledged by assuming a position beyond oneself, but without actually being there, as is the individual who is designating the 'you'. It also promotes a penetration further toward the self. More important, it is not altogether detachable from the self.

Wittgenstein says that if one were to close one's eyes on being asked to locate a pain and then were to touch the body of another, one would thereby show that it is possible for one to feel another's pain. This is surely mistaken. Wittgenstein makes no allowance for the fact that a pain is inseparable from a self engaged in identifying it as that which belongs to it, and then only as mediated by a me. There is a great difference between alighting on the body of another and feeling something then—it would be the feeling of what it is to touch another—and alighting on one's own body, for this involves the acceptance (by an I) of the me as that which belongs to and mediates a penetration toward the I. We identify our pains at various places in our bodies, not as if our bodies were somehow alien, and simply coordinate with or together in some public space with other bodies, but as bodies which we move through from within, approach from beyond, and penetrate toward the self.

'Movement', 'penetration' and cognate terms are offensive metaphors for many. Only bodies, it will be said, can move; penetration requires permeable objects, or a power to pierce. The irritation can perhaps be reduced by referring to acts of attention having an origin and a terminus, not necessarily separated in time nor identifiable as at different parts of space, and by replacing 'penetration' by 'attentive to what is being presupposed, or to that on which something depends'.

The acknowledgement of oneself as a me does not presuppose that there is another I, or that one in fact assumes the position of another, even that other in the guise of one who is a you for oneself. One need not be faced by another in order to be able to assume a position beyond one's body and from there attend to oneself as a me which is inseparable from an I. The me is double-faced, inseparable from the I which accepts some exterior position, as well as from a reference from that exterior position.

When one remembers, there is a reference to an I which accompanies what it is that is being acknowledged. The object of
memory thus is no mere object contemplated now, but content
inseparable from a self attending to it. That self is identical with and
yet different from the self that is now present. It is identical with it
in being, for it is I who remember what I experienced or encountered; it is also different, because the past act of experiencing or
encountering is distinct from the experiencing or encountering in
which I am now involved with present objects. I face something
present with me in the very same sense in which I had faced
something present with that which is being remembered; at the
same time I distinguish the act in which I now engage from the act in
which I had engaged. I now, therefore, am involved in two acts. In
one act I do something similar to what I had done, and face something as an object of experiencing; in another act, occurring at the
same time, I distinguish that facing from the facing in which I had
engaged. What is faced may be identical in both cases, and since the
self is identical in both cases as well, the difference between them
necessarily lies in the act relating self and object.

When I was experiencing something before, I was present as a
self, but that self is not an object of my memory. I do not remember
myself as being identical with myself now, except of course as
having such and such an appearance, views, having engaged in such
and such similar activities, and the like.

The identity of a self is not an empirical matter; it can not be
reduced to the ability to remember or to any other empirical
activity, since it is presupposed by them. The self as having been
engaged in an act at some previous time, of course, is not in the past,
though it was present then as engaged in such an act. I now, as this
self, identify the self as engaged in a particular act in the past
terminating in certain content, as that which is not only distinct
from the self as engaged in some other act now but from the self
which grounds both acts. I accept the act in which I had engaged as
the act of the self which is now engaged in some other act, and in so
accepting it distinguish that act from the one in which I now engage.
I, therefore, am able to assume responsibility for it, and to claim
that what I now take to be remembered was remembered in fact.

Might I not now be dreaming, or imagining an occurrence
which never did take place? I might, and indeed sometimes do. I
can not tell merely from the fact that I accept myself as having acted
with respect to an object, the same or different from that which I

now confront, that I did in fact so act. What I am sure of is that as in the past I did act in a way that is distinct from that in which I am now acting. I determine that what I take to be remembered is remembered by noting that the object is more determinate than an object of imagination or dream can be, that it has an objective relationship to the content I now confront which is not possible to what I imagine, and that I find myself with content now that is like what I imagine but which it is referential to what is more determinate than itself.

The degree of determination characteristic of an object of direct experience, is perhaps less than that in an object of memory, without being equatable with an object of imagination. We can add to the memory, but we can not, by merely exercising the imagination, produce the kind of content which now makes up my present memory, or the referent of that content which now is the object referred to as having been experienced. I see at once that the content is not applicable to what is here and now; in remembering, I immediately refer the content of my memory back to the past—the future requiring less determinate content, and the present excluding both. In making that reference, the content is here and now in the present as that which is the object of an experiencing self. It is here and now displaced, referred back to the past where it is made more determinate by being made the terminus of a particular act by the self at that time.

I become aware of the unreliability of my memory when I find that the object presumably encountered in the past could not, by any known processes, have given way to or have preceded what is now being encountered, and particularly what I now can explain and understand. I remain confident that I have remembered correctly just so long as no conflict arises between what I now confront and what I take myself to have remembered to have confronted.

The self that is now present was present in the past. But it is not a self as in the past to which I now refer as the correlate of what was then encountered. The self that confronted something in the past, via a particular act of attention, is as particular as the act, and is strictly coordinate with the object. The self I now am is the ground of what I now do—encounter something now, entertain remembered content, and refer the remembered content to the past where it is related to the self as engaged in a particular act of confrontation. Since it is I who now remember and therefore who now refer the content back and accept the past confronted object as that which I did confront, the self as engaged in a particular act of confrontation in the past is one which is identified as a particularized correlative of the particular content confronted, as well as a particularized form of the self that I now am. I now, as a self, take my confrontation in the past to be engaged in by a specialized form of myself, a specialized form which at that time required the presence of the self.

I was present in the past in a double sense: I was present in the guise of a particularized self which was involved in a particular act of confrontation, and I was present as that which was being particularized and thereby involved in a particular act of confrontation. I therefore come to know myself as one who engages in a plurality of exclusive particularized acts requiring exclusive particularizations of myself.

When Buddhists and some Whiteheadeans maintain that the self perishes at every moment, though inheriting what it had undergone in the past, they also give up knowledge through memory, for they have no self in which the particular acts in the past could be grounded. They can say only that such and such an activity had been engaged in the past by a self which is now somehow encompassed within the particular self which is now acting. They would still have to distinguish the particular present self as now confronting something, and that self as referring some of its present content back to the past where it had been confronted by another self. They could not say that any thing is really remembered, but only that what had occurred in the past is making a difference to or is retained and distinguished within a present particular self.

If we are engaged in particularized acts which have as one term a particularized momentary self, there is then a question as to the bearing that self has on the persistent self that is being particularized. Is the particularized self a kind of me? Or is it an I, delimited? If I know the self via the particularized selves, it would seem as if the latter were kinds of me's; yet it is an I which knows, experiences, and confronts.

Since we do not approach particularized selves from the outside, from an exterior position, they are not me's. We know them as specializations of the self, expressing it in a specialized form. We refer to the more basic self via particularized selves by grounding them, possessing them, taking them to be identical in their source of power, in responsibility, in ultimacy, and yet different, as beginning distinctive acts of confrontation.

A note to philosophers: the universe is at least as diverse, interesting, and active as any university.

There is no 'we' peculiar to philosophers. Each is an I, belonging together with all mankind. Their common technical competence and possible audience enables them to sharpen up the differences in their methods and conclusions from those of all others, and from those of one another, but they have no common doctrine or standing which would justify them in taking them to constitute a distinctive we. Philosophic associations are occasions for social activities, for knowing about jobs, or at best for keeping current with some trends. This states a partial truth only; if all philosophers are engaged in discovering and saying what others do not or can not they constitute a group, a 'we'.

*   *   *

The self (or I) accepts particularized versions of itself, (which serve as the beginnings of particular acts ending in particular objects at particular times) by a process of intensive, possessive self-identification. It accepts the particularized versions as expressions of itself in the very act of specializing itself so as to produce these. Specialization of the self is part of the expression of the self; as it occurs it is countered by a reverse movement by means of which the resultant particularization is accepted as one's own. A man is responsible for his particular acts, but he is responsible not simply as one who then and there did what he did, but as a self which expressed itself as a particular self engaged in that particular act.

When it is denied that there is a self, or that a knowledge of it is possible, and recourse is taken instead to a community, society, state, or other group, one is still left with the problem of who it is that affirms this fact, who it is that accepts the outcomes of the workings of these groups, who it is that criticizes and sometimes opposes them. Even common language has to be understood by individuals by themselves; and they may produce novelties in it which are accepted by the rest. A community account, moreover, can not do justice to the idea of responsibility; it can get no further than accountability, the crediting of someone publicly with the import of some act, whether or not he is a source of it, intended it, or even knew about it. One can be made accountable for negligence, even when it is the case that one has taken every imaginable precaution, provided only that it is the intent of the society to see that the victim is compensated, or blame is imposed.

We do not have a direct acquaintance with a self; we must at the very least mediate it by a me, or recognize diverse particularized selves to be so many specializations of the selfsame self. A self, despite the fact that particularized selves specialize it, should not be viewed as something general or generic. It is even more intensive, unified, powerful than the particularized selves, but only as the locus of rights, individuality, and so forth, and not as an object decorated with predicates, and not as an isolated unit, a hard core which somehow expressed itself without being affected by anything that is done. A self, in accepting particularized versions of itself and the acts which start with these, reidentifies, reindividualizes itself; it takes back into itself through possession and control, through the assumption of responsibility, through dedication, through its assessments, what it expressed in particular acts, and by its assumption of distinctive roles as mind, spirit, and so forth.

One can take a self to continue through its expressions, into and beyond the body, until it terminates at what is maintained apart from it. But one can also, with equal warrant, take a self to be a center—and also, for everything beyond this, to be making itself available as a me. The one position is assumed when we view a self as a source of acts and therefore of particularized selves; the other is assumed when we take a self to be the outcome of a process of self-identification and self-individualization of what is available to it as material to be used and solidified.

Evidently, a self engages in two distinct kinds of intensifications. There is the intensification which results when it pulls on its own expressions and solidifies them as expressions for which it is responsible, even when unconsciously produced; and there is the intensification which results when it takes into itself what is intruded on it, so that it can be inwardly what it has been outwardly conditioned to be and, therefore, is able to avoid being divided against itself or to be only adjectival in some respects to what is final. The one intensification ends with the self as a dense intensity, the other with it as able to have various roles because it is in the locus of individuality, rights, rationality, distendedness, and value. The first form has to do with its own economy, and is in effect the completion of a circle which begins with the self and ends at it through the intermediation of what the self is expressing. The second form has to do with its dignity, its ability to be at once an instance and an irreducible opposite of the finalities. A self, in engaging in the first, takes advantage of what it is as the second; in its expressions and consequent acceptance of them as its own, it exhibits itself as a reality with individuality, rights, and so forth. Behind every expression there is, for example, a claim being made; the claim as expressed is taken back into the self, in its particularity, to be solidified with other expressions.

A self does not just express itself or make itself into an instance opposing the finalities; it also enables a body to be in a world of actualities in a distinctive way, as an organic, human body for which there is responsibility and which will mediate irreducible, native claims. What is thereby expressed is also possessed and internalized. In addition, other actualities affect it; they make a difference to its bodily functioning. They modify the body. If a self is to be selfsame, these modifications and alterations must be reduced by it to the selfsame, identical self.

Despite the fact that a body changes and a self expresses itself in multiple ways, there is an identity to the individual because the self makes what it expresses and what affects it reduce to the same unitary dense result. It is, consequently, responsible as involved in a cosmos governed by the finalities and as involved with other actualities which may or may not be backed by selves. A self is no Platonic pilot in an indifferent bodily ship; it is no incomplete substance awaiting, with St. Thomas, the resurrection of the body on the day of last judgment so that it can be completed by something other than itself. It has no necessary existence before or after death, but this does not preclude it from being selfsame throughout a life from birth to death. Men are identical despite change; all are responsible despite a state's incapacity to get beyond accountability; all are expressive and affected and yet, despite this, are persistent, able to act in specific distinctive ways at different moments of time.

April 19

The acknowledgment of actualities is made from a position where use is made of all-encompassing categories referring to those actualities as together in various ways. The acknowledgment of those actualities, though, is only as a base for the counterparts of those categories. The categories are mediated by the actualities, and are thereby enabled to refer to the expressions of the finalities as in fact governing the actualities as together. To come to know the finalities better, one must ignore the intermediaries and proceed symbolically with the expressions toward the finalities as they are in themselves.

A converse situation holds with respect to the categorical knowledge of the finalities. The initial category used when we attend to the finalities is that of 'actuality', a variable. That category enables one to face the finalities as loci of diversifications. The initial category faces the finalities, but it is directed at the diversity of content which the different finalities sustain. To come to know actualities better, it is necessary to ignore the finalities and attend to the diversification as having its roots in actualized differences, which is to say, in individuals which are the loci of intensifications of those differences.

In each case we face an intermediating support of what is at best only a faint version of the proper object of the categories which we are employing. We are always beyond the categories, always beyond the intermediate sustaining reality, always beyond that which they sustain and which is the proper object of the categories we initially employ.

There is no necessary use of categories when we are practical, and involved with some particular actualities, making and remaking, adjusting ourselves in order to avoid distress and perhaps achieve some object of desire. The equivalent with respect to finalities of this practical involvement with actualities is submission or self-abandonment, where we present ourselves, some claim, or some symbol to the finalities for acceptance.

Empiricists attend primarily to actualities or their appearances. Some of them become aware of the fact that the language, categories, outlook, mind, or self of which they make use is itself beyond knowing by the agencies by means of which the actualities or appearances are first faced as constituting a single domain in which they are inseparably together as actualities or as appearances. Sometimes a correlative acknowledgment is made by those who are concerned with transcendentals; these begin by acknowledging finalities from a finite position, whose nature and existence they can not then account for. Such considerations, of course, apply to the facing of actualities or appearances as within inclusive domains, and to the facing of finalities from finite, contingent, limited positions; when, instead, one attends to a particular appearance or actuality, the position of a domain is adopted in place of a category, and attention is directed to a portion of it which is being maintained in contradistinction to the whole.

The acknowledgment of particular actualities thus takes two steps, one in which, through the help of a categorial finality, actualities or appearances are faced as together, dominated by a controlling encompassing unity, and the second which involves the acceptance of that unity as the area within which a focussing on distinctive particulars occurs. The initial category is not constitutive of the togetherness initially faced, but merely enables one to acknowledge it; the togetherness which is allowed to replace the initial category is double-faced, since it is the terminus of the category, and a control over the items which it unites.

When we attend to the evidences that all actualities or all appearances as together sustain, we do not take the second step. Instead of taking the domain as an area within which we will focus on particulars, we take it as the beginning of a progress into finalities, the proper object of the categories we originally assumed.

It is harder to see the correlative state of affairs, involving the use of a finite position in order to approach the finalities. The acknowledgment of the finalities as loci of diversification is followed by the acceptance of some diversification as providing a position from which one can see the differences unified in a finality.

A particular actuality and a finality are reached in two ways. Each is the outcome of the use of the first step, the object of a category, to allow for a division or a unification, respectively. Each, too, is the outcome of the use of the first step as evidence leading to the proper counterpart of the category with which one began.

All this is most obscure, perhaps artificial, and might well be entirely in error. But it does seem to be the case that we arrive at particular actualities via them as together and therefore subject, cognitively and objectively, to the finalities. It seems, too, that there should be a corresponding arrival at the finalities via them as diversified and therefore subject, cognitively and objectively, to actualities.

An interesting way in which these considerations come into play is presented by social contract theories. A modern form of such theories is given by Rawls, who asks one to assume an original position where one abstracts from all the differences between oneself and others and then tries to envisage what principles and rules a rational man would accept. Putting aside the supposition so evidently in operation here, but also present in the older theories, to the effect that what is subsequently achieved after the aboriginal state is abandoned is somehow accidental and merely overlays the initial stage (rather than transforming the individuals radically, and therefore making the conditions accepted initially not valid any longer), the view starts by assuming that all men are intrinsically equal to one another. This is true, but it is not more true than that they are affiliated and disaffiliated—the latter being expressed by Hobbes's account of men as enemies of one another, while the former is maintained by Locke with his supposition that they have some positive involvement with one another; that they are structurally and intelligibly connected, particularly by virtue of their ages, sex, assumption of responsibility, and above all by their native constitution with its native aptitudes (and therefore different capacities to enter into the original position and move from this into a political organization); that they are effectively united through work and ability, interest in and occasion to work, to work with, and to work for; and that they all possess values which are necessarily comparable, enabling them to be parts of a single harmonious value with the least possible modification. All these could be said to be 'original' positions. But all in fact are the ways in which men are together 'transcendentally,' and in terms of which we must understand them as politically or empirically together.

An 'original position' is reached after assuming the category of some finality—Rawls opts for Being—and then dealing with them as distinctive beings (and thus as distinct from and oppositional to the Being with respect to which they are equal beings together). Having identified men as so many separate beings all on a footing of equality (as beings always are), they are then dealt with as subject to empirical unities, that is, to political wholes where the men are at last allowed to be and function in their full concreteness as actualities, and no longer as mere beings which are at once equal and together under the aegis of Being.

In passing from the stage where men are equal and together as beings to where they are in a political system, one can pass either to them as still equal and therefore under the dominance of a special form of Being, or to them as interconnected in new ways. One can, for example, go from a supposed original position where men are beings together all equal in status—idiots and infants, the perverted and foolish apparently, as well as the ordinary, mature men, which Rawls seems both to permit and not to allow—to the men as together as richer beings, or as closely affiliated, or as making up a single economic force, and so forth. There is, in short, a distinction to be made between justice with respect to men in an original position and justice with respect to them in the condition they have in a state. One can treat them, as members of a just state, as necessarily equal because they continue to retain the natures they had in the original position, but to require legal agencies to recover that equality when one brings into account their actual divergencies from one another. But one can also take them, as members of a just state, to be not merely equal, but to have definite economic roles and (as in the Indian caste system) to have distinctive tasks to perform if they are to be just in a just state.

There would seem then to be a number of 'original positions' and a number of political states of affairs in which those original positions are qualified by the actual differences that exist amongst men. Which of the first and which of the second are especially to be identified with 'justice' or 'justice as fairness' is an open question. There is a reasonableness to the supposition that the first is one where the men are taken to be equals, but equals as together, and not just as units entirely disconnected—for them they would be incomparable. The second position involves some difficulties. If we say that in a state men are to be acknowledged to be what they are in their full concreteness, they can not be taken to be equal beings there without abstracting from their actual differences (and thus returning one to the first position), or without allowing them to be in fact unequal but tolerated because this is allowed by the principles assumed in the original position. That alternative is what apparently is intended by Rawls. As a consequence, it is being supposed that the principles which are operative for equal beings in the original position are the principles which must operate in a state, but on individuals acknowledged to be unequal there.

If principles which are forged when the men are taken to be equal are allowed to be in control when they are subsequently acknowledged to be in fact unequal, they are to be governed by what is controlling in the original position. This will mean that if they are originally merely beings equal together, then their status, as let us say workers who are unequal and together, is to be kept subordinate to and subject to a conditioning which is defined for them, not as workers but merely as beings. In effect, this means that the ways in which men are in a state are to be subject to overriding principles which were forged by the men as merely beings equal together. Not only might one justifiably contend that the original position for workers should not be of them as merely beings equally together but of them working maximally well together, but one can also justifiably insist that even if they are initially taken to be merely beings equally together, once we take account of the fact that they are workers, the principles that were formerly operative would now be ways of bringing about injustices. The injustices would arise since the principles ignore or transform what the men in fact are, workers who are involved in different tasks within a single economic whole, requiring them to assume different roles, regardless of their individual desires.

Contract theories of the state suppose either that men are originally—or are assumed to be originally or natively, or for the sake of a theory—in an impoverished (Hobbes) or in a better (Rousseau) condition than they are when they are citizens. The advantage of Rawls's approach is that it allows one to see that the initial state of affairs is not an empirically, or even a supposedly or imagined empirical condition, but a metaphysical one in which men are viewed as under the direct aegis of one finality. Not only, as was just suggested, might this finality not be Being, it is even conceivable that in the initial position they are under the aegis of all the finalities together. Indeed, this is the most reasonable supposition of all. Not only does it accord with what has been independently found to be the case with appearances and actualities, but it allows one to do justice to the fact that, even when we abstract from the transient differences which distinguish men empirically, they may have intrinsic differences which enable them to have different roles while they are together in other ways, besides that of being together as equals, More, it allows one to see that they might then even be envisaged to be mere units which are not merely coordinate, but are affiliated, rationally connected, dynamically interinvolved, and assessed. They would then all be on a footing, not because they were beings, but because they were just units in maximally perfected totalities of affiliated, rationally connected, dynamically interinvolved, and valuational items. On this last suggestion, the original position is one where unit men were maximally together under the aegis of all the finalities, and the fivefold principles which then could be said to govern them would be carried over in a single move to operate on what men in fact were like now, to make them conform closer to what they supposedly were in the original position. In any case, one would start with a metaphysically defined position and then, in the empirical situations which confronted one, use the principles that were justified by the metaphysically defined position.

The consideration of men apart from the actual groups in which they are in fact need not take one to another period in history nor to some other conceivable empirical grouping; instead, it should free one from empirical considerations altogether and make one face a metaphysical situation where men are viewed as governed solely by the finalities and whatever principles these warrant.

Abstraction from an empirical situation need not force one to consider men as in fact denuded of the very particular transient features they are acknowledged to have in the empirical situation, but merely to have those features directly subject to the finalities. We need not suppose that the men are without age or gender, for example, but only that these are being dealt with in terms of the universally applicable conditions provided by the finalities. One would then be engaged in something like the shift from a consideration of physical particles in some limited situation to those very particles in a cosmos without any subtraction from what they in fact had been found to be. They might have features in the limited situations which are to be abstracted from, but what is left over would then be the particles viewed first as they are in fact related to certain others, and then as subject to comic laws. A woman would be taken to be equal to a man, under the aegis of Being, not by abstracting from the fact that she is a woman, but by taking her to be subject in a different way than the man is to the operation of Being so that she then is his equal. When one moved back to the actual situation, her distinctive way of being, and not the fact that she was a woman, would be the new consideration that would be brought in and which the state would have to deal with and reduce to equality, by making use of the principle it had presumably received or adopted from the original position.

If the foregoing approach be rejected, what is one to say to the suggestion that we should think of humans in the original position not as distinctive kinds of actualities but as merely complicated animals or machines? Why retain any distinctive human traits if we do not also hold on to their distinctive sex, age, and perhaps even color, intelligence, diligence, and so forth, and so forth?

By a roundabout route once again we come to the question of the difference between men, animals, and machines. Concentrating on the extremes, we can, in the attempt to overcome any supposed differences in kind between them ask if machines might not be conscious, and if men can not be understood to be merely complicated machines.

To the first question, it would be proper to say that though it is conceivable, logically possible, imaginable that a machine might be conscious, think, philosophize, invent stories, or be a kind of autistic man, unable to bring to expression what is going on inside it, the supposition is idle. We have no evidence of any kind that machines are conscious, and we can make no use of the supposition that they are, unless it be to say that there is no radical distinction in kind between men and machines. But that radical distinction can also be denied by going in the opposite direction and maintaining that there is nothing about man that might not be duplicated in a machine.

It is conceivable that we might not be able to distinguish the products of a machine from that of a man. This is in effect what the Turing experiment is designed to show. But just as it does not follow from the fact that one may not be able to distinguish an original from a copy that there is no distinction between them, so it does not follow from the fact that we are unable to distinguish the products of the machine from those of a man that there is no distinction between them. But is this not to entertain another idle supposition? On the contrary.

I can intellectually distinguish an inscription, a sentence, and a statement, the one consisting of the marks on paper, one of which is a dot after one of the words, the second being a unit which ends in a period, and the third of which is a claim to truth that is being made to function as a unit in discourse and logic, and allows for presentation in a number of different sentences. I may not, when presented with the letters of the alphabet grouped together in various ways be able to determine whether these were placed in this way by a machine and were only inscriptions, or whether they were set down by a man and were sentences purporting to express propositions.

But I know that I can produce one or the other—the inscription by just using some instrument, a sentence by attending to the rules of grammar and usage, and the statement by assuming responsibility for the truth of the claim that is conveyed. I have no evidence that a machine or even an animal can do this. I therefore take the supposition, that they can, to be idle, a 'mere' imagined possibility.

If I can not be sure that what is before me is an inscription or sentence, and that the latter purports to express a statement, I can not be sure that it was produced by a man. If someone I take to be a man presents me with a grouping of groups of letters with a dot at the end, I do not know if what I face is anything more than an inscription. I do not know, so far, whether or not it was put down by a man functioning in a way not possible to the nonhuman. If I know he is a man I allow that he can speak and perhaps write sentences and express statements; if I know that he is expressing statements and speaking sentences I know that he is a man. But if I am doubtful of the one or the other I can not decide the issue, unless I have some other way of knowing that what is before me is a sentence expressing a statement, or that the actuality before me is a man and not a machine. I decide by seeing what follows and what preceded, and how its presence coheres with the occasion, and so forth; by seeing if I can be in sympathetic accord with him; by trying to converse with him; by seeing if he can produce new sentences which are germane to what was already produced; by seeing if he treats me as a 'you'; by noting the way he works with me, defies me, denies me, speaks to me, just as I decide whether someone is a copyist rather than an original creative artist by seeing what else he does, how he goes about producing his works, what happens after an interval, and the like. If I am denied these further tests, the issue is left undetermined, not settled. The Turing experiment supposes that what is still undetermined at a particular moment is equatable with what is decisively determined; it takes an incapacity to differentiate the work of a man from that of a machine to be equatable with the lack of any difference between those works.

Each type of investigation has a closure point. There comes a time when we will decide that something or other is the case even though it is logically conceivable and may in fact turn out that we are mistaken. But we need not decide anything more than that a decision can not be made—and this is the case when we are confronted with the Turing situation. Similarly, we may not be able to decide whether or not a fetus is human, a plant feels, a virus is living, or a man is fat or bald. If we have nothing but the public expressions of a man, we have something which might be duplicated and which could conceivably have issued from him without thought or human surveillance. But we can conceive of situations where we can tell the difference. We could try, in a Turing situation, to engage in a conversation with the unknown man behind one door and the unknown machine behind the other, and on the basis of the responses decide which is the man and which the machine. The dead products of them both may not provide enough data to enable us to know what the data were when or if they were parts of a living discourse.

When I come to know when or if something is part of a living discourse, I go beyond bare data and attend to the source of an utterance to see if it is in fact responsive to what I say and do, and whether or not a unit utterance conveys claims that are in fact sustained. I will not be content with seeing if it can produce signals. An animal can perhaps be taught to hold up a sign 'hunger' when it is hungry, but this is not yet enough to allow us to say that it is using a language, for the sign says no more than there is hunger somewhere or other. It is not enough for it to say 'I', or even 'am', or to say these in a series. What is necessary is that it be able to say 'I am hungry' and understand this as a single unit, and thus as a claim to truth, and whose verbal rejection entails another claim that the rejection is mistaken. Should there be apparent humans who are not able to get this far in discourse then, apart from our ability to be with them in other ways, we will be forced to say that we can not yet determine whether or not they are in fact human.

A machine might be so made in the future that it is an apparent human; when that time comes, we will then, apart from the ability to discover what is the right answer in other ways, not then be able to determine whether or not we should say it is not only conscious but is to be included in humankind. We may have put it together so that the relation of its parts is external to them, but this does not preclude their then providing an occasion for the intrusion of a unity which gives those parts an internally connected status in addition to the external one, somewhat as the living body provides an internal connection between the heart and the liver even while they are at a distance from one another and detachable one from the other and, so far, externally related.

Whether or not one can make evident that men are distinct kinds of actualities, it is surely right for Rawls and other students of political and ethical theory to attend to them as the irreducible realities with which a political organization is concerned. But there is more than one alternative to the 'utilitarian' view which Rawls opposes. There is, for example, the absolutistic ethical view of Kant and the absolutistically grounded view of Hegel. To understand what men ideally ought to do in a state, one can justifiably attend to what it is that they severally and together ought to have and do in order to be excellent, and then look to the state as an instrument by which one can attain the desired result to some extent. It is not possible to reach that ideal fully through the agency of a state; a state is an imperfect instrument able to consider and satisfy only viable rights which have come to expression in good part because of historic exigencies, and not because they were discovered by reflection. Even if one were to have no other objective but to see what a state in the interest of fairness can and ought to do, it still is the case that this must be measured and directed by what it is men ought to achieve. It is not what they are able to formulate or contract for in a condition when the state is not in existence that is to be attended to, but the ideal existence of men together. This ideal, of course, is to be realized by starting where one now is.

What the state ought to do, in order to take us at least partly from where we now are to the ideal condition, can not be laid down in a single block or policy; the state, as only one instrument, must be adjusted to other instruments. If the state be taken as the locus of political justice, these other agencies will be the market, education, society or human interinvolvement, and a sense of commonality or peace. Each of these is a value and has some independence from the state itself; the state can promote some part of these; reciprocally, they can help promote the activity and functioning of the state as an instrument for the achievement of ideal results. Granted, then, that one can say exactly what should be done in a state in order for it to be the locus of a fairness—that is, everyone treated with impartiality—and a justice—that is, everyone being given his due—one will, if one seeks to be concrete, have to take account of other agencies as well. The hard question that then arises is whether or not one of these agencies, at least at a particular time, ought to be dominant and to dictate to the others, or whether it makes sense to allow them to function in considerable independence, with the expectation that they will adjust to one another and make it possible for them to be maximally effective together.

April 20

The orchestra of a symphony, the actors, director, playwright of an acted play, the choreographer and the various dancers in a dance, like the various contributors to the making of a film, are these all artists? They are more than craftsmen, merely making something of instrumental value. But they need not be artists. If they are not, we have the paradox that the outcome of their activity might be a work of art, and therefore that a work of art might not be produced by an artist, and yet not mechanically or through the adventitious operation of nature. All the men would be deliberately acting to produce a work of art, but no one of them would produce it. The issue can be dealt with in a number of ways:

A] One of the contributors is in fact an artist—the conductor, the choreographer, the leading dancer, the director—and the others are subordinate to him. In *Cinematics* I explored this possibility and came to the conclusion that though there is no one such individual having the others as mere assistants, there can be cinematic works of art in which one man functioned as a leader for the others. It was not clear there whether or not the leader was supposed to be an artist and the others not, or whether all of them were artists but with different roles, some of which were subordinated to others so as to attain a certain kind of result. If one of these men is supposed to be an artist, there is no reason why the others may not also be thought to be artists. One would then be left with a form of the original question, since one would still have to explain how it is possible for different artists to make a work which can not be credited to any one of them.

The various contributors could all be said to produce aesthetic objects, which is to say items that have been cut off from the rest of the world and presented for acceptance in the way they present themselves. One of them could have the responsibility for converting into a work of art the aesthetic objects that the others produce. No one of the men would be an artist; but, also, no one of them would be only a craftsman.

B] One can take the various contributors to be members of a community to which the production of the work is to be attributed.

The community is here granted a reality of its own, somewhat as we grant reality to a single organism, to a state, or to a work of art. The community might embody some overall rule or meaning which will be incarnated in the work through the efforts of the various members of a community, somewhat as a man may express himself through the use of his hands or eyes.

How would a community acquire this overall guiding unity? It might be credited with it by one or more of the members, though there seems to be no evidence of that. The unity might be brought about by the ways in which the various members function together, thereby enabling a final unity, perhaps that of Existence, to be exhibited and specialized there. The supposed community, in the present case, however, seems to come to be and pass away with the production of the work of art, and thus is hard to dinstinguish from a merely verbal reformulation of the problem. We make sense of an appeal to a community when we find ourselves able to characterize it in distinctive terms, to follow its career, to see it operate even in opposition to its members, and often in opposition or in coopera-tion with other communities.

It does make good sense, though, to speak of a symphony as being the product of an entire orchestra, of a dance as being the product of the entire dance company, and of a film as being the product of all the main contributors to it, but this is not yet to credit a community, standing in contradistinction though not entirely separate from the members of it, with being the author of the work. And it begins to sound implausible if we go on to say that the community alone produces a work of art and is therefore alone rightly to be called an artist, in good part because there seems to be no direction, no emotion, no intention, no deliberate making which can be traced to a community.

C] One of the contributors could be said to have a double role. He might be the source or backing for the governing unity, as well as for a work of art which is produced not only by the others but by himself as well. After all, a member of a pair may lead both; the Supreme Court, acting under the Constitution, can interpret (and therefore be above or apart from the Constitution) and find itself subject to it in ways which it itself alone enunciates; a magistrate might find himself guilty of a violation and subject himself to punishment. Some such view can be taken to lie behind the 'auteur' theory of the film, to the effect that the director is the main film maker. While functioning together with others he will be *the* artist because he is the source of and remains in control of the idea that is to be embodied in the work, and which enables this to be an excellent unity. As a maker of a film he will not necessarily be superior in role or function or importance to the others; but as the origin, locus, representative of the meaning of the whole and the source of the insistence that the meaning be incorporated in the work, he will stand above the others.

D] Each of the contributors could be said to express, maintain, or even insist on the unitary meaning which is to control and dictate what is to be done so that the result is a work of art. Each, since he has a different task to perform, will of course himself exemplify and interpret the unitary meaning in a distinctive way. But we have no surety that all the workers will intermesh. Despite the fact that they are being said to be dealing with the selfsame unity, they will still possibly be only an aggregate of men, in no way able to insist on a single unity, constitutive of a work of art.

E] All the different workers might acknowledge the very same overriding unity. They might follow the same score, choreography, design, and so forth. Any specialization of this which they inevitably introduce would be subordinated to the common unity and be adjusted to the specifications that the others introduce.

What is to assure their introducing subordinated specifications and adjusting themselves to one another? Must it not be that they can constitute a single body of workers on the same enterprise only so far as they in fact acknowledge the same unity, which may have been formulated by one of them, or introduced even (as is the case with a musical composition) by someone outside them all? Must not the adjustment be made in terms of the demands of that very unity to be maximally realized, that is, in the most subtle, dramatic, nuanced ways? Each of the workers will face the selfsame unity as overriding, and from his angle realize it to the fullest possible extent so far as this is consistent with the others producing a similar realization. But surely in the case of the film, and perhaps in the case of the other arts as well, some of the contributors do not know the overall unity, do not know exactly what the others contribute, and do not know how to adjust themselves to the others. One would have to have recourse to a director whose task it was to see that the overall unity was conditioning, and limiting their different tasks (and his own as well, so far as he was working with and not merely for them). Or some other worker might assume such a task—a scriptist or a montagist might take the job many now hold to be properly assigned to the director.

F] Each of the contributors represents them all, and therefore realizes the selfsame unity but in a distinctive way. Each will be an artist but engaged in producing a work of art of a special kind, illustrating the very same principles that the others do. This alternative differs from the previous one in emphasizing the selfsame unity in contradistinction to an emphasis on different specializations of it; it also allows one to speak of the different contributors as artists producing works of art which mesh together to yield the single work of art of the symphony, dance, film, and so forth. One still has not assured the concurrence of the different artists and has not shown that they work in harmony. It is possible to have a number of works of art which together do not make an artistic whole, even if they all embody the same meaning in the best possible way. Some parts of a work of art may have to be muted so that the whole can be excellent. (This alternative could perhaps be combined with C.)

G] Each of the workers can take on the responsibility of representing the whole from his angle and, therefore, produce a work of art, but in contrast with the last case, allow it to be reordered, modified, muted, subordinated, or utilized by the others. If the men work in sequence, this is a possible view; but if they work together, as they sometimes do in a symphony or a dance, functioning as an ensemble and not carrying out solos for a while, it is hard to see how they could be offering something for the others to utilize. Yet if each utilizes the others in his own way, there is no reason to suppose that the result will be a work of art.

H] In *Cinematics* it was held that there were five basic varieties of film art. In each, some one contributor had a leading role, but in such a way as to allow maximal independence to those who follow his lead. There could be a film made under the controlling meaning of a script, another under the controlling meaning maintained by the director, and so forth. Similarly, there could be a symphony where the conductor was primary; another in which the violins were, another in which the flutes were—somewhat as one might have a *Hamlet* where the primary focus was on Hamlet and another where it was on the different women in the play. Each could be a work of art with a controlling unity, but it would be a controlling unity which was concretized in a distinctive way, depending on which of the different contributors was allowed to have ascendency over the others.

*   *   *

The questions I raise and discuss in this work sometimes arise in the course of my teaching. Sometimes they develop out of the discussions I have with my younger colleagues. Almost every Friday I have lunch with Jack Boudreaux, Martin De Nys, Tony Cua (when he is here), and sometimes with John Driscoll and Dominic O'Meara. Occasionally we are joined by Father Sokolowski. The other members of the department have so far not accepted the invitation to join us.

Usually I ask the pivotal question, a question which was raised in class, or which is a narrowed, perhaps linguistic or logical specialization of one of these, or which may be the outcome of a reflection on something I had thought about on my walks or even in the course of writing. The discussion of the other day about machines and consciousness was based on what was said during one of those Friday luncheons. The discussion of film, instead, was an outcome of some questions I put to myself and my Philosophy of Art class. I there confessed an inability to provide a good resolution to the problem at that time.

Usually when I am trying to get some issue in focus, some question becomes prominent. I jot down in shorthand a number of alternative answers that occur to me, and try to think through to the proper final one. Does such an answer solve or dissolve problems? I do not think it dissolves any. If it solves them, what happens to the claim that we not only begin philosophy in wonder but that we end it in wonder, perhaps even a wonder deeper than before? The two are compatible if it be realized that the solution of a problem takes us into the universe on a deeper level, where the problem appears again.

The answer originally provided is adequate to the original formulation, but not adequate to the problem found on a deeper level. How do these problems differ? If they differed merely in the greater intensive, objective content which is encountered on the deeper level, the original solution would seem to be adequate, and the wonder would be directed only at the fact that it was being sustained on a level more concrete or intensive than that at which it had originally been framed or encountered. Instead, it seems that we must say that the problem and the solution, available initially, are altered in being embodied on a deeper level. There will be new factors introduced; the problem will have new facets, factors, angles that had not been present before. A solution of the problem of how one could have a single work of art produced by an orchestra will not entirely answer the question of how a single work of art can be produced by a company of dancers; a solution of the general problem of how a number of men can produce a work of art which requires the independent but conditioned functioning of others will not be adequate to either of the previous specific cases. The solution of the general problem still leaves over how, in the case of the dancers, for example, the choreographer, or the soloist, or the duet could have ascendancy over others who also contribute to the making of the single work of art.

There is no reason why a multitude of problems may not be solved, and even why some of them might not have to be dissolved as without intelligibility or importance. The thesis that one ends with a greater wonder than one had when one began pertains only to metaphysical issues.

Wonder is a primal emotion directed at what is ultimate. The wonder is increased because one returns to the position from which one had started out: A] with the accumulation acquired in the course of a movement from that starting point to its return, and B] confronting the very reality which had provided the occasion but was not the object of the initial wonder. If the initial wonder was directed at the presence of attenuated forms of a finality, the wonder one returns with is directed at the actualities which make it possible for the finality to be diversely exhibited. From such a base one can engage in still another wonder which is directed at the finality as a reality which is both by itself and is involved with actualities. The terminating in actualities or a finality with the emotion of wonder always leaves depths which we penetrate toward and never fully encompass. What is left over are greater intensities than those at which one terminates. The 'new' wonder will not be different in kind but will terminate beyond the point where it had terminated before. There will always be an inexaustible object of wonder; but the kind of wonder which will be exhibited will be directed either at actualities or finalities in their depths, after one had passed beyond the wonder directed at the evidences of these.

April 21

Collaboration can occur with men working concordantly or sequentially. When they work sequentially, the results achieved and, therefore, the way in which some overall principle and meaning was incorporated, can serve as a guide for subsequent activity. The precedent could be produced with some awareness of the role that the successors will have, and therefore it may be other than it would have been had it been made without regard for the role the work has for the successors. But each will be an artist just so far as he produces something excellent without regard for what the others might do with it. There is no need to neglect the fact that the others do have a role. When that is taken to account there is not much difference between a sequential and a concordant collaboration. The sequential is one-directional and the concordant is reciprocal, but in its one-directionality the sequential can be in accord with the concordant.

In an ensemble, in an orchestra, and when performer and director are interplaying there is a concordant collaboration. The most conspicuous case of such a concordant collaboration is in acting on the stage, for an actor properly understands his role when he deals with it not only from his own position but as that which is being faced and dealt with from other positions as well. He is somewhat like a man who knows himself as a me from the assumed position of another you, without abrogating the fact that he is also an I.

An actor's concordant activity involves two stages: A] it allows for the positions of the others as constitutive of the role that he is then filling out, and B] it accepts his own position as being constituted by the others. Each stage is schematic, general, with a position that is to be filled out in a specific way by some other actor. The actual performance of a play involves the concretization of a role which is modified by the way in which it is allowed for by other roles, and is carried out so as to allow for them.

A concordant collaboration can evidently be achieved by actors. Each can engage in his own role excellently, not simply as it is marked out in a play, but as the locus of a schema inseparable from other roles. At the same time it will have a primary value which the actor carries out. Even if instrumental to the carrying out of the roles of the others, he will remain within the orbit of his own role. The fact that his role is partly defined by the others, and that what he is to do is in terms of what his role means from the position of others does not hobble his freedom. Nor does the fact that he acts in such a way as to provide a schema for the others which those others sustain mean that he is functioning just as a means for those others.

What is true of concordant cooperation is also true of the sequential. Each can provide a schema for the rest to begin with. But the initial workers, say the scriptist and the performers, in contrast with the montagist, not only provide very slight indications of what the montagist is from their angles but are not provided for by the montagist when that scriptist and those performers actually engage in their work. A good montagist, nevertheless, will make allowance for them. His subsequent efforts will utilize their achievements in such a way as to make them in fact provide schema for the work he does. As a consequence, he will provide the kind of schematic role for himself that they would have provided had they been artists concordant with him. If this is done the collaborators can all function as artists, each producing an excellent, self-sufficient work. What is used later will incorporate within itself the import that the earlier has for what is to follow after.

A member of an orchestra usually carries out both types of collaboration, with an addition. He collaborates concordantly with others then performing, and he collaborates sequentially both with reference to those who had performed earlier and with reference to those who will perform subsequently. The notes he now plays are notes which allow for the playing of those (or related) notes at the same time, but in such a way as to take account of what had been played and what is still to be played. Each member of the orchestra presumably knows the entire score and, therefore, what is before and after what he himself is to do. He also knows something of what other players—even of instruments he has not mastered—are to do and therefore of the conditions they will mutually impose on general conditions to be filled out by each in a distinctive way.

A system of checks and balances which is sometimes said to characterize the United States government, with its independently functioning and yet mutually referential Congress, President, and Supreme Court, is one in which no account need be taken of the other roles, and all effort is directed to the carrying out of one's own in the light of what the others had done and might be expected to do. It is system of adjustments, not designed to produce something excellent, as a collaborative artistic enterprise is, but something effective, peaceful, useful. Each factor gives up something of its own objective or claims in order to avoid conflict with the others. It does not provide a schema within which the others are to operate and which qualify the controlling unities that those others will concretize, but it does react to actual or expected actions on the part of those others.

It is questionable whether a system of checks and balances is the system under which the United States operates. The idea smacks too much of the free market concept also entertained by its defenders—pragmatic, roughhewn, without ideals or objective but that of having different parts function in independence of one another, and accepting the outcome of their effect on one another as the only fair or proper result.

The United States Constitution lays down the different roles that the different branches are to play, and each not only assumes the roles that are then assigned but is aware of the roles that the others are carrying out as well. Legislation is passed with an eye on past and future legal decisions and the President's possible veto; the President knows that he must contend with Congress and makes his judgments in the light of what he expects the Court will do; the justices have been appointed by a President who, though he may no longer be in office or may be defied by them, still has an affect on them as maintaining some principle which they presumably are to exemplify. The justices, too, for the most part, try to accommodate the intentions of Congress, consistently with what they understand previous legislation, its certification in previous decisions, and its sanction in the Constitution to be. More important, each branch understands itself not only to be covered by some provisions in the Constitution but to be exemplifying that Constitution in a limited area. As such, the branches are concordant and sometimes sequential collaborators, each carrying out its role while constituting a schema for the others.

The United States Constitution can be said to be expressed by all three branches, each having its distinctive, defined role, which is to be understood as grounding a schema for the other roles, themselves realizing conditions which the schema qualifies. The three branches, so far, are like collaborative artists. Still, they are not artists; they are not concerned with the production of an excellent work of art. Instead, they are more like interdependent workers, each occupied with making the Constitution effective in a society over which the state is imposed.

A state is inseparable from a government and therefore from officials who have specific tasks to perform, all carrying out more or less well-defined structures, demands, routines. A state by itself is the officials and their decrees and acts as imposed on all the others as well as on themselves. A society has no such fixed structure; it is a domain of lived interinvolvement, of adjustments, of checks and balances, limited by tradition and the prevailing myths. There can be a nation without a state, since it requires only a sense of identity amongst the members of the society, promoted perhaps by the sharing of a controlling language, tradition, and myths which a society might minimize or let slip away. But the existence of a state promotes the achievement of a nation, since the state has a structure and power, and imposes sanctions authoritatively expressed and insistently maintained. It makes the society be a nation, at the same time that it transcends the limits of a nation; it is able to take over nations and societies by conquest, and can allow for the presence within it and protect the rights of slaves, aliens, children, and visitors. It may have a duration which is shorter, equal to, or longer than that of a nation or a society; but it can not be entirely cut off from a society without being reduced to a set of formal principles without efficacy, or being arbitrarily imposed on a people who are so far only hostages or subjects, and not citizens.

A state is a legal entity, a society is an historic unit; a nation ideally is the two together. The legal dimension of a nation may be muted and subordinated to and perhaps even distinguished by the historic dimension. Both society and nation may be modified by the intrusion of factors which function in some independence of them—the formalistic dimensions of the language, history, and so forth.

I return to the question formulated yesterday, which raised the issue as to whether or not a work of art could be produced by a group, and if so, how one could then speak of a work of art as being made by an artist or artists. The account of collaboration with the assumption of roles, and the constitution of schemas which play a part in defining the roles that others will assume, shows that there can be a number of distinct artists each carrying out the same overall idea, both in the guise of particular roles and in the guise of those roles as projecting toward and not being subjected to and separable from the schema. The carrying out of the roles are ways of epitomizing the overall idea; the having of those roles together with the schema imposed on them and which they impose on others, are ways of expressing the meaning of the overall idea that the final work exhibits. A work which has only the first will have excellent parts that somehow fail to give full value to the entire work; one which has only the second will limit the freedom of the different collaborators too much. The ideal is where each has maximal independence but is occupied with giving maximal value to the entire work and, therefore, with subordinating what is independently achieved.

In architecture, and sometimes in sculpture, we have many workers. In these cases there is an artist and various craftsmen who carry out his intention. There is an asymmetrical assumption of a role by the artist; he provides a schema which defines the work of craftsmen, and does not, except so far as he deliberately accepts it as part of his own enterprise, attend to what they do. Though there are some who speak of musical performers as having this role with respect to musical composers, it seems quite clear that both can be artists, engaged in different arts.

Could one take musical performers to be sequentially collaborative with a musical composer? There surely can be compositions made with such an idea in mind, but it is not necessary in order to have a fine composition for a performance to occur. Nor need a performance provide a schema for a composition, or a composer attend to any such schema when producing a composition. The most that could be argued for is that a composer writes for a possible performance and therefore provides a general schema overlaying the specifically defined roles that the performers carry out. Such an idea is to be distinguished from a closely related one to the effect that performers take as part of their roles the positions assigned in a composition; in the latter case, there need be no projection from composer to performer, but only an adoption by the performer of what he takes the composition to be.

Might this not be what is done in the making of a film? Might not a montagist just assume the work of a performer or a scriptist or a cameraman, or all of them together, as a condition? If so, we approach the positions that film encompasses a plurality of arts, just

as music does—musical composition and musical performance
(Nine Basic Arts)—each occupied with the production of a distinctive work.

No one would deny that Beethoven was a great artist. That
judgment is made on the basis of his compositions, not on the basis
of any playing by him. Yet music is surely what is heard. The fact
that a musical performance follows a score does not invalidate its
independent status as an art. Similarly, a great montagist, like a
great violinist, could take his start with the artistic achievement of
another artist engaged in doing something else—performing before a camera, writing a script, filming, and even directing.

Could the idea of concordant cooperation be introduced into
the problem of the way in which the finalities by themselves, or
together with the actualities, might be a unified Many? Since the
finalities are independent, and are not concerned with the realization of anything beyond themselves, the first of these alternatives
would not be pertinent. But if we consider the finalities and the
actualities as providing conditions for each other, it is plausible to
suppose that each provides a schema for the other which that other
fills out in the course of its career. But it is also true that actualities
and finalities are not engaged in carrying out some role; they are
just actualities and finalities. Nor do they affect one another or
make use of one another for the sake of achieving some desirable
end, particularly beauty. There is an ideal which is pertinent to
them all, but it is not entertained or pursued by them with regard
for what is done by the other.

April 22

Dying is a lifelong habit.

Preshrunk: One who is about to consult a psychiatrist.

When in doubt, a politician evades, a logician distinguishes, an
impulsive man acts, and a fat man eats.

One thing seems never to die: man's belief in immortality.

I know that I am an unduplicable individual in a world with
others. Conceivably there might be worlds exactly like this in which
I and everything else are completely replicated, with nothing left
out and nothing added. Such worlds would be disjunct from ours;

their members could not be encountered in ours. They would not be together with me in a single totality.

I know that I am an individual because whatever I terminate in, perceptually or conceptually, is a limit toward which I have thrust myself. I am at the center of that world. Were this all, the result would, of course, be solipsism, for there would be nothing else which was faced as individual in contradistinction from and independently of me.

I know that there are other individuals for I do not simply stop at the limits of myself. I penetrate beyond those limits toward other centers which possess the limits from their side and thereby enable me not only to terminate at the limits but to face the others as being present to me.

I do not arrive at other centers; I never find anyone as irreducible as myself. But I do reach beyond the limits of my percepts and thoughts to what holds on to and presents the limits at which I terminate. I must learn, over the course of time, through the use of other penetrations, reflection, and the discovery of how little I know of myself when I approach myself from the outside through something at those limits—my body, possessions, and so forth—that others learn truths of me as I do, by moving beyond the limits at which my attention ends. Later I may approach myself and others from the vantage point of a single primary Being. I will then be aware that we are coordinate individuals on a footing as realities, though not necessarily as agents, thinkers, or workers. To know myself I approach myself from the position of other individuals and therefore come to myself via what I am for them.

Individuals are the outcomes of solidifications and intensifications of at least one of the distinctive qualifications they suffer because of the finalities. The finalities must be credited with a power for fecund proliferation. We can make no sense of this except so far as the outcome is distinguished from the finalities themselves.

Difference is the border line between an individual and the finalities. It is the diversification of the finalities as maintained apart from them; equally, it is an individual at his most attenuated, subject to and possessed by the finalities. An individual is one who has turned a qualification, due to a finality, into an intensive instantiating center which stands away from all else and radiates outward endlessly, without letting go of what it expresses. What it expresses, nevertheless, is maintained apart from it. Each finality accommodates all the actualities to make them into a single fixated unity together. The objective difference that the individuals permit is thus matched by the objective unity of actualities which the finalities provide.

This is not yet exactly right. Another try:

A] Self-expression is a self-diversification, the exfoliation of an undifferentiated unit into a plurality.

B] Without any support, self-diversification is simply a set of fulgurations which vanish as they appear.

C] Expressions are distinct only as maintained against their source by distinct powers.

D] Expressions of a finality terminate as distinct differences because they are maintained apart from their source.

E] Differences are not individuals but expressions of finalities, held in contradistinction to those finalities. Their acknowledgment presupposes agencies which can maintain them. Those agencies are not knowable from the standpoint of the differences; the agencies are nevertheless inferable since they convert a diversity of expressions into a set of sheer differences.

F] A plurality of expressions of a particular actuality and the expressions of different actualities are maintained apart from the actualities—see A–C.

G] A plurality of expressions of actualities terminates in a plurality of distinguishable nuances maintained together apart from the actualities.

H] Distinguishable nuances are not the finalities, but expressions of actualities held in contradistinction to those actualities. They presuppose agencies which can keep them together. Those agencies are not knowable from the standpoint of the actualities.

I] There is no stop with just differences or nuances. Ontologically and epistemically, there is a thrust beyond them into what is not known from the original position.

J] What comes to expression in the guise of externally maintained differences is accepted by actualities as content for individuation by intensification. That which individuates is what had maintained a difference apart from the finalities.

K] What comes to expression, in the guise of externally maintained nuances together, is accepted by finalities as content for solidification. That which solidifies is what maintained the nuances apart from the actualities which are their source.

L] Individuation begins with differences which owe their origin to the finalities' expressiveness.

M] Solidification begins with a set of nuances which owe their origin to the expressiveness of actualities.

N] Individuation begins with differences approached from a side opposite to that from which the differences originate.

O] Solidification begins with a nuanced whole approached from a side opposite to that from which the nuances originate.

P] An intensification of differences occurs beyond the control of the source of those differences; a solidification of nuances occurs beyond the control of the source of those nuances.

Q] The accounts from the side of actualities and from the side of finalities are reciprocals.

R] The finalities solidify the nuances, and in that act of solidification make them less and less distinguishable.

Individuals are thus accounted for by starting with finalities, as fecund, expressive, self-diversifying realities; the expressions must be sustained apart from those finalities. The sustaining is by actualities which add intensifications to what they sustain. Reciprocally, the concreteness of finalities is accounted for by starting with actualities as fecund, expressive, self-attenuating realities, and recognizing that the expressions must be sustained apart from those actualities. The sustaining is by finalities which bring the sustained expressions of the actualities closer and closer together in solidified unities.

It is not customary to suppose that there is a dual problem raised when one begins to look for an explanation of individuals and individuation. Normally, it is taken for granted that the finalities (or as is usually supposed, one finality, God, or the Absolute, or Nature) are self-explanatory, or beyond explanation with no content originating elsewhere. (Whitehead is an exception here, for he does try to account for God's consequent nature as being the outcome of content derived from the world of actual occasions; but Whitehead also supposes that his God is an actual occasion, merely contrasting with the rest, and not a radically distinct kind of reality.) But one could just as well, as nominalists must and do, take individuals to be self-explanatory or beyond explanation. The two positions are the outcome of the same supposition—some kind of entity is taken for granted and no explanation for it is given, in part perhaps because it is feared that it will then not be acknowledged to be irreducibly real. But an explanation is not a deduction, a derivation of what is being explained; instead, it approaches the explained from a position outside, and attempts to show how a basic truth can be dissected and some of its components traced back to other sources.

Individuation comes to be an outstanding problem because language, ideas, principles, and science are all occupied with universals, while we know that we ourselves are irreducible and unduplicable. If finalities had no commerce with the world of actualities, and were just presupposed by them, we would have to accept them as inexplicables. They would be arrived at last in knowledge but would be first in reality, to be accepted as prior to all accounts and the source of all explanations. But without denying that finalities have a content of their own (any more than it is denied in providing an explanation of individuation that actualities are individuals in themselves), one can give an account of that content by understanding it to be the outcome of a solidification of the expressions of all of the actualities.

Individuals are accounted for as the outcome of self-individuations which begin with given differences. Similarly, concrete universally pertinent finalities are accounted for as the outcome of self-solidifications which begin with given nuances. But the differences and the nuances themselves can be traced back, the one to expressive finalities, the other to expressive actualities. In tracing back the differences, one progressively loses their diversity; in tracing back the nuances, one progressively loses their union. The loss in the diversity is one with the attainment of a primal unity; the loss of the union is one with the having of a plurality of actualities. Since we can get to the unity only through its aid, the unity must have power and content of its own. And since we can get back to an actuality only through its aid, too, it must have a status apart from other actualities and all the finalities.

The finalities are other than one another. They can not properly be said to be individuals, lacking as they do a power to preserve differences by merely introducing intensifications into them. Nor can they properly be said to be universals, lacking as they do a power to multiply themselves. (To say this is to go counter to the attempt in *Beyond All Appearances* to differentiate the finalities in terms of the ways in which they combine individuality and universality.) They can not be differentiated from the standpoint of actualities except as providing different ways in which the expressions of those actualities are solidified. If we are not to take the finalities as merely givens, or as merely the termini of the use of evidences found to have been intruded on actualities, we must explain their difference from one another by attending to the ways in which they can be said to take account of what the actualities express.

There always are finalities and actualities. Each provides a One for the other as constituting a Many. The many finalities have many Ones in the form of the loci of their diverse expressions. Each locus is converted from a 'One of' the finalities into a 'One for' them by an actuality in its full concreteness, and thus as at least a substance. The many actualities have many Ones in the form of the loci of their diverse expressions. Each locus is converted from a 'One of' those actualities into a 'One for' them by irreducible, insistent final realities. Actualities function as many different Ones for the finalities because they are, at least, so many different substances. Finalities function as many different Ones for the actualities because they are so many different kinds of irreducible, fixed realities.

All actualities are substances, to be accounted for as the outcome of intensifications which go beyond the localization of the expressions of the different finalities. The finalities are different basic types of unity and are to be accounted for as self-determining unifications of the multiple expressions of the actualities.

Both actualities and finalities are affected in persistent and in transient ways. The finalities affect actualities always in the same way; but actualities come and go and affect one another differently at different times. An actuality's intensifications yield a constant result, enabling the actuality to be selfsame over the course of its career. A finality's is diversely affected by actualities; each actuality provides it with a different nuance, and at different times provides it with different nuances. At the same time, the finalities are affected by one another in constant ways.

Finalities do not directly receive the expressions of actualities. Those expressions are first part of a single Context. That Context, to be sure, is an attenuation of the finalities; it is only as nuanced that it is different from moment to moment.

This account is accurate, I think, when it deals with the actualities. But I think there is something strained, obscure, and perhaps missing in what is said of the finalities. This may be due to a straining to make the account of the finalities be correlative with that of the actualities; it may be due, too, to a lack of familiarity with the finalities, or to the fact that most of our language and thought is directed toward actualities.

April 23

Yesterday I did not keep in mind a number of distinctions that I had made earlier. As a consequence, I mistakenly spoke as though individuation had its correlative in a nuanced Context solidified in a finality. But such a Context has to do with the encompassment of a plurality of exhibitions of actualities together, and not with the affects which actualities have on finalities.

Finalities affect actualities severally and together. The problem of individuation has to do with the first type of affect. Does the correlative problem—unnamed as yet—have to do with the affects of actualities, severally or together, on finalities? I now think, both. Actualities in their severalty affect the finalities, but the finalities as all-encompassing make those affects be together, though not necessarily in the best possible way. Each finality reorganizes the affects, dividing and realigning them so that they are maximized together and, as such, are assimilable within the finality.

How does the assimilation take place? What is achieved by it? Is it similar in all the finalities, or does each finality bring about an incomparable result?

Actualities affect Substance by introducing oppositional positions into it; Being by independent positions; Possibility by distinctive positions; Existence by self-maintaining positions; and Unity by assertive ones. In order to be self-sufficient, a finality converts all the positions either into an affiliated, coordinated, rationalized, extensively connected, or evaluated totality. Self-sufficiency is achieved by each of the finalities by its subjugating the different positions, which have been intruded on to it, to make them into single harmonies. The limit of the conversion, the attainment of perfect harmony, is one with the reassessment of the positions so as to make them into the very being of the finalities. The finalities make themselves be self-sufficient by absorbing the positions into powers of affiliation, coordination, rationality, connection, and evaluation within which the initial positions are at best abstractions which are dispersed and set in contrast with one another.

Individuality and self-sufficiency are to be explained in similar ways. In each case we look to another type of reality for the material which is to be internalized. In neither case does a deduction of the result occur; nor is there any precipitation of individuals or self-sufficient finalities from the other. From the very start there are individuals and self-sufficient finalities. But each can be explained by acknowledging the other type of reality as being the source of differences of positions. The differences are intensively internalized by the actualities. The positions (demarcations or boundaries) are harmonized by the finalities in acts of intensive internalization.

April 24

A machine could be made which   A] rejected anything or some things that it had accepted before,   B] marked it with the date on which it had been accepted, and   C] marked it with the date on which it had been rejected. Would it have a memory? I think not. There would still be no reference to itself. That reference would be lacking even if the machine recorded with each rejection, "I had encountered this before." Nor would the fact that it had put aside what it had recorded and then was able to make use of it later show that it had a memory. A 'memory bank' is a reservoir, and the utilization of its content is but a later use of it. But what is remembered need not be used.

If an animal were to reject and then do so with the irritation, annoyance, or fear, which normally accompany this in men, and were these even to be like those that had previously been present with the acceptance of the rejected items, there would still be no memory involved, but only a repetition of behavior on the occasion of a similar experience. Indeed, it would be less than what our supposed machine was doing, for the machine is rejecting what it had before accepted, perhaps with different accompanying activity. We could say that the animal had learned from experience, that its behavior had been modified, that what it had undergone makes a difference to what it does, but there would not yet be a reference to an I or self which was engaged in an act of acknowledgment that precluded the same kind of acknowledgment of something else.

Memory does not even require that one confront something external which is then rejected. It has to do with something now before the consciousness or mind which is denied the role that something present has, and is referred to another time in which it could have been present.

Can an autistic child do this? A congenital idiot? A hopelessly senile man? Apparently not. Why then do we take them to be human? Is it merely that they look like other humans? Is it that the difference between them and the others is apparently only a matter of degree? Is it that we can discern dimensions in them which are peculiar to man? Is it that in some cases we have been able to bring them to the stage where they are unmistakably like the rest of us in functioning, understanding, discourse, and the like?

Our acknowledgment of them as human is too immediate, too ungrounded in experience, reflection, or knowledge, to make it possible to account for their acceptance as humans in these suggested ways. We sympathize, we are emotionally disturbed, we are responsive to their inadvertent movements of eyes, hands, body as the kind of movements the rest of us make. Those we have not been able to reach in these ways, we still continue to respond to, apparently in response to very slight clues and penetrations into them.

The Nazis were able to look at, speak to, and attend to other humans whom they nevertheless proceeded to kill as vermin, beasts, subhumans. Did they recognize them to be humans? Did they then go on to suppress their flickering grasp of the condemned individuals, under the pressure of more conspicuous insistent principles, conditions, and commands? If so, might it not be the case that we are in the same position with respect to animals, and even machines? Might they not have memories, and thus not only entertain images and ideas, but take these to be excluded from presence in the world now encountered, and identify them as having had such presence before? The supposition is to be dismissed as idle, because we have no evidence that they have selves. Though we may not be able to tell in the case of some humans whether or not they are self-aware, at least to the degree of being able to acknowledge something as having been encountered by a self before, we think we have other indices or even a direct grasp of the fact that each has a self.

Memory requires that something be now before the mind which is being excluded by something having an objective, independent status. The object of memory is not simply denied that independent status, but is taken to be excluded by what has such a status, and to be sufficiently determinate (perhaps only because of its reference to an act of the selfsame self) to require it to be referred to the past and not to the future, or identified as a mere fantasy. We do, of course, imagine events which never happened; we confuse what we fantasy with what is remembered. Evidently in this case the fantasy is determinate enough, or the remembered is indeterminate enough to make possible the inability to tell one from the other. Is it not the case, then, that it is the exclusion of the referential act by something objective that is at the heart of the act of remembering? If so, in the act of remembering there are two acts of the self, in one of which we have an 'intentional' object which finds rootage in what is now external, and in the other of which we have an 'intentional' object for which no rootage is now provided.

When we dream, we are not usually aware of the fact that there is an I which is engaged in the act of dreaming. When we remember that we had dreamed, we are aware of the fact that there is an act of the self now being excluded. But, instead of, as in the case of ordinary memory, claiming that one of the acts terminates in an intentional object which had a rootage in something external to us, in remembering our dream we acknowledge it to be an 'intentional' object which had not been externally sustained. Even if we subsequently find that the dream had an objective cause, such as smoke or fire or a crying child, we identify the dream as content for the mind which is not only now excluded from an external status but for which no external status is claimed.

Evidently in what is remembered we are not only aware of an intentional object which can not get a footing in the present, but as that which had such a footing before. The remembered, then, must have a texture marking the fact that it had been part of an external world, just as now, when we confront anything, we are aware of it as having a side which is being maintained against us and gives status to the object we have in mind.

The object of memory is tinged in a twofold way. It is the terminus of an act of the self which is now acknowledged to be other than the act of the self involved in a direct confrontation with something in experience; and it has a texture which marks the fact that it had been part of an objective occurrence. In the present moment of perception, we should say, therefore, that we not only face or experience something, but that this is doubly oriented—toward ourselves as engaged in a specific act of perceiving, and toward an object which is maintaining that experienced content apart from us.

In *Beyond All Appearances* I remarked on the fact that when we perceive we impose boundaries on what is confronted, and that we are aware of the fact that the content is being held away from us in defiance of those boundaries. The boundaries are the outcome of an act in which the self engages. The remembered, too, is confronted as that which had been bounded by us, and as that which is independent of those boundaries; but it is not now withdrawn from them, as are the objects of present perception.

It is possible to remember with our eyes closed, concentrating on what had been before. We seem here not to be excluding the remembered but, instead, to be excluding a present experience. But in that concentration we are aware of ourselves being engaged in an effort directed at the object of a previous encounter. We know we are now concentrating, trying to remember. (If we are trying to merely recollect, we would have already attended to something remembered, which was lacking details that we are now trying to remember so as to add to the remembered item.)

Each of us can know that he is remembering, and can remember that he has remembered. This claim will not be accepted by radical behaviorists, by positivists, by any who demand publicly available evidence for anything acknowledged to occur in private. These men deny that one can confirm what one is claiming to remember, and in any case that there is any evidence, which another can use, to substantiate the supposed fact of memory and other intentional acts.

I can check my memory claims by attending to historical evidence, that is, to evidence of what had been, of my presence there, and the way my conclusions cohere with what is now known. Another may not know that I am remembering or just what it is that I am remembering, but he can know that I can remember if he can know that I have a self and what this can do. And that knowledge he can acquire by knowing, through a sympathetic encounter, that I am human, and by a speculative reflection on what it is that a man is and can do.

There is no logical deduction of the nature of man that is needed here; the question is not what is conceivable, but what coheres with what else we know. We can not rest with the rough reports of common sense without accepting error and superstition and confusion mixed together with truth and reliable reports. But we can not abandon common sense either; if we did we would not be able to distinguish philosophy from fiction or even from fantasy. Philosophy holds to as much of the commonsense world as it can. It subjects everything to critical examination. The doubts it raises and the questions it asks are not merely concerned with what is logically possible. The doubts and questions, which the accepted data itself elicit, are undergirded by a wonder that goes beyond the data and leads to the formulation of accounts serving to articulate what is there encountered. The articulation, if it keeps close to the encountered, is not altogether irrelevant to the data with which one began and which is accepted in the course of the wonder. Wonder, and other deep philosophically pertinent emotions, are not detached from an experience with the world.

A philosophic account which goes counter to long entrenched commonsense views need not be without other types of support. If its speculative results cohere with and make intelligible the termini of deep emotions which had been elicited and partly satisfied by the arts and in religion, a warrant is provided for rejecting the commonsense contentions. There are some who would go further. They allow for the dismissal of all that is commonsensically contended, on behalf of what is discerned or what is claimed to be discerned in what is eternal. But such dismissal makes one give up the very occasion for the supposed advance into what is ultimate, and thereby the warrant for the starting point. It could be argued, of course, that as one goes on one comes to see the defects in one's starting point. But then it must also be granted that the method of attaining to the final result is tainted, since it is not altogether separable from the starting point. If the final position alone is allowed, it becomes difficult to see how, granting that reality, anything else could have appeared.

Philosophy tries to accommodate two distinctive kinds of articulation: a generalized, rectified version of common sense, where the more obvious errors, confusions, and superstitions are eliminated, and a speculative, systematic formulation of what is arrived at from the former as well as by means of the basic emotions that are elicited in the course of an experience with particular art objects and religion.

Since this allows one to deal with only two finalities, Existence and Unity, it requires supplementation by references to other finalities reached, not only by starting from these two, but directly by the use of evidence available in daily experience, and through the carrying out of emotions which terminate in what affiliates, coordinates, and structures. Suggestions pertinent to these last are offered in *Beyond All Appearances* in the chapter on the Assessment of Men, but it is not altogether clear that emotions terminating in these other finalities are elicited in these ways. Is there, for example, a distinctive kind of emotion awakened when dealing with logical and mathematical matters, which continue to operate after the engagement in the logic and mathematics is over, and which terminate in the finality, Possibility? Or does one terminate in this, as well as in Substance and Being, in other than emotional ways? A negative answer to these questions would lead one to attend first to the finalities, Existence and Unity, and on the basis of these, and along the lines followed in *Modes of Being,* derive accounts of the other three finalities. Were this the only way to proceed, one would be left with the perplexity as to why, if all the finalities are equally ultimate, and all are equally involved with actualities, it is not possible to arrive at all of them with the same directness and effectiveness. That perplexity would not affect the fact that one could nevertheless come to know and articulate the natures of the three finalities. What one would lose would be a direct encounter with them which was coordinate with the encounters one in fact has in art and religion with the finalities, Existence and Unity, respectively. A derivative knowledge of the other finalities would, though, provide a check against a retreat into fantasy when one had come to the point where some commonsense views had to be abandoned. In the course of its own development philosophy finds itself forced to face issues and work out solutions, some of which are either irrelevant to or go counter to commonsense attitudes, acceptances, and beliefs. If it can find its articulations about what is finally the case to be sustained by what is directly encountered, or what can be inferred from what is directly encountered, it has a means for remaining in touch with reality, particularly if it then goes on to see how the result can help explain the initial commonsense data and what underlies and is presupposed by this.

April 25

Last night Jack Boudreaux's paper on sortal terms and individuals was the topic of discussion in our bimonthly Thursday evening meeting. In part, as a consequence of what was said there by others and myself, and in part, because of my reflections on the discussion today, I can see that there are at least seven distinct characterizations of 'this' that are worthwhile making.

1] 'This' is a universal. It is evidently so as a term in language, evidently so as referring to the object of any one of a number of concepts, and evidently so as emphasizing a common dimension of diverse objects. The universality of the 'this' was recognized by Hegel and put to special uses by him in the *Phenomenology.* The fact that there are other, at least equally basic senses in which the term is used, shows that there is no need to follow his lead. Even if 'this' were taken to be only universal, and then in his sense as expressing less than what one means, and thus to be just an 'abstract' universal, it does not follow that what was not said is what completes and eventually concretizes the abstract 'this'.

2] 'This' is a designator. That sense is dominant in logic and linguistics. Though it does not of itself point out anything, such a 'this' is the verbal accompaniment of a pointing out. An actual pointing out requires gestures and sometimes an actual laying hold of something. But when we gesture and lay hold it is not yet made clear just what the object is that is being designated. Is it the whole or only a part of that which one has in hand or is pointing toward?

A designator is vague. It is not general, for it is not directing one to something which is to be specified further, but to something whose borders are not clearly determined. Normally, though, our interests, practices, conventions enable us to be quite accurate in ascertaining what it is that someone is designating when he uses 'this', or its cognates.

3] 'This' is an incomplete symbol. It is part of the single complex 'this-x', where the 'x' refers to a kind of thing. This is what I took it to be in *Reality;* it seems to be the position which Boudreaux is taking now, but for different reasons. He holds that we could not find the object of a 'this' except under the guidance of a sortal term, that is, a universal which allows for countable instances. If one takes his position, it appears that though the 'this' and the 'x' are linked, the 'this' will proceed in advance of the 'x', after the 'x' has preceded it in marking out the area in which the 'this' will operate. One is then prompted to distinguish three cases: A] where the 'x' precedes the 'this' to which it is linked,   B] where the 'this' precedes the 'x' to which it is linked, and   C] where the two are on a level, constituting a single name. Case A is Boudreaux's primary sense of 'this'; he does not allow its use except as guided by a concept or universal. Case B is the case where we recognize that the 'this' marks out a value of a variable, an item to which a predicate is to be ascribed. This seems to be what is intended by the authors of *Principia Mathematica*. Case C is the case I emphasized in *Reality* and have attended to again on subsequent occasions. The 'this-x' is an adherent name. Judgment separates the components and attempts to unite them to yield a unity which matches what is objective. Not altogether separable from some of the other cases, one has to determine whether or not the 'this-x' stops with the surface of the object, is intended to envelop it entirely, or is supposed to have some penetrative value and thus to have a depth to it. If these cases are distinguished from one another we have a number of other subordinate cases to consider.

4] 'This' refers to the object as absenting itself, escaping from the boundaries we are instituting when we focus on something. The 'this' here thrusts beyond the bounded content to attend to what is capable of escaping our epistemic conditions. It takes us away from discourse and reference to make one attend to what is substantial. One makes use of such a 'this' when one is expectative, acknowledging a source of predicates or expressions or occasions for the use of the 'this' in other senses.

5] 'This' reaches to and continues to maintain a hold on the retreating object. It is penetrative, with an intensive depth. One here does not simply acknowledge a source of predicates but shares in it to some extent, gives oneself to it, stands on its side, but not in entire detachment from oneself as making use of the 'this'.

6] Father R. Sokolowski remarked on the fact that we sometimes use 'this' without any concept or predicate (see 3), particularly when we face something important, overwhelming, which makes itself conspicuous. I think this is a special case of the next sense of 'this'.

7] 'This' acknowledges the presence of something, of what is insisting on itself, which is 'this-ifying' itself. The absenting object does not merely possess the content that I bound for my own use; it does not merely provide a texture for what I distinguish; it insists on itself, thrusts itself forward, possesses the content, not in the sense of retreating from the boundaries I impose but in the sense of bursting them, forcing me to attend to the content as it in fact functions as present to me in a world of other objects which insistently affect it while it insistently affects them. Here, more evidently than in any of the other cases, 'this' is a term of certification, or of submission.

Where 'this' is a designator, we moved out toward the object. Here the initial position is with a concept for which one seeks a grounding in a particular value. But when 'this' is a certification, the reverse movement is to the fore; the object is insistent and we are receptive. The 'this' now serves to mark the fact that there is something which has an integrity, power, independence, which is obtruding itself, making us pay attention to it. This making us pay attention is most evident when we come to the important and overwhelming, but it is characteristic of every object we confront.

The very same content which is being presented to us is what we bound and which at the same time is kept apart from us by a possessing absenting object, defying our control. The object that presents the content is the very object which absents it; in the one way the content is distinguished by the object from itself, while in the other the content is held on to and away from our attempt to deal with it apart from the object.

Do all types of object present themselves in the same way and to the same degree? It seems to be the case that when we perceive we confront equally insistent objects. We are not forced to attend primarily to men or animals; there is no compelling of attention to these. But we do not always just perceive; when we perceive we note, sympathize, feel, are emotionally involved, become attentive, watchful, alert, practical, concerned, indifferent, and so on. When we speak to a man we do not simply perceive him or just await a reply from him; we find him coming out toward us, making his presence known. He makes us alert to him, insists on himself, makes himself a primary 'this'. He makes himself stand out as a man by his look, attitude, attention, movements, often directed toward us. A thing is present *ipso facto,* but a man is present, in addition, as one who is making a claim to be heard, with rights, truths, demands, and a self which I am forced to note.

As has been remarked, we may not be able to make contact with some presumably human beings—the hopeless idiot, the senile, and the autistic, but we can sometimes note a flicker now and then which allows us to discern the distinctively human side of these. And where we do not, we make use of a principle of continuity, taking the senile to be a continuant of a state when he was evidently human, the idiot to be toward the limit of a continuum of grades of men, and the autistic to be merely incapable of making his desires and intentions manifest, but showing other characteristics that only humans possess. The Nazis did not recognize the humanity of these. They also did not grant the humanity of others who did communicate, respond, and act as men do. How was this possible? Is it not that under the influence of some principle or ideology, under the pressure of practice and passion, or because occupied with the pursuit of some goal which does not depend on the presence of certain men, one can fail to note that which one otherwise would?

Must we not say, therefore, that our acknowledgment of men as having a depth to them where they are in possession of rights, exercise a mind, and the like, is a weak, perhaps tentative, readily obscured act? Indeed, is it not the case that every once in a while someone whom we well know will call attention to himself because we have been negligent of him as just that presence? We normally know that men have rights and dignity, that they have centers of their own because we penetrate beyond their surfaces, at the same time that we are made to attend to content as that which the men have in fact made present to us.

The Nazis were surely aware of the insistent presence of those they exterminated—at least those with whom they were directly in contact. If they really hated them they would have penetrated them as well. Hate, though, is an unmodulated emotion; it is not contoured to the nuances of that at which it is directed. Still it penetrates, and penetrates into men. The Nazis knew that they were hating men, and they were faced with the men's insistent presence. It would seem then that the Nazis knew them as men with rights and dignities, and so on. Must we not conclude that they did know those they destroyed to be men, just as the rest of us do, but that they lived under the control of a principle which allowed them to see any man, themselves included, to be expendable? If we take this tack, we are led to say that the Nazis followed a principle which they applied with fairness, that is, impartially as rightfully determining what should be done with men who are defined or assessed to be corrupt or vicious and the like, somewhat as a hangman who, on behalf of the state or justice, despatches the defined criminal, and somewhat as a soldier does who shoots his supposed enemy on behalf of the future of his state, values, community, and family.

What is present is another as a 'you' which is being insisted on by his 'I'. I face it as that which is being presented. As a me I interact with it; as an I something more is done—I accept him as one who is making himself present for that I. While remaining private and self-centered, not fully reached by the other, each of us presents himself via public content to the other as an I. Each, as it were, says to the other, 'this is my me', a me which is being insisted upon and which is to be dealt with as an avenue to what an I is in fact.

April 26

'This', though it may be pertinent to a large, indefinite territory, is primarily directed at actualities. When an entire region is being dealt with, it is a region as an object, as standing apart from oneself and locatable within a larger region. If we are to deal with contexts, conditions, evidences, or finalities as having their own integrity, we must turn in the opposite direction, to the counterpart of the 'this'. Once again, a number of distinctions are to be made. However, there does not seem to be a single term which is used in different ways, but only a number of different terms with not altogether clearly distinct uses:

1] All terms in discourse are universals, and therefore all the terms to be subsequently distinguished can be said to have a universal use. But there is also a generic meaning, a meaning common to them all that can also be expressed in language. Perhaps one can use 'partici-pation' in this way, with the subsequent cases all being taken as specific ways in which the participation occurs.

2] The mere acknowledgment of a domain, perhaps after a begin-ning with some particular localized item in it, as a consequence of the use of evidence, or merely as the outcome of a confrontation with what conditions anything we might wish to designate with a 'this', can be acknowledged by remarking that one is 'involved with' something. The involvement is perhaps understood and used only when accompanied by some indication of the kind of entity or attitude that is to be acknowledged. This need not mean that the

reference to an involvement is incomplete, in the sense of requiring some other term in language, since all that may be required is that one occupy a certain position and attend to what is to be discerned from there.

One withdraws from practical affairs and an interest in particulars to turn toward a condition. The transcendental deduction of the categories by Kant (strangely misstated by me in *Beyond All Appearances*) is occupied with just this issue. Starting with experience, Kant tries to reach to the synthetic conditions of unification which this presupposes: his deduction begins with a dim grasp of the unity of apperception which he comes to know better and better as he progresses toward the categories.

3] One sometimes speaks of being 'into' something. As expressing a position, which is distinct from that which one might be said to conventionally occupy, the 'into' is an incomplete symbol, requiring supplementation by religion, art, and the like. Here there is a precedence given to the encompassing domain. One can use the 'into' with various emphases, all the way from a beginning in an enterprise to a deep immersion in it, emphasizing the 'into' as a kind of movement toward, or emphasizing the domain as that which governs the 'into' at the other end. Is there a position where the two are coordinate? This seems to be where one stands when trying to communicate to another what it is that is taking one away from daily affairs.

4] A domain (to use this for a moment to refer indifferently to rules, principles, evidences, finalities, societies, states, and prescriptions) is always beyond anything we can grasp of it. It, too, is absenting itself, a fact which we try to convey in some such expression as being 'caught up in'. Here there is a strong emphasis on the power of the domain, as holding on to us and thereby making evident its escape from any kind of limitation which we do or might want to introduce. The domain is an ever receding horizon which is grasped as receding when we recognize ourselves as being caught up in it. That recognition requires us to maintain a hold on ourselves; we see that we are caught up in it, and that we are so far not entirely absorbed in it.

In this, and in the previous cases, reference is made, not to content which is distinct from ourselves but in the control of an absenting actuality (as was done yesterday), but to ourselves as being subject to the control of an absenting actuality. To make a parallel, one would have to refer to the evidences one is using. These evidences are not altogether separable from ourselves. An occupation with encompassing domains requires a reference to us and not merely to content which is being encompassed.

5] Domains are not merely surfaces, but have a depth to them. When we concern ourselves with them we penetrate them to some degree. The penetration makes us be involved with them, to partake of them to some degree, to yield to their influence. But no matter how far we penetrate there is always a reality beyond. A mystic claims that he can penetrate far enough to lose himself, but that can be far short of the domain in itself. Indeed, his recognition that it is something in which he has lost himself, and that it is something to which he might be able to return again, would seem to indicate that. If he could get to the very center of that in which he was losing himself, it is hard to see how he could ever return to the position he had originally occupied. And, since the centered reality is insistent on itself, it is hard to see how he could possibly arrive at its center except so far as that center itself transmuted and transported him.

6] Those who are occupied with transcendent realities, and thus with the finalities and evidences and specifications of these, functioning as encompassing conditions and controls for particulars including the individuals, take those realities to be of great importance. They sometimes speak of themselves as immersed in the pursuit of them, or as preoccupied with them. But this way of speaking places too much emphasis on themselves. The overwhelming importance of a domain is better expressed through the help of emotionally loaded terms such as 'awe' and 'reverence.' (In *Beyond All Appearances,* I take these and 'openness', 'humility', and 'interest' to specialize an 'appreciation'; the distinctions these underscore must be maintained, I think, though better terms may be found to replace those I chose.)

7] We sometimes speak of ourselves being 'caught by' something. We then try to convey the fact that a domain has thrust itself forward, laid hold of us, insisted on itself in such a way as to dictate to us. The 'awe', 'reverence', and other cognate emotions which the different finalities elicit and control, are now taken to be special cases of more commonplace and constant emotions. 'Openness', 'humility', and 'interest' do more justice to the present case than 'awe' and 'reverence' do; the latter two should here be replaced by others, and the other three replaced by three others in 6. More important than the choice of terms is the fact which they should convey: a finality is not something which is to be arrived at, as though it were passively awaiting out activity. It is insistent on itself, not only in the form of imposed conditions and qualifications, but for us as being able to attend to them. They do not simply intrude on us and are internalized; they force themselves on us, demanding our attention.

Men rarely pay much attention to the presence of domains. Wittgenstein speaks as though domains defined the areas within which we could speak and think, and supposes that there is no possibility of referring to them. He fails to see that one can take up the position of a particular without attempting to know it, and that from such a position one can confront a domain, and even, as in the present instance, find that it is making demands on oneself. Were this not the case, how could one know that there was a domain? How could one ever come to occupy it and therefore come to know actualities?

How does one know what a domain is like? It makes sense to say that it can not be known if all knowledge is necessarily directed at particulars, for then it would be that which is necessarily presupposed but, by definition, beyond comprehension. What does it mean to hold that something is presupposed but can not be known? Do we not, when we refer to something presupposed, take a position at the presupposing item? Does not Wittgenstein in effect deny the possibility of a transcendental deduction, without adequate grounds for maintaining this? Does he not unwarrantedly deny the possibility of psychoanalysis, religion, political theory, as well as metaphysics?

The very fact that the preceding discussion is so awkwardly developed, and follows rather slavishly the divisions which the 'this' so evidently requires, gives some plausibility to the thesis that perhaps domains are beyond the reach of knowledge. And when one adds that language has been forged, apparently in the interests of practice and the experience of particulars, leaving over nothing for what else might be supposed to be, except metaphors and exaggerations of particulars, one is tempted to stay with the Wittgensteinean thesis, paradoxical though it be. Yet it is a fact, as the suggested terms at least adumbrate, that even in the course of daily life we constantly speak of domains, and acknowledge that we encounter them as at different positions from us, not only absenting themselves but insisting on themselves and making us submit to them.

We are affected by both actualities and finalities. At the same time, we confront them as distinct from us, where they not only maintain a hold on anything we might mark off in them, but insist on themselves, making their presence evident. In the case of the finalities, the insistence does not stop with the making of them present to us or for us, but with a subjugating of ourselves, making us share in them. That we may not note them, or that we may even resist them when we do note them, but points up the fact that we are primarily turned toward particulars, or that, once we do yield to them, we immediately turn around and from that position attend to the particulars.

Do finalities insist on themselves only for a man in the grip of basic emotions? Do they not have any affect on the speculative man? Does he merely arrive at the finalities as abstract entities, and hope that they will find a grounding, or that he will be able to supplement his abstract conclusions by the final termini of art, religion, and so forth? To say so is to make the speculative man too detached from the object he seeks to know and to separate him entirely from the life which the artist or the spectator leads. It would be more correct to say, I think, that speculation is grounded in finalities which initially are recognized to be absenting themselves and later recognized to be insistently demanding of men that they yield themselves and their claims to those finalities for adjudication and acceptance. The termini of the emotions, which the arts awaken and which continue after the experience with the arts is over, allow speculative thoughts to have the role of articulations of those termini.

To speak of the finalities only as termini is to neglect their insistence, their thrusting themselves forward, demanding, absorbing, controlling. The finalities to which the arts lead force one to attend to those finalities. The elicited emotions do not merely terminate in the finalities, but are pulled toward them. Those finalities govern the articulations of the metaphysican, forcing him toward the very realities which are emotionally faced after an encounter with particular works of art, and also after being seriously involved with rituals, community activities, celebrations, judicial decisions, and intellectual work. A metaphysician is only faintly controlled, the others more strongly. He mediates a confrontation of finalities by an articulation tinctured by wonder; they mediate the confrontation by an experience tinctured by a sense of something forever basic and powerful. But if metaphysical speculation is to get support from the achievement of art (or the others), and if we are to know that art (or the others) arrives at what is final, it must be the very finality, at which art's (or the others') elicited emotions arrive and which insists on itself, that is articulated by speculation and which insists on itself at that articulation.

The finality, at which the emotions aroused by art arrive, is the very finality which is insistent in an articulation of Existence; the Existence which is articulated is the finality that insistently claims to pull on the emotion which an experience of art leaves in its wake. Standing neutrally between art and metaphysics, therefore, we must affirm that a finality insistently thrusts itself forward to the emotion left over after one has experienced a work of art, at the same time that it insistently thrusts itself forward as the presence of what is articulated and thereby controls the emotion of awe or terror which can not be entirely expunged from a metaphysical quest and formulation.

Such an account makes emotion to be present both for the product of artistic experience and for the speculative metaphysician. Is it also true, that an emotional confrontation of a finality due to artistic experience has something like an articulating role for the finality? If so, an experience with art will have a didactic consequence, enabling us to know something about the nature of the finality in the very act of coming to it emotionally. Such a supposition goes directly counter to the contentions of most of those who have acknowledged a direct emotional involvement with some finality in religion and in art. But is this not because these men are anxious to overcome the separations and diversifications, the abstractness and intellectuality of thought and discourse? Is it not true that one not merely comes to a final object of awe but judges it, mediates the object by some kind of acknowledgment, not altogether nonverbal, not altogether unarticulate? If this is allowed, then the well-formulated articulation of speculation with its base in an insistent finality is matched by a poorer articulation which rides on the back of a confrontation with the finality. In the one case, the articulation is to the fore and the finality almost veiled; in the other, the finality is confronted but not without the presence of an intermediated, hardly attended-to articulation.

April 27

In dealing with a thing in itself a number of traps are to be avoided:

1] A thing in itself must not be taken to be cut off from all else. If it were, it would be radically indeterminate and so far would not be different from any other thing in itself. A thing in itself stands away from all else because it maintains itself against them.

2] A thing in itself must not be taken to be static, without any career, sunk within itself. It is a pulsational reality which is self-diversifying and self-solidifying in turn. It expresses itself but holds on to and integrates all its expressions. It is a turning point between an outward and the inward movement. That turning point is not prior to or subsequent to the movement outward or the movement inward.

The diverse expressions of an actuality can all be viewed as a thing in itself, but as less intensive. Each expression is an attenuation of the in itself; this in turn is an intensification of all. The different expressions could be said to differ from one another in degree of intensity or, equally, in the way in which a common degree of intensity is set in contradistinction to the source of them all. A thing in itself, when expressing itself, does not become diminished, any more than, when it pulls back the expressions into itself, it becomes enriched.

The entire pulsational whole with center and expressions, is the thing in itself. But the expressions are contrasted with the center only so far as one attends to the ways in which other realities impinge on the expressions and thereby set a task for the center in its act of self-solidification.

3] A thing in itself is with other actualities, and it is involved with the finalities. As having solidified its expressions as affected by intruding actualities, it expresses itself and terminates in expressions which receive determinations from the finalities; as having solidified its expressions as affected by intruding finalities, it expresses itself and terminates in expressions which received determinations from the actualities.

The determinations imposed by the finalities are constants; the determinations received from the other actualities are transients. As made determinate by other actualities, an actuality pulls back into itself to make itself be a distinct being; as made determinate by the finalities an actuality pulls back into itself to make itself an individual, more or less enriched, depending on its grade. A thing in itself is at the limit of the influence of the other actualities and the finalities. We can say that it is then indeterminate, but indeterminate relative to the determinateness for which it is the limit.

4] Explication and explanation are not derivations. When we attempt to make evident the nature of a thing in itself we approach it from a distance where we make use of other kinds of concepts. The explication and explanation tell us what the thing in itself is from exterior positions. From the standpoint of a finality, a thing in itself is a locus of the differentiated finality's expression; from the standpoint of another actuality, a thing in itself is a locus of that other actuality's effective insistence. The differentiated expression is individualized by being internalized; the effective insistence (by being internalized) is reduced to a self-maintained identity.

None of this is altogether clear. I think this is not due to the impossibility of becoming clear about a thing in itself, but to the difficulty of attending to it, free from associations with other states. There is also the difficulty of making sense of the sheer differences which result from expressions on the part of both the actualities and the finalities, perhaps due to the temptation to deal with expressions apart from the loci of their terminations.

A mere act of expression is diversified or not, depending on the perspective. From the standpoint of an expressive being, expressions are itself manifest, with none of the expressions held away from it or one another; from the standpoint of that on which expressions have been impressed, expressions are diverse, and the loci in turn, as enriched by those expressions, are different from one another.

Differences are the termini of expressions of finalities as externally sustained; distinctness is the character of expressions of actualities as externally sustained. The sustaining in both cases is by actualities, as having material to utilize, the one in order to achieve individuality, the other in order to achieve a center which is maintained against other actualities.

What must be avoided is the attempt to deal with actualities or finalities as though they ever were without affect on one another. Yet, at the same time, an account must be given of the fact that they are distinct, irreducible realities. Even those who would avoid any reference to things in themselves are faced with the problem of giving an account of the entities which they initially assume to be distinct—'each impression is a distinct existent'—or to be united. (The values of a variable are said to be distinct, but we know them only via the use of a common variable, a common 'this', and repeatable gestures.)

References to things in themselves are the outcome of a resolute attempt to deal with entities apart from all exterior determination. The most that one can do is to grant that that which is making use of the exterior determination is, relative to this, indeterminate, but not absolutely so, since it is in the same continuum with the determination and is indeterminate only as a limit. But once the limit is recognized to have some integrity, as individuality and identity require, the traps discussed earlier become operative. A limit, as outside and contrasting with determinations and determined portions of an actuality, is still relative to other actualities or to the finalities.

The closest we can come to actualities in themselves from the outside is as indeterminates relative to exteriorly imposed determinations; as self-diversifying; as self-solidifying; as self-maintaining so as to be able to be the loci (of the expressions of finalities) in the guise of different instances of the same condition; and as individuals so as to be the loci (of expressions of other actualities) in the guise of distinct recipients of external, particular influences. When we imaginatively place ourselves at a thing in itself, we place ourselves at a pulsational reality. This expresses itself. It also solidifies those expressions in an alternating rhythm with other solidified expressions which were transiently determined by other actualities.

When we attend to the double fact that things in themselves must be individual and distinct, we approach them from the position of imposed differences and imposed disturbances, and attend to the pull of the thing in itself on the differences and disturbances. The differences and disturbances, in turn, can be accounted for by looking outside an actuality to finalities or other actualities and acknowledging that self-diversifications of these are sustained by the actuality. The diversifications of the finalities and other actualities, by being sustained, become differences and distinctions.

Difference intensified from within is individuality; distinctness diversified from within is self-maintenance. The 'within' does not follow in act on what is different or distinct; all are analytic factors within a single interlocking of actualities with one another and of all of the actualities, severally and together, with the finalities.

*   *   *

This morning the gas in my apartment was turned off, and I was unable to make my usual cup of coffee. How much of the unclarity of today's discussion can be credited to that fact I can not say. Only one who knew how to compare different unclarities might be able to distinguish the present from others, and trace it back to my failure to have my normal stimulant. If there is a difference, it should now be overcome, for I have now had lunch and coffee.

A solidification of the affects of others makes the center of an actuality be the beginning of an insistent outward thrust toward the finalities. That insistent thrust comes to an end at a counter-insistence, which adds determinations to the other. At the same time, the permanent determinations, produced by finalities, are solidified as the center of the actuality, beginning an insistent outward expression toward the other actualities. Each solidification reduces to the selfsame result. Each insistence, too, is necessarily diversified, thereby providing occasions for the production of differences and distinctions.

For the moment what I find hardest to focus on is the diversity in the expressions of finalities and other actualities before they are in fact united with the loci that actualities provide. I am supposing, without sufficient examination and no justification, that a dense reality, when it expresses itself, disperses the import of that reality in various less intensive forms. This seems to be getting something for nothing, if it is being supposed that the actualities are in no way diminished; it also leaves over the question as to how two expressions differ. Do they have the same intensity? Do they necessarily have different degrees of intensity?

I think we must say that a center is diminished, but that the actuality in itself is not, so far as its expressions are recognized to be fulgurations which have not yet been sustained or made determinate by anything beyond themselves. But if they are not made determinate, they would seem to be as indeterminate as the center is. We would then have a plurality of indeterminates whose intensities differ in depth from the center's; we would not yet have shown in what sense the expressions differed from one another.

Nor will we have shown that there must be more than one expression.

Would it not make sense to say that every expression has less intensity than its actuality, but that the actuality, in order to have this be its expression, must make the expression represent it in a distinctive way? The expressions would be the actuality self-articulated, with the diversity expressing the meaning of the actuality for itself. Those expressions would not differ from one another until they were sustained from the outside by other realities; before that time they would be the actuality externalized for itself, nuances in a single act of exteriorizing.

Were an entity to remain unexpressed, it would not be anything for itself and, so far, would be at a disadvantage with respect to others which might at least isolate an aspect of the entity. Is not the fecund superior to the inert, as is supposed by romantics and by theologians who explain creation as the outcome of God's gracious giving of Himself?

To have some degree of value is to make it available to others. As merely available it is an expression of exuberance, overflowing, spelling out, placing intensive degree alongside intensive degree until the totality equals the original single intensity. There must be more than one expression, for no one of them is adequate to what the entity is; all are needed so that it could be articulately what it is densely. The components of the articulation are distinguishable, precisely because no one of them can be identical with its source, and a number are needed if there is to be an adequate presentation of that source. But until they are embedded elsewhere, the expressions are not different. For the expressions of a reality to be different, one from the other, there must be a reality which contrasts with the first, and can sustain and thereby add to what an expression was as belonging to the source. Until then, the expression is only distinguishable and not distinct from other expressions. As still part of the reality, expressions are only nuances in a single totality, components in a 'subject', where before they had been sunk within a 'substance'.

April 28

Suppose there were just one entity. This, apparently, would be Parminides' One. It would not be characterizable in any way, for characterizations require a distinction between themselves and that to which they are applied. We could not even say that the entity was simple, for 'simplicity' is a characterization, and requires a contrast between itself and 'complexity', if it is to have sense. The entity could be said to be indeterminate, where 'indeterminacy' is a limiting term, the boundary of an infinite series of less and less determination; but such a characterization, again, is not possible except so far as one approaches the entity from a position outside it, though, on the hypothesis, there is no such position.

I have argued as early as 1938, in *Reality,* that such a single entity is identifiable with nothing at all. The argument, though, depends on the prior identification of indeterminacy with the object itself. I went on to hold that 'nothing' was a self-contradictory idea, since it was then supposed to be determinately indeterminate. This argument, though, presupposes that the indeterminateness of the nothing or of one entity stands in contrast with something else. Instead, it might be maintained that a single entity could no more be indeterminate than it could be determinate; surely it could not be said to be either.

I have subsequently maintained, as late as last year in *Beyond All Appearances,* that a single entity would necessarily burst into fragments. The position presupposes: A] that a unitary entity is somehow held together by outside force, B] that a dispersal of a unitary entity ends in parts actually detached from it and one another, leaving over no residuum, and C] that the entity does not continue to lay hold of what is being dispersed, pull it back, and solidify it in itself—activities which, of course, could not be distinguished and are not in fact distinguishable. (Leibniz's monads are not properly said to be simple, if 'simple' requires a contrast with 'complex'; nor can his monads be rightly said to have many perceptions within them or to envisage a temporal sequence of occurrences within themselves, for these require a distinction between the monad and transient phases of itself with which it is able to contrast itself so as to have them as objects for its knowledge.)

The fate which awaits the supposition that there is just a single entity seems also to await the view that there are things in themselves, for each of these is apparently as much an isolate one as the supposed single entity is. The position of Parmenides is not dependent on the supposition that there is only one entity, but only on the supposition that we are attending only to a one—which could be the center of an entity.

There are many ways in which it is possible to deal with the difficulty. One can maintain that the supposition of a one is idle. Not only is a man now being asked to envisage it and thus to have it as something over against himself, not only does he discourse about it and thus have it over against himself, language, thought, and other men, but he arrives at the idea only by ignoring or canceling a plurality.

With Hume, one could say that a single entity (if an impression) is simply given, or is outside the reach of any understanding. Still left over is the question of the sense in which an impression is simple or single.

One might, with Kant, deny that there is a warrant for speaking of a single entity, particularly of 'a mere subject which was never a predicate' as though it were simple, substantial, and the like, because it is not available for such characterization. A self, according to Kant, is therefore not an object about which one can discourse or have knowledge, even though it might be said to be presupposed in ethics. But, surely, if it is presupposed, we are able to understand it; if we can postulate it, we must have some understanding of it. It may not be the object of a direct confrontation, without intermediation, but this observation is not equivalent with the contention that a self therefore does not exist or can not be known, once granted that its status by itself is what it achieves through the use of what is impinging on it.

Must an entity express itself? Is it necessarily fecund, expansive, insistent, diffuse? If these questions be taken to presuppose an unexpressed entity closed up in itself which then engages in expression, our initial questions will rise again when we come to consider the presupposed unexpressed entity. An entity that *must* express itself is one which never is without expression. Yet if it is single, its expressions can not be set over against it. Its reality must consist in the entire set of expressions as not sunderable from one another or their source.

Because it is taken for granted that a single entity is simple, the question is not usually asked whether or not it is homogeneous. 'Homogeneity' seems to involve some acknowledgement of a plurality. There are in fact at least two kinds of homogeneity which permit of conceivable pluralization—a homogeneity of intensity, encompassed within a single intensity of more than minimal degree, and a homogeneity of kind, toned or nuanced throughout.

A thing in itself as present is insistent, assertive, with a degree of intensity greater than any concept of or claim about it could possibly have. Such an entity could diversify itself without dividing itself, by laying intensity alongside intensity. We come close here to Hegel's idea that the absolute has the cunning to present itself to itself in the guise of an other. But that idea leaves open the question as to why it should do this, and how it could actually face what is other than itself if that other is in fact itself and never allowed to stand away from itself as an independent entity.

Might not an entity have only a minimal degree of intensity, precluding a nuanced diffusion in degrees of intensity alongside one another? No matter how much we suppose the intensity to be reduced, there is always a smaller degree. To be is to have an intensity which is infinitely distant from nothing at all, and reducible beyond any assignable degree. The diffused nuances of an entity, consequently, will have nuances which themselves have intensities that can be diffusely expressed, each of whose nuances is itself capable of such expression, and so on without end.

An entity will never get to the end of an expression of itself, if a degree of intensity greater than a minimum requires that it be diffusely expressed in the form of intensities alongside one another. If it must express itself so as to lay out alongside one another the intensities which it now has solidly together in the guise of a single intensity, diffusion upon diffusion will cascade from it, without end.

A Leibnizian would hold that diffusion occurs 'within' the entity; an Hegelian that it is set in 'logical' contrast with the entity; a materialist, that it is set in a preexistent space or ground for the world. But it makes sense to say that expression is itself a way of producing the very domain within which it occurs. When an arrow is shot outward from the edge of the universe, to use Lucretius's illustration, it creates the space that relates it to where it had been. But, if as is the case here, there is no detachable arrow but an unsunderable expressiveness with terminating expressions, the diffusions will not be alienated from their source but will still be continuous with it. It will then be correct to say that the original dense intensity, together with all the diffused expressions of this, each with its nuances, is still the thing in itself. Even apart from any pulling of the expressions back into itself, the entity will remain undivided.

We are here close to the Neoplatonic idea of a primal One

which proliferatively descends until it becomes a primal matter, except that what is now being maintained is that there is no final position that can be reached. The Neoplatonist, as Lovejoy has made evident, takes his universe to be a plenum, with every possible degree of reality filled out. The thing in itself, and a supposed single entity, can also be thought to produce such plena, though without the supposed last term. If, in contradistinction from Neoplatonism, it is also contended that there is more than one thing in itself, these will have to be said to provide stopping places for one another's diffused expressions, thereby enabling those expressions to be located at those others and there achieve the status of being different from one another. Each entity will put a stop to the diffusive action of the other, going through an infinite number of expressions, each of more than a minimal intensity, thereby enabling the expressive being to have a different expression there from what it would have at some other entity.

The very insistence of an entity on its own expressions will put a stop to the expressions of another at some degree of intensity which is theoretically capable of division into a plurality of intensities of lesser degree. One could then maintain that if the original entity is a finality, its expressions will be stopped at the same degree of intensity by all the actualities. Or one could hold that different kinds of entities, or even different instances of the same kinds, provide stops at different points. Mine is the less bold supposition, grounded in the idea that all the actualities stand in contradistinction to all the finalities. This is consistent with the idea that each of the finalities provides a different stopping point for the expressions of other finalities, and with the idea that different grades of actualities provide different stopping points for the expressions of other actualities. The difference in the stopping points, here being considered, will consist in their bringing an end to a series of diffusive expressions at intensities distinct from that characteristic of other stopping points.

A single entity endlessly proliferates itself and yet never gets beyond the stage of being just that entity in itself and, therefore, not being explanatory of this world of ours where there is plurality, defiance of instrusions, and interaction. Why is it, though, that there is not just one entity which has expressed itself in a cascade of expressions, each of lesser degree than those before and within which there are nuances, the source of subsequent diffused expressions with their own nuances? Perhaps there is a self-contradiction in the idea?

A single entity would be endlessly expressive and never get the length of having expressed itself. It would be expressive in order to give full value to the different degrees of intensity which it has solidly together, but it would fail to attain the position where it could have the degrees of intensity alongside one another, each maintained in contradistinction to the others, all to itself. Stopped by nothing, it would fail to achieve what it was endeavoring to be—become something for itself or at the very least articulate itself and thus give full value to its own dense intensity. But there is no self-contradiction in the idea of a failure, or in the inability to provide a satisfactory articulation for itself, though there is a contradiction in the idea that there could be such a single entity in this world of which we are a part. If so, must we not also say that the idea of a thing in itself is self-contradictory for, as was already remarked, there is no difference in principle between the problem that such an idea raises and that which is raised by the thought of a single entity alone having reality, since each thing in itself is an entity away from all else? Not, if it be recognized that the thing in itself is not a point of origin, but is instead a position enjoyed as a pivot between A] an outward expression toward the finalities, with a coordinate absorption of expressions that had been directed at and been affected by other actualities, and   B] an outward expression toward other actualities, with a coordinate absorption of expressions which had been directed at and affected by the finalities. Each thing in itself extends as far as its expressions; but these, as located at other entities, and there functioning as differences, are also distinguishable from any and all of its expressions.

The objection to the idea of single entity as alone real, to the effect that it is blocked by the fact that there is no evidence for it, that there are men who are thinking about it, that there now is a plurality, is a strong objection, but it surely does not go the length of showing the idea to be self-contradictory. It is tempting to say that we can not make sense of it, knowing that we exist, and that there is a plurality of entities in the world with which we are familiar and from the perspective of which we entertain the idea of a single entity. Yet we can think of ourselves as no longer existing. This is not yet to think of ourselves as not being able to exist, which would be the case were there only one entity, and no way of obtaining a plurality from it. Must it not, therefore, be concluded that since we exist, it is self-contradictory to suppose that there could be an entity which would make it impossible for us to be? And does not a single entity, which can not get the length of having a plurality independent of and facing it, have just this nature, making it impossible for us to be?

There is a plurality of entities; therefore it is self-contradictory to suppose that a plurality is impossible. But a plurality would be impossible if there were only a single entity, since this can not pluralize itself.

The fact that there now is a plurality, even though every item in it is contingent, shows that a plurality is possible. That possibility is denied by the supposition that there could be a single entity, even one which proliferated itself endlessly. A plurality, at the very least, requires one to suppose that every thing in itself is terminated in its expressions by what is beyond itself, and that only as so terminated and determined does it have the comparative status of an undetermined center which is the source of the expressions that are being terminated.

Can the contradiction be avoided by supposing that there are two things in themselves? I think not, unless it be allowed that the things in themselves terminate one another's expressions and thus have a bearing on what the things are for one another. Two things in themselves, if entirely unrelated, could not be two. To be two, they must somehow be addable and therefore together. Things in themselves are not equatable with single entities wholly self-enclosed; they are together with one another, each providing a base for which the other could be a locus of a distinctness; they are also affected by the finalities and provide the expressions of these with a requisite sustaining.

Since I am now awake it is possible for me to be awake; it is not now possible for me to be asleep, since that state is now being excluded, not only as a fact but as a possibility that could be realized now. Yet it is now possible for me to be awake. This is only to say that being awake and being asleep are contingencies, and that the realization of one contingency may involve the exclusion of the other. The possibilities remain; what is contingent is the realization of this one or that.

Might not the existence of one entity and the existence of a plurality both be contingencies? The fact that there is a plurality now would not, therefore, mean that there can never be a single entity. Might it not have been the case that there once was just a single entity? When it was present, there would be no plurality in fact and none then possible, but there would be possibilities for both the entity and the plurality apart from the contingent fact that the one or the other was realized.

Might not the contingent presence of a single entity precede or succeed the contingent presence of a plurality? The question takes us into a new area—the realization of exclusive contingencies, each without antecedent or consequent, and thus as mere actualizations of possibility. We would have to hold, not only that actualities are contingent but that the entire set of them was and, like a single entity, or any thing in itself, that each was an occurrence whose presence could not be explained.

We are left with two alternatives: either there is no accounting for the fact that there is a set of actualities (just as there would be no accounting for the fact of a single entity, were there such) or we can account for the set by showing that a single entity is impossible.

April 29

Behind the almost universal rejection of the ontological argument is the conviction that existent entities can not be derived from ideas or meanings. As directed to an 'argument', the rejection concerns itself with what is cognized; but it could be given an ontological import, and be taken to reject the idea that from Possibility one could obtain instantiations of it. If one takes that line, one should also go on to maintain that it is not conceivable that instances in thought or in fact can be obtained from Substance, Being, Existence, or Unity. (The position that one is committed to something outside logic or language if one makes use of such expressions as 'there exists' or 'always' is, is the ontological argument in a poor moralistic disguise. When it is further maintained that 'existence' is not a predicate, what presumably is meant is that the existent is something quite other than any predicate or set of predicates.)

These objections are sound, I think, so far as they relate to actualities or even to any or all of the finalities. What remains over is the question as to whether or not it is sound with respect to all that is, and whether or not this is itself a totality, all of whose parts might be contingent, but which is itself necessary. The necessity here would be a concrete necessity, and contain within it all possible meanings as well as all other items, precluding the possibility that there could be anything less. For the moment, I will not pursue this question, but, instead, will return to the problem of the contingent existence of a single entity or of a plurality. The following cases seem worth considering:

A] The existence of a single entity is contingent. It has no cause and can not be derived from the idea of itself. We must say that it just is, and leave it at that. To say that it is perfect, that all plurality is negatively achieved, that it is a self-caused, and the like, not only has difficulty with the presence of other entities, such as ourselves, but with the fact that it allows for no way of showing that the entity is or is not perfect, simple, without determination, or self-caused.

B] The existence of this or that single entity is contingent. This is possible even if it were true that some single entity or other necessarily is.

C] A set of entities could be contingent, even if it contained all the finalities or all the actualities, or all the finalities and all the actualities together. The last supposition opposes the supposition that the totality of all that is, is necessary.

D] The particular set of entities that now make up the universe could be said to be contingent, even if there be a necessity that there be a totality of some kind. After all, actualities come and go, so that if there were a necessary totality, it would not necessarily have the same membership always.

E] A single entity could be the contingent outcome of some previous activity on the part of some other single entity or on the part of a plurality. Once it had been produced it could be forever. Or it could just succeed some previous unity or some previous set of items, and then be forever or give way to something else. (The 'forever' here would have to be understood in nontemporal terms to mean that there would be nothing succeeding on it, not that it was necessarily existent.) This alternative is occupied with the realm of existents, and attends only to the presence of some entity in relation to some others that might have been in its place. These other entities are not mere possibilities, but entities on the same level with it, which are able to exclude its presence.

F] A plurality of entities could be the contingent outcome of some previous activity on the part of a different plurality, or on the part of a single entity. Once it had been produced, it might be forever, or

give way to some other plurality or to some single entity. Like the
previous alternative, this also remains within the realm of existents.

A Humean would take the antecedent and the consequent in
the above two cases to have no necessary connection; a single entity
or a plurality might then follow or precede a plurality or a single
entity, not only because the plurality and the single entity are both
contingents, but because there is no compulsion which either imposes on the other. What is, is disconnected from anything else that
might be; it can vanish without anything else being affected; it could
give way to something like itself or to something quite different.

G] A universe in which there were both finalities and actualities
could itself be the contingent successor of one in which there was
only a single entity, only actualities, or only finalities, different
from or identical with any or all of those that now are. This case
differs from that in which there is a single entity, or a plurality as an
irreducible fact having no predecessor or successor. The latter has
contingents which just are indefinitely; the other has contingents
which are encompassed within a larger domain, logical or temporal,
where other entities exclude them.

H] A single entity or a plurality might be the necessary outcome of
some activity on the part of some predecessor, but might not itself
be something necessary, either as single or as a plurality.

The very fact that there are these various alternatives points up
the incompleteness of accounts which are content merely to acknowledge certain items, a One or a Many, this or that kind of
plurality, or this or that kind of One, without further ado. Yet this
procedure is most in accord with the current temper. The dominant
philosophies of today—linguistic, phenomenological, Whiteheadean, existentialistic—are all content to describe; they eschew
dialectic and a justification for their assumption that this or that is
the case, even in the face of the denials by other equally well-
trained thinkers.

Let it be granted that every item in this universe is contingent.
Its contingency can mean: A] some other items could be rather
than the ones there are;   B] the plurality might not have been, for
there could have been only one item;   C] an explanation for the
presence of whatever items there are may be logical, without
thereby making the explained a derivative which could be deduced,
for it might just be something presupposed by what is itself contingent;   D] an explanation for the presence of whatever items there

are may be causal, either in the sense of merely having an antecedent associated with it by a Humean habit; as following on a necessary but not sufficient condition, (since the process of causation or the self-achievement of the effect may also have a contributing role); or as following necessarily on what is itself contingent.

If it be granted that every item in the universe, including the finalities, is contingent, and might not have been, even if some had no antecedent and will have no consequent, this does not justify a purely descriptive philosophy, not only because there should be some assurance that one is describing what in fact is present and only that, but because explanations are still significant within that frame. One could start (as I have tried in *Beyond All Appearances*) with actualities, not this or that, or this particular set of them, but with any set of them that may now be, have been, or will be, and show that they presuppose five finalities. Each of the finalities is outside the domain of the actualities, though not at a spatial distance from them. No finality is caught up in the extensions governing or characteristic of actualities. A finality neither comes to be nor passes away.

Once one arrives at the finalities one can go on to account for the content that serves to make individuality possible, as well as the beings, natures, identity, and values of the actualities, and in that way provide explanations for the actualities.

The finalities, as arrived at from the vantage point of the actualities, would have to be occupied before one can get an explanation for their self-sufficiency, produced by possessing the expressions intruded by actualities. The positions of the actualities, also, have to be occupied before one can get an explanation for their individuality, and so forth, produced by possessing the qualifications imposed by the finalities.

An explanation which starts with actualities, or strictly speaking, with qualifications found to have been imposed on actualities, arrives at what the actualities presuppose. The finalities are arrived at from the position of particular contingents; they are presupposed by any set of actualities, and not simply by this or that set of them. But the qualifications, and thus the possible ontological achievements of actualities, resulting in their being of different grades, depends on the prior operation, not of any conceivable set of finalities, but only of those that are in fact presupposed by the actualities.

It is impossible that a single entity alone *must* be; the present existence of a plurality precludes this. Those who maintain that there is or was such a single entity, sooner or later have to explain away the world, with which they start, as a world of illusions, nonbeings, facets, and the like, and therefore must deny that there is a world of genuine realities engaged in trying to get to that supposed single entity.

It is not impossible for there to have been a single entity which preceded the presence of a plurality, but it could not have caused that plurality, except as supplemented by a process of causation (or self-causation on the part of the supposed effects) enabling the effects to stand away from their presumed cause. Nor is it impossible for there to be a single entity later which succeeds the plurality that there now is, though its causal coming to be requires a process of causation (or self-causation on the part of the entity).

Both a plurality of actualities and a single entity could replace the other if that other could vanish and the replacement could occur, both without cause. However, if a plurality of actualities could be simply replaced by a single entity, the finalities themselves would have to be denied the power to intrude qualifications on actualities, and to affect one another. And, if a single entity were simply replaced by a plurality of actualities, the plurality would necessitate that there be finalities which in turn necessitated that there be the actualities on which they could intrude.

A replacement of a single entity must either be another single entity, or a universe of actualities and finalities. A replacement of a universe of actualities and finalities might be another universe of actualities with the same finalities (where the actualities function in relation to the finalities as the others did), or a single entity. The various alternatives with which the present account began thus reduce to: 1] a single entity being replaced by a universe of actualities and finalities; 2] a universe of actualities and finalities being replaced by a single entity.

Since a genuine plurality can not be produced out of a single entity, and since a plurality requires a status where it stands away from any unity, and this can not be provided by a single entity, one would have to suppose that if a plurality came after a single entity it replaced this without reason. One would then gratuitously add to the acknowledgment of the universe of actualities and finalities, even if contingent, the supposition that it had a predecessor with which it was not in fact connected. And since, as has been argued in *Beyond All Appearances,* there always is an ideal perfection which stands in opposition to the actualities and finalities as opposed but concrete and interacting, the ideal would have to vanish with the vanishing of the actualities and the finalities. Such vanishing, if it was followed by a single entity, would bring this universe to a close without giving an entrance into the other that replaced it.

Granted then that the universe of actualities and finalities is not necessary, able not to be, the supposition that there could instead have been a single entity is gratuitous. The alternative supposition that there might eventually be a single entity, in place of the universe of actualities and finalities, would require that the finalities be able to vanish, even though they are not in time and, though reached from the base of transient actualities, are independent of those actualities and capable of prescribing to them. It would also require that it be possible for there to be nothing at all, or that the replacing of a single entity be necessitated, either by the vanishing or by the nothing which ensues. But if the single entity is entirely self-enclosed, its presence can not be dependent on the vanishing of something else; if it were so dependent, the negation of a plurality will yield it, and it would have a logical or causal connection with that plurality. If its presence is contingent, it might not come after a presumed vanishing of the universe of actualities and finalities. To suppose that it *will* be is gratuitous.

The universe of actualities and finalities, if contingent as a totality as well as in its parts, might conceivably be preceded or followed by a single entity; equally it might be preceded or followed by nothing at all. In either case there would be no accounting for its presence. Whether then one supposed that it had been preceded or followed by a single entity or by nothing, one would be left with the irreducible fact that though presumably contingent, it nevertheless now is, might always have been, and might always be and, in any case, contains within it finalities which are not in time or causal processes, and presupposes actualities to provide all of them with Ones so that they can in fact be a Many.

Granted, then, the contingency of the universe of actualities and finalities, there might instead be (antecedently, presently, or subsequently) nothing at all or a single entity. Only if one can show that nothing at all is impossible, and that this is not the case with a single entity, could one hold that in place of the universe there could be a single entity. Though both the universe and the single entity would be contingents, they would be as red and non-red are—mutually exclusive, and together exhausting the possibilities. With nothing else available for explanation, the fact that one of those contingents was realized and not the other would be inexplicable. If, then, the universe of actualities and finalities is contingent it is no more (but, of course, also no less) inexplicable than either nothing or a single entity would be.

Taken each by each, things in themselves are unities pulsationally involved with incipient pluralities which attain the stage of actual pluralities only because there is a real plurality of sustaining entities external to them. They are then like the finalities where these are seen as so many Ones for the many actualities.

By another route, we have once again arrived at the conclusion that actualities are instances of the finalities. Just as the finalities pluralize their expressions through the help of the actualities, so the actualities pluralize their expressions through one another's help and the help of the finalities. Any supposed single entity would be unable to achieve a real pluralization, or would be a thing in itself or a finality which could not get the length of having anything pluralized.

Throughout the above, the idea of vanishing has been used without examination. It is the reciprocal of a radical coming to be of something from nothing. The distance here is infinite. Theologians have long insisted that if there were nothing actual, it would require infinite power, that is, God, to make something be, no matter how feeble or low in value. Nothing springs from nothing. But if this is so, there can be no vanishing except with God's help, for the distance from something to nothing is as great as the distance from nothing to something.

Things do pass away, but passing away is not identical with vanishing. Not only does material and/or energy continue in the physical world, not only do the intruding items continue to be, but the outcome of these, particularly as distinguishing the present from past and future, is preserved in the past, where it is factualized, deprived of its constituents. What is, on passing away, is dispersed, not annihilated.

The universe of actualities and finalities can no more issue out of nothing than it can return to it. But, Hume's impressions pop into existence and out of it; they make an infinite jump, not once but twice. Kant allows the jump only one way—or rather he thinks that one can reach utter vanishing by going through degrees of intensity, but does not raise the question as to whether the reverse is possible or not. We take our death to be an extinction but see our birth as having an explanatory cause. Though the achievement of a unique personality or identity is no further from nothing than the loss of it is from something, we usually take the latter to be a loss only of a foothold in the present, while the former is taken to involve the coming to be of such a foothold. The foothold is seen as merely replacing something not itself.

The present is new because there is something new in it. To say that the novel component is preserved in the past is not yet to account for the fact that it has come to be for the first time in the present. But this, too, can be accounted for by attending to the future, where the novel item is to be found to have a generic guise. If so, novelty in the present consists in attaining specificity; the specification is a novel outcome of the way in which the generic item becomes present.

Items in the present yield a new feature which specifies a possibility in the future and continues to remain, detached from its present occasions, when the present becomes past. A present insistence specifies what is future and leaves over a determinate husk to constitute an item in the past. Given the universe of actualities and finalities there would be no coming to be of it out of nothing and no passing away of it into nothing. Before it is present it is future; after it is present, it is past.

But is not time within the universe, and not characteristic of it? If so, the universe can not be said to continue to be in some form in the past, except so far as actualities are in the past and thereby help constitute a totality which differs from the totality now present.

April 30

A replacement of a single entity by the universe, and conversely, involves inexplicable jumps from something to nothing and from nothing to something. But this still leaves over the alternatives that one of them may be the source of the other, in one of two ways:

A] One of them might be the cause of the other. Such a cause will require the achievement of a present status by the effect, with the reciprocal passage of the cause (as having that effect) into the past. The effect will be able to have the presence that the cause itself once had because the process of causation will involve the attainment, in the effect, of the independent reality of the effect. That process of causation could be attributed to the effect—as Whitehead does. Whether this is done or not, the question still remains as to how the effect obtains the status of a present occurrence excluding and being excluded by its cause.

If a cause is a single entity, a process of causation can not be part of it, without making it multiplied, or by making the causation not able to yield something exterior to the cause. A process of causation is one over which a change in status of the present cause and the prospective future is achieved. It is either added to the former or to the latter, unless the cause itself can diminish itself to allow for the process of causation and the presence of the effect.

That there is more to a cause-effect situation than just terminal points, and that a process of causation is not reducible to either, I have argued for in *Nature and Man*. The account there, however, does not enable one to understand how a single entity could have a prospective effect before it, or could continue to be a determinate past item, lacking something that it had when it was present, or how, if it is the effect of the universe of actualities and finalities, it could have that universe as its past.

B] The second way of taking either the single entity or the universe of actualities and finalities to be a source of the other avoids the causal view and, with some cabalistic writers, maintains that the source diminishes itself so as to allow what it makes possible to have a reality of its own. If one starts, as those writers do, with the idea of a single entity, this must be taken to undergo an act of self-sacrifice, a making of itself less, in order that there be a world in addition to it. Without adopting their view of God, or the supposition of a creation, one can, with them, hold that the very reality of a single entity is inseparable from a self-diminuition and the allowing of its diversified, nuanced expressions to exist apart from it. It will reduce itself, withdraw within itself, or decrease its own intensity so as to allow for the presence of what otherwise could only be an aspect of itself, undetachable and without distinct parts. If one is to avoid causal and temporal notions, the diminuition would also have to be integral to the entity's very being; its very status as a single entity would be inseparable from its status as one among the many which it has allowed to be. However, if the single entity is not in time, as thus divided against itself (as entailed by the first alternative), it will be eternally against itself, with a self-enclosed nature at the same time that it was diminished and coexistent with the items which had been an integral part of itself.

If there were a single entity, which was produced by the universe of actualities and finalities diminishing itself, that single entity would be coexistent with the universe, unless the universe not only diminished itself but reduced itself to nothing. The single entity, as alone, could not be the outcome of a simple preceding diminuition on the part of some other reality.

The discussion can be summarized:

1] There is now a universe of actualities and finalities. This could not replace or be replaced by a single entity, all alone, without an inexplicable jump over the distance which separates something from nothing. Even if the universe and the entity were contingent, and therefore conceivably might not be, their non-being can not be identified with an inexplicable utter vanishing.

2] The universe can not be the effect of the single entity, without making the latter be in time and thus connected with a future prospect and an actual effect. It would also require the occurrence of a process of causation which encompassed the change of status in the entity, from one which was facing a prospective future to one which is past to a present.

3] A single entity could not be the effect of a preceding universe without having that universe as its past; nor without there being a distinction between the single entity as a prospective future item, and itself as concrete and present (and therefore not a genuine single entity, all alone, like a Parmenidean One).

4] A single entity could not yield a universe by atemporally diminishing itself without also dividing itself in two. Both parts would exist at the same time, one being the entity all alone, the other that entity diminished and together with the other for which it made room.

5] A single entity could not be the result of an atemporal diminution of the universe, without requiring that universe to extinguish itself totally. Otherwise the universe would be together with that single entity, precluding this from being all alone.

6] If the universe of actualities and finalities is contingent, what could be instead of it would be a different plurality of entities, and not a single entity, all alone. That plurality of entities will be: A] a set of actualities,   B] a set of finalities, or   C] a different set of both altogether—a different type of universe.

A] A set of actualities is exactly what we do have at different moments of time. The difference in the actualities does not affect their possible grades, or their governance by the finalities.

B] A later set of actualities could conceivably have its members be together in ways totally unlike those that now prevail. They might not be subject to the same local conditions of space, time, value, and so forth, or they might not be subject to such conditions at all, but to others quite unlike these. If they were not subject to the same general conditions, the finalities could still be those I have distinguished, but their properties would be different from those now acknowledged. The metaphysics would be different in detail, not in principle, from that which I have been maintaining.

C] If the actualities were subject to quite different conditions than those that now prevail, those conditions would be inexplicably operative or would have to be accounted for as some consequence of the principles that now prevail. In the latter case, finalities would have to be temporal or atemporal sources of other finalities; or the present finalities would have to alter. On either alternative, they would change the kinds of expressions to which they subject actualities and their expressions. The present universe might, for example, be the source of or change into one which required actualities all to be melded together and then to separate out as atoms, again and again.

Not only might the finalities be different, but the actualities which they affect might be altogether unlike the substantial entities that are now members of this universe. The present universe would then be the temporal or atemporal source of a universe with different particular items and different all-encompassing final ones. And, of course, the present universe might have such a different universe as its source.

The contingency of this universe (if it be contingent!) allows for its having a different pluralistic universe as a temporal or atemporal source or product. Anything else, the current discussion indicates, would require one to assume a number of unnecessary inexplicables. But, then, a universe of particulars and finalities is necessary, generically; the specifications of it, including the present ones, all have the status of contingents. Not yet accounted for is the fact that the necessary pluralistic universe is contingently specified in the way it now is, and not in the other ways which are conceivable.

Are we now not back at the old traditional position with its supposition of a necessary being who is the source of this contingent world? No, for at least two reasons: A] what is contingent in the traditional view is only the world of actualities, whereas (I am maintaining that) what is contingent is the particular actualities and finalities that now constitute the universe;   B] the necessary, on the traditional view, is a reality, individual, perhaps conscious, but definitely not generic, whereas (it is here being maintained) what is necessary is a generic, pluralistic universe.

A generic necessity is inseparable from a concrete specification. The specification exemplifies, sustains it, as any actuality exemplifies 'actuality'. A universal might have some reality, and might be specified by what stands in contrast with it, but a generic item has no status apart from some specification or other. The present universe, therefore, could be said to have a necessary 'form' with a changing 'matter', where 'form' is less than an essence, and 'matter' is more than an indeterminate potentiality.

'Red' and 'green', it might be held, are universals; or alternatively, only particulars. In either case, they are distinguishable from 'color', as the specific from the generic. There is no mere 'color'; there is always this or that color. But this or that color is *a* color; it specifies generic color, not as something which has a prior or independent reality, but as that which can be abstracted from every particular color. This is not nominalism. Nominalism denies the reality of universals and the control that universals, particularly in the form of principles, conditions, and prescriptions, can exert.

To hold that a generic item is necessary is to maintain that there always is an instance of it. It is a primary category which is empty or verbal, only when treated in abstraction from a particular instantiation. Yet, fixated on, as it has now been in the course of the examination of what might conceivably be in place of this particular universe, the idea of it is not evidently meaningless or unimportant.

By another route, and with different results, I have now arrived at something like one of Kant's positions. With him, it is being maintained that there is at least one inescapable category, but that this has a meaningful use only when it is united with what in fact is. He, to be sure, has nine or a dozen categories, takes them to apply to the raw stuff of experience, supposes that they help constitute an experiential world, denies their application to finalities and even to actualities as substantial beings with an inwardness of their own, and makes them the creatures of judgment. None of these ideas need be accepted.

I haven't thought of the matter for decades, but in *Reality* I tried to show how one could start with a single category. I took this to be a category for knowledge, and used it as a base for the derivation of other categories. The present account, in contrast, is ontological in import; its reference to a single category is to what is isolatable. It may not have a specific, delimited application to the items within the universe. If, in consonance with the view in *Reality,* one were to suppose that the primal category was the law of contradiction, this would now have to be understood as initially requiring an opposition between actualities and finalities. But it still is too accommodating to allow it to be interpreted in that way only; the law of contradiction has application to numbers as well as to existents.

It could be argued that if numbers are abstractions, they are precisely what the law of contradiction does not deal with. Abstractions are universals, that is, generals, and generals, as Peirce remarked, do not allow for an opposition between their conceivable alternative specifications—'man' is neither male nor female. The law of contradiction, if it applies to numbers, will apply to them as distinct items in the realm of Possibility. If the law applies to all (and only to) actualities and finalities, must they not be where it is sustained and specified as a generic category?

The 'is-not' or 'is non-' of the law of contradiction is specified by an actual relation of otherness operating between the actualities and the finalities. When the law of contradiction is utilized to refer to what is not an actuality, it deals with a finality or some subdivision of it—usually a delimited possibility or meaning within the realm of Possibility. Such a use requires that the distinguished possibility have a boundary enabling it to be set in contradistinction to other items; a reference must be made back to actualities as the only agencies by means of which possibilities can be demarcated one from the other. The category applies, not only to the entire universe of actualities and finalities, but also to what these make it possible to separate out of something general. Such a general is subject to the law because it stands in contrast with other generals. The items which may be subsequently separated out of it are not (until the separation occurs) subject to the law of contradiction, not because of any defect in the law, but because there are no distinct items within the general to which it could be applied.

The general, as that which allows for no separation of items within it, and the generic, as that which is abstractable from particular cases, are obviously different. The law of contradiction, identified as the generic category always governing the universe, no matter how different it may be from what it now is, is exemplified in the opposition of actualities and finalities, in the opposition of actualities to one another, and in the opposition of finalities to one another.

Can the generic govern? Only so far as it was abstracted from the universe, and made to apply to delimited portions of it.

Still unanswered is the question as to just why one contingent exemplification of a necessary law prevails rather than some other. We can not answer this except by referring to some other contingent or to something necessary. The one reference leaves us in the same situation as before; the other leads us to consider a necessity which is able to act, and then to seek a reason why it acted in one way rather than another. If the question can not be answered, a metaphysics should concern itself only with what is required by the necessary dimensions of the contingent universe of actualities and finalities that happens to be the case now.

If a plurality of items requires a One, then a plurality of one actuality and one finality will require a One beyond them. If there were two actualities and one finality, the latter would be a One for the two; if there were two finalities and one actuality, the latter would be a one for those two. Only if there are at least two actualities and two finalities can each pair be a Many, for which each finality and each actuality, respectively, provides One.

A cautious metaphysics would allow for no more than two actualities—which does not seem to make any significant difference to the understanding of the universe—and no more than two finalities—which would require one to hold that three of the finalities might not be. The finalities, of course, do not depend for their reality on actualities, but the evidences we have for the finalities depend on their having certain intruded features and relations that could not be accounted for in any other way.

Two actualities could conceivably be affiliated and coordinated; affiliated and rationally related; affiliated and located; affiliated and evaluated; coordinated and rationally related; coordinated and located; coordinated and evaluated; rationally related and located; rationally related and evaluated; located and evaluated. I now see no way in which to choose amongst those; the two actualities could be connected by and subject to any of these ten pairs of ones. But if any of these couples alone could be, why are there five finalities now?

May 1

If, to the coupled finalities listed yesterday, one adds the triplets and quadruplets that can also be distinguished, we get (together with the five finalities together) a set of twenty-six cases where we have at least two actualities and at least two finalities. If the twenty-six cases are all that there can be, we have the following three necessities:

A] A generic necessity for a pluralistic universe having at least two finalities and two actualities.

B] A disjunction of twenty-six ways in which the generic necessity can be exemplified.

C] A particular exemplification, one of the twenty six, in which the generic necessity is in fact present.

Each of these alternatives deserves some consideration:

A] The formal necessity, I have suggested, has the shape of the law of contradiction. Though not dependent for its validity on any particular alternative, it nevertheless requires an exemplification, for it to have any status at all. Following the lead of Frege, but abstracting from his emphasis on truths, one can define "x presupposes y" as "x could not be unless y were," and then note that the law presupposes the exemplification rather than the converse, for unless there be an exemplification of it, it would not be. Viewed in this way, the law has no prescriptive power; it is a variable, not assertible. One might write it with mere place holders, and thus without the terms which enable it to be true or false.

B] The supposition that there is a disjunction of twenty-six cases, which exhausts all the possible universes, sounds mad, willful, perverse. But, of course, if there be an exhaustive set of items which satisfy the generic law together, they will come to an arbitrary number. It is to be noted, too, that the number abstracts from the consideration of how many actualities above two that there in fact are. The twenty-six disjuncts are distinguished only by the number and kind of finalities they embrace.

The law of contradiction, stated as *"x* is not (or is other than) non-*x"* allows the *x* and the non-*x* to be exemplified by single entities, combinations of entities, and disjunctions of entities. If the law is the primary category, it will not only always be exemplified—the third alternative—but there will be twenty-six cases excluding one another. Such a disjunction is still abstract, differing from the law in giving values to the *x* and non-*x* in the form of disjunctions, each of which is related to the rest as strictly other than this. The understanding of the twenty-six cases as exclusive disjuncts requires the application of the law to the set of them; the set illustrates the law without exemplifying it, giving the place holders in the law an imagined filling.

c] The universe is one of the twenty-six distinguishable illustrations of the generic law, differing from all the others in the fact that it occurs. In addition to excluding and being excluded by (as in B) what is on a footing with it, it excludes all the others with an additional force, making them logical possibilities that can not then be realized.

As exemplifying the law of contradiction, the case that in fact holds will have a necessity to it which is sustained by actualities and finalities standing in opposition to one another. Since one of the twenty-six cases must in fact be and preclude the others from being, its presence also involves an exemplification of the law of excluded middle (or as modern logicians like to say, the law of bivalence, though this, for them, is restricted to statements or propositions as true or false). The law of excluded middle gets application only when we have distinct items, and thus only after we have descended from the law of contradiction, or even from the twenty-six alternatives, to the having of one of them maintained against the others.

The exemplifying case excludes all the others. They can not in turn be said to exclude it in the same sense. There is a reciprocal exclusion only so far as all are on a footing. But the exemplifying case, as that which is or is necessary, has an excluding force not possible to what is excluded. This consequence has importance for modal logics, which seek to keep in accord with the nature of things and are not content merely with abstract formulations.

If one were to identify a thing in itself with a finality, or at least allow it to function as one, despite its possible transcendence and incapacity to govern an objective cosmos, one would, according to the foregoing account, have to hold that there were at least two things in themselves standing in contrast with at least two objects.

May 2

In part of yesterday's discussion I seem to have been following out the lead of two conflicting ideas.   1] Exclusion was seen to be a symmetrical relation, and as a consequence I held that past and present excluded one another.   2] The present was seen to have a power that was greater than that which it excluded, and, as a consequence, I said that the present excluded the future, but did not go on to say that the future excluded the present. How are these to be reconciled?

One might maintain that the exclusion is always symmetrical, and that the asymmetry, which involves the acknowledgement of the distinctiveness of the present, is but a way of remarking on the contrast between the past and the present as involved with its future, or between the future and the present as involved with its past. But this does not take account of the fact that it is the present, by itself, which is so distinctive, with a presence which has a definiteness and force not possible to the past or the future.

A better alternative is one which takes exclusion to be symmetrical in both cases, but contrasts one exclusion with the other. A present item would exclude and be excluded by both the past and the future, but as excluded by both it is more than either, in power and presence. Such a view would seem to require   A] that if the past and future excluded one another directly, this would be in a different way from that in which they excluded one another through the meditation of the present, and   B] that the present be divided against itself, be that which merely is, and also be in one relation of exclusion to the past and in another to the future.

A] There is nothing surprising in the idea that if x excludes both y and z, these may not exclude one another in the same sense that x excludes both. Courage is a virtue which excludes both cowardice and foolhardiness; these are both vices and may both occur together. Both the present and the past are determinate relative to the future; both the present and the future are indeterminate relative to the past. The present, in contrast with both, can be relatively determinate and indeterminate and, so far, have a power which they do not.

B] The present is divided against itself just so far as it is a term in relations of exclusion; but it also exists apart from such relations. The power that it exerts is the power to sustain itself as a term in two different relations of exclusion. The past and the future are only terms, but the present is also a source of itself as a term related to each.

If past and future are only terms in a relation of exclusion, in what sense could the one be determinate and the other indeterminate with respect to the same present, or with respect to one another? Also, as mere terms in the relation of exclusion, they seem to lack an existential thrust away from themselves or to be able to suffer one issuing from the present. If so, the past does not appear to be an operative cause or condition, and the future does not seem to be prescriptive, restrictive, conditioning.

The indeterminateness and determinateness of the future and past are abstracted from in their roles as terms; they are then just units excluding and being excluded both from one another and from the term which the present provides. The present is not divided, but it enters as a term into two different relations.

I am not divided because I am small in relation to one man and large in relation to another. The thrust of the present depends on its being present, and not on the way it excludes past and future. Its concreteness involves the possession of its relativized forms. The being of that, which is small in relation to this, and large in relation to that, is of such and such a magnitude; small and large are attributable to the being from different positions, and reduce to the same magnitude in the being.

A past and a future item, no less than a present, are more than terms in a relation of exclusion. Each has relations to other items in the past or in the future. When each is directly related to the other it is as a term in a relation, distinct from that which each has to the present item.

A past item is more than a term in a relation of exclusion, but is never as concrete, as rich, as powerful, as insistent as what is now present. Both have reality, and both have a forcefulness greater than that expressed when they function just as terms. Relations of exclusion are not merely formal.

Present, past, and future items all exclude and are excluded in more than formal ways. The present not only formally excludes the past and future, but forcefully maintains itself against them; its maintenance is not different in kind from that which characterizes the maintenance of the past and the future against it, and perhaps also against one another. Past and future items, though, could be said to be nothing more than single meanings which all relativized terms express in different ways, whereas a present item must always be more than such a meaning. A present item possesses its relativized terms, reducing them to itself; but past and future items are not relativized by the present, for it can neither reduce nor possess them.

The present offers itself in the guise of a plurality of terms and, in this guise, makes it possible for the past and future to have the roles of terms in opposition to it. Apart from a present item, a past or future item (abstracted from the relations it has to others, also past or future) would just be, the one a fact, the other a possibility. There would, of course, not be a sequence of the present functioning as a term and then the past and future doing so. A present item, in addition to functioning as a substance expressing itself and possessing what it expresses, enables past or future items, by means of its expressions, to be in a relation of exclusion to the present.

Past and future, though, are not only excluded and exclude; they also make a difference to the present. The present is not cut off entirely from either; it is that which issued out of the past; it is what it is because of the past; it is now functioning in terms of what is possible to it in the future. These considerations support the view that past and future items have some status of their own, and are not merely relativized terms. The exclusion of the present is met by exclusions which are more than formal. Those more than formal exclusions, which are due to the past and future, are elicited by the more than formal exclusions now being expressed by a present item.

To speak in this way is to seem to hold that the past and the future depend on the present before they are able to function. It should not, therefore, be said that the past and the future have roles as excluding items which are dependent on the present, since this would allow them to be excluded before—if only logically 'before'—they exclude. All three—present, past, and future items—function together, excluding and being excluded in more than formal ways. But the present alone is active with respect to its status as terms, since such terms are inseparable from it as expressing itself, whereas past and future are not active at all.

At the end of yesterday's discussion, it was said that if things in themselves were taken to be like the finalities, they could be set in contrast with bodies or external objects. The matter was not pursued because, most uncharacteristically, I suddenly became very tired and was unable to think further, even though I had before me a good part of the day, had slept well the night before, and was well rested.

If things in themselves are endowed with consciousness, they are not the loci of categories which illustrate a primary generic category; such categories apply to the total complex of finalities and actualities (or, as restricted to the present question, to the complex of things in themselves and what was external to them, whether these be bodies that are conditioned by those things in themselves or are objects which have a greater independent role). If the generic category were given any function it would be something like that of a Kantian unity of apperception, and not like an Hegelian mind, since it would have no reality of its own. But unlike a Kantian category, and more like an Hegelian one, the exemplifications of the generic would encompass both a formal or abstract principle of unification (similar to a Kantian category) and the world which stood in contrast with this (a world which neither the Kantian nor the Hegelian allows for as that which in fact exists apart from any application of a category, whether this be sustained by a human mind or by an all-encompassing one). The mind as employing epistemic or constitutive categories could be viewed, though, as epitomizing the category which in fact encompasses both it and the objects with which it is concerned. Categories, as epitomized by the mind, on this supposition, would not work on raw material, a manifold, but, instead would be agencies for a judgment of what had already been categorized by a part of an original all-encompassing category.

Such an abstract way of dealing with the mind, or the self, even when these are identified with things in themselves, or at least with men in themselves, does not do justice to oneself as normally known. We come to know ourselves first by becoming aware of a slightly nuanced feeling, which spreads throughout the body; normally there is an emphasis on the termini of the feeling, where the differences in the nuances become evident, often simply by means of the attention that is directed toward them. With pains, pleasures, itches, some termini come into sharp focus, flooded with additional feeling. The termini are known by a double contrast—with themselves just before, and each with the other termini that also are felt, though in less emphatic ways.

There seems to be a kind of normal or even normative feeling; it is habitual and hardly noticed. That feeling has the same roots as those which accompany the use of distinctive organs, particularly those used in perception. In the case of perception, the feeling is partly spent in the use of the organ; as a result there is some awareness that the eyes, for example, as Whitehead constantly remarked, are being used. But much of the feeling remains inconspicuously expressed, to be elicited into greater expression when, by means of the organ, there is a termination at what is not simply a terminus, but a limit, maintained by something not in one's control. At the very same time that one is having a nuanced feeling of one's entire body, there is a limited expression of feeling in the use of an organ. This may be followed with an emotional involvement with what lies beyond the terminus.

To arrive at a terminus of perception is to be caught up in controls beyond one's power to modify or to eliminate. In sympahy, and surely also in anger, hatred, and when in the grip of similar strong emotions, one penetrates (beyond any preassignable degree) past the terminus into the object, which provides one with a maintained limit. (Anger, hatred, unlike sympathy or the feelings and emotions evoked by art, are unmodulated, and overrun, distort, and make us misconstrue what is being encountered.)

We can perceive our own bodies; we can look at our hands, touch our thighs, smell our toes, taste our lips and fingers, hear our stomachs and our voices. We then function as we do with respect to other perceptual objects. But we know that we are perceiving *our* own bodily parts because the feeling which is being expressed in the perception is countered by the normal feeling that we have. We are self-aware because we confront perceptual content with the normal feelings of ourselves as centered and expressed at the surface of our bodies.

Tom might claim that he felt Sam to be providing Tom with a locus for Tom's pain. Such a claim is on a par with Tom's claim that he is made of glass or is invisible. The acknowledgement of a pain as located at some place requires a meeting of the individual with the pain. He then attends to a location at his body. Were this not true, it would be a mystery why even a dog knows where to scratch itself, and why we know where to direct the doctor, where to apply lotions, and the like. Though our locating is not precise, we do attend to an area where a felt public location is countered by a felt accentuation of a nuanced feeling.

I call something 'mine' when it belongs to me in fact or by right. I can apply the expression to many different kinds of entities:

A] What I constitute—dreams, beliefs, hopes.

B] What I constitute in part—memories, sensations, experiences.

C] What I vitalize—my body, particular organs, and what these affect, such as work or actions.

D] The terminus of my attention, as that which stands away from me, which terminates me.

E] What conditions me—my past, my future, my ruler, my experiences, my parents, my traditions.

F] What I am entitled to, because of what I am, because of what had been given to me, or because it had been prescribed as that which ought to be given to me or recognized to be mine.

G] What is mine by nature—my ways, my inheritance, my diseases.

H] What I have acquired over time—my habits, dispositions, temper, character.

I] The beginning of a movement into me—my name, my appearances, my look, me from your standpoint.

J] A subdivision of ours, my share in what is common.

K] What I claim, even though it may not be honored—my sweetheart, my country, my friend.

L] Where I had once been a part—my college, my country, my city.

M] Where or with what I now identify myself, accept as an object of loyalty—my team, my friends, my family.

N] The not-mine. It is *my* not-mine, a not-mine relative to me, possessed by me as that which is my proper other.

O] What distinguishes me from others—my body, my accomplishments, my reputation, my style, my manners.

P] What is recognized to be independent of me but yet to have a special relationship to me—my children, my parents, my cousins—even though that relationship may also, though with a different stress, characterize others as well.

Q] What I own—my clothes, my money, my typewriter.

Some of the illustrations show that a number of these headings are too inclusive. It would be desirable to have a systematic way of deciding such questions, for that would help us determine whether or not something had been omitted.

All of the cases together make evident that an I or self is not only at a boundary where a not-mine is maintaining itself and perhaps opposing me, but is also possessing all that is on my side of the boundary, and thereby incidentally making what lies on the other side of the boundary be a 'my not-mine'.

In 'my x', the 'x' is something distinct from the 'my', and therefore from the self. When I speak of 'my self', the 'my' serves to distinguish rather than to mark out a possession. The distinction may serve merely to contrast other dimensions of myself with the self, or the entire self from other selves.

Whatever possesses, and thereby makes something be mine, is itself not possessed. In contrast with most of the other senses of 'mine', possession is determined from the standpoint of a public world. When 'mine' refers to a portion of the 'ours' this meaning is also touched upon.

I speak of mine when I want to distinguish it from what could be or might be claimed to be yours, or, though it might not be claimed by anyone, is something which I want to claim. 'This is mine; I created it'; 'that hat is mine'. 'Mine' here expresses the fact that I have reached out, if not into a public world, into one where I want to put an emphasis on what could conceivably be ignored, alienated, possessed, or claimed by another. The mine is what is to be qualified by my self, or 'I'.

When I speak of 'my self', a distinction is evidently being made between the subject speaking and the object spoken of, even though the intent may be not to allow any kind of division between them. The 'my' approaches the self from an area where it is or could be together with other entitites, in fact, in imagination, or in thought, so that in speaking of 'my self' I am using the self as an I to deal with it as approachable via a 'me'. Though I may be reporting the result of an introspection, I nevertheless speak from a position where the self can be known, approached, understood, or addressed by another as well. When, instead, I speak of my dreams or thoughts, I make the approach from my own center, even though the language and the communication may presuppose the presence of myself with others. If I say 'that was my idea', 'I had that thought' I do not reach back to my self but, instead, affirm that the thought or idea already acknowledged is qualified by my private self. Though something is mine only as reached from the self, I acknowledge the self only after I identified something outside it;

though I may acknowledge something as privately constituted and possessed, I distinguish and remark on it from a position external to the self.

May 3

Though 'you' are acknowledged by me, just as are things that are mine, I do not say 'my you'. I do say, 'you, my partner', 'you, my friend', 'you, my support'. The 'you', as not tolerating a 'my', points up the fact that you are acknowleded to be coordinate with me. Exterior things that are mine are known in perception to be absenting themselves; they are also had as objects claimed because they are known to stand away from us. The 'you' emphasizes the absenting, the standing away, the having of a status apart from the relativization that 'my' involves. References to you as a partner, friend, support, and the like, recovers the position of you as related to me. If, as I have argued, Being dictates that entities are equal in status, the acknowledgment of you is one with the acceptance of a dominance by Being.

'You and I' also takes us to be coordinate. But unlike the previous case, where the coordination was merely that of granting the other the status of a reality in itself, 'you and I' takes us to be together in a way which preserves our irreducible separateness. There is an intimacy adumbrated in the expression, even if it is followed by '. . . are enemies'. We are thought to have an involvement with one another for the moment, as realities which nevertheless are distinct. 'You and I' seem to reveal the dominance of Substance.

'They' and 'the others' do not grant that anything else is on a level with us. They emphasize the difference between ourselves and other men. This is even more obvious when we speak of 'they and us' 'we and the others'. We do not simply stand away from them, or take them to be apart from us, but to be at a distance, and perhaps to have some effect on us, or for us to have an effect on them. Evidently, the expressions point up the dominance of Existence with its characteristic extensions.

'We', particularly when used authoritatively (a use not altogether absent in the other case), is assessive, demanding, subordinating, normally requiring a lower status or role for that to which it is addressed. One can, of course, in an act of submission, allow that another or that others are superior to oneself. And, in a generous act of accommodation or encompassment, one may allow for the addressed to have the same status as oneself. But it is the 'we' which ascribes to the others the status of being inferior, superior, or equal. 'We' marks the presence of an evaluative power, expressing the finality, Unity.

'You', 'I', 'they', and 'we', if entertained together, make up a set of meanings whose interrelationship to one another is presupposed in the examination of them severally. Such a set is governed by Possibility, or Meaning. The relations amongst the members of the set are initially formal in character. An examination of these pronouns perhaps properly begins with such a formalized set.

Terms such as 'me', 'he', 'us', 'them'; the special uses of the term 'you', referring to a number or used to demarcate; 'we', as merely collecting a number of I's; and I, as a subdivision of 'we', will, if the foregoing be taken as a base, have to be understood in terms of it, specializing, modifying, limiting or extending it. 'Me' could be said to begin with the 'you and I', 'he' to be a subdivision of 'them', and both to presuppose 'the others' or 'them'. 'Us' is the correlative of 'them', the locus of the several 'I's' or 'me's', and 'you's'. With some justification one could maintain that 'us and them' is even more primitive than 'I and you'. That would lead to a change in what is to be set under the heading of a dominance by Being.

There seems, though, despite some plausibility and even insight which such an approach promotes, to be something artificial to the entire procedure. For the moment, I am not confident whether this is due to the fact that I have dealt with the several pronouns, not in terms of their familiar grammatical uses but in the light of what I had already concluded about the various finalities and their effectiveness, or whether it is due to the fact that the approach is unfamiliar. Perhaps something of both. (I found the five categories of great value in structuring the book on the film.)

If the metaphysics, which yields the finalities as unavoidable conclusions, is sound, the finalities should provide a good base in terms of which to deal with primary distinctions. To this contention it might be objected that empirical enterprises do not necessarily have neat divisions; that the ways in which we use our language and pivotal terms may answer more to our practical and communal needs than to any primary set of categories; and that the election of certain terms or areas as topics, just because they serve to illustrate primary categories, is a way of keeping inquiry within the confines of an abstract account and thus precludes creativity, novelty, chance, and history. Similar objections could be made to logic, theoretic cosmological physics, and even to such a table as Mendeleeff's, or the classifications of botanists. For their own purposes, these various enterprises abstract from aspects which might be of primary interest for other purposes, and attend to what will enable them to bring an intelligible order out of what had been a miscellany. Some of them could justify themselves because of their success in predictions, the deduction of various laws, and the like. Such a defense, though, is not open to classical symbolic logic, which can be said, even less than metaphysics, not to be bothered by the higgledy-piggledy miscellaneous character of the familiar world.

The finalities need not be acknowledged as they are in fact functioning with respect to the actualities of the world. It is enough if they serve as guides leading one to see how various items always stand in relation to one another. The items examined may well have a multiplicity of features of little importance in practical life and daily experience; yet these might be emphasized on behalf of a systematic understanding which attends to the most persistent and well grounded aspects, taking all others to be specialized forms of these, complications of them, or irrelevant accretions, reflecting something of the incoherence or contingency of the world.

There is a risk in proceeding in this way, but there is also considerable gain. Egyptian geometry was empirical, and attended primarily to actual measurements made on the earth. The Greek mathematicians broke geometry off from its empirical moorings and, though they did not rest it on prior metaphysical speculations, proceeded to deal with it in terms of ideas somewhat remote from what was obtrusive in daily experience—points, lines, straights, planes, and the like. No one can tell in advance whether the losses that result from such an attempt will be greater than the posibble gains.

If there are five finalities affecting the actualities in the ways I have described, their influence in every domain should be detectable. If they do not in fact isolate what is of paramount concern in a particular discipline, it could well be that the discipline is not yet in a fully matured stage. But one need not go this far in order to defend the attempt to deal with a field in the light of what one has learned in a metaphysics. Nor need one woodenly apply metaphysical distinctions. One can use them as agencies for ferreting out essential divisions that otherwise would be obscured or unnoticed, and checking (in the double sense of testing and braking) them by what one is able to see is functioning as pivotal, primary, or dominant. There is no reason why categories, rooted in an understanding of what the finalities are and how they function, may not be used loosely and tightly at different times—loosely when one is attending to actual occurrences, tightly when one is trying to systematize, conduct an orderly inquiry, uncover hidden dimensions, and be in some consonance with what has been or could be discerned in other enterprises.

There might not be anyone other than myself. Nevertheless, I can say 'we' with justification. If the 'we' is not to be a mere area in which I find myself, it must stretch to a possible other 'I', or to a 'you', understood to be that which is maintaining itself on a level with myself. In claim, expectation, or supposition I take there to be something which can be an I (as I am) within the 'we'. That we is a condition, with a power and a status greater than I alone have, even when the 'we' is used, as an editor might, to express nothing more than what he alone holds.

Socially minded thinkers would maintain that one must begin with some socially determined notions. For them 'we' has primacy over 'I' and 'you'. But though there are senses in which 'we' is primary, there are also senses in which it is not.

It could be that an individual finds himself to be an 'I' only after he has shared in a 'we', and located himself within it. But it is also true that one can begin with an 'I' and see this as extending toward a position where there could be another 'I', which is being accommodated at the same time that it is being assessed from the position of one's own 'I'. One can also start with 'you and I' and then speak of a 'we'. When this is done, emphasis is placed on the 'and', with the speaker abdicating his authoritative role, but not wiping it out entirely, since it is he who is putting the union of the two in place of their interaction.

Suppose one starts with 'you' and belatedly changes to 'we'? Here one seems to be including oneself subordinately, as though one were filling out the position which one's 'we' permitted him to assume, with him in an authoritative position. The situation is quite close to that in which one submits to an authority, where the act of submission itself involves, by virtue of its origination with oneself—even where compelled by another—an attitude of superiority. By the submission, one allows the other subsequently to enjoy a primary evaluative role, and thus to be the 'I' about which the 'we' primarily pivots. Because it always allows a place for another 'I', 'we' weakens the force of an initial 'I'.

The kingly 'we' is more objective, more anonymous, more authoritative, but also less idiosyncratic, less personal, less private than, and thus without the expressiveness of the imperial 'I'. The 'we', even though expressing just an 'I', is set away from it, given a public status, made authoritative in a world. One can even start with it as authoritative in a world. A legal partnership is a 'we' where no partner need have any priority over any other. The 'we' here is uttered, as it were, by another 'we', the legal system, or the state. The initial evaluation is made of the different individuals, faced as primarily different 'you's' and 'me's', that is, as in public, and not as primary 'I's'. That evaluation carries out, within a restricted area, the authority of a primary legal or political 'we'. The evaluation does not necessarily instance the latter; a legal or political 'we' merely determines how a 'we' or a 'you', or 'others' are to be used within its frame.

A partnership of two is a 'we'. It is neutral to both of them, without authoritative force. It does, though, obtain a force from the legal 'we'; this specifies just how the partnership is to affect the partners and others. The legal 'we' has here usurped the place of the 'I' which is operative in the ordinary use of the 'we', and which provides the 'we' with its authority.

At least as impersonal but less imperious is the 'we' which expresses or represents some special inquiry, some group, with which one has identified oneself. We speak of 'we Americans', 'we who are rich', 'we scientists' to refer to what has the force of a fact compacted out of the conjoint activity of a number, perhaps also with the addition of what has been accumulated from the past, and the kind of ideal which is being pursued and perhaps realized. There is an authoritative force here, but it is not due to any of the members, or to the speaker. It expresses the overriding nature of the conjoint fact, its ability even to be diversified amongst the various members. One might come to the recognition of this 'we' from the position of an 'I'. But the 'we' can also be the outcome of an acceptance, with an 'I' only later acknowledged. This use is rather close to that of the legal 'we'; it is distinctive in that it allows for the acknowledgment of oneself as a part of it. A state is imposed, at least in part; a group is shared in.

'We Americans' may refer to what is a creature of history in which we participate. It may also refer to a domain of interaction, where the various individuals help constitute the very 'we' that is conditioning them. Each contributes his share to an encompassing 'we' to which all are subject, if only for the possession of certain traits, or tendencies, or responsibilities.

All men are part of a single humankind. This may be understood as the entire set of men, as set over against all other types of actualities; it may refer to a single community tied together by a common acceptance of themselves as distinctive, or even as the loci of truth; it may be taken to refer to a common culture or civilization of which all are at least in principle a part; it may refer to what has had and continues to have a single history. All of these, like the previous case, are constituted by the interaction of individuals to which every one contributes, and to which everyone owes something distinctive, particularly since mankind has a history. Unlike 'we Americans', it is inescapable precisely because it is all-embracing. It, too, may be taken to be prior to every individual, and to subject them all to itself, even though they constitute it. It will then have an authoritative force which comes from its own nature and career, helping to determine some of the features which every individual will possess. Such a 'we' could be taken to be prior to every other, and every other expression. In a limited form, this is what is maintained by those who submit themselves to the dictates of common sense, a common language, a form of life, a conventional outlook, or a view of truth. On this view, an 'I' would have meaning only as a contracted form of the 'we' or as that which is made the bearer of certain traits.

The 'we' of mankind, some selected segment of it, or some expression of it, is authoritative as a matter of fact, because of its encompassment, because of its power, because the various individuals are found subject to it, because the acknowledged traits are delimitations or consequences of it, or because of its effective control over its members. In acknowledging it from the position of an 'I', I yield myself, accepting whatever features or position that then accrue to me. I enter into it, not as one who is empowering it, but as then able to share in and use its authority by accepting what it requires of its members. If it is not entered into, and there allowed to dictate to me what I am and what I can claim, I take it to be a projection from myself but with terminal points which have already been filled out by other 'I's'. The submission in which I then engage is considerable, for I come without authority of any kind, but obtain it instead from the 'we' in which I participate.

The 'we', then, has an authority which it owes to individuals, to a power beyond it, or to itself by virtue of its all-encompassing, possessive, determining power. Though, as the last, it is prior to the 'I', the 'you', and the 'others', though it has a longer duration than any one of these, and though it may even be the aboriginal fact out of which everything else was eventually precipitated only to come back to it again in acts of submission, it may have a minor role in the actual speech, thought, and practices of men. Even if it be supposed that 'we', in this sense, is prior to all the other senses in which 'we' is used—logically, historically, epistemologically, and ontologically even—it still may be that the other terms have an independent role and stand on a level with it in power and import. Though, for example, I might discover myself to be an 'I' only after I found myself within a world of men, I may find that I had had an unnoticed 'I' all the while, and that I could have and now certainly can and shall use that 'I' independently of, and sometimes perhaps in opposition to, the common 'we' in which I participate.

May 4

When a beginning is made with 'we', the 'I' is a limit, a construction, a presupposition, the 'you and I' an articulation, the 'you' a possibility or a subdivision, and the 'others' possible projections or contrasts. When, instead, a beginning is made with 'you and I', the 'you' and the 'I' are granted reality at the same time that they are taken to be constituents of a 'we' resulting from the way in which they are together. 'We' then becomes a consequence of the emphasis given to the 'and', or the way, or the fact that the 'you and I' are together. 'You', here, could be singular or plural; in either case, even while it is conjoined with the 'I', it contrasts with that as an other. The 'I' and the 'you' are independent, joined together, but in opposition and subordinated to a single 'we'.

If a beginning is made with 'you', once again there is a duality; the 'you' is relative to an implicit 'I', and stands away from that relativization as another 'I'. As standing away, it is an other; as a relativized term, it is joined with the 'I' to constitute not a neutral 'we', but one constituted in an act of attention.

By attending to a 'you' I set the two of us away from all the rest. If the 'you' is multiple, I face it as a 'them', which may or may not be acknowledged to subdivide into a plurality of individual 'you's'. If I take myself to be functioning as an authoritative 'we', or as a 'we' produced by an act of attention, the 'them' may be only something projected, and not actually present.

If a beginning is made with 'them' or the 'others', there is an implicit reference made to an 'I' or a 'we' to which the 'them', 'they', or 'others' are relative. We have here something analogous to the case where we begin with 'you', with the difference that we do not yet necessarily acknowledge that there are distinct 'you's' or even a collective 'you' which is maintained against an 'I' or a 'we'. It is possible for there to be subdivisions of the 'them', but no claim about this made. The 'others' are faced as standing away, opposing, contrasting. They may be faced by an 'I', a 'we', or even by a 'me'. If we begin with the others, it seems as if there is an implicit reference, at least, by each of us, to a 'me', since we then envisage ourselves from the position of 'others', or take ourselves to be limits, constructions, or sustaining sources of the 'me's', then accepted as in effective involvement with others which are kept away from the 'me's'.

If we start with a set of these terms, we obtain them in their severalty by separation, abstraction, or emphasis. Each is given full weight when it is recognized to have a function not expressed by a mere unit in an aggregation. It could be said to be a construction or a limit from the position of a set, though from its standpoint it will be a member of the set only as an abstraction, not exercising its characteristic functions. In the previous cases, the abstraction begins at different points in the abstracted entity.

There are five possible beginnings, each of which allows for a distinctive way of getting the others. There is no reason to believe that there is an empirical priority enjoyed by any one of them. The doubtful case, perhaps, is where we have an aggregate of all of them for, on the one hand, the aggregate seems to be for some 'I' or 'we' and, on the other, seems not to be an empirical occurrence. In the preceding cases there was a realistic dimension to the item selected as a beginning, but this does not preclude an empirical confrontation.

There is some justification even for supposing that the realistic

uses of terms, with their ingredience in actualities and as involved
with actual functionings, is not possible until there has been an
understanding of how the terms are used in an actual language. But
there surely will have to be an 'I' at work, making the identification
and benefiting from the meanings in the language. The 'I' can, from
this position, be taken to be a kind of subterranean force which
achieves intelligibility only after it has made use of public meanings;
it will not be reducible to a function of the public meanings without
making its activity and its ability to stand away from public involvement be beyond comprehension.

The realistic import of the various terms can be understood in a
number of ways. A 'we', for example, may be the 'we' of a cultural or
societal interlocking of individuals; of a domain of distinct individuals each with his privacy and dignity; of a common human
nature which has a core of constancy even when specialized in
diverse and even antagonistic ways by different individuals; of an
historic mankind which has made itself what it is over the course of
time; and of a civilization with its ideals, hierarchy of values, and
inherited treasures, vices, and equipment. A 'you' may be insistent,
imperious, basic, the Freudian father; a locus of rights and duties; a
distinctive mind; a listener and speaker; an interacting other; a
source of evaluation; or an object of evaluation. 'You and I' may be
involved in vital relations of attraction and repulsion; stand in
relation to one another as worthy of the same degree of respect,
responsibility, privileges, rights; be units of a world of men or some
subdivision of this; be basic interactive elements in a social system;
be a primary condition (as Buber insisted), which does not allow for
a genuine separation of the 'you' and the 'I', but also not assimilated
to a 'we'. 'They' or the 'others' may be taken to be a primary basic
reality to which we must adhere in order to achieve power or
standing; it may refer to an as yet unexplored set of beings like
ourselves, or to a set of beings who are, as under the aegis of the
'them', so far on a footing; it may refer to a domain of language,
custom, or practice in which we must share if we are to be able to
understand anything. It may be that which we are required to
understand to some degree if we are to be able to understand
anything else or to do anything intelligible; it may set the condition
for our functioning, defining what we can and can not do, accept, or
believe; or it may be a ground of the values in terms of which we
assess everything, including ourselves. And, finally, inside lan-

guage, the different terms may be so many different adherent names; the primary semantic referents for our discourse; the primary subjects in discourse; the primary denotatives; or the loci of primary values.

All of these uses, evidently, can be combined with one another to yield a large number of complex cases. 'You', as an adherent name, for example, could be used for the locus of rights and duties, a source of evaluation, an insistent substance, an interacting other, or an acknowledged user of a mind; it could refer to one of the units in an attraction-repulsion, or as an other which is conditioning us, and so on. Or one might take a stand with one of them and see the others as somehow accommodated, assimilated, modified by it. 'You', taken as an object of a denotative, could be dealt with as accommodating or being accommodated by the 'we' in the guise of a culture, human nature, and so forth.

There is something amiss, however, in any attempt which fails to take account of the 'I' in as explicit a manner as the 'we', 'you', 'you and I', or 'them', even if we were to grant that we come to it late, understand it as a limit or construction, and find it overlaid with what had been produced by a society. Even if an 'I' be taken to be just a subterranean force which could not be characterized as it exists in itself, but only in terms derived from elsewhere—which I do not believe is the case—we come to know it as distinctive, with an insistence, feelings, nuances, activities, issuing from itself. It may have obtained these, qualified these, been able to understand these only after it has been involved with other entities, but there is no question but that they are now present, and it is conceivable that what was obtained from other entities provides an opportunity to discover that they are already present.

Instead of taking 'you' alone as one of the pivotal terms, one might take 'I or you', and supplement this with 'I and you', 'I interactive with you'; (instead of 'they or others') 'I prescriptive for or prescribed by you'; (instead of 'we' and in place of the aggregate of terms) one might take 'I implying a you, and you implying an I'. One can move outside a complex set of terms to consider the individual items, the 'I', and the 'you', and then the kinds of connections they have with one another. Or—or, in addition—one can deal with the 'I' as involved with the finalities, or with complex terms, viewed as special cases of those finalities. Thus the 'I' might be considered in relation to a common human nature, and the question then asked as to just how men affect one another, and the kind of difference they make to one another's functioning. Once such a question is raised, we are soon aware that the body makes a difference to the self as surely as the self makes a difference to the body, and that such matters as differences in gender, color, and age assume a special guise.

Is gender or color solely a matter of the body; does it get a differential meaning solely from culture, history, training, tradition, and habit? The acknowledgment of the equality of all individuals and the knowledge that there has been prejudice and discrimination practiced without any apparent warrant tempts one to answer such questions in the affirmative. But then one tends to set the self on one side and the body on the other, or to assimilate the self to the adventures of the body in society. But if the body is quickened by the self, if the self possesses that body, and if that body is at once a continuation of the individual and part of an external world of society and nature, we can not stop short of an acknowledgment of gender, color, and age as having some bearing on the functioning of the self, and perhaps also on its nature as the self of an actual individual in this world.

Are gender, color, and age to be thought of an intermediaries, ways in which the world is transmitted and translated for the self? Do they enable the self to function together with other individuals and perhaps with other beings in nature, and even with the various finalities?

It is imperative that we not fall into the trap of breaking mankind up into intractable subspecies; it is also imperative that we do not minimize the bearing of gender, color, and age on individuals. The question has not been faced by philosophers in good part because they have, since Aristotle, been inclined to define the essence of man in terms which refer to what is presumably identical in all—animality, rationality, toolmaking, speech, and the like. (Yet, even Aristotle took some of the differences to be crucial and perhaps even intrinsic, since in his theory of politics he held that some men were by nature slaves, and that women naturally had an inferior role.) A scientific account loses none of its objectivity or exactitude if it takes account of such differences. This is what current sociologists and psychologists do, though they, of course, have to be content with showing what empirically discovered differences seem to be associated with one or the other of these bodily differences.

Even if every individual be granted to be equal to every other in substantiality, rights, nature, presence, and value, it still could be that gender, color, age, and perhaps even experiences, weight, strength, and health may make a difference to what the self does. Differences in these respects may require different efforts in degree and kind on the part of different selves so that they can be reduced to the selfsame result always and for every one. Two individuals who differ in gender will then be faced with the problem of making themselves representative of mankind, responsive, or valuable, by starting from different positions. Those positions might be incomparable, equal in importance, be related as more or less effective or desirable; whichever they are, they would present to the selves the same problem—the reduction of them to the same value intrinsic to the self. Each self would be faced with different content to reduce, and would have to produce the reduction in different ways.

A man lives in his body and lives through it. Even apart from societal conditioning, he can maintain an identity in himself only so far as he takes a different accounting at different moments of what his body is and does. We are not inclined to dismiss his laxness, his acts of wrongdoing, his indolence, his aggressiveness, his vital giving or withholding of himself, his cowardly turning away, or his brave facing of danger, as though they had nothing to do with what he in fact is. But all of these may be affected, and surely are nuanced and changed in rhythm by his gender, age, experiences, and perhaps color, size, weight, and musculature. If they are to be credited to him, and not merely to his body set in contrast with him, and not solely to his body when this is taken to be him exhaustively—the one because he is a man in the world, and the other because he is one who can intend, know, plan, reflect, and may sometimes be subject to bodily conditions over which he has little or no control—they must be acknowledged to have some role in his total economy and yet to be capable of a reduction to him as one who is completely on a footing with all others.

This result can be avoided by holding that men are equal in rights and duties, but are not necessarily equal in other ways. The difference in gender, and so forth could be said to be unbridgeable, and to make a difference in different areas. Childbirth, great achievement in sports, and resistance to certain diseases are functions of differences in gender, age, musculature, color, and so on. These could be said to be basic and not reducible matters of fact; nevertheless, it may be denied that they affect other equally basic facts, among which is the intrinsic equality of all men, particularly in the area of rights, duties, and opportunities. But one will still be left with the problem of the unity of all these, and why different achievements, which are grounded in different bodily traits, powers, and structures, should make a difference to the nature of the individual. To this it might reasonably be countered that the difference lies solely in the complex individual as involved in a public world, that the intrinsic equality of men lies in what they are in themselves, and that it is the task of a just society or state to translate that equality into equal viable public rights that continue to prevail, no matter what the individual is capable of doing or what his experiences are.

This is surely a cautious way to deal with the issue. It allows for a variety of human beings, without denying their equality before the law, ethically or spiritually. It keeps gender, color, and musculature where they were found, in the body, and allows them to play a role in what the body does. When moral questions are at issue it takes that body to be just an intermediary between a responsible self and the external world, and to be praiseworthy or condemnable only so far as it is taken together with the self that is quickening and directing it. Gender, color, and size will then all be entirely a matter of genes, heredity; they will play a role in experience, habit, and accident, without being granted an overriding status with respect to what men are intrinsically, not because the self is detached from all else, but because the intrinsic features of a man lie beyond public determination, even while governing public acts.

An individual does not reduce what his body is or undergoes, or brings about, or expresses. He enriches the body with intent and will, and so far is responsible for it, or will find it functioning with traits not within its provenance to control or alter. Some account has to be given of a man's failure to express an intent and will, and thus of his leaving the body undirected, a creature of passing conditions and aroused emotions.

A question remains: why should the equality of men, why should the demands of justice, override or be indifferent to what individuals bodily are or bodily can do?

May 5

Ideally, justice abstracts from the gender, personality, size, weight, and color of men, but not always and not entirely. Wards, the insane, the criminal, the senile, the alien, and the indigent receive special treatment. This takes account of their differences from the rest. One can argue that the special treatment is designed to compensate for discrepancies so as to make it possible to equate all, but then the idea of equality is used not to override differences of various kinds but to justify a consideration of them with a compensatory addition. The working hours for women were legally modified in order to protect the women. Here gender was a factor considered, and not simply abstracted from.

There are other situations where gender, color, and the like are taken into account. Insurance companies attend to differences (in the average mortality rates) between men and women; sports, such as football, do so as well; models, adoptions, friendships, clothing are attuned to gender, color, size, and other differences.

If men are dealt with as constituting communities in which they directly interplay with one another to constitute more or less close-knit unities, then personality, ability, concern, sociability are pertinent factors. If men are dealt with as legal units, justice and equality are pertinent. If they are dealt with as vehicles and sustainers of a common language or truth, their imagination, articulateness, knowledge, intelligence, and dedication are factors. If they are dealt with as interactive, their willingness and ability to work, compete, cooperate, to oppose violations of territory or customs, their openness, and their health must be considered. Dealt with as units of value, their virtues and vices, their achievements and dedications are pertinent.

If 'you' is of primary concern, personality mediated by gender, appearance, color is not to be abstracted from; if 'you and I', then an equality which a state should attempt to defend and promote in public ways; if the aggregate of terms, or language, then truth or knowledge, and its dependence on native endowments of mind; if 'they', 'the others', then their possible threat or support, and (on our side) the ways in which we can together interact with the others; and if 'we' as authoritative, its nature and operation, and the values they determine. In each case, the other terms will have subordinate roles. Once, for example, legal demands are satisfied, there can be activities in which the factors it ignored are allowed free play—in the family, in sports, in friendships, in compensation for different kinds of work or responsibility, and so on. Consequently, there will be a number of systems in which each term will have a role, but only one in which it will be pivotal or primary. There will also be one in which no one has a superior status. This will have to be distinguished from the case where we have all of them together as units in a langauage.

I am now close to the schema which governed the writing of *Cinematics*. There the film was viewed as the product of the working together of different types of contributors. Each was taken to represent and guide the rest, and also as the pivotal figure, with the others creatively working under his aegis. I also considered the cases where only one of the contributors was granted creative rights, and went on to deal with different types of film—propaganda, educational, documentary, disclosive, and experimental— as illustrating such distortions. With that as a model one would be led to say that if we begin with, let us say, 'you', we will have to view 'you and I', 'they', and so forth, as having independent areas of influence, but under the final governance of the 'you'. Denied independence, each will yield truncated or unsatisfactory cases.

Film already exhibits some approximation to the case where all the contributors work in harmony, with no one in a fixed dominant position. Is there anything here analogous to the use of the pronouns? The living language is an obvious answer, leading to the examination of the best modes of communication, where this includes discourse, recording, the preservation of truths and beliefs, and the sustaining of insights.

A language in which 'you' is the dominant factor, whether it allows for or excludes independent roles to others, is different in use and value from one in which 'we', instead, is dominant. But other terms are also important; to neglect these is to deal only with a language of pronouns. And, unless one yields to the view that language constitutes or defines what alone can be or be known, one will have turned away from the realistic sides of the various expressions, except so far as they are entailed or presupposed by the need or fact of communication.

Mankind is many things. One thing it surely is is the totality of men as together constituting a single historic people, whose nature, value, promise, and achievements are being defined and redefined every day. If there is anything that could be said to be the result of the interplay of all the different pivotal stresses I have distinguished, and the many more not yet attended to, it would be a perpetually self-making mankind. But if this leads to the neglect or minimization of the role of the individual, one will end with just a universal history, or sociology.

The importance of the pronouns, even the 'we' and the 'they', is that they reach outside the totality of men to distinctive, irreducible individuals. If this fact be taken into account, one attends to individuals in their privacy, the individuals as together, and the ways in which these two dimensions interplay. One can go on to assess an individual as a person, as a character, or as having style or personality in terms of the way in which he is in accord with the trend of mankind, contributes to it, resists it, is molded by it, interacts with it, or stands away from it.

I am evidently at a loss, groping, floundering, jumping from issue to issue, place to place, looking for a purchase from which to begin a study, whose nature and direction I have not yet got into focus. The struggle can not be avoided. Hiding its existence would defeat the intent of this work; it would also make any eventual starting point and perhaps development of a systematic position seem to start and perhaps develop without warrant, or without false but revealing moves.

Using the structures of previous studies as a guide involves both a gain and a loss. The gain is in the availability of categories and patterns which have proved helpful, and which may with some pertinent alterations prove useful again. The loss is a restriction of the imagination, a possible confining of one inquiry within limits appropriate to others, an overlooking of distinctive dimensions in the new enterprise, a neglect of opportunities to discover what may have been limitations in the previous enterprise and what may be new categories and dimensions that might illuminate what else is to be investigated. One sees such losses in the work of those with whom one disagrees, particularly those who, in their development of a philosophy, confessedly lean on the achievements or outlook of the sciences or arts or history. But there would be an even greater loss if one were to be content with one's own categorizations, instead of with the publicly available, multiply tested, highly successful ones that are sanctioned by the practices, methods, and achievements of the sciences, arts, or history.

For some time, I have had in the back of my mind the idea of writing a book to be entitled "You, I, and the Others." This has prompted some of the recent reflections; it may also be responsible for the confusions and lack of focus which have accompanied these, since the topic may itself be an arbitrary segment of something larger which I am preventing myself from seeing.

There is considerable difference between following the lead of a particular enterprise, and following the lead of a metaphysical account claiming to encompass within a set of unavoidable categories all that there is or can be known. A particular enterprise should be guided by a more inclusive enterprise. Of course there is a danger in following this course. The more inclusive may be in error; the specializations of a particular enterprise, not accounted for by the other, may be what is most of interest; the categories may be dealt with woodenly, mechanically; one may do nothing more than give concrete content to the primary categories without making anything else more intelligible or interesting. To know of these dangers is to be put on the alert, and to be in a position to avoid them. They are dangers, in fact, to which nonmetaphysical or nonphilosophic thinkers are most prone, since their implicit, fundamental views are not examined and may—and undoubtedly do—contain regrettable unexamined errors which pervert their grasp of whatever it be to which they attend.

At a minimum it seems that we must acknowledge a number of encompassing and controlling conditions, as well as a number of entities to which they apply. If the entities be 'you', 'I', and the like, the encompassing and controlling conditions will include mankind, nature, history, and the finalities, each affecting the entities in a distinctive way. Each entity will have a role to play with respect to those conditions, resisting them, qualifying them, and assimilating them.

Faced with such an array, my initial response is to see if the items do not fall under divisions previously made, particularly in the metaphysical studies; to see if, should there be less than five conditions considered, one or more have been overlooked; and to see if, should there be more than five, there has not been an unncessary duplication.

Mankind, nature, history, the finalities seem to be specializations of Substance, Possibility, Existence, and Unity. A specialization of Being is missing. Is this 'communion' what I have been expressing before with such terms as 'you and I' and 'we'? If so, a distinction would have to be made between encompassing conditions and what is subject to such conditions. The personal, private component in these, their unavoidable involvement with an 'I', even when they reach out and encompass a number, makes evident that 'communion', and 'you and I' or 'we', are to be contrasted as the encompassing and the encompassed.

Communion, mankind, nature (as a system of intelligible laws), history, and the finalities are all involved with men as irreducible actualities taken severally, or as joined together in various ways. A distinction still has to be made between the men as joined together apart from these conditions, and as a consequence of the imposition of the conditions. There is, for example, a difference between 'we' as a product of an acknowledgment of individuals by one another, and 'we' as the outcome of the operation of history on the previous 'we', on individuals separately, or as together in other ways.

Now the net is evidently too wide, at least for a single work. The finalities, moreover, in their bearing on actualities and even on men, have been dealt with in *Beyond All Appearances,* and need not be examined again. The history of man, and the ways in which men are subject to the universal intelligible laws of nature, also, are large, distinct topics. And mankind, taken as the totality of individuals, all on a footing, seems to have only a minimal import for individuals in their severalty. This leaves 'communion' as the primary representative of the finalities, and particularly Substance, to be dealt with as conditioning, affecting, and being affected by individuals in their severalty, and as together in ways which are not a consequence of the operation of a communion.

There is at least one oddity here. I made the original selection of the pronouns in the light of the five finalities. I now end with these being the entities on which a specialization of one of the finalities is to operate. This is the kind of situation which is close to that characteristic of idealism, where a single operator is understood to work on a specialization of itself. The fact that the operator here works on specializations of other possible operators will not, I think, affect the similarity, with its danger of making what in fact occurs to be nothing more than a local instance of some universal condition. But there is no need to succumb. In any case, there is no need to restrict oneself to five kinds of entities, and no need to overlook the fact that each makes a depth reference.

A communion does not float or exist on its own; it involves men. This should cause no difficulty in the use of it, provided attention is paid, not to its membership, but to the feature it has. A communion has an established interlinkage of roles, positions, and dignities; an inherited tradition of requirements to which all are subject; a mythology with its idealized heroes and villains, guiding the practices of individuals; established customs, territory, and work; crucial events, such as birth, rites of passage, death. Each of these has a prescriptive role, and the individuals, severally and in various combinations, are unavoidably qualified by them, internalize them, are caught up in them, and interplay with them.

This approach is different from that which was also considered today, where something like the structure of *Cinematics* was entertained, for here there is no set of more or less independent conditions or agents which creatively produce something but, instead, a number of distinct situations, all examined in relation to a single governing factor. That factor, I suggested just now, has a number of distinct roles; these can be dealt with in the manner pursued in *Cinematics*. The major emphasis, however, will still remain on the ways in which the various subdivisions could function as creative powers collaborating with one another in various ways and degrees.

May 6

Descartes, knowing that he doubted, knew that he existed. He said he knew this when he was doubting. He should have held that he, a *doubter,* existed when he was doubting. But he went on to maintain, without justification being offered, that his I was a thinking, believing, and so forth, I, that it was always in such a 'cognitive' state, and that it was something more than any of these or apparently all of them—a substance in fact.

It takes a mature man to reflect on the fact of doubt and to conclude that he is a doubter; it takes ingenuity and hazardous inference to go further and to claim that a doubter is a substance able to engage in other cognitive activities. One is no more daring if, instead of following Descartes's route, one were to conclude that one exists because another is: 'You are, therefore I am.'

Does not the 'You are' here contain a claim to existence? Is the Cartesian attempt not directed at deriving an existent? The sense in which a you is, however, is not necessarily the sense in which a Cartesian I is. All one need intend by 'You are' is that a you is confronted or acknowledged. That you is present and is undergirded by an I. We penetrate toward this I, and acknowledge it as being beyond any point at which we reach. But so far as the

Cartesian 'I am' is concerned, all that is needed is a you as the object of an as yet unprobed and uncharacterized I.

Sartre claims that I come to know myself through shame, and that this presupposes a you. It still will be the case, though, that the you which is making me ashamed is a you for me, a you directed at me, a you acknowledged from the standpoint of an as yet un-examined I. The shame will be a consequence of my approach toward that I from the position of a me, approached from my acceptance of the position of a you, itself presupposing the func-tioning of an I.

Does a child come to know itself as an I only after it has felt a tinge of shame? Does it not, rather, start with an awareness of a you? I think that its own I, though presupposed, is not initially known. A child is initially directed outward toward a you before it comes to grasp itself as a me (from the standpoint of some you).

The I reaches to you in an act of attention. The I and the you then either   A] have to constitute the connection between them, or   B] act within the frame of a prior connection. The alternatives are not incompatible. It is possible both to act within the frame of some connection and to add to it. In fact, it is necessary that there be some connection before there can be a constituting or adding, for otherwise there is no reason why an I should be able to find a you, be able to make contact with it, or be able to have it as a counter-weight in the guise of an I which is taking me to have the status of a you for it.

A child usually, and an infant surely, knows nothing of the interlinkage of roles; it does not start with a grasp of itself in relation to a parent; it has not yet come to know the traditions to which the members of its family and others are subject; it knows nothing of a common mythology; it has yet to learn how crucial such occur-rences as birth, rites of passage, and death are for itself and for the community. The connection that it has with others is spatial, but not simply mathematical. The space between itself and others is charged, vibrant, territorial, with various routes which it quickly learns to follow or avoid. It does not know this initially; it discovers, and then without reflection, that its movements, cries, wettings, feet have their own courses, and that their production or its actions with respect to them are accompanied or followed by desirable or undesirable actions by some you. It does not deduce that its mother is a you, or compare her with itself; it confronts that you from various starting points in itself, at itself, and over various routes. It finally faces that you within a limited area where both it and the you are confined and related.

The common condition to which both you and I are subject is not simply yielded to. Each individual internalizes it in his own way, making himself able to plan, anticipate, and adjust to the circumstances in which he will in fact operate. Such internalization is rarely deliberate, but it is also more than a shift in the location of conditions. The internalization of the conditions which connect I and you requires learning, maturing, the effort to become internally what one is socially.

Why does an individual not just habitually proceed along whatever routes it has been accustomed or trained to follow? What need is there for it to make internal what is externally conditioning it? A behaviorist would deny that any internalization occurs, except in the sense of habituated conditioned actions on the part of a body. His account seems reasonable and adequate when one considers the nature and achievements of animal training. To extend his views to humans, however, one would have to equate learning with training. This, of course, is what a behaviorist would like to do. To learn, though, is not merely to become able to do something but to master it, to be in possession or control of conditions under which action will occur.

Men expect, anticipate, plan, intend. Sometimes they do not act in accord with these. Others know only of those activities for which some evidence is publicly provided. But each of us knows that he can formulate intentions and not carry them out. It could be argued, and it has been argued, that such intentions are unintelligible, meaningless, nonexistent, except so far as they are formulated in a community's language. But this is to ignore the fact that just as the body may be tensed in a certain direction, so an individual in his privacy, without any reflection or thought, may be disposed in a certain direction and yet do nothing further.

A disposition is a consequence of the effort of an individual to maintain himself even while involved in a world beyond. He internalizes the conditions to which he is publicly subject in order to be able to maintain himself as he was before. The difference between one grade of animal and another is inseparable from a difference in its capacity to be within what it is being conditioned to be from without.

To learn from experience is to internalize the conditions to which one is being externally subjected. The 'internalization' obviously does not depend on a prior knowledge of the conditions, even on the part of those who are in a position to acquire it. It is, instead, the outcome of an act of adjustment which goes further than merely allowing action to proceed smoothly.

Internalization occurs both when public actions are easily performed and when they are difficult. Dewey thinks that thought begins with the attempt to find alternative routes in frustrating circumstances; if he were right, those who immediately adjusted themselves to the prevailing conditions would not think. They could not be said to learn anything, but merely to function smoothly. Yet accomplished craftsmen can sometimes communicate what it is they have been doing; they can rehearse what they will do, and along the lines that they previously followed.

To learn from experience is to be experienced; to be experienced is to be able to project what it is one might subsequently do. The internalization by a learner is one with his act of self-recovery, his achievement of an original position of self-maintenance within situations where there is an external, effective control. What is learned is not the actions which one had gone through—training takes care of that—but the conditions to which the actions are subject. Having adjusted oneself so that conditions are now part of oneself as standing apart, it is possible to initiate actions which are in consonance with the conditions—rather than, as was the case before one learned, initiating actions which are subjected to conditions over which it has no control.

An internal subjugation to conditions requires that an individual place his self under them. Instead of moving outward from a privacy into a world in which there are conditions to which his body is forced to submit, he places himself, as not yet active, under the governance of those conditions. This is possible if the conditions have a generality and detachability from the public situation, allowing them to be operative on the individual as he stands apart, or if he places his private side under the same governance as that to which his public side is subject. In the second way he intends that he himself be publicly governed, accepting for himself the conditions to which he will be subject.

To have learned the course of custom is to yield to the conditions that prevail, not simply as a body but as a privacy inseparable from that body. To have learned to deliberate, to reconsider, to access, it is necessary first to attend to the conditions, with a possible subsequent submission to them in privacy, and thus with the consequent formation of an expectation, plan, purpose, or intent. One is then able not merely to function under the governance of conditions, but with reference to those conditions.

Initially outside the provenance of conditions, a self accepts them as governing its actions and itself as well. Instead of simply expressing itself in action, it gives itself to the conditions. It yields to the conditions, not because it intends to be publicly governed, but on the contrary, because it is engaged in producing an intention by subjecting itself to the very conditions which govern its public body or actions. Its intention is a consequence, not a precondition; it intends by accepting the conditions governing the activities of the body as its own conditions, and thereby makes itself function as a single being with a self which is continuous and in consonance with its body as involved in a public state of affairs.

Custom acts on the individual, not as the active on the passive, but as the publicly effective to which one is privately accommodating oneself. The private accommodation can be achieved by a relaxation of the insistency of the self, so that one just inwardly accommodates what the body is subject to. This is what happens when we come to prepare ourselves to do routine or habituated things, such as stopping at a red light, swimming, typing. The accommodation can also be achieved by a deliberate effort to make the not expressed self accept the conditions which now govern the body. This is what happens when we deliberately plan. In either case, the individual goes beyond simple conformity to the conditions that govern the way in which he is to face another. He thereby makes himself one who is inwardly as well as outwardly a socially conditioned being. And what is true of the individual who is confronting a you, may be true as well of the confronted you.

The inward acceptance of publicly prevailing conditions may be more or less successful, more or less complete. An I and you, while interlinked in customary ways, may not intend to continue to be so subject, not because they have in fact entertained the prospect of doing something else, but because they have failed to give an adequate place within to the conditions which are operative without. Later, they may perhaps attend to the conditions and attempt to modify them, replace them by others, or defy them. Long before they are in a position to do this, however, they give variant concrete import to the common conditions, by expressing the selves which had accepted the conditions in diverse ways and with individual modifications. The result is that you and I are privately and publicly more or less adjusted to one another as units within an established customary way of being together. Equally, we are privately and publicly together in specialized forms of a customary connection.

The privacy of an individual is not exhausted in the act of accepting some common condition as its own; the I that does this always remains outside of itself as subject to the conditions. No individual, consequently, is ever completely socialized, not only in the sense that each is always more than a socialized body, but in the sense that no acceptance of social conditions is so thoroughgoing as not to leave over something still able to withdraw from what had been accepted, to modify what had been accepted, and to engage in other activities besides that of making contact and interplaying with another.

No one confronts the I in its absolute self-centeredness, but another can know that it is there, because wherever he stops he finds that which retreats before him, holds on to what he is attending to, insistently expressing itself, defying and qualifying whatever may be intruded on it. Without that I there would be no native rights or identity over time. But, as has been remarked before, there is no need to suppose that the I is static rather than pulsational, or that it is self-enclosed, neither affecting nor being occupied with the possession of what is externally presented or externally conditioned.

The involvement of an I and you with one another, both publicly and privately, not only does not reach to the center of either individual, but may involve more than customary connections. Eventually, the established hierarchy of roles and tasks, the inherited tradition, the mythology, and the crucial events characteristic of their community will also play a role in the ways in which they interact with one another; it will affect the nature of their private intentions and the ways in which they express themselves in the light of these. Nor are the individuals without affect on the conditions which in fact govern them. The customs which prevail change as the men change in their ways of acting.

The governance of custom is tight enough to make men engage in private acts of adjustment to the prevailing conditions so as to be in harmony inwardly and outwardly. What is done is usually what is acceptable; what is intended is often what is done. But the governance of custom is also loose enough to enable men to escape a complete conformity to what had been done, and to allow for alterations in the customary ways, and thereby determine the nature of the customs that will prevail in the future. Though an individual or pair of individuals rarely makes much of a difference to the customary ways, over the course of years customs change, and subsequent individuals are conditioned as their predecessors were not.

In addition to the ways in which an I and a you are conditioned together within a customary frame, and the ways in which they privately adjust to it (and thereby modify what its import is for them and make possible a modification of what the custom will subsequently be), each individual brings beliefs, experiences, knowledge, attitudes, and hopes to bear. He thereby either alters the patterns he will follow, or he evaluates them as more or less in consonance with what he is bringing to expression. In addition, a mature man will engage in complex activities in relation to the prevailing tradition, mythology, and so forth, and thereby make a difference to what he does within the area of communal custom.

Individuals in all their complexity can provide the authoritative force behind a 'we'. They are also affected by any authoritative force that a we may have achieved from others, or which it has a solidified unity with a career and import of its own. That 'we', as having a solidity, career, and import of its own, may itself be nothing more than a specialization of the customs which govern the interplay of individuals. Such a social 'we' may be produced by the individuals in interplay, by one of them, or by both accepting the result as its representative. It could itself be the outcome of custom. Custom may institute a 'we' in the form of set of linkages between individuals. This social 'we' will add to the custom an extra dimension of demand, assessment, or pressure which makes some ways more important than others. The adjustment of the individuals and the ways in which they interplay will be affected by the 'we' and the difference it makes to the established customs.

It is possible to isolate the customary ways by noting the conventional routes along which action takes place; a 'we' will then be discovered, not by seeing how well or poorly individuals conform to custom but by noting the kinds of rewards and punishments they undergo when they conform to or go counter to the demands of custom. Related observations are to be made with reference to 'others', to the 'mine' and the 'ours', as involved with the established interlinkages of the community.

May 7

The discussion of yesterday points up a number of basic distinctions:

1] Each human enters into an area already governed by established, customary ways. At the beginning and occasionally throughout his life he finds that the customary courses dictate to him what he is to be, do, and say.

2] Each individual is prescribed to by custom; this dictates how he is to function in relation to other men, things, animals, and himself.

3] The process of conforming to prescriptions is adjustment. It is promoted by admonitions, punishments, rewards, frustrations, and achievements. Others correct, redirect, accelerate, and hobble the individual's activities—usually when he is not conforming to custom, but sometimes even when he is. The latter case occurs when others are opposed to him, misconstrue custom, or are themselves in the process of altering the customary ways.

4] Training is the habituation of individuals, initially so as to have them adjust to established requirements in certain circumstances and with respect to certain objects.

5] A trained individual yields to customary requirements. The yielding brings his self under the conditions that govern his bodily acts. To yield in this way is to become experienced.

6] An individual may maintain himself apart from governing conditions. He then leads a life of reverie, self-enclosure, reflection.

7] To make himself inwardly what he is being conditioned to be outwardly, the conditions governing the latter must be internalized. Such internalization is learning.

8] A practical man accepts, with minimal qualification, the conditions that govern him.

9] In learning, an individual may modify the nature of internalized conditions, interpreting them in a personal way.

10] Accepting the conditions, a man may nevertheless occupy himself with activities which are primarily governed in other ways. He then occupies himself with nonsocial matters.

11] Planning, practical programming, rehearsals of what a man is about to say and do, intentions to act in accord with the learned courses of action, involve a reflection on the conditions he has accepted, with a consequent possible assessment, and a readiness to think and act in accord with the result.

12] One initially acknowledges a you as a source of the conditions to which one is being subject. The you has the power to force one to be trained. But it is known to be a source of training only so far as a distinction is maintained between the habituation of the body and a self that is beyond this.

13] A man can be forced to learn so far as his public activities are met with opposition not then overcome. Without error, there is no learning.

14] To know that I am being trained is to be aware of myself as having conditions imposed on my self. That self is continuous with or in possession of a body.

15] Another is acknowledged as a you from the position of one's self. The other, because accepted as a source, is faced as a you continuing in depth, toward an effective I.

16] An acknowledged you may not be entirely identical with the you which is a source or support for conditions to which one is submitting. The you, therefore, is more than a social reality, for it is inseparable from a self, an I.

17] The adjustment and the learning which another has undergone may not be consonant with what the social conditions require.

18] An I and a you, facing one another, may produce a modification, or may counteract the influence of the custom to which they are subject. Specific meetings are not always in consonance with what is customarily required.

19] Either the I or the you, or both, may be trained or may learn to function under other than customary social conditions. They may interplay in terms of legal, conceptualized, mythological, or evaluative prescriptions.

20] The expressions of a self are modified by the ways in which various conditions affect one another. Expectations, plans, and so forth, directed at performances under customary conditions, are modified by the effective presence of other kinds of conditions—and conversely.

21] 'We' makes explicit, though normally only in special cases, conditions governing a number of individuals.

22] A royal or authoritative 'we' produces or expresses or supports conditions which govern individuals as publicly together.

23] A connective 'we' allies the initial speaker with others, and contains an implicit reference to still others.

24] An authoritative 'we', though imposing conditions on others, itself functions within a socially conditioned situation.

25] A collective 'we' may relate individuals in accord with socially established conditions. Whether it does so or not, it functions thereafter as an authoritative 'we'.

26] An authoritative 'we' may produce new conditions or may alter prevailing ones; it always presupposes social conditions under which it functions authoritatively. There is always a 'consent' of the governed, if only as enabling the authoritative 'we' to be expressed and be acknowledged.

27] 'You and I' makes explicit a limited, collective 'we', emphasizing the irreducible coordinate status of two or more individuals.

28] 'You and I' cancels the anonymity of a 'we', replacing it with an ambiguity regarding the dominance of the 'and'. The more there is a stress on the 'and', the closer is the approach to an anonymous 'we'; the more there is a stress on the 'you' and the 'I', the closer is the approach to what is being conditioned.

29] The 'you' and the 'I' in 'you and I' are not entirely symmetrically related, for the 'I', in acknowledging the 'you', brings it under the conditions to which the I submits and to which it may contribute. An I makes itself be with someone else. Since a 'you' may be the source or support of conditions under which an 'I' operates, the acknowledgment of the 'you' may yield nothing more than a coordination of it with the 'I'.

30] 'Others' are active or passive. As active they are the anonymous source of the conditions to which one must conform; as passive, they are the anonymous subjects of the conditions that 'I' or 'we' are sustaining and which they may help constitute and alter.

31] 'You and I' removes another from his position of an other, and allies it with an 'I'. It is a 'you-I', or better a 'you'd-I'. As allied with an 'I', the 'you' faces the same others that the 'I' does. The differences in specific perspectives, content, opportunities, obstacles is abstracted from, or is generalized, so as to be pertinent to the 'you' as well. The 'you' of the 'you'd-I' has been made to vanish into a concordant I.

32] If the 'you' in 'you and I' is an active other, the conditions governing the way in which it is together with the I remain, but are supplemented by those which relate the 'you and I' to others.

33] I can ally myself with others also by taking myself to be coordinate with the others as already allied with one another. I then join them.

34] I may fail to penetrate a confronted you beyond that minimal which enables me to face it as a 'you' and thus as that which is sustained by an 'I'. The failure may be due to me or to a resistance encountered. In the latter case I become conscious that I am. The consciousness that I am is the outcome of a resistance encountered from beyond a 'you', directed against my effort to penetrate.

35] The consciousness that I am is distinct from self-consciousness. Self-consciousness is the outcome of the acceptance of the position of a resistant other, and the approach from there to the self, via a confronted me.

36] One becomes conscious of the self by attending to it from the position of the conditions to which it is being subject apart from the body. To know that one is learning or is resisting learning is to become conscious of the self.

37] I can be conscious of my self as one who does or does not fit himself in intent within the customary, within the scheme of justice, as intelligible, as effective, or as having a distinctive value.

38] The expressions of the self, when found inappropriate to what is confronted or for the conditions that prevail, may be rectified by the self before they come to completion. If completed, they may be supplemented by rectifying expressions. The rectifications involve an assessment of the original expressions as unsatisfactory.

39] An assessment may be made in the course of the rectifications, or may precede them. If it precedes a rectification of an expression, it attends to what is required by something external to the self. Attention is provoked by the insistence of the external and the conditions to which one has not yet conformed.

40] A person, etymologically, is a mask, a part carried out in the world, or something to sound through. He is a you inseparable from an I but not a you reached from the position of another.

41] Personality is the effective presentation of a person. If a fetus is a person, it still does not have a personality.

42] A personality changes at different times and in different circumstances, while the person remains selfsame.

43] Character is a person as persistently embodying and expressing approved principles. A noble character is involved with trans-social ethical principles; a good character is involved with socially endorsed principles.

44] A life-style is an exhibited character quickened by a distinctive self.

45] A signature is a life-style expressed in something produced.

46] Achievements are in part a function of the body and circumstances. Diverse achievements may have the same signature.

47] Differences in gender, color, intelligence, age, and so forth, make a difference to achievements, not to signatures, lifestyles, or characters. The difference in the achievements is in part due to what custom supports, discourages, and permits.

48] Gender and the like are occasions for signatures, life-styles, and characters. Social conditions turn them into conditions for a personality.

May 8

Individuals have positions of importance relative to one another. Their status is only in part due to the customary values which are put on their appearances, familial position, work done, achievements, attitudes, gender, age, and so forth. In addition to these, there are the individual decisions of others, and the new assessments that have to be made because of new roles, tasks, and work. The person, personality, character, and related dimensions of the individual are (contrary to yesterday) properly understood only when these considerations are taken into account.

Others neglect, help, hinder, reject, blame, praise, compare what one does, how one acts, how one looks. Sometimes a frown or smile, sometimes violent acts bring home to a man just what he is taken to be by others. He may be assessed in comparison with his judge, or in relation to a number who are being judged. Whichever it is, he comes to know of it when he finds himself assigned an importance relative to others. His coming to know is a kind of learning, not in the sense of achieving an inward state of practical preparation, but in the sense of achieving an awareness of the status that has been granted him in relation to others, assessed in terms which are taken to govern still others as well.

One can be mistaken as to just what status one has. The status one takes oneself to have might be that which one has only in the eyes of some other man, whose assessment may have no other import than that of revealing his dispositions or attitudes. The error and the peculiarities of the assessment are to be discovered by attending to a more objective, broader ranged evaluation of what one is, does, and accomplishes. For this to be possible one must see oneself and others as being subject to common evaluative conditions.

Privileges, denials, ignorings, rewards, punishments, approvals and disapprovals may be held to be unjustified. The individual then views himself in a double light. He sees his self to be assessed in terms derived from a particular publicly operative hierarchy of importance which attends to what is being publicly manifest, and takes the assessment to be distortive, limited, or applied incorrectly. He therefore knows himself to be assessing in terms of a different set of principles, or in terms of a different application of them. He may be deluding himself; the initial judgment may be correct. Whether it is or not, he sees himself as one who is assessed by others in one way (an assessment which he himself learns to attend to apart from them) and as one who is assessing in another. Normally he will take the assessments of others together with his own, and end with a complex assessment resulting from some combination of both factors.

Each man sees himself in the light of an externally imposed assessment combined with another which appeals to some more impersonal set of values. The combination varies in degree, often during the day and always over the course of a life. One's opinion of oneself, as a consequence, fluctuates. Rarely does it coincide with the assessment of others. If the fact is ignored, there is a possible self-delusion.

A man can be trained to take a particular position within a hierarchy of positions; he may function there with ease and self-satisfaction at the same time that he accepts the position as proper, deserved, inescapable, or more or less desirable. The caste system in India is hierarchical; there is a condemnatory note in the acknowledgment of a low-caste status, since this is thought to be the deserved punishment for what was done in a previous life. Judg-ment of oneself there, as living in the present time, is confined to the assessment by others and oneself as to how completely and nondistortively one accepts the position into which one is born.

A child is helped to function in ways that a position demands in relation to others, in part by being trained to follow customary routes and practices. He can also learn how the position is assessed, and thereupon assess himself as a type (the specific assessment taking account of the way in which the type is accepted and carried out) when, because of error, with the accompanying chastisement, frustration, admonition, and other aids, he is redirected. His self, held away from what his body is and does, then adopts for itself the condition to which that body had not been adequately subject.

Customary ways may remain unchanged but the various posi-tions which they define, and the ways in which these are required to interplay, may have different relative values at different times. Without changing the kind of work women or children do, that work may acquire a new importance at some stage in the society's development. Conversely, the same scale of relative importance may continue to be accepted, but the roles that the individuals play may change. The dancer may have a constant relative importance in some society, but the nature and the occasion for dances, and the training and use of dancers may undergo drastic modifications. The customary and the evaluative are evidently independent, even when the latter is initially a product of the former, or conversely.

One learns of public assessments somewhat in the way one learns of the nature of customary conditions. Both are first met with as operative in particular situations; it is their insistent presence on the failure of their operation that prompts a man to learn what he is to do if he is to be able to function with maximum approval, acceptance, and success.

How does a man come to entertain another set of values in terms of which he may judge that the previous set is to be ignored, discarded, or modified? The principles may not be embodied any-where; the individual may even grant that he does not live up to them, even while he takes the prevailing public assessments to be unsatisfactory.

Any particular position in a hierarchy may be filled in more or less adequate ways. The degree of adequacy is measured in terms of the position, or according to the way in which the position is scaled in the hierarchy of which it is a part. The one concerns the individual and the other contains a unit in a more or less fixed structure relating different positions. In both cases there is a comparison made between a fact (the carrying out of the position or the nature of the position itself) with a set of possible facts (other ways of carrying out the position or the set of positions). In the former case, the position itself is an area within which a plurality of relative stands can be taken; in the latter, the position is itself one of a number of relative stands in another area. In both, the individual initially becomes aware of the difference in status between where he then is and possibly better or worse standings.

Whether or not better or worse is justifiable on purely objective, impersonal grounds, initially it is known by the ways in which one is received by others. So far the emotivists in ethics, who take ethical statements to assert in effect that what is done is being approved or disapproved, are evidently right. But they overlook the fact that the approval and disapproval with respect to either hierarchy could itself be objectively evaluated in terms of the other, and this whether or not one approves or disapproves of that other's conditions. The position that is being adequately filled now can be assessed as itself not adequately meeting the demand that a position should meet—for example, doing justice to man's potentialities, happiness, promise, and so on; and the manner in which a position is being carried out can be assessed as failing to do justice to the requirements of that position.

In the course of maturation, an individual changes his standing. Even in a caste society, he moves from the position of a child to that of an adult while remaining fixed within the caste. He becomes aware, consequently, that there are other standings within a given position, and sometimes even that there are other positions in a hierarchy that he can and does occupy. He also becomes aware of the difference between his own standing and position, and those occupied and taken to be higher or lower than his own, judging from the rewards and punishments, the acceptances and rejections that accompany them. As a result, he becomes aware of two sets of virtues and vices. One set involves an assessment of his character in terms of the adequacy with which a position is filled; the other is an assessment of his importance in terms of the ranking that his position has in relation to others.

A man can have little importance and a fine character. He can have great importance and a poor character. Both the importance and the character may be evaluated by him in one way and by others in other ways, and then independently, or in the light of what had been decided by the others or by himself. Most men are less important than they think they are. Nor are their characters as noble as they suppose them to be. It is hard to know what is the most important position—not in a society or a state, but absolutely—and hard to know whether or not a position is not merely carried out in the best possible ways under the circumstances that prevail, but is the position which rightfully is to be carried out.

Judgments of worth by oneself or by others, made explicit in evaluations or exhibited in acts, are rooted in the acceptance of what is neutral to both oneself and any others. The complex hierarchy within which one is to find a place, both as a character and as of importance, even if grounded in social custom or based on an authority figure, is operative whether or not one approves of it, defies it, or tries to alter it. It has its most adequate embodiment in a comprehensive we, a we in which every individual has a place, and to which each submits as distinct from himself and every other.

Morality is an actual we dictating to every I. Ethics is the we sustaining principles which every actual we is to exemplify. Initially one begins with a limited moral we, the we of a particular community, and gradually works himself to the position where the range of that we is extended indefinitely beyond a particular society. But the judgment of worth, and eventually the judgment of the prevailing morality, depends on the acknowledgment of the ethical we, and the principles which it sustains and prescribes to all.

Not many take account of the ethical we. Even Aristotle went no further than a moral we in the guise of the best men in a Greek state. Yet, by his adoption of the moral we by his self, in the endeavor to make himself be in consonance with the public world where the moral we is operative, a man inevitably becomes aware of a distance between himself and that we. Due to the difficulty he may have in adopting the moral we without distortion, he might ask himself why he should adopt it, even if in that way he was able to be inwardly what he was outwardly required to be and do. Had Aristotle not fitted so neatly within the moral world which encompassed him and others, or had he not found it comparatively easy to adopt the moral we as a guiding principle for himself, he might have questioned its ultimacy.

To accept the ethical we is to see oneself as subject to the conditions of an absolute assessment. The moral we need not then be ignored or opposed; a moral life is one of the requirements of ethics. To attend to the ethical is to allow oneself an opportunity to evaluate the moral, to judge its assessments as being relative to an established society and, consequently, to deny its ultimacy.

An ethical we is presupposed even by a Kantian kingdom of ends, where each individual is irreducible, self-legislative, more than a means only. To get to the Kantian kingdom of ends, provision must be made for a plurality of selves, each subject to the very same ethical conditions. The ethical we is the locus of the conditions to which, according to Kant, each individual self is subject. His neglect of that we makes his assumption, that all selves are subject to the same ethical conditions, arbitrary. Only because the different selves are recognized to be separated epitomizations of the ethical we, can one say with confidence that each individual self is subject to the same ethical requirements. It also justifies a nonselfish, individual opposition to the demands of the moral we, for an individual can set himself in opposition to those demands on behalf of the ethical principles he, as a unit within the ethical we, is able to take as pertinent to himself.

A kingdom of ends is a universe of I's, each within and subject to an ethical we. Each is self-legislative, and thus occupied not with others, but with determining itself to be in a certain state, preparatory to action. Action is outward-moving; it may terminate in others as you's. But it is not the others as you's with which the individual as ethical is concerned, but only with them as together with him. A plurality of ethical I's is outside the domain where individuals and positions are ranked—or more precisely, it is a domain where there is no ranking, but which is reached only because another domain, the moral, where rankings occur, has been faced as requiring a ranking of its own. Though a kingdom of ends is not subservient to any other domain, it is reached by starting with a moral we (itself reached after one has been subjected to assessing others or you's), moving from there to an ethical we, and then explicating this as a set of equal, self-legislative selves. One can then return to the moral we and recognize this to be made up, not of so many equal selves but, instead, of I's and you's.

Though the moral we changes only slowly, it is nevertheless affected by the men it governs and with whom it interplays. Resistance to its demands, changed circumstances, failure to live up to its requirements, loosen its hold. Its general demands are specified in gradually established, effective ways; the nature of its hierarchy, as that which is backed by the actions and judgments of most of the community, is altered. The ethical we, though, is beyond alteration, except so far as it is understood in its distributive sense, as divided amongst a multiplicity of different I's, for each of these lays hold of the common principles in distinctive ways and with distinctive force, thereby altering the meaning that the we has for them as equally ultimate coordinate selves. Each, even though self-legislating, does so with a different insistence, to make itself more or less clearly a private distinct locus of inescapable principles governing all. As a consequence, the we is constant in structure in its undivided unity, but with a changing import because of the ways in which actual selves in fact assume the positions of distinct units for it.

May 9

Yesterday's reflections can be developed and the results stated with some precision:

1] An authoritative we and an assessive we are distinct. The one demands, commands, exerts physical or suggestive force; the other prescribes, attracts, or repels. The one is hard to escape, the other is often ignored and set aside.

2] The same individual or group may express an authoritative and an assessive we at the same time and in the same circumstances. There will then be an authoritative we by right, and an assessive we backed by force.

3] An authoritative we without the support of an assessive we is arbitrary; it may be variable, inconsistent, and perverse. An assessive we without the support of an authoritative we may be unknown, dismissed, unapplied.

4] An assessive we may originate with an individual, and be offered projectively to include another.

5] An assessive we may originate with a group and may exclude or include, and then derogate, honor, or position one or more individuals not then in that group.

6] An assessive we may already include a number, and refer to what its members or other individuals are or do.

7] An assessive we may be represented by an actual or possible plurality of individual selves, each of which may represent it.

8] An assessive we, used by individuals to evaluate the nature or actions or outcomes produced by others or its members, is a moral we.

9] To enable him to be inwardly in consonance with the prescriptive principles governing him in relation to others, a man endeavors to internalize the prescriptions of the moral we. So far as he succeeds, he intentionally plans to act in consonance with the morality of his community.

10] A person belongs to some assessive we.

11] A moral personality makes evident in act and speech his acceptance of some assessive we. From the standpoint of another assessive we, he may be immoral. The same man can, therefore, be a moral personality for one community, his own or some other, and immoral from the standpoint of a different community, some other or his own.

12] To have character is to carry out persistently the intention to do what is morally prescribed by some particular, assessive we.

13] An assessive we ascribes positions in a hierarchy, and measures the degree to which one lives in consonance with what the position demands.

14] A morality with its hierarchy of positions can itself be assessed from the standpoint of another morality. From that standpoint, the other morality may be condemned, at the same time that individuals may be differentiated as having better and worse characters, even while taken to be immoral personalities.

15] A morality can be assessed in relation to other moralities from the standpoint of an ethical we. The ethical we orders various moralities, with their hierarchy of positions, in terms of their degree of conformity to a kingdom of ends.

16] A kingdom of ends is all the I's which make up a single assessive we for all mankind, but encompassing no ranking and thus no moralities.

17] Each member of a kingdom of ends represents the assessive we in terms of which all moralities are measured and, derivatively, where all characters are reassessed in terms of their conformity to what the kingdom of ends requires.

18] Individuals are assessed as more or less noble in terms of their conformity to what a kingdom of ends requires.

19] A morality is ethically assessed in terms of its instrumental value in producing and sustaining noble individuals.

20] The assessive, ethical we may be discerned in the course of the individual's private accommodation of the demands of a moral, assessive we.

21] The assumption of the role of a representative of ethics or morality is not usually constant. A dedicated man is a constant representative.

22] To accept an ethics or a morality is to be dedicated.

23] Dedication is a matter of degree, and may have longer and shorter spans. The constancy of a representative has a longer or shorter duration depending on the remoteness of the attainable goal.

24] A dedicated ethical man is a representative of the ethical throughout his life.

25] Dedications differ in intensity as well as range. The most intensive dedication requires the self to function only as a representative; the least intensive yields a general frame within which individual intentions are expressed.

26] The degree of dedication makes a difference to the nature and career of the self, and the actions and work for which it is responsible.

27] The character of the moral we is affected by the manner in which individuals in fact exhibit morality in their actions and work.

28] The operative nature of the ethical we is affected by the role it is given in the individual's assessment of his own and others' intentions, actions, and work.

29] A state ideally stands between the ethical and the moral we. It functions in some consonance with what justice demands and what the community does, expects, and demands.

30] Native rights are the possessions of the members of a final ethical we.

31] Endowed rights are those which the state bestows.

32] Acquired rights are of two kinds: native, which the state acknowledges because of an urgent insistence by the community that they be legally expressed; and endowed, which are given by the state at some particular time. All endowed rights are acquired rights, but some acquired rights are merely legally affirmed.

33] A state provides public, formal, and effective translations for native rights in consonance with the morality of the community.

34] A dominant myth is a prelegal expression of the consonance of native rights with the prevailing morality.

35] A representative official intends the myth.

36] A representative official is morally criticizable for departing from the prevailing morality; he is ethically criticizable for not living up to the demands of ethics. He serves as an instrument for the realization of the ethical in a society through the mediation of rules.

37] The mythical stands to an actual society as the ideal stands to that which is guided by it.

38] The deeper the emotions the less subject they are to conditions imposed on the body or its actions.

39] Emotions, not in consonance with what is occurring and will occur, leave the individual maladjusted.

40] Emotions, involved in maladjustments, need rectification and redirection.

41] Expressed emotions are rectified and redirected by deeper lying emotions.

42] Freedom of the deeper lying emotions from control by what is publicly dominant allows them to be at the service of intentions, dedications, and representativeness.

43] The proper terminus of the deepest emotions is in what is irreducibly real, the finalities. One of these, Unity, is the ground of all value.

44] An ethical man inwardly subjects himself to conditioning by that at which his deepest emotions will be able to rest eventually.

45] A free expression of an emotion, directed toward Unity, is in consonance with ethical principles.

46] An emotion, that has not reached its proper terminus, is a turbulence. Turbulences occur within the body as disturbing feelings.

47] A disturbing feeling is exteriorized at the body in the form of a grimace, an outcry, an aberrational act. To confront another as grimacing, making an outcry, acting aberrantly, is to reach toward him as a frustrated I. To do this from the position of an assessive we is to distinguish what a man is in fact from what he could be, since it involves the acknowledgment of emotions which have not yet reached their proper termini in appropriate ways.

48] The assessment of others is accompanied by sympathy or

repugnance; they are agencies by which one penetrates to them as intending in consonance with a morality or ethics.

49] An acceptance of a morality or ethics permits of an assessment of a rule or custom as more or less good; an acceptance of a rule or custom permits of a dismissal of the moral or ethical as more or less irrelevant to what must now be done.

50] The acceptance of a rule or custom, with its consequent determination of the relevance of the ethical or moral, is the acceptance of a principle of assessment which itself needs assessment. The acceptance of a morality or ethics, with its assessment of customary ways, is the acceptance of a control whose social value has yet to be determined.

51] The neutral evaluation of a combination of the demands of custom and those of morality and ethics, is to be made on noncustomary, nonmoral, and nonethical grounds— economic, rational, religious, historic.

As was the case with the set formulated the other day, this combines some clear and pivotal notions with others which are more obscure, and which perhaps may be only incidental. A probing in a number of directions, carried out first in independence and then in their bearing on one another, should make possible a better justified and sustained account of each. It is desirable to oscillate from highly general and even vague ideas, embracing a multiplicity of items but doing some justice to the total complex of individuals, to more specific, isolated, and sometimes overspecialized considerations of the individuals in their severalty, and to the various limited principles governing them and sometimes all of the individuals together in special situations. At one extreme, there is an entrenchment on areas governed by principles distinct from those governing the areas with which one began; at the other, there are special cases where isolated principles, or even a multiplicity of them in highly restricted forms, may be at work. The oscillation is unavoidable in the beginning of an inquiry not overly abstract or particularized. But, in the end, the nature of the extremes must be fixated, and an account given of the proper ways in which they are to be interrelated. This must be done, I have just said, 'in the end'. When is that?

Every artist is confronted with the problem of closure—when has he come to the end of his creative activity in that work, so that any additional work will result in a spoiling, distortion, corruption, a slicking over of what had been achieved? His problem is not different in nature, though different in locus and quality, from that which confronts the theoretician in science, history, religion, or philosophy. The decision is properly made in the light of the kind of closure the work itself requires; with that in mind one must still engage in a psychological closure, but with an implicit judgment of one's own competence. In any case, others will be in a position to judge whether or not the psychological closure came too soon or too late. Eventually, one may be able to attain the position where one can make about as good a judgment as they can. Whether this occurs or not, there comes a time when one is forced to make a decision that the outline and pivotal ideas are sufficiently well in focus to justify the abandonment of undisciplined reflections in order to engage in systematic writing. And there, once more, a similar problem of closure will arise.

Success or failure with respect to one type of closure need not imply success or failure with respect to the other. Also, the preliminaries may have been well taken care of, but the systematic work still not properly completed; or, alternatively, the systematic work might be properly completed, though the preliminary work was sketchy or overextended.

One may fail to produce a satisfactory closure of either type. The second is the more serious; the first is engaged in for the sake of the second. Still, much may be left out of the second which had been focussed on or hinted at in the first. (There are some—Lewis Hahn, now in addition to Tom Prufer—who think that this is what occurs when I move from this work to more systematic technical presentations. For them, this is more suggestive, valuable, interesting. But I am inclined to agree with the others—my son Jonathan included—who think that systematic presentations are what one should finally strive for. I do not agree with the latter—but also I do not oppose them, for I really am not sure—that my own systematic writings are on all counts superior to what is achieved in the course of the oscillations characteristic of this work. In any case, they could not, I think, be written were it not for it.)

May 10

Another set of distinctions has to be made when one turns from the customary, moral, and ethical, to work, interaction, creativity, and manipulation by or of others:

1] 'They', 'them', 'that', 'those' refer to what is other than oneself, not necessarily human or even alive.

2] The conditioning by things and animals is not entirely unaffected by custom or even ethical considerations; their functioning is normally kept within limits that are dictated by what has been done in the past and what it is right to do now.

3] No human conditioning entirely obscures the nature which an entity itself has, or the functioning of which it is itself capable and to which it is necessary to attend if one is to act on it effectively.

4] A man expresses himself so far as he makes manifest in his bodily movements and changes the feelings, thoughts, intentions, attitudes, beliefs, and expectations that he privately entertains.

5] A man moves or publicly alters so far as his body changes in position, nature, or direction.

6] A man acts if he makes a difference to some other's nature or functioning, actual or possible.

7] Reaction is an action elicited by the action of another.

8] Response is the action elicited by the action of another having relevance to what that other did.

9] Work is action, viewed from the position of some other which has been made to change in nature or functioning.

10] Work may or may not be morally acceptable.

11] Work may or may not be ethically acceptable.

12] Work has economic value if morally acceptable.

13] Work has nobility if ethically acceptable.

14] Economic value is determined in partial independence of moral demands, on the basis of acceptable exchange. The rate of exchange may fluctuate while the moral demands remain steady; or it may remain steady while the moral demands change.

15 The economic value of work provides a partial determinant of the relative position that a man occupies in a society.

16] The outcome of work is a function of energy and skill expended, and of the resistance and pliability of the objects on which they operate.

17] One learns what work is economically viable, and to what degree, by discovering its exchange value. This requires that the product be permitted to be part of a world encompassed by other men. The carrying out of the exchange makes both sides part of a common economic we.

18] The economic we expands and contracts as more or fewer men become part of it, as a consequence of the acceptability of their work for exchange.

19] Unlike the ethical we, the economic encompasses only public individuals evaluated in terms of the economic value of their work.

20] A productive, economic we is the totality of individuals accepted as a source of what is exchangeable.

21] The status of individuals in the productive economic we fluctuates in accord with fluctuations in exchange values.

22] The need for what can be obtained through exchange ideally determines the work that individuals will attempt.

23] Were a man able to satisfy all his needs without exchange, he would stand outside the economic we.

24] In order to produce what has exchange value, it is desirable for an individual to incorporate the economic we privately.

25] A private incorporation of the economic we is anticipatory of what is to be made public. Ethical demands do not anticipate what will in fact be done in public.

26] Individuals who take account of economic conditions, independently incorporate established, customary ones as well. The union of the two defines positions in an economic society.

27] The requirements of economic and customary conditions may conflict, leading to antisocial economic acts and socially wasteful ones.

28] There are as many economic we's as there are independent systems of exchange.

29] From the perspective of a particular economic we, others break up into sources and possessors of products with which to exchange.

30] A plurality of economic we's coexist within a particular community. Each individual, then, not only is able to exchange within a limited group, but can represent that group in exchanges with others outside it.

31] Economic we's may extend beyond the borders of a particular society. The exchanges will then be governed by a nuclear morality common to the different societies.

This vein has petered out rather quickly, and has veered over into limited economic questions too soon. In part this may be due to the fact that the distinctions were not preceded by an overall, general examination.

A man finds himself with appetites and needs which he strives to satisfy, only to find himself limited by the possessions, demands, obstacles, and attitudes of others. His effect on the objects, and sometimes on the individuals he encounters, is a function of what he himself sets out to do, and what is permitted him by the customs, by the natures and functioning of other individuals, and by the objects on which he acts.

A man's needs, being practical, require him to yield himself to the conditions that prevail. Consequently, he makes himself submit to the others until he arrives at the point where he is no longer set over against them, but with them constitutes a single we. Within that we he is able to satisfy his needs by exchanging what he himself produced for what is then available.

Individual needs and appetites are sustained from within, even when they are satisfied in purely bodily ways. But the individual stands outside the public sphere as expectative and anticipatory. He does not oppose the dominant we, but stands away from it in the attempt to make himself a better functioning part of it.

Both as engaged in satisfying needs and appetites and as attempting to function with a minimum of frustration and punishment, the self is anticipatory of what will publicly be the case. Though the self may then be qualified to some degree by moral and ethical considerations, it is directed at what is being dealt with in other terms. Even though moral factors operate to dictate what a man will be able to do publicly and what will be publicly available to him, the emphasis will be on what is to be done to satisfy his needs and appetites.

What is owned, taboo, privileged involves a relation which leads to others as private beings. Work yields a public product, but ownership, taboo, and privilege orient the public product in private individuals. Possession is a matter of fact and can be countered by force and other means of dispossession. But ownership and the others are a matter of rights, identifications, and status. These are known only by making reference to individuals or to a set of conditions other than those which govern the ways in which objects are now possessed and used.

An individual enters into the arena of a publicly defined economic we, only to find that what he needs is held away, not only as objects possessed which must be dispossessed, but as objects which are inseparable from the privacies of others and must therefore be dealt with in consonance with moral and ethical requirements. Possession and dispossession, however, are not altogether separable from moral and ethical conditions. A dispossession must follow sanctioned routes. But different routes are involved in a dispossession of what is and what is not owned, privileged and not privileged, and the like.

Where there is ownership, rights must be satisfied. Though those rights may have public forms, and be defined by public bodies, they are traceable to individuals standing outside the public setting, if only as individuals who are able to have their public positions altered.

A dispossession which conforms to social demands conforms to conditions socially sanctioned; the possessor is then denied those uses which possession alone permits. When, instead, there is a change in ownership, no change in use may be involved; a limit, though, is set to the period of use on the part of the continuing possessor, and certain uses denied to him. A possessor dispossessed can not do certain things; transfer of ownership denies to the original owner the right to do certain things. As the source of what can be done, which can take account of penalties if it is done, a man is dealt with as one who is not altogether manifest in public.

Ownership could be said to be a purely social or legal matter, not involving any reference to a private self. An owner would then be one who was privileged to act in certain ways with respect to various objects, not necessarily in his possession, and to have that privilege supported by public force, actual or threatened, officially or unofficially administered. It could be said that he is just a body with multiple potentialities which will be expressed on different occasions, and that some of those expressions will be backed by public force. Individuals, as capable of having their public positions altered, will of course not be identified by those public positions, but that will not require one to refer to them as private realities, but only as public ones with public capacities.

Rights of ownership could be endowed. The endowment might be made in the light of what other rights or status the individual had, some of which might even be traceable to the individual in his privacy. Whether or not such tracing does occur, the rights of ownership will not, on the present interpretation, force one to take account of anything but public individuals. A change in ownership will involve a change in the locus of the acknowledged publicly expressible rights, and will not require a reference either to the original or the subsequent owner's privacy and native rights.

So far as no reference is required to anything private, one remains in the realm of the impersonal, the others, them. One's submission to the impersonal, his functioning as a part of it, and thus as a member of a single we, makes him be a part of what is not only set in contrast with other we's of similar impersonality, but which has its own characteristic mode of dividing into a plurality of units and becoming solidified again. Economically viewed, this is the market—an open market if its nature and functioning is determined by the independent actions of the units within it, a controlled one if these are determined in other ways, for example, by the society as a whole, by the state, or by limited groups or powerful individuals who determine what is to be available, and under what conditions.

It is possible for individuals to avoid functioning within an economic system for indefinite periods of time. They can gear their actions to be more or less in consonance with its requirements; they can assess it even when they conform to it. One may be forced to work by necessity or by punishments, actual or threatened. One may give oneself to work, lured by the prospect of rewards, actual or illusory. Room is still left for the passing of moral and ethical judgments on what one is doing, and on the demands that are being made and met. Such judgments can dictate a modification, a redirection, and even an avoidance of the work that is economically viable.

May 11

If every emotion has a proper terminus, where it is articulated and thereby satisfied because multiple dimensions are distinguished and allowed to be sustained and enriched, malfunctionings involving the emotions could be taken to miscontrue their objects. The overcoming of the malfunctionings involves a reassessment of oneself in relation to what is beyond, and the finding of something which will enable the individual to be properly placed and, therefore, able to express his emotions properly.

Freud seems to hold that malfunctioning is due to a force behind an emotional expression, reflecting something which had been denied expression. The therapist is to discover that force and disassociate it from the expression. What is left is taken to be 'natural', or 'native'. But this can lead to a malfunctioning of men as they actually are in societies. A proper functioning of social men requiries modification and redirection of the 'natural'.

Instead of rejecting or transferring the force behind an emotional expression, there is warrant for not analyzing the expression at all, while trying to find a better object for it than it had before. Instead of weakening the force of anger, anxiety, fear, love, or hate, one might try to have the individual change his focus. This could be done in part by training or habituating him to follow new directions, or it could be done by his learning with some self-determination. Instead of freeing a man from the emotions, and thereby leaving him bland, remote, and insensitive, the emotions might be diffused over a larger area and thereby enabled to be articulated as they had not been before. Improperly expressed emotions override what is present, and do not enable one to be adjusted properly to what else is there. If faced with appropriate objects, a man will find his proper relation to them as a consequence of the fact that what earlier had not enabled him to deal properly with what was before him, is now lived with in accordance with its own diversity and nature.

To reach the proper object of an emotional expression, there is no need to recount past experiences or to employ other devices by which one is able to locate the additional force which presumably was distorting one's expression. One might, with current sex therapists, try to get back to the beginning of some practice and build up a more effective expression than had been previously exhibited. This will require a man to give up his usual activities. The expression will still be faced with the same objects it had faced before, but now supplemented with others. The supplementation could be provided by associations, trainings through rewards and punishments, learnings with the help of advice, admonitions, suggestions, or opportunities for approaching the original object from new positions and with the help of agencies from which it could not be readily separated. It would require the therapist, teacher, or guide to know the appropriate objects for different emotions and how to make the move from inappropriate to appropriate objects.

A possible method is suggested by an experience with works of art. Here the emotions are elicited by what in fact spells them out, but in such a way as to leave residua of the emotions directed at what can properly satisfy them. What is left over, after an experience with a work of art, is what permits one to reach beyond that work. After an emotional experience with a work of art is over, one is directed at the proper object of the emotion but with less vitality than was involved in the experience with the work of art.

The proper object of the emotions is learned through residual emotional experiences. What is needed is an emotional involvement with that object with all the vitality which an experience with art requires. One must try to find a way of reaching the ultimate object of an emotion, and thereby satisfy it. This is possible if one could direct the emotion at such an object, without any intermediation.

The proper object of an emotion, at its most intensive and powerful, is an irreducible ultimate at the edge of actual experience. To do justice to that ultimate, the emotion needs both the kind of articulation which art provides and the driving force which the emotion normally has in ordinary experience, but too often there exhibited in distortive forms. Art leads one to sense the nature of the relentless course of the universe, and ultimately yields a sense of its tragicomic state. But a direct experience of the object of emotion, as it is expressed without the benefit of the articulation that art provides, enables one to experience the universe as tragic, comic, all-powerful, promising, frightening, perverse, evil, or good in relation to the experiencing individual. He reaches it as a finite being whose emotion it satisfies, and whose existence it is thereby seen to condition.

Art, of course, is not the only agency for articulating emotion and satisfying it to some degree, leaving over a residuum directed at what is ultimate which one may learn to face directly without the mediation of art. Religious ritual and prayer have a similar function; craftsmanship another; communal living another; confrontation with other men and objects as obstinately maintaining themselves in opposition to us still another. Each spells out emotion; each leaves over a residuum directed at some particular dimension of the universe. The nature of their termini is a topic for metaphysical inquiry, but the termini do not need its help to have a bearing on the emotions and the individuals who express them.

Final termini can be arrived at with full emotional intensity in religious and natural mysticism, through communal identification, and by yielding to a persistent determinant of the import of one's finitude. When religious reverence, for example, has given way to awe there is a direct emotional involvement with the object of religious worship. But one need not go this far. Fear and terror take one to the same terminus as awe does but, unlike it, do not over-stress the terminus.

What is sought is an understanding of those emotions which mediate an individual and what is ultimate. On arriving at what is ultimate the emotions are satisfied in every part, leaving over a drained relationship between the individual and the ultimate real-ity. The more basic and disturbing the emotions, the more defi-nitely must they be brought to their proper termini. When they occur on a less disturbing level, one can rest with less basic or encompassing termini, particularly when what is wanted is not a satisfactory answer to the emotions, but an avoidance of a malfunc-tioning with respect to particular items in experience.

If this view is sound, one accepts the individual in his full emotional reality and seeks at first to find what else can be added to initial objects so as to provide for a more adequate expression of the emotions that had been expressed with reference to those objects. The emphasis is on the objects and not on the individual; he is to find himself by achieving satisfactory emotional termini. The ter-mini will enable him to free himself of that portion of the emotions which he had kept within himself, in part because he had not found what was appropriate to it.

The movement that is required is to larger and larger areas, more and more comprehensive, with natures which are indepen-dent of the particulars which fall under them. At best, the emotions which were initially inappropriate, will then be freed of undue reference to the expressing individual, at the same time that they are freed from a focussing on some particular item or items which can not satisfy what is directed at them. Without loss to their power, without denying them legitimacy and place, the emotions as they had originally manifested themselves, though in inappropriate ways, will be granted satisfaction, and make room for the expres-sion of other emotions which properly come to rest at, and are spelled out by other particulars.

May 12

The interval between one creative work and another is lived through in a distinctive way, to make the work at the end of the interval have a character which could not be determined apart from that living through. As a consequence, not even the most slavish disciple or the most ingenious forger is able to know what the next work will be like. Something similar occurs when one shares in an artistic work; instead of, with the unperceptive man, attending only to sounds, objects, solids, the aesthetically sensitive man also gives artistic weight to silences, empty spaces, holes. Something similar, too, occurs when one moves from self to body, and from body to perceived or penetrated object. The interval is not skipped over but lived through emotionally.

An emotion prevents the mind from functioning without regard for the body, or the body functioning without an accompanying awareness. Unexpressed, it leaves one unattentive to what is without and to what is disturbing within. The expression, though, may be explosive, raw, brute, misdirected. The individual is then freed from the disturbance, only to find himself maladjusted and a possible prey to the emotion again, since he knows nothing of its cause, or of what would make its recurrence, in something like the original form, unlikely.

The cause of an emotion is an object which alone allows the emotion to be expressed in such a way that the individual is freed from the emotion and yet enriched because properly related to what lies beyond him. Particular objects and occurrences provide occasions for an emotion to be evoked; if the emotion is directed at them, left over will be a diluted form of the emotion, directed at an appropriate object.

Is it possible for one to learn to direct emotions to their proper objects without mediation? This the mystics attempt to do. A metaphysician is like them, except that what is ultimate is not taken to be singular, involves emotions diluted by the insistent presence of thought and argument, and does not deny the legitimacy of the satisfaction which the emotion obtains in particular situations and from particular objects.

Wherever one rests in inquiry, knowledge, experience, and

participation, one is always also beyond that point, emotionally involved in what is then both absenting itself and maintaining itself in opposition to what would intrude on it. The dismissal of the emotions as without epistemic value or, even worse, as having negative epistemic value, serving only to distort or falsify, subjectivize, or obscure, has prevented thinkers from recognizing that they themselves are thrusting beyond what they are entertaining, knowing, considering, or experiencing. They have, therefore, overlooked the need to and the possibility of penetrating into what is retreating. This has led to the paradoxical result that, though they have denied that it is possible to know what is ultimately real and have held that what is known are only appearances, they have taken those appearances to be bedrock. In effect, they have treated them as realities, beyond which no one can meaningfully go.

To acknowledge that anything is an appearance is already to acknowledge it to be known to be sustained by something other than itself. Either that something is known in some independent way and then may well be that which has nothing to do with the appearance, or it is reached, via the appearance, as the reality for it. An appearance is known not only as being sustained but as being constituted, at least in part, by what is beyond it. This beyond can not be a human mind without giving this a reality and substantial power for which there is no warrant.

To maintain a hold on an objective world, a human mind will have to share, at the very least, in something more universal, objective, and depersonalized. There is no need, though, to suppose that what sustains and contributes to appearances is a mind, individual or cosmic.

An appearance does not necessarily presuppose a consciousness, a rational operator, judgment, or knowledge in order to be present. Nor is it necessary to hold that the object of an emotion is necessarily an emotion or a feeling, or anything of that order. Emotions, such as dread and fear, are appropriate to what is nonrational, relentless, overwhelming, brute. There is a cognitive dimension to an emotion, but this, too, need not terminate in what is itself cognitive, though it does focus on and isolate what is structured, rational, intelligible. Is the remainder without a mental dimension? If it were, it would not be an emotion, but pure physical energy. The sheering off of a cognitive dimension from an emotion, and having this terminate in appropriate intelligible content, leaves the emotion impoverished, but not changed into physical energy. Instead, a new equilibrium between the mental and the physical components of the emotion is achieved.

An emotion is not the outcome of the yoking of two disparate sources. It is an indivisible union of body and mind. The isolation of the cognitive dimension does not leave over the physical, but an emotion weakened, just as a physical action which is isolated as the expression of an emotion leaves over, not something mental, but the emotion weakened from another side. It is an emotion, denied its violence and abrupt unsatisfying expression, that terminates in what is ultimate.

Dread, fear, terror, anxiety seem to be emotions which make us withdraw and not to penetrate, not to reach toward their source. We do withdraw into ourselves, we do try to avoid making contact with anything beyond when we are beset with these emotions. But then we do not satisfy them. These emotions, in fact, have objects into which we can penetrate, but only so far as we continue to maintain ourselves as having a status and dignity of our own. Unlike ecstasy and love, and perhaps anger and hate, each is expressed properly only so far as it has a double referent, toward oneself and toward an object. Its proper terminus is the object, but as that which is set in contrast with oneself as finite.

What lies beyond the point at which we rest in perception, cognition, action, and penetration resists at the same time that it attracts, lures, pulls us. The resistance expresses the fact that it demands that we proceed under its terms. It is inseparable from a pull toward itself.

Everything seeks to maintain itself, to be its own incommunicable singularity. This does not mean that it opposes the entry of anything else, but only that it opposes that entry on any but its own terms. The deeper one penetrates, the more is he required to abandon his own bias and to assume that of the other; one stops at the point where one's self-abandonment becomes intolerable.

It is the aim of some Eastern religious leaders to make one willingly abandon oneself. The tendency in the West, instead, is to insist on some modicum of the self and, therefore, to refuse to continue a penetration into ultimate realities beyond the point where one has some self-awareness. An emphasis on practice and on empirical or positivistic publicly verifiable ideas, has led a good number to stop far short even of that characteristic common Western limit, with the consequence that not only metaphysical realities, but the inwardness of men cease to be available.

When existentialists insist on men involving themselves with one another, they move toward a rectification of the bias so characteristic of thinkers who suppose that they are showing their modernism by taking scientific knowledge, logic, and technology alone to be basic and sound. Since the existentialists are content with descriptions, and since they define themselves to be in opposition to the prevailing trends, they end by isolating an additional or larger domain, which they leave to the others. Some, to be sure, have gone to the extreme of maintaining that their approach is alone basic or allowable, and dismissing the others as abstracted, mistaken, and arbitrary. But this is to overlook the fact that these others know truths which the existentialists presuppose—such as that there are real things, a universe, other men, and an objective causation.

If articulate knowledge stops at some point, and an emotional move goes on beyond this, how can one come to know the latter? The knowledge of the latter is, of course, not known so far as knowledge ends at the point where the pentration begins. We are now in a position to speak to Spinoza's contention that when we know, we know that we know, and so on without end. He would be right were knowledge, as he took it to be, clear and distinct, without anything left over into which one might be able to penetrate. But knowledge is part of a larger activity in which there is a thrust beyond the point where the knowledge arrives, and a knowledge of that knowledge takes account of this fact.

Knowledge of knowledge takes that in to which one pentrates to be something known, but with a different modality than the knowledge which had originally stopped where the knowledge of knowledge began. It knows the penetrated as that which is being dealt with in a distinctive way. It faces the knowledge and the penetrated as relative to one another, at the same time that it thrusts beyond into that which relativizes them. The higher up one goes in the hierarchy of knowledge the deeper one reaches into what is able to present itself relative to what is known. Reality allows itself to be known both in the guise of that at which cognition rests and in the guise of that which lies beyond this.

But now it seems that one is caught in an infinite regress, coming to know only what is relativized and what engages in a relativization of itself. Yet that which engages in a relativization is so far not relativized. Cognition of it takes account of it as relative to a cognition on a lower level, but there is also a movement toward what is a source of, and not relative to that content.

Descriptivistic accounts are buoyed by grounded awaitings, themselves affected by emotions, and inevitably point beyond themselves into depths which they do not deign to consider. Their descriptions would otherwise be haphazard, ignoring any regularities, repetitions, structures, unable to distinguish the important from the unimportant, the adventitious from the regular, the random from the ordered. There is no escape from penetrations beyond the point where we take ourselves to rest in description, perception, thought, belief, acceptance, or practice, for every one of these is a moment in a longer-ranged emotional move toward what maintains itself against all else.

May 13

Much of what I know of myself I know in the same manner that others do. I attend to what I am publicly, and even assess this in terms which others use. Of course, it is *I* who do this. This obvious truth is apparently neglected by those who insist that all that one can say of oneself is what is known in public. It is the private individual who makes use of public language, public paradigms, public assessments.

I know about *me*. But if I know that it is I who know, do I not know that I, only as a kind of me? Is it not something approached from outside itself, from a distance, from the side of public manifestations? It surely is distinct from the I which knows it; it is something known, and does not know in the way in which it is known.

The I that knows what is me and what is I, and what these do, is in the position of a knower concerned with what confronts him and with a source beyond this. The I confronts what has a role as a source or ground or condition in relation to other content. The me and the I are related as confronted and relativized conditions, from the position of a more basic I. But in the case of a knowledge of actualities or finalities, the complex, faced on a higher level of knowing, is also rooted in something more basic than either component, and is indeed the source of the relativized components. Is there a similar base for the I in a relativized position to a me, faced by an I which comprehends them both?

Two special cases will help clarify the question: A] the confrontation of some created work with the desire to understand oneself as a creator, and B] the change in one's ways in order to be in consonance with another's judgment.

A] A work of art not only leads one toward more comprehensive realities—the object of the residuum of the emotions which had been spelled out in the course of the experiencing of the work of art—but also toward an understanding of its creator. Every work of art is autobiographical because it is the outcome of the creative work of an individual. The fact can be admitted without leading to the intentional fallacy of trying to understand the work in terms of the artist's supposed intention, or to a subjectivizing of the work of art as nothing more than the expression of some impulse or desire. There is a distinctive signature and style to it, which makes it possible for a forger to produce another work that seems to exhibit the same signature. The fact that this can be done stands in the way of a ready reading of a work as revelatory of its creator, for a forger deliberately hides himself, and leads one to misconstrue who in fact produced the work.

It could be argued that a forger does nothing more than find a pattern in extant works, and exhibits that pattern once more in a new work, but with less of a modification than the original creator might have provided had he in fact produced such another work. The fact that the creator can produce a new work which the forger can not anticipate shows, though, that the pattern which is incarnated in the works that had been produced is no distillation but a governing, controlling power which achieves a distinctive rhythm and punctuation in being exhibited. His signature, as involved with the content, provides a clue to the creator.

The problem raised by a forger is avoided when one attends to something that one has created. The work is then looked at as the outcome of the union of the creativity, with its characteristic individual signature, and the content on which it is being imposed. A man comes to know what he is, as a creator, by taking the created work to be an outcome in which content is united with an established pattern in a distinctive way. It is that distinctive way which reveals what the individual is as a creative individual—the content providing the occasion, and the signature providing one with a base in terms of which the contribution of the creative act can be understood.

B] Sometimes when a man finds himself approved for being of such and such a nature, he makes an effort to be so. Said to be diligent, the child works a little harder; said to be kind, he is inclined to do some kindness. Sometimes, viewed as being harsh, mean, disagreeable, unreasonable, one shifts to make oneself be so. These changes may be only in degree, but they can also be radical. The outcomes may not ensue; men can not be reformed by the simple device of crediting them with the virtues one would like them to have. But when one alters so as to be in consonance with the way he is known or judged or spoken about, he receives another man in a way that he had not before. Another's insistent confrontation of oneself is accommodated; what another abstracts from the public manifestation of oneself is not merely presented for acceptance, but is adopted, allowed to be part of oneself as maintained apart from the other.

In perception we insistently confront what is being insistently presented by what maintains itself apart both from what is presented and from the confrontation. The perceiver moves into the sustaining content and beyond this into the reality, but under conditions that the reality sets. But when one confronts one's own creation, or reorganizes himself in order to conform to the judgment of another, what is known is just more deeply grounded.

When I come to know myself through the mediation of me, I insistently confront myself with the same power that I insistently confront external objects. Once I arrive at an actual or supposed you, I must change direction in order to approach myself from that position. The me that is then confronted is the manifested outcome of an insistence. I insist on myself, and thereby sustain a me on the inside. That me is produced by my insistence as met by others. In knowing me, I stop an intrusion into another in order to turn about and begin an intrusion into myself at that me. The me, consequently, is insistently dealt with in two ways—once as the manifestation of the I and from the side of that I, and then as a manifestation of the I faced from the position of some other, external to it.

The I insistently expresses itself, both to give the inward side of the me, and to deal with the outside of the me from the position of some assumed or actual you. But it does not stop at the outside of the me; it penetrates toward the I which is expressing itself as the inwardness of me. What it rests with when it penetrates is an abstraction, but it is one which is continuous with and intensified by the I.

In ordinary perception one ends with public content. That is true even when one attends to himself as a me. One ends with what usually is not merely the complementary public dimension of what is being insistently presented, but with something much less than this. What is known is part of an external object; as part of that external object it achieves a supplement which may require the known to be considerably modified before it could be integral to that object. But when one knows oneself via a me or a creation, or alters oneself to accommodate the judgment of another, the known is met with by its proper complement.

When I know myself via me, I encounter me in its complete-ness, as at once constituted from the outside and approached from there, and as produced from the inside and maintained from there. At the same time, I thrust myself toward the I as that which is producing the me from the inside. It is absurd, therefore, to sup-pose that I could feel the feelings of another, or that I could, by closing my eyes and trying to touch a troublesome spot on my body, touch the body of another and take this to be the locus of what I am feeling. What I feel is a me which is complemented by the me which terminates the inward insistence of the I.

What is the 'I' that lies beyond both the inward and the outward me? What is the I that touches a me complemented by an inwardly expressed me? Is it not an I which was divided and now is one? It was divided so as to be able to provide the inward side of the me and to be able to approach that me from the outside. It is undivided because the me arrived at from the outside is the complement of the me which is being insisted on from the inside. Because the outward me is completed from the inside, I know myself to be completed by the I that is insisting on itself on the inside. When I approach myself from the outside I divide off a portion of myself, to end with this reunited with that from which it had been isolated.

When I try to understand myself as a creator, I do not in fact find the complement to a creator expressed in just that work; I envisage myself as one who provided the union for the pattern there dis-played and the content in which it was displayed. When I make myself be in accord with the estimate of another, I do not provide him with the perfect complement to what he has focussed on, but merely minimize the discrepancy between what he publicly faces and what it is that I am producing. It is only when I am attending just to myself that the match is perfect. I know only part of what I am, but in knowing this I become aware of it being sustained and completed from the inside. The me, as a consequence, is full-bodied, a me that is not merely something approached from the inside or outside, even by myself, but which allows for the distinguishing of both an inward and outward me.

A me which I have come to know is a substantialized appearance, in a double sense. It is the possession of an I, shorn of whatever features it may have accrued from others. (We are dealing here not with those objective appearances which are constituted in part by the finalities as well as actualities, but with those objective appearances that are constituted by interplaying actualities.) Each of the appearances is overlaid with subjectively introduced factors, but these can in fact and surely in principle be abstracted from, to leave over appearances which are the product of an inwardly maintained thrust outward, and an outwardly imposed addition. This is substantialized as an appearance.

A self is not exhausted in an insistent facing of itself as a publicly manifest me with a penetrative movement beyond that point, and an insistent expressiveness terminating in the inward side of that me. It lies beyond both, since it is undivided; it is that which they dissect and exhibit in diverse but complementary ways. It is an undeveloped me continuous with an I.

The complementary character of the two me's, an inward and an outward, is not equatable with two disparate items which happen to fit together; each needs the other, is sustained by the other, and is able to have the status of a me because of the other. Together they are rooted in a substantialized me, sustained beyond itself by an I, a self.

A self knows its substantialized me as that which it sustains, and knows itself as so sustaining it. When a self has that knowledge it still remains beyond the me. The source of the knowledge and the energy of insistence by which it meets what is available, a self never exhausts itself in knowing itself—or anything else.

How does one know that there is a self beyond a substantialized me, or beyond any knowledge that one might have of oneself? It is not enough to say that one penetrates beyond the knowledge, for the self is always beyond the point to which one penetrates. There is no clearly demarcated point at which a penetration ends. What one finds is a continuum of increasing density ending in a vague area where one can not differentiate oneself as engaged in knowledge from oneself as the ever-retreating source of the complement of what one knows. Should one fixate any point, one will find his self retreating beyond it. Were the attempt to fixate given up, one will find himself eventually in a position where he can not distinguish himself as knowing, nor what he knows, from himself as retreating from that knowledge while accommodating what is known of himself.

I always find something more than I know, but when I attend to it, I find that it still leaves over more than I know. What is left over is encountered emotionally, but the emotions do not come to a stop at some particular part of the self that is known. They terminate in it, when the self is an object which I know; at that terminus, though, is exactly where the emotions are taken over by what satisfies them, and makes them into separable components of the whole in which they are satisfied.

What satisfies an emotion is integral with it in a larger whole. There is not first a headache and then the pain of it, not first the eating of an apple and the pleasure of the eating, not first an annoying man and then the annoyance, though to be sure there may be incipient occurrences, objective observations, abstractings, and ignorings of factors. The headache is painful, the eating of the apple is pleasurable, there is annoyance with the annoying man. The emotions reach to and permeate their objects, terminate in them only in the sense that they come to an end.

We can properly speak of an emotion having a terminus only when we are able to identify that terminus apart from it and recognize that this provides a satisfaction from the emotion when the emotion reaches to it. As emotionally felt, it is permeated by the emotion and gives the emotion its distinctive modality. But if this is so, no distinguishable emotion awaits an object, or moves to an object, or is directed toward one; it has its object in the very moment that it exists as just that distinctive emotion.

One consequence of these reflections is that the emotions provoked by art, and which continue to function after an experience with a work of art is over, are already at their appropriate satisfying objects beyond. What happens after the experience with the work of art is over is that one has a clear case of an emotion no longer unduly restricted to some particular object. There is no shift from one object to a larger or more basic one, but an intermediation by one object, the work of art, and a final unmediated involvement with another, a finality or an actuality in its depths.

An undivided self, which is the source of both of the insistence that terminates in the inward side of a me, and of the insistence which approaches and ends with me on the outside, is also discerned beneath both of these. And not only does it allow for the achievement of a knowing of all this, but it is known in still another way. All the while, there is no doubt but that there is an I doing all these things, unique, persistent, with a distinctive tonality that continues to be known—apart from all knowing, one is almost inclined to say. From the very start the I meets with resistance by the body, by intruders at and into the body, and by intruders which emotionally and insistently move toward the I. All are resisted, countered, reordered, absorbed, and subjected.

I know myself when I confront something in perception; I am aware of myself as countering what is now defying. I know myself when I confront any facet of myself, any intrustion into myself, any effort which allows for it to be confronted, abstracted from, or judged.

I have a reflexive knowledge of myself, a knowledge not mediated by me, a knowledge not directed at myself, but given to me by being defied. I know myself as the other of the others, as that which counters them, as that which is a vital unconquered opponent. I am I because everything else is for me, before me, distinct from me, defied as surely as it defies me. I penetrate toward the defiance of the others, but all the while I defy a penetration into myself, not passively by holding my ground, but insistently, by making myself into a condition to which all else will yield, if not in act then by leaving behind a bounded portion of itself, an abstraction for me to use as I would. But I scientifically, linguistically know it, except in the more limited term that a knowledge mediated by a me permits. Once I have that knowledge, I can say what I always knew.

At every moment I know myself as that with which I was always familiar, in contrast with anything else. I am the other of the others and of every distinction I make within myself, and with respect to myself. But I do not await those others; I other them and in that act make myself the other of them. The resistance they offer me leaves me with a sense of myself that I continue to maintain at the core of everything I do and know.

Sometimes I am bewildered, at a loss. "Is this me?" I ask. But even then I have myself as I always had. For the moment, I am unable to say anything about it; I am in a setting about which I know nothing; I have lost the familiar side effects which for the most part content me in my usual acceptance of myself—the feeling in my arms and legs, tongue, stomach, head. But still I, who ask the question, am the very I who will answer it, and who before did not raise it.

How do I know it is the same I? Only because whatever there be, I other. I neglect the details of that other, its claims, its familiarity and similarity, its usefulness, its threat, and its value or disvalue, to face it as that which I other, and thereby face as an other of myself.

Was the same I yesterday? If so, how could I know this, if I am fully here today? The questions are sometimes taken to point to the ruination of any view that allows for a private language or a private self. But surely the acceptance of a public language or of a public me, of criteria and paradigms, is a present act by myself, never to be repeated, and never ever publicly checkable. I am the same I because I ground the same othering, an othering of all the rest, holding them away from myself.

May 14

The act of othering, which is at the base of the self, is not directed at particular items. If it were, it would involve distinctive efforts, and the self would not be the seat of anything permanent. Even if the act of othering were directed at the finalities, it would have to function in a distinctive way with respect to each of them. It would engage in such tasks persistently, but its othering— abstracting from its othering of the actualities—would be subdivided into independent modes. There would not necessarily be anything common to those modes. Or, if there were something common to all the different ways of othering finalities, it would, in any case, not have the dynamics of the particular acts which together were supposed to constitute the self.

The act of othering involves a projection of the self outward, the demarcation of an area, which so far as that self 'knows', may or may not be filled out by anything. And surely, so far as othering is constitutive of an area which is to be occupied by men, there is no surety that it will be occupied. If this is so, the act of othering is something like the projected we in which an individual engages, apart from any knowledge that there are other men. Evidently, a projected othering is not the only mode of reaching outward.

The acknowledgment of the projection of a self, in the guise of a we, on a footing with the projection of the self as an othering, and thus as projection of a singular, self-separated I, alerts one to the prospect that other projections may be being produced as well. The earlier reflections in this book and in *Beyond All Appearances* (as well as in the almost final draft of "First Considerations") point up a need to distinguish three more projections—a conditioning, which is ready to bound, focus on, and abstract from what is confronted; a control to which the self submits so as to be subject to it as well; and a 'gestalt' effort to anticipate what will in fact provide it with a satisfactory supplement.

Whether or not all five projections be admitted, or one remains with only two—the projection of otherness and the projection of an assessive we—the question arises as to how these are together. Were they to be merely aggregated, they might not be so aggregated at some subsequent time. An aggregation lacks a dynamism of its own, and exerts no control over its members. Were the projections amalgamated, there would still be the possibility that the amalgamation might not last, and might lack a dynamism and a power to control.

Unlike the aggregate, an amalgamation could be credited with a distinctive character. There is no warrant, though, for supposing that this character is a constant. An amalgamation, too, allows for the dominance of one of the projections at one time and a different one at some other time. Instead, I think what we must conclude is that no one of these projections is basic, though more basic than any particular act in which the self might engage with respect to any particular item or any finality.

At the root of all the different projections is a single, basic, persistent insistence, a sheer projectivity marking out an area which can be filled out in distinctive ways and by independent objects. The persistent sense of the self is its way of projecting, a thrusting outward which proliferates into the five distinct modes. The persistent, single projection is soon hidden by more specific modal projections, by specifications of these in the body, and by the differences which various objects make which limit and thereby affect the import of the projections and their specifications.

Our daily awareness is an awareness of different parts of the body, and sometimes of the body as a single unity. To get beyond that point, it is necessary to become self-conscious in the sense of getting to oneself via one's me—a self-consciousness itself analyzable into five distinct strands, depending on whether one is approaching oneself in an assessive, othering, abstractive, controlling-yielding, or completive effort. Having arrived at that position, one must then attend to it from a more fundamental position and note that the nature of the projection that is then involved is more specific than is appropriate to the self.

A man internalizes the qualifications to which all the finalities subject him. The internalized result of the qualifications is man as an individual, a locus of rights, a test of truth, the self-identical, and an eternal value. This is an ontological result, occurring without consciousness or awareness, or sense of self. Starting from there, how does the next stage arise, where a man has some self-awareness of himself as projecting an area where other entities will have the status of being others, intelligibles, and so forth, in relation to him?

The individuality, rights, and so forth, of a man are not self-enclosed units; they thrust outward to make him not only be on the inside what the finalities qualify him to be on the outside, but to instance the finalities and thereby once more be conditioned by them. The projection of himself is a merging of himself with the conditions. In that act he makes himself relevant to everything, and makes the conditions limited to what comes within his use of them. His self-awareness—a most unsatisfactory expression—is the outcome of his act of completing his internalizations by coming to the end of his projection.

The merging with the conditions which have affected a man has two parts: as an individual he expresses the very conditions which he has internalized, and that expression is caught up in the conditions which are operating on him. As a result, those conditions are directed outward from him. His individuality then becomes one with Substance as a power for affiliating other items with him; his rights become one with Being as a power for coordinating other items with him; his status as the test of truth becomes one with Possibility as a power for structuring other items and the relations they have to him; his identity becomes one with Existence as a power othering what else there be; and his eternal value becomes one with Unity as a power for assessing all else. The resistance he encounters from the conditions when he merges with them, together with the resistance that is felt through those conditions by the particulars (which are conditioned by and sustain them) awakens his sense of self as that which is persistently projecting itself in the fact of those resistances.

Do other actualities also have selves? If not, why not? Not having internalized the qualifications due to all the finalities, none of them is able to be as rich internally as the human being is. All lack native rights, though all are qualified by Being and thus have qualified, conditioned rights. None is subject to the same shock that a man receives in his juncture with conditions and the conversion of these into his projections. But there is enough weight to the inwardness of the higher animals to make possible an approximation to the self-awareness that is man's. At the lowest level, that of a brute thing, the automatic thrust outward in which it engages on having internalized qualifications due to Substance (the only qualifications it internalizes) is absorbed into the Substance, leaving behind nothing more than a minimal kernel of intensity.

Apart from all cognition and knowing, apart from self-consciousness and the mediation of a me, a man finds himself resisted by the very conditions with which he is merging himself on the inside, and which he is thereby invigorating and turning into a projection. His failure to make a smooth juncture reflects his independence, and the independence of the conditions. This gives him his sense of self as an irreducible, unduplicable, private reality. The act occurs below consciousness, and in fact has consciousness as one of its products, for consciousness is the outcome of a self's merging with conditions stemming from Possibility. It occurs also below self-consciousness, for self-consciousness is the outcome of a merging with conditions stemming from Existence. If so, what warrant is there for speaking of a sense of self? Is there anything more than consciousness and self-consciousness?

When we are conscious of something we may become conscious of ourselves. If, from the position of that something, we approach ourselves we become self-conscious. Though we may become aware of ourselves and what we are only after we have found ourselves assaulted, resisted, imposed on from without, the awareness we have of ourselves is carried out from within and maintained apart from what else there be. When we are self-conscious we reach to something else and find ourselves taken up by it. The act of self-consciousness, therefore, is not only something which the self institutes, but which terminates in that self as instituting it, sustaining it, and supplementing it with other acts.

Self-consciousness reaches to us as beyond and prior to it, as that which must be if there is to be a self-consciousness. Since it is insistently maintained against the resistance of that to which it is joining itself, it could also be called an awareness. Self-consciousness is a felt undergone tension between the self, as internalizing and inward, with itself as expressive and merging with what has a standing of its own and which is, therefore, resistant to the expression and the merging.

What is being said today is in advance of what has been said before, though it is consistent with and in fact carries out the principle that one always thrusts beyond the point at which one stops. The present view, instead of resting with an acknowledgment of the privacy of actualities, toward which one is forever approaching via the thrust of a continued symbolization, attends to what in fact is already there, the privacy or centered reality. It takes into account the fact that this is not only the limit of an internalization, but also the beginning of an insistence. That insistence both merges with a resistant condition and converts it into a projection of an area.

A projected area can be occupied by others. When occupied, it suffers resistance and thereby affects the way in which the insistence of the self is exhibited. A sense of self is one with an insistence resisted, an internalization externalized in controlling conditions, the self maintaining itself against the very projection it has made possible through an invigoration of the conditions.

One's identity is not a core maintained apart from all else. Nor is it merely the outcome of a process of reducing what is encountered to the selfsame result. It is also insisted on in the form of a projection defining an area where what is other than oneself is to be. This is a specialization of a more primary projection, itself analyzable into a center and a condition, the one of a product of an internalization, the other of an intrusive power. The two are turned outward through the insistence of that center.

A projection which is achieved by insistently joining up with the prevailing conditions, and thereby making them become conditions under which items will be faced, requires that one fend off the demands of the body as that which is to be directly vitalized by the self. So far as a projection is concerned, the body is to fall within the area that the projection marks out. The self, though, is already involved with that area. As a consequence, the self holds itself away from the body while it engages in a projection. This requires it to change its position with reference to the body. Instead of expressing itself in and through this, it will either treat it as a conditioned object or try to transcend it. In either case, the self will be faced with the body as resisting it, in the one way as a specialization of a projection, and in the other as that which is already involved with the self. As a consequence, one becomes aware of oneself primarily as embodied, as toned by the way in which the body resists the effort of the self to become united with a condition and thus be able to project itself as an area in which items will have a certain type of role.

The self withstands the body in a triple way: it reduces everything it encounters there to the selfsame result; it transcends the body by involving itself in a projection; it insists on that projection against the resistance of the body. But it is not occupied with the task of dying, of letting the body go. Its ability to be involved in a projection makes use of what it obtains from the reduction, and that reduction needs that body. It vitalizes the body, makes the body be its agent, and identifies itself with the body as standing with it in contrast with all else.

May 15

Can there be any surety that the self is selfsame over time? Obviously, the self can not be at any time but the present, when it is making a judgment on this matter. It is in the present that it remembers or attends to what it had been in the past.

Those who rest content with the decisions or practices of common sense, science, or a language community tacitly hold that these are steady, self-identical over time. On the base of that self-identity they are able to compare different items that are subject to it. The answer, I think, points in the right direction, but it falls short in its neglect of a need to show the constancy of the accepted base, and in its refusal to allow for any other constant bases.

A self can record the difference that different items make to it, and recognize the ways in which they differ and agree. Conceivably it might be only relatively constant, constant in relation to more rapid changes. Everyone of us changes over the course of our lives, so gradually and imperceptibly at each moment of it as to make us unaware of the change, and sometimes to be incapable of knowing what state we had been in much earlier. How can one tell whether or not the self remains selfsame? We can not, evidently, find out by inspection; the past is gone. We can not, evidently, find out by memory, for the memory itself might be unreliable. There can be no way, I think, but two, and these supplementary.

One can note how, on attending to the same external objects, the self confronts the same contents, and becomes aware of itself as contrasting with these. And one can engage in a speculative account about the nature of the self and come to see that its self-identity is the outcome of an internalization (of Existence) and is maintained as the initial term in a projection of otherness.

To "the self seems to be selfsame over time" it is normal to add "because it in fact is the same." Something similar is done when we use a ruler and suppose that it does not shrink when we lift it up to set it down at the adjacent extension. Because it looks to us as if it had not changed, and because of what we understand about con-tractions and their causes we add "because it in fact has not changed." When we lift up the ruler, anything we might have made coincide with it might also shrink with it. If we supposed that everything in the universe also shrunk, and proportionately, no pragmatic difference would be discernible. But it might be the case that the only things that shrunk were the ruler and anything made coincident with it. There is no logical contradiction in the idea. We dismiss it because we support the apparent constancy with sup-posed laws which justify the claim that there is an actual constancy.

Our selfsameness over time, as held against and othering all else, moreover, is concurrent with a selfsameness in which we provide that which is to fit with others, which is to be coordinate with them, which is to isolate intelligible aspects in them, and which assesses them. Were one of these to change, it could be noted against the background of the constancy of the others. Even if those others were to change, if they did not change at the same rate, they would enable us to know whether some one mode of maintaining oneself while producing a projection was relatively selfsame over time. And beyond all these different modes, is the self-maintaining of oneself while producing a sheer projection, not yet divided into these different modalities? This makes possible the recognition that when one of the modalities is in the ascendancy again and again, it has the same affect again and again. Relative to those modalities, the self is unchanged. Were it in fact changing, but at a slower and even imperceptible rate, it would still allow us to know what changes, if any, are made in the specification of the projections, and in the determinations which the projections receive from the particular items that fall under their conditioning. But this prospect of a change sufficiently slow to enable such other changes to be sensed is of no interest if not supported; it becomes untenable once the opposite alternative is supported by speculations which have a systematic character, not designed to uphold this particular result.

It is also true that the self is constantly changing. This apparent contradiction of what has just been maintained results from the fact that the self is not an isolable core, standing away from all else, including its body, not only because it is engaged in a perpetual reduction of what impinges on it, to make it one with itself, and not only because it projects outward by dynamically identifying itself with prevailing conditions, but because it has variable limits, at the different items that are other than it.

A man points to his body and rightly says "Here I am." His self reaches to the limits of his body; he is an I up to the point where he backs a public me by a privately supplied complement. As embodied, his self has powers and abilities it does not have as standing in opposition to his body. The question, then, as to just what the self is and where it is, depends on the role one is considering. Its root role is that of a reducing, self-maintaining projector. But it is also integral to a living sensitive body, and is even present, through projections, in what one is producing, creating, and claiming by right.

When the self is taken to extend to the limits of the body or to the limits of one's claims of ownership, it is obviously caught up in changes which are not characteristic of it when it contrasts with all else, including these. Still, as maintained against what else there be, and as occupied with what else there be in a distinctive way, despite all changes in the body and things, such an extended self will be unchanging. If this is so, might we not then rightly go on to say that the self, as detached from the body, as that in which items are reduced and which projects outward by merging with prevailing conditions, is constant only in the sense that it is engaged in a certain type of activity persistently?

Without going to the extremes of the process philosophers and maintaining that there is nothing but a process in which the self momentarily comes into being (by reducing all else) and which expresses the result (by a projection), one can reject the idea that the self is a substance—if that means it is a unit closed off from the body, the world, and outside knowledge—and also the idea that it is a changing mass which exhibits a constant type of functioning. One can then hold that the self maintains itself at the point between where all else is reduced, and where it merges with the conditions that govern it and others. It will be central point only while it is functioning as the locus of reductive convergencies and as the source of the transformation of conditions into projections.

A difficulty still remains. I have said that the self merges with various conditions and thereby converts them into projections. But I have also maintained that there is a primal, unspecified projection which underlies all these different projections. That primal projection is evidently not a product of a dynamism and prevailing conditions. As a consequence, it is desirable to speak, not of a primal projection, but of a primal thrust or insistency which becomes specialized in the form of projections when that insistency merges with the different conditions that the finalities produce.

Each man, it can now be maintained, asserts himself in a persistent way, and is thereby able to remark on the similarities and differences in the diverse things he encounters, experiences, undergoes. His persistent activity has a self or I at one end, and is diversely specified at another. The end where it is an I has an indefinite extent—from that of a mere sheer point to the very end of a projection. At the other end it contrasts with the particulars which are governed by it, though not without resistance by them.

Might not you and I at the root be the same, mere fragments of a single cosmic mind or spirit? Or not even fragments, but that very cosmic mind, differentiated, not by our insistencies (for these would be identical) nor by our projections (for these, too, would be identical since they would result from the insistency as merging with constant conditions) but solely by the kinds of particulars which the projections in fact governed? (The question is related to that which epistemologists sometimes raise: might not the sensation that I have of what both of us encounter be quite unlike yours, so that you subjectively feel or sense or know green, while I instead feel or sense or know red?) The question supposes that there are real particulars which could produce such a differentiation. If this were so, what stands in the way of the acknowledgment of distinct individuals, particularly since each of us faces the other as an other? What, indeed, stands in the way of the acknowledgment of distinct data being used by the different individuals? Why suppose a number face the same object and diversely sense or internalize it?

If there be—and there is—a position from which it can be said that you and I are fragments or arbitrarily demarcated units, it is one which does not preclude the existence of us as really distinct. The position where we are somehow one is the position where we are subject to finalities; the position where we are distinct is where we are engaged in insisting on ourselves and therefore in imposing ourselves on conditions governing all that is. I am extensionally related to other actualities, but at the same time I occupy a place; I am that which can be there only because I am not identifiable with that place.

You and I may merge in a we, but at the same time you and I also now have different values and stand in opposition to one another. Indeed, it is because you and I are self-maintaining individuals that we are not just absorbed by pervasive conditions, but make a contribution to them, and to the finalities at their base.

Might there be a possible world where I am once again, with this selfsame insistency? Such a universe would have to be distinguished from this, and would so far, be related to it by opposition. But it would be different from this universe only if something in it were different. If the universes were in every way identical, in what sense would there be two? There are numerical differences in the sense that there can be more than one item with the same predicate or universal, or with the same set of predicates or universals, but that is because there is more to an entity than its predicates. Numerical differences are specified from the outside, and point beyond their predicates to actualities as distinctively insisting on themselves.

May 16

A method that I have been pursuing—isolating intruded conditions, moving through them toward their source, and reflecting on the import of there being something luring and pulling beyond the point at which we stop—has some affiliation with that followed by the advocates of social contract theories in politics. They start with man as already in a state and, by an act of imagination, endeavor to understand what the men are like apart from the conditioning to which the state has subjected them. Once these theories arrive at that point, however, they are inclined to ignore the original intruder and, instead, try to see what would have to be done in order to produce a better state than that which now prevails. How could such a better state, or indeed the original state come to be? A number of answers are possible:

A] There is a kind of platonic universal 'state' which descends or is exemplified with more or less adequacy at different times. It is not clear why, on this view, the state is not always exemplified, and everywhere. Platonic forms are superior in power to anything else; nothing apparently can dictate to them and therefore determine just when they are to be exemplified. Nor is it clear why it is that the form of the state is not perfectly exemplified everywhere. The history of the state, in fact, and the particular individuals and leaders that it has do not here get the recognition that actual states and leaders in fact have received and sometimes deserve.

B] There is an absolute mind or power with its own interior dialectic which in due time exhibits itself as a state. This is the Hegelian and Marxian view. It takes account of the historic fact of the state, but minimizes the role of the individual leaders of it. It also makes the state a creature of powers, that of the Absolute or of an economics, and therefore fails to allow for the state's apparently adventitious appearance and disappearance at different times, and the laws and history it has. It is a view unable to accommodate what is produced through the interplay of multiple contingent forces, not entirely cognizant of one another or aware of the result they are bringing about.

C] There are not other powers but those which individual men have; these alone suffice to account for the creation and continuance of a state. The men, on behalf of some ideal or common objective, give up power to some one or a few of their number, and submit themselves to this. The state is the product of an abnegation of empowered rights, privileges, opportunities, freedoms by some or all men for the sake of realizing some such good as peace, prosperity, efficiency, or protection. A question remains: how could those individuals have come together and acknowledged a common ideal? How could they transfer or abdicate power in such a·

way that it could be used to contain, suppress, and govern them?

D] Men could be recognized to be together in a society. After all, no one grows up by himself. All are brought up within families, groups, tribes; all are influenced by their peers, teachers, elders, the myths, practices, traditions, and values that others insist upon. A society has a status apart from, and in contrast with men. It is on a different level of existence and action, somewhat as the organic body is on a different level of existence and action from the blood and electrons which are within it. When various alliances are developed, or some individual or individuals receive prominence in a crisis, there is the beginning of a move toward the distinguishing of leaders and followers, and the eventual development of a political governance.

Even if a government were the historic product of some traditional mode of governance, it would, on its arrival, introduce new powers and ways. States, too, can be arbitrarily imposed, forced on a society against its wishes; sometimes (as was the case on the eve of the French Revolution, and apparently the Russian as well) contingent events interplay with one another, and yield a new governing agent. No individual self-abdication is required; the outcome is one which might allow men to be as they were before, but now within a new compass, where of course they will subsequently be found to have fewer, more, or quite different roles and privileges than they were able to exercise before.

E] A state is a specialization of some more basic power. It does not result from the unfolding of that power in dialectic time, but rather from the ways in which men function together in a society and thereby are able to interplay with the basic power. On this view, a state has a power which can not be altogether traced back to the men, severally or together; it also has a nature and a career which can not or at least need not be a specialized part of some more basic power. Still left over is the question as to how and when and why the specialization occurs, and why it is that the power of the state is never entirely cut off from the power of individuals, from power which the entire society has, and from the power of the rules that the individuals and society support by a readiness to yield to them.

F] Individuals project governing conditions, and thereby provide areas within which other individuals can be in the roles of affiliates, coordinates, intelligibles, others, and values. The reciprocal presence of a multiplicity of projections constitutes a single total condition under which everyone falls. Each institutes a 'we' extending over a number of others. When the others reply in kind we have a single governing unity. This is not yet to say that the result is a state. We have here an account of a society, or a club, or some historic union of individuals, but no necessary legal joining, no governance through a government, no power to make war and peace, to have a treasury, to go counter at times to what the individuals, or a society of them, may require, or desire, or demand.

G] There are many societies—families, clubs, tribes, classes. When the classes come into conflict but are unable to suppress or control one another, they adjust to one another, and thereby produce a traditionalized way of funtioning together. This becomes the concern of one of those classes or of some new class. We have here a kind of social contract theory transposed from individuals to classes of them. It takes the state to be the outcome of impersonal forces, recognizes the role that classes have, and is able to explain the origin of the ruling class and its occupation with the agencies of government. An emphasis on classes, though, seems neither justified by history nor required by theory. There is no explanation, either, of the way in which a class is able to stand apart from all the others and take as its concern the forces, rules, traditions, and interests which govern all the others. What governs it?

H] A more flexible account recognizes that one of the various societies which interplay in some region for a while may produce a set of conditions that governs all. But the application of those conditions must be under the control of someone if the governance is not to fluctuate, with variations in relative power amongst the subordinate societies, and if there is to be an adjudication amongst the societies and their competing demands and claims.

I] A class, a subordinate part of one, or even an individual may assume the task of applying conditions and adding others, the subtracting from those that prevail, the modification of tradition, and the keeping abreast of changing situations. It may be designated to do this, or do so deliberately, or because it has been placed for a moment in a position of prominence or dominance. We have here a basis for an explanation of why states reflect the interests of certain classes more than others, and how they might arise because of the desire that societies be at peace with one another, because there are men who set themselves to have political power, or because there is a need to anticipate particular eventualities. But no account is yet given of the fact that a state is concerned with individual as well as with class and other societal interests.

J] Individuals are often treated by states as though they were mere delimited portions of societies or classes. It is an old saying that there is one law for the rich and another for the poor, even though nothing is officially said about a distinction between them and even though such a distinction may be expressly forbidden. It is one of the virtues of the social contract theory that it attends to individuals, but it also has the correlative defect of overlooking the role of societies.

K] A state is needed not merely to regulate the ways in which societies of various kinds and sizes are to be related to one another, but to attend to individuals, regardless of the society to which they belong. Even when states are primarily occupied with the privileges, duties, and rights of nobles, soldiers, craftsmen, and the like, they also attend to privileges, duties, and rights of other individuals, and therefore give some attention to murder, mutilation, to birth, death, marriage, and rites of passage. We do not have a state until all the individuals are dealt with in terms which have application to all, though perhaps in a differentiating way. There may be a fine exacted for manslaughter which differs in amount from one group to another within the state, but we have a state only when there is a common penalty imposed, even though only for the members of a subclass. There may be only a few items or acts which are covered, and it is conceivable that the rulers might themselves define themselves to be exempt from the provisions. But some items must be covered, and the exemption of the rulers will have to be understood to involve an identification of them with the state, or to follow from their being above it altogether.

A state, on this view, arises when different we's, which characterize different societies, are not simply subordinated to some one or combination of we's, but when this one or combination is dealt with as applicable to all within its range. There will not only be an acceptance of the we which results from the reciprocal presence of a number of individuals, not only an acceptance of a we which results from the acceptances of a number of the outcomes of the previous junctures, but an acknowledgment of the projections of each individual. A state arises when there are conditions governing societies, at the same time that account is taken of the individuals who made such conditions possible.

An analogue: Suppose there were two couples sharing the same kitchen. They would have to learn to adjust to one another. Suppose one person assumed or was designated to see that something like a successful adjustment was formulated, and had, was granted, or assumed the power to punish violations. He would provide something like an analogue of the state only if he went one step further and dealt not only with the couples, but with the individuals as well. Each of these would be envisaged by him as projecting an area which includes the others, the member of his own pair in one way, and the members of the other pair in another. He would see each member taking on the role of projecting a we which was as comprehensive as the we which results from the combination of the pairs, and which he had taken as his responsibility to express and promote.

On this view, a state includes a plurality of societies, which together constitute a single we. This the state not only formalizes and promotes, but takes each individual to project from his own side. If the state orders various classes in hierarchy within a single we, it also takes each individual to project that we. The individuals may differ in the ways in which they fill out one another's projections, and may be dealt with as belonging to one class or another, but the projections will still be taken to reach to all the others.

For the state, each individual within it is a projector of the we which that state formulates and protects. The state then has a unitary meaning which it applies distributively in the form of a set of irreducible forms of itself.

May 17

Yesterday's account of the way in which the position of a neutral governance was achieved is not altogether satisfactory. It does not clearly distinguish between the case where there is a codification of custom, and one where a position is assumed which may go counter to custom. Nor does it take proper note of the fact that some individual might take himself to be the model for others.

When different individuals act on one another, and particularly when they encompass one another within the area of some projected condition, they together constitute a changing conjunct of their diverse and independent efforts. Someone coming to the result from the outside could take it as a topic of discussion, and may find it not too difficult to codify it, though he will then surely run the risk of codifying it in accord with his own practices and categories. If a man were to try this from the inside, he would be somewhat in the position of one who tried to formulate the grammar of the language which he speaks. This has been done, but rather slowly with many errors; it could be conceived to have been done by one looking at the language that had been used, and thus approaching it from the outside. A codification will, of course, be of more than theoretical interest if it applies to something which has more than momentary duration. And it will, of course, fall far short of the laws of a state with their intent to prescribe, sometimes in opposition to the custom.

A craftsman has one of two ways of teaching his apprentice. The craftsman may take himself to be a model and help the assistant follow the pattern which the craftsman is to spell out. Or the craftsman may attend to an ideal way of proceeding, which he himself may not carry out perfectly, and in the light of this, help the assistant to achieve a result that may be superior to the craftsman's own, or at least avoid the errors that the craftsman habitually makes.

The first of these alternatives allows for the carrying out of specific step-by-step procedures along the lines of a projection. The craftsman here holds his own projection steady as he proceeds to help the assistant function in conformity with what the projection demands. On the second alternative, the craftsman himself gives up an emphasis on himself to become one with the projected condition as then applying to himself as well as to others. It is the second alternative which provides a clue to the manner in which an individual (or individuals) responsible for a projected condition may carry out that condition as governing not only others but himself as well.

When an individual merges himself with a condition, and thereby imparts to it his insistence, he continues to function as a private self. He is, of course, so far not distinct from the projection he is producing out of the condition. But no one can merge completely with a condition. Not only is he involved with his body and a world beyond, and not only does he internalize what is qualifying him, but he has a density which can not be exhausted by his persistent insistence. He may fall outside the provenance of the projection, and function as an authoritative we for others; he may, with others, be subject to a common condition and there have the status of a unit related to those others; or he may work outside the scope of a condition, insisting on himself and even projecting, in interplay with others who are also insistent and projecting.

To achieve this last position, he must move toward the midpoint of the condition he is vitalizing in the form of a projection, and thus keep it vitalized, but no longer as that which originates with him as an area within which others can be. Both he and the others will be within the area of the condition. As under that condition, both he and the others will make a juncture of their selves with the condition, and project this as an area within which still others can be. As a consequence, he will have accepted a condition which governs not only himself and others as projecting insistent selves, not only the area which results from the merging of their selves with the conditions, but the outcome of the juncture of their diverse projections. Like the craftsman, who is teaching in the light of what ideally ought to be done, he will approach himself and others in terms of a common condition which may diverge considerably from the condition that is constituted by the interplay of himself with others. As falling under the same condition that others do, he will be on the level of those others, and thus subject to a special case of Being.

There are, then: A] the qualifications of a man by the finalities—a special case of Unity;   B] the internalization of the qualifications—a special case of Substance;   C] an acceptance of oneself and others as instances of a condition—a special case of Possibility;   D] the dynamic infusion of a condition by the insistence of the self—a special case of Existence; and   E] an acceptance of a common governance by a condition—a special case of Being. Each of the five finalities yields a distinctive condition.

There is no need for one to be conscious of the nature of Being, or of some special limited form of this, in order for him to make use of it as the condition under which he and others function as interacting projecting selves. To know Being, or a special form of it, he would have to have it as an object. This requires him to stand away from himself at the neutral equilibrium point of the condition and to be subject to it.

Recurring to the simpleminded illustration of yesterday, one of the members of a pair moves to the position where he makes the condition apply to all, including himself. He does not engage in the difficult task of codifying the customary ways in which he and the others act, but faces himself and the others as on a footing. He will be able to see all of them function as pairs and as such constitute a single adjusted customary pattern of behavior, but this too will be envisaged from the very same position where he sees himself and others to be on a footing. The customary pattern of their conjoint behavior will be assessed as more or less adequate because more or less in consonance with the position accepted.

The discussion so far speaks as though it were concerned solely with a single individual assuming the position of a specialized form of Being; it seems to make no provision for the assumption of different roles or even for a hierarchy of roles under the aegis of a common governing position. The fact that a position assumed is neutral with respect to all the individuals, however, allows for any number of them taking that position at the same time. The common condition has the individuals as coordinate entities; it does not preclude either their diverse social functionings or the assignment to them of distinctive, hierarchically ordered roles.

The ability of the individual to stand outside a common condition, and himself as subject to this, is common to the speculative thinker and the legislator. Both envisage conditions and that which stands apart from the conditions but which the conditions govern; both do this from a standpoint which has the conditions as well as the conditioned as objects of knowledge. The ordinary legislator, just like the ordinary philosopher, however, instead of taking this standpoint, works on the results that others have achieved, spending his energies in modifying, criticizing, and supplementing.

So far, the discussion seems to do justice to some such institution as the United Nations, and not to actual states with their power to coerce, punish, reward, and effectively keep subjects constrained and even forced to change their customary ways. The common condition seems to lack the support of power, and expresses more an ideal than the structure of an actual state. Does the power issue from the individuals and groups as not yet involved with conditions and one another? Are these made to function on behalf of an acknowledged neutral condition? If so, a neutral position will not be simply arrived at, but will be backed by what is at the root both of the conditions and what they govern. But what is at the root of these is ultimately private; public support is needed.

A governing power assesses, modifies, and restrains the actual social interplay of individuals and groups. Some or all of these individuals and groups themselves provide the power to which they are politically subject. Or, more precisely, political wholes which might be supported by a social interplay which the wholes themselves control, must in turn support any larger whole that controls them. What is to be subject to the governance of common neutral conditions must provide the power behind that governance. A state intermediates between two roles of a customary society, one of which exercises power and the other of which is subject to that power. The proportions between these will vary, and there need be nothing steady in the way they are exhibited. The stability of the state lies not in its control but in its demands which require only that there be some control.

The achievement of a neutral position, particularly when this is supported by formulations, provokes a division in the energies of the society, leading it to support the neutral position and to function under the governance of that neutral position. The fact that there is an intermediation by means of the political structure makes it possible for the society to lend a power to that structure which can be directed toward the restraint and alteration of and even an opposition to the society's normal functioning. The manner in which that power is added, and the way in which it is applied and resisted distorts the initial, pristine coordination of the individuals who are subject to the political governance.

Such a supposition allows one to avoid the extreme of absolute sovereign rule and that of the consent of the governed. The intermediation of the neutral condition allows for the separation of the ruling segment of the society from the ruled. This makes it possible for the state to function in opposition to the interests of the governed society, as well as to function poorly because not well sustained by the society, not merely in the sense that it is not obeyed, but in the sense that it is not properly supplied with the requisite power. The separation may originally occur along class lines. Both when it does and when it does not, it may result in class divisions between that segment of the society which is functioning to empower the state and that segment which is being subjected to it.

Is not the societal support here being put behind a neutral condition? Has that condition any other status but that of being produced by an individual arriving at the neutral point of a condition which he has been projecting? Societal support can be provided for what governs society only if that governing condition is as public as the society.

The condition which is projected, and in which one can reach a middle position is an expression of the finality, Being. This is specified by the society and finds partial satisfaction there. It is as public, therefore, as the society, but not as fluctuating, and not wholly dependent on it. Being is not in a position where it can be specified by an actual society until a number of individuals have made it their concern. But once they have, it is brought to bear on the society in such a way as to require the society to back the individuals who are urging that condition.

Using our illustration once more, one of the members of the two pairs takes up a mid-position in a condition of coordination of them all; applying it to them, he specifies it as the rule for them all, in such a way that one (he or some other) or more of them backs the application of the rule to just the four of them.

May 18

Attending to a special case may help give precision and clarity to the rather general discussion of yesterday.

Somewhat arbitrarily, let us consider space. A man occupies a region of space which is continuous with the space beyond this. He is affected by the region which he occupies; the space is his but it is nevertheless continuous with a space which is not his. The occupied space is a qualifying space. That space is internalized by him as that which he holds apart from the rest of space in such a way as to make it an integral part of whatever else he might be internalizing. At the limit of internalization he turns the opposite way, and expresses himself in the form of an insistent projection which requires that whatever there be, be the other of himself at a distance. The projection is the outcome of what he is as apart from the space internalized and of a region of space larger than that which he in fact occupies. The projection makes use, then, not simply of the space that affects him or which he internalizes, but of that space as part of a larger. That larger is not the whole of space, but it is also not a well-demarcated portion of it. It extends clearly for a short distance and then gradually fades off, to become a condition which can be filled out, not by all the actualities that there are, but by an un-specified limited number of them. Though it allows for no actualities outside its range, it is indefinitely extendable, as that which applies to any item of which one might be forced to take account. No set of individuals, even if their projections reciprocally match one another, need therefore be said to project themselves only up to the limits of their society.

A projection involves the identification of a man with a condition in such a way that he stands away from it as an individual. The identification with the condition is produced in an act of insistence. It may run from the extreme where the insistent self is at the beginning of a projection to the extreme where it is at the end. If at the beginning, the projection is his own, his claim, his way of envisaging what else there will be and (in the particular case being considered) his way of being occupied with a territory in which others will be related to him. If at the end, since the projection has no well defined terminus but fades out, the man will be insistently concerned with a region at some distance from himself. If, instead, he is able to stand somewhere in between, he will insistently impose a space which is pertinent to himself and others.

The in-between state at which a man might reach on insistently merging with a spatial region is that with which empiricists with their space datum, Leibniz with his theory of space as a confused idea, and Kant with his pure intuition of spatial extension begin their accounts. Only the first of these is ready to allow that the entities which the space is to encompass are already spatially together, not to be sure in a neutral space, but in a space which is constituted by the ways in which the diverse individuals in fact have their projections overlap and intermesh. When men remain at the beginning of their projections, the projections constitute a social space which fluctuates in character with their interplay. The interplay yields a single complex neutral space to which no one of them attends but in which all can be located. (That social space is not identifiable with the space which is insisted on by a man who is at its equilibrium point, with himself no less than others subject to the space.)

To be at the equilibrium point of a vitalized, not well-demarcated region of space is to be involved with a condition which is part of the expression of a finality, Existence. It is to take oneself to be urging the claims of territoriality, to which oneself as well as others are subject. This is most readily done by taking the conditioning space to be occupiable by oneself at any position there. In freeing oneself from the projection of a space, one does not then simply remain an occupant of it, but deals with oneself as a possible occupant of any portion of it. This could also have been done when the space was being projected, but then the other positions which one might occupy would be dealt with as positions in contrast with the present.

The achievement of a position of territoriality is the achievement of the standpoint of a spatial condition to which one sees oneself able to be subject at any point. Equally, it is the achievement of a spatial condition in which one allows for the occupation of the space by other entities. I live in Washington, D.C. I call it 'my city', I say I live in it, even though I never occupy more than a small segment of it. But it is 'my city' as long as I see myself unaltered in any part of it; I call it 'our city' so long as I see myself coordinate, spatially located and conditioned with other entities by that limited territory. I can do this because I am able to identify myself as an actuality who can occupy a spatial region, and can set myself in that role against the vitalized insistent fact of the region as comprising me at any number of positions, or as comprising me together with others at other positions. As at the positions, I and others stand away from the territory; it is a prescriptive condition for us.

There is a difference between my being in Washington and my having Washington as my city. The first occurs when the city is a territory and that is all; the second occurs when the city pertains to what is constituting an actual spatial configuration with others. Because I am socially connected with others, by residence, work, voting rights, shopping, dining, and a thousand other ways, 'my being in this city' is abstractable from 'this being my city'. Indeed, it is my city even when I am not in it; I am then related to others by habit, custom, rights, by having a residence there, by having it as the point of my return journey, and so on. In contrast, there are those who are in the city but for whom it is not 'their city', because they do not constitute it socially, in the sense of helping constitute a somewhat stable or at least slowly changing spatial complex of intermeshed men.

A territoriality which applies to socially related men in a space they then and there constitute would have only a geographic import were it not backed by a power which forcefully imposed the territory on the society. I move freely in and out of the city, but it still demands special taxes from me. Its forceful application to the socially determined space of myself and others involves an insistence on certain conditions which are to be imposed on what is socially constituted. That forceful application does not reach to every dimension of the individuals within the confines of the territory. Some of the social relations have to do with men outside that territory; some are confined to the family or the home outside the reach of the conditions expressed by the territory.

A territory subordinates a social situation and also is in part defied by it. In order that the defiance not make the application have only a geographic import—as the street a half mile away does—the territory must be backed by a force which will subject the society to constraints. If that force is applied from the outside, without regard for the constrained society, it is arbitrary, dictatorial. Only if the society itself provides a good part of the force to which it will be subject, do we have a territory which effectively relates individuals in ways that do not go wholly counter, are indifferent to, or are not entirely in consonance with social relations.

A territory must be backed by force. If that force is not provided by a part of the society which is constituted by the men who make use of an applicable territoriality, it will have to be accounted for by making reference to what is not to be found within that territory. In that case, a territory will subject individuals and a society to what may require radical alterations, abstractions, or the application of additional force before it can persistently constrain them.

The forceful application of territoriality bears on socially determined spatial connections among the items there. Some of these are the constituents of the social whole—projective individuals who intermesh. But some are just located units there; they may be man, animals, or things. As merely located they are the very entities which were initially just qualified, mere occupants of limited portions of space, within a larger space. Even if those very occupants also provide the force behind the application of a common territoriality, the application of this will be constraining, alien, not imposed on what has the status of belonging to a larger space. Only socially constitutive men belong to the space they together produce; only they are subject to a force which is more or less always compatible with the social space, and with them as involved with this.

Territory, as neutrally maintained, is an extensive othering. Each individual is encompassed by it. Each internalizes it, instantiates it, applies it, submits to it, or is qualified by it. One who had projected the territory and then assumed an equilibrium point at it also falls under it; he maintains himself as an other, as engaged in an othering, as accepting himself as conditioned by it, as located within it, or as enabled to occupy it.

A territory is insisted on with respect to some actualities, either as units or as socially constitutive; these provide the force behind the territory's application to them. The territory is then set in opposition to a larger space or to other territories outside its confines. What comes within its confines is brought into relationship with all the others within that territory; it is given the status of one who belongs, or who is an enemy or an alien and is therefore subject to constraints not applicable to the others.

A territory, and the social space of the actualities within its confines, are intensified versions of an actual space which relates all actualities. That space is specialized as the result of the individuals identifying themselves, in part, with a limited portion of that space, and helping to constitute another space, not altogether alien to, but still not identical with the former.

Some of the higher animals live in territories. They not only function there according to habit and custom, making use of familiar cues and conditions, but some of them are 'territorial-minded'. These assume for themselves the task of guarding and insisting on the territory. Within its confines a territorially minded animal distinguishes subregions where it and others might be. The territory evidently, even for the animal with its limited imagination, is held in contrast with the animal as in some particular place. But unless the territory is only for itself, the animal sees other places as occupiable by others with which it belongs in some kind of grouping.

The territory that an animal takes to be its own is not only applied to the social space it helps constitute with some others, but is backed by a force to which the others also contribute. How does it differ from a government or a state? So far as we have now gone, there seems to be no difference. The difference, I think, lies in the permeability of the intermediate territoriality. The backing which this has imposes it without residue on what is socially together. Men in a state go further; they fixate the territory, insist on its integrity, and keep the force behind it under constraint so that it is contoured in accordance with that territorial structure.

A territorial man maintains a territory by utilizing social force on its behalf, even to constrain and alter a society; a territorial animal, in contrast, makes use of it solely to provide a means for differentiating a social function—confining from being confined. Man is able to rest at a point between. If he insists on it too much he will abstract it, formalize it, make it inefficacious. If he does not insist on it enough, he will, like an animal, be part of a social group that is maintaining its territory, and not be able to stand away from that social maintenance; he will not evaluate it, and in terms of this deliberately alter it.

Territoriality is a we, either as authoritatively insisted on through a projection, or as neutrally applied to oneself and others. The former might be allowed to be possible to an animal. The latter can not, without stretching credulity. Is this not because we suppose that an animal is resting with that neutral we and maintaining it in contradistinction with the force that is behind it and the social space and its occupants on which that force is being imposed?

There is no reason to suppose that an animal acknowledges only a territory projected outward from itself. There does seem to be some recognition by it that its young and others of the same group belong to the same territory. There must, therefore, be a neutral way of dealing with the territory by the animal, as an area within which it is together with the others.

Whatever strain the idea puts on credulity is perhaps due to the supposition that a reference to the we credits an animal with self-consciousness, an ability to deliberately transform an I into a we, or an ability to formulate that transformation. Of course, if there is a supposition that an animal is contemplating the idea of territoriality and insisting on it in contrast with the force with which it is applied, or the group on which it is applied and the social territory that is occupied in fact, we would be crediting the animal with a power of detachment, for which we have no warrant. There is a neutral way for the animal to deal with a territory, but this requires only that the force applied serve to overcome any bias that might have been exhibited by a projection.

An animal's neutrality, on the last suggestion, is a consequence of the way in which a force, derived from a social group, permeates a projected territoriality and thereby enables the animal to view the territory as common to itself and others. But its neutrality would be wholly a matter of social pressure and experience. Men, in addition to being subject to these, have the power to consider the territory itself and to insist on it in its neutral form, and thereby make use of the social force on behalf of that neutral form. An animal, because it has no neutral form with which to rest, necessarily varies in the degree of neutrality which it gives to a common territory, depending on its experience, its place in the group, and the pressure that is being exerted by the rest.

A state, with its formal structure, gives men an opportunity to free themselves from the direct influence of social pressures, since these are mediatable by the state; it also allows them to reflect on the state's structure and to draw implications regarding what it can and can not do. It is a resting point which, in the course of history, has been found to have the value of enabling one to make use of social forces (and not merely to be subject to them) and to maintain a distance from the society on which those forces are applied.

Each animal achieves more or less of a neutral position because of the social pressure to which it is subject, but a man achieves a neutral position also because he is able to take a stand with a condition at the same time that he places himself under it.

May 19

Today I am seventy-four years old. Autobiographical remarks, even at the risk of repetition, are appropriate.

I was born on Avenue D in New York City. My father was a Hungarian from near Budapest. He had been a wandering tinker and left for America to escape service in the army. My mother was a German, from Eisenach, the daughter of a small manufacturer of sausage containers. She was a servant girl when he met her. I was the third of the children (six boys in all), the first having died before I was born, another but younger brother when I was very young. I was three years younger than the oldest, and five years older than the next. Only my youngest brother, Arthur, seven years younger, is still alive. Both he and the oldest became salesmen, the oldest, Ervin, quite successful. The one after me, Milford, had a comparatively short life, part of which was spent in petty thievery and the rest as a self-employed stone blaster, improving the appearances of buildings.

When I was about six we moved to Yorkville. My earliest recollections begin about this time. I remember that my father had to take off a day from work, and go to school when I was in the second grade. I was apparently misbehaving. He took me out of my seat and spanked me before the entire class. I was transferred to another school where, awed by the larger boys, I immediately began to behave myself and was soon doing quite well in my schoolwork. I skipped two classes and was graduated at thirteen. I think the trouble in the earlier class was my showing off before the girls; the new class and school were solidly male.

My father, Samuel, was a little under six feet (I am five feet, five and one half inches, down from five feet, six inches), swarthy, black-haired, strong. About the time we moved to Yorkville he became a coppersmith. Previously he had been a tinsmith, and a construction worker (he had worked at the construction of the World's Columbian Exposition in 1892); a little later he became a foreman in a boiler factory, supervising some half dozen to a dozen Bohemians and Hungarians making large copper drums for beer manufacturers. My mother was a little more than five feet, with red hair. He was quiet, she talkative; he had hardly any interests, going early to bed every night (he worked from eight to after five, I think it was, and half a day on Saturday). Sunday afternoons were spent with his Hungarian cronies playing cards at a coffee house; Sunday morning was spent reading the newspaper. He read Hungarian and German, but had difficulty with English. She, on the other hand, took every opportunity to see operas, plays, and to read the latest books. I thought her too noisy, and liked him more, but in retrospect I can see that she was a lively, imaginative, intelligent woman who had married a man who could not match her in spirit or intellect. But he was steady, hardworking, with firm moral standards. We had a broomstick with three knotted leather thongs hanging on the back door of the kitchen. He used it on the boys occasionally, but never when we did not deserve it. I never resented his using it on me.

We lived in a railroad flat on what is now York Avenue at 86th Street, from about the time I was eight to about the time I was seventeen. It was heated by a stove in the kitchen. There were five rooms—the kitchen where we really lived, three bedrooms, one for my younger brothers, one for my older brother and myself, and the third for my parents. Beyond them was a "front room," with our only good furniture. This was closed at all times except for use by my father on Sunday mornings, when we were allowed to come in and fool around with him for a while, and when, which was very rarely, we had visitors. But if we heard a fire alarm, we could without permission run into the front room to look out.

Most of my time was spent on the street. It was comparatively quiet, mainly Jewish and Italian families on our side, and some Irish families, and a few high brownstones occupied by professionals, on the other side. A gangster's family lived across the way. When the gangster was killed, there was a large funeral procession many blocks long, with a number of carriages containing nothing but flowers; this was one of the outstanding events of the time. Around one corner were tenement houses, many stories high, filled with immigrants more recent than my parents. We occasionally bought things from the stores there, but for the most part we kept aloof. Around the other corner were Irish, of whom we were terrified. A half dozen streets down was a Bohemian district; a dozen streets up was an Italian. Though I wandered all over the city, and skated as my fancy dictated, I never wandered far into Harlem, or into the Italian district.

I was run over twice, had blood poisoning from a broken blister achieved by swinging on a roped swing, was subject to bad burns when I suddenly slipped into the tub as my mother was pouring in a boiler full of hot water (and had to go to the hospital for a few weeks), had diphtheria, mumps, and other childhood diseases, all treated in a clinic nearby. But from the time I was thirteen or so I have been almost without any illness or disturbance except for colds, the removal some ten years ago of two hernias apparently acquired in childhood, and the extraction of the rest of my teeth last year.

I have just had my yearly checkup. My health is as it has been for the last six years. My blood is 100/70, and my sugar, and so forth, is well within the proper range. I weigh 131–133 pounds, stripped. I do not smoke (I smoked both a pipe and cigarettes until I was about forty-five, when I stopped instantly on being told to do so by my doctor), and now drink only when I find it the more convenient thing to do in social gatherings. I have always been a walker, but now walk more than I had six years ago. If I have a school day I walk some four miles to the main post office downtown (since I was mugged three times I avoid any but the well-traveled streets where governmental buildings are), and then take a bus to school, reversing the process after class. On other days I walk anywhere from six to eight miles without stopping.

I have tried to be alert to the differences age has made. I think I now walk about a minute a mile slower than I did four years ago—when my rate was four miles an hour. I think I have a little harder time remembering names than I had before. And I do find that I must sleep ten hours a night if I am to be fully alert the next day.

When I awaken I do thirty push ups, thirty reachings over toward my toes, and thirty bendings over from an erect position. I then squeeze some fresh orange juice and grind some coffee. If it is a school day I may add some eggs to my breakfast. When I return from my walk, I lie down for from five to eight minutes, and then sit down to write, usually something along the lines of what I had written the day before, what I had touched upon before falling asleep, and what I considered during my walk. At noon I make a light lunch, and then continue to write for the next hours. Sometimes I paint of an afternoon—perhaps once or twice a week at most. Around four or so, I either read or, about once a week, go to a movie. I make my own dinner, usually chicken, liver, or some other single course, which I might follow up with some sweet cake. I get to bed, if all goes well, at 9:30. This is my pattern, day in and day out.

After I was graduated from P.S. 77 at 86th Street and First Avenue, at the urging of my elder brother I entered the High School of Commerce, taking courses in commercial drawing, commercial Spanish, shorthand, typewriting, bookkeeping, practical arithmetic, chemistry, and English. My work was not good. It got worse every year. By the time I was in my third year, I was working during the summer as a kind of secretary-stenographer-bookkeeper in a fountain pen company—Salz Brothers—and my mother encouraged me to continue working there. I today remember nothing about bookkeeping or Spanish, remember a few tricks in practical arithmetic, and nothing of the high school chemistry. But I still write shorthand—a modified form of what I was taught, since I tried to improve my skill by including some of the shortcuts used by court stenographers. I typewrite at a great rate but very carelessly.

I learned my shorthand well, for I thought of myself as having a poor memory, and decided that I had to memorize my lessons if I was to pass the course. I have the impression that the teachers of English and shorthand both thought very well of me.

I stayed with Salz Brothers for a year or so, and then had a series of jobs, all of a minor sort—stenographer, usually, but once also as an assistant to an advertising manager for about four years or so. Then I joined my elder brother, for a year or so in his freight-forwarding business; after that I became a secretary to a lawyer. I spent my evenings (from sixteen to nineteen) standing on the street corner, ice skating, or going to occasional dances. Then I began to spend more and more time at the libraries, and a good deal of time reading at home. I remember, while I was going to public school, I spent many afternoons in the library of the Hebrew Association at 92d Street. Much later I spent a good deal of time in the public reading rooms of the New York Public Library, reading books of proverbs. But I do not now remember if I interspersed this reading with street corner standing around or not.

My mother died when I was about sixteen, my father when I was about eighteen. The four of us then lived together, first in Yorkville and then in Manhattan Beach, under the governance of my elder brother. I began to go to night school to make up my needed high school credits, and then, at the suggestion of a Japanese salesman who worked for my brother soliciting freight-forwarding accounts, enrolled at City College at night. I took three courses in philosophy, at seven, eight, and nine, three times a week, I think it was. One of the students in the class was Eliseo Vivas. At the end of the year—with my work as secretary for the lawyer suffering considerably, since I was often quite tired, for I arrived home after school at about 11 P.M. and got up before 8 A.M. to take a subway to work—I responded to the teacher's (John Pickett Turner) announcement that a prize was offered for the best essay in philosophy. I spent all my spare time writing an essay—just on what I have forgotten, though I do remember looking at it with some horror a dozen years or so later. When I was awarded the prize jointly with an undergraduate, Milton Steinberg (who later became distinguished rabbi), Turner suggested that I enter the day session. I appeared in the fall as an undergraduate student, with about a year's high school credits still to make up. I was twenty-three.

Since I had not had elementary geometry, I had to make up that work; at the same time I took Morris R. Cohen's class in logic, which was thought to be the hardest course in the college, taken primarily by seniors who prided themselves on their intelligence. I made out better with Cohen than I did in the elementary class in Euclid. (Cohen reasoned with you; the teacher in the high school—Townsend Harris—yelled at you if you said you didn't see the proof.)

Cohen had a tremendous reputation among the students at City College. He was quick-witted, had a very wide range of knowledge, and since he taught the same courses year in and year out, knew exactly what questions and responses to expect from most of the students. He was sharp, hard on every one, but just what bright, ignorant, immigrant sons needed. Later, when I began to study logic, I was shocked to discover how little he really knew, and how arbitrary he had been. He was not a great man, not even a great teacher; instead, he was a splendid goad, challenge, and disciplinarian.

I remember one heartwarming incident. Cohen was very frail. He spent his lunch hour usually by himself, munching a sandwich and reading some book. A number of us had tried to read Spinoza without success; we asked him if he would help us. He generously allowed us to come in during his lunch hour and helped us get a fine beginning in the text. In such a situation he was splendid. But he could not stand not being in a dominant position; if one visited him he was most gracious and helpful—until someone else came in, when he would turn nasty and sharp, evidently to show the new person that he was in the dominant position. One admired him but did not love him.

I spent many luncheon hours discussing, arguing, disputing with equally fervent and ignorant fellow students. We read widely and even wildly; we had little knowledge of foreign languages and none of the classical—I speak now of the majority. We were all quite poor, and almost without exception had to spend time after school to earn enough money to keep body and soul together. Some of the students supported a mother and younger children and worked at night; others (like myself) were more fortunate and needed money only in order to pay rent and buy food. I taught English to foreigners, and later took charge of a number of boys in Manhattan Beach once a week. I took them on trips to the zoo, on the subway, and the like. Twice a week I helped them with their schoolwork.

I continued my interest in philosophy during my undergraduate days. I also edited the college literary magazine in my senior year, won the prize in logic given at graduation, was elected to Phi Beta Kappa, and received, I think, some other award as well.

Toward the end of my junior year I met Victoria Brodkin. She was the youngest child of four; her mother was a widow who could not write her own name, but managed to have all her children well-educated. For a time two of them, the son and Victoria, were placed in an orphan asylum, with no effect apparently on the son, but with permanent ill effect on Victoria. Her life there was traumatic, and was always remembered with shock and hurt. Victoria went to Hunter College where she did not do good work. But she was imaginative, free spirited, very intelligent. When, on graduation, I decided to go to Harvard to study with Whitehead, about whom I had heard but whose writings, particularly on extensive abstraction, I did not understand and which no one apparently could teach me (and also to avoid going to Columbia where most of the young City College philosophers went, but where they seemed to continue the incessant arguing which characterized them at City), she took a job as a schoolteacher. I borrowed something like $75. and went off to Harvard, not quite sure just what to expect.

At that time, Harvard was a place for rich undergraduates, and for graduates who came from colleges all over, but rarely from City College. In any case, I was an oddity; I was poor, badly dressed, with a New York accent, a loud voice, poor manners, somewhat smelly, half educated, but evidently hardworking and not stupid. No one could make much sense of me; none of my teachers apparently had had much or any acquaintance with the sons of Jewish immigrants from the lower East Side. Harry Wolfson was a colleague (though, to be sure, he had gone to Boston Latin and Harvard College) with an accent worse than mine, and even more involved in Judaism than I was, but I don't think he impinged on the others. But Evelyn Whitehead (redheaded as my mother was—Victoria had black hair) took an interest in me.

The Whiteheads had lost a favored son in the war; they had a marriagable daughter; they were intrigued with the new country; they, and particularly she, were interested in anything different that seemed to mark off the United States from England. In any case, Evelyn, particularly, seemed to be most interested in George Morgan, a handsome Southerner with splendid manners, and in me.

Soon she was urging me on all the colleagues and all the colleagues' wives, until I think she made a nuisance of herself, and did not make them want to have much to do with me. But all that was to the side. In most subtle ways, with kindness and thoughtfulness, shrewdly and sensibly, she constantly edged me toward more and more civilized behavior. I was intrigued by her; she was opinionated and lively, widely read in literature, with independent views and forcefully expressed opinions on politics, people, and literature.

Victoria came to Harvard a year after I did. We were married soon after. She there had a brilliant career, coming out with the highest marks in her graduate examinations, and being sought out by Whitehead and others again and again. Her opinions were shrewd and bold; she had a brilliant mind. Victoria began a thesis on Leslie Stephen which she never completed; I read some of it and did not find it very good. But in conversation she was perceptive, original, daring, mature, radically honest, and easily the intellectual equal of anyone with whom we came in contact. Victoria and Evelyn became fine friends, and I think Victoria soon became closer to Evelyn than I ever was.

I took courses with C. I. Lewis, R. B. Perry, Langford, Hocking, Gilson, and above all with Whitehead. He had incredibly blue eyes, a melodious somewhat high-pitched but very clear voice. Yet when we first met one another I could not understand a word, in good part because his syllabication and mine were so different. He, as he told me later, had equal difficulty in understanding what I was saying. (Evelyn and I had no difficulties with one another.) It was evident to me at once that he was an entirely different kind of philosopher from any I had encountered. He was ruminative, given to asides, indirect replies, odd ways of expressing what he had in mind. The classes were not too well attended, and though a number of students, particularly undergraduates, seemed to be aware of his distinction, he seemed not to have made much of an impression on his colleagues. They would never discuss the issues we would bring to their attention after a session with Whitehead.

The Whiteheads had open house on Sunday evenings. The first of these in the fall term was filled with colleagues as well as with students. As the term went on, fewer and fewer came. If the evening was rainy, sometimes no one but Victoria and I and George Morgan would be present. If there were many present, Evelyn would sit in one room and Alfred—she called him "Alty" and after a year or so, when I continued to call him Mr. Whitehead, she asked me to call him "Alty"; I found the change very difficult to make, and never managed to get further than "Alfred"—in another. Sometimes Jessica or "Jessy" would be at the center of a third group. The Whiteheads would change places after a while. Some of us, a minority, would sit with Evelyn to begin with. But though she was witty and worth being with an entire evening, it was Alfred who was really exciting. When I came home after a Sunday evening I would often toss and turn a good portion of the night stimulated by what he had said. My thoughts, more often than not, did not turn in the direction of the conversation but toward something hinted at or perhaps only awakened by what he had said.

Whitehead was very courteous, charming, gracious; he was overgenerous in his praise, but always alert, never caught off guard. If he was confronted with a bore, he would quickly direct the conversation toward some political matter, usually remote from the present. He would not allow anyone to question him on particular passages in his books, or even to remain long with something he had said or had done. The conversations were about people they had met—if the students or others brought up their names—about what was happening in the United States, especially if it contrasted with England, about the ideas of historic philosophic figures such as Plato and Leibniz, about current thinkers such as Dewey, Santayana, Bergson, Russell, Moore. He was never mean or petty, never personal (she was), but sometimes quite sly. He had a remarkable wink, in which his eye would come down a fraction of the way, so that one was never sure if he had seen it or not.

I felt that I knew Evelyn, but that neither I nor anyone else outside his family ever really made contact with Alfred as a person. He had a way of escaping any attempt to elicit personal responses. In the classroom he seemed not to be very well prepared, not to know the names of students, and not to have a program in mind. Yet what he said was almost always unusual, illuminating not the questions one had in mind or which one had asked or the issues which an assigned reading may have focussed on, but something quite different which one sensed was even more important than what one had been directing oneself toward. He had a graduate seminar in what he called 'logic', but it was not the logic of the *Principia* or in any way related to this so far as I could see. It was surely alien to the logic that was being taught by Lewis, Langford,

Sheffer, and Eaton. In his course in metaphysics he would make references to Plato, Aristotle, Leibniz, and Kant, but for the most part his were large-scaled criticisms directed at the entire view.

I was convinced at the time that Whitehead was by far the outstanding philosopher in the English-speaking world. The view was not shared by most of the graduate students, and evidently by none of his colleagues, with the possible exception of Sheffer. I was constantly surprised and annoyed to find that he was not mentioned in the indices of the books in philosophy which were then appearing but that, instead, Russell was being quoted and discussed on every side. Though I thought that Russell's *Principles of Mathematics* was a brilliant and original book (a view which I modified when I came to review the second edition years later), I thought Russell's philosophic views far too simpleminded and surely far less viable than Whitehead's. The so-called process philosophers have now swung too far the other way, I think, and have exaggerated Whitehead's philosophic importance. Nor did I find that the book *Conversations with Alfred North Whitehead* did justice to his genius. I think the author blanked out the most searching and original comments as perhaps too ridiculous; in any case, I found too few of them in this supposed verbatim report of many conversations.

C. I. Lewis did not like me at first, and stood in the way, I understand, of my getting a scholarship at the end of the first semester, despite my good marks in all the courses and my passing all the examinations in preparation for the Ph.D. But I think his opinion changed soon after, in part because of my industry, and in part because of what he had heard and then later seen of my work on Peirce.

I had come to Harvard with some knowledge of Peirce, for I had read Morris R. Cohen's *Chance, Love, and Logic,* which collected some of Pierce's papers. One day I heard that Charles Hartshorne was working on the Pierce papers; I volunteered my services. He gladly accepted, for no one apparently had paid any attention to him or the papers since he had assumed charge of them a few years previously. Full of energy, with some knowledge of logic, at least more than Hartshorne had, I used to go to the room in Widener Library almost every day to help Hartshorne edit the papers. He quickly turned over to me the papers on logic and mathematics. To my astonishment and delight he soon asked me to become a co-editor, and after the first year at Harvard was over I received a telegram from Lewis, the chairman of the department at the time, or at least the person in charge of the Peirce papers, asking me to work on the Peirce material for the summer, for $500. I gladly accepted.

The collaboration with Hartshorne was a very happy one; he was a most congenial person to work with. We were left entirely alone to organize the material as we saw fit. Hartshorne already had a plan about the publication based on the three categories which Peirce took to be central. With some modification (due in good part to my insistence that we publish entire papers and not simply extracts from them, or little snippets of wisdom—which had been Hartshorne's original idea, in good part dictated by the supposition of the department that the Peirce papers should appear in only two volumes) the six volumes of the Peirce papers that appear under our editorship follow the rough outline he had then developed. (I have given a more detailed account of the ways in which the Peirce volumes were edited in the interview that Richard Bernstein conducted for the *Peirce Transactions.* Since it has already been published, I will not go over that ground now.)

C. I. Lewis was modest, quiet, earnest. His class in logic was somewhat routine, but his seminar in epistemology, based on his reading of what was to be his *Mind and the World Order,* was very stimulating. I was impressed with his honesty and simple clarity. It was my intention to write my dissertation with him, but was finally persuaded by Victoria to work instead with the person whom we both thought was a great man—Whitehead. I think Victoria also had more practical considerations in mind, believing quite rightly that Whitehead's recommendations would carry great weight. Lewis was not brilliant but he was careful, thoughtful, and patient. I think every one of his students admired him; I spoke of him quite often to the Whiteheads, who did not know him well, for he would retreat to his home in Lexington and avoid social contacts. I think he thought of the Whiteheads as too elegant for himself and his wife; in any case, he did not mix with them or with any of his colleagues so far as I could see, devoting his spare time to his family and his photography.

One day Lewis called me into his office and said, "Paul, I want you to do me a big favor. Someone has left us a sum of money which is to be spent solely on clothes. Will you do me the favor of going to Hart, Shaffner, and Marx, and using up the entire sum?" It is hard to believe, but I said I would, confident that I was doing him a favor, and certainly not doubting for a moment that there was such a fund. Years later, after I had been helping some student, suddenly it occurred to me that the entire matter had been contrived, that Evelyn had persuaded someone to see to it that I had clothes without stains and tears, and shoes without holes in them. The scheme had been conceived to avoid embarrassing me. It succeeded admirably; I remember coming back proudly to Lewis to tell him that I had managed to spend almost the entire $100, and had bought a suit and an overcoat and some shoes. (This all occurred I think in the first semester when I was at Harvard, February–May 1927.)

I took Gilson's courses in Descartes, Leibniz, and Thomas Aquinas. I had never imagined that history was so important, that anyone would be so much the master of his material. The course in Descartes was especially impressive. Gilson would fend off our criticisms by making references to letters, secondary literature, and other works of Descartes until he had made evident how superior Descartes was to anything we were supposing him to be. In the Leibniz course on the *Discourse* we were each assigned one of the page-chapters. It was our task to provide a better translation, and to trace back the references to such basic terms as monads, God, and so forth. I prepared for an entire month and then, to my astonishment, found Gilson correcting my translation, and piling reference upon reference to texts which I had somehow ignored or slighted. I saw then that the history of philosophy was not, as I, a kind of logician at that time, thought, something easy which evaded the basic issues, but profound, searching, illuminating, requiring much preparation, thought, and knowledge.

Gilson himself was rather rough in his ways. His criticisms were direct, hard-hitting, serious, and almost always telling. I met him once again, just a few years ago, to find him almost the same. He and Evelyn spoke French together (she had been for a while in a French convent) and seemed to have made contact; otherwise, I think, Gilson had no friends at Harvard and was treated by the department more or less as a foreigner. I, for one, never forgot many of the things Gilson pointed out in Descartes and Leibniz. His course on Aquinas, however, was quite routine. It was taken by teachers of Latin, Catholic students, people wanting some official statement, and he dealt with Aquinas in some accord with their needs. Years later I read his book on St. Bonaventure and was very much impressed with what I there learned. I wish he had given a course on him; I found and still find Bonaventure to be a source of brilliant insights into dimensions of the universe others neglect.

Hocking I found to be acute in criticism and arbitrary in his own claims. Perry, whom I admired for a kind of Puritan honesty, could be said to have lived up to every requirement in a book on pedagogy. He knew the names of every student, had jokes for all occasions, provided a fine bibliography, seemed to know the literature, and got everyone to participate. And yet the course was dull, dull, dull; I think everyone was bored. There was no insight, no vision, no understanding of the depth or the breadth of the universe.

Sheffer was away when I came up for my Ph.D. with the "Nature of Systems," a piece which showed more industry than intelligence or ability. It had been turned down by the department once, though I had presented it with what I had thought was Whitehead's endorsement. When I came back to him, he suggested that I include my published paper on the "Theory of Types" as an appendix. He made a few other suggestions, all of which should have been made before. I was allowed to pass, I think, because of the work I had been doing on the Peirce papers. (Yet, later, the department tried to deny credit as editors either to Hartshorne or myself, until I protested and, with the help of Perry, persuaded the department that we deserved to be termed the editors.)

On receipt of the doctorate, I received a second-level scholarship for traveling abroad. Victoria and I went to Berlin, and there, on the urging of Jacob Klein (later Dean at St. Johns) who was a splendid companion and friend to both of us, went to Freiburg for a term. I there heard Heidegger, whom I did not understand very well, and who, when I approached him, brushed me off with a scornful look, because of my ignorance, German, or appearance. I visited Husserl who greeted me with the remark, "Oh, you are an American. I suppose you think you can come here and study for a year or so. It should take a lifetime." I attended seminars with Becker the logician, who had many original things to say, and with Ebbinghaus who, holding that Kant was right on every point, illuminated and clarified a great deal in defending that impossible thesis.

After a term in Freiburg, we went to Paris and the Sorbonne. We lived the life of students, studying advanced French, reading and discussing, but learning little. We returned to Cambridge, Massachusetts, where I had a post as a one-year instructor at Harvard and at Radcliffe. I taught logic at both places. My teaching at Radcliffe was a disaster. I had been told by some young teacher that one merely went over to Radcliffe, said one's piece, and walked out. I did that, but I also sat tight in my chair, held my hand over my mouth, and mumbled. This was pointed out to me by Victoria when she went to visit my class one day, and from that time on I have walked about, raised my voice, and have gradually become a fairly good teacher. I also tutored at Harvard. No one had told me how to tutor; I hurried, I spoke too loudly, I insisted, and all in all was a very poor tutor. None of this, so far as I could see, was known to the department.

In the meantime, Evelyn was urging members of the department to hire me. The total effect, I think, was to stiffen opposition. It was a relief to all when I was offered a position at Bryn Mawr. I had not known that Mrs. De Laguna, the head of the department, had already consulted the Whiteheads and that they had recommended me. But as she quickly told me, they already had a Jew in the department, and she did not think that it was possible to have two. (I notice that the most liberal of places always sees every group but white Protestants to make up a segment in which there could not be more than a few members. They would not allow a department of more than two or perhaps three Swedes, Hungarians, Greek Catholics, Buddhists, no matter how brilliant, how divergent their interests and background and personalities; but that there is no limit to the number of white Protestants that can be tolerated, all the way to the limit of having only these.) Having spoken to Feigl, I called her up the next day to tell her that Carnap was on the way to this country and that he was a very able logician. (She had wanted a logician, hopefully one who also knew some history of philosophy; Carnap qualified more on the first count, I on the second.) She told me that they could not employ a foreigner. When she went back to speak to the president of Bryn Mawr about her "dilemma," she was told to make the decision herself. After a night's struggle with her conscience, she decided that it was possible to hire a northern Jew since this provided a sufficient contrast with the already hired southern Jew (Milton Nahm).

Victoria was very unhappy in Bryn Mawr. They would not give her a job, and she had few friends. The academic women took themselves (often with justification) to be superior to everyone else, teaching or not teaching, in the community. In any case we were from a different world, with odd manners, background, interests. I loved it; my students were exceptionally keen, hardworking, already on my side. They liked me and I liked them, and to this day can count as friends those I taught even in the first years.

In the meantime, I had taken with me the manuscripts of the Peirce volumes which I was to edit, and while Victoria remained in Cambridge—a mistake, we both subsequently agreed—trying to finish her degree, I spent almost all my spare time finishing my work on the papers. When they were out of the way, at Victoria's suggestion, I gave up writing articles and began work on *Reality*. She read every word of it, and made me explain and clarify what was not evident to her. Unfortunately, she was too intelligent, and much that she understood others did not. At any rate, the book never did sell very well. I found it hard to get a publisher; finally at the urging of Ted Greene who was eventually to be my colleague at Yale, Princeton University Press accepted it and managed to sell some 750 copies over some ten years. I still think there are splendid things in it. But like most of what I have written in philosophy since then, it did not make contact with the larger philosophical community. My things have rarely been directly dealt with as pivotal, as requiring discussion, as grounding theses or books. I do keep abreast of the literature, I think, and do think I am attending to central issues, some not too far from the basic views of the great thinkers of the past. But somehow what I have said sounds too alien, nonsensical, undeveloped, arbitrary, or unfruitful to elicit continued interest by a large number.

I do think of myself, though, as an unusually fortunate man. Not only has my health been good for decades, not only do I have the freedom to think and write every day, not only am I now not troubled by money matters or a possible penurious future, but I have been able to investigate multiple fields about which I have had some curiosity and very little knowledge. Those about which I have been most ignorant to begin with—art and sport—have been dealt with by me apparently in such a way as to convey something of the excitement of discovery and the freshness which my initial ignorance made possible. I have had splendid serious colleagues, good students, and boundless opportunity. Whatever defects and limitations there be to what I have done and what I am can be attributed only to myself.

I wondered why, when I was in Bryn Mawr, I had so few

invitations to speak elsewhere; why I was not offered other posts; what it would be like to have a good number of graduate students. But I never let such thoughts disturb me. My rise there was rapid; I was a full professor at top salary—at that time $5,200—by the time I was thirty-seven, I think it was. I was publishing; I had just finished a book; the Peirce papers were out of the way, I was (by 1939) the happy father of two children who, although not always in the best of health, were bright and attractive. My teaching was a pleasure; I had many friends among the students, though few among the faculty; we had a place in Vermont to which we would go every summer and live a nonacademic life for a few months. We visited the Whiteheads for a week or so at the Pickmans' every summer—the Whiteheads had asked for us. That was a most civilized, delightful time. The Pickmans were incomparable friends and hosts, and the Whiteheads were delightful, stimulating friends, conversationalists, and guides.

In 1945 I received a call from Brand Blanshard at Yale. He needed someone to substitute for him for a term while he underwent prostate surgery. (He had tried Otis Lee without success.) I turned to Victoria to ask her opinion; she told me to accept it. After I did, I was astonished to hear her say that she would remain in Bryn Mawr with the children. I then went to see the president of Bryn Mawr. I was shocked to hear her refuse to let me go, on the ground that I would never come back. After some reflection, I told her (Ms. McBride) that A. Cameron, a friend from the Greek department, was about to return from the army, and was most anxious to teach philosophy. He could take over my undergraduate history of philosophy course, and we could omit my logic course for a year as well as my graduate seminar. In that way she could save my entire term's salary, not having to pay for any replacement. That persuaded her.

I have now been typing without interruption for hours—a little more than four, I think, and I am getting tired. I do not find it particularly enjoyable or profitable to write autobiography. In any case, if I think I ought to continue, I will do so tomorrow. Now I will take off a moment or two to continue some of the reflections that I have had about some of the things said yesterday.

*   *   *

A condition which issues from a finality applies to all actualities; it has power. There is, therefore, no need to have a man get to an equilibrium point before the condition applies to all actualities equally; nor does it depend on a society for its power to govern. The attainment of an equilibrium point and the need for power have to do, not with the condition as produced by a finality, but with the condition as delimited to a society. The equilibrium point is achieved after one has started from an insistence and moved into a projection, and then it has to do with a condition as governing that individual and an indefinite but limited number of other men. The power which the society introduces into the condition gives the condition boundaries, to make it a condition for the society. Otherwise the condition would extend beyond it, be a condition which a finality indifferently imposes on all that is available.

May 20

At the time I left for Yale for a semester's substitute teaching, I was head of the department at Bryn Mawr, succeeding Grace De Laguna. I was a poor head of the department. Not only had I not been getting along too well with my colleague, Milton Nahm, but I was too brusque, too quick, too insistent, too much in a hurry to change things, presumably for the better, too thoughtless to be little more than an irritant to him and to the more junior people. He had been a Rhodes Scholar and had accepted many of the English manners and a few of the mannerisms; he was interested in aesthetics, read widely, had some knowledge of the classics, was relaxed in his manner, easy in his ways with students, on the whole quiet, reserved, quite the opposite from me. My being promoted before him, despite the fact that he had been appointed a year before, exacerbated whatever tension there was, though he never complained or gave any sign of annoyance.

Dr. De Laguna and her husband had been the department of philosophy for years. I had met him once; he made some perceptive, judicious remarks to me about a paper on logic that I had read at a philosophical association meeting. She was intelligent, genuinely interested in philosophic thought, but rather uptight, and in any case could not compete very well with the attention that the girls gave and the interest they showed in the two young men, even though neither of them was particularly attractive or virile.

I came to Yale as veterans were returning from the war. They were older men, some of whom had attended Yale before, and now had returned, sobered, serious, matured, after some experience in the armed forces. I made a great impression on them, in part perhaps because I was seen to be somewhat irregular in my ways, thinking, and speech. I found out later that a number had written to the dean and other university officers urging that I be kept.

The necessary expansion of the department required by the sudden influx of students made it desirable to hire new people. F. S. C. Northrop was one of my strong backers. He had been about the first of Whitehead's American students, having gone to England to study with him. Imaginative, freewheeling, open to new ideas, Northrop made many of his university colleagues not only aware of the importance of philosophy but led them to believe that they themselves were doing philosophy in their own ways. From the beginning I liked Northrop, and was glad that some time later I had the opportunity to dedicate one of my books to him. He was a master of Silliman College, and during that first semester let me have a suite in it, and the privilege of dining at the college. He had touted me, on the basis of my knowledge of Peirce and of Whitehead, as an expert in American philosophy (which I was not), an area which the department could well take seriously.

Before the semester was out, Northrop quietly told me that the department was thinking of hiring me permanently. I almost precluded the appointment, for I made too many inquiries and raised too many questions, with the consequence that Brand Blanshard became increasingly reluctant to have me given a permanent post. At one time he asked me whether I would consider an associate professorship. I hesitantly answered, in part because I was not sure whether or not I should take it. But that hesitance was in conformity with typical academic politesse; he took it for granted that I would not accept anything less than a full professorship. In the meantime, two retired professors, Bakewell and Sheldon, heard about the impending appointment, and went to President Seymour, I subsequently learned, to tell him that, like all Jews, I was merely verbal, and that there was nothing of substance in what I was writing. He told someone that this was a charge that was always being brought up, but that this time he had decided to ignore it. In any event, by December I knew that I was being seriously considered, and somewhere around February or so, after I had returned to Bryn Mawr, my appointment was confirmed.

It was a splendid move for Victoria. She immediately made

friends with intelligent, interesting women, and we came to know a number of couples and families. My children, though, were denied the run of the Bryn Mawr campus with its many available babysitters (who were easy for me to get, since they took quickly to my open shelves of books, particularly the Henry Millers). Still, in 1945 they were ten and six, and were in a position to benefit from an urban community and what a university town had to offer in entertainment, schools, and culture. I liked the large graduate classes, and liked the variegated, vigorous interests of the undergraduates.

We had had open house at Bryn Mawr for many years to which the students trooped in considerable numbers, week after week. We lived a distance from the campus in New Haven, but this did not deter students, reluctant though they usually are to walk more than a street or so, from coming to our house on Friday evenings, again and again. Many of them came, I am confident, because of Victoria, who was particularly interested in literature and in the young poets and writers at Yale. The house was often very crowded, with students standing around the walls, sitting on the floor, and remaining for many hours. It was eminently right, when Victoria died, for the college newspaper to publish a special editorial on her, though she had no official connection with Yale. (During the term when I was in New Haven by myself I also had a kind of open house, but I found that it is hard to carry out such an open house if there is only a single focus. There ought to be at least two people who have something to contribute.)

I was quickly made a member of the Elizabethan Club, and I think it was at that time that I became a member, too, of the Aurelian Society, both providing me with opportunities to meet the liveliest students at the university. I think it was not until I arrived, as a tenured professor in 1946, that I was formally admitted to these places.

It is hard to believe at the present time, but in the 1940s and a good part of the 1950s Yale was rather anti-Semitic. It had had Jewish students, mainly from New Haven, but all, I think, were excluded from the eating clubs, fraternities, and senior societies. There had been a number of distinguished Jewish teachers in the law, medical, and graduate schools, but there had never been a Jewish full professor appointed to the undergraduate school. Those who had been appointed to the graduate and other schools did not teach undergraduates as a rule; and, if they did, they were not members of its faculty. Many of the faculty were fairly well off, had been graduated from Yale, and had a social life amongst themselves. All the while I was at Yale, there were many houses to which I never was invited, in part because I was so outré, I think, but also in part because of the latent anti-Semitism. A splendid exception was Mrs. Coffin, who was the widow of a philanthropist, and the mother of William Coffin—whom I knew as a student, came to know as a friend, and who subsequently became chaplain of the University. Mrs. Coffin had parties every few weeks or so to which Thornton Wilder and other luminaries would come. We (and after Victoria's death, I) were frequently invited, and had an opportunity, therefore, to share in some of the vital exchanges which take place in a great university town.

At Bryn Mawr we had a somewhat similar experience, for though we never had much of a social life, we were frequently invited to parties given by Miss Donnelly, the head of the English department, and Miss Edith Finch, who is now the widow of Bertrand Russell. We met many interesting people at the Donnelly/ Finch home; whenever Judge Learned Hand, and particularly Bertrand Russell came, we were invited, sometimes as the only other guests.

Judge Hand was rather pompous and self-important—it is an occupational disease, I found, when I came to meet more judges, though I do think Judge Charles Clarke was an exception. Judge Hand listened to disagreements with irritation, and did seem to need adulation and confirmation over and over again.

Bertrand Russell was an exceptionally witty man. Looking a little like the mad hatter in the Tenniel cartoon in *Alice in Wonderland,* he seemed unable to comment on anything without making a clever, sometimes malicious, and occasionally a perceptive observation. He was gracious and always alert. I do not remember him ever saying anything that was probing, pivotal, or which opened up new territory. But as a dinner companion and afterward, he was a delight to be with. Miss Donnelly and Miss Finch were excellent hostesses; I think Victoria and I were invited not only to the Russell evenings but to others, because of Edith Finch's good opinion of me. Mrs. Coffin, I think, perhaps was not quite as intrigued, but I may well be mistaken, for there was nothing she did or said that would justify such a judgment.

Thornton Wilder was, to my disappointment, a rather tedious man; his observations were banal, and his thoughts commonplace. I heard him some years later give an address before the Connecticut Academy of Arts and Sciences to which I then belonged—any member of the Yale faculty could, without difficulty. He spoke in a prissy manner with minor comments apparently directed at school-teachers. But as he went on he began to say more and more insightful things; the speech was brilliant, and worthy of the man who wrote the *Ides of March,* and rewrote *The Man from Yonkers* to make a splendid play.

One of the visitors to New Haven was Henry Miller. I had corresponded with him some years back, and he visited us in Bryn Mawr (where he met Jenny Lepska whom he eventually married, and whom I had a chance to meet again with considerable pleasure when I was out in California four years or so ago). I had been urging Miller to see Jasper Deeter who had been running the Hedgerow Theatre near Bryn Mawr. I had written a paper on pacifism which some members of his cast found congenial, and I had been invited to visit them. After the play, invited back with the cast, we found ourselves in the midst of a most congenial company. Sometimes they would spontaneously act a portion of a play for us, as a gesture of friendship. Jasper, a warm, friendly, easy spirit, in love with the theatre, was such an unusual person in his thoughts and ways, that I was sure that Henry Miller and he would admire one another. I was right. Henry Miller speaks of his experience in (I think) *I Remember to Remember.*

Henry Miller was not particularly arresting as a person, as a speaker, as a thinker; he was then more or less at the stage where he was surrounded by sycophants and it was not easy for him to be with someone who was not one. Miller's ways, though, were easy, his views somewhat off the beaten track, and many of his actions spontaneous and generous. Years later I was asked to contribute to a book in his honor; I praised him, but also made some criticisms. These were not well taken by him or by his friends, though my paper was favorably remarked upon by a number of critics.

Apart from Northrop, and a junior man, F. Fitch, an expert and an original in logic, my colleagues in the department had all come to Yale in recent years. Hendel preceded me by about three to six years, Blanshard by one. T. Greene had been appointed when I was. We came as full professors with some confidence in what we were individually doing. Meetings were good spirited, and everyone seemed to be concerned with improving the department. Hendel gave himself unselfishly and without limit to the daily work of running it. He had started as head of both the graduate and undergraduate sections, but we persuaded him to give up one of them. It was his constant concern with the department that made it become nationally recognized in a few years, and begin attracting students from all over the country and sometimes from abroad.

Greene had come from Princeton with the reputation of being the greatest teacher there. He had been urged on the department by President Seymour who had him in mind to be a master of one of the colleges—he eventually succeeded Northrop. His field was aesthetics, but it was an aesthetics focussed on classical works, with no tolerance for modern things—"Picasso," he said, "was all right for ties." He was not as effective a teacher at Yale as he had been at Princeton, perhaps because his colleagues in the department and outside it were excellent teachers too.

The man I had known longest was Blanshard, since he and I belonged to the Fullerton Club when he was a professor at Swarthmore, before coming to Yale. But though when at Yale we had him to dinner a number of times, and he had us to his home even more times, and though we met together at the department meetings and elsewhere, I never advanced much beyond the initial contact I had made with him when he was in Pennsylvania. He was always self-possessed, somewhat austere, clean-looking, moderate, modulated, very academic in his manners, attitudes, and values. His wife had been a dean at Swarthmore; they had no children and he, at least, had little interest in the arts, though he did profess to know T. S. Eliot, and did make a number of references to literature. One respected him, but so far as I know, no students and no members of the faculty went beyond this. He just never seemed to allow or to want human intimacy, even of the kind that the ordinary professor has with colleagues and students. In meetings he was reasonable, conservative, displeased with what was unusual, either in idea or in behavior.

R. Calhoun was a professor of theology with a remarkable memory and a wide knowledge of the history of thought. He gave the undergraduate course in the history of philosophy, without notes, and with an intelligence and a flair that made him one of the really popular teachers. He and Northrop were my strongest supporters, both at the time of my appointment and later. Calhoun was caught between two luring extremes. He had a gift for clear presentation of what, though not profound, was nevertheless sound and educative. But he wanted to be a great scholar. As a consequence, he would not allow himself to publish what would have been a good intermediate work on church history, much better than McGiffert's but considerably below the classics. Like Northrop, though, he was open to new ideas, had firm opinions, and was attracted to distinctive people. He sent his students and his sons to attend my classes; their good opinion I think helped solidify his own about me.

I was not voted to be a member of Silliman College. Fortunately I was taken in by Jonathan Edwards. As a result, I belonged to Yale right from the start, for without a college affiliation one was denied contact with a diversity of people. One of the other members of Jonathan Edwards was Hindemith, with whom I would sometimes speak about questions in music that were troubling me. He—as I found to be true of other distinguished musicians—could not believe that anyone was as ignorant as I was telling him I was and revealing myself to be. Painters, dancers, architects, and sculptors, I have found, understand the desire to know on the part of someone who is honestly inquiring from a position of genuine ignorance, but musicians, perhaps because they have themselves undergone such a long period of disciplined training—though I suppose dancers have been at it as long and with as much seriousness—seem unable to grasp what it is that others would like to learn from them.

In my first year I had a graduate student, Eli Karlin, twenty years of age or so. He was brash, bright, independent. Convinced that I was the greatest philosopher since Aristotle, he told everyone that he was my disciple, and that I was a philosopher of exceptional stature. He wanted me to start a periodical devoted to my thoughts. I did not approve. But I did say I would be willing to start a periodical devoted to aspects of philosophy that were being neglected today, providing that I could be assured of financial backing. He told me that his family would guarantee the finances. Somewhat naïvely I accepted the assurance and launched the *Review of Metaphysics* the next year. It was hard to interest people in a periodical with that title—deliberately chosen in fact as a challenge to a positivistically dominated philosophical world. It took some five or six years before the periodical was able to pay for itself. I asked for money in various places and managed to scrape by until the time came when it was self-supporting.

Karlin wrote his thesis with me, and he took charge of managing the *Review*. But, suddenly, without notice, he and his family left the United States, with a host of bills unpaid. There was a period when I thought that I would have to take out another mortgage on my house in order to pay the bills and keep the periodical afloat. I consulted Judge C. Clarke who recommended a lawyer, J. O'Keefe. He wrote Karlin a number of letters and eventually managed to get back the sums that were owed the *Review*. In the meantime, I had appealed to Louis Rabinowitz, a benefactor of the library, who made up the difference. When Karlin eventually paid, Rabinowitz refused to take back the money he had lent me; that laid the foundation for the accumulation of funds for the *Review*—which came to over $30,000 by the time I gave up the editorship.

In the beginning, I asked passing graduate students to put the issues in envelopes and to help with other chores; some of my colleagues took out life subscriptions. With the help of these and some university subscriptions at higher than the usual price the *Review* managed quite well. I soon found that there were quite a number of thinkers here and there who needed the periodical as a rallying point. (I had the idea of such a rallying point in mind when, much earlier, I suggested the founding of what finally became the *Journal of Symbolic Logic*.)

It soon became clear to me that there was a place for a society where the great problems of philosophy were treated as of primary concern. With that in mind I called a meeting of the Metaphysical Society of America—an institution which is still flourishing but which does not seem to me to be as much occupied with deep and central issues as it had been in its early days. Hendel, with his verbal support, and Hocking, with a letter, made it possible for the society to become a member of the Learned Societies of America. I represented our society at the LSOA at the beginning, and found the meetings to be so interesting and important that I decided that others should have the privilege, too, and decided, therefore, not to be a representative for more than one term. I have tried to make it a tradition of our society that it change its delegates after each term. A similar policy was instituted in connection with the *Review*'s managing editor. I alone was the editor and made all the editorial decisions; the managing editor was in charge of seeing the periodical through the press, the bookkeeping, and the circulation/advertising. As soon as he learned how to do the job well, I would ask him to leave so that another young person could learn how a periodical was published. This amateur emphasis, I am glad to say, is still characteristic of the *Review,* though there is now an inclination to keep a good man at the post longer than I did. My idea was to adventure, to dare, to experiment constantly.

Henry Luce, whom I had solicited by mail, soon became much interested in the *Review* and me; he gave the *Review* some *Time* stock. When I asked, he gave me good cautious advice. I met him, too, when I was in Italy years later at the time that his wife was the United States ambassador to Italy. She was lively but quite superficial; he, on the other hand, was modest, retiring, simpleminded even, but sincere, genuinely concerned with America, an average Yale student who had accumulated years without much additional wisdom or insight. He visited me every once in a while in New Haven, came to the party given me when I retired from the editorship, answered my solicitation for financial help for a student, and contributed when I campaigned, without much success, for money for the *Review.*

The reputation of the *Review* grew rapidly; its circulation began to approach those of the *Philosophical Review* and the *Journal of Philosophy*, published decades and decades earlier. The department began to be known to many, I think, as essentially metaphysically oriented. This did it little harm. Students kept coming from many places, and many of them were antimetaphysical in interest. Most worked with others. To counterbalance the influence I was exerting through the *Review* (but not I think through my own publications), I made an effort to see that we hired philosophers with persuasions quite different from mine. I called the attention of the department to, and helped secure the appointments of, C. Hempel, A. Pap, W. Sellars, R. Brumbaugh, and, when the emphasis began to be felt the other way, J. Wild.

When I first began to dine at Silliman, I met Richard Sewall. We soon became good friends. We had lunch together at least once a week for the twenty-odd years I was at Yale. No two people could have been more dissimilar in obvious ways. He was the son of a minister, quiet, careful, at work for almost his entire career on a life of Emily Dickinson (his book on that life won a National Book Award just this year). When he became master of Ezra Stiles, I left Jonathan Edwards in order to take up residence there, helping him with decisions on new fellows and the like. At lunch we would discuss or interchange opinions, on literature primarily, but also on university politics and issues, personalities, and students. He knew a great number of students, and was also on good terms with a great number of the faculty. It was never exciting, but it was always pleasant to meet with him.

Yale had invented a Scholar of the House program—I think it was Dean W. De Vane's idea. Excellent students could offer a project which they would carry out in senior year, free from all classes, but under the supervision of a faculty member. I had students in the program very early. I was also invited to attend the regular meetings that were held for all the students and their supervisors. By the time Richard Sewall took charge of the program—the third director I think—it had developed a good routine. He improved it further. Students and their directors met once a week at dinner; one of the students would read from his work in progress; this was discussed by the others. Sewall had me come every week, whether or not I had a student in the program. I functioned as a kind of devil's advocate, raising difficulties and pointing out directions not considered by the student or his director. We made a good team I think. Some day the enterprise may be written up; an interesting chapter in American education should be the result.

Victoria died of lung cancer in 1953, at the age of forty-seven. She had become a heavy compulsive smoker in her later years. Evelyn Whitehead had been a heavy smoker too, but the smoking apparently did not affect her. I had planned to go to India with Victoria on a sabbatical, supported in part by a grant. With some misgivings, but with the approval of my children and at the urging of my colleagues, I decided to go, and break the pattern of my life with Victoria. When I got back I sold my house and took up residence in Jonathan Edwards. There is no need to go into the details of the trip and associated matters; I have dealt with them in a diary, mimeographed copies of which are somewhere about.

Somewhat after that time I was invited to join the New York Philosophy Club in New York. It was not until such junior men as John Smith and Carl Hempel had been invited, and who were shocked by the fact that I had not been, that the invitation came. I found the meetings not very profitable. A dozen or so sat around a table, each offering a comment, kept to a limited number of minutes, on some paper which had been written and read by one of us.

My life at Yale is too recent, and in any case would be better dealt with by someone else who looked at it within the larger context of a department or from another angle, to make it desirable for me to dwell upon it, any longer. One thing is clear: it was a time when I had a chance to try out ideas with good students, and sometimes with colleagues.

The spirit pervading the department was one of mutual respect and decency. Later, with the departure or retirement of the senior people, followed by the scandal of Richard Bernstein's being denied tenure, the reputation of the department began to fade. I think it lost, too, from its no longer being the home of the *Review,* though at the time it was thought to be a gain. (Bernstein had taken over as editor just before he had been denied tenure, and I saw no reason why he should not take the periodical with him wherever he went.)

I was due for retirement in 1969. The inquiries and offers I received about that time from Kansas and Texas, among others, were for too short a period. I wanted one for of at least five years' duration. That was the offer I received from the Catholic University of America. When I came down to meet the members of it, I was impressed with the way in which Dean Jude Dougherty conducted the meeting, the quality of the faculty, and the pleasantness of the campus. It was a wise decision, though it took me a year or so to get back into my usual rhythm of reading and writing, and thinking.

I have rarely looked back; I never think of myself as a retired Yale professor; my attention is directed here. I do not attend general faculty meetings, but I do attend the department meetings, and have more committee responsibilities than I ever had before—though they are not very great. I live near the center of things in Washington, within walking distance of the museums, most of the movie houses and theatres, the Kennedy Center, the White House (where I have not yet gone). I will reserve my evaluations of colleagues and department of the school and the administration for some later anniversary.

*   *   *

The examination I was conducting before I interrupted myself with these two days of autobiographical remarks dealt with the way an individual vitalized and also allowed himself to fall under a condition which had application to others as well. It recognized a variety of ways in which one was able to be together with those others, and thus dealt with those others as so many acceptable but separate actualities. But there is another way as well in which one deals with others—by exclusion, rejection, repulsion. The former allows them all to be under the governance of a single we; the latter takes the individual, or the we that he might help constitute, and sets this in opposition to others, by placing them outside that governance. How is this possible?

Repulsion is the other side of the act of self-maintenance, the holding of oneself to oneself, but set at a point beyond oneself, in terms of which the maintenance is established. There may be nothing at that point. So far, the situation seems to be quite like that which is produced when an individual projects himself outward in the guise of a possible we. But where a projection involves the use of a condition under which individuals are to come, a repulsion is directed at individuals or at a position where there might be individuals, without regard for the conditions which might bear on them and oneself. Or, if there be individuals there, they are faced directly as 'others', as them or you, repulsed, not to be encompassed within any common condition that is being vitalized at that time, but to stand away from it, placed outside its provenance.

There appear to be as many basic types of repulsion as there are types of encompassment—we repulse those that are not to be affiliated in some special way, not to be coordinated within a frame, are not intelligible according to certain demands, are not to be in our territory, and do not fit in our scheme of values. It is not that we first consider a mode of encompassment and then reject something as not subject to it—though this is of course possible—but that we just repel in one of these ways.

A repulsion is possible even under an encompassment, and may be independently expressed in different modalities. One might even encompass another as capable of affiliation, and at the same time repel him as not capable of affiliation in some other way. More often, though, a repulsion is directed at actualities not then taken to be within the compass of a vitalized condition. The repelled is then set outside the boundaries of the condition, and thereby helps to define it.

In order to internalize a condition, an actuality sets itself in a repulsive opposition to others; it maintains itself in that way during the entire process of internalization, and also when it reverses its direction to produce a projection. An individual always stands in repulsive opposition to others even when it ends with a we under which those others are brought into connection with itself. He becomes aware of himself when he makes a juncture with a condition, but it is an awareness which involves a repulsion of others at the same time. As a consequence, he becomes aware of himself both as an I who can make a we vital, and as an I which bounds itself away from all others. He comes to the condition as an I which has held off others and is therefore aware of itself as having a dimension other than that which the condition could provide. At the same time, he repels the others while making himself part of a we, and thereby deals with the others, not as a mere individual all alone, but as one who has already in principle allied himself with others.

May 21

Mr. Duckett, who is in charge of the archives of American philosophy at Southern Illinois University library, came by this morning. He plans to take my correspondence (up to about 1969), copies of manuscripts, and related material, both what is here at home and at my office at The Catholic University. My current correspondence, and of course the books I am now working on, are not to be touched. In addition, he is taking two of the four manuscripts which I now think should never be published: a rapidly written commentary on Kant's first *Critique*; another equally hurried commentary on Hegel's logic from the *Encyclopedia*. He is not taking an intricate, dialectical, worked-over discussion of categories, or the running notes made for "You, I, and the Others." Apart from this work, that leaves "First Considerations" (which is now being revised while awaiting criticisms from various philosophers), and the manuscript, "You, I, and the Others"—still somewhere in the back of my mind.

Mr. Duckett suggested that I make this work attend more to my daily activities, make it more of a Pepys diary. To follow his suggestion will require some change in outlook on my part, but I think there will be nothing amiss in my trying to do it. He regretted that I had not made the attempt years before, but he thinks there is some value in my beginning now. There are few philosophers, he says, who have the range of interests and the kinds of contacts that I have; in any case, my reactions to daily events, entertainments, and experiences might be of some benefit for those who might look into my *nachlass* years later.

Last week I bought tickets for the American Ballet Theatre performance at the Kennedy Center. I had tickets for last Tuesday, Wednesday, and Friday, and for last night. The much-publicized Baryshnikov and Kirkland were to perform, as well as Makarova. I am not very knowledgeable in the dance, not having seen all the famous dances, and few of them more than one or two times. I can not tell the difference between the excellence of a Kirkland and a Makarova. But, at the same time, I lose interest in dances which put too much emphasis on the story line, in which the dances are mediocre, and where there is an attempt to be humorous, topical, or acrobatic.

The *Giselle,* which I had seen performed once before some years ago, was as delightful and as emotionally stirring as any dance I had seen. Baryshnikov is all control and grace; apparently he can do almost anything with his body. Last night he performed in every dance but one. *Vestris* had him dancing alone; *The Young Man and Death* had him with Mathis. He leaps with a smooth, easy movement, and changes direction, emphasis, and gesture with startling but masterly abruptness. The critic in the *Washington Post* this morning thinks yesterday was an historically memorable day, and could not find words strong enough to express his admiration of Baryshnikov. But I was disturbed by the emphasis on acrobatics, mime, and tricks; they took away time and even emotional involvement with the dance, to leave me with admiration for a dextrous, fluid body, but without excitement or the feeling I had seen *the* dance performance. There is no doubt but that Baryshnikov has incredible suppleness, that he can command himself to make the most startling moves without apparent preparation, effort, or attention. His leaps, though not high or overly long, moved off the dance floor and returned to it in a continuous movement. I have seen dancers who have appeared to hover longer in the air, but none who left and returned with such ease and grace.

I liked Kirkland even more; she is a consummate dancer, with a lithe body which moves with both precision and dexterous charm, even with some daring. I saw Makarova last week, and was taken with her dancing too—and also with some of the others. The *corps de ballet* also was splendid (the men excepted); at every performance the *corps* was at once firm, gentle, simple, and direct in its movements.

My theory about dance says that the dancer occupies the entire dancing space. I think I see that to be the case, but I am not altogether confident that I *really* see it. I liked the free dance more than the ballet, until this last week; I have been soured by too many *Swan Lakes* seen amidst a sea of children and guiding mothers. But I never have seen a company as well disciplined and polished as this. This time, though, there were not many moments when I was completely caught up in the dance, though my attention rarely wandered; it was too often a spectacle, something to enjoy or approve rather than to live through and with. After my four days of viewing dancing I felt that I had been neglecting this side of my life too much; at the same time, I was glad that I was not seeing any more dances for a while, and that I would now return to my thinking and writing.

Yesterday, David Slavitt's *Vital Signs: New and Selected Poems,* arrived, with his salutation, "For Paul, with affection." I have always thought that Slavitt was too clever for his own good. His novels are bright, sprightly, ingenious, and witty, but never deal with any basic issue in a serious manner. All turn about some tricks. They exhibit facility but no depth. But I am surprised, delighted, and impressed with his new book. So far I have not read more than some thirty pages; there seems, though, to be no question but that he has both a mastery of the medium and an ability to do justice to poignant situations and to many emotions. While he brings in no new perspective, no new, successful poetic forms, presents no theme of a fundamental sort which is sustained over a long period, his *Vital Signs* is poetry, and poetry of a high order, better than most of what I see today, and far better than what I had expected or even suspected that he might do. Sensitive to his own feelings and the feelings of others, particularly of women with whom he is involved, he is most of all acute about his own feelings in relation to the women seen as already affected by and involved with him. I will continue reading in his book with high hopes.

It is a pleasant and rather unexpected experience for me to look forward to reading a book of poems. I do read poetry every once in a while, but in a kind of passive state awaiting to become involved. Slavitt made me be involved.

Two philosophers at Harvard have suddenly made a considerable stir—Rawls and Nozick. I read about a quarter of Rawls's book, and gave it up bored, for he seemed to me to assume so much arbitrarily, and to argue without taking sufficient account of what appear to me to be equally plausible alternatives. Nozick does not agree with him, but to judge from the reviews I have seen, shares the same common outlook.

I have just bought Nozick's book mainly to see what the method is, and why it is that it has received such acclaim. The thesis is most implausible—that government is best which governs least. It is, of course, an old thesis, but I see by glancing at the book that he is approaching it in a fresh way, with new arguments somewhat attuned to the present-day discussions. I will begin it this evening.

*   *   *

Rarely does it occur to me to look at anything from a fivefold point of view until, for some reason, I have come to consider one or more alternatives to some given account. It is then that I ask myself whether or not the few alternatives that I had considered, prompted usually by recognizing that the original view was not able to take care of some obtrusive fact, should not be supplemented by others. I follow this by asking if I had not stated the original set incorrectly. These reflections are pertinent to what was said yesterday after the autobiographical comments, when I spoke of two kinds of negation or opposition, an inclusive and an exclusive, a holding away and a repulsion, a setting something outside the provenance of an I or a we.

A repulsion, even though direct, without any apparent reference to an overall condition or a projection, appears to instance Existence, with its extensional possible subdivisions outside one another. An encompassment, even one which is in the form of an othering, operative on entities that are one another's others, illustrates Substance, with its possessive, affiliative, grounding ultimacy. This suggests that there is also a kind of opposition reflecting the nature of Being, another reflecting the nature of Possibility, and a third reflecting the nature of Unity. Is not the one instanced by the mutual self-enclosure of actualities; the second by alternative bases for truth; and the third by an evaluational ordering in which actualities are related to one another but only as also being encompassed? The original pair was thought to have five different modes; if this is also true of the latter three, evidently there are twenty-five different cases in which an individual stands as an I, or as part of a we, in contradistinction with others:

1] Encompassment has   A] a substantializing mode at the same time that it illustrates the finality, Substance. The accepted condition affiliates whatever items fall under its governance.   B] There is also an encompassment which requires the items to be coordinate with one another; another,   C] connects them by means of a rational principle or rule; a fourth,   D] relates them as at a distance in an extensive field; and finally,   E] an evaluational deals with them in terms of some comprehensive value.

2] Mutual self-enclosures may concern distinct entities in the guise of   A] qualities,   B] units,   C] meanings,   D] positions, or   E] values. Each item stands apart from the others, and though all presuppose Being as a condition under which they function together, each merely maintains itself in one of these five guises.

3] Each individual either provides a test of truth or accepts some other as the test of truth. In either case, that truth has an   A] aesthetic,   B] ontological,   C] formal,   D] criteriological, or   E] measuring role.

4] The direct repulsion of entities by the others also has five forms: A] repugnance,   B] alienation,   C] contradiction,   D] antagonism, and   E] conflict. In all, the entities directly reject one another without regard for any encompassing condition. The operation, however, presupposes that there is such an encompassing condition, enabling an individual to approach the others in any one of these five modes. If he stands at an equilibrium point he can subject himself to the condition at the same time that he imposes himself on others with the support of a social force.

5] Finally, individuals encompass one another in ordered relations. They   A] form some kind of harmony,   B] have unit values,   C] comparable values,   D] are irreducible, or   E] contribute to a final total value.

Not only do I now seem to have gone to the opposite extreme, with an ungainly set of distinctions, but some of the terms used to mark them off seem rather arbitrary. I have done little more than set down headings. Until they are filled out they can do no more than offer suggestions as to where one might look for important differences.

The first and fourth five have previously been touched upon, making it desirable to begin an attentive examination with the second and to proceed to the third and fifth:

An individual brings his internalization of what is qualifying him to a close, not simply by having the qualification sunk within his dense center, but by keeping it there, and this apart from a thrust outward. It is not that he just encloses himself, but that his internalization is completed in a self-enclosure, immediately balanced by a thrusting outward.

A self-enclosure bounds a quality in the sense that the result is an intensive whole, a qualification given depth and tone. It can be said to end in a mere unit, in that the outcome is a real being on a footing with any other. As self-enclosed it is, of course, not together with the others; but also, it is not self-enclosed except so far as it closes itself off from others, equally real. A self-enclosed individual is also a meaning in the sense that he is a possible object of thought, and explanatory of what else he might do. His self-enclosure is also a way of occupying a position in an extension, where he remains apart from the rest. Finally, his completing of the act of self-enclosure is the completing of himself as a value within which all that is being internalized is made to fit. The self-enclosure in all these cases occurs independently of any acts on the part of others; indeed, regardless of whether there are any other individuals. When there is a multiplicity of individuals, each engages in an act of self-enclosure under the aegis of the conditions provided by Being.

The third set of cases is harder to deal with. In *Beyond All Appearances* I offered a defense of the idea that an individual is a test of truth, and tried to show that this did not lead to a personalism, pragmatism, or solipsism. But I here go further and recognize that the individual may take, not himself, but some other to be the test of truth—as is sometimes done in verifying some hypothesis.

The schema suggests that truth must not be treated as though it pertained solely to statements which are of interest to logicians. There is an aesthetic 'truth' in the sense that other items are to be accepted or discarded according to their degree of harmony with it. An ontological truth is what the existentialists call 'authenticity', the living in accord with what one in fact is, and not in terms of some alien principle or custom or society. A formal truth is the familiar truth that concerns the logician. As I have tried to make out again and again in this work and elsewhere, that truth is not to be simply identified with the truth which attaches to an assertion directed at some matter of fact. The truth in formal statements takes a ninety-degree turn from that, and is related to some other formal statement. The former is semantic, the latter syntactical. A criteriological truth, in contrast with the others, has to do with what is in fact accepted as the sufficient warrant or evidence for admitting some other claimant to truth. Finally, an individual can set himself as the basis of truth, or at least provide that standard in terms of which all truths are to be determined. This case differs from the criteriological which looks outside some claimant for its warrant.

The fifth set has to do with ordered values rooted in Unity. That Unity, dealt with as a kind of Substance, orders values in accord with the ways in which they together produce a harmony. Each individual is also a unit, incomparable value in its own right. As subject to an encompassing rationale, under the aegis of that Unity, the values are comparable in accord with some principle. As mere occupants of an extension, each value is irreducible, a localized item. And as contributing to a final all-inclusive value, each has a position in a hierarchy, depending on how much it must be altered in order to be assimilable within that totality.

The account is still too hurried. It does not make clear in what sense there are modalities falling under the five headings. Why, for example, should an individual repel others as contradictories and as antagonists? And if they do so repel one another, why take them to be under the governance of a single, generic repugnance, illustrating Existence? Is there always a repugnancy operative? Does it always proliferate into five modes? Does it always operate concurrently with the other four operations? What kind of operations are these? Under what conditions do they themselves operate?

May 22

When I awake in the morning, I turn on the radio while I do my exercises. In the evening I used to turn on the television for the seven o'clock news broadcast. In these ways I dispensed with the reading of newspapers, except to see what the entertainments were, to note special occasions, or to scan particular items of news. While I dress and make breakfast I listen to the hi-fi, which is set at a classical music station. After that I am ready for my walk. If I stop in at a drugstore I may glance at the obituaries and at least look down the index of the *New York Times*. On Sundays I make up for the deficiency somewhat, for I buy both the *Washington Post* and the *New York Times*. I read the book reviews, the news summaries, the magazine sections, and the art sections. I have subscriptions to *Time* and *New York* magazine. These help me keep abreast of current affairs.

I keep reading in a number of books at the same time. I am now in the process of reading Slavitt; Nozick; W. Kaufmann's translation of Buber's *I and Thou;* M. Friedman's translation of selected essays of Buber, *The Knowledge of Man;* Lincoln F. Johnson's *Film;* F. Alluntis and A. B. Wolter's translation of Duns Scotus's "The Quodlibetal Questions," *God and Creatures;* and G. Roy Levin's *Documentary Explorations: 15 Interviews with Film Makers.* I have just finished Lee Gutkind's *The Best Seat in Baseball, But You Have to Stand.* (I find after I have written a book on some field, in good part in order to get a better understanding of it, I have a strong desire to read books in it, to supplement what I have said, and to get a better understanding—not possible before.)

Gutkind's book tries to report the actual conversations of a number of umpires of baseball with whom he spent a good deal of time. The umpires are revealed to be exactingly, painfully honest, but also vulgar, chauvinistic, narrow, with no interests outside of baseball. Umpiring is their pleasure and their life, despite the fact that it takes them away from home for long periods, and that they suffer pains and sometimes danger from pitches, hits, and fans. They live in a world of their own, uninterested apparently in other sports, or in any questions which do not impinge on their work and game.

I also finished Paul Sylbert's *Final Cut,* the making and breaking of a film. This is a bitter recounting of his adventures with producers and their representatives by a director—film writer whose work was, in his opinion, badly mutilated by incompetent, untrustworthy, insensitive people with full authority to decide what is to be finally retained and therefore made available to the public. Sylbert thinks that his contribution was so badly treated as to make the outcome an inevitable failure. His writing is strident, single-toned, throughout condemnatory, but it does confirm other judgments one has heard made of some of the powerful men in Hollywood. Sylbert mentions the villains of his story by name, and recounts the incidents with an anger which apparently has not yet passed away—quite a while after the damage was done.

I do not notice that my readings in the different fields, or my writings for that matter, have much affect on my thought in philosophy. When I try to organize what I would like to say in these other fields, however, I do find that my reflections in philosophy provide structures and sometimes yield insights which were denied to me in the reading of books or in the seeing of films and games. (I used to see a game or so a week on television, but now I look only at crucial games in basketball, football, and sometimes track events.)

The wide range of interests answers to my temperament. I think that when I was a young man I was what some psychiatrists would call 'manic'; I was beset with a multiplicity of thoughts, darting in many directions, which I could not bring into focus or order. Even today, I may have to go through as many as a half dozen heavily rewritten drafts before I have something like a coherent account, over which I will have to work some more in order to take care of errors in syntax to remove confusions and contradictions in thought, and to increase the clarity of the discourse. Today the thoughts are not as many or as vagrant as they once were, but they still take me in many different directions, if only for short periods.

I do not find it hard to drop the reading of one book and to take up another. The lightweight books are particularly good to read at mealtimes and when I am tired. I reserve the philosophical works for periods when I am more alert. More often than not, though, I reserve mealtimes for the reading of periodicals and mail. I attend to the answering of letters usually in the afternoons, a time I also reserve for painting—which I now do with less and less frequency, at least for these last two months.

I have written these few pages just after breakfast. I will now go on my walk, and see if I can get in focus the way the individual self functions in relation to others.

*   *   *

It is tempting to credit all powers, actions, conditions—even laws, history, and political might—to individuals. We can see the individuals functioning, and can account for their cooperation and the controls they exercise in unison by referring to their habits, dispositions, and even agreements.

Nozick, in his *Anarchy, State, and Utopia* says: "But there is no *social entity* with a good that undergoes some sacrifice for its own good. There are only individual people, different individual people, with their own individual lives." I may want to comment at length on his book when I have either gone further into it, or have finished it. I think, though, I have gone far enough into it to see that it suffers from the besetting sin of philosophers—cleverness. I think I, too, am inclined to be clever, but I also do my best to inhibit the tendency. Cleverness ruined A. J. Ayer and, so far, it has shown itself to be an obtrusive, destructive factor in Nozick's work. He says many disconnected things, in a style which changes constantly; there is a great deal of reading behind what he says, but it is of a miscellaneous sort, and is rarely backed with a concern with the reflections of great thinkers of the past. His book sounds as though it had been written in a hurry; it would have benefited greatly had its ideas been 'filtered'—his word—until the important ones were together in some systematic arrangement. As it is now, we have a series of salvos, some arresting suggestions, and a good deal of dogmatism of a positivistic, nominalistic sort.

I refer to him now because of his express denial of the reality of social entities. Were he right, what has a social and political history? What has political might? What does injustice to people? What is legislation, precedent, the power to make war and peace? I do not know what answers, if any, he will try to provide for these. They are matters to which I, in any case, must attend, while giving as much weight as possible to the idea that there are individual men.

One might think of a number of individuals being together in such a way that a distinctive pattern emerges. A family is not the individual members; it has characteristics and implications of its own. This Nozick would allow. But that is still to fall far short of what is required, if there is to be a history. One might take a history to be made up of short-spanned events; these might have or exhibit an overall pattern which we will be able to dissect serially and speak of in temporal terms. The history will then be a sequence of disconnected or constantly constituted events with a nature and a course distinct from any of its members or from some other organization of them. Problems arise when account is taken of the fact that an event or other whole within which individuals interact limits them, controls them, subjugates them. Can this fact be reduced to the utilization of tools, materials, places, and energy by one man, or by a number of cooperative ones, to which the rest yield in order to avoid difficulties, punishment, or penalties? Can the subjugating individuals themselves be subject to others who are exercising other powers and making use of other means? Should we put the bureaucrats and the government on one side, and the rest of the people on the other, and then view the bureaucrats and government, together with some of the people, as subject to some other individual or individuals, say those who control the media? The result would be a complex scheme of things constituted by the interlocking of a number of subordinating-subordinated groupings. The political world would exhibit one such grouping, the media and educational worlds two others, the scientific community still another, and so on, all of them together constituting the historic, customary culture of a people.

Left over will be the problem of explaining the togetherness of even two individuals without making reference to an overall unity of them together. That unity is not explicable by taking account of each of them, even as projecting one toward the other and being countered by the other so as to produce a single frame larger than either, and neutral to both. This is the alternative I entertained in *Reality,* but which I had to give up in order to account for the prescriptiveness of ethical principles and for the contemporaneity of individuals, since these require that there be something determinative as well as common to the individuals.

It seems obvious that men are together in a common space. From their diverse positions they act and take account of one another, but the commonality of their common space is not yet explained. In the last week or so I have been holding that individuals could be taken to vitalize a common condition and thereby turn it into a projection of themselves, under which other individuals might fall. Such an account not only presupposes the independent reality of the common condition, but requires a contrast between the projecting individual and the others who are subject to the projection, or between the individual by himself and the project he makes possible. If there is no acknowledgment of an independent, common condition which functions as a one for a number, that number can not be added, make up a single number of them.

From the very first, there is something not constituted by the members of some group, but which makes it possible for there to be a number of members *of* that group, even if it be as small as a pair. One could, of course, suppose that there are nothing but aggregates, and that the having of this and that rather than some other entities in a given aggregate is a matter of applying some rule or principle by an individual mind. Such an aggregate, since it would depend on the use of an idea, could not be identified with a society or a state, for we find these already functioning in some way, with members already belonging to them somehow; they are not dependent on our understanding their members as being together in an arbitrary aggregation.

Granted, though, that a togetherness of individuals presupposes there is a One for them, independently operative and not constituted by them, it could well be that any other togetherness might be a product of their intermeshing as habituated individuals with various dispositions. Were there not attentive individuals, were no one to do anything, the state or society would simply exhibit some pattern; it would not evidently be a special case of some constraining way of having individuals together. The actions of some one or a few individuals might well trigger actions on the part of the rest; the one or few might act with reference to others in other groups, and might elicit supportive actions from the members who are together with it, all helping constitute a common structured grouping, itself having no distinctive role or status or power.

If one could not get beyond this point, it still, of course, would be true that individuals are related to one another in receptive, coordinate, explanatory, repugnant, and hierarchical ways. These would have to be explained either by taking account of some controlling condition, or as the outcome of individual acts which somehow reach to others, and are often countered by those others with equal and opposite force. One would have to maintain that, in the absence of the controlling condition, they accidently mesh in perfectly reciprocal ways, that the reciprocity is a matter of more or less, or that it is a statistical result, but in any event, something which need not continue. The individuals could all have their habits forged under similar circumstances or under the same human limitations and were therefore able to keep in some consonance.

One might think of various individuals facing the same serious threats and satisfactions in nature, and building up habits which enable them to intermesh with one another in these various ways. There would be a neutrality provided by nature, maintained with respect to all of them, and in terms of which they could function as so many units in relation to one another, reciprocals more or less. (The common world or nature, which was neutral with reference to them, would have to be said not to have a power which it was imposing on them. Otherwise, we would run the risk of surreptitiously introducing the idea of a powerful society or state under the guise of a presumed asocial nature.) The men would confront a world from their different angles and there would find common objects to which they would react in similar ways (due to the men's similar constitutions) and would thereby be in a position to function within a limited orbit, and therefore also with reference to one another as in that orbit.

The world of nature, on this last supposition, would have its own integrity. It would even have a compulsive or prescriptive or conditioning force with respect to the individuals. One would then not have given up an acknowledgment of something other than man, which was governing them, but would merely ascribe this to a nonsocial nature that the individuals severally faced, and thereby acquired similar traits and the ability to interplay with one another within the area that the nature permitted. No longer would individuals alone be considered, for though the nature to which one was now referring might itself be understood as nothing more than a multiplicity of individual entities, as functioning with reference to the individual men it would have a single import, making it possible for those men to have similar kinds of traits. Scientifically oriented thinkers would find such a consequence agreeable; they do not mind endowing nature with powers able to constrain and control individuals, particularly since those powers might then be expressed in terms of laws of nature and in other viable scientific ways. But, it is to be noted, the affect that that nature has on individuals is not purely physical. It accounts for their habits and dispositions. One might, of course, go on to contend that these eventually will be shown to be the products of purely physical forces, but for the present it will have to be affirmed that one is acknowledging a nature which is pertinent to men as able to be made into social beings in interplay.

A nature which operates on individual men so as to make them able to acquire habits and dispositions which are in some consonance with one another, if only as repugnant others, is not the nature at which scientific investigation is directed. Instead, it has a human import, being but the common condition for the individuals' mutually pertinent habits and dispositions. Is it anything other than a society whose articulations and transactions are dictated by various natural occurrences? Is there anything different in principle here from a society that intermediates the workings of that nature by acts which originate with the men whom the society embraces? What role is to be assigned to the laws that govern the course of that nature? Will it be different in principle from the conditions which a society imposes on its members? I see no difference.

Sooner or later we have the case that now prevails, where we do not have the conditioning of men produced by the nature which they severally face, though in similar ways and under similar circumstances, but the society operating, in independence of what is happening in nature, according to established rhythms of its own. Even if we start with a society grounded in the workings of nature, we have to end with one which is functioning apart from it. As functioning apart from nature, it can not be anything but the creature of men who might be responsible for its working, or who might impose the societal pattern on the rest or perhaps on all of them, themselves included.

The addition of a government, with legislature, courts, and the like does not force us to consider any new principle unless it be to take account of the idea of justice and the rights which men have. Long before we come to that issue, long before we have an opportunity to see what a state should do with regard to men's rights, we have the men functioning together under the governing aegis of a society which is distinct from all of them, and not reducible to a function of them as acting with reference to one another, or a nature beyond them.

In dealing with society and the state from the position of projections of individuals, I ignored the possibility of accounting for society and state by reference to a sustaining nature, to which individuals might severally respond in rather similar ways. The two ideas are not incompatible. Either, though, could be thought to be presupposed by the other. If we start with nature, we can think of individuals being conditioned by it, and then turning the conditions into projects. If, instead, we start with individuals as conditioned perhaps by delimited versions of the finalities, we can speak of them involved with nature in common ways because of the manner in which the conditions have been used by them with respect to one another. In the one way, nature dictates the common ways; in the other, common ways dictate a common approach to nature. The first, one might suppose to have been the original way in which society began; but the second is surely the way in which men now function within a society. We are social beings before we are natural beings, or at least no later than we are natural ones. But if that is the case what role do projections play?

Even when we are firmly organized according to the dictates of nature or a society or a state, we form we's which may have a more limited subordinate scope, an independent and possibly a greater range, or which could coincide with the society, even making use of the conditions it provides. The we's enable one to become self-aware as embracing and being subject to conditions, first oriented toward oneself, and then eventually in a more neutral form. When the latter prevails, one is able to see oneself as well as others to be subject to the same neutral vitalized conditions, which are empowered by oneself and/or others, and imposed on oneself and them as forming one group.

We fit together with some men more readily than we do with others; they and we constitute a we having the encompassing powers of something like Substance. At the same time we constitute a we in which we are coordinate with others. The membership of this second we may be the same as, may overlap, or may be quite different from the first. As a consequence, the society we form in the second way may be the same as, overlap, or be entirely differently constituted from the society produced in the first way. What is true of these two modes of encompassment is true of three others as well, in relation to one another and in relation to each of these two. We are members of five different societies; these rarely coincide in their membership; but they rarely have an entirely different membership, in good part because of the limited number of individuals with whom one can be involved. The five societies overlap; the result is a single society in which there is a limited number of men who are related to one another in a fivefold way, and in which there are various junctures of men related in one or more of the five ways.

No matter how intimate men may be, they also repel one another in various degrees, preserving some kind of reserve about themselves, pulling into themselves at the same time that they set themselves in opposition to one another, pushing them aside, denying their impingement or presence or value. The very same individuals whom they may accept as most congenial in a fivefold way, they may also keep at a distance in order to be able to be themselves the individuals who are being congenial. Such repulsion, I have already suggested, also has a fivefold character. Some individuals may be repelled in a fivefold manner, and some may be repelled in a fourfold or fewer ways. The repulsion may keep within the confines of a society defined by the ways in which the individuals fit together, or it may have a shorter or a greater range.

Can a society be constituted by individuals who repel one another? According to Hobbes, this would be a primitive nonsocial state of affairs. It also seems to be the kind of society envisaged by optimistic anarchists who think that men prosper together when left strictly alone by any outside force, and who as alone insist on leading their individual lives.

What role does Existence, or some specialized form of it, play in what seems a direct relationship of the individuals to one another? Is the Existence specialized in the form of condition when the repulsion occurs, or does the repulsion presuppose that it is operative and controlling? The answer to that question will allow one to get a better understanding of the other ways in which individuals are interrelated, and how their interrelationship stands with reference to that which does explicitly occur because they are encompassed by some condition exemplifying Substance.

May 23

A year or so ago I was invited to attend a preliminary meeting set up by some psychiatrists to see if one might not arrange interdisciplinary seminars. I thought the venture unpromising because it seemed primarily designed to stimulate the psychiatrists, also because there did not seem to be a clear idea of what was to be done. I have been invited from time to time to attend some of these seminars but have not gone to any. Last night, J. Williman, who is in charge of the seminar on humor, asked me to go with him. The meeting was at Judith Viorst's home. She is an accomplished writer of light verse; her husband wrote the account of me that had been requested by the Sunday *New York Times Magazine,* but which, because they finally did not want it in the form presented, ended up in the *Washingtonian.*

The meeting was attended by three psychiatrists, a teacher of education, Williman, Viorst, Mac Isaacs from the Catholic University speech and drama department, and me. For the most part the talk was anecdotal. I tried raising more and more basic issues; they were never discussed, except for some occasional asides. But I did come home with an awareness of aspects of the problem of humor, jokes, and the like which I had not previously attended to.

A joke is a completed whole. It needs an introduction in the form of an atmosphere, an attitude, an appropriate occasion. Otherwise, it fits into normal settings as badly as a lie does in a context of truths. Usually it is more conspicuous and more readily rejected than a lie is. That is why there are few, if any, jokes presented in the course of a serious treatise in philosophy, science, history, and other basic disciplines. At best, one can use a joke in an introduction—particularly when the introduction itself is outside the main business—and wants to relax the audience. Or one can bring it in at the end, to offer a relief and perhaps even another way of focussing on what had been said. It jars when put in the text itself.

Humor does require receptivity. It is defeated if the time is one of great seriousness; should it have any effect, it will often have one quite out of proportion to what is said or to the degree of humor. It releases tension; reactions to it are not modulated; as a consequence, the speaker and others may sometimes find themselves unable to contain their laughter, echoing and reechoing one another until they end exhausted. It is contrary to what is wanted from a serious work, for this is to be spelled out in accordance with a cold objective relationship holding among its ideas, details, and pivotal positions.

In a play, even one with a strong persistent tragic theme, humor can be brought in, even coarse and blunt jokes, partly as relief, but also in a controlled manner, eliciting emotions which are subject to artistic control as surely as those which the tragic aspects produce.

What is true of the theatre is not true in the dance. I, at least, resist attempts at humor there; I feel pulled away, diverted from what I want to see. This may be due to my comparative innocence about the nature of the dance, and an inability to grasp the humor as a part of it. Perhaps I am reacting, not to a humorous touch, but to broad attempts at humor, accentuated sometimes by peculiar costumes, mimes, acrobatic stunts, supposed asides to the audience. These, I think, are intrusive on the dance. But it should also be possible, following the lead of great dramatists, to bring in humor in the course of a dance, a humor which is consistent with and even vital for producing necessary nuances, pauses, 'empty spaces'.

Wit is another matter. A work of great seriousness can be written with wit. Bertrand Russell could do this; Schopenhauer could, too. Here the emphasis is on the use of words, on associations awakened, on the fact that the reader is alerted to something relevant, having a bearing on what is as important as the topic directly dealt with. Wit seems rarely to be out of place. But though there are many witty men, there are not many who are also serious thinkers. I do not know if the proportion of witty men among the serious thinkers is less than the proportion of witty men in the general population, but it does seem so. The fact, if fact it is, may be related to the matter of cleverness touched upon yesterday; wits tend to be clever, and cleverness stands in the way of a persistent, penetrating occupation with inquiry and truth about what is fundamental and important.

    *   *   *

There are a number of distinct cases which could easily be confused, but which, if the current discussion about projections, repulsions, and so forth, is on the right track, should be clearly set apart from one another. When this is done it may perhaps become more evident just what a self is and can do, the ways in which 'we', 'you', and 'others' can be used, and their ranking in importance.

We have   A] an encompassing Existence under which individuals are related by affiliation,   B] an encompassing Substance with individuals opposed to one another,   C] individuals repelling one another as existents,   D] individuals repelling one another in the guise of repugnants. Each of the encompassments can be considered in terms of the condition which originates with a finality, or in terms of some specific delimited form of the condition; and the individuals can be taken to be dealing with one another regardless of grade, or to be men only. The present concern is with the specific delimited forms of the conditions, and with humans dealing with one another.

A] A delimited version of Existence used as a project may be sustained by the normal operations of nature; it is a region which is pertinent to a number of men. Those men may, while subject to that condition, be multiply related. One way might be by affiliation. Then, the individuals will approach one another or allow for their relation to one another in space, time, or causality, at the same time that, as individuals under these relations, they will ally with one another in various ways and degrees. Their alliances will be independent of their being in a relation of opposition, due to the individuals being subject to the controlling condition, or to their own individual self-enclosures. The alliance and the self-enclosure will be alternative modes in which the Existence is occupied, fragmented, or intensified by individuals.

B] Instead of being encompassed by Existence, it is possible for individuals to make projects of the condition which Substance makes available. Encompassment is an instance of the kind of power that Substance exerts; but a substantializing encompassment is a mode of encompassment as such. That mode is coordinate with an existentializing encompassment, as above, in A. Under the encompassment, the individuals are in various relations to one another; one of those ways will be opposition. The individuals, then, while being affiliated by the governing special case of a substantial condition, will stand apart from one another, enclosing themselves in opposition to those others.

C] Without attending to the encompassing condition, individuals may directly repel one another. The primary emphasis here is on each enclosing itself, holding itself away from the others, each functioning as a distinct occupant of an extended limited region. They will not do this except so far as they are together with those others under some condition; but, instead of, as in the previous cases, operating as under those conditions, the individuals here will be directly concerned or related with one another. The governing condition is either ignored or modified; its power is limited and perhaps even completely countered. They are 'psychologically' not sociologically in opposition.

D] Instead of repelling one another as so many distinct existents, they might do so as natures or meanings. These are like complementary colors which deny one another to yield one in which neither can be found, or like a man wrongfully depriving another of his rights. The conflict is independent of their status as mere occupants; they may or may not repel one another as existents.

The first and third case can be brought together, by taking the third to differ merely in stress from the first, since it does not deny the presence or operation of Existence, but only the degree of control it in fact exerts, and the prominence given to it in one's thoughts and actions. This is particularly the case when the first is restricted to a delimited Existence in which the individuals who are subject to it repel one another, and are not affiliated. What we would then have is individuals in the first case considered as directly related in any one of five ways. One of those ways is recognized in the third case. We should therefore make allowance for cases where individuals directly affiliate, while presupposing a possibly ignored encompassing Existence. The fourth case is of a different order, since it is concerned with a mode of repelling, which is alternative to the third.

It is now possible to put all this in a better way:

1] Existence and Substance provide distinct modes of encompassment, which we can use as projects or deal with at some neutral position so that we, too, are subject to them.

2] Under both Existence and Substance are different modes of direct relationship, where the Existence and Substance, and special cases of these, are not psychologically, and may not even be ontologically, of much effectiveness.

3] Each type of direct relationship—affiliation or repulsion—will pertain to the individuals as substances, beings, natures, existents, or unit values.

An individual makes a juncture with all forms of encompassment—those provided by Being, Possibility, and Unity, as well as by the Existence and Substance mentioned in *1*. These in turn are more or less effectively, and more or less neutrally, imposed on individuals. Under each type of encompassment the individuals will have any one of five ways of being directly related, and then in such a way that the encompassment will have any one of an indefinite number of degrees of efficacy. As a consequence, we have twenty-five different ways in which individuals are directly related, regardless of how they are encompassed or the effectiveness of that encompassment.

An example: a man is in a relation of repugnance toward others, disaffiliating himself from them. That repugnance, though, may fall under any one of five encompassments. He may have that status while he is in fact being subject to some kind of harmonizing with the other. He may be brought into the same room, club, or workshop with others where he may work cooperatively with them at the very same time that he holds himself apart. The two kinds of connection, in one of which he is being subjected and confined by the condition which Substance makes possible, and the other of which he produces—without reference to the condition—may have various degrees of influence on one another. The former not only allows for the presence of individuals as terms subject to it, but dictates to those terms how they are to function with respect to one another. This does not preclude their also directly acting on one another, regardless of that determination, or in some opposition to its demands. They function as controlled terms, but also as units which operate in some independence of that control. At one and the same time, they could be affiliated and be directly repugnant; and, of course, they could be opposed because of their governance by a condition rooted in Existence, and opposed (or affiliated) independently and possibly in some defiance of that Existence.

If an encompassment has the status of a common social condition, individuals will be socially related to one another as well as psychologically, at one and the same time. As distinct individuals they will be occupied directly with one another and in such a way as to make a difference to whatever condition is in fact connecting them, unknown or unnoted though it be. A given social context will then confine and control them at the same time that they will independently illustrate it, or some other way of being directly connected with one another. While subject to an affiliative condition, they will repel one another in five ways, and thereby limit the effectiveness of the affiliative condition. They will repel one another in a similar five ways, too, when subject to a different kind of conditioning besides affiliation. Under each condition in fact, there will be five forms of repelling.

All the conditions are operative at the same time. Is this also true of all the forms of direct relationship, such as repelling? Since the direct relationship of repelling occurs independently of the condition that is dominant, and also independently of the condition which the direct relations in fact presuppose, and since the repelling has to do with different aspects of those conditions, evidently all five can occur at the same time, regardless of the encompassing condition.

The five ways of repelling, one can say, are qualified by the nature of the encompassing condition with which they interplay. If so, we need to consider only those five ways of repelling; we can take the increase to twenty-five to be a derivative complication, explicable in terms of the ways in which encompassing conditions operate. This will still leave over five ways in which the individuals are directly affiliated, coordinated, rationally connected, and hierarchically ordered.

An individual can be directly related to another as a being capable of affiliation with it, at the same time that it repels, is rationally connected, and so forth. Its being will not be divided; it merely assumes the different roles at the same time with respect to the same individuals. Consequently, it must be allowed that a man, at one and the same time, may have all twenty-five relations to the same individuals, and with these be variously subject to all the encompassing conditions. Their direct relationship will presuppose encompassing conditions which they may not attend to, but those conditions will nevertheless make a difference to their functioning. The conversion of conditions into projects, and eventually into neutral controls and governances, has evident repercussions on individuals, enabling them to become self-aware, but this is not a prerequisite to the functioning of the conditions, particularly as grounded in nature or as part of an established traditional setting.

The fact that individuals directly act on one another, without attending at all to the condition that is presupposed, or to their role in a self-awareness, is apparently what has loomed overwhelmingly conspicuous in the minds of those who attempt to understand we and societies and states solely in terms of the interactions of individuals. They overlook the full number of ways in which individuals interact, choosing one or two out of the twenty-five (which are equally fundamental, and apparently always present) and entirely ignoring the presupposed common conditions and the ways in which those common conditions are made into projects, neutrally applied rules, and socially effective forces operating on the source of the social effectiveness. Even individuals who are repelling one another are not only under common conditions, but constitute a social group which is able to provide power to the condition, at the same time that it and the individuals within it are effectively governed by the condition.

It now seems that we is a limited condition, initially projected, and then perhaps neutralized and empowered; I is a vitalizing individual; I and you are individuals falling under the condition; I (or we) and the others are individuals directly related to one another. We reflects the dominant influence of Substance; I, of Unity; I and you, of Being; and I or we and the others, of Existence. This leaves Possibility unaccounted for. For the moment, I am not now sure whether or not it would be an evasion to say that Possibility is reflected in an account which considers all of these in their intelligible interrelationship. Possibility would then seem to allow one to start with any one of these as primary and to derive the others by making explicit what they presuppose, or how they are to be obtained.

If one started with the we, the common condition, before it had been vitalized by a projecting individual, it would have to be recognized to function in advance of an acceptance of it. This would involve an even sharper break with an atomistic, nominalistic approach to society and politics than a mere acknowledgment, that there are common operative confining conditions, does, since it involves the use of a personal pronoun. It gives reality to what would normally be thought to be a derivative indexical term, and seems, therefore, to be at once willful and unnecessary. Still, men are parts of a family, a tribe, a group, a minority, and a nation before they are aware of or even have accepted these as conditions under which to operate and which they might help vitalize.

To begin with a we in which no I is a clear component is to begin sometime after one has actually begun with it, for it is a we which occurs before one has been able to know, and thus to begin an account. It is a we that has already included oneself within it, which one finds already in operation. It is a we, then, in which one is a component, but a component which has not yet come to know itself as I. It is a we in which one has been pulled in as a you, perhaps a you acknowledged to be backed by an I, but still a you in which one does not enter on the strength of his own I, but because others enable him to do so. Of course, they who constitute this we can have and usually do have some sense of themselves as so many I's. But what is true of me with respect to the we, into which I eventually find myself to have been a part for quite a while, was also true of them, not with respect to just that we with its particular components, but with respect to a we which is continuous with it.

There are, then, two possible beginnings. In one, there is an acknowledgment of something which preceded oneself and one's knowledge of oneself, but which is nevertheless not known until much after that self is known. In the other beginning, there is an acknowledgement of the I and a consequent production of a we, which may function as the first of these beginnings for other individuals in the future. For the first beginning, we move into the future to find out what had been operative in the past; for the second, we move toward ourselves as at a moment in the past to base a discovery of what is now the case. But, of course, other beginnings are also possible. A beginning could have been made with a direct confrontation of oneself and a you, or of oneself with a you in an oppositional relation to some other you, without recognition of what is then being presupposed. Such beginnings could be known at the same time that they occur; they would be present and known in the present, even though they might be preceded by an unknown we, and perhaps even the discovery of oneself as a component or factor in the projective use of that we. A similar beginning could be made with oneself as together with others.

A choice must be made between beginning with what preceded anything I might know now and beginning with what is in fact now (or which at some other now had been within my purview). The first is alert to the fact that I am already molded, no matter when I start to investigate, and molded by that which I am here trying to investigate; the second is alert to the fact that what I now know I really know, and do not have to infer, even to what I depend on. The one allows for the world out of which I issue; the other allows for a genuine irreducibility of the present. Ontologically, the one is first, epistemically the other is. The ontological first is a first *for* knowledge, while the epistemic first is a first *for* what is to be known as real, objective, apart from the knower. In each case the 'for' follows on material to be used on what is presupposed, a beginning discovered after one has in fact begun.

May 24

Yesterday, after writing, I thought of death. It is not a topic that comes to mind often. I suppose the fact that Mr. Duckett, the archivist, was here and took most of my things, dating way back to 1928, my photographs, copies of manuscripts, indeed everything but what could be thought current, the fact that this is the age when it seems so many intellectuals die, and that I was feeling tired, may have something to do with my thoughts turning in that direction.

What did I think? Not much, hardly more than the hope that when it came it would happen quickly, without pain, in the middle of the night; that I, though still struggling, still thinking, still wanting to know, still looking forward to the next day and the solutions to what I am now bothered by, have nothing to regret and in truth am grateful (to whom?) for having had the opportunity to think and write, year in and year out, what I thought I should. I am satisfied that I had sufficient opportunity to revise and revise. The archivist was surprised to find a manuscript entitled "fourth draft" heavily overwritten; it is not unusual. I think, though, were I not geared to a poor man's economy, I would have ordered sets of galleys after sets of galleys, changing and changing until the result was exactly right.

In the evening, I read some more in Slavitt; he is a very likeable poet, with considerable grace and deftness, neat turns, much humor, and a surprising melancholy and recurrence to disillusionment and pain. They are poems I would like to read many times.

And then I read some more in Nozick. I doubt whether I will be able to finish the book, it seems so willful, arbitrary, and careless. At times, I think it might well be called, "Why in the world should there be unions?" or "The outrage of the checkoff system." He does not, so far, mention the labor unions, nor show any sign that they were ever needed, or why it is they demand that even those who do not belong to them must contribute to their support. He does not seem to see that men may need to come together to constitute a force and a world from which all benefit, because they then together are able to work under conditions and at a pitch they could not individually or even as a collection demand, maintain, and improve. He seems to think that rights are wholly civil in nature; he takes them to be 'permissions', but gives no indication as to who gave the permissions, just what those permissions are, how absolute they are, or what their import might be when men exercise their permissions together. He speaks of men being guilty of crimes, as though this were an absolute, and already settled before the men were tried, and thus as if these were determinate features of individuals apart from any legal system.

Men might be guilty in terms of some transcendent absolute, but the problem of the state requires not the acceptance of that fact but its translation into politically viable forms. The adversary system of the law is a method for making determinate what is politically or legally indeterminate.

Nozick is evidently bright, clever, trying, but he seems also to be singularly ignorant of various lines of thought, and singularly unaware of significant alternatives to what he is saying. Crucial issues are settled by fiat. Rights, guilt, responsibility, the nature of collectives, the difference between society and state, constitutional and subordinate laws are hardly noticed. He expresses his views somewhat in the spirit of the present work; his book is more a series of asides than a sifted product of long reflection and rewriting. I will continue to read in it for a while, in the hope of catching something of the spirit of its thought and something of its method.

I see in Nozick overtones of Wittgenstein's conversations, positivistic analyses, some language analysis, and the discussions of his teachers and his own in the classroom. To judge from the attention it is receiving, it seems to answer to some of the current attitudes among the younger and perhaps among some of the older philosophers in the United States and England.

*   *   *

In the last few days I have been writing right after breakfast for an hour or so, and then going on my walk. I continue following this new plan.

*   *   *

It would not be correct to start with the acknowledgment of the setting into which one entered as an infant or at any earlier time than this; that one did so, and what the setting was like, should be shown. Nor would it be correct to start with the acknowledgment of oneself as involved in a projection if by that one intends to refer to something presupposed by one's experience today. But it does make sense to start with either if one can find oneself undergoing the experience of entering into an impersonal we, or producing one. It would make sense, too, to start with oneself facing a you or with others, if one can find this taking place now.

The time has come, it seems, to look at present experience and, with theoretical distinctions in mind, see what can be discovered and explicated. Without the theoretical distinctions there would be no way to know in what direction to proceed, where to look; but if the theoretical distinctions be followed slavishly, the experience will be subject to a possible regrettable distortion. Experience must be attended to, but sections should be marked out with the help of a theoretical guide, and then examined with care. This should be followed by the examination of other sections to which the theoretical discussion has made one alert. After one has explored the experience, discovering perhaps that the theoretical discussion is inadequate, it is easier to see how all the sections hang together and thereby constitute an actual experience, and could conceivably make a possibly different kind.

1] The Impersonal We: I awaken every morning to a surrounding of things, some of which belong to me and some of which do not. Without thinking, there are various things I do not do; I do not make loud noises, bang on the walls, jump from my window, expose myself to the street. Instead I fit myself into an ongoing scheme of things in which there are rules, ways of functioning, eddies and crosscurrents to which I give heed, and adjust my acts to accord. When I go for a walk, I keep my distance from others, I wait at a red light, I make myself conform to the speeds of cars. Occasionally, I may see a policeman or someone else who will limit what I and others might say or do. Again and again, I yield to the governance of what functions indifferently or neutrally with respect to me and a few others. The governance is not entirely alien; as I submit, I accept it as something I then help constitute. What governs is not a set of entities but a way in which they are together, and as such dictate to others severally, and to me as well. I adjust myself, and in that adjusting help constitute, and perhaps even alter a little, an impersonal we whose presence I help perpetuate and make applicable to others.

The impersonal we, because impersonal, is alien to me; because it is a we to which I, too, can contribute, and do so just by my acting in accord with its established demands, it is a genuine we. As alien, it demands and functions without regard to my rhythms and in apparent indifference to my existence. It may be found to have been long established, but there are times—on a line waiting to buy a ticket, in a famous restaurant, in a strange neighborhood—when I may find the impersonal we suddenly solidified, almost foreign. Only with some difficulty do I manage to become part of it. It is strange, but not really antagonistic, rejective. Sometimes, because of the way it changes and sometimes because of the way I do, and usually because both occur at the same time though in some independence of one another, I find that I not only become a part of the we, though perhaps in a minor way, but that I always had been. There was only a difficulty in meshing with the stabilized patterns and ways, both on my part, and on the part of those who were constituting and being subjected to the we.

The language I use, no less than the streets, the public vehicles, the bridges, and media, help make up a large, somewhat amorphous, impersonal we. I contribute to them, I help make it a we to which others will conform, at the same time that I, by and large, keep in accord with them. Some referents of the we, particularly as reaching to a few men, and then as casually together, come and go quickly, and change from moment to moment. This readily leads to the belief that that delimited we, and perhaps a larger which embraces more individuals in more stable and important ways, is nothing more than the summation of men's habits and dispositions. But some habits and dispositions are geared, not to actions directed at other individuals but to an adjustment of rhythms and directions in accord with the structure of the we.

2] *The Biased We:* It seemed to me that, when I entered a strange setting, the people there constituted a we from which I was excluded, and to which I could enter only by yielding to the pattern they had instituted. But I also find that I sometimes just do not know how to become a full constitutive part of a we to which I had already conformed, and to which I had in fact already contributed indirectly by helping constitute an even larger we of which the particular impersonal one is a part. There are times when I see that I do not in fact belong to some we, and that I can not belong until I alter my ways to make them conform to its demands. Other individuals may project themselves toward me, and encompass me when I make myself available or alter myself in minor ways. But they also may not even take account of me; I, in order to be part of their we, not only try to conform to its demands but try to accept those demands as not alien.

The bias of a we may be exhibited in the way it applies to me, favoring others rather than myself. (Sometimes, though, the reverse occurs for children, the sick, the dying, and it may at times be biased in my favor.) Or the bias may be the result of the fact that it was constituted by others without regard for me and my needs, reflecting what they desire, need, and insist upon. In either case, it is extended toward me, and I may in fact be made not merely to conform to it, but to be a contributor to it, who at the same time makes himself be under it.

Children rebel against the yoke of the family; they do not recognize that they belong to it, help constitute it; they note only the bias of the we, and not the we which is biased, and which they, too, help constitute. It is the kind of we from which the most radical anarchist can not escape since his actions also involve a constituting and yielding to the demands of a common language, habits, customs, truce, decency, and a tissue of interlinked rights and duties.

The impersonal we, though it does not expressly concern itself with the interests of anyone, may itself be biased toward some men more than others. The point at which absolute neutrality is attained is not sharply set off from all other points; an emphasis, at best, hovers near a center, and seems more or less to govern me and others in the same way. Our peculiarities and idiosyncracies are then ignored; we are dealt with neutrally only as abstractions, not in our full concreteness. In our full concreteness, the same conditions may operate to the advantage of one and to the disadvantage of others. If there is favoritism shown to me, even to the disadvantage of those who had constituted the we, it still is a favoritism which they exercise on my behalf, and not the result of an indifferent working out of an impersonal we. If there is no favoritism exhibited toward any of us, it still will be a biased we if I do not help constitute it as others do, either by occupying a somewhat neutral position or by matching their bias with my own individual stresses.

3] *The Personalized We:* I start a conversation, I smile, I watch the path of the fire engines, I kick aside the broken glass, I pick up the fallen tricycle. In these different ways I not only act, but act as part of a larger whole which embraces others. I start a conversation with someone present, but I kick aside the broken glass though no one is about, and thus reveal myself to be one of the constituents of a responsible we, made up of adults, thoughtful men, or even busybodies. I may bias the we toward myself in the sense of having it reflect my dominant interests, or by having it apply to me in a distinctively advantageous way. I turn it into a kingly, an authoritative, an editorial we, not by such a bias—for these we's may favor others more than they do me—but by becoming the exclusive source of its application. There may be no others who are in fact constitutive of it, or who also fall under it, but it still is a we and not an I. It expresses not myself but something of which I am only a constituent, and to which I am perhaps also subject. It is not an impersonal we, precisely because I am then and there constituting it.

A biased we could well be a personalized we, constituted by others. But this need not be the case; a biased we may come about by implacable forces which somehow catch up a number of men and have them constitute a single demand. Nor is it necessary that a personalized we apply to me; it may, in an authoritative manner, be constituted by me alone, but applied impersonally, and then only to others. It is personalized, despite its apparent objectivity, for it exists only because an individual has projected himself in the form of an encompassing condition which others might sustain as well, whether or not it also applies to them.

In the constituting of the personalized we one has the most direct and clearest awareness of oneself as at once distinct from but engaged in vitalizing a condition which others might also help constitute. It is a we in which there can be a stress on the constituting individual or a stress on the possible other constituents, or a stress somewhere between. The different stresses are due to the individual who is constituting that we; wherever the stress is put, that we is still personalized, a we which is to be acknowledged only together with the acknowledgment of a contrasting individual I.

I lend myself to the constituting of the personalized we, but never entirely. I leave myself still distinct from it, and as distinct, aware of myself as making some available condition into a more limited, humanly oriented demand. It makes no difference how objectively and majesterially that we is expressed; the fact that I project it and stand away from it at the same time keeps it personalized. It is never reduced to an impersonal we—except, of course, for those who are subject to it and were already to some degree constituents of it.

A personalized we does not lose its character because others share and personalize it; it can be multiply personalized, personalized by many individual I's. An effective leader may start with a personalized we extended toward others, and end with that we sustained by those others, each personalizing it from his side. The result is a complex, multifaceted, personalized we, expressing the temper, spirit, consensus, or common outlook of a people.

4] *The Structured We:* A number of men may constitute a we not merely by bringing in their personal notes, but by accepting certain rules, requirements, conditions as pertinent to them all. They may view those rules as having different kinds of application to different individuals or at different times. They may never in fact conform to those conditions; they may leave them stated as noble ideals which everyone ignores. Any we may be feeble, but it is more likely that the structured we, rather than any of the others, will be without efficacy, since, unlike even the impersonal we, it may not have the backing of habit and tradition.

Men live by rules before they attend to them as rules. The rules are implicit in, buried within the we's to which the men might be subject. But the rules also stand out at times. Men learn to belong to special groups by grasping the principles which guide them; procedures are slowly learned, step by step, until they, too, are sunk within the anonymous impersonal we that the men help constitute and to which others may later conform.

Does every people formalize some rules, make a formalized we, at least with respect to some enterprises? Is this one of the ways in which men differ from animals? Or do some people learn the steps of some difficult enterprise, in which all share and which expresses what they are together, by imitation or by rote? I do not know. If I attend to my own experience, I find that I can not get back in time to any period when I did not know some rules, some principles, some explicitly formulated set of prescriptions, which lacked the human dimension which is present even in the impersonal we, and stood before me as an express demand.

A mere demand, of course, is not a we at all, but a statement, a claim, even an insistence in a formal guise. There is a structured we for me only if I accept it as my own, prepared to be and act in consonance with it. The grammar of a language is hard to isolate; few of us know it; most of us conform to it by training and habit. But because I use it, that grammar, with its own rationale, becomes mine without ceasing to be not mine. It is the we of all the speakers formalized, that which enables them to be together in a language whose words they connect in acceptable ways. The fact that I take myself to belong to a state with expressly formulated laws points up my being one with common formal conditions to which I am submitting.

5] *The Diversified We:* I share a common territory with others; I live through a common extent of time; I share in the same causal patterns with them. There is a common, limited portion of Existence to which I not only submit, but which I help constitute by the way in which I stand in it, apart from, in opposition to all the others. I am an occupant of limited extended regions, which are extensionally related to other regions where there are other occupants.

A common existence does not have the guise of a we until it is held away from nature, even while continuing to be rooted there. It is a we only so far as it is also ours—the we referring to it as primarily relating the occupied regions, and the ours to it as governing the occupied regions. The we, here, is double-faced; it is sustained and has a career which is dependent on the functioning of nature, and it is taken to be our own by right, by claim, and by possession.

In all the previous cases the we was a unifying reality; here it is essentially diversifying, existing only as that which is in fact being diversely occupied and divided. Its diversification, however, does not destroy its unity; if it did, there would not be a we at all, but only a plurality of individuals or locations. It is the we as a single extended domain which is diversified in the very act of existing and thereby becoming the common extension for a plurality of occupants. It is to this kind of we to which I refer when I recognize myself to be a member of a nation, or even of an ethnic group, and surely of a people living at a particular time in a particular part of the globe. I and others are neighbors, part of one society or tribe, belonging together under the governance of a we which is dynamic, historic, and geographic in nature, and which each of us, in sharing in it, diversely exhibits it while being still connected to one another by means of it.

In this case and all the others—not only in the case of the personal we, as the isolation of the discussion there would seem to imply—I can become directly aware of myself. The impersonal we challenges, and I become aware of my lack of it; the biased we comes to me from the outside and thereby makes evident that I am singular; the formalized we in its very anonymity makes evident to me how I, with my feelings and emotions, differ from it; my occupation of this position in space, time, and causality enables me to stand in contrast with the common we of inclusive extensions.

Each one of these we's, too, the theoretical reflections suggest, should allow for the distinction of the I and the you, of others, and finally of these together with the I and the we. These, as together, deserve to be looked at in detail and in the heart of experience. But for the moment, it should be observed that each we has a fivefold form, since each functions to affiliate, coordinate, make intelligible, extensionally connect, and assess what comes within its provenance. And all of them will have application to individuals who interplay with one another while maintaining themselves in opposition in multiple ways.

* * *

Last words:
"Damn it, just when I was getting the hang of living."
"There's something wrong; finitude is not the same as brevity."
"All my life has been a rehearsal for this last scene."

"From the light into the dark is a step everyone learns to make, and that without any learning."

"Everyone is cheated of death; when it comes he is no longer."

"How remarkable to be able to move an infinite distance, from something to nothing, in a finite time. I wish I could understand it without having to go through it."

"Since I really do not know just where I have been, will I be able to know where I am going?"

"To say that death stings is to make a typographical error."

"If I am going, what are you doing? Standing still?"

May 25

I have not finished W. Kaufmann's translation of Buber's *I and Thou*. I had found the book almost unpenetrable when I read it some years ago; I find it so now as well, with the exception of a passage here and there which seems to me to be both perceptive and sound. But almost every one of these passages which I now understand says roughly what I had also already come to hold. It may be that I will not understand Buber until I have myself come to understand on my own what it is he is saying; but it could also be that there is nothing more there for me, and that I might even be reading into the text what is not intended. I pause in this evaluation because of the number of people who take Buber seriously and find him to be a source of insight and inspiration. He does write somewhat as the wisdom writers of the East do, but I find that I get much more understanding, at least of what they intend, from them, than I get from him. Neither explicates; neither makes all the distinctions one would like to have drawn; but the Eastern thinkers, whom I have read with profit, point me in a direction and point up reasons for going in that direction, which Buber does not. It is not that Buber is a Westerner trying to convey essentially Eastern ideas, for he is much concerned with preserving the status and identity of man, whereas this is minimized by the others. In fact where there is an attempt on his part to convey the import of Eastern thought, it is less successful than Schopenhauer's was.

There is one idea of Buber's that seems to me to be important and which I, for one, have not attended to sufficiently: individuals are not merely present but present themselves, make themselves stand out away from the nature in which they are immersed. The other comes to us, he makes himself distinctive, not merely as that which is available for us to attend to or focus on, but as a man. As I read Buber, he puts a greater emphasis on self-presentation, on a thrust away from nature, than I had ever envisaged. In any case, whether it be his idea or not, I think it sound and illuminating.

Every occupant of the extensional world not only fills out the extension it occupies, intensifies it, masters it, makes it its own, but, with this, sets itself away from all others. The self-enclosure of a man is more extreme and involves a greater internalization; his, and the self-enclosure of others, concerns not merely what they are in their privacies but what they are as concrete, full-bodied, extended realities. That is why men are able to face one another in a society across the indifferent space of nature, ignoring distance, territoriality, their accompanying maintenance of their privacies, and the constitution of an encompassing we.

The idea is close to Schopenhauer's in his ethics, which lies behind the so-called mysticism of Wittgenstein. The sympathetic bond between men and also, in a different degree and manner and with different values, between certain types of subhuman beings, does not depend on their reaching into one another as though they were initially confronted as bodies or as purely external, but involves an acceptance of them as distinctive units. They are with one another immediately, and their antagonisms, hatreds, loves, fears, cooperations, indifference, and the like are to be understood as somehow falling under this acceptance, or as involving a reassessment of the men as somehow immersed in nature.

That men are immersed in nature is, of course, true, since they do act and live subject to its laws and influences. But from the position now being adumbrated, this is self-abstracted from, or is maintained despite the other, sometimes as subordinate, sometimes as superior, sometimes in consonance, and sometimes in opposition to it. Such an account comes close to making man primarily spiritual or at least on a par with the body as an item in nature; this will lead to the usual difficulties associated with mind-body, inner-outer problems. The difficulties can be at least minimized if one takes the individual to provide a juncture point between two sides, in one of which he stands out from all others, and in the other of which he is together with all others within the scheme of nature. Other ways of being together might overlay either one of these sides; and so may various ways of being opposed to one another.

To the fact that men are insistent in opposition to the expressions of finalities, that they internalize qualifications, and that they thrust outward with projects, it is therefore necessary to add that they also assert themselves, make themselves stand out from nature. It is also true that they absent themselves from the appearances which are bounded by knowers. In their full concreteness they are part of nature and assert themselves apart from it, at the same time that they distinguish themselves from any appearances that might be externally bounded by knowers.

Other actualities also assert themselves; the tree so evidently says "I, I"; even a sheep, so subject to a we, stands out against all the others. But if this is so, what is left of nature? Everything seems to stand away from it. The ways and the degrees in which they stand away, though, differ for different kinds of actualities. Men stand away with a fullness not possible to any other actualities, because of the richness of their internalities due to their ability to take account of qualifications originating with all the finalities. And, on the other hand, even though all actualities stand out as distinct assertive entities, there are pervasive features and conditions to which they are subject. All remain within the same space, time, causal extensions, and are subject to cosmic laws at the same time that they present themselves to one another directly as units. But it is only in their direct presentations of themselves that they show what they individually are, after the common cosmic conditions act on them all as together and on each one as an extended region within which there are smaller actualities.

The assertive presence of individuals, each by itself and yet available for one another, takes place within the frame of nature; it also takes place within other frames expressive of finalities other than Existence. The fact provides another set of considerations to be set alongside what is acknowledged as a we. But before going into a discussion of those individuals, the distinctions made yesterday, among the various types of we, require further refinement, qualification, and supplementation.

The impersonal, biased, personalized, structured, and diversified we's may overlap in range. They may encompass only some men or they may range over all. And though we can find rather clear cases where there seems to be one of them without the others—an impersonal without a personalized, for example—they seem not to be altogether separable, and in some cases—the structured with the others—seem to merge. It is plausible to suppose that there is a single we which has a plurality of statuses and constricted uses, and which at times can be subdivided into subordinate we's, emphasizing one or more statuses to the comparative neglect of the others.

The status of a we is independent of its tonality, that is, of the type of unification it exhibits—affiliation, coordination, rationality, interaction, or evaluation. These types are independent of one another, but compatible. A we may require that individuals be at once coordinated and affiliated, that is, affiliated as so many independent entities, and even to be rationally related, dynamically connected, and at the same time occupy positions in an evaluative hierarchy. If this complex of all the tonalities be taken to be the norm, or source, or primary form of the we, different, distinct tonalities can be viewed as special cases. The single we within which the various tonalities are to be found, varying perhaps in dominance over the course of time, may fluctuate in range. One of the tonalities in it, too, may be more pertinent to some subdivision of the range than to some other.

The structure of the we, also, may have a number of ways of being exhibited. It could be in the form of a traditionalized tendency, express the equality of a multiplicity of independent entities, be merely formal, be sustained in habitual practices, or reorganize that over which it ranges. Once again, these may be prominent with respect to different individuals and may overlap in range. Since they seem to be compatible with one another, they allow one to view the structure of the we as a complex of a number of subordinated structures, which may or may not have the same range of application. Which of these substructures will dominate over the others is a matter determined independently of the determination of the status or the tonality of the we.

A we, too, may have any one of a number of natures. It may be intensive, fragmented, rational, extended, or ordered. Each of these is independent of but compatible with the others and may operate over different ranges. An intensive we has a singularity to it; a fragmented we is hardly more than an area occupied by distinct entities; a rational we is dominated by an intelligible structure; an extended we occupies a region of extension; an ordered we is hierarchical.

Finally, a we may introduce a distinct kind of value. It may emphasize clustering, independence, rationality, cooperation, or harmony. Once again, these may be restricted to limited groups;

they may be exhibited together; their ranges may overlap. This type of we is independent of, but compatible with the others, and may itself overlap their ranges, or achieve prominence with respect to them at different times.

If one were to follow this lead, the distinctions in types of encompassment (the 'tonality' indicated above) would be a derivative secondary matter; so would distinctions in power, and the rest. But there would still be five basic we's that were being distinguished. Are these specializations, derivatives, subdivisions of a more fundamental we? Such a we, though never possible without the existence of individuals who provide it with a pertinence to men, and thereby differentiate it from a complex cosmic condition which operates indifferently on all actualities, has a reality of its own. That we is a specialization of the common, complex, cosmic condition which governs all actualities.

Men, it might be said, when they individually thrust themselves outward away from nature, inevitably thrust still further in the form of mutually supportive expressions which together constitute a single, multifaceted we. This is intensified and specialized by the men as they in fact interplay with one another, thereby providing a we to which others, or they themselves, or some combination of these may be subject. It is a nuclear, root we, the surface of which is being dealt with when one faces a biased, affiliative, reconstructive, and so forth, we.

Were this suggestion followed, distinctions among the various we's would all presuppose a primal we. That primal we would, of course, not be grasped in experience, except so far as an occupation with any one of the specialized cases was inseparable from that which it specialized. But even then we could not immediately consider it, but would have to move to it from the position of at least one of those specialized forms. Beginning, for example, with an impersonal we, one might attend to it in depth and there note that it is inseparable from a constant we which was expressing itself collaterally in the form of a personal we, and so forth, as well, and was supplementing these with various tonalities.

The very fact that one inevitably contributes to the constitution of a primal we requires him to stand away from it as well, and thereby become aware of himself as standing away from the we of which he was a part. The awareness becomes more acute, has sharper and sharper focus and a noticeable quality, the more attention is directed to one of the specialized forms of the we. The specialized forms provide occasions for an individual to become aware of himself as one who is intensifying a more basic, primitive self-awareness of himself as distinct from a primal we, to which he had, by the very fact of his existence, contributed.

What is true of the I, is also true of an I and a you, and of the I (or any particular we) and the others. There is then a complex array in which there is a primitive we, I, I and you, the others, each specialized and intensified in multiple ways. All of these dimensions are present in a primal complex situation, out of which, by delimitation and intensification, one can derive specialized forms. The discovery of that primal complex can take place in either of two ways: it is discerned behind any one of the specialized uses, mediated by a primal form of that special case; and it is discovered (as it is here) by reflection on a plurality of cases and the way they can be considered together. The first of these is experiential; the second speculative.

A speculative method, no less than an experiential, has to start with the limited, intensive, specialized experiences of every day; it also takes account of a more persistent, underlying primal situation. But instead of trying to penetrate into that situation, it takes the special cases to be in such a common primal situation. In the light of this it attempts to provide an intelligible explanatory account. The methods should support one another.

What is the most obvious or common type of experience involving the we, I, I and you, and the others? Is it not one where we have A] an impersonal we, B] dependent on interaction, C] sustained by habitual practices, D] extended, and E] harmonizing; where the I becomes conspicuous by its self-enclosure; where the I and you are conspicuous by their assertiveness; and where the others are conspicuous by their independence of the we or the I?

Is it correct, though, to distinguish five different dimensions of the we, each of which has five variants, and only five dimensions of the I, you and I, and others, without any variants? Is not the I known as individual, irreducible, rational, insistent, and evaluative, with one of these prominent at some moment, supplemented by the others, and all of them rooted in a more primal I? And is not something similar to be said about the I and the you, and the others? If so, the I will have to be characterized, not only as standing away from the we, but as withdrawn, spontaneous, localized, and a measure of the values of others. The I and the you will also have a plurality of ways in which they assert themselves in relation to one another, and the ways they severally or together face the others. Is it worth outlining these various cases now? Or would it be better to grapple with the complexity of the we, and only then face up to the nature of the others as they are to be understood in the light of what that we is normatively in experience, and in its primal form? For the moment, the latter seems better, since it provides a setting in terms of which an approach to the others can be made, with details and consequences that could not be known until one had seen exactly what the we is like. There is no question but that the I, the I and the you, and the others are known as early as any we. But is it possible to say which of the many possible emphases they can sustain is normative, or even conspicuous, until we have fixated the nature of the we?

It seems just as true, though, to say that I know myself, or that there is an I and you, or that I (or we) face others, well before we have fixated the we, and surely well before we have made sure just what variant is present, and what the primal form is. But is this more than to remark that we start with an impersonal we, and therefore with a contrasting sense of ourselves, as selves by themselves, related to other selves and to contrasting others?

May 26

L. F. Johnson's *Film* is a book which would have helped me had I read it before writing *Cinematics*. It contains many of the distinctions and divisions that I found essential to make, supplementing these with accounts of films, adding photographs, and going on to make subdivisions and sometimes distinctions of which I had no inkling. He has no theoretical base, and some of his distinctions could be ignored without injury. But he is at home in the field, with its vocabulary, technical methods, experiments, and achievements. His is a solid, factual book. There are too few of these in this field. There are, though, many technical treatises, many more recountings of the plots of films, and quite a number of journeys through the process of film making. In his, almost all the dimensions of film are set down in a straightforward, sensitive, and sensible account.

It is not satisfactory to do what I did yesterday, and slip in the comments about I, you and I, and the others, at the end of a detailed discussion of we, and be content with remarking on the fact that there will be a similar multiplicity of cases to consider. Each of these should be examined carefully as it makes itself manifest in experience. The various types of we could provide a guide, however, to the examination, for even a direct confrontation of an I and a you is carried on against a background where they are both together.

A we is a unity in which the contributions of its constituents are merged together, are kept on a footing, are rationally related, fragment it, or are effective in different degrees. (This way of referring to the tonality of the we attends to it without regard for anything else but its constitution.) In any one of these forms, it may function impersonally, personally, in a biased way, as formal, or as diversified—what I had called its 'status'. It will be effective as a governance—what I have taken to be its ways of being exhibited; it will have one of five different guises—a 'nature' I called it; and it will be a ground for values. Does the I come into prominence in all of these different cases? And when there is a direct relation to a you and to others, might this not fall under a we for which that relation is not pertinent, thereby making them face it as impersonal or biased, even though the relation is formal or even legalistic? These questions arise because I do not yet have the entire situation in clear focus. A direct consideration of the I may help also in making more evident just what exactly should be said about the we.

1] I always remain outside a we, even one which I myself vitalize and impose on others in an authoritative fashion. Every we remains to some degree impersonal for me, with a structure and career that I do not control and which contrasts with me even when I most conform to it, allowing myself to be and to function in accord with what it requires. Because there is always a difference between the I and a we, every we as in some degree an impersonal we. For an individual to take upon himself the task of projecting a condition so that it applies to others, and thus to put the entire force of himself behind it, is still to leave the individual over as a substantial reality, able to repeat the act again, to deny it, to withdraw from it, and to engage in other tasks as a limited particular actuality.

The most personalized we leaves over an I with which it contrasts. That I, because it contrasts with a part of itself, serving to vitalize and project a condition, is different from the I which is being reached toward by a biased we, which falls under a common structured we, and which requires that I to stand at a distance from other I's. The difference amongst these is in the content which is alien to the we. Since the we may be in more or less marked contrast with the I that remains outside it, a particular content characteristic of the I may still vary from moment to moment, depending on the sharpness of the discrepancy between them. A personalized we, for example, though constituted mainly by an I, may be turned away from that I completely—as it does when it is functioning authoritatively in relation to other we's. Or it may function as a continuant of the I that is outside it, with the individual not altogether sure just where he or the we begins.

Evidently, there is a singularity to the I which contrasts with a we. The greater the contrast the more acutely is one aware of oneself as a singular. As a consequence, one is led to suppose that the less the contrast the less aware one is of one's singular self. Is this true? A king may lose himself in his roles, in his authority and decrees; so far, he will leave over only a minimal content. He may see himself, nevertheless, as one who is most subject to the decrees, at least in the sense that he holds himself responsible to carry out all that they require of him. He will always have some independence of the we he makes possible, and will always have to make himself conform to its demands; but his task will be of minimal difficulty so far as he, in constituting that we, has the self, which remains outside it, be continuous with that we. This is done by approximating the state of being just an instance for that we.

2] The we is always *my* we, even when it is one with which I had not been familiar, had not known I was a part, did not know exactly how to conform to, or found to have been operative in my absence and even before I was born. The 'my' here is ambiguous. It is the my of right and not necessarily of possession. The family into which I am born is my family; I am part of the single we characterizing that family; I helped constitute it when I was an infant, and even when I was a fetus. The others may have granted me the status of being a part of the family, but even apart from that granting I was already a constituent of it. Even a biased we, which reaches to me from the position of someone else who is projecting some condition in his own independent way, already has me as part of it, not to be sure as I exist as an actual man, but as that which is within its range, as that for which there is already a place to which I can contribute, perhaps as

much as the others do. I know that I, as standing away from a we, am continuous with a constituent of the we. I belong to it and it belongs to me.

There is a tension between myself as standing apart from a we and myself as a constituent of that we. My acceptance of the constituent as myself in a special role is one with the awareness of myself as a substantial, possessive unit. I find it more or less difficult to overcome that tension by making that we fully my possession. Sometimes it is not hard for me to fit in with an impersonal we; the tension is minimal or I quickly reduce it by changing my attitudes and actions. Sometimes it is hard for me to fit in with the personalized we; the tension between myself as a singular, standing apart from the we, and myself, as the main constituent of that we, sometimes is very great, or, though slight, is beyond my power to reduce further. I speak with the voice of authority, but I am myself meek perhaps or fearful, or I find that there is a resistant streak in me which leads or tempts me to defy even what I myself prescribe, not only for others but for myself as well. My identification of myself as standing apart and helping constitute the we evidently varies in tension and reducibility, and this whether the we be personal or impersonal, biased, and so on.

3] Even where I am most responsible for the constitution of a we, even when the tension between myself and it is minimal and easily overcome, I find that it is not entirely congenial. Anything smacking of a juncture with others, any loss of my own ego, any way of functioning together with others, necessarily conflicts with what I am. An alien, impersonal we could well be more congenial than one which I myself am most responsible for. I fit into it, or I want to fit into it, perhaps because it is of long standing, or more inclusive, or more powerful than the one I am most responsible for. The congeniality of the very same we over time may vary considerably. My interests, my purposes change; I become more or less involved with myself than I had been.

There is a pull to a we even when it is I who am vitalizing it. It may not function neutrally with respect to me and others; but, whether it does so or not, it congeals away from me, to be just a we, and it is this which I find more or less congenial. I sometimes like the fact that, together with others, I constitute something which is different from any one of us. But sometimes I dislike it precisely for that reason. A radical individualist claims to be in the latter position constantly; a radical collectivist goes to the opposite extreme. But they, too, with the rest of us, find that they vary in their likes and dislikes, and then with respect to we's which are personal, impersonal, biased, formal, or evaluational.

I become aware of myself not merely as identifiable, not merely as distinguishing myself as apart from what I am as a constituent, but also as an I which is other than the we. The contrast is not between myself in my privacy and myself as a public being. The I that I am insisting on may well be myself in my full concreteness, standing away from all else, and the we may well be a kind of spiritual bond which operates primarily on and is constituted by individuals engaged in some intellectual pursuit or who are inspired by a religious insight.

At different times and under different circumstances I may find the same we congenial in different degrees. I doubt that it is ever absolutely uncongenial, that I ever want to have nothing whatsoever to do with the constituting of a we; even the individualist would like others to be individualists with him. I doubt that it is ever absolutely congenial, that I ever want to give myself to the collective spirit, without residue; the collectivist is clear that the outcome of an immersion in the we brings happiness to each.

4] A we extends over a region but without losing its integrity. It may encourage its own fragmentation into distinct areas each of which is allowed to function apart from, independent of, and perhaps even in conflict with the others. But it is a we only so far as it remains single and extended, bridging a distance, a way of relating what is distant and independent. The individuals to whom the we applies stand away from one another, and they do this no matter how intimate they become, or how much they want to merge, sympathize, or be in harmony. Each occupies a position within the orbit of the we that it maintains against the we, even while it is being related to the others by means of that we. It is in fact related to the other by a more cosmic condition, by the very extensions of nature, in ways which lack the unifying power and specialized intensive form of the we. Each can also directly affiliate, be coordinate, have rational connections, or be in a hierarchy all the while that it is being faced with a we which extends over them all, but without regard for the ways in which they are directly related. Conversely, individuals are related in space, time, and causal processes, at the same time that they were faced with an affiliative, a coordinating, a structuring, an extensive, or an evaluative we. In either way, individuals help constitute a we in which the different constituents are bound together, while they are themselves directly related to one another.

Whether the we itself has its constituents bound together affiliatively or in the other ways, while individuals directly affect one another, in matching or in other ways, the two have more or less independent careers. A we which stresses the equality of men, affirming the rights that each will have, may be set over against men who are actually in possession of such equal rights; or it might be set over against men who are just allied with one another in various degrees and kinds of affiliation, and so on. In either case, the individual will know himself as a unit in a direct relation to others in contrast with a demand that such a relation prevail. He will or will not fulfill the demand, and will do so with more or less adequacy.

5] Men make different contributions to the constitution of a we, even one which demands that they be coordinate. And no matter what the we demands, the men themselves assess themselves and others by what they desire, what satisfies them, or what they take to be the good, or what ought to be. They may maintain that assessment as more basic and right, no matter what the others may demand; or the men may yield their assessments for reevaluation by the we. In either case, the demands of the we, and their own assessments of what they are and ought to be in relation to one another, will be more or less compatible. The incompatibility, in the end, comes down to the ways in which the standards for individual assessments mesh with the standards set by the we, even though the former are often tacit and the latter expressly stated or habitually manifested. We have here the root of a possible conflict between the morality of the we and the ethics to which the individual in the last resort appeals, though perhaps in a misconstrued form, to justify his taking his pleasure or independence to be of primary value. Such a possible conflict may arise even when the we is mainly constituted by oneself; and it will vary with time and circumstance.

Though what has been set down in these five sections is not, I think, entirely satisfactory, it does point up the fact that the I recognizes itself in multiple ways and with multiple emphases. The I is in itself, is involved in various we's, stands away from them, and is able to take account of the difference between itself and them. As in itself it is, of course, not yet brought into relationship with any we or with anything else. Brought into relationship with a we and with others, both in that we and directly under the aegis of a common condition or a specialized form of it in the shape of some we, it will exhibit a plurality of aspects, tensions, qualities, and contents.

A we presupposes an I as one of its constituents; an I presupposes a we as that which enables it to become aware of itself. That self-awareness, in the end, rests on the fact that the I has an integrity of its own, which it is maintaining in the face of roles it might exercise and of the we which is distinct from it. Without an I there is no known we, and without a we there is no known I; but there can be a we and an I which are not known, each multiply faceted, capable of being expressed in limited situations with specialized, more or less transient features, qualities, and strengths.

The present accounts of the we and the I have not apparently been exactly parallel. The we seems to have been considered as an entity by itself and then as having various roles in relation to the I, while the I is dealt with as something known by virtue of a contrast with itself in some role, or with the we. Should the we be dealt with first so far as it is known, perhaps through a contrast? Should the I be dealt with as having various roles, such as maintaining itself, asserting itself, understanding, interacting, and constituting a we? The we, as entering into experience, and therefore in relation to an I, is parallel to the experienced, the self-known I. That we has its own nature and standing, and that I has a reality in itself. At least, with some tinge of doubt, this is how it now seems to me.

Perhaps still another venture, with an I and a you together, dealt with as far as possible as a dimension independent of a we or the self-known I, will help clarify what has already been examined, particularly since it will set up, in contradistinction to the we and to the I, another set of factors, and require these severally and perhaps together to be involved in additional relations, and possibly even to be altered in nature and role as a consequence. This will have to be followed by an account of 'others', whether these be others with respect to an I, a we, or an I and you. Then, perhaps, it will be possible to envisage a complex matrix which can serve either as the frame in terms of which a study is to be made, or as initial material which is to be dissected into various components, identical with or somewhat similar to those now being isolated and examined.

*   *   *

More last words:
"Well, here's an invitation it is never too late to accept."

"It's getting colder. There must be a door open."
"Am I being called, or am I being tempted?"
"Advance or retreat, it still ends in a defeat."
"At last, to be known as I am."
"Forever? That's a bit too long."
"Take your time about coming; I can wait."
"How quiet it is; I can hear a finger beckoning."
"Goodby body; hello . . . ?"
"I live, therefore I pay taxes. If only I could get the converse to be true."
"And now for one last step, all by myself."
"Goodbye body, I think I am losing my grip."
"My poor soul, now it must answer for what the body did."
"It did seem amusing from afar. Now it is not even interesting."
"Of course I hear you calling; I'm trying not to listen."

May 27

You and I are directly related to one another, as well as being under the governance of some common condition. Each of us, as in that relation, also grounds himself as apart from that relation.

1] In a direct relation between us, the you may be impersonal, someone out there, an indeterminate unspecified individual. Conceivably, there might be more than one. I make the reference from my position, calling on others to assume the role of a you with respect to me. The situation seems close to the one in which I project myself. The two differ in that the latter is directed at another or others as filling in, as being subject to a we which I help constitute, whereas in the present case I directly refer to someone or other, perhaps for help, to blame, or from whom I am awaiting a response. The reference is to someone who will perform some role, more or less expected, more or less consciously entertained.

When I awaken, when I am alone, I am still assertive; I stand away from the things about, and with them stand away from the course of nature, but I am rarely altogether oblivious of the possibility of others impinging on me. Well before I learned to expect the possible presence of others, I was readied for the acknowledgment of a you. In my earliest thrusting outwards I encountered others whose responses were satisfying or dismaying, wanted or disagreeable. I not only found myself coming to be accepted by what became more and more evidently a we, that of my immediate family perhaps, but also independently of some particular you, or of a kind of you. Instead of awaiting someone who might be subject to the we of which I am a constituent, I directly await someone to terminate my direct reference to a responsive being. The two may be the same, of course; I sometimes await someone who will sustain and be subject to a we which I am insisting on, at the same time that I direct myself toward him. When I do both at once I find that the two are not in consonance, and that I in fact require a constituent and a subject of a we different in nature, functioning, and relation to myself from what I directly require as a respondent.

When, under the governance of a we, someone is related to me, he is being subjected to a condition which, though he may have helped constitute it, prescribes the kind of relation which should hold between us. The relation that the two of us, under the controlling we, may have to one another, is independent of the we but oriented toward it and assessed in relation to it. It is a different relation, therefore, from the relation that the two of us directly have, apart from the we. I would like someone to see what I have painted; I await a critic or an appreciator of the painting. Another may look at it indifferently, but still as within the compass of a personalized we which I am instituting. At the same time, I may take up a direct relation to that you, first in anticipation, awaiting him as one who will give me an independent judgment perhaps, and then standing away from him, or interacting with him as he independently functions.

2] From the very beginning of my consciousness I am aware of many different you's; they come and go without my knowing how or why. They differ in their demands, their acceptances of me, the way they attend to me. I find myself oriented by them, taking up their positions, but not yet attending to myself. I am caught up in the world of others. But they are not simply with me, distinguished from myself. I am too unaware of myself for that to be the case; instead I pivot about a you.

I am not always clear as to whether a you, about which I pivot, is one or many. I find it hard to know at times whether or not that you is urging a we on me, and asking me to join with him more expressly than I have; I am not sure if I am or am not being required to attend to the you within the provenance of some we. Sometimes a particular you or a number of individuals constituting a single you stands out conspicuously, either by virtue of some activity, or as attending to me in terms I don't altogether understand. I am affected by the presence of others; they are orientation points, standpoints from which an insistent relation is being sustained in relation to me, even when no attention is apparently being paid to me. I am faced with assertive individuals, and I am aware of that fact even apart from and perhaps even before I am aware of myself as also assertive. Those individuals may be primarily assertive with respect to something which I also confront, or with respect to something which I can not discern, but I know them as you's because they provide a vector which I must reciprocally supplement in order to be in relation to them.

I am, of course, already related to others, in nature and in a we—by affiliation, structurally, and so on. I learn of this much later, sometimes long after I have accepted a you as a pivot, as the biased determinant of my status, my range, or my value. The you here is primary, dominant, orienting, but it is still a you in relation to myself. It could not be otherwise. I could face others who have nothing to do with me; but though the you which I acknowledge may in fact be occupied with something other than myself, it is a you in relation to me, inevitably inviting, luring, compelling me to be directed at it. There may be no noticing of me, but this does not affect the fact that the you is functioning in relation to me. You and I here are initially in an asymmetrical position; the initiative is all on the side of the you; the you defines what I am to be and do. This state of affairs could not have arisen had I not independently already faced that you. The you may awaken my consciousness of myself, make me self-aware; but well before and surely independently of that possibility, I face that you as primarily determining how I will face me. Or I find that I had already directed myself toward that you in a more primitive way, after I find myself being directed toward that you under conditions which that you provides. The you is initially a you for me, but I know this only after I find myself in the role of a referent for that you, and then use that you to help me refer back to myself.

3] You and I, consciously and deliberately, sooner or later, and also initially but unknowingly, stand on a footing. We are related to one another impersonally, coordinately, neither as two I's, nor as two 'you's', but just as two units, two individuals, who stand away from all else together. We make a bond, we are linked, excluding all others. We may, without losing that situation, also attend to something together, stand away from a particular object, or from others, but without forming a we. It is just ourselves as a set or aggregate, functioning independently but yet related to one another. We may both be looking at some scenery, strangers to one another perhaps, but still united and without any apparent relation to anyone else. We may also be related under some we, even an impersonal one, such as the law governing the ways in which one remains within a fence, respects property, and avoids littering. But now, as looking at the common scene, paying no attention to one another, but still being together, we are impersonally related, each of us an I for a you and aware of one another as being I's as well as you's.

The impersonal relation I directly have with another is evidently highly complex. It is a relation between two I's, standing independently of one another but directed at something common; a relation of two you's facing one another as strangers; a relation of my I to another's you, about whom I am somewhat curious; and a relation of his I to me in the guise of a you, because he is curious, and even when he is indifferent to me but somehow aware that I am there. I can not say that I know that he is an I or what his I is like; I can not even say that I am aware of myself as an I. But this lack of awareness is not absolute. We are together in the guise of I's because I am, with him, facing the same scene from within. It is not that the scene is an other for both of us; it may be something we are subjectively enjoying, with its status as other radically reduced. He and I function primarily as I's; the direct relation which we bear to one another is sustained not by us relative to one another, for we are radically independent of one another, unrelated, except as being together, and with a side connection to one another as functioning I's who are primarily directed elsewhere. Despite the fact that both of us are I's, our relation is impersonal, since it is merely sustained by those I's as they function, not with respect to one another, but with respect to something else. The relation we have to one another, despite our status as I's, is here a consequence of the fact that as I's we are not involved with one another.

I am also like him in having the status of a you. We are two you's, not knowing what we individually intend, not interested in what each is to himself or how he is enjoying what he sees. I detach myself from myself in order to stand there as a you which is primarily a you with respect to him, but which I also will continue to be with respect to any other stranger who might appear. Each of us sees the other as a you, and presents himself as a you for that other, someone of whom he is to take account from the outside, but as a person, as someone in direct relationship to him. I suppress my I, or detach it, and stand together with him, each a you for the other, knowing him as a you for me, and allowing or expecting him to face me as a you for him.

These two stages, where there are two I's and where there are two you's, fluctuate. As a consequence, I find myself at moments in the role of an I related to a you, and then myself as a you related to him, acknowledged to have an I. But it seems just as correct to say that I am constantly interchanging my role and so is he, and that at one moment I am functioning as an I for a you, and at another that I am functioning as a you for an I, and that we arrive at equilibrium points, for longer and shorter periods, where we are both I's and both you's. This formulation seems to answer to experience better than the first. I insist on myself as an I directly with reference to another in the guise of a you, and at the same time I find myself functioning as a you for someone whose attention, interest, respect, and judgment is being elicited. The seeing us both on the same level, either as I's or as you's, is not only something achieved later, but appears to require the achievement of an equilibrium in the ways in which we face one another.

The social contract theories of the state which are being revived by Rawls and Nozick (who rightly remarks that Rawls starts with groups—minor we's) try to begin with men imagined to exist apart from the state. There is a stress in these views not on some overall we—which is nevertheless presupposed—but on the individuals or groups as bearers of rights. It is difficult to determine from these writers whether the individuals are so many I's or so many you's, or so many different complexes of I's and you's. Apparently what is intended is a multiplicity of I's, separate or collected, I's which nevertheless have *civil* rights and abilities, and powers that they do or can exercise with respect to one another, as well as possessions, privileges, advantages and disadvantages which they will ignore, want to preserve, or would be willing to give up for some other good. These writers suppose that all rights are fixed and that none are given existence, discovered, or made determinate by a just state. The state for them is just only so far as it abstracts from everything about men, to consider them only as coordinate possessors of equal rights.

If rights are civilly exercised in the area of property or self-defense or work or health, and there come in conflict with the individuals, as outside the state, possessed of unequal opportunities or quantities of these items, a just state will convert some of these inequalities into equalities, mediated perhaps by an open market, by definite, prescribed rules of distribution, or by continuing to maintain itself apart from the distribution and attending only to the justice of the manner in which the distribution is to occur.

If it is as unequals that individuals entertain the prospect of being in a state, it will not be in order for them to maintain the inequalities that they had before, but to achieve an equality either in abstraction from or by acting on the inequalities. The rights that the individuals have apart from the state are not given to the state or held in opposition to its attempt to possess those rights; they are rights which forever remain outside the provenance of the state. Were a state instituted by rational men (and therefore in abstraction from all the ways that they are together as I's and you's, and we's and others), they would not enter it with their differences, but as equals. The problem then will be to see how far and in what way the state will then function so as to convert or make use of the inequalities of the men as they are apart from the state, possessed of native rights and perhaps also rights which the men acquired in the course of time because they achieved higher degrees of intelligence, self-awareness, or came to react in similar ways to the dangers of nature or the course of experience.

4] You and I face one another at a distance, even when intimate, clasping one another, involved in one another's affairs, sympathetic, in love. The distance is physical, but it is also ontological, that is, a distance between entities which maintain themselves as bounded off from all else. But while at a distance we are also together, sometimes because we are directly affecting one another, interacting with one another, or producing something between us in which we partake in different ways, such as works of art, products, or language. Each of us, as involved in his own space, time, and activity, or as centered in a self-enclosed limited region, is an I. Each of us reaches the other as a you. In addition, each of us suffers the actions of the others, directly or mediately, as so many different you's, the exchangers in a world of exchange, not necessarily of goods, but perhaps of opinions, beliefs, and attitudes. We are adjustive beings, beings at a distance who take account of one another as independent, but yet making a difference to one another.

We know ourselves to be I's, and we come to know others primarily as you's. But in the world of interaction, of exchange, or of interplay, we move beyond ourselves as I's. We may attend to the fact that others are dealing with us as possessed of such I's; we may assume the position where they are and, like them, see ourselves as me's. But as merely interacting with the others, we are, with them, just you's together. This fact we learn somewhat later; initially what we see is that a number of others are functioning as you's with respect to one another. When we take the place of one of them, we function as they did, and know ourselves to have the status of you's with respect to other you's. Behind each of these you's is an I, from which it can not be entirely sundered.

Interchanges could occur with individuals functioning as mere it's, as entities which merely provide a place for something that is being exchanged. There would then be no purchasers or sellers, but only impersonal loci where the objects of exchange are placed. We have here a limited form of an exchange where others are bargained with, judged, taken into account and where the goods exchanged all have value because of the ways they make a difference to the relative status of the different individuals, initially as you's who are together, and perhaps eventually when they withdraw from the situation to make private use of what they had publicly obtained. The you-you situation here is distinct from that which, in the previous case, might be reached by achieving a midpoint between a stress first on the I and then on the you, or conversely. In the present situation, the you's sustain what relates them; each presents himself as the position at which their relation comes to an end. They are terms for one another, no matter what else they may be either for one another or themselves.

5] Each of us, whether in the guise of an I or a you, contributing to a we, or being subject to one, has a value in terms of which other items are assessed, whether these be men, animals, or things. The value is usually exaggerated and distorted, particularly when it is placed on a scale relative to the others. But it is also beyond all such exaggeration and distortion in the sense that it is at once incomparable and maximal. It is incomparable so far as it expresses what I am in myself; it is maximal in that everything whatsoever is to be assessed in terms of it.

My value is maximal, and yet I do want to get more than I have, not only of external things from which I then extract something for myself in privacy, but of things which I alone will enjoy. The apparent contradiction is avoided with the recognition that the maximal value which I have is one which nothing else can exceed, but which I nevertheless can add to, intensifying and enriching it. And others, too, can contribute to such an addition. The maximal value I now have is not one on which an advance is not possible. At the same time, the value that I have is determined by others. I find myself judged by them, and not unfairly. They assign me a lesser rank in relation to others, sometimes using standards that I myself would use on myself. There is a standard for all of us, and any one of us could use it, but there is a little more hope for objectivity and surely for a redress from my excessively high opinion, at times, of myself, in the use of the standard by others.

I am usually assessed, and I usually assess, on the basis of what is done. But an assessment rarely stops with the body, or the hands, or the tools with which something is done. It penetrates beyond any present you to the I which supposedly intended the act and, in any case, gives it a value because issuing from a maximal-valued self. I and you, though both assessive, maximal-valued selves, do not exchange judgments; nor need we share in the use of a common standard. Each of us begins in the same way, but from a singular beginning, to see all others from its perspective. I grant that the others, as apart from any public manifestation, may be no better or worse than I, members of an atomistic kingdom of ends, but the assessment I make is direct, and begins with myself from within, reaching to the others as you's. Via these, I reach toward but never arrive at the I's which are bases for assessments of myself and others.

Neither here, nor in the other cases, do I stop with a bare you. I either penetrate to some degree beyond this, toward another's I, or I turn about and face myself as a me, and thereby grasp what I am, more or less, from the position of another. I face another as a you'd-I, and face myself as a me'd-I, all the while insisting on myself as an I who assesses what is true of the you and the me, and of the I's which are continuous with these, but which, as maximal, can not be reached in these indirect ways. If I am to acknowledge an I behind a you to be of maximal worth, I must not try to get to it by going through the you. I must face it via a condition which permits it to be on the same level with myself. This is the we I help constitute and which applies to both of us as equal, self-maintaining, and irreducible, but together.

The I and the you, despite their direct relationship independently of anything else, are separately and together subordinate to a common we which neither one of us, or only one of us, may acknowledge. The way I and you separately and as directly related conform to any particular we leads to a new set of relations. Consideration of these perhaps can await the distinguishing of 'others' from myself, from you, from the you and I, and from any we which we might constitute. My awareness of myself and my functioning need not, of course, await anything more than an immediate sensing of the discrepancy between what in fact is occurring and what the we is demanding.

May 28

Elementary psychology: If tissue paper keeps absorbing water, that shows it has been conditioned by the water it has already absorbed.

Elementary sociology: If a black and a white man are walking in the rain in Harlem, the white man holds the umbrella. Fifty years ago it would have been the reverse.

Elementary linguistic philosophy: 'Yes' and 'no' have many meanings. So does that statement.

Elementary biology: Be wary.

Elementary philosophy: It's not necessarily so. Nor is it necessarily not so.

*   *   *

You have others; so do I; so do you and I; and so does every we. The others may be animals, or things, or other men; they may be faced or merely anticipated; they could be thought to be in the past. And they may be faced in a personal, biased, impersonal, interactive, or evaluative way.

Both from the side of the others and from our own the relation may be direct or indirect. If indirect, I may face others which are the others of those with whom I am now making myself help constitute a we. I may also acknowledge others beyond the others to which I am attending. They will be others about which I may know nothing more than that they are the others of those I am acknowledging. They could conceivably be like the ones I am acknowledging, or like myself, you and I, we, or you; they could, so far as I know, be quite different from any of these.

1] 'Other than' is a symmetrical relation. But it may also be asymmetrically instituted, by an act of rejection, dismissal, or withdrawal. The symmetrical relation arises when the others are, as it were, at rest, having a status of their own, and thus can be met directly, without having first been made into 'others'.

The instituting of an othering relation by me, by us, by you and me, or by you (as intermediating me) puts a personal emphasis on the others. They are my, your, or our others. If you are instituting an other by rejection, or by related acts, if that other is an other which has been personalized by you, it is possible for you to go on and identify it with, or make it be an other for me. But the other that you are instituting might well be yourself, or something identifiable by you through claim or possession or use, which you are then placing in the position of that which is other. Such cases set the other in the realm of the personal, but only after it has been characterized in other ways.

A personalized other is relativized toward myself, toward a we of which I am a part, toward a paired you and I, or toward the you who is functioning as my agent, making himself transparent in the very act of acting with respect to it, so that I can be directly related to it. This last case is to be distinguished from that in which the you (and of course you and I, or the we) occupies itself with an other for itself, and then makes it available in the same or an altered form for a direct confrontation as an other. The personalized alternative is an other which is directly confronted, but through the agency of someone who is functioning for me somewhat as my arm or my knife is.

The fact then that a man may consciously be occupied with something which is other than himself does not entail that it is an other for him. He may in fact so use his own hand that it is unknowingly presented as something which is not to be touched by him. The world about is not my other except and so far as it in fact makes me be its other. Until then, it is something distinct from me, to which I might turn in an attitude of othering, or acceptance, or which I might ignore altogether.

When there is an emphasis on myself (or on the we, or the you and I, or the you), there is always the problem of how there can be anything else. Subjectivists suppose that the emphasis on oneself necessarily taints everything confronted, and indeed reduces it or even constitutes it to be a continuation of oneself. But then there is nothing found, discovered, nothing obstinate, resistant, going its own way, and even producing or facing what is other for them and also for oneself. The Kantian, instead, recognizes that there is something obstinate to the world, and makes it into his other by introducing his own categories into it. The recognition of that obstinate content is, of course, a problem for the Kantian. It is not one for ordinary men, for they find themselves presented with what is already categorized by what is an other for them. The Hegelian recognizes this, and sees that the other is our or my other, something inseparable from and instituted by us or myself. But, though he avoids the subjectivist impasse of supposing that the other is a continuation of us or himself, a mere projection, he does so only by somehow getting the othered content to turn around and face us or me as an opposite.

Othering can be projective, a special way of imposing a condition, and thereby assigning to any particular within its compass the status of an other with respect to the projector. But othering can also be direct, a thrusting outward in an act which requires that at which it terminates to remain at a distance, not because it is caught within the process I am instituting, but because it is already there. It is a place where the othering which I am instituting can come to a rest with what then and there, in the act of sustaining my othering, functions as my other.

The most compendious statement is also the most exact: A personal other is instituted by an I (oneself or another), a pair, or a we, in the double form of a condition under which opposing items fall and of a direct repulsion which may not terminate in anything. The two dimensions occur together, but not necessarily in perfect consonance. It is possible to institute an othering and at the same time directly face an other, with the first encompassing much that the second does not terminate in. An othering, in this crowded world, usually terminates in a resistant object directly faced, and in what is governed by a relation instituted primarily by the individual directly engaged in an othering. But here, too, the other entity may be different in the two cases, despite the fact that the encompassing and the direct othering are not distinguished. And of course one may move along a condition and utilize it in a neutral way while continuing to be the source of a direct othering, not only of other individuals, but of things, nature, finalities, or prospects.

2] An impersonal othering is imposed or preconditional, as the space, time, and causality of nature are. I am kept apart from others and they from me; and what is true of myself with others is true of the we, the you and me, and of the you functioning away from me. The world into which I come when I am born, and on awakening, is not only diversified but is distinct from me in nature, role, action, and place. I am with other things only as that which is at a distance from them; they oppose me in a setting which keeps us distinct. I make myself be an instance, a unit which is within the range of that othering, and am thereby connected with them, via an encompassing othering, within a single undivided stretch. Were I to other or to be othered, or to other and be othered at the same time, all directly, without being subject to an impersonal other, I and the other would not be in a single extended whole; any extension that might be between us would just keep us apart. There would be no common ground between us or, if by chance our diverse otherings meshed in reciprocal ways (an idea which I entertained in *Reality* in connection with space), there would not be any necessary persistence to the union; it might not have a distinctive character, and it would not, if it had such a character, govern us, make us be part of the same territory, period of time, or causal whole.

I hold myself to myself even when I thrust myself outward. A governing other adds an intensity to my self-containment, supplementing my self-bounding with the power of the self-divisiveness of an extension. The extension is not divided but unitary; nevertheless, it is self-divisive, supporting and strengthening the self-enclosures of whatever entities it governs. I close myself into myself without regard for other entities, but a governing otherness makes the result be related to the other entities. The difference it makes promotes my self-awareness, just as surely as the resistance, which my personal othering meets, promotes it.

An impersonal othering is not identifiable with a self-diversifying condition to which I am subject. Were it so identifiable, this present case would reduce to one of the special forms dealt with under 'we', having the peculiar tonality of an extension. Not only may an otherness operate apart from all extensions, having to do with tempers, natures, roles, dignities, but when it does operate I directly deal with other entities as my others. This direct dealing is neutral to both of us. Initiated by me, or at least emphasized by me, it is an other in which I am in a symmetrical relation to others. I feel its force; I see the others as the others of me. But I do not experience the way in which they are suffering the otherness or the way in which they are directly utilizing an othering with reference to me. The thrust of the otherness against me, however, is not possible except so far as I also thrust equally forcefully, even if not noticed, against others. Sometimes I note that somebody acts as though he alone were the source of all alienation, distancing, othering, but also see that others are reciprocating, and that all of them are being subjected to forces which divide them, for example, in a disaster.

3] No matter how concerned I am with myself, how grandiose my ideas of myself or my power may be, I am faced with an overwhelming world which not only goes its own way but keeps me within a restricted place, not merely physical but bearing on my status, power, control, and duration as well. I am subject to a biased other of the world at large, and also by the several objects in it. That world at large is the sum of all the items that there are besides myself, but it is a sum which also has a structure and mode of action that can not be expressed as the aggregate of all the items, and the way they act. The world is not a blur of particulars; it is those particulars, each functioning on its own, and what they are, with me, subject to—the laws of nature and the energy and paths these govern.

Normally, I attend not to the world at large, but to a segment of it. It is an insistent other, a biased other, an other which compels, limiting my movements, determining the possibilities that are now open to me. I am alienated by what is already alien to me, by what is insistent on itself and therefore functions not simply by excluding but by thrusting me aside. If it just excluded me, I would be free from it, able to function without regard for it; but because it thrusts me aside, others me from its side, denies me place and scope and opportunity, forcing me to call upon additional energy, to make extra effort in order to make myself effective, I find myself subject to an alien, intrusive, determining other, allowing me to act or to consider it only on its terms.

The stronger and large the we, the more confident I am that an othering by what is not human can be effectively countered. But that we, too, is small and weak, pushed away by a large, humanly indifferent, but nevertheless insistently effective world. And a you and I, because often more intimate than any we, each directly involved with one another, but possessed of less power than a we which is backed up by the individuals to whom it in fact applies, is at once more thoroughly overwhelmed by others and yet more vigorously defiant of them.

A biased other has its own strength, occasion, ways of functioning; it is at once encompassing and direct, subjecting me to its conditions and thrusting toward me without regard for what I am or do. I am not only required by it to stand away; I am pushed away directly by whatever may be constituting the encompassing, subordinating otherness which takes me as a term. Since I am othered by everything else in this double way, I am a most intensive other, an other which is at the focus of a multiplicity of entities. The more I am aware of this, the more I am aware of myself as a singular, able to sustain a plurality of thrusts and indeed to give them a unity they do not otherwise have. To be rejected from every side is to be credited with the dignity of being able to provide a unity at which they all can converge.

4] Othering has many degrees and forms. The relation of otherness is constantly fluctuating in nature with different strengths at different times. A fine craftsman works as much with the wood as against it; a poor craftsman works not only against it but despite it. The outcome of both is something made which stands in contradistinction with him. Bearing his imprint, it is his other at the same time that it is other than what he has impressed on it. As other than what he impressed on it, it is the wood it was before; opposing him as it had before, but as together with what he impressed on it, it is an other of him, now unified and thereby opposed to him in a new guise. The work of the poor craftsman also bears his imprint and stands away from him as sheer wood. What he has impressed makes a unity with the wood, 'botched work', a unity which not only opposes him as an actuality, but opposes him as one who intends. The good craftsman relocates the object of his intention; the poor craftsman does not.

You and I together interact with an other in ways in which we individually can not. We supplement one another, and in that supplementation face the other with a nature and force neither could before. If the other is human (and sometimes animal) it may counter with actions which may increase, reduce, or maintain the same degree and kind of opposition that had occurred earlier. So far as our otherness depends on the reaction of others to what we are and do, we are like good or poor craftsmen, facing objects which are the others of us intending actualities.

United as a we, others are approached as opposed to us in that guise. We act on them as a single unit, backed by our several supplementary powers, while they, as singulars, paired, or constituting a we of their own, act on us. The interaction determines whether we remain undivided unities, or are split into a number of levels, which, as was the case with the poor craftsman, have oppositional roles. Each of us, in the interaction, may reach to the other and transform it into a remote continuation of himself. The otherness of that other will not be abrogated, for no matter how closely it may be made to conform to what is working on it, the other will remain that which has been worked on, a reality still other, though with a nature which may be merely differently located or functioning, rather than with a nature which is also different in character. (There is something wrong here, but I am not sure just what it is, except that it has to do with the nature of the opposition between what has been transformed in accord with an intent, or on which an intent is not impressed but which still bears the marks of the action of the other.)

5] Even in the narrow world of the family or a tribe, there is a plurality of values operating. Each individual is assessed from the position of many different value schemes. In the end, each is assessed from the position of a final value. Initially, that value is in an individual; derivatively, it may be maintained by a pair, by someone viewed as a you, or by a we. Each of these makes shifting demands, and assesses in the light of these. Some of the demands are basic, intrinsic, flowing from the nature of the assessor; some are transient, expressive of passing appetites and needs. Measuring what is other, they may end with these having a value, greater, lower, or equal to the assessor's, for what is other need not be, nor be taken to be of a higher or lower value than oneself without precluding the recognition that all are equal.

By another route we come back to questions at the root of contract theories of the state. Rousseau, with his doctrine of consensus, is concerned not with the establishment of a state, but with that of a society. In such a society all are equal in having a voice, and whatever other inequalities there be are governed by the operation of that single voice. In other social contract theories one moves directly to the state from the position of distinct individuals, each concerned with his own advantage, or functioning as purely rational beings. But a state rests on the existence of a society, with a multiplicity of independent cross-evaluations, in which men have different advantages and positions. To abstract from their evaluations and advantages is to pass at once from the individuals to the state. But just as a society has, and even depends on individuals in different positions and thus as evaluated in different ways, while allowed in some respects to be on a footing in value, so a state allows individuals to be unequal in some respects, and equal in others. It is as occupied with achieving equality that it decides to accept, ignore, transform, or reassess the inequalities.

Let it be supposed, though, with Rawls, that we have a number of rational men together who ask themselves what a just state would be like, once regard is taken for the contingent distribution of goods that in fact prevails. Rawls thinks that the men would all agree to a state in which existent advantages were retained but under the condition that the disadvantaged would be helped by the use of those advantages. This, in effect, is saying that advantages, or their consequences, belong to the entire state, and what is wanted by the state is a way of distributing the goods that result from the exercise of those advantages.

A just state for Rawls is one in which distribution is such that rational men, before joining, would find it the best possible way in which they could be together with one another, no matter what their diverse advantages. But to speak of advantages is to speak in terms of a standard; not all that is seen to be an advantage from one position is so from another. A life of leisure, with health, money, and respect, seems ideal to the academic, but is not recognized to be so by the adventurer, the soldier, the aggressive man. Not every slave wants to be a master. Advantages enjoyed are not so many beads to be separated off, but are part of a constellation, constituents of a unity which one would not want to give up, precisely, because it is familiar and shared with others. Rational men, even if they could conceivably move as singulars into a just state, will be concerned, not with what are later taken to be advantages in a state, but with the kind of equality which a state permits, and the ways this equality will function in independence of, and with reference to the differences characteristic of a society. In any case, all advantages and disadvantages presuppose the existence of a standard and a norm from which these deviate.

I have now come to the point, I think, where I should produce a matrix of the main cases, and then proceed with the writing of a systematic work. I leave in a day for Hungary with Marcia and Michael. She has a grant to investigate and evaluate the work of schoolchildren. I will spend the time in going over this manuscript, correcting its typographical errors and its grammar, and cutting out the passages that seem hopelessly muddled; I will plan also on rereading and perhaps partly rewriting "First Considerations." When I get back toward the end of next month, I hope I will be in a position to work on the two works systematically and persistently.

June 24

It is now almost a month since I sat down to anything at all. I spent most of the time in Budapest and Paris, where I went over the preceding pages, correcting the typos, grammar, and annoying illiteracies. I now find it very hard to get back to thinking and writing. I am relying on two devices to help me. One is to continue to work on "First Considerations," and thereby gear my mind to the kind of thinking which I wish to pursue; the other is to write in this work so that I recapture the connection between brain and fingers.

The travel books say that Budapest is almost entirely unchanged from the Empire days. I was not there then, but I was struck with the Vienna-like flavor of the city, its ease (compared with Bulgaria), and the lack of restrictions in movement. Hungary has experimented with a decentralized social system, in which almost everyone has a job of some kind. This has resulted in some freedom for the expression of initiative; it also has produced more workers than are needed for some jobs—sometimes many salespeople stand about doing nothing, though ready for any customers. I have read reports that there is some question as to whether or not the decentralized social-economic system should be continued, since it was found to be inadequate for export demands and a balancing of the budget. There is a tendency on the part of bureaucrats to meet requests with an instant "no," readily changed, though, at the slightest show of hesitation, doubt, or resistance.

Budapest is a pleasant, inexpensive city with a few reasonable hotels and restaurants, some of which are in some accord with what they were like some fifty or more years ago—baroque, overelaborated, many waiters, an indifferent cuisine. I do not think it is possible to spend more than a week in Budapest without being thoroughly bored, unless perhaps one knew the language. I had no difficulty with English, pieced out again and again with German, and found an occasional film to which I could go where the original English speech in the American film was retained and the Hungarian was used for subtilties.

Paris looked about as it had some twenty-odd years ago, though somewhat improved, since the buildings had been cleaned, the dogs kept on leash and not permitted to dirty the sidewalks, and some of the old subway cars replaced. In compensation for the marvellous advantage I enjoyed in my student days, back in 1929, when the dollar was strong, Paris today is not only undergoing its own inflation, but the dollar is falling relative to the franc. Food, fresh and cooked, is as excellent as ever. I did not go to shows, but roamed the streets, saw some American movies, visited shops, and did some desultory reading.

I had a vacation, one of the longest I have ever had, but now I am back and regretting every minute in which I am unable to think creatively. I have not yet been able to find the clue to the book on the we, I, you, and other, but am hoping that I will soon. I know that this can not be done by insistently looking, but it may be helped by my trying to set down the main outlines in charts and tables. I made such charts and tables in connection with other books; some of them I discarded, but others should be among my papers now in the Southern Illinois University Philosophic Archives.

Michael Guttentag, who was with us abroad, is staying with me until Saturday. He is a very intelligent, engaging, lively, happy young man, and despite our sixty-year difference he and I seem to get along amazingly well. We seem to enjoy many of the same things—circuses, films, puns, friendly tussles, and the like. I have, of course, not involved him in the things he does not really care for—going to museums, seeing dances, operas. There have been tensions and disagreements, but I have tried to make these occasions for me to show self-control, maintain some discipline, be understanding, flexible, and warm. It seems to work. He is in the same room with me now. Normally I work without anyone being present; I find that it is not easy for me to work with him here. I am reminded of the story told of Carlyle who complained first that his wife was interrupting him with her occasional remarks, then that she was disturbing him with the click of her knitting needles, and finally that he could not bear to hear her breathe. Michael is as silent as the tomb, but I nevertheless hear him rolling toy cars across the table, and can catch him from the corner of my eye. He is, of course, not the cause of my being unable to get back into a mood of creative writing, but he may be a deterrent to some degree. Nevertheless, I am glad that he is here. We go out together, and occasionally see a film—we both enjoyed *Jaws,* an excellently presented adventure which is a great success, with long lines waiting just to buy tickets for some subsequent performance. He occupies the painting room, and that makes me even more reluctant than I otherwise would be to begin to paint again, despite the fact that I have no classes and no obligations, and therefore apparently plenty of time. But I do have much material that has accumulated over the month, some of it periodicals, some of it recommendations, articles to referee, and the rest of the familiar material with which an academic has to occupy himself some of the time.

One idea that I have been toying with is that of making five twenty-five squared graphs to represent the different pronouns with which I am concerned, and then just going on to deal with each of the five times twenty-five distinct items, after which relations amongst them might be examined. The result would be a rather large work broken down into a multitude of discussions of distinguished dimensions and interrelationships. Is it important to do this? Would it be of interest or value to anyone? Would I learn by doing it? Is the doing of it in this way an evasion of the problem of finding a basic systematic approach, perhaps dialectical in some extended sense, which would lead me inevitably from one distinguished item to another?

June 25

Every theory of knowledge must face the question as to whether or not there is a given, and what it is like. Analysts, linguistic philosophers, phenomenologists, and idealists, who allow only for what is encompassable within and exhaustively explicated by their categories, must either deny that there is such a given, or confess that their position rests on the assumption of an entity whose presence, nature, and functioning they do not and can not understand. For them there always will be something to which they must adjust, but which they can not comprehend, or they will have to deny that there is anything which serves to confirm or sustain the categories used. Since these different thinkers deny that there is

anything which stands away from the entire world of particulars—
some idealists even tend to speak of their absolute as though its
reality was exhausted in the history of the universe and had no
reality in reserve—they have no other recourse but to move to the
position of a Fichte and claim that the given is itself a product of the
same source as the categories. This solution is at the heart of the
idealistic view of the nature of the empirical or at least the particularized world. A variant on this position is to be found in Peirce
who holds that there is nothing which is absolutely given, and that
any particular which is supposed to be so is in fact the outcome of
some previous relative given, and so on without end. But Peirce
also held that there was a 'secondness', a brute factuality. What else
is this but the 'given' in another guise?

One possible solution: every category faces a given. But what is
given for it is itself a category for what had initially been a category
for it. Categoreality and givenness would then be dimensions of
every item, each dimension being relative to some external given or
category. Each item, by itself, would be the identity of a given and a
category (Schelling's view) or an identity in difference of a given
and a category (Hegel's view). But this is only to push the matter
back a step, for the item itself would be some third thing, a given or
a category. Hegel maintains that the item is itself something to be
related to some other having, relative to it, an oppositional status;
there would, for him, not be anything which was to be understood
as more than or other than a related given and category. On that
view, a given and the category would both either be analyzable into
a subordinate given and category, or would be abstractions from a
more basic reality. The first of these alternatives means that we
never come to an end in analysis or construction; the second
requires one to make an exception for that from which the given
and the category are derived. Hegel, I think, prefers the second, at
least with reference to his final Absolute. The inexplicable Kantian
given is then replaced by an inexplicable Absolute, beyond the
reach of any categories and any knowing.

The solution which is suggested by *Beyond All Appearances* takes
the given to be either an attentuation of a reality, that is, an
exhibition of an actuality, by itself or in interplay with some other
exhibition, or to be the product of such an interplay. There will
then be a given   A] which is an actuality made manifest in a limited
form,   B] a manifestation of an actuality as caught up in a con-

textualizing manifestation of a finality, and C] the product of the actuality's manifestation with the contextualizing manifestation of the finality. The first two of these alternatives are analytic results of the third. On such an account, what is in fact given to us for knowledge is an appearance, itself to be analyzed into two factors, one of which has the role of a given for the other.

Men categorize appearances by 'idealizing' them, in that they impose boundaries which make the appearances be defined and possessed by a knower. But the appearances, all the while, are also possessed by the actualities and finalities which interplayed and thereby constituted them. The givenness of the appearances for the knower is here due to the fact that the categories do not control the adventures of the appearances. Is this not to return to the older view with its given that is used in knowledge but which has a status apart from it as well, and which so far is not known? I think not. 1] The boundaries are not put around something given to a knower; instead, in the very act of acknowledging anything he imposes boundaries and thereby has content which is known. 2] The content that the knower has brought within the confines of his boundaries which here have a categorial role, has another career as well. This is not given to the knower, but it does enable the content known to have a status apart from the knower, which of course is one of the roles that a given is designed to play.

An exclusive emphasis on epistemology makes necessary an insoluble problem of the given. One avoids such a problem by recognizing that one is always involved with a reality, an aspect of which is a constituent of an appearance. That appearance is 'subjectivized' in perception through the imposition of boundaries, but it is not first given to the knower to be so categorized. What is categorized is constituted by the categories or boundaries in the very act of being categorized; but this which is categorized is found to have a career of its own, and thus to be given in the sense that it has been taken away from an objective appearance which stands apart from the knower.

June 26

Atomists and monists set themselves in opposition to one another, but each tacitly accepts what the other insists upon. The atoms are acknowledged to be together in some field, itself not an atom or a function of them; the single reality of the monist is reached from the position of some one or more limited particulars with characters and careers distinct from that of the supposed single reality.

Once this fact is acknowledged, interesting questions come to the fore:

1] What is the nature of the 'atoms', or more generally, the particulars? Some identify them as sense data; others as molecules, ultimate physical particles, things, persons, objects of perception, impressions, commonsense objects, words, truths, the products of some mind or theory—and this surely is not the end of the list. It is the vice of reductionism to insist on one or a few of these pluralities of acknowledged units and to deny the others. The particulars are of many different kinds.

It is philosophically immature to denude the universe on behalf of some methodological principle.

2] How are the different pluralities of particulars related? We can classify them as epistemic or ontologic, and then reframe the question as to whether one of these lays the ground for the other. I have tried to show, since the days of *Reality,* that philosophy is a great circle in which epistemology grounds ontology, and conversely. If this be admitted, there will be subordinate questions about the various pluralities included under the two headings. The solution to these questions will depend on the grasp of what is basic, grounding, presupposed, and what is derivative, secondary, localized, limited, specified. This distinction in turn is a function of the seriousness with which one takes action, motion, emotion, distance, and value, and the degree to which one accords an antecedent but not absolutely privileged position to commonsense objects and experiences.

3] Can the single reality or dimension that contrasts with the plurality with which one begins or ends be discerned when one is confronting a particular or a number of them? Some hold that it is an object of inference only, or that it is to be arrived at by engaging in some special kind of activity, altogether other than that which is characteristic of those required in the acknowledgment of particulars. One must, they think, move to a mysticism, natural or supernatural, or make use of some special intuition, to be achieved only after one had gone through some ritual, purgation, withdrawal, denial, inspiration, or unusual experience.

Neil Welliver came by yesterday. Our conversation turned toward this topic. He thought that politicians, businessmen, and many others, were unable to discern anything beyond the particulars with which they are daily occupied, but that artists discerned it most of the time, and that some people discerned it always. I objected, since this would seem to divide mankind into two species of men, those who and those who do not and perhaps can not discern what is beyond the particulars. It seems more correct to say that there is a continuum, at one end of which there are men who are always alert to what lies beyond, and at the other end of which there are those who are alert to it only occasionally, perhaps when subject to some deep emotional experience, but that even these have a vague, dim grasp of it always, even though they may act and speak as if it were not there, and may deliberately set themselves against the acknowledgment of it.

4] Does what lies beyond affect the particulars? The easiest supposition to make is that the particulars merely lie in a field, and are simply together as an aggregate of independent items. But this precludes their being subject to controlling conditions—spatial, temporal, causal, evaluational, affiliating, coordinative, structuralizing—and thereby compelled to be together in distinctive ways not explicable by a consideration of the particulars themselves or their placement in an indifferent field.

5] Do controlling conditions have a status apart from the particulars controlled, or do they exhaust their being and power in such control? The latter alternative has difficulties with the fact that the world continues beyond the present. The controlling conditions must be understood not to be exhausted in their present and past activity. But might they not be exhausted in the course of history? This is surely possible, but it does presuppose that there is some neat adjustment of the conditions as not yet expressed with the conditions that will be expressed. It makes the conditions oriented toward the particulars and thereby gives the particulars a kind of preconditioning status for them. In any case, before the entire universe has run its full course, there will be a conditioning which is rooted in something other than the particulars and which is capable of standing apart from and operating on those particulars.

6] Might the conditioning control be exerted by a mind? Yes, if the mind be given universal scope, and not identified with the mind of this or that particular man. But this is tantamount with giving the mind an ontological status, indistinguishable, I would think, from what I have called a finality.

7] Is it necessary to go this far? Might not the primary condition be logical, mathematical, or linguistic? I think not. The first two are too formal, and involve no control by themselves, requiring in fact the mediation of a power which applies them—unless they themselves are already identified with the structure of the supposed universal mind operating on those particulars.

8] Is there only one conditioning control that is being imposed on all the particulars? If the particulars are of many different types there may, of course, be different types of control and perhaps conditionings pertinent to them. If so, the different controls and conditionings will have to be related to one another. But the question now raised is not about such a plurality of sets of particulars, each with its distinctive kind of imposed unification, but with respect to the most basic set of particulars—actualities, substantial entities. It is the almost unanimous opinion of philosophers East and West over the decades that there is but one ultimate controlling condition. But in order to maintain this they have been forced to ignore the occurrence of a number of independent modes of conditioning control to which the particulars are all subject. Law, for example, operates independently of a source of value.

One finds men quite ready to acknowledge that there is something discernible, more or less dimly, beyond the particulars confronted every day, no matter how these be classified as data or things. An occasional few find it not difficult to credit this discernible with some reality. What seems hard for most is to acknowledge that the entity has a career of its own, that it is not like some particular, enlarged and ennobled, that it governs but does not entirely control or possess or master the particulars, that the particulars themselves always have and use a power to resist it, and that the particulars and the entity interplay. What is apparently taken to be untrue by almost all is the view I have been urging to the effect that the actualities, which are the most real of particulars, and roughly identifiable with the things, animals, and men encountered in daily life (though as purged of the accretions with which one ordinarily overlays them) are distinct from, resistant to, and interplay with a plurality of distinct, final, conditioning, controlling powers acting on all the actualities at all times. The major obstacle (which also confronts those who attend to only one finality) is produced by the great tendency to think and speak as though the powers were particulars, but of larger scope, rather than quite distinct from particulars, in kind and nature, and yet capable of being known, without recourse to intuitions, insights, or the achievement of special states of consciousness.

I sometimes speak of the powers as 'conditions', though this does seem to make them be essentially oriented toward the particulars, and suggests a kind of mind which imposes limits. I refer to them also as 'controls'. Though such a term also has similar unfortunate associations, it does lead one to recognize that the source of a control has a status of its own, and is able to insist on itself and even resist any intrusion which might originate with the actualities. A reference to conditioning controls leads to the acknowledgment of their sources, the finalities themselves.

9] Are the finalities discernible? They must be if they are continuous with the conditioning controls, if they are those controls maximally intensive, maximally remote, and maximally self-centered. And yet, because they have a standing in and of themselves, what we discern of them must fall short of them in their full concreteness, not because the discernment stops at some particular place to leave an unapproachable reality beyond, but because discernment itself has degrees. Though the discernment can not be said to stop short of a finality as it is in itself, we are unable to distinguish different degrees of it beyond some point. We discern the finalities in themselves, it could be said, without knowing that we do, unable as we are to note the difference between the degree of the discernment that reaches to the finality itself and that which falls slightly short of it.

The discernment of finalities does not preclude a knowledge of them through an inquiry which is based on a consideration of what must underlie controlling conditions, operating everywhere and always.

*   *   *

There are at least three kinds of nobodies:
There is the nobody of whom nobody says he is a nobody. There is the nobody of whom somebody says he is nobody. And there is the nobody of whom everybody says he is nobody. The first is unknown, unrecognized, unacknowledged. The second is the

object of jealousy. The third is one who once was somebody but is this no longer.

June 27

A conditioning control can be understood in three ways. It refers to what is then and there being expressed, without residue; the conditioning control is then countered by what will also have the role of a sustainer for what the conditioning control intrudes on it. The conditioning control also stands away and has some reality apart from the exercise of the control; it is a general, a prescription, a demand, not exhausted in any particular expression or particular act of control. Thirdly, a conditioning control is vitalized, maintained, possessed, to be understood as continuous with a reality which remains, regardless of what there might be conditioned or controlled. It is not possible to remain with only the first of these senses, without making it conceivable that, at the next moment, whatever there be may be subject to an entirely different set of conditioning controls. The guarantee of any degree of persistence to the nature of the world is the presence of a condition which is a priori in the sense that it dictates to whatever might come to be. Such a condition has no reality of its own. It also lacks intrinsic power. If it were real, it would be able to impose itself on what is conditioned; if it had intrinsic power it would be able to interplay with the very entities for which it provides a condition. It is equally true that the condition is not without all reality or power, since it is continuous with, being an attenuation of a finality. As continuous with the finality it is real and powerful; as pertinent to the world of actualities or appearances it defines the limits of their activities; as actually applied to that world it is distinguished both from its source and from the items in that world. Indeed, it is specified by those items so as to constitute a qualification of them or of the relationship which interconnects them.

Most philosophers seem to take their stand with something like the second of these senses. They recognize that there are general conditions, rules, laws, contexts, fields which impose some limitation on and assure the togetherness of a plurality of entities. They know, too, that the conditions must somehow be imposed. They think that they are cautious when they attribute the conditions and the imposition to a mind, individual or cosmic, to a linguistic community, or to the use of a convention. But it is hard to see how one who stops with an individual mind can avoid solipsism; how one who stops with a cosmic mind can avoid idealism and the reification of a Reason; how one who takes a linguistic community to be primary can avoid the solipsism of a community, cut off from all others; or how one who accepts a convention as basic can avoid adding to such a solipsism the extra limitation of an arbitrary assumption.

It is sometimes thought that an escape from this kind of problem can be achieved by appealing to history. It is some such attitude which makes companions of Hegelians, Marxists, pragmatists, and students of the history of ideas. Or is it perhaps the case that all of these are variants on the same position, an idealism which is always on the go, always mastering whatever it confronts only to find still further content to be mastered?

I have myself been urging that there is always content beyond any point at which we are compelled to stop in thought, perception, awareness, symbolization, emotion, to which we might move later. Such a view is somewhat different from the one now being examined, for on my view the 'historic' or temporal move is a consequence of the fact that there is always something beyond, which one may or may not want to reach, whereas the view now examined supposes that if there is something still beyond what has been mastered, there is either a subjective or an objective necessity that it be mastered. Inquiry on such a view has its own dynamic persistent thrust; the cosmos, too, or the fundamental reality beyond this, is also supposed to have an insistence to it, demanding always that whatever is not mastered be mastered and finally be entirely absorbed.

Another difference is that the activity of knowledge (on my view), no matter how completely it encompasses and explains without residue whatever there be, always leaves over the reality which is known. This difference is not allowed on the other view. It argues that if there were such a residuum it would, by definition, be outside the purview of knowledge and therefore could not even be said to exist. Yet knowledge is not just abstract meaning; it *is*. The utilization and embodiment of the conditions of knowledge presuppose that there is a state of being, or of having or using conditions. This evidently can not be known, unless one were able to approach knowledge itself from a position outside it. Such a position is provided by the reality which is being known. The utilization of the reality of what is known as a basis for a knowledge allows one to know the fact of knowledge, just as a knowledge of an external reality allows one to know that external reality. In each case the reality remains outside the knowing, and accounts for the fact of the knowing.

This is not exactly right, yet it suffices to make evident that the historic view has to face up to the fact that something 'given' at each moment has to be brought under the control of the historic rules or the historic process, and that the historic rules or process do not account for that given, since it is a given for it.

*   *   *

The expression "nobody says that x is nobody" is ambiguous. It may mean that x is so unmistakably and universally acknowledged to be important—Newton, Einstein, Jesus, Moses, Buddha—that he never is dismissed as insignificant. But it can also mean that the individual, x, is so insignificant that no one attends to him; he is not even dismissed from some level where one is termed 'somebody'. Of course, to have picked out x is already to have given him a significance which is greater than that which he has as one who is entirely ignored, and thus not even designated. One must, as it were, acknowledge him in a glancing way, pass beyond him at the very moment that one is attending to him.

"He is a nobody," we might say pointing to some derelict. Should we stop with him, treat him as more than an illustration, we will already have made him into somebody. 'Nobody' must be prevented from being a classification or a name, and just be allowed to mark off that which is not to be designated, or is to be designated as not to be given any further name or dignity. Do we here not have a situation similar to the acknowledgment of a fact apart from all theory, of a given apart from all conceptualization, of that which is meant but not said?

June 28

Every view is confined within two presences—its own and that about which it discourses. Neither presence is then part of it. A presence must either be said to be unknown and therefore not even to be known to be there, or there must be some way in which the view accommodates it, or confesses that it is inadequate, incomplete, not yet a full-blown philosophical account.

A philosophical history, of which Hegel's is the model, also has to be confined within two presences. If it be allowed that the course of the history consists in the absorption of the presence which is to be historically mastered—whether this be supposed to be originally a product of the history, a kind of projection forward at each stage requiring still another stage, or to be found available and given importance or dignity by the historic process—there is still the fact that the history itself is present, but not to itself. The attempt to deal with this issue by referring to a 'self-reflection' merely pushes the issue back a step, for the self-reflection has a presence as well as a content which is present to it.

1] One solution is to suppose that history oscillates between the two presences. Starting with one presence it encompasses the content before it without residue. It then produces the other from within itself and, by occupying this, encompasses what had been operating on itself. From the position of each presence the other is no longer, being absorbed; but in order to account for its own presence, it finds it necessary to give that which was absorbed the status of a presence. The solution makes each presence be a product of some other actual presence, but a product which allows one to take a stand with it. Putting aside the supposed necessity of a perpetual oscillation, the view not only makes each presence a product and therefore supposes that there is a 'double cunning' at the heart of things, but has yet to account for the presence of the oscillating whole.

2] A second solution begins with the acknowledgment of a single all-inclusive power which is present. This assumes one position having another as a counterfoil, and then takes up the position of that other with the first as a counterfoil. There is a perpetual oscillation between these positions. Each absorbs the presence of the other, assimilates it without residue on its own terms. This, though, would not eliminate it entirely since it would still be insisted upon by the primary power. And the primary power would itself be present, oscillating from one position to the other.

Neither of these solutions has been stated with sufficient clarity. But I think it is sufficiently clear that they will not do, since they do leave over the presence of the agent, whether this be identified with what is at one position or the other (as the first solution supposes) or what is able to occupy the positions in turn without exhausting itself in that act (as the second solution supposes).

3] Philosophy is not a substitute for the universe. Nothing that the philosopher can conceive can replace what is present for him. His conceiving, as well, is other than that which is being conceived. Nevertheless, there need be nothing that must be termed absurd, unknowable, or even merely projected or supposed. Presences can be acknowledged to have depths and to be known, and so far to be absorbed within the knowing situation, without being denied a place in a continuum of greater and greater depth. We always reach to a depth beyond the position at which the knowing attains, but as that which is conquering us, making us conform to its career and demands.

In fact or in imagination it is possible to occupy a depth which one has not yet cognitively reached, and from that position turn back to understand the position initially entertained. The presence of that initially entertained position is a depth into which one penetrates at the same time that one articulates the position in terms of the position occupied. There will be no position and therefore no presence not reached into. None will be forever beyond the power of an articulate judgment to represent. None will be replaced by any thought or view. But none, too, will be necessarily unexpressed. The entire philosophic system will itself of course be present, and will as such not know itself; but it can say that it is present, understand what it means to be present, and end by allowing its presence to be envisaged from the position of some other enterprise, such as science or history or art.

We know that a thought or system is present; we know that it is occupied with mastering something that is present for it. We know, too, that no thinking or any other act on our part can produce, annihilate, or substitute for the presence of that which it understands, and that it must itself be present if it is to function. The two different contentions seem to be in opposition, but the foregoing discussion neither clearly shows the opposition nor overcomes it.

How do we know that a thought is present? Is it not because it is effective, operative, insistent in the face of what is resisting it? If so, we know that it is present because it is in interaction with some other presence. Presence is twofold, and to be aware of one presence is to be aware of it as at least contrasting with some other.

Thinking, judging, knowing are acts. That means they occur in the present. The concepts, categories, assertions with which thinkers are occupied are but the termini of such activities. The presence of a theory is the activity of the theorizing, with an emphasis placed on the terminus. The terminus is reached from a depth beyond it; as a mere terminus it is an abstraction, and is in fact available only as part of a present act.

In using the terminus, we entrench on the presence before us. In organizing material for the terminus we always leave over something into which we have penetrated but which we have not included within the organizing unity of the terminus.

We know what is present to us by bringing it within the confines of what we are using as concept. We know that there is a presence for us because the action of the concept involves a delimitation and structuring of what continues to function apart from this. We also know that there is a presence to our thinking because that with which we think is continuous with the presence of that thinking.

We become aware of ourselves as presently thinking by finding ourselves producing a concept. The awareness that we are producing a concept is inseparable from that concept, not in the sense that the concept is applied to the production, but in the sense that the concept is not except while being produced. Do we know this because the concept itself points back to the production of it? If so, the concept would also have a different meaning as referring to what is beyond it, and in effect would be two concepts. It is more correct to say that there is a structure to the entire process of producing a concept and that this structure solidifies into a kind of concept of the process at the very same moment that another concept terminates that process.

In the activity of thinking one generates a concept of it which applies to that process, and has it in contradistinction from the concept with which the process terminates. The first of these, a concept used in self-awareness, is part of a circular activity, in which the concept is applied to that which makes it possible. The circular activity has, tangent to itself, the concept which is to be used. This concept, in turn, has tangent to it an objective circle in which there is an intelligible form of an objective presence percipitated by that presence and turning back into it.

A concept is flanked by two intelligibilities, each of which is involved in a circle where it is precipitated out and refers back to that from which it issues. It is the maintaining of the concept as a distinct item which allows us to distinguish the two presences, each of which is self-intelligible, the one a self-awareness of the act of knowing, the other the rationale of a presence given for knowledge. It is possible, therefore, to speak of a concept being environed by a concept of a process of knowing and by a process external to a knowing, or by two presences, or by one presence and a concept. But it would be more precise to say that it is environed by two self-intelligible activities. In using the concept on the self-intelligible activity which is present before it, that activity is subject to the concept and thereby made part of knowledge. Since it is a self-intelligible activity, by making one's concept identical with its intelligibility one makes the concept part of the self-intelligible activity and thus allows it to be able to function as though it were the precipitate as well as the structuralization of what is before one. The concept then becomes identified with the presence of another without ceasing to be the terminus of a present act by a knower. It is, of course, not caught up in the activity of the object; the dynamism that it needs in order to be a proper substitute for the structuralization of what is present, it obtains from the activity by which it is produced.

The presence of this entire enterprise, in which a terminus is flanked by two circles, each of which can be described as a precipitated intelligibility referring back to itself as an activity, is expressed in a concept inseparable from the two intelligibilities which flank it. The concept is then not only a product of our activity and may substitute for the intelligibility of what is beyond, but a juncture of two intelligibilities, each in a circular relation to a subordinate presence.

June 29

When we perceive, and even when we make use of concepts and proper names, we penetrate beyond the point where the percept, concept, or name comes to rest. We are then, with the percept and the others, subject to the entity into which we have penetrated. It is then not the case, as is usually assumed, that we actively impose concepts, ideas, or judgments on something beyond us which passively receives or is unable to allow for it. Instead, the concepts, ideas, and judgments are subject to what is beyond and are thereby transformed, if need be, so as to be accommodated by it. What we attribute remains exactly as it had been, but only from the perspective of ourselves who introduce it, not when it is caught up in the object. I think some of this thought is behind pragmatism with its acknowledgment of the transformation which abstractions undergo by being made part of something beyond them, and having their proper meaning thereby determined.

As individuals, of course, we are not absorbed in the objects we know. What is taken over is ourselves as penetrating not ourselves as we are in ourselves. We are made alert to the course of nature, to the career of that which we are endeavoring to know, not simply by seeing that it does not conform to the implications we can draw from our concepts, but by seeing that new consequences are being produced, not envisagable from the position of what we entertained or apply. Our concepts are not only transformed but made to be acceptable by the objects to which they pertain.

There are two degrees of acceptability. An idea is acceptable in the sense that it is possessed by, subject to that into which we are penetrating from the standpoint of that idea. An idea is acceptable, too, as that which is being transformed so that it is able to merge with the very meaning of the object, a meaning which is at the midpoint of the course of a circular return of the object to itself. We are aware of both acceptabilities only so far as we can hold on to the concept in its initial form and also be with the object as it is possessing and altering this. The penetration is emotionally toned, and is usually kept confined to the vital activity of the object, while the concept is brought into consonance with the intelligibility which the object is expressing and repossessing in the course of a circular movement.

A concept is not only directed at an object, where it is confined to its surface (and there functions as an agency for bounding the object, thereby enabling one to have the object in the role of something within knowledge), and also is more or less transformed, accommodated by the intelligibility of the object, but is the terminus of an act of knowing, not entirely separable from that act. I know that I am knowing (that I exist as one who knows) because I have the concept at the limit of my act of knowing.

Subjectively, a concept is not separable from the act of knowing as at once present and dynamic and intelligible. So far, the concept is just mine. As such, it differs from the concept in the role of a concept-of-something; it is the terminus of the full presence of myself, a presence which takes the form of an expression which is taken back into itself. By means of the concept I have more or less of a grasp of the meaning of an object at which the concept comes to rest, at the same time that it is pulled on by the object within which I have become subject, via the content reached through a penetration. By means of that very concept I also have a grasp of myself as a present knower who is distinguishing and solidifying the intelligibility of his knowing with his presence as engaged in the knowing.

The Cartesian 'cogito' is already on the side of the 'sum'; it merely characterizes the way in which one is. Instead of 'cogito' Descartes should have started with an idea, perhaps the idea of God which is so essential to the development of his view. That concept he should have considered in three ways: by itself, as an idea, something in mind, something which he was going to use as a claim; as the terminus of his thinking; and as that which was referred to and there maintained and possessed by the object of the concept. Every concept, in fact, has all three roles at the same time, though we emphasize sometimes one and sometimes the others. Inevitably, we face a presence which we must somehow make intelligible. If we can get a concept at an exact equilibrium point, we will have it inseparable from our own presence as knowers, and from itself as that which is being transformed into the intelligibility of the presence of the object. The concept then will be the presence of oneself in an attenuated form and the intelligibility of the presence of the object as that which has already accepted a penetration into it.

The entire complex of concept flanked by two presences, one of which it terminates, and the other of which it more or less adequately expresses and thus is maintained apart from the knower, it itself present. That presence is given intelligibility by the concept as held apart from the knower and the known. The more surely that the concept functions within the concrete situation where it at once unites and separates two distinct presences, the more does one depart from the overall presence of the entire situation of knower and known related by concept. We thus are confronted with a choice—having a concept of the overall presence of the complex situation, or having the concept mediate between two presences, one of which it expresses, and the other of which, under transformation, it shares in as its intelligibility. If the first of these be accepted, the concept functions with respect to the overall presence in the way the intelligibility of the knower or the known functions with respect to their presences—it is part of a single circular movement in which what is present expresses itself as an intelligibility which it takes back into itself in the course of a circular movement.

A concept as the expressed and possessed meaning of an overall presence can be identified with the known meaning of an historic occurrence. There is, though, no need to suppose some grandiose historic movement or dialectic at the service of some absolute, helping one solve all philosophic problems. An historic occurrence is merely a new kind of presence produced through the interplay of present entities whose juncture provided the intelligible meaning of the overall presence within which the other presences could be located.

How does such a view differ from the idealistic, in which some ultimate reality is supposed to produce its own opposite and then take this back into itself? Firstly, it gives priority to a presence and not to a reason or mind; secondly, the idea or intelligibility is not held to be the opposite of the presence; thirdly, the idea is recognized to have two sides or roles, in one of which it is the expressions and in the other of which it is the possession of the presence; fourthly, the single presence considered is punctuate, individual, distinct from case to case; fifthly, it allows for the genuine presence of a distinct individual's knowing distinct objects, each with its own presence, in no way to be swallowed up in the single presence; sixthly, the single presence can be considered to be both prior to and subsequent on the subordinate presences—the one when the knowing or historic situation is viewed as issuing out of a more fundamental nature, and the other when it is viewed relative to the concept or event that is produced as the juncture of the subordinate presences.

There is something present or given only for a meaning (structure, concept) which that very presence or given produces or accommodates. It produces it ontologically; it accommodates it epistemically.

June 30

It can be said of the knower and of the object that each has a meaning which is the meaning of its existence—and an existence which is expressed as that meaning. The observation brings one close to Thomas's formula about God: God's essence is his existence. For Thomas, of course, the essence gave the full reality of God, for God, unlike ordinary things, did not have an additional matter in which an essence was introduced or with which it was united. Since God's essence was the essence of a perfect reality, the formula also permitted the use of an ontological argument, could one but know what the essence was. But in the present account, the meaning is not identical with the existence, and does not allow a deduction of it, even for one who knew the meaning thoroughly. The meaning epitomizes the existence, brings it into a focus; it is then the existence or presence epitomized, without being separated from that existence or presence. It could be said to report or represent the existence, but only from the standpoint of that existence, which takes it back into itself in its own way. It could tell one about the existence only, as it were, from the position of the existence itself.

The existence (or presence) contrasts with the meaning in which it terminates on the way to a return into itself, and also has that meaning and therefore itself as contrasting with that meaning. In the first sense, the presence exhibits itself as a meaning which returns to it in a return where that meaning is absorbed, and not merely sustained. In the second sense, it is the presence of the entire circular totality of presence exhibiting and absorbing its own meaning. For a Descartes this would be the existence of the entire complex, "I think therefore I am."

A concept (which is at the terminus of a knower's act) also epitomizes the complex of present knower and object. It can be brought back into that complex and can be understood to be the expression of it in somewhat the way in which a meaning is brought back into the presence it expresses. A concept, however, differs from a meaning in that it can be used to refer to what is beyond the knower; it can be brought back into the lower only by an effort, and refers, not to the existence of the knower alone, but to the existence of that knower as expressing and recovering his own meaning apart from that concept.

There is still left over the presence of the entire complex of knower and object, with the concept as their mediating juncture. The presence of the entire complex can be said to exhaust itself in the concept as that which is in fact a mediating juncture. The act of exhausting itself is the act of being present; the exhaustion is the factuality of the being present, a factuality which is all that remains when one refers to it as in the past. The reference is in the present and depends on the present. That present is not then encompassed but, like the passed-away present, can be the object of a subsequent knowledge.

Still left over is the awareness of the entire complex as present. This is achieved in the very act of finding the concept unsustained by a presence and therefore become identical with a past fact. We are aware of the present in which we and the objects we know (as well as the concepts which are at the juncture of the two) are all components. We are so aware in the act of attending to any of these components, for we then have the encompassing present in contrast with the subordinate presences and with the concept which is one with the factuality of what had been present.

Being present is never reducible to anything known, but it is not beyond all grasp, for in knowing anything we already have it as a contrastive factor, as that in which we are sharing, at the same time that we stand away from it by attending to the concept and that to which it refers. This in effect is to say that the presence of the entire complex is itself the contrastive ground for whatever we may acknowledge as a concept, or as a concept united with the knower and the object known.

It is also true that, in the case of the knower and object, there is a contrast between their meaning and presence, which is felt when the circle reaches a midpoint at the meaning. Conversely, it is also true that the overall presence is epitomized in the triadic occurrence of a meaningful present knower conjoined through a concept with the meaning of some present object.

An individual knower begins as a man who is present within the larger present of a world. He attains the status of one who is in the knowing situation by an act in which he epitomizes his presence together with the presences of others. The outcome is a concept which is at once inseparable from himself and from a meaning beyond him and the concept. He is aware of being within the larger present by the contrast that is set up between that present and the epitomizing concept; he comes to know of that present by referring the concept back to its source in a process in which that concept is submerged more and more in the source.

The contrast between the individual or a situation as present and what is focussed on is not identifiable with a relation of opposition, not only because the former but not the latter is asymmetrical, but because it is a relation of more to less intensive, of that which is at the beginning and that which is at the end. And though it is true that the meanings and concept are at once distinct from and express a presence, they do not represent the presence in an abstract form; they are it in a transformed though attenuated guise. We can not know, by examining meaning or concept, the nature of the presence they express; to find that which they express, one must see how they are altered in being absorbed.

We are aware of a presence in the very act of being directed toward the expression of it, and thereby forced to contrast the presence with that expression. We know what the presence is by seeing how the meaning or concept is transformed in being brought to bear on the presence. We lose the meaning or the concept in the presence; that presence, which is then outside the reach of the meaning or the concept, is already involved in another expression. As soon as we have mastered a presence in an awareness and a knowledge, we are involved in a process where what is present is expressing itself in a fresh way. The reality, in its full concreteness, is thus known in one sense and not known in another, for it is that which is grasped in awareness and concept and which is reached by means of these, at the same time that on being reached it is found to be engaged in a new expression, and so on without end.

July 1

In place of the traditional form and matter analysis of an actuality, or the later analysis into essence (with its meaningful juncture of a form and a matter) and existence (presumably derived from God), the foregoing discussion leads to the view that every actuality pulsates between the extreme where it is primarily a meaning which is more and more intensified until it terminates in a sheer dense presence, and the extreme where it is primarily a presence which is more and more expressed until it terminates in a sheer meaning.

Is the mind of man to be identified with the meaning of his presence? The supposition that man is a rational animal and that his mind is the very embodiment of his rationality would encourage such an identification. But if it be recognized that man has other powers, and that a mind is one of the expressions of the self, that identification is not plausible. Instead, one must hold that the meaning of a man has a thickness to it, and that his mind involves the isolation of a portion of this in the form of a structure which is to be vitalized and particularized in inferences, thoughts, beliefs, and concepts. To know a man's mind is not yet to know the full meaning of his presence, but it is to know part of that meaning, a part which has been held apart from the rest of the meaning and placed in the service of the production of thoughts, concepts, and whatever else is involved with the meanings of other actualities.

Men entertain many concepts, some of them obviously pertinent to what is before them, some of them apparently irrelevant to anything past, present, or future. The fact that there are many concepts makes evident the impossibility of identifying any one concept with the meaning of the individual, or with his mind, since these are singular and undivided. How then account for a concept? And for the emotions? And the self?

A concept expresses some of the meaning of a man as together with his presence; it is the terminus of the expression of himself as a meaningful presence. But that terminus is only one of many possible; moreover, it does not express the full meaningful presence, at least to the degree that an emotion does.

So far as concepts are elicited by what is confronted, their diversity can be accounted for by recognizing them to be in part a function of what is being experienced. But there are concepts which are freshly produced. Though these are never so alien to what is beyond as to be unable to be absorbed there after a transformation, it is still the case that they are produced by the individual apart from what else is there.

A self is the inward equilibrium point between an individual man's meaning and presence; they have equal weight for the self, and can be taken to be part of one expression of the self. That expression, as distinct from it, goes through a pulsation from the extreme of being almost all meaning to the extreme of being almost all presence.

A self expressing itself directly—but inevitably, also—in part through the mind and the body as a presence, is the self making itself emotionally evident. It makes use of a mind in the guise of particular concepts by bringing to bear some of the presence, rather than allowing that presence to be together with the meaning—as it does when in itself or when expressing itself emotionally. A concept is thus part of the meaning of the knower vitalized and particularized by an expression of the self.

*   *   *

On Friday I attended the funeral mass of Dr. Roy R. Bode, a colleague. The mass was in the crypt of the Shrine, co-celebrated by about a dozen priests. It was a moving, impressive ceremony, in part because there was an evident consciousness of the fact that it was a friend and colleague who was at the center of the activities. I had once attended an Episcopalian ceremony (for Dr. Urban at Yale) and was left unpurged, dissatisfied, because a ritual had been gone through in which the name of the deceased was inserted at various places, but nothing more was said or done about him as an individual. Here, instead, there was a homily, a consecration over the coffin, honorary pall bearers—colleagues (I among them), students, the President of the University—and references again and again to Roy.

Roy was one of those teachers who devote themselves entirely to students; he was always available, and spent hours upon hours discussing philosophy and other matters with them. He never came to our philosophic discussions in the evenings, and when he attended lectures it was mainly to see that the machinery of slides, doors, and the like was functioning smoothly. He was always pleasant, kind, open, friendly, but I for one never really got to know him, in part because he was absorbed elsewhere, as I was, and in part because he and perhaps I avoided the kind of contact which might have led to the embarrassment of finding that we had no way of making contact in the realm of ideas. Yet I felt deeply at the mass, conscious that it was Roy, and maintained that consciousness these last days. Though I do not agree with the Catholic view about the immortality of the soul and the resurrection of the body, I did find that the ceremony made me acutely aware of the spiritual side of Roy, and the fact that the body's death left over the meaning of his life, and a sense that what he was and did was not entirely extinguished.

In this same period I have been reading *Alive!* a book about the survivors of a plane crash in the Andes. It is a book which brings the adventure and the hardships clearly into focus. But what is most remarkable, I think, at least for me at the present moment, is that it is about a group of rather devout Catholics. I think some of their hardiness, cooperation, confidence, and eventual survival was due to the kind of training and faith they had received in their Catholic schools. Bravery, of course, is not limited to any particular religious group, but the kind of cooperation which enabled them to survive, and the confidence they had in God's concern for them did, I think, add an extra dimension to what else was there natively or was the result of their secular adventures and life. Having said this, and combining it with my increasing respect for the quality of the spirit my colleagues in and outside the department show again and again, it still is the case that I haven't the slightest inclination toward their faith. Nor do I have the slightest inclination to practice any other. I feel no call to pray, to hope, to participate in religious ceremonies of any kind.

I have begun anew to read *Gravity's Rainbow* by Thomas Pynchon, in good part because I am challenged by the extraordinary praise that has been bestowed on the book. I have read almost a hundred pages, and find it somewhat disconnected, not particularly insightful or arresting. I will continue for a while and then, if there is no change, give it up as not worth my time.

It is now quite a while since I drew or painted. I feel no urge to do either. I have had no sense that I had something to express. No vagrant images, suggestions, or thoughts about what I might like to do—which in the past have prompted me to spend some time drawing or painting—have come to me for some time. It may be a question of age, of a tiredness which follows on a day of thinking and writing, or (as I think) of my having at last come to the end of my abilities in this field. I do not regret the fact that I do not do any work in this area now, but I can not help wondering what it means, whether or not it is temporary, and whether or not it imports anything for the rest of my activities, particularly those relating to philosophy.

*   *   *

On the present account there are no detached forms, Aristotelian or Platonic. The closest I come to the acknowledgment of such forms is in the view that there is a finality, Possibility. But unlike the Platonic Good, or an Aristotelian active reason, which it most resembles, this is but one among many ultimates, and always has facing it real actualities (without which it could have no instances) which it serves to unify and control, severally and together.

Does this mean that the meaning of actualities depend for their presence on the action of Possibility, and therefore that the pulsation of the actualities between the extremes of meaning and presence does not occur except under the influence of Possibility? That would be most implausible.

Just as actualities are distended apart from the influence of extensions grounded in Existence, so actualities have meaning or intelligibility apart from the rationale they receive from Possibility. Meaning or intelligibility is inseparable from the presence of an actuality and is grasped only via a concept which is transformed so as to become homogeneous with it. The imposition of Possibility's expressions on the actuality bring the intelligibility of the actuality into relationship with the intelligibility of other actualities, apart from any concept or knowing.

The distendedness of an actuality is one with its presence, so that the operation of Existence on the actuality in effect relates the presence (which before was entirely involved in a pulsational activity with respect to the meaning of that actuality) to other presences via a mediating extension. This is but to say that there are other presences in addition to actualities, in the guise of spatial, temporal, and dynamic relations. The presence of an extension, relating the presences of actualities, converts them into presences that are continuations of the presence of the extension.

Does the extension have a meaning analogous to the meanings of the actualities? I think not. A relating extension is not an actuality or a fragment of one. To understand it, we must not analyze it the way we analyze actualities, but must, instead, approach it from the perspective of other finalities, particularly Possibility. The cosmic extension of space, time, and causality, and thus their presence as the field in which actualities cosmically interplay, is a condition expressing Existence; it can, therefore, be understood in the same way that other conditions can, as the intelligible source of limitations, determinations, and connections amongst the actualities and the appearances.

July 2

Unless 'presence' be understood to refer indifferently to the existence, the inwardness, the reality, and the irreducible value of an actuality, a contrasting of it with meaning or essence will unduly narrow the actuality—as in traditional approaches. If, instead, 'presence' be identified with existence, we should go on to say that the pulsation of an actuality occurs among a possessive individual, an intelligible meaning, a primary reality, a distended presence, and an irreducible value. No one of these will be more basic than the others, though for special purposes one will want to attend to one of them rather than the others. For the special purpose of knowledge we push meaning to the fore and contrast this with presence. A similar interest in knowledge would permit a contrast not with presence, where this is identifiable with the distended existence of an actuality, but with the possessive individuality, the singular reality, or the irreducible value of the actuality. But one need not place emphasis on the meaning of an actuality at all, or even attend to it as standing in contrast with what else is emphasized. It is possible to contrast the inwardness of an actuality with its reality, presence, or value; the reality of an actuality with its inwardness, presence, or value; the presence of an actuality with its reality, inwardness, or value; or the value of an actuality with its reality, inwardness, or presence.

When meaning is contrasted with inwardness, reality, or value rather than with presence, the same kind of situation remarked on in connection with the contrast with presence prevails. There is once again an identification of a concept with the meaning of an external actuality, and a continuation of the concept with the knowing individual.

Instead of taking a meaning to be the dimension of the pulsating activity with which one makes contact through the use of a concept, one can take a meaning to be the base. This is to be grasped through the agency of something homogeneous with what contrasts with that meaning. We here invert the previous situation and through action, respect, acknowledgment, or assessment produce the analogue of a concept and thereby have a mediator between a man and an actuality lying beyond him.

When meaning is set aside—whether as something which is to be grasped through the agency of a concept, or which serves as a base for what is grasped through action, respect, acknowledgment, or assessment—individuality, reality, presence, and value can be contrasted with one another. If individuality is what is contrasted with a base in these others, it is mediated by an action. That action will then be something which is directed at what is real, existent, or of unit value.

If the reality of an actuality is contrasted with an individual base, distended or evaluational, it is mediated by an attitude of respect. This reaches the actuality as standing apart with a dignity of its own, in such a way as to enable the respect to become identified with the reality of the actuality.

If the presence of an actuality is contrasted with the other dimensions, it is mediated by an attitude of acknowledgment, the facing of it as something distinct, at a distance, with its own distendedness. The acknowledgment mediates the individual's presence with that of the actuality.

If the value of an actuality is contrasted with the others as a base, it is mediated by an assessment. That assessment has the same role that a concept, an action, an acknowledgment, or respect has. It mediates the value of the individual with the actuality he confronts, and enables the latter to be grasped via the value which the assessment mediates.

These contrasts are here stated as though they occurred in pairs, and as though there were distinct cases where we had a meaning, presence, and so forth, set in sharp contrast with the others. The primary fact, though, seems to be a fivefold dimensionality of the actuality into which it expands, and out of which it is solidified. The nature of the solidified result is to be understood from the perspective of one or the other of the results of the expansion; it is the other dimensions undistinguished and functioning as a base. Could it be understood to be the unity of them all? I think not, without introducing over and above all the dimensions another factor, their unity, and thereby repeating the unity expressed in an assessment and making this primary; making one rest with an unintelligible unity; or taking the unity to be due to a finality and thereby in effect denying the ultimate integrity of the actuality.

There is never a stage in which all the dimensions are entirely separated out from one another, and there never is a stage where they are all so completely solidified that no one of them can be distinguished from the others. An expansion never loses a reference to the base in which the different dimensions are solidified; a solidification is never so complete but that there is an expansion. An expansion is of the solidified; the solidified has itself expanded into distinguishable facets. A pulsation is not between extremes which exclude one another, but between a minimal and maximal occupation of those extremes. Pulsation enriches the one without absolutely impoverishing the other.

Still left over, apparently, is the total complex of expanded and distinguishable dimensions with the base in which they are all solidified. But an actuality itself is never just one complex whole; it is in a perpetual state of expansion and contraction. We have such a total complex as a unit only from the standpoint of something outside it. The complex is the actuality as something acknowledged, and thus the actuality as primarily a presence contrasting with a solidification of the other dimensions.

The various finalities are not actualities, nobler, more refined, united—though each does accommodate them all even while it governs them. The question, nevertheless, remains as to whether or not the kind of dissection just offered with respect to the actualities has a counterpart in connection with the finalities. They are, after all, known, and the knowledge one has of them is not identified with them. How then are they to be analyzed, from the position of that knowledge? How, from the standpoint of an action, respect, acknowledgment, or assessment?

Perhaps the reverse is true, and the actualities as I have described them are truncated limited cases of the finalities? I have spoken of them as being distended, intelligible, and so on. These seem to be features much like those of the finalities. In making reference to the distendedness, and so forth, of actualities, however, I was trying to point up the actualities as they stand apart from all finalities, in a position to be qualified by and to interplay with them. To be distended, real, and so on is to be so subject to the finalities that an actuality is able to master its parts and be in a relationship to other actualities beyond it. It is only after an actuality has been qualified by a finality and has internalized what it can of the qualification, that it matches the finality. It then instances the finality while continuing to remain defiant.

The finalities are radically independent entities which nevertheless affect one another and permit of a grasp of one another from a perspective that reflects the nature of one of the finalities. When use is made of any of the finalities for the sake of dealing adequately with actualities, one engages in something like action toward the finalities; in symbolization there is something like respect accorded them; in evidencing there is an analogue of conceptualization; by approaching the finalities from the position of actualities there is something like an acknowledgment; and when one deals with any from the position of the others, one produces something like an assessment of it. Each one of these has its primary use with respect to one of the finalities. By staying with a primary use, one makes oneself and one's claim most acceptable to a particular finality.

When we come to know a particular actuality, the mediator we provide—concept, action, and so forth—is homogeneous with one dimension of it as contrasting with other dimensions. But when we come to know a finality, we not only do not provide a mediator but offer a beginning which the finality adopts, not as that which is homogeneous with some dimension of itself, but as homogeneous with it in its full concreteness.

An actuality pulsates among the various distinct dimensions of itself; a finality is all of a piece, with any distinguishable aspect being distinguished as merely less intensive than others, or that which has been dealt with from the position of some other finality. Knowledge of a finality is always via Possiblity; knowledge of that finality is one with the having of a claim homogeneous with Possibility itself, and thus accommodated by it. Knowledge, in that pristine sense, can not be had of the other finalities, but they can be reached with the same directness through the agency of symbolization, use, naming, or a standard of value.

A pure, cognitive presentation places primary emphasis on Possibility and what this enables one to know of the other finalities. That knowledge, though, is not altogether separable from a grasp of other finalities in other ways, or from the grasp of an actuality as pulsating between the intelligibility of itself and the other dimensions.

July 3

A distinction between conceptualization and emotion is obviously inadequate to take account of the different ways in which different finalities are to be reached. In *Beyond All Appearances*, I distinguished openness, reverence, humility, interest, and awe. If these distinctions be accepted, awe will be understood to express a deep emotion, elicited by the arts, and reaching to Existence after the experience with an art is over, while interest will involve thought and a minimal emotionality, or at least an emotion which is qualified by thought. Reverence is evidently an attitude which is most appropriate to Unity, particularly when this is understood to be evaluative and all-absorptive. This would leave openness to be associated with Being, and humility with Substance. But it is also said in *Beyond All Appearances* that this openness "goads speculation." That would seem to confine the idea to what can be thought about, unless speculation be deliberately restricted not to thoughts, systematic or otherwise, about the finalties, but to a primary sympathetic contact with that ultimate inwardness which is Substance.

I recur to that classification, not in order to insist upon it or even to build upon it, but to point up the fact that the various finalities are to be approached in different ways, all illustrating a primary appreciation. Instead of referring to the various approaches as special cases of that appreciation—'emotional vectors' I called them—it would be better to take some such terms as 'sympathy', 'submission', and 'susceptibility' to be coordinate with these others, but not entirely independent of them. A similar set of distinctions will have to be made to take account of the richness of an actuality. Its presence, as was already indicated, should be analyzed into a number of other factors, contrasting with one another and with meaning.

It is not surprising that there should be a paucity of terms appropriate to this discussion, for the fivefold nature of actualities and the five finalities, together with the ways in which speculation and the emotional awareness elicited by art supplement one another, have been overlooked in the literature. I, too, as the last weeks' discussion shows, have not always been alert to all the distinctions, leading me to try to deal with some such question as 'the given' as though it presented an issue which was simply set in opposition to conceptualization. Once the distinctions amongst these various dimensions are kept in mind, it becomes more evident that what I have termed 'action' these last days functions coordinately with conceptualization and the acknowledgment of a presence. But for special purposes—such as bringing out the difference between thought or meaning or essence and other dimensions of men and other actualities—it suffices to emphasize one of these dimensions and to set it in opposition to all the others, taken as a single unit, provided only that one continues to recognize that that unit is in fact constituted of four distinct dimensions, interplaying with one another and with the emphasized dimension in independent ways. Once this is done, one can go on to emphasize some other dimension and set it in contrast with all the others, accepted for the moment as constituting a single contrastive element.

Dualism is the outcome of an insistence on contrast, the setting of everything else over against some emphasized factor. It is legitimate just so far as the contrast is of major interest. An Hegelian acknowledgment of a 'third' does not actually take one away from dualistic considerations, but merely to another level where the dualism operates once again. A Peircean acknowledgment of a 'third', however, is set in sharp opposition to a dualism—indeed, this could be said to be a degenerate case of the third, or at any rate to be embraced and made possible by it. But not only does the Peircean view end with 'thirds' and therefore overlooks further equally valid distinctions, but inevitably fails to explore the various kinds of thirds which a fivefold outlook is able to acknowledge.

The acknowledgment of thirds has been taken by both Hegel and Peirce to involve one in the realm of thought or reason, progressively pushing one toward what is ultimately true and real. Not only is there no necessity for this, but there is no necessity that the fivefold distinctions which I am urging in place of it be understood to be anything more than the outcome of a distinguishing of factors which are always present and which need not serve the purpose of the achievement of some absolute truth, dialectic, method, or anything else. Of course, if the distinctions are legitimate and basic, they will have to be taken account of in any enterprise which seeks completeness, and refuses to blur together items that are as independent and as basic as any which need be emphasized for some special purpose.

If one were to distinguish psyche, reason, mind, sensibility, and spirit as diverse expressions of the self, which not only contrasts with but can be combined with the existence of the body, one can take reason to combine with presence so as to yield the distinctive kind of thought which is concerned with Possibility. One can then go on to hold that the psyche and the bodily presence unite to yield the humility appropriate to Substance, that a mind unites with the body's presence to yield the emotion which reaches to Existence, that a sensibility unites with the body's presence to yield an openness appropriate to Being, and that a spirit unites with the body's presence to yield the reverence appropriate to a final evaluative Unity. On such an account the thoughts involved in speculation are either just as much involved with the body as the emotions are, or make use of the body in order to sustain the creative activity of reaching the termini of the evidences of the finalities. The latter seems to be the alternative to take. Each one of the factors which is set in contradistinction with the existence of the body is expressed together with some of the body's existence. Only in the case of the emotions directed at Existence does there seem to be an equal involvement in both dimensions. Speculation involves the least amount of bodily existence, with the others somewhere in between.

Suppose there was a minimization of the body's existence in the awe which is directed at Existence; suppose there was a maximization of the body's existence, parallel to that found in the emotion of awe, in connection with efforts at reaching Being, and so forth? Do not such suppositions answer to the ways in which the finalities appear when we approach them in terms singularly appropriate to only one of them? When we speculate, we are most clearly directed toward Possibility, and come to know the other finalities under the restriction that they are to be grasped as intelligible. The restriction requires that the bodily involvement in the use of reason be greater than that which is required and used when one attends to Possibility. Similarly, when there is an emotional approach to the other finalities, instead of having the body involved to the extent it is when we are attending to Existence, it will be involved in lesser degrees to constitute distinctive ways of being involved with the other finalities.

I have also urged (most recently in "First Considerations") that actualities are reached emotionally. But this, too, should be expanded, and room made for the juncture of a bodily involvement and some other dimension of the self than that of thought. But if this is done, it seems as if there is no difference between the ways we reach actualities and the ways we reach finalities. But there are differences: we get to the finalities via the production of an evidenced claim, and to actualities by starting with a facet of them; the depth of the emotions and other ways of reaching finalities is far greater than that involved in getting to actualities, for they presuppose radical withdrawals into oneself.

Is the difference then only one of degree, of the density or intensity of the emotions? In one sense yes, for the difference is dependent only on the effort made by the knower. In another sense no, for the occupation with actualities is with distinct, limited, finite particulars whereas the finalities are universal, final, and forever. We urge ourselves on actualities, but the finalities take over both ourselves and our claims.

Strictly speaking, there can be no reverence for an actuality but at most respect; no humility before it but only a yielding; no interest but only an acknowledgment of its intelligible presence; no awe but only sympathetic participation; no openness but only a receptivity to what might be present.

Does this not mean that actualities are the finalities, limited, particulate, weaker? No, the very concern for actualities which the various approaches specialize is different from the appreciation which leads to finalities. Whatever the terms used, actualities and finalities are to be understood to be independent, opposed, interactive, reached through different agencies and the exercise of different powers.

July 4

Men are equal in many ways. All are actualities, all must die, all are brought up in communities, all belong to one humankind. And all have rights.

How much of this would be denied by a Nazi? By a sceptic? By a nominalist?

A Nazi would want to deny that Jews and Poles had any rights. Yet no matter how brutally they treated these men they did not treat them as animals; they separated the sexes, respected their fear of death by telling them lies, recognized their role in the economy, and so on.

A sceptic would not, by his methods, be able to locate any rights and might even hesitate to say that all men must die. His scepticism, though, is either gratuitous or logical, or is grounded in something. It is an abstraction or a product. If the former, it merely restates the fact that it is difficult and perhaps even impossible to prove that any of these are necessary; if the latter, the scepticism is the outcome of some kind of reasoning based on accepted data, a reasoning which is presumably being offered for any man to acknowledge. It presupposes a community of thinkers who agree on what it is to be valid and true.

A nominalist has no way of acknowledging a plurality except on the basis of a resemblance and a need to classify. But he, too, thinks he speaks the truth and he uses the ordinary accepted reasoning.

At the most, these various approaches take some men to be possessed of rights, and thus to constitute a single group in which the members all have a status that is denied to others. This does seem to be the view which once prevailed in despotic and slaveholding countries, and in a sense still holds in a caste society. The difference in rights is held by these to be the consequence of a difference in virtue, intelligence, fortune and the like, to be the outcome of legal ordinances, economics, or war, or to be privileges accorded and not demands which should be acknowledged.

If all men are of a kind, and if rights be identified with claims justly made on behalf of essential features, all men can be said to have the same rights. But such rights have at best the status of a measure or a condition for the rights that are publicly viable. These are of two kinds—those that are in fact and those which have yet to be sustained by whatever society or state there be. A transition from privately possessed rights (which answer to demands made on behalf of the essential features) to publicly supported rights can be said to be mediated by a right to be publicly viable. That right can be understood in a number of ways: to belong to a unit coordinate with all the others; to belong to one able to acquire power enough to function as such an equal unit; to belong to one for whom others use their special privileges and opportunities in such a way that the outcome is an equal distribution of goods; to belong to one who is dealt with impersonally in terms of needs and deeds; or to belong to one who has a place amongst all the others in accord with his ability, intelligence, diligence, or accomplishments.

Social contract theories take all men to have the same rights, not only intrinsically but with respect to the outcome of any public agency they make possible. They might set apart some one or more individuals as the instruments by which the rights of others are assured. On such a Hobbesian view, the individuals who are set aside are no longer included within the common frame, but stand apart from it as a condition for the satisfaction of the rights of the others. But the individual or individuals set aside can then be only abstractions, whose human nature is ignored. Were a state a final reality, it might be impossible to get beyond that individual's or those individuals' identification with the power of the state. But a state is a limited institution, and the individuals who function as the state are also to be understood within a larger frame where they are on a footing with others.

What right do all men have with respect to any organization they may institute? Is it the right to be able to function as a unit there? That would still allow them to be given differential treatment. Is it the right to have a power equal to the others, at least in the functioning and in the benefiting from political and economic conditions? This would allow for an unequal distribution, since a number can together operate to the disadvantage of some others; the power, too, could be misused or not exercised. Is it the right to be considered by others as one who is to be brought to and kept on a footing with them, should it be the case that one is underprivileged or has been denied the opportunity from which the others benefited? This makes the right limited, being credited only to the underprivileged; it presupposes another which requires a consideration of the other men. One could conceivably think of all men making this one demand, and then subsequently discovering that some are privileged and others underprivileged. The right would then be that of becoming equal to the others in the public arena. But in what respects—economic, educational, in dignity, before the courts?

Each individual enjoys in private whatever rights he has; they are viable only if translated into a public form. Apart from a state or society, each demands that the equality, individually and privately maintained by virtue of his ultimacy and essential nature, be given a public translation. Each offers himself as the locus of a plurality of distinct rights, and demands, in addition, as his right, that they be given publicly sustained roles.

Each has the same right to demand of a public agent, purporting to encompass him and others, that his native rights achieve a public translation, support, and satisfaction. This single right is a function of the fact that each enters the public arena from a private position. On such a view the state or similar organization is at the service of private individuals, enabling them to be publicly together, possess-

ing the counterpart of their private rights. The demands each makes
on behalf of his essential functions are then turned into demands
against others or the totality in which they are. Such a translation
leaves the individual one who remains thereafter a public being
involved in expressing and satisfying his publicly formulated rights
(or having them acknowledged and satisfied), or who then translates the satisfactions of his publicly expressed and acknowledged
rights into the private satisfactions of the native rights which had
been behind his single right to function as a unit in the state.

It is still not clear just what the single right demands—equal
treatment, equal privileges, equal satisfactions, equal opportunities, or equal results. Does one want merely to have a full unit share
in the state, to be dealt with in the same way as any other, or to have
the state and its subordinate economic and educational systems so
function as to overcome whatever privileges may have come about
by accident, endowment, history, and the like? There is no sense in
appealing to random men for the answer, for few have reflected on
the question. Nor is it enough to ask what fairness or justice or
efficiency or an actual state allows, for what is being sought is
something which answers to the right that men have to obtain a
proper public translation of their native rights.

The social contract theory presupposes that each individual
wants to be treated as a unit by all the others, and that he in fact will
be so treated. If we make those presuppositions, there is no necessity that one then move to a social contract. To want to be treated as
a unit equal with the others is but to want to be a man together with
them. This want could be satisfied by simple social respect, interchange, and acceptance as a locus of truth, individuality, identity,
mentality, and value. No voting or concurrence in opinion will be
required; one will present oneself to the others in the hope that he
will be equal to them in whatever enterprise or situation there be.

Beyond this one might, with Hobbes's men, want protection, or
some way of distributing and using limited resources. The protection needed may differ from person to person; the different individuals, too, may have different needs because of their different
constitutions and situations. If there be a minimal protection and
satisfaction which everyone needs, this could serve as a base line. A
minimal and necessary state could then be said to be one which sees
to it that the minimal protection and satisfaction is guaranteed. This
leaves over a large area where individuals contrast with one another

materially and spiritually in radical ways. It is not enough to enable men just to live or even to live at some ease, if others are able to live a fuller, richer life, or at the very least are able to obtain from the public world what they will be able to internalize as the satisfaction of their privately enjoyed native rights—unless it be the case that those others are in fact superior to and not equal with them.

Instead of providing for the bare minimum for everyone, it would be better to provide for that minimum which permits everyone to benefit from the knowledge, tradition, culture, and discoveries of mankind. Each individual would then be taken to be equal in deserving to be brought to this stage, and that state would be best which in fact did bring them to that stage. Whether the opportunities were utilized and how would be left to the individual. If one were to take this to be the basic demand that each individual makes as he comes into a world, each could be said to be equal to the others in his right to have an opportunity to benefit maximally from the attainments of mankind. This opportunity presupposes that all have been brought to a position where they can take advantage of those attainments. The function of the state then would not be simply to satisfy men's minimum need to live, but to provide them with that status where they are able to take advantage of civilization's achievements. That will require the state to see that they have economic goods, education, health, a proper environment, and freedom of speech and thought.

There will be those who will not be able to be brought to a level where they can benefit from civilization. They will be like the infants, insane, the senile, and mentally defective today. The rest will have to act as guardians for them, and serve as mediators between the goods they in principle ought to have and the goods they have the capacity to make their own.

Looking at men from the outside, and therefore ignoring any native rights they may have which answer to essential divisions of them, each is to be credited with the right to be in a position where he can benefit maximally from civilization. Public agencies, of which a legally functioning state is one, will be so many different devices by which he is brought to that position. What kind of right is this? Is it not the right of an incomparable individual to become a contributing unit in a civilized totality? Is it not in effect the right of an individual to be fully in himself one who has made himself part of civilized mankind?

An individual by himself is incomparable, but not yet a full man. His completeness requires that he epitomize the totality. His right is a mediator between what he is and what he needs in order to be complete. Various agencies are justified just so far as they promote that completion. Some of the agencies, like the state, will have the task of bringing each individual to the stage where he can attend to that completion; others, like the school, will provide the material to be used in the completion. But the completion, in the end, will be due to the individual himself. The agencies are justified so far as they provide opportunities for everyone to reach the same final end. Those opportunities presuppose that the men have had basic needs satisfied and are then enabled to face and realize the final goods they need in order to be completed.

The right each has to benefit from the achievements and prospects of mankind is the distributive meaning of mankind, as the locus of civilized achievements and openings. It belongs to each because each lives within the frame of mankind, which has a richer meaning the more civilization, achieved and prospective, is integrated with it. Instead then seeing the state as an agency for protection, for the promotion of justice, or as the guardian of economic health, one will on this account see it as an agency working both on behalf of civilized mankind and on behalf of individuals. It may allow some privileges to some. It may tightly control the economy, or allow it considerable freedom so that it can approximate the ideal state of a free market. It may extend or limit the vote. The value of these decisions is to be determined by their efficacy in enabling each man to be enriched by his incorporating and thereby epitomizing what is there for all.

July 5

Ideally, work is a means by which one not only produces what is valuable for others, but in the process enhances himself. Such work might be expected of everyone, benefiting each and all. But there is no escaping the fact that there always is some drudgery, some sheer hard labor or monotonous activity required if only in order to get to the position where one can do meaningful work. If there are individuals who, because of circumstance or lack of training or ability, are permanently assigned to such meaningless, 'alienating' work, evidently they will not be given an equal opportunity with others to benefit from a participation in civilization with its inherited goods and benefits, its privileges, rewards, and opportunities.

Either such work should be distributed so that everyone engages in it to the same extent, or compensation should be provided to overbalance the loss involved in a concentration on such activity. The former alternative is not feasible, because even drudgery sometimes requires persistent presence and attention, some degree of training or habit or skill. In a highly developed industrial world there are minor and major jobs to be done, in which the minor no less than the major require some persistent attention. The only alternative appears to be that of compensating those involved in the drudgery for the fact that at that time they are engaged in activities that do not benefit them, do not benefit them as much as other work might, or do not benefit them maximally. The compensation is to be expressed in wages only when this is the best means for obtaining the compensation that ought to be provided. That compensation could be directly given in the form of privileges and opportunities—free health care, free entertainment, free education, free homes—toward which the so-called welfare states of New Zealand and Sweden are now moving. In Hungary there is now an effort made to give workmen's children special consideration when determining who shall be admitted to the university. Libraries, vacations, and adult courses have already been made available to the members of some of our own strong and long-established unions. The unions, like a state, here take over the role of governing, distributing, and providing a kind of compensation for the comparative meaninglessness of daily work. All are to be given equal opportunities as their right; as a consequence, when any are deprived of such an opportunity there should be compensatory opportunities provided at other times. Such an idea is only approximated, and in a negative spirit, by the western world today. Welfare, medicare, child support, workmen's compensation, unemployment insurance, and the graduated income tax are conceived, not as providing compensatory opportunities, but as humanitarian devices to prevent the underprivileged from falling below some acceptable humanitarian standard. Free education for all through college is at best a hope in most countries, and in ours is available in only one or two places.

I think Aristotle is right in thinking that all men seek what they take to be the good, but that some misconstrue this, and others lack the self-discipline to persistently work on its behalf. Others unduly narrow its range so that its realization involves a benefit only to themselves or to some limited few. One need not go as far as Socrates did and hold that evil and ignorance are one, or are linked as effect and cause; one can go further than Aristotle and maintain that virtue and vice are more than habits. In the end one comes to free decisions whose realization must be prevented and whose expressions in public must be used as an occasion for correction and redirection of the individual.

There are some who are not only unwilling to work, but who have set themselves in opposition to the rest, depriving these of possessions, safety, and even life. There are lazy, indolent, selfish, self-centered, malicious, reckless, and inconsiderate men. It is not possible to avoid some kind of agency for punishment and, at the very least, some control over their actions. Punishment can be taken to be a public way both for assessing incorrect behavior and redirecting the individual. It is a radical form of education which involves a freeing or purging from established or wrongly conceived procedures, and the redirecting of the individual along paths where he benefits both himself and others. In some cases, the current way of viewing punishment, as matching improperly achieved gains, has some justification—where money is equated with time lost—but this is evidently not appropriate to acts of violence, particularly those which result from passions, irritation, or insufficient concern for the rights of others. What is needed is not a shift to a concern for the whole society of men, as apparently is the intent of communists as well as fascistic states, but a change in the conceptions and actions of each man so that he benefits himself and others as well.

A concern for a state at best is mediating, giving attention to a power which presumably is to be used in order to enable individuals to be and function at their best. Crimes against the state are never wholly justified because the state is an instrument that must be used to attain the goal men ought to reach. It alone has the power and reach to make possible the provision of opportunities for all. There is, though, some justification in crimes against the state, just so far as it is a poor instrument for attaining the goal and to that degree stands in the way of the achievement of it. The crimes are to be assessed by weighing the degree of need for a political instrument in relation to the efficacy of a particular state to bring men to and sustain them at the goal.

Government officials are instruments working on behalf of an instrument; the fact that they are not engaged in heavy labor, receive kudos, do stand in the doorway permitting some and excluding others from entering into areas where privileges and opportunities are available, should not preclude an understanding of them as only remotely benefiting themselves and others. The power, status, privileges, and opportunities they have should be viewed as compensation in part for the losses they in fact suffer because of their devotion to their particular jobs. It makes no difference, I think, if we here attend to the highest officers of the government rather than to their underlings.

There is no need to look for a principle or ground of evil any more than there is for a principle or ground of good. Nothing is natively geared to bring about the ideal goal of a civilized mankind which is to be epitomized in each. Neither nature itself, nor the history of men, neither the individual body, nor its desires, neither its impulses, nor its responses point to or lead one to the place where all ought to be. Everyone must undergo training, education, adjustment by himself and in relation to others in a world where few have the ultimate objective in mind and where perhaps none know exactly what it now requires.

What men do today is in part conditioned by and partly accumulates what had been done before. Men are historically conditioned; the problems they face today are different from those which had been faced before because they are in part a consequence of those previous problems and the kinds of solutions these had received. Nevertheless, no mere historic approach can be adequate, if only for the obvious reason that an historic view is itself ahistoric, or is caught in a relativism expressing merely a position valid for the present day. The ahistoric factor is that constant generic element which is to be found in the partly accumulated and transformed past which is making a difference to the nature and course of what is present.

*   *   *

I have now completed about a quarter of Pynchon's book. So far it appears to be little more than a series of loosely connected incidents, presented in a slightly offbeat manner, with some humor and amusing turns of phrase. But there is no pressing need to continue, and I am therefore putting it aside.

I am well into S. Bellow's *Herzog*. He stands somewhat between Dickens and Dostoyevsky. His canvas is not as large as either's, but his primary figures are more believable. Like theirs, his are robust and distinctive, with peculiarities which in minor forms are present apparently in everyone. There is a vigor and assertiveness to his Herzog (as was true of Henderson the Rain King) which is not as overlaid with quirks as Dickens's characters are, and not subject to the kind of frenzy that marks so many of Dostoyevsky's.

I have gone fairly far along in my reading of the translation of J. Hyppolite's *The Genesis and Structure of Hegel's "Phenomenology of Spirit."* I am surprised to find that there is so little here which I had not understood before. What are difficult sections in Hegel for me, he too finds difficult. More important, there seems to be no awareness of the multiple turns taken by the dialectic. He rightly says that Hegel's is a magnificent work but does not succeed in showing that it is or why. I think Hyppolite will not help one much if he has not read the *Phenomenology* or if he has read it with care. It is a book which might be used to introduce one to the *Phenomenology,* provided that one was already convinced that it was important.

The *Phenomenology,* I think, is one of the very great works in the history of the world, mainly for the brilliantly original ways in which it faces such questions as the relation of inside to outside, the existent and the ideal, the claims of rationalism versus those of religion, man, and nature, knowledge and the object known. Its primary failure is its inability to grasp the difference between the object known and the object itself, the ways these are related, and how that relation can serve as a paradigm for other oppositions and problems. The Hegelian scholar, of course, will, with Hyppolite, want to know how the *Phenomenology* fits in the larger system, and whether or not it is supposed to restate the course of philosophic or cultural history. I treat it as an independent work, perhaps prefiguring the entire work to follow, using the history as a framework and for illustrations without making it the topic of the work or even allowing it to govern the organization of the whole. Here I think I am one with Hyppolite.

There has been too much emphasis by most commentators, I think, on the chapter on Master and Slave, in part due to the influence of Marx. It is a many-faceted chapter, only part of which is utilized by the Marxists. It impressively shows how consumption is inferior to work in that it fails to put the impress of a man on what is and remains exterior to him. But this is no simple conclusion for Hegel; it is one turn only of the dialectical involvement of men with one another, and with a world, indifferent to life and mind, which is beyond all men.

The fundamental drive and ultimate outcome of the *Phenomenology,* in which self-consciousness self-consciously faces itself as its own other, is appropriate to its beginning, with its endeavor to make what one means identical with what one knows. That Hegelian objective is rooted in Kant. Kant could not acknowledge anything unless it had a categorial ground in mind. But if one necessarily always thrusts beyond what one knows, always means more than one says, and yet can nevertheless always say what one had meant, and can mean even what one now knows, there will always be something beyond knowledge from which knowledge itself can never be entirely separated, and which can always be reached and even known.

July 6

There seems to be a contradiction in saying both that there is no necessity that one produce a state, given the presuppositions that men want to be and are to be publicly equal, and that crimes against the state always lack some justification since the state is a necessary instrument for the achievement of the publicly attainable end for men. It surely is true that men without contradiction can envisage circumstances where they are fulfilled without the aid of the state. There was a time when the state was not. Evidently, then there is no absolute necessity that a state be. Yet once we have a state we have the best known instrument, and indeed the only instrument which seems able to lead to the production of other effective instruments for the attaining of the end. The utopian alternative conceived in the first of these alternatives is logical, able to be set alongside the presuppositions, without engendering a logical contradiction. But the state as it now exists is a realization of the presuppositions, one way in which they have in fact been brought into existence in an historically conditioned world and which therefore can not be just canceled out but must be overcome by that which it makes possible. This would seem to argue against the right of revolution. It does, in the sense of maintaining that revolutions themselves are never fully justified, and that they must, as a consequence, make good the loss of the value that the preceding state had incorporated. On this account, there is nothing like an absolutely corrupt state whose extinction is all gain. The most ruthless despotism produces some cohesiveness, peace, order, continuation. When a despot is as mad as Caligula, the state still preserves some kind of order and solidifies a ruling class, thereby producing a possible protection against the ruler and the populace. It may be necessary to engage in violence to achieve another way of having the state, but the violence has to be justified by the excellence of the replacement. Indirectly, this points up the value of the preceding state as that which is being violated. The state, one might say, always has some minimal rights.

Are there native rights? Are they the same in all men? Does everything have rights? Is there a right intrinsic to a state and every other governance? Are a man's native rights coalesced into a single public right to benefit as an equal unit from public existence? Is the right to be an equal unit benefiting from public existence one which requires for its satisfaction that each man epitomize civilized mankind? How does one prove that a right is a justified claim?

If the term 'property' be disassociated from the notion of 'goods', one could be said to have a right to what is one's property, whether or not one is then in possession of it. If it be the case that each man is necessarily related to mankind as that which completes him, a right can be defined as a necessary reference to a component which is to be incorporated in the individual. Such a statement, though, leaves out of consideration the difference between mankind as such and civilized mankind, and of course deals with rights as apart from any consideration of what the law is or does.

Native rights are not claims necessarily sanctioned or supported by a state, for the double reason that a state is only an instrument and that states are rightly judged to be unjust if they do not support the rights men already have. The reciprocal of a right is not a duty, but rather the right of the ideal to be realized. Each man has both a right and a duty toward the very same ideal, the one being defined in terms of his claim to realize that ideal, the other in terms of its claim to be realized by him. It is therefore best to begin with the right of mankind as directed at each individual, demanding of him that it be realized, and to credit each man with a right to maintain himself in that realization. The right of mankind demands the right of each to be himself so that mankind can be realized in every one.

I have now shifted the question from the justification of the rights of individuals to the right of mankind. What justification does it have? Is it not the justification of a good which is not as good as it can be? And does this not require that mankind be realized, not merely in each individual but in its richest possible form? Mankind makes a claim to a double intensification—to an enrichment by civilization, and to a multiplication and concretion by distinct men. All men are equal from the position of that single generic demand by mankind; their coming out into the open is one with their having a place inside mankind where they are to act on one another and other entities in such a way as to realize that mankind in all. To say this, though, is still not to consider the right of mankind to be enriched through the civilized achievements of men. Must we not divide the rights of mankind into two—a right to be enhanced as an ideal, and a right to be realized in and by every man? I think so.

Mankind stands in between the state and Being (or an Absolute which might be substituted for this). It has a greater reach and a longer history than a state, since the state not only deals with only some men, but comes on the scene late in time. Mankind also has a smaller reach than Being, for this applies to other actualities as well. Like these others, mankind has some power, but it has less than either. As that which is to be realized by and in every man, it is already a part of each, functioning there as a semidetached universal. This is its role as a species, and is so far like the species of other living beings. Each species is made up of distinct units which are subject to and incorporates it, without exhausting it.

One difference between men and all other kinds consists in the fact that this role does not exhaust the species of man, as it does for other species. Mankind always awaits enhancement as well as realization in a plurality of individuals, each of which specifies it in a distinctive way. In the case of the subhuman the unrealized portion of the species is but the possibility of other distinctive specifications; in the case of man it is also the locus of the achievements and prospects, and thus of an intensification which is acquired over the course of time. The subhuman does nothing to make the species character have a greater import or content or intensity than it had before, but men are faced with the right of the species character to be so enhanced.

The realization of a species character by subhumans leaves over a general, common trait, because the specification of that character merely fills it out. In the case of man, the specification is held away, set in opposition to the character, thereby giving this the status of an opposite. An animal becomes just an animal, leaving over nothing else which it ought to be; but a man in becoming a man leaves over the status of a man which he still is to realize. That which he is to realize is man as an excellence, man, not merely as that which is pluralized and localized, but which is to be realized in each case in its full universality. Such realization requires the taking into oneself the meaning of the universal in its universality. This is an achievement beyond the reach of any ordinary man, a fact underlined in the view that Christ alone is a true man, full man, man in its perfect universality at the same time that he is an individual. For ordinary men, the universal has to be made more specific, detailed, and that is what the achievements of civilization do to it.

The realization of man to the full in every individual awaits the realization of man in the guise of a multiplicity of biological units, which then are faced with the task of realizing the universal man that they have set in opposition to themselves. That realization is possible only so far as the opposed universal man is filled out with specific achievements in which the individuals can share and thereby realize the universal man in each of them. The species man has the right to be enhanced as an ideal civilized mankind because only in this way can it be realized by men. Its primary right to be realized requires the transformation of it into a civilized mankind, which alone is within the power of men to realize.

A man in himself faces a common species character, has localized it, has it as an opposite to himself in the guise of a common universal man, and faces it as a common civilized mankind. So far he is like every other man. But, strictly speaking, he can not yet be said to be equal with or like every other, for equality and likeness presuppose the use of a common measure. In himself each merely points to something from an incomparable private position.

We rightly speak of the equality of men only when we approach them from a common position with respect to which they then function as mere units. We can then read back into each in his privacy the equality each had as a mere unit under the aegis of a common character, each needing the common character and so far having a right to it as that which is required for completion. Each is obligated to realize the common character as that which had been set in opposition to it—a realization which requires a filling out of the character so as to make it capable of being shared in and thereby adopted by any man.

There are native rights because there are native intrinsic claims directed at the common character which is needed for completion. The rights can be said to be the same for all men only if the men are approached from a common position, and what they then are as public units is read back into them as private. Every entity can be said to have rights because every one is necessarily related to something common, but only some actualities have those rights internally possessed, and only men have them in relation to civilized mankind. Every state and governing control has a right just so far as its very presence is inseparable from what can diversify it and thereby enable it to be effectively operative in each.

The right to benefit from public existence is the right of a unit defined by the common nature of public existence. Each individual can be said to have such a right intrinsically only so far as one reads into him the power of internally sustaining it. Each needs to have his right as a public unit to be realized together with his fulfillment of his obligation to a common enriched human nature, for the two are part of one reality, tensed and oppositional with respect to one another, and so far making claims on one another.

A justification of a claim is given by showing that what in fact is not possessed is nevertheless possessed in meaning and nature. One rightly claims what belongs to one, and what belongs to one is what is essential to integrity, completeness, and self-identity. It is just as true that mankind makes a claim on individuals to realize it in diverse ways, as that they make a claim on it to become integral to them as units, and as realities which internally sustain those units.

*　　*　　*

I have now completed my eighth revision of "First Considerations." I am very much disappointed in it. I had wanted it to lay out most clearly and with well-demarcated arguments all of the essential points in the views I have been developing over the years. But too much is taken up with distinctions and definitions, and too few places are supported by argument. It is now presumably being read by a number of philosophers, and they will undoubtedly enable me to focus on the major unclarities and incoherencies. But the whole I think must be rewritten from top to bottom. Have I been in too much of a hurry to get this work out of my way?

I am somewhat astonished to think that I have written over twenty books. I never intended to be so prolific. I work over and over manuscripts; no one demands that I publish. I work on a vein in order to become clearer, to carry through some inquiry, and find that I do this best when I write and rewrite. After a time, it seems to me that I can make no further progress and the whole seems as if it might be of some interest to others.

I am not being contributive to current philosophizing. I am not altogether sure just why. Is what I am saying not viable, or not fashionable, or have I failed to make connection with the primary, or better, the indispensable ways in which men today are approaching basic issues?

A philosopher must keep himself free even of philosophic fashions, but if he writes and publishes he should also do so in such a way as to make contact with others. Those others need not be those who are now receiving most attention, but it surely should be those who are seriously interested in fundamental philosophic issues. Since I am dealing with such issues, the view that what I am saying is not really contributive must mean that there is a truth in what is now going on with which I have failed to mesh. If so, perhaps the comments of others will enable me to discover it. In the meantime, without striving to be original or different but merely to follow the logos wherever it may lead, I struggle with what seem to be central questions. I think *Beyond All Appearances* profited from a comparatively long incubation. I think I will try to have "First Considerations" given the same amount of time to become strong and evident. As a first step, I am having it retyped, for I find that a clean copy enables me to see more readily the areas that deserve to be attended to more.

July 7

In *Beyond All Appearances* it was said that the rights men have are due to the internalization of the qualifications to which Being subjects them. But the rights I have now been speaking of concern man in relation to humankind, enriched by civilization. The latter seems to be the equivalent of the former; mankind enriched conveys the import of Being, the limited range of man-

kind being compensated for by the intensification which civilization provides.

Because of Being, every actuality has the right to be self-
complete, to be itself as together with all the others under Being,
but actualities below men are unable to make that right into an
integral part of their substance or of any other dimension. Being is
never internalized by any of those actualities, and a qualification
produced by it is within the compass only of a man's internalization.

Mankind is inseparable from each man. Being has a status of its
own, but mankind is only so far as there are men, each of whom has
it as a distinguishable but inseparable universal. As a consequence,
each is able to concern himself with its further realization, a realization which needs the mediation of the very civilization which makes
that mankind have the same import that Being had for him.

Men are distinct, not only from Being, but from Substance,
Possibility, Existence, and Unity. Do these have rights? Are there
surrogates for them, as mankind is for Being? Are they enriched by
some intensification which also serves as an agency for sharing in
such surrogates, just as civilization is an agency for sharing in, at the
same time that it intensifies and enriches mankind?

To speak of rights is to speak from the position of Being or of
what is affected by Being. It is therefore correct to say that men
have other rights than those which are directly due to Being. The
other finalities, should they have more particularized forms, as
Being has in mankind, would also have rights to be realized. But it is
also true that one can envisage Being and what substitutes for this
from the position of the other finalities; indeed, whatever conditions are traceable to any one finality are not only directly manifested but are mediated by the other finalities.

The kind of relation which an individual man has to mankind,
viewed as a species character, he also has toward the community,
taken as a locus of immediate relations involving sympathy and
requiring cooperation; toward language, taken as the locus of the
meanings he is able to use by adhering to the established rules and
using the established vocabulary; toward work, taken as the outcome of the expression of the individual within a single relevant
nature; and toward value, as the locus not only of the measures in
terms of which items are ordered, but of their distinctive values
viewed as forming a single whole. These various terms, however,
are not on a footing with mankind, but only with mankind as

enriched in special ways. That fact requires one not only to take mankind to be a generic notion which is inseparable from these others, but to view 'civilization' in contradistinction from them. If civilization be viewed as the intensification of mankind, serving with it to produce a surrogate of Being, it should be understood to include, not these others, but only the knowledge, art works, ideals, traditionalized cohesion, and achieved mutual acceptance of men. This allows us to go on to speak of mankind as having other dimensions, such as community, language, work, and value. But one can also take civilization, like mankind, to be highly generic, and to have specifications which enable one to provide adequate surrogates for other finalities by having those specifications introduced into the generic mankind. Perhaps the problem is verbal only.

What is needed is a recognition of all men being subject to a universal from which they are inseparable but which has to be intensified if that universal is to function as a surrogate for a finality. Since there are five finalities, there would have to be five distinct modes of intensification. The relations which the individual has to the various forms of the intensified mankind will, properly speaking, not be simply subsumable under 'rights'—or, if this term be employed, it will have to be understood in a generic sense, leaving over the need to distinguish special forms relating to different intensified forms of mankind. One might speak of the right to equality as being coordinate with rights to dignity, consideration, functioning, and status; or, alternatively, one might take rights to mean equality, and see men, as in relation to the other types of intensification of mankind, to have interests, liberties, entitlements, and dignities, all viewed as types of claims which are satisfied by their participating in the intensified mankind in different ways and degrees, and thereby enabled to make an enriched mankind an integral part of themselves.

Least confusion is perhaps achieved by starting with the idea of a generic mankind to which an individual is related by a generic claim-demand (the claim expressing him as insisting on himself against the other, the demand expressing mankind as insisting on itself against him). The intensification of that mankind will have a fivefold form, involving a fivefold division in the claim-demand.

Why should there be a mankind? Why are there species? What kind of connection is there between the individual and the species—is it necessary or contingent? Are "this-cat, Mabel, is a cat" and "I am a man" necessary truths?

Most logicians would say that it is a necessary truth that "this-cat is a cat," because they take 'a cat' to be an abstraction, an aspect of 'this-cat'. Even if they were right, the abstraction is distinct from the concrete individual. The relation is not a simple identity or implication; at the very least it is an identification across a difference, a uniting of disparates so that they become one.

"I am a man" or "I am a member of mankind" is a much more difficult expression to analyze. 'I' normally refers to the individual by himself, and most accurately to one incomparably private, and self-centered, but 'a man' is a universal, applicable just so far as an individual is a locus of a universal and perhaps even localized within the range of that universal. Since we also say "he is a man" and "you are a man" and intend no less than what we intend when we say "I am a man," it is plausible to suppose that the 'I' does not refer to the individual in his privacy but to him as a unit who is related to others, though there seems to be no commonly accepted way of expressing this. Since we cannot entirely free 'I' from its reference to a private individual, in this particular case it must be allowed to be doing double service, referring to a related unit which is being sustained privately.

Why should it not be the case that I and every other entity, living or non-living, are actualities together with others, and that all other subdivisions are just arbitrary cuts made for certain purposes? Or if it be claimed that mankind is a necessary subdivision of the realm of actuality, might it not also be maintained that 'black' and 'male' and 'intelligent' also are? Is the primary set of subdivisions man, higher and lower animals, vegetative living beings, and things? Why should this be, if in fact it is the case?

The obvious answer is that the primary divisions are the outcome of biological study which takes account of the genesis, interbreeding, blood, articulation, and structures of entities, and even explains their diversity as the outcome of the induration of what was accidently achieved. But such a study abstracts from substantial individuals, to deal with them as instancing the common species. Each individual is more than this; at the very least, he stands in opposition to the species and gives it details and lodgment.

If the only genuine members of the cosmos are the irreducible particles of a cosmologic physics, then complexes of these, organic and inorganic, will have to be dismissed as mere constructions by us, taken to be dependent for their presence on the operation of some such limited universal as a species. On this view each species will be inseparable from a particular individualized type of organization. The organization will be distinctive in each individual case, as set in opposition to the species, and yet common to all, as that which is involved with the species. There will be species common characters, because organizations of parts will have substantial grounds, and so far are made to function as complex units. Species characters are necessary because they are the unavoidable correlates of the integrity of a unit organization. The relation of the two is one of identification across difference, pursued both from the side of the species and of the unit. In the case of humans, the species character 'man' has a thickness to it which is beyond the capacity of a mere life to exhibit; the character must therefore be mediated by intensifications—civilization, community, language, and so forth—which also enrich that species character.

The relation between a unit and a species character is a necessary one; it is also dynamic, and varies consequently from the state where the necessarily related terms are distinct from one another to the state where they are intimately involved with one another. Subhumans are intimately involved with their species characters; but men, at the same time that they are so involved, also have that character remote from themselves and must therefore mediate and thereby enrich it to make it equivalent with the finalities which those men internally instantiate.

'Black', 'female', and the like can not replace mankind in the way this can replace the finalities, unless they can be so intensified that they thereby become equivalent with an enriched mankind and therefore with the finalities. Only if there is some way of becoming a complex unit which is to be identified with 'black', and so forth, that has been so enriched that it is substitutable for civilized mankind, will it make sense to take these limited universals to mark off distinct groups within which the units can be fulfilled. This can be thought of as a challenge; to take some subdivision of man as a proper ideal counterpart of oneself, and therefore to be that in terms of which one is to have rights, identity, and so on. Success requires one to enrich the subdivision so that it is the equivalent of a fivefold civilized mankind, and of all the finalities themselves.

Limited groups—family, society, teams—differ from 'black',

'Jew' in that they are structured, intensified, with historic accumulations, and contrast with what are local units rather than just instances. They can, though, be taken to be the outcome of intensifications of regions, or even of such limited universals as 'black', and so forth. 'Black', and each of the others, refers both to the individual and an unstructured universal. A society can be taken to provide a structure, intensification, and mediation for the universal. If the result is a limited whole which is intensified by its encompassing the vital interplay of individuals (as is the case with the family and the tribe), this could with some justice be said to be the equivalent of the more impersonal, longer ranging civilization which enriches mankind.

Does it make sense to speak of a family or a tribe as the equivalent of a civilized mankind? Is an individual, taken primarily to be a black, an Indian, or a female, when integrated with its tribal or similarly limited universal, as fulfilled, as completed as one who is the guise of a human is integrated with civilized mankind? Are these outcomes competing alternatives, each as valuable as the other? If they were, we would have to say that a man can be as perfected by being a member of a family or a tribe as he can be by being part of civilized mankind. Perfected in the one guise he will function not as a unit man but as a unit member; perfected in the other guise he will function as a unit man but not as a unit member. Or is it not the case that each of these alternatives lacks something the other provides, and as a consequence we all, more or less consciously, want and need to be members of a family, share in a society, be part of a language group, be directed at an ideal, and function as participants in a civilized mankind? If so, we must sacrifice a complete immersion in one of them for the sake of getting some of the goods possible only in the others. The solution to the problem of living in the best possible way will lie then in a decision as to just when one must give up being primarily involved in one of these and instead become primarily involved with the others, each for a time.

In these various cases what is lost in range on the part of the universal has to be made up in intensity. Can the idea be extended to cover the realm of economics and the individual men occupied with having a place in it? To cover politics, inquiry, art, and religion? Is each of these a delimited intensified equivalent to a finality but never entirely satisfactory, requiring one to turn from it to others which are equivalent to other finalities? Must an individual find his own way of having all five alternatives by trying to bring together as much as he can from all of them? For the moment, it seems to me that these questions can be answered in the affirmative. As a result, there can be any number of distinct lives which are of equal value. One man might be occupied with civilized mankind for a while and then with a life of inquiry within a small scientific community; another might be occupied with a life within a family for a time and then with one involved with economics. These need not be taken to occur in sequence; they can be interspersed. Also, a man need not remain with only one equivalent of a particular finality; he might give up participation in one of these for a participation in another. The same finality's significance may be recaptured now in this context and then in that. Of course, if the various universals deserve to be enriched and concretized, justice will not be done to them when attention is directed elsewhere. A man's fulfillment will still leave a multitude of universals unfulfilled, and he will therefore be criticizable as one who has failed to do all that he ought. There is some justice in the criticism made by the socially or politically minded of an artist's social and political detachment, and some justice in the artist's criticism of them. It is right to criticize one who fails to devote himself to either, with all his spirit and attention.

'Enrichment' and 'intensity' are terms not here analyzed. Why should, how could, an increase in intensity make up for a loss in range? How does one measure a difference in extension by recourse to an intensity? The problem looks insoluble only when it is forgotten that a range is single, possessed as a unit, and in this sense is itself an intensity. Enriching it, giving it more intensity is one with making it more specific, with distinguishable areas.

July 8

The various universals which men embody in intensified forms are we's, each with its rights, and each impersonal. As intensified, each is the locus of residual you's, you's that have expressed themselves in acts and works. The realization of those we's enables one to become one of those residual you's at the same time that these are all epitomized by and in a vital I.

Is war an intensified universal? Does it, too, have a right to be realized? It is a universal, but not one that is to be realized, since its realization involves its division into separated parts, opposed to one another. Each part could be said to be a realizable universal with rights, involving as it does a unification of men. War as so divided exhibits in an acute form the defects of all limited universals; one can not remain with their realization without standing opposed to other realizations of other universals. Where a family or science may keep men away from the realization of art or philosophy, in war they are not only kept away from an alternative realization of a similar universal but so act to preclude its adequate satisfaction. Paradoxically, the realization of the universal 'war' in one group usually promotes the realization of a similar universal in another, but in such a way that the other values achieved through other realizations of other compatible universals are jeopardized and perhaps destroyed.

The necessary link between the individual and the universal which both need to have shortened so that each side is integral to the other and thereby with it makes a single complexity in which each component is at rest in the other, is also the locus of freedom. Freedom in each individual and for the universal is the activity of bringing what is claimed and needed within the compass of the claimant. For the individual it is a freedom directed, not at other actualities or for the bringing about of something in the world, but for the carrying out of his duty to realize and satisfy the universal. The outcome is an enrichment of him, with a consequent capacity to act with respect to other actualities.

Over the course of intellectual history, men have fastened on different universals and have urged their claims to the exclusion of others. They were wrong to insist on those exclusions, but they were justified in urging the claims of their chosen universals. Those who have defended science, religion, language, politics as deserving realization in men, have not always been aware of the necessity and freedom which their views involve, but they have made evident how the realization of their chosen universals completes the individuals who realize them, and bring them together within the orbit of those universals functioning as regions for all. When and as each freely gives concreteness to the common universal, that universal remains over as the region within which they are all together.

The polemics of philosophers exhibit the virtues and vices of war. Each side seeks to realize its appropriate universal made most intensive, but each does it in such a way as to demand that others give up desirable goods—such as the status of being a respected or right-minded philosopher, clear and not confused, fruitful and not barren. Fortunately, philosophy is not the possession of any individual or group, and the demand that others be taken to be incompetent because they are excluded by some particular realized universal can be safely ignored. The realization of some particular limited universal, when it has been so enriched that it is the equivalent of every other, still leaves over the rights of the others to be realized as well.

A philosopher has only one recourse: he should intellectually realize the most inclusive of universals and do what he can to realize intellectually as many as possible of the more limited universals. The most satisfactory philosophic system is one in which the more limited universals have a place. If an individual philosopher can not himself give realization to those universals, he still has to make allowance for them. A metaphysical system is to be counterpoised by specialized studies, each of which has an intensified universal whose import is the equivalent of the metaphysical.

There is always an historic dimension to philosophic systems, reflecting the intensifications which other you's introduced into the universal that is being realized. The you's provide the most comprehensive of universals with content which enables the universal to function as the equivalent of all the finalities; the you's also enable the individual to get a purchase on that universal. Instead, though, of taking account of the you's which are exhibited in the form of intensifications of a comprehensive universal and are without vitality, one can begin with the vital intensifications they are now producing within some such limited universal—for example, present common experience or discourse—and use it to enrich the comprehensive universal. One then makes use of a systematic philosophic category not merely as that which is reached from the position of available evidence or by abstraction, but by turning it into a proper name of what is ultimately real. The realization of that category will, on the side of the individual philosopher, involve his identification with that name and thus enable him to be in a position to symbolize the object of that name.

Epitomizing requires the carrying out of a role as implicated with other roles within a common domain. A model for this is an actor. The part he is portraying is properly carried out only if it is also envisaged from the position of the other parts. He is not merely an architect but a brother to that sister and to that brother, a son to that mother and father, and so on.

Instead of epitomizing some limited universal, a man can instead treat it as providing him with a position where he can epitomize a set of limited universals all contained within some more inclusive domain. In place of an epitomizing of governmental activity in his assumption of some bureaucratic role, he can realize the meaning of government as implicated with the education, religion, economy, and so forth, of the country. If he does this, he will have no need to give up his involvement in a limited area in order to do justice to other limited areas, but will instead, as in that limited area, bring in the import of the other areas.

Mechanical work is detached work, unit work which is not dealt with in its bearing on other kinds of work or other goods. It is unrealistic to say to one who is spending his working hours adjusting right front fenders that he should envisage this in its relationship to the production of cars or the promotion of transportation. But the work can be organically related to other activities within the domain of a union, a social organization, a team effort, and thus as the occasion for an epitomizing of a larger universal than that directly involved in the particular work that is engaged in.

Intensification enables a universal to function not merely as that which is common, but as a domain in which an individual can find a place and from there epitomize the whole. Without the intensifications, the universal would be only what was pertinent to each without having any other status than that of being able to be pertinent to still other entities. Its range would depend on the particular items over which it could stretch. Intensifications turn it into an area in which one can function and thereby act as an individual at the same time that he is benefiting from the whole.

Might it not be possible for an individual to epitomize some limited intensifed universal at the same time that he epitomizes a larger within which the other functions as a part implicated with the rest? Might one not only be a scientist who sees his particular work as interlocked with the work of other scientists and therefore is able to epitomize the realm of science in carrying out his limited tasks, but also is able to take the whole of science as itself epitomizing the realm of truth? A scientist can, I think, imagine doing both, but he can not live through both at the same time. Living will require the expenditure of his freedom within the area of the necessity of one or the other enriched universal.

To epitomize, one adopts an undifferentiated universal and enriches it with other universals. If a man accepts as a universal what is to be enriched, he cannot then also accept it as that which is being realized through the epitomized use of some particularized localized portion of it. To epitomize, one must get an undifferentiated universal and enrich it by others; the outcome is a single self-enclosed union of the epitomized differentiated universal with the individual. If this is correct, one has a choice of epitomizing an enriched mankind by identifying himself with some limited role there, or of taking such a limited role to be a domain within which an epitomizing position can be assumed. A man might function as an artist within mankind, or as a poet among other artists. As the first he will understand other activities and achievements as sustaining and being sustained by art; as the second he will understand poetry as sustained and sustaining other types of art. But must he not be a poet or a sculptor or some other particular kind of artist if he takes the first alternative? If so, how can he differ from one who takes the second? Will not his concern in the first be not so much with the production of great works but with the exemplification of the kind of devotion and attention to ideals that mark the artist? If so, how could he have such traits except by being a poet devoted to his poetry?

There is a difference in the two cases, expressed in the content which is being epitomized. To epitomize mankind is to contrast and relate the virtues and achievements of various types of endeavor, with one of them at the center; to epitomize some limited universal, such as poetry, is to contrast and relate special ways of exemplifying a particular type of virtue and achievement. The latter ignores the former. A poet who is a spokesman for poetry has taken the former alternative; a poet who is working at his poetry, the second. Each objective can be realized maximally only if it is made the object of full devotion. Yet each deserves realization. A man can choose either as having as much value as the other, but his choice will involve his neglect of values which deserve realization, and any attempt to pass back and forth between the alternatives will end with neither being realized to the full. Only one who is concerned with the realization of the largest ranging universal will be in a position to appreciate the rights and values of forms of life other than that with which he has identified himself.

A man may, of course, gladly grant that there are other and perhaps even equally valuable forms of life besides that with which he has identified himself. Such tolerance falls far short of what is needed in an epitomizing, for this, as has been remarked, does not simply leave a place for other forms of life, but vitally involves those other forms with an accepted form so as to enable the latter to become the locus of an epitomizing of the universal which encompasses all them.

The only kinds of universals which are involved in these considerations are those that constitute domains where individuals which epitomize them are able to be together. Unless those universals are given a fivefold intensification, we will have to acknowledge clusters of five universals all of which have the same range but are intensified differently. There will be as many clusters as there are different ranges for universals. At one limit will be all-inclusive fivefold clusters, and at the other there will be many fivefold clusters of universals, each of which is a domain for only two men but which can be intensified and epitomized to yield the intensifications and epitomizings equivalent to the largest ranging universals. All the universals will make demands and all will be met by the claims of individuals.

*   *   *

I have made two changes in my habits of writing. The first, made some years ago, was the abandonment of the practice of writing triple spaced (so as to make the pages self-deceptively pass more rapidly). The second was made these last weeks. I now sit down to write immediately after breakfast before I go on my six-to-eight-mile walk. I type some 700 to 1,000 words (for the time being in this work), and then carry on the thought while I work. I find that I am able to think with some freshness before the walk and am able, while I am walking, to see the implications of what I had written. It would be interesting to see if a difference can be detected between what I have set down before and after the daily walk. I have not marked off the places where I stop and where I begin again (usually after lunch); if there is a difference of any significant degree, that place should be evident. The matter, of course, is of little import except for one who might be interested in noting the difference a change in physical condition and state of rest makes in the pursuit of some such creative enterprise as this.

July 9

The smallest ranging universal which can function as a domain and be epitomized in an intensive form is a pair—partners, a couple married in accord with ritual or law, or a worker and his assistant. Since there are many different individuals who can form such pairs, there is a multiplicity of possibly equivalent realizations of universals having the same range and type of intensification. Each, of course, will be intensified differently because of its different history, and will be epitomized differently because of the differences in the epitomizing individuals, but these will be differences in tonality and not in comparable worth.

The acceptance of one of these pairs as the domain in which to try to achieve maximum fulfillment is a challenge which is fully met only if the result is equal to the value of a mankind enriched by civilization. Only then can one justly speak of a world justly lost for love, and the like. It is doubtful that the challenge can be fully met. The enriched universal 'mankind' is not only always present and for all, but serves as the measure of the success of the more limited universals in which extra effort must be made to make up for their limited range. But men cannot carry themselves for long at such a high pitch, though there may be a few moments in which they are able to match the value that is enjoyed in a participation in the goods of civilized mankind.

In a somewhat similar way, a limited philosophic position is measured by a comprehensive system. The acceptance of this measure, and even the perfect realization of it, does not eliminate the legitimate demands of other universals, any more than the use and satisfaction of the demands of a civilized mankind eliminates the demands of other goals. A universal does not deserve less effort at realization merely because its range is more limited than others. When most fully a part of civilized mankind, when most surely in possession of a comprehensive philosophic system, a man fails to do much that ought to be done, for he necessarily neglects to satisfy the demands of other more limited universals.

In *The Making of Men,* I claimed that production, service, and the like did not provide as complete a life as a man can and ought to have. That view is being questioned here. I am now maintaining the opposite, and contending that not only such lives, but a host of others as well, are capable of being as complete, since they can make up in intensification what they lose in range. But if this is so, no one, living as a full functioning member of the widest ranging universal, could have as intensive a life as one who kept himself within the confines of some more limited universal, such as a marriage or a partnership. Yet there seem to be men who exhibit great passion and devotion to some large-scaled cause, who give themselves entirely to a life of religion, culture, the cause of peace, and the like. What they have to epitomize is so vast and intricate, however, that they succeed only in achieving a position from which such epitomizing might be achieved. It is difficult enough to do justice to the role of another in relation to one's own without attempting to do justice to a multiplicity.

One might with considerable warrant maintain, therefore, that all men should exhibit the same degree of passion though not necessarily in the same ways, when they attempt to realize the universal within whose limits they endeavor to live at the same time that they incorporate it as part of themselves. The effort that is needed just to make possible the attainment of an epitomizing position by one concerned with the largest ranging universal seems to be about what is needed in order to epitomize a much more limited universal. The satisfaction of the demands of civilized mankind needs concurrent actions on the part of all men, whereas the satisfaction of the demands of a limited universal can perhaps be satisfied by one alone and surely completely satisfied by the epitomizing activities of a few. An individual engages in the act of satisfying a universal by himself, even when this requires the support of other concurrent acting individuals. But the satisfaction that he can provide for a limited universal with its limited number of interlocking roles takes into account the import of other roles to a greater degree than is possible for one involved with larger ranging universals.

Nothing has been said so far about the difference between one who vigorously makes himself a part of an intensified universal, so as to benefit from what it then is, no matter what the range, and one who makes himself a part of that universal as a domain to which he will contribute. The former is a precondition for the latter. One enters into a domain that has been established and meets its demands by epitomizing it at the same time that he accepts it as a domain in which he will interact with others.

There seems to be no limit to the intensifications that can be introduced by new specifications and which are appropriate to the individual claims others present—and others still to come—may make. Does this mean that one who devoted himself to a cultivated life, a life in which he enjoyed the available past achievements, would be inferior to one who contributed to such a life? Is every cultivated man inferior to every artist? It does not seem plausible to say so. We might credit the artist with a greater dignity or value; we might esteem him more; but we can not rightly say that his life is richer or more complete than the other's.

So far as richness of life is concerned, it is more within the grasp of one who enjoys the fruits of civilization than of one who is concerned with contributing to it. But this is true only up to a point. Each individual needs to benefit from the achievements of the past and each needs to build on this in order to make himself as completely fulfilled as it is possible for him within the domain of the universal whose demands he would satisfy. The point at which he should give up enjoyment for contribution each must decide for himself, and determine it in terms of his abilities.

Suppose there is someone who has minimal creative abilities and another who is overflowing with them. Does it make sense to demand of the one that he eventually give up his full enjoyment of a cultivated life and make some contribution, and of the other that he restrain his creative urge and devote himself for a while to intensive enjoyment? I think not. But that does not mean that they will then have lives as rich as those who are able to have both careers at high pitch.

A great creative man deserves to be honored, but this does not mean that he is living as full a life as a man can and ought. We ask him to cut short his creative career only by leaving him with even less than he otherwise would attain. In compensation for a failure to live as richly as others do, who are, nevertheless, less creative but more able to enjoy what had been achieved, a creative man, through his accomplishments, becomes an integral part of the intensified universal which others will realize. He is fulfilled not in himself but in and through them and then, of course, not as a living individual, but as one of whom account is taken by others. He is fulfilled via the epitomized roles which are carried out by others, somewhat as a man continues to be part of his family and community when he is honored and remembered after death.

It is not necessarily the case nor even always the case that the shorter the range of a universal the less nuanced, the less diversified into multiple roles it is. But the relation seems to hold for the most part. It is easier, therefore, for most men to epitomize some limited ranging universal than one of unlimited sweep. They are able to give more of themselves to the limited role they have accepted, and thereby find a greater completion, satisfaction, and meeting of obligations there than they could otherwise. The fact, though, that others may be calm, rational, deliberate in the ways in which they occupy their positions within a universal functioning as a domain, does not mean that they are without passion in the sense here understood; the passion is expressed in their commitment, that is, in their tenacious continuing in that role in the face of temptations and obstacles.

The *Gita* is surely wrong in equating the life of a warrior with the life of the contemplative, unless by the former is meant not the warrior in opposition to others, but a focal point in the solidification of his own community. In any case, one should add to these alternatives a host of others, which is in fact what has been done by some Indian thinkers. Is this not a way though to encourage complacency, and at least the acceptance of the 'station' in which one happens to be born? Unless one could show that the 'station' is merely the outcome of the moral status one had achieved in some previous life and, as a consequence, the only position which one could in fact occupy, one must reject the castelike view which tells everyone to be content with his lot.

Though every type of life could be taken to be the equivalent of every other, when the universal is properly epitomized, it still is the case that for some men one universal is more congenial than others. A caste view denies to men the opportunity to carry out lives which in fact they might be able to carry out more successfully than those which had been assigned to them through birth. Every man should have the liberty of deciding which universal he will obligate himself toward and thereby fulfill himself, and where and when he will shift from an enjoyment of its achievements to making a contribution to it himself. The more he creates the more he is to be taken account of by others when they epitomize their common universal.

The glory of self-sacrifice is in its making one a vital factor in the lives of others; its defect is that it precludes a justifiably equal satisfaction on one's own part. A life of pleasure is not necessarily inferior to one devoted to the welfare of others; what the sybarite lacks in richness because of his failure to become a vital factor in the lives of others is matched by the humanitarian's failure to complete himself as much as possible by benefiting from the very universal which is being made to benefit others—the matching, of course, being possible only so far as they are occupied with the same universal.

We have, then, a multiplicity of universals of differing degrees of complexity which are to be epitomized in men, at the same time that they function as domains to be enriched in subsequent acts. The individual must not only make a choice of the universal he will be involved with, and for how long, but must decide when he is to change from a participant into a contributor to its richness. The ideal, not possible of attainment, would be to realize all universals and then in such a way that one both benefited from and benefited them maximally.

Left out of this account is the relation of the individuals to one another under the aegis of their common universal. Each man has the obligation to preserve and possibly enhance the values of others. Since those values are in the end the outcome of the ways in which the individuals epitomize a universal to which they also make contributions, the task of each with respect to the others is that of enabling them to share in and contribute to the same universal. This means that each must make himself available to them in a double way—as one who makes for their maximum embodiment of the epitomized universal, and who helps them contribute to its richness as well. One can be said to be still working on behalf of the universal, since what one is doing on behalf of other individuals enables the universal to be embodied in them in the richest possible way. This is also to say that to act so with respect to others enables those others to be fulfilled in themselves, for the full satisfaction of the universal in them is inseparable from the full satisfaction of each at the same time.

Offhand I can think of two modern men who seem to have made the right decisions for themselves as to the universals they should realize, and who have made good decisions as to just how much of their time and energy was to be spent in profiting from that universal and other men, and how much in contributing to it and them. In different ways, J. M. Keynes and A. N. Whitehead were cultivated and contributive, occupied both with limited and with wide-ranging universals, to which they attended with sufficient dedication and effort to be able to enrich themselves and others, about as much as others do who attend to only one of those universals, as participants and contributors.

There is, as historians of thought are quick to remind us, no incompatibility in benefiting from what had been achieved and being creative at the same time. Indeed, it takes creative activity to be able to make maximum use of what had been achieved. One need not, they would insist, have to give up a participation in order to be creative; indeed, to benefit properly one must also benefit. But this creativity is quite different from that which produces new significant positions in a common universal—unless the historic figure itself be taken as a universal to be intensified and epitomized and made into a domain. And then, of course, there are historic figures who have been neglected and who equally deserve to be dealt with as universals to be intensified and epitomized.

As a universal, a chosen historic figure will have a different status from that which he has as one who is taken account of by others under some other universal. That he has this latter status can of course itself be made the object of an historic study; that study will not be of that figure primarily, but of the universal—the history of thought or philosophy or the nineteenth century, for example— in which he has the role of one who must be included in an epitomizing of the universal.

A great hero and a great villain make a difference to history; one must take account of them when one shares epitomized universals with them. But the mode of epitomizing in the two cases must be different. Since a hero adds to one's value and a villain subtracts from it, the latter can be accommodated only by being compensated for by the epitomizing individual. He is to use the epitomizing as a guide for determining acts which make good the losses in value that the villain produced.

There is a creativity involved in epitomizing a universal, and another in enriching the universal and thereby providing others with what is to be considered in their creative epitomizing of it. The latter creativity is to be contrasted with the participation of those who put primary emphasis on benefiting from the universal they are realizing. That creativity, once carried out, leaves content in the universal which the creative individual can himself take back into himself in the way others do. As a rule, though, he finds it tasteless and profitless to do so, even after he has ceased being creative, because, even if he sees the way it is involved with the achievements of others, he does not know how to make it the focal point of an epitomizing in which those others are grasped in relation to his own contribution. If he could do this, he would be a critic or historian who was not only on a level with himself as a productive contributing individual, but who approached his own work from the vantage point of the contributions of others. To be creative as a critic or historian, one must reach a position other than that which he had creatively enriched with his works.

July 10

It was about a week ago that I took up the question of rights. The discussion that followed expanded on that question, and opened up new areas. I summarize some of the main contentions:

1] There is a multiplicity of universals, each of which is intensified as a nuanced domain.

2] Every such universal makes a demand on a man to epitomize it, and thereby make it divided into a particular role implicated with all the others that can be carved out of the other nuances.

3] The most encompassing of universals is that of mankind; it is intensified by the contributions of civilization.

4] An enriched mankind is the available counterpart of a finality as pertinent to individual men.

5] All other universals that can constitute nuanced domains are delimited forms of an enriched mankind.

6] Some of the delimited forms of enriched mankind have the same range.

7] Universals with the same range, if they are equally complex, are divided into five distinct kinds answering to the types of union they provide.

8] The universals are related to individuals by demands.

9] The individuals are related to the universals by claims.

10] Demands and claims constitute necessary unions between individuals and universals.

11] The bringing of universals and individuals more closely together is the work of an individual's free act, along the lines of the necessary relation.

12] A participant in an intensified universal epitomizes it by embodying the roles of others in terms of their import on his own.

13] A contributor to a universal epitomizes it by enriching the roles which epitomizing others will take to be implicated in their own.

14] The less complex a universal the more—as a rule—will the universal have to be intensified by a man's creative energies.

15] Any universal can conceivably be epitomized so as to yield a life which is equivalent in value to one that epitomizes civilized mankind.

16] Civilized mankind is the measure of the excellence of the epitomizings of other universals.

17] No human life can be all it should be, since no one can meet the demands of all the universals.

18] Neither the life of a participant nor of a creator alone adequately enriches a universal.

19] There is no rule by which one can determine when to shift from participation to contribution.

20] There is no rule by which one can determine when to abandon the task of satisfying the demands of one universal and take up the task of satisfying another.

21] The decision as to when one should shift from participation to contribution, and from one universal to another is to be made in terms of an estimate of success in approximating the epitomizing of civilized mankind.

22] Mankind is a species-character; other types of living beings are faced with different species-characters.

23] A species-character is always realized as a governing universal in individuals, leaving over a residue to be realized by others.

24] Mankind differs from all other species-characters in continuing to demand realization by every individual. That demand requires it to be enriched by the creative assumption of a role or by creative contributions which others are to epitomize.

25] Individual rights are privately sustained by native rights, which answer to a man's essential needs.

26] An individual's basic right is to occupy an epitomizing role in civilized mankind—or an equivalent of it.

27] Roles are related in ways which match the operation of all the finalities. As a consequence, individuals not only have equal rights but comparable values, and so forth.

28] The task of the state is to enable justified roles to be sustained and fulfilled.

29] A role is filled by acting on other individuals and the world about.

30] The perfect filling of a role results in the enabling of others to embody their elected universals maximally.

31] One usually has a choice between accepting some role within a domain or using that role as a domain within which a subordinate role is assumed. The one is implicated with other roles within a domain, the other attends to a more limited number of mutually involved roles.

32] It is wrong to extend a domain to include roles which cannot be filled without involving a reduction in the value of those who fill them.

33] One who gives himself to a life of service may live as rich a life as any creator—contrary to what I have long contended.

34] An ethical man—one who does all he ought for the universal and for others within its range—is the fulfilled man, and conversely, not because virtue is its own reward or because happiness is added to it, but because the satisfying of the universal is inseparable from the satisfying of his essential claims.

35] A man must enrich his own role but in such a way that other roles are equally enriched. Each is then able to epitomize maximally, since each will then bring maximal content to bear on his own role, through the determination of the nature of roles which are as valuable to fill as the chosen one. The first of these aspects is of primary concern to a participant or to one who faces a universal which has no well-stabilized structure or fixed roles—friendship, love, celebration; the second is the outcome of the contributions one makes to a domain, and is pertinent most to those who are engaged in creative work there; the third concerns both of these, since it relates to the maximization of a domain by allowing it to function on behalf of a multiplicity of roles, all of which together maximize it by allowing it to be epitomized from multiple positions.

If someone occupies a comparatively simple domain, he neglects many roles and individuals who are encompassed only within a more complex and articulated, and usually wider-ranging domain. If all men were to occupy themselves with comparatively simple domains they would all be together only by accident; they would form groups, say of Epicurean friends, each group in its own garden, leaving open the possibility of conflict should they come in contact, making no allowance for the groups to benefit one another.

Were there someone who was concerned with an all-encompassing domain within which the simpler domains were fulfilled, he would have to take the simpler domains and not portions within them as defining the kind and locus of the intensification he is to provide. If the simpler domains were those within which men functioned as friends, one who was concerned with a domain occupied by all friendly men would adopt a position in which friendship was treated as a role implicated with other similar roles.

*   *   *

There are two splendid styles of writing which cannot be substituted for one another. One lucidly moves among established categories; the other forges categories. The second has difficulty with knowing the limits of the categories and how they are related one with the other. The achievements of neither are to be minimized, for most others seem to move woodenly among established categories, or to obscure as much as they illuminate in the areas of their primary discoveries. The second rarely, perhaps never, becomes the first, because he never or rarely achieves the position where all his categories are clearly demarcated and articulated.

July 11

A universal, which is a domain, is to be realized in two ways: it is to be made internal to the individual through epitomizing and is to be enriched as a domain through deeds and works. The latter continue within it as nuances, and become available as roles for whatever is within that range.

There are universals which do not function as domains; color is specified as red or green without also standing away from these and the specifying entities. A universal capable of functioning as a domain imposes a condition on the specifying individuals, under which various features and activities occur. So far it functions as a species. Mankind has in addition the ability to stand away from the species role and to contrast with the individual as one who is to give residence to the entire universal in all its diversity. Subhuman beings leave over a species-character which is to be specified in similar ways by other similar living beings, but humans leave over a character which demands that it be fully realized in all its diversity in each of them—and that requires epitomizing.

Because mankind requires realization in each individual, it has to be enriched by their deeds and accomplishments, for these enable individuals to lay hold of mankind via epitomizing roles. It also makes it possible for the whole of mankind to be the equivalent of the finalities—if to the degree that mankind falls short of the scope of those finalities, it is enriched in a fivefold way.

The species-character of a subhuman group can be viewed as a degenerate form of the kind of nature possessed by mankind. Or it could be held to be like mankind, but to be pertinent to beings which are unable to satisfy it in such a way as to enable it to still stand away from them and therefore able to be enriched. The latter is the better alternative, since it points up the comparative excellence of the human being, with his ability to forge a private life for himself. The more surely a man forges a private life the more he sets himself in contrast with mankind, not as a mere species-character, but as a domain which is to be enriched and then epitomized.

On the second alternative, the groupings of complex individuals are specialized ways in which individuals are subject to the finalities. Each specialized way provides a controlling limit for each complex individual, dictating the kind of constitution it has and the manner in which its parts are interrelated. Men are able to have still another status because of the ways in which they can go beyond such a point and become self-centered. It is as so self-centered that they face mankind as a domain to be enriched. Taking enriched mankind to be a measure, they can then go on and provide equivalents of it in the form of more intensive, though less diversified domains.

A universal, such as color or green, extends beyond but is inseparable from particular instances of it. A species-character, in addition, has a power, enabling it to constrain and govern what occurs within the limits of its instances. Is it sustained apart from all its instances? Where does it obtain its power? Unless one supposes that there is a history or an evolutionary force or an absolute at work, there would appear to be nothing which sustains a species-character apart from all its instances. The process of generation would then have to be understood to involve not only the production of individuals but the presence of that species-character.

The power to govern is derivative from the power of finalities.

Species-characters govern limited groups of complex actualities by using the power (that is connecting all actualities) to relate a limited number of them in the same way, but more insistently. A species-character needs enrichment because the increase in intensity of the ways in which its governed entities are related occurs without regard for the entities involved. Enrichment provides a place in which, and by means of which the different complex actualities can be fulfilled. Subhuman beings are unable to be anything more than interrelated instances of species-characters, but men, because they can enrich theirs, can be individuals who can be enriched by the universals within whose confines they are and function.

A man in his actions with relation to other specific individuals turns a domain into a 'fixed variable' that is, one which is restricted to him and those with whom he interplays. But what he fixates at one moment he may allow to be loose at another, or may fixate in a different manner. The habits he has, in contrast, can be dealt with as 'floating constants'. These, like a decimal point which makes a positive or a negative tenfold difference depending on which direction it is moved, add or subtract from that to which they are applied. Administrative work in academia, curiosity, ambition, poverty, are floating constants; they can be goads or hindrances to the successful carrying out of the work that should be done.

Why does it not suffice to refer to the intrusive presence of the various finalities, without having recourse to the idea of a species-character? After all, a finality, such as Substance, affiliates actualities in multiple ways. Why may it not affiliate all cats with an intimacy that it does not give to the cats with reference to anything else? Putting to a side the question as to whether or not a finality acts on complex actualities or only on ultimate particles—I have wobbled on that question, since it does seem as if complex actualities are in the cosmos, while the laws which govern the cosmos concern ultimate particles—and recognizing that a species-character does involve reference to those other species-characters which characterize its enemies, prey, parasites, hosts, and the like, one must affirm that Substance and the other finalities affect distinct actualities and provide conditions for their interrelationship. But this is only to say that the finalities provide necessary and primary conditions for actualities severally and together.

Species-characters mark groups off from multiple others. The sun affects all actualities but only the members of some groups attend to it or function in terms of it. The stars, the bottom of the sea, bugs in other continents, have only the relevance a finality makes possible, and then only for the actualities severally and not as members of a group. Species are cut off from most of the other species and the actualities within them. It is that cutting off, the existence of a functioning group interplaying with only some groups and individuals, that must be accounted for. This is done by turning away from the indifferently operating finalities to limited universals which make up in controlling, confining power what they lose in range.

I keep being nagged by a consequence of some of the previous discussions. I somehow allied creative men with men of service, though they are usually and correctly contrasted. But the two are not in conflict. Both make possible the enrichment of the roles of others, in quite different and even opposing ways. A creative man concentrates on what is a limited part of a domain and only incidentally attends to other parts; a man of service reverses this stress, attending to other roles and only incidentally to the vitalization of a particular one. A propagandistic artist begins to imitate the man of service; an inventive man of service functions creatively in his particular role. The ideal, of course, is a position where one does maximum justice to one role while giving full value to all the others which can be carved out of the nuanced domain common to them all. That ideal is approached by the artist who is also concerned with communicating what he does, since he then gives some weight to the relations which his role has to others. It is also approached by the man of service who is concerned with the kind of conditions which other roles impose on his own. In none of these ways does either fulfill himself; such fulfillment requires them to make the universal domain, with its distinguished roles, an integral part of themselves, while still leaving it to function as an actual domain within which they act. The latter presupposes the former.

Is enrichment of a domain eventually justified because it enables men to be fulfilled? If it were that alone, there would be no value in an enriched mankind existing in contradistinction to the individuals who may participate in it, and thereby incorporate it. The greatest creative works in art and history, in religion and science would all be held in reserve within civilized mankind for the use of individual men, to make themselves be individually fulfilled. Civilized mankind has no reality apart from men. Even though it stands in contradistinction from all of them, it is still inseparable from them. But precisely because it stands apart, it has a value regardless of what good it might give to men. They are obligated to realize it for its sake, not their own; but the richer it is the better is it able to satisfy their claims for their sake and not its own.

If this is correct, men at least stand in contrast, not only with the finalities with which they are to interplay, but also with a limited equivalent of these, intensified mankind. By internalizing the qualifications imposed by the finalities, they are able to be individuals with rights, identity, and so forth; by epitomizing mankind they are, in addition, able to be allied with other men, each of whom is fulfilled because epitomizing their common domains. The finalities and the actualities can never lose their independence of one another; they affect one another, and they together constitute appearances. Analogously, civilized mankind and incomparable men never lose their distinctness from one another. But they, too, affect one another. Together they constitute transient human acts.

Human activity, if it were just the counterpart of appearances, would provide a means of penetrating to the individuals on the one side and to civilized mankind on the other. As the product, though, not of an interplay of the insistencies by two ultimate kinds of reality—as appearances are—but of private epitomizings of men, transient human activity is ingredient in them. It is as if the appearances of an actuality were not merely credited to it, but were ingredient in it, and thus as if the appearance were not together in a context with other appearances but existed independently of them.

Men make an appearance, apart from other appearances, because they individually interlock with civilized mankind. Civilized mankind, unlike a finality, functions both as a contributor to the acts to which men also contribute, and as the context in which the acts are related to the acts of other men. Such acts are appearances, different from those which exhibit attenuations overlaid by a counter thrust; they are appearances of men, each externalizing what he has epitomized. They are close to what I have termed their 'exhibitions', ways in which men make attenuations of themselves available to a context. Acts differ from such exhibitions in having a moral import, since they reflect the degree to which men have done justice to the demands which civilized mankind makes on them.

The reciprocal, the expressions of mankind, as quickened by the deeds and achievements of men, are the categories of human intercourse—familial, social, political, economic, and historical. These differ in range and complexity and the kinds of interplay they permit and promote.

July 12

If epitomizing individuals and enriched domains both express themselves, their juncture will be the counterpart of what I termed 'appearances' in *Beyond All Appearances.* Unlike the appearances of actualities which result from the interplay of the actualities with finalities, with the actualities having a more effective role, the counterpart in social intercourse will result from the interplay of actualities and domains as already enriched by the other. These counterparts are social occurrences which come to be and pass away depending on the continuance and cessation of a particular social category and mode of action. As a consequence, their duration is indefinite, not to be measured by the occurrences which result from the direct interplay of actualities and finalities.

Social intercourse, history, economic exchanges, political activities are appearances. This does not mean that they are illusions or have no rootage in realities. They are in fact inseparable from the enriched individuals and domains that help constitute them. But it does mean that they do not have any causal power of their own, and that their coming and going, and the items which precede and follow them are to be accounted for, not by invoking the laws and energies which pertain to items in the cosmos, but by making reference to the ways in which one set of interlinked expressions of individuals and domain places limitations on and make a difference to other interlinked expressions.

Cause and effect in the social domain, on this account, are quite different from cause and effect in the cosmos, where what is present is engaged in making indeterminate possibilities determinate. Their relation is also quite different from the kind of relations that appearances have to one another, for appearances are all inert and depend for their connections and their coming and going on the realities which constitute them. Domains retain the increases which they owe to the individuals who distinguish nuances within them and fill them out in the form of interlocked roles, but the contexts in which the exhibitions of actualities occur are indifferent to those exhibitions, merely interrelating them when and as they occur.

Because this country is arming, the other is beseeching its allies; because the members of this group are being denied jobs, there is an increase in violence and discontent; because children are being brought up in fatherless homes, they are maladjusted. These seem to be cases of causality, contrary to what was said just now. There is, though, a difference between a cause and a because, though no necessary incompatibility. In the social realm the becauses are effective, have a kind of causal power; in the cosmos, the causes are rationally connected with their effects and thus have an explanatory value. The causal power of a because, however, lies in the connection which the domain permits, while the power of a cause lies in that cause as making use of the formal connection. The causal power of a because is in the additional determinations which a domain achieves because of the way it has been enriched; the power of a cause lies in the way in which it makes use of the connection between itself and the possibility it confronts.

Yet it would seem, as I took to be the case in the examination of history, that history has a teleological character, and what happens is in part determined by the insistence of a prospect, and not simply by the additions made to a relation between one enrichment and another. The two accounts, though, can be reconciled by recognizing that a relation not only connects a relevant enrichment with what is now enriched, but gives the former a directive role.

Have I not now obscured the fact that social occurrences are subject to contingencies, chance, and unpredictable moves on the part of individuals? I think not, for the ways in which the relation is realized is dependent in part on the activities of individuals which, though confined within the area where the relation occurs, are carried out with a consciousness of that relation. In a causal situation the action of the cause is one with the concretization of the relation and the determination of the effect; in a social situation, there are instead actions (which can also be understood in causal, nonsocial terms) which are confined within a teleologically limited situation.

When it is said that "because this country is arming, the other is beseeching its allies," it is not yet clear whether one is referring to the acts of a country; to the teleological linkage between their enriched domains, in which the need or demand of the beseeching country to be at peace or be victorious limits the ways in which the arming of the first will be carried out; or to their combination. The first of these alternatives obviously has to be dealt with in the usual causal way; and the third must give some room for such an account. The contrast between physical and social events is to be found in the presence of the teleological linkage focussed on in the second alternative, whether or not that linkage be utilized in the causal activities of men and their instruments.

Teleology is the successful resistance which a part of a domain offers to the alteration that a change in some other part requires. That resistance can be credited to tradition, indurated habits, or to the integrity of the part. It need not, therefore, be identified with some good supposedly operating backward in time. And it can be understood to have degrees, and even to vanish with an increase in the power of the initial part. A maximum degree of teleology is achieved when a part resists all change despite radical alteration in others and therefore in what they require of it.

In a causal situation a man gives a possible terminus a teleological import through his dedication. In a teleological situation a dedication could lead to an insistence on a course of action which is not sustained by the rest of the domain. A proper dedication should be in accord with the degree of successful resistance that an accepted part of the domain achieves. A man's activities will then enable him to fill a role excellently. But in the ordinary course of a dedication, which provides a kind of subjective teleology, success could end with a man not being able to take full advantage of what is in fact available in a domain.

When attention is turned from general issues to specific problems, such as abortion, behavior modification, cloning, and the like, one seems to move into what is completely alien. But if the general issues be kept in mind, it then becomes apparent that these specific questions are in fact multiply faceted, and have no simple answer. The question of abortion has to be faced in the context of a mother and her possible child, a family, a society, mankind. What might be right in one of these domains may not be in the others. As has been observed, a rich life is possible within the confines of a limited domain allowing for only a few individuals in distinctive roles. Such a life could be equal in value to one which was occupied with filling out a role within civilized mankind. But unlike the latter, it leaves over the question as to how the limited domain is related to other limited domains. If it conflicted with the others, it would have the virtue and vices of a war, which usually solidifies a people at the same time that it opposes a similar solidification produced by others. Subjectively viewed, any one domain could yield the same degree of fulfillment as any other; objectively viewed, it may require a minimization of the values attainable by others.

Each domain has its own integrity and rights; in an unriched form it is a subregion within the unriched domain of mankind. Satisfaction of it in the former guise does not cancel its needed satisfaction as part of mankind, both when this is functioning as a mere species-character and when it is enriched as a civilized whole. A solution of the problem of abortion which took account only of the realization of an excellent family would still leave open the question of what it imports for the mother and father, for the mother and other children, for the children together, and so on, as well as of what it imports for the society as a whole and for mankind. The issue can be settled by one who is occupied only with a self-fulfillment within some one domain. But the outcome will still leave over the question of what must be done on behalf of other domains, and how the abortion affects the realization of these. To say this, of course, is not yet to face the question of the right of abortion, but only of its justification in this and that domain.

The realization of a civilized mankind provides a measure in terms of which other realizations are to be evaluated; such a measure can be used, not only to evaluate epitomizings of different domains, but the loss involved in making those subregions function independently of one another. These subregions are best which, with the least alteration in themselves and their implications, can be made integral to mankind and there enriched. The evaluation of an abortion then requires a reference not only to the subjective fulfillment, let us say of the members of a family, but to the way that family must be altered so as to become a subregion within mankind, where it will be enriched together with all other subregions. The family, in turn, provides a measure of mankind, as requiring the family's transformation if it is to be integral to mankind. What may be best for a family may in fact so close that family off from all else as to make necessary a radical alteration of it before it could be an integral component of mankind.

We now seem to be brought up against a universal relativity with various domains offering measures for one another. But they measure different things. Civilized mankind measures the value of separately functioning units, regardless of their intensifications; an intensified family measures the value of a single mankind, not yet intensified, in terms of the alteration required of that family in order for it to be an integral part of mankind. As unintensified they are related as subdivision to whole; as intensified they are distinct, each with its legitimate demands and capable of providing full satisfaction to the epitomizing individuals within its range.

An absolute measure is provided in the idea of a civilized mankind in which every nuance can be turned into an intensified independent sub-domain, without distortion to its structure or implications. A justification of an abortion will require the demonstration that the family which is best realized by that act is just a detached portion of a single civilized mankind. Nothing need be said about the rights of the mother or the unborn since those rights are publicly significant only in relation to a domain. It must be shown that the best realization of the kind of family (or other limited domain) that is most readily assimilable to civilized mankind requires the abortion. In the absence of such a demonstration one can do no better than try to approximate it. This will always leave an area of controversy. The issue can not be conclusively settled, except of course by those who put an absolute value on the life of the fetus, which nothing is to be permittted to reduce. But such a position, apart from its unsupported supposition about the person of the fetus or divine laws, attends only to the supposed rights of fetuses in and of themselves, and not to those rights in relation to the rights of others, or to other types of publicly significant claims.

The primary fact is a plurality of distinct, independent, intensifiable domains which are to be identified with the nuanced subregions embraced by a maximally intensified mankind. The warrant for lives lived within limited confines is given by the different domains; those lives are to be evaluated by the ways in which their domains fit within intensified mankind without distortion.

An earlier conclusion must be modified. There is a multiplicity of distinctive domains, each of which is to be intensified and epitomized. All occur within the provenance of civilized mankind with whose nuances they are to be identified. Those intensified universals which can not be so identified are distortions of those that can. Only those are genuine realizable domains which are detached, bounded, and intensified cases of the nuances of mankind at its most complex and intensified. He who uses Plato, family, community as a domain is right to do so; he who uses Protagoras, his acquaintances, the passersby gives to them an intensity which belongs only to the former. Only the former are genuine universals functioning as domains; the latter are used as domains, but their incapacity to be identified with the nuances of mankind reveals this to be an error. There are multiple types of lives men can live, but only those ought to be lived which epitomize enriched domains identifiable with the nuances characterizing an enriched mankind.

July 13

Both roles and domains are identifiable with nuances in civilized mankind. Roles are occupied in relation to other roles; individuals ideally act in accord with the relation which connects their roles as ingredient in that domain. The domains, in contrast, are to be identified with nuances in civilized mankind; they are areas in which limited roles are carried out. As has been noted, one can sometimes take an historic figure to be a role which is to be vitalized in relation to other roles implicated by it, or as a domain which is to be articulated through the carrying out of more limited roles. The latter, though dealt with in independence of any other domain, must of course harmonize with others which, like it, can be identified with nuances in civilized mankind.

A domain is a kind of we, and a role a kind of I, but an I not enjoyed in private but merely vitalized from there. Civilized mankind is the most comprehensive we, allowing for the independent functioning of subordinate we's and for the independent occupation of the position of public I's in relation to other positions which can be independently filled by other public I's. Since both the I's and the subordinate we's must be carried out in such a way as to harmonize with others, no satisfactory account of either can be given without making reference to their bearing on other I's or we's.

Though one can deal with the problem of abortion within the compass of a family or a community or a state, and though all of these may be capable of being intensified and epitomized to provide the same degree of completion to the individual members, the result must still be measured by the way it coheres with the richest possible satisfaction of other domains. Such a statement, of course, presupposes that domains are not merely identifiable with aspects of a larger, but that they have an integrity of their own with their own demands so that, unlike the roles in civilized mankind, they are not implicated in or by other domains.

Roles are carried out somewhat like inferences, presupposing as they do a rational connection between them. Domains are like so many inferential rules, each of which can be utilized independently of all the others, but which must cohere within a more comprehensive set of distinguishable but not distinct rules. This does not reduce such a question as abortion to a matter of logic, but points up the fact that it requires a reference to acts within structured situations, themselves having structured relations to others.

This is not yet to attend to what many take to be the central issue—the rights of the unborn. Whatever there be has rights in the sense of making native claims on behalf of essential features. But they are rights which are to be understood in terms of demands by domains, or they are merely privately enjoyed, to which nothing can make a difference. The issue evidently concerns the first alternative, even though it may be backed by an acknowledgment of the second. The problem of abortion, like every other problem of viable rights, has to be dealt with in terms of the satisfaction provided, not only to the bearer of the rights but to other individuals as well, and to the domain within whose confines they all are. Granted that the unborn have no more and no less rights than adults—a questionable assumption—it still is a question as to how those rights are to be satisfied coherently with the satisfaction of the rights of others within a particular domain.

The obvious answer to this is that abortion does not deny certain rights but life itself and thus the totality of rights of a certain kind, and therefore the right of the unborn to have a position within the accepted domain. Unless life is sacrosanct and can never be sacrificed, jeopardized in war, brought to a swift close in a terminal and horrible illness, it may at times have to give way to other claims. A very large family could be a domain where no provision can be made for the continued living of the fetus under horrible conditions involving sickness, deprivation, and a painful death. In such a case what is at fault is the kind of family in terms of which the decision has to be made. Such a family may itself be traceable to a larger domain, and eventually to a civilized mankind. This, as now attained, will then have to be acknowledged to be less than it ought to be. On such a view, the defender of abortion has as his task the conversion of current civilized mankind into one in which the satisfaction of the demands of families—to use that example—will not require a denial of life to some of the unborn.

An approach such as this avoids dealing with the question purely from the side of the unborn, and purely from the side of the mother. It does, though, allow one to deal with the issue from the side of the mother and father, taken as a domain of parents. The kind of parents that the present civilized mankind allows to be a domain, or the kind of parents which those particular individuals now are able to be, will both have to be taken into account, the one in order to determine what parenthood demands, the other to determine how well they do what they ought.

Might one, instead of dealing with the issue in terms of what a certain kind of family (taken as a domain) requires, deal with it in terms of the capacities, intents, and behaviors of that particular family? I think not, unless we are to change policy to accord with the ineptitude, failures, and vices of individuals instead of continuing to impose on them the demands of a domain, whether this be thought to be that of a family, without qualification, or of a family of such and such a size and nature—both of which could be domains compatible with the nuances of civilized mankind.

There are three formidable objections that now arise.   *1*] If it be permitted to distinguish large and small families as separate domains, what is to prevent a distinguishing of large families of blacks with educated parents living above the poverty level and so forth, and so forth, from other large families? What is to prevent one from continuing on and on until the domain is no larger than a particular situation?   *2*] Why suppose that a family is a domain, and not an arbitrary subdivision?   *3*] Why place such emphasis on a domain, impersonal, indifferent, abstract, instead of on actual human beings?

1] The first objection is to be met somewhat the way in which one meets the objection to a view which acknowledges a limited number of realities at the root of all else—by taking account of 'floating constants'. The determination of a domain is not to be made after the fact, in the light of particular details, but in terms of the nature of civilized mankind. (Only those features, too, are to be considered which are relevant to the problem considered.) When details are brought in to particularize a situation, those details have a negative, prejudicial value; if brought in initially without regard for the particular situation and on the basis of what the nature of the domain requires, they have a positive value. (When one lays down that the universe has three or four or five basic realities, rather than discovering that this is the case, a 'floating constant' is used with an opposite import, for the prescription arbitrarily elects some one of all possible numbers, while the discovery merely finds the number that in fact is there.)

2] A family could be said to be, like a large family, or a prescription about the number of fundamental realities there are, the result of a bad use of a 'floating constant'. Perhaps the ultimate unit is a tribe, a community, a state? To answer this objection one must turn to history. Civilized mankind as the product of history, and the do-mains and roles it allows are determined by the enriched nature it has acquired over the years. Were one to aim at a civilized mankind which had no room for nuances that could be expressed as families, it would have to be done via the present civilized mankind that provides the only arena in which action can now occur.

3] The emphasis on a domain does not exclude consideration of individuals, but in fact is essential to them. To know what is to be done by, to, and for them it is necessary to refer to the domain they are to realize and thereby perfect themselves and others. This answer does not cover the entire situation, for the claims of re-vealed religion and absolutistic ethics have been abstracted from. Revealed religion finds answers in the commands of God, and an absolutistic ethics takes account of what the ultimate, irreducible ideal of excellence demands. But their existence and their demands do have some weight in historic civilized mankind, where public practical issues are resolved.

Is it true, though, that families, tribes, communities are domains identifiable with nuances in civilized mankind? Is it not rather the case that civilized mankind is the outcome of the deeds and achievements of men in the arts, sciences, work? Or is it not that there are two ways in which mankind is enriched, one by deeds and achievements, and the other by established ways in which limited groups of men interplay? The last I think.

Mankind as a species-character allows for at least two levels of intensification, the one expressing the ways in which men in fact function together in various subgroups, the other expressing their deeds and achievements. Many of the achievements and deeds are dependent on the men functioning in subgroups. The deeds and achievements become part of a single civilized mankind at the same time that they belong within an emphasized nuance. This can have a distinguished status as a domain enriched by those very deeds and achievements, so far as these are confined within the domain. What is part of the intensification of civilized mankind becomes the whole of the intensification of some delimited portion of it. The family has to be reckoned as part of civilized mankind because it is one of the important agencies through which some of the goods of mankind—moral education, fidelity, dedication, love—are nurtured and produced.

July 14

Large families, or the families of immigrants or farmers, could be said to make distinctive contributions to civilized mankind. Perhaps they take care of the young, the elderly, engage in work, educate, and so on, in distinctive ways. If they do make such contributions, they are rightly said to be domains, but this will be not because we have as a matter of fact found that their members act in such and such ways, but because we see that they implicate and are implicated by other areas of civilized mankind. We commit the error of improperly placing a 'floating constant' when we try to decide the question of whether or not we have a true domain by attending to particular activities rather than to the nature of the enrichment by a part of mankind with which the supposed domain is to be identified.

We are now forced back to the consideration of the nature of an enrichment as an organic intensified addition to a domain. Because painting went through a period of postimpressionism, an historian of art might say Dadaism was made likely, and that when Dadaism was a fact the two types of painting were interlinked. The historian of art is undoubtedly alert to the historic occurrence of both types of painting, but what he seeks to show is that they have a relationship as distinct domains because they are already interlinked in a larger. Otherwise, he would have to be content with merely chronicling the fact that at such and such a time the one occurred and that at another time the other did.

History differs from chronicle not in supposing that there is

some far-off event which controls the occurrences that take place in
sequential time, but in involving a domain where distinguishable
parts are relevant to one another. Postimpressionism has a different
import after Dadaism appears. The latter affects the former. But
since the former yields only in part to the pressure that the other
imposes, the latter so far functions as a limited controlling condition on the course of the former.

Philosophies of history are tensed between the need to acknowledge the exclusion of the past from the present, and the need
to acknowledge its influence in the present. The latter can not be
simply reduced to the remains of the past that are now functioning
in the present, for the influence of the past is also in the guise of it as
distinct from the present and yet effectively braking and redirecting
it.

It is possible to distill an explanation of this double fact from
Whitehead's cosmology. He holds that the past has its repercussions on God who utilizes it to provide a new influential future for
what is present. Translated into the present discussion, this would
be tantamount to holding that actual occurrences affect the nature
of a domain, and that this, as a consequence, affects the nature of
particular occurrences. Putting aside the fact that Whitehead makes
provision for only one all-encompassing domain, God, that no
provision is made for smaller domains, that particular occurrences
have no duration and therefore no capacity to act or move, and that
he takes God to do no more than rearrange a preexistent fixed
number of abstract possibilities, his view is faced with the difficulty
that domains are enriched, and are not merely avenues for the
influence of what had been on luring possibilities.

The involvement of portions of an enrichment with one another
can not be deduced from a consideration of their abstract meanings;
nor is it merely a summation of what in fact had occurred, somehow
preserved or transmuted. A domain has its own integrity. Whether
or not it distorts a portion of a more inclusive domain, it plays a role
in the individuals' perfecting of themselves. It is itself not another
actuality, grander and more persistent, but a controlling condition
needing and providing satisfaction to what needs and provides
satisfaction to it.

Is it not true, though, that after the fact one can always find
supposed implicative connections among the various items on
which one focusses? Is it not the case that had Dadaism followed

after action painting the historians of art would have seen a connection between them? Yes. But not because the connection was read into the situation, but because such a Dadaism and such an action painting would be different in nature from what they are now. The techniques, arrangements, colors, and experiments they incorporated would be different from what in fact occurred.

The connection amongst the distinguishable factors in a domain is not a merely logical relation of implication, and is not merely accidental or adventitious. What is already part of a domain makes a difference to the way in which a subsequent addition to it will fit within it. To determine whether or not large families are a constituent part of an ideal civilized mankind one will have to see if they are accommodated differently from the way in which small families are, and if they make a difference to the ways in which other contributions to civilized mankind are accommodated. The accommodations are made independently of what is occurring amongst particulars, and can therefore serve as a guide and measure of what these do.

The large family, it could be said, because of the limitation in the size of dwellings, available land, food, and work, all of which are involved in the enrichment of mankind, has an import for that enriched mankind that the small family does not. Such a contention is partly based on what is learned in the course of experience, but it also takes account of the nature of the large family within civilized mankind. At present, civilized mankind, one might say, is where men have limited resources, not enough living space, and the like. In such a domain the large family makes a difference.

To bring matters into sharp focus, let it be imagined that no matter how one imaginatively expands and contracts the family one can find no involvement with music, no matter how this idea be varied; nothing, we find, is changed in the ways in which family and music are affiliated, coordinated, structured, positioned, or evaluated. Let us also suppose that no matter how far back we go we always find that music is produced, cherished, and made available only in large families. We then will be forced to conclude that this is an adventitious occurrence, and that any attempt to make a domain out of the combination of music and family will distort the domain in which they both are.

But is it not the case that civilized mankind is an achievement, and that the interplay of large families with music is, on the hypothesis, taken up into that domain? I think we must say so. But we need not suppose that the two of them are taken up as intimately related. They are able to contribute to mankind in their separateness. Their conjunction, on the hypothesis, is contingent, traceable to the ways in which particulars interplay with one another. In the domain they are independent, a fact which reflects their indifference to one another there, and consequently the distortion that results when anyone tries to combine them.

Do not the accepted common procedures of social theorists conflict with this way of thinking? Having noted the high incidence of cancer of the lung among smokers and the low incidence among those who do not smoke, they have come to the conclusion that smoking (or more precisely, the tar in the cigarettes smoked) is a cause of cancer. If the conclusion be granted—though it is one which the physical scientists have long ago found to be of the kind they did not care to trust—it will at best show that causal relations are not necessarily preserved in the enrichment of a domain. If the domain be one dictating the positions of items in space, time, and causal chains, the causal relation will be part of it, but not otherwise. Consequently, the fact that a causal relation is found to exist— granted that the high correlation shows this—still leaves undetermined the answer to the question as to whether or not the items involved are mutually implicated within a domain, for the mutual implication may concern only the ways in which the items are affiliated, coordinated, structured, or evaluated.

If it be granted that the high correlation of large families and music in our supposed case provides sufficient evidence of a causal connection between them, and if the two are in a domain which unifies nuanced items in a fivefold way, we have to conclude that at least in one way the two are relevant to one another—in the domain so far as this relates its nuances in a single dynamic unity. When that way is to the fore, the large family and music of our supposition will have to be considered to be relevant to one another. But the relevance will not be a consequence of the fact that they are part of an empirical causal sequence but of the fact that the domain in which they are relevant is one which dictates that they are causally connected.

This result depends on the supposition that causal relevance within a domain has to do with the very same items which are in fact dynamically connected as items detached from that domain. This may be doubted, either on the ground that the dynamic connection between items detached from a domain are not there distinguishable, or on the ground that a domain has degrees of density, and allows for the dynamic connection only on the most superficial level. The latter alternative allows one to say that every kind of occurrence has a role to play in the final domain of civilized mankind, but that only certain items are able to diversify it as a primary condition. Civilized mankind can then be said to allow for the causal connection between large families and music, but that this connection and those items are indistinguishable the more closely we come to mankind as a permanent, final domain. Large families and music will be taken to be relevant in the dynamic world but only in abstraction from a more basic dynamism which connects items in which either or both large families and music will be only aspects. On either alternative, though, the fact that large families and music were actually in a causal relation would not go to show that they were causally relevant to one another within the compass of mankind.

If this is correct, there is evidently an important difference between domains and finalities. We come to the latter by noting that actualities and appearances are subject to compelling conditions which we then trace back to their sources. But domains are themselves sources of the compelling conditions which enable us to understand and assess particular occurrences. The reason for this is that the unions which domains provide operate not on sub-domains or roles which stand apart from the domains, but on the enrichments of these domains. Were one to begin with the deeds and achievements of men and note that these become subject to unifications and thereby become enrichments of a domain, the domains would be dealt with in the way the finalities are; we would come to know of their power by contrasting the distinct products of men with the compelled conjunction of these by the domain, which they thereupon enrich. Conversely, if one began with contextualized appearances or with a cosmos, one would begin with unified particulars, which could be taken to provide a base for determining the contextual or cosmic promise of the particulars as they stand apart from one another. Connections amongst those particulars, which were empirically discovered and which were not in consonance with the connections characteristic of the context or cosmos, would then be credited to chance or accident (even if they persisted), traceable perhaps to some other condition (than that provided by the context or cosmos) such as the independently produced actions of actualities. It is as if, when we were faced with the constant conjunction of large families and music we took their accidental conjunction to be the outcome of their independent operations.

July 15

Last night at the Kennedy Center I saw *An Evening with Margot Fonteyn and Rudolf Nureyev.* It was the first time I had seen either on stage, though I had a glimpse of her on some TV show some time back. The first dance, "Marguerite and Armand" has an uninteresting choreography and there is comparatively little that either dancer has to do. One had no opportunity there to see anything really distinctive in Nureyev's dancing. Fonteyn is a remarkably fragile, graceful, delicate dancer; her moves are airy and appealing, but the result a warmth for her rather than for her part, a share in the sad event portrayed, or pleasure in the dancing. "The Corsaire" danced by Nureyev and Karen Kain allowed one to see the effortless, intricate, vital nature of Nureyev's dancing. But Kain, a rather unattractive looking, tallish and even awkward looking dancer, overcame her handicaps in a superbly controlled complex set of dances. The highlight of the evening was "Songs of a Wayfarer," danced by Nureyev and Paolo Bortoluzzi. This is a sad and moving dance. Here Nureyev, well matched by Bortoluzzi, showed a range and a power that makes one understand and endorse the reputation that he has here and abroad. I became involved with both of them, though not passionately or purgationally but with admiration and concern. I left before the final piece, "The Moor's Pavano," to make sure I could get home in time. A slow dance as this, though, could not have changed the fundamental tone of the evening—intellectually rather than emotionally satisfying, beautiful, masterful, by experts.

I have been reading Locke's *Essay,* a book I have hardly looked at since my undergraduate days. I am surprised to find how likable and even persuasive it is, despite its well-known faults and the movements which have, since Locke's time, taken us far from his position. There is a vigorous honesty to Locke which makes intelligible why he had such a great influence on mature men who did not claim to be professional philosophers. He faces his issues straightforwardly as a reasonable person. Subtle alternatives and even a careful consideration of opposing views are avoided. Yet one is left with the sense that he is unusually fair, careful, judicious, and sound.

In between times I have been reading Dostoyevsky's *The Book of the Dead,* and rereading *Crime and Punishment.* The first is strangely inert; it is hard to get a sense of what the prisoners are like, how they interact, what they in fact do with their time, what they are thinking about. Again and again, Dostoyevsky is content with telling us that they are surly, quarelsome, and the like. There is no mention, as far as I have gone, of homosexuality, masturbation, and other similar activities that we know occur frequently in prisons. *Crime and Punishment,* in contrast, is vibrant, tense, perceptive, powerful; there is excitement on almost every page. Though I know what is to come I await it with anticipation and some emotion. How much of the difference between the books is due to the translators I can not, unfortunately, say, but I think it may be due to the fact that the one is an early and the other a later work.

In a few minutes I will be off to the annual meeting of the Philosophy Education Society, Incorporated, which is the corporation that publishes the *Review of Metaphysics.* I am a vice-president. At the meeting we discuss financial affairs, listen to the report of the editor, consider problems of price increases, advertising, the raising of funds. It is the only connection I have with the *Review.* I scrupulously avoid looking into the office, and at most, occasionally point out to Dougherty the occurrence of an excess of typographical errors. I think the *Review* today has too many historical articles; it is hard to believe that there are not as many good, original pieces now available as there had been in the beginning. A periodical, such as this, is most justified when it serves as a means for encouraging the writing of fresh papers which break new ground. Almost without exception, the historical papers that are published there are excellent; the occasional original papers are too often long-winded and could have benefited from editorial criticism. The strongest part of the *Review* is in the long Summaries and Comments section, where new books are carefully, intelligently, and ably examined soon after publication. I know of no other periodical which reviews so many works of so many diverse sorts with such skill and decency.

I have now returned from what became a rather long meeting, in good part because I raised a number of difficulties and pointed up errors in the accountant's report. While I was abroad, the available members of the board decided to raise the rates for the *Review* again. I was disturbed by the fact that the rates for students and for individuals were increased. Not only are the number of subscriptions in both categories, here and abroad, falling off, but one of the ideas I hoped would be cherished by the board is that the *Review* has an educational purpose. It is desirable, both for its present impact and future circulation, that the numbers of students and individual subscribers be increased. No one seemed to know whether or not the decrease was due to inflation, lack of interest, shift in the temper of American philosophy, and so forth. That question will be reported on at the next meeting. The value of the stocks has fallen, and so has the reserve, but last year a goodly profit was made. Still, prices for printing and mailing are going up, and these costs must be met.

The meetings are well conducted; every member is conscientious and concerned, more than those on the boards that the Society had in the past—perhaps because I then usurped most of the functions, and was thought to be almost indistinguishable from the *Review,* and even from the Society.

*   *   *

Every domain has the character of a we for each I that is involved with it, either in fact or prospectively, as a past or as a future contributor to its enrichment. But not every we is a domain. It may express merely the will of a single despot. His we is his I made objective, impersonal, controlling. Unlike a domain it is produced by an individual and expresses him.

Might not a we be conceived as a domain by virtue of the fact that it is commanding, demanding, controlling? It will then, though, be a we which does not encompass the individual who is insisting on it, but only others. It will be a we not for an I, but a we which absorbed or abolished an I. It is as if an individual in a domain were to meet the demands of the domain without providing any satisfaction for his own claims. Such a man would have sacrificed himself for the sake of the domain and eventually for others who will benefit from it.

Does it make sense to equate a sacrificing man in any way with a despot? Yes, a despot may be benevolent, generous, self-denying. But whether he is or not, he is caught up in power, and so far neglects himself as an individual who might be subject to that power. In giving himself to the vitalization of the we, he makes himself part of the enrichment of it.

Every we, in fact, has as part of it something of an I. To that degree it is unlike a domain, which stands in contrast with the individuals who are to assume roles, except so far as the domain has as part of its enrichment the individual as expressed in his deeds and achievements. A 'we' always remains a personal pronoun, never entirely freed from an individual person, even when it refers to an area within which individuals, including the one who has vitalized it, will interact. And so far as it is functioning as more than a relatively depersonalized expression of the I, it will also have as part of it the you's which it encompasses. There is evidently an intimacy between the we and the individuals embraced by it, making it an enriched domain for them. In giving themselves to the constitution of a we, men make it an enriched domain, and do not face it as a domain to be enriched, though of course an enrichment may be added subsequently.

If a we is to be treated as a kind of enriched domain, a distinction should be made between it as already benefiting from an I, and as merely allowing for its contribution. In the latter case, with respect to that I, the we is like any other enriched domain under which one might assume a role; though, of course, with respect to the individuals who are then vitalizing the we, it will be an enriched domain, with which they are so far identified.

July 16

A we incorporates one or more I's, and this even when it is somewhat impersonalized, and its range is as large as all mankind. It is, therefore, an enriched domain. Does such an enriched domain have a counterpart in epitomized I's? Do the two interact to give us something like an historic event? The answer is yes in both cases, I think.

To be a responsible social being is to govern oneself by the meaning of the entire we which encompasses him and others. He assumes a role understood in its bearing on the roles that others might assume. In himself he meets the demands of the social whole by making this give the meaning of his acts.

A responsible social being is like a man who has internalized the qualifications of the finalities, differing only in the limitation, concreteness, and particular roles that the former involves. The two internalizations in fact occur together, the first presupposing the second. Without the first a man would act solely as one among others, without any special reference to other men and without regard for the demands of any particular community.

A responsible man, interacting with the we that he had epitomized, functions as a pivotal member of an actual social group. Some who might be equally responsible fail to interplay properly with the we which they had epitomized; others who give themselves to a social life may fail to make themselves responsible beings and consequently may not publicly act in terms of what they internally made themselves to be.

If the we is as large as mankind, it is identifiable with that mankind as enriched, not fully or by achievements in the arts and the sciences, but by men vitalizing it in the course of their reaching toward one another, apart from and indeed as one of the conditions of their acting as members of one mankind, which is more than a mere species-character. A responsible man, on behalf of a closer union of men, justice, truth, a common environment, or comprehensive value, epitomizes that vitalized mankind; he assumes a role which is grasped in its interlinkage with the other roles that others ought to assume within that mankind. A responsible man, when he acts on others, does so under the aegis of a vitalized mankind; he becomes a pivotal individual, one from which major lines of activity originate, and in which they terminate.

The truly great men of history are neither those of outstanding virtue, nor those who affect the lives of a multitude; they are not the accidental products of the course of history, nor men of destiny who dictate the course of mankind. The truly great men have first made themselves responsible epitomizers of mankind and then carried out their responsibilities. Men of outstanding virtue might remain closed in themselves; those who affect the lives of a multitude may do so to their injury, or (where these others are benefited and deliberately produced) those benefits may be provided without a conscious personal grasp of their value.

It is no surprise, therefore, to find the figures on whom historians fasten so often to be men of limited intelligence, dignity, virtue, or self-control. They occupy pivotal positions and there may function to enhance the lives of a multitude. They might conceivably even have a good idea of the way in which mankind is to be significantly enriched. Usually, though, they act without regard for anything other than the multitude then living. And where they pay regard to the promotion of truth, justice, and the like, these demands are slighted in their own individual lives, not because such a slighting is needed in order that the demands be publicly satisfied, but because they are not made integral to the individuals as responsible social beings. The great historic figures might even, as Napoleon did, concern themselves with the promotion of certain areas of knowledge, regardless of use.

There is a paradox latent in these observations. A Napoleon is here being taken to be inferior to a Mao, because Napoleon but not Mao promotes a knowledge not kept within the limits of mankind's demands. But not only may a Mao himself not epitomize a we any more than a Napoleon might, a concern for knowledge, not confined within the limits of mankind as it now is or might be envisaged to become, seems to have an importance and an eventual value that a more limited practical concern does not.

It need not be said that Mao is a man of greater personal virtue than a Napoleon in order to acknowledge the more humane interests of the former. Nor need the acknowledgment of the value of truth or knowledge preclude a consideration of the nature and demands of the we or mankind as it is now constituted. As individuals, both a Napoleon and a Mao might be equally virtuous, equally responsible as social beings—these are illustrations, not historic judgments or comparisons—and their achievements might result in about the same benefit to mankind, the one indirectly, the other directly. But much of what either does must be adventitious because carried out without their first having made themselves properly epitomize a large-scaled we.

A Confucius stands opposed to both, for he seeks first to epitomize the we and then to carry out the epitomized result. But he insists that one first epitomize smaller ranging we's before moving on to the larger. There is wisdom in this, for epitomizing is no simple act dependent on will. It involves habit, adjustment, control, and attitudes, assumed and carried out with reference to others.

Action is of three basic kinds: directly in response to what is being confronted; inseparable from the effort to epitomize; and at the service of an encompassing domain. The three, of course, can be combined in pairs, or all together, and with various stresses. Ideally all three are united but with distinctive functions. What a man confronts has its own integrity and demands apart from any domain; his effort to epitomize requires adjustments in his body and in the relations he has to what else there be; and if he is to serve an encompassing domain, he must carry out the role which is identifiable with a distinctive nuance within it.

An encompassing domain can be vitalized in two ways: one can give oneself to it, turn it into a we, or merely contribute to it, make available what is capable of being assimilated to a domain, given the particular structure and content that this already has. But even in such a case, there often is something personal which clings to the actual product and this makes a difference to the domain, tinging it with an I, and therefore giving it so far the nature of a 'we'.

This discussion in effect provides a philosophical base for social thought. It avoids the extreme of trying to deal with this area by accepting the categories and methods there used, merely clarifying, ordering, and explicating them (the extreme which most philosophers of science embrace); and the extreme of intruding philosophical categories and problems with minor changes into another area (the extreme which most philosophers of art embrace). Instead, it keeps in mind basic categorial distinctions justified in a philosophic speculation but as transmuted, specified, and given new roles so as to be in accord with what is otherwise known of the major practices and results in the field.

July 18

Discussions by historians and philosophers of science in the last years hve focussed on an issue somewhat related to the present discussion of civilized mankind, domains, and we. On one side are those who hold that the major developments in science are cataclysmic, revolutionary, involving quantum jumps; on the other side are those who insist on a gradualism, a continuity, a maintenance of the old with additions, subtractions, and modifications. Both sides work within the provenance of the same error: they deal with the issue in abstraction from the consideration of a constant scientific domain, with its stable view of the meaning of theory, hypothesis, law, verification, experimentation, and above all, with its place for such instruments as telescopes, microscopes, pendulums, scales, pressure chambers, and the like. Quantum jumps could go from one place to any other, having nothing to do with the first; they are significant for a history of science only because they are quantum jumps in science. The continuity which the others emphasize, too, is a continuity of scientific effort, not a continuity in the use merely of a technical language, of established mathematical formulas, and techniques—though it is these also.

Once a common scientific domain is recognized, it becomes evident that the two sides are compatible. Every new discovery of magnitude affects the others; it gives them a new import with respect to that discovery and often makes a difference to what they will then imply. But every new discovery is also made within a large established area, and this has an inertia, limiting the affect of the discovery, and with it constituting a new domain, in which the older views could still have somewhat the same import that they had before. A new discovery makes a difference, but that difference may be slight or it may be great, depending on the resistance of the established areas.

What is hard to know is just what a domain is like. Men differ in their understanding of the nature of civilization, of such sub-domains as states, societies, and families, of what is great or pivotal in history, and the kind of difference which a new discovery makes. But there is an established way of dealing with what is to be understood as established—there are certain figures and events that are primary and pivotal. To deny that they are so is to speak of some other enterprise than an actual historically developed science, art, politics, philosophy, and so forth. No account of the domain of literature makes sense if it leaves out Aeschylus, Shakespeare, and Dante; a domain of painting must include Michelangelo; a domain of philosophy is misconstrued if it has no crucial place for Plato, Aristotle, and Kant. Let it be supposed that at some future time it will be universally agreed that no one of these is a pivotal, primary figure in the relevant domain. It still will be the case that these men belong to the domains that now prevail. Those domains are completely self-enclosed, or they are related to radically new domains within a still larger domain such as civilized mankind.

The most that can be said at the present time is that a view of science which takes Newton, Darwin, Einstein, Pavlov to be pivotal scientists expresses an elitist, conventionalistic, arbitrary view. It still will be the case that science today is inseparable from a domain where these men have primary, pivotal roles. To deny this, is one with a refusal to use the language of educated discourse; it is, therefore, in effect to avoid sharing in the larger domain of civilized mankind. Left over still is the question as to how to assess different parts of the scientific domain in relation to one another, after it has been granted that they are primary and pivotal. How important is Shakespeare or Newton? Suppose one were to urge that Goethe or Galileo was more important? Will not the resolution of the argument depend on the determination of the changes which other parts undergo as a consequence of the achievements by these different men? If this be the case, do we not ignore the lonely towering figures in the history of thought whose achievements are as great as the others but who, because of the quirks of history, have not had the same affect? Yes. The issue is not who is the greater man, but who and what is important for and in an established domain.

　　Once there is an agreement on the primary pivotal figures, and the major ways in which they affect the rest of their domains, there will still be areas of dispute. Men will honestly differ on the importance of Chaucer and Spenser, Faraday and Mendeleeff, Vermeer and Picasso. If a distinction be made between deeper and superficial aspects of civilized mankind or some other enriched domain, one can find a core of agreement on the deeper level, while leaving undetermined the question as to just what is the case on other levels. The fact that the issue is undetermined does not mean that all opinions are equally good. Opinions not only anticipatorily determine the outcome, but themselves need grounding and justification. The situation is somewhat like what occurs in the interpretation of poetry. Every idea, every nuance of meaning that is elicited is legitimate, even if not seen or understood by its author; but there are controlling meanings, central meanings, to miss which is to miss the poem. Those central, controlling meanings are urged by the establishment of college professors and literary critics, but this does not make them the product of an establishment; they are the establishment's justification. We who attend to what the establishment urges can see for ourselves whether or not the supposed pivotal meanings are so in fact, and that other meanings are peripheral and depend on them. If we fail to see this, we could conclude that the establishment is mistaken, but then, of course, we will be speaking of poems as in a different domain. This is not yet to show that the poems are not also in the establishment's domain nor does it go to show that the establishment gave the poems the roles they have. An establishment of critics and professors is itself one of the factors in a domain with the poems it assesses.

Both sides in the controversy on the nature of historic scientific discoveries accept somewhat the same data; they even evaluate it in the same way. They differ primarily in stress, the one attending to the novelty of the great discoveries, the other to the stabilized character of what had already become known. By attending to what both contend, it is possible to move toward the position where full value is given to both factors, at the same time that those factors are understood in relation to one another.

July 19

If science is brought under the aegis of civilized mankind, must not every other discipline be brought there, too—religion, metaphysics, and even common sense? Do we not then accept an absolutistic conventionalism, analogous to that adopted by the linguistic philosophers who understand everything to be confined within a language with its conventionalized structure and use of words? I think not, for two reasons: *1*] Civilized mankind is but a special case of all the finalities taken together. Those finalities are not subject to but, instead, subject civilized mankind to forceful constraints.   *2*] Civilized mankind encompasses the history of science, art, metaphysics, and so on, and not their truths.

But do we not know the finalities in the course of an historical investigation? Are not the truths of the various disciplines achieved in and tainted by the actual course of historic efforts? An affirmative answer to these questions, though correct, can not be sundered from a reference to what lies outside the historic course of mankind. Science and the other disciplines make a contribution to mankind, but only because they deal with what lies outside mankind's conditioning. The very knowledge of mankind's conditioning, in fact, involves a knowledge of what is outside mankind's conditioning, just as an absolutistic conventionalism is nonconventionally assumed to be the only or the best or the proper position to take for understanding all else.

July 20

A central problem in Spinoza is whether the attributes of God are objective or subjective. If they are the former, since there are an infinite number of them, God becomes infinitely divided. If they are the latter, the attributes, though they all equally exhibit or contain the essence of God, will tell us about men rather than about God. I think there is a way of being on both sides of this controversy, and by that very act avoiding the difficulties each entails.

The attributes as distinct, held apart, contrasted with one another, are subjective, reflecting a man's emphasis. The attributes as objective, instead, are not distinct, but only distinguishable; they are nuances, abstractable aspects, somewhat as a cherry's size and mass are not distinct but only distinguishable aspects of it. In himself, Spinoza's God is simple, undivided, though allowing for an infinitude of distinctions. Each distinction provides a special way of acknowledging God. We, according to Spinoza, are able to focus on only two of the attributes, thought and extension.

Spinoza says that there is an infinitude of equally basic attributes; if the present interpretation is correct, this claim must be understood to mean that an infinitude of attributes could conceivably be distinguished, though we now know no way to do this. God's full reality is such that this distinguishability is possible, not actual.

Since each of the finite modes is a delimitation under the two attributes which men are able to distinguish, we should go on to say that every mode, too, allows for a conceivable distinguishing of delimited forms of the other attributes, as well, though, once again, we do not know how to distinguish them. We know that there is such an infinitude of distinguishable facets because we know that the modes are delimitations of the attributes, and we know that the distinguishable attributes are infinite in number—even though we do not succeed in distinguishing them—because we know that God is perfect, infinite not only in each attribute but infinite in the number of attributes that could be distinguished.

When it is said that the attributes are conceivably distinguishable, the statement must not be identified with one which says that they are separate or even distinguishable in God, but only that we can conceive of men or other finite beings understanding God from the position of an infinite number of distinct 'subjective' attributes, all of which are indissolubly united in God.

* * *

If God did not want us to wear hats, why did he create us with heads?

What is being assumed here? *1*] That heads have an essential or primary function, *2*] that the wearing of hats is such a function, *3*] that we are created, *4*] that creation is designed to sustain the essential or primary function, *5*] that if an essential or primary function is not carried out, God's intention is frustrated.

Nothing is changed in principle if we turn from this absurd example to some more congenial one such as: if God did not want men to think for themselves, why did he create them with minds?

July 24

Every me has three dimensions: A] it is that at which one arrives from an outside position, B] it is expressed as feeling and terminates at the former, C] and it underlies and is articulated by these other two.

A] From an outside position one arrives at one's body. But the me is not identifiable with that body as arrived at; it continues indefinitely beyond that point. To arrive at the me is to penetrate toward the I that engaged in the act of assuming another position and from there moved back toward the me at and beyond the body.

B] The me is also oneself as countering and involved with the me reached from the outside. Though it is I who feel, the feeling itself, as being countered by a me reached from the outside, terminates in a me. A me thus has two termini. Those termini are joined, but are yet distinguishable. Both depend on action of an I, but in each case the action is distinct. The feeling of a pain is not identical with the pressing of the spot where the pain is being approached from the outside.

C] The me, approached from the outside, is met with a me, approached from the inside. Together they constitute a single unit. But a man remains a me apart from such conjunction. Such a me is substantial, the individual as grounding a multiplicity of successive junctures of distinct feelings and identifications of himself from the outside. That substantial me could be known by one who was able to use the two joined me's as components in a judgment, or who was able to penetrate toward their sustaining ground. Whether this be done or not, the substantial me is continuous with the I which expressed itself in the diverse conjoined me's.

What is not yet clear is whether or not a me approached from the outside is continuous with the substantial me and, through the help of this, with the I itself, or whether or not it is continuous with the I without any mediation. I think it is the former. Though there is no stopping at the substantial me, and though there is no acknowledgment of it or apparent awareness of it when one refers to oneself from the outside, or when one is aware of oneself as reaching toward the body in a feeling, the existence of a substantial me becomes apparent when it is realized that an I unexpressed is cut off from all else. A man, as one who is in the world with other men, is a substantial me, ready to be involved in this or that relation with this or that part of his body, through feeling and through a reference from some outside position.

To these three me's one should perhaps add a me that is produced by the juncture of those distinguished under A and B. This me, which comes and goes, is an experienced me, a me which has a different import over the course of time, and which could be identified with oneself as the object of awareness, mediated by both an inwardly and an outwardly reached me. It is that experienced me which the Buddhists apparently have identified with the self; they have therefore concluded that there is no persistent self. To explain the continuity of the individual, and the actions which are apparently grounded in and affected by past activities, these thinkers say that a later version of the self inherits something from earlier ones. For such inheritance to occur, however, there must be something which engages in the inheriting. Evidently, a newly constituted me at each moment is inseparable from an ontological base which, for these thinkers, is not a substantial me but the course of the universe. They in effect undergird experienced me's, not with individual substantial me's, but with a cosmic course of diversified inheritances from the past.

Some of the Whiteheadeans hold, instead, that an actual entity in coming to be takes into itself what it is to inherit from the past. The past as available for such inheritance would seem to be a kind of dead substance, and the process of coming to be a kind of conversion of that substance into what Hegel would call a 'subject' and into what Whitehead calls a 'subject-superject'. It appears that these Whiteheadeans are Hegelians, writing small.

* * *

I have been neglecting this manuscript in order to concentrate on getting the earlier portion of it ready for the press and, also, another revision of "First Considerations" ready for another typing.

Suppose one were to find that in all these volumes I never wrote on such and such a date? Suppose, further, that this was a date of importance in the history of philosophy—perhaps the birthday of someone with whom I profoundly disagreed or with whom I almost entirely agreed? Would one have a right to say that I deliberately avoided writing on that date? Not if my own denial is accepted as honestly made. Might one go on to say that the omission was made unconsciously? Not yet. One would need collaborative evidence. This fact is sometimes overlooked by psychiatrists. They forget that their probing to the unconscious on the basis of a patient's present reports is supported by other things that the patient thought about and did before. Were a patient entirely well, there would be no confirmation of the supposed unconscious motives which were supposedly being reached through 'analysis'.

Might one perhaps say that the very fact that one went to see a psychiatrist is already evidence of an aberration, and that this could support the probing? Perhaps, but only if the kind of 'sickness' which the visit indicates is of a piece with the kind of aberration that allowed the psychiatrist to probe to the unconscious motivation.

July 29

I saw *The Skin of Our Teeth* last night, for the first time. It is astonishing to see how like Thornton Wilder the play itself is. It is banal, obvious, boring at the beginning, and then builds up until at the end one becomes aware of insight, understanding, and wisdom. It is warm, naïve, pleasant, humorous in turns and, at the same time, wilfully tries to disrupt ordinary theatrical conventions without making any particular point in doing so. There is really only one good part in it, that of Sabina, with the children not well understood, the wife conventionally treated, and the intrusions of the stage manager somewhat foolish. It made for a pleasant but not memorable evening.

I have now finished my rereading of *Crime and Punishment.* There are a surprising number of set scenes, wooden portrayals of women, snide anti-Semitic remarks, and yet a strong emotional drive, sustained particularly by a complex psychological grasp of Rashkalnikov. I don't think I will read it again, and as I think back on it I do not see that I have gained much insight from it either about crime or about any of the characters. I will reread *Brothers* one of these days again, to see if my high opinion of that work can still be maintained.

I picked up S. V. Benét's *John Brown's Body* to see if it would be worth reading again. I could not get started. There was a flatness and obviousness to the lines that made me put it aside at once. I remember, though, when the book came out, Evelyn Whitehead was so excited by it that she bought many copies and gave them to her friends. My copy is a gift from her. She thought it caught the distinctive sense of America as nothing else did. But it is not surprising, I think, that the book has dropped out of the world, unquoted, not referred to.

It is a long time since I read any of Kafka. I have pulled out *The Trial,* and will begin reading it on and off, as I continue my revising of "First Considerations." I veer from thinking that that manuscript must be rewritten from top to bottom, to believing that it can be made into a significant work by careful revision. I am now revising it at something like twenty to thirty typed pages a day.

Though I can not persuade myself that my paintings have any distinction or importance, I have heard again and again from men who have devoted their lives to painting that I am 'gifted', and that some of my paintings are excellent. I wonder whether these judgments are not merely ways of saying that my paintings are somewhat unusual in color, design, execution, and impact. I do not conform to conventional canons, not because like Thornton Wilder I know them and then set about deliberately to break them, but because I do not know them, and have not sufficient mastery of technique to be able to do much more than to content myself with simple ideas, designs, and colors, and to take advantage of accidental results discovered a little later when I look at what I had done.

August 1

The depth delvers—structuralists, psychoanalysts, Chomskyan linguists—rightly look beneath the obtrusive phenomena for the controlling, unifying features of myths, social practices, and languages. But it is not altogether clear just where they are probing. Is it the individual, groups of individuals, or something beyond all individuals and groups of them?

The dominant thought seems to be that the basic controlling structures issue from individuals, but only so far as those individuals are alike. The position is question-begging if the likeness of the individuals is identified with the supposed common structure they are producing. In any case, what they must mean is that the individual gives special impetus or makes particular use of something which is not identifiable with him. And that is the second position.

On the second position, what is being brought to the surface is a 'collective unconscious', a shared way of being or doing, something transcending the individual, perhaps in the form of a society or a history. Does such a collective have power? A distinctive nature? Does it make itself manifest through individuals? Is it irresistible? Is it qualified and modified by what is encountered in the individual and in the world outside the social group to which he belongs? What is the source of the differences amongst various groups, and the particularities of a group? Are these traceable to individual men? I have not yet found answers to these questions in the writings of the delvers.

The third alternative is one which I have been urging over the last years. It refers us to a transcendent reality operative on all actualities. The shape it has with respect to a plurality of men is due to the ways in which those men respond to it. Each yields to it to some degree, thereby making them all appear in common guises; and each insists on himself and thereby qualifies and personalizes the result. The common condition is internalized by men who therefore are in a position to express its import from within.

The term 'structure' and the reference to grammar support the supposition that the condition is an expression of Possibility; the reference to myth, supports the supposition that the condition is an expression of Unity; the reference to social practices and the emphasis on dichotomies support the supposition that the condition is an expression of Existence; the reference to particular societies, kinship, and distribution of work supports the supposition that the condition is an expression either of Substance or of Being. There is no more justification for bundling all these expressions together and contenting oneself with a reference to a depth, even in individuals, than there is in bundling together a man's rights, identity, individuality, value, and beliefs.

Structuralists are particularly occupied with attaining a position from which a multiplicity of phenomena of different kinds can be explained. But the fact that these all may have a depth grammar does not go to show that they all originate from a single source. To this it will be answered that there are too many similarities in the phenomena of myth and kinship, for example, to allow one to rest with different depth references which pertain to them in their severalty. But may these similarities not be due to the fact that the various phenomena are dealt with on different levels of abstraction?

The finalities express themselves independently of one another with distinctive results. Each, too, is affected by the others, and each provides a way of dealing with what is primarily produced by the others. Thus, we can look at Substance and the results it produces from the position of Unity or value, with the consequence that we will be able to speak of what is possessive and possessed, affiliating and affiliated in terms of values, ordering the two in relation to one another, and assigning them a place on a scale with the other finalities and their products. But in this way the nature and the primary role of what is being dealt with from the position of some other finality will be obscured.

It may well be that myth, grammar, and so forth, are all the outcome of the use of a single internalized condition. If so, we should look to other phenomena for the beginning of probings into other conditions which also have been internalized and expressed. The depth delvers have either wrongly brought together different ultimate factors, or they have failed to take account of other ultimate factors which are at the root of different clusters of phenomena—or both. I think the last is the case. Law, for example, is to be traced back to an expression of Being, coordinate with the source of grammar or myth or kinship, and at the same time is to be dealt with together with economics and ethical principles such as the Golden Rule, all expressing Being. Being would here be seen to make itself manifest in the cluster of law, economics, and so forth, which it sustains alongside the independently sustained cluster (by Possibility) of mathematics, logic, grammar, and science, at the same time that the law was being contrasted with only one of these, grammar, in the specific guise it has in some particular society.

August 6

It is not possible to make a single totality out of all the actualities and finalities. The most that one can do is to approach the actualities as a plurality from the vantage point of the different finalities, each having the role of a one for that many, or to approach the finalities as a plurality from the vantage point of different actualities, each having the role of a one for them.

I am somewhat inclined to think that these approaches to one type of reality from the vantage point of another functioning as a one for it is to be identified with a process of naming which never gets the length of becoming or achieving a name. If that supposition is justified, we would have to say, among other things, that the use of transcendentals reflecting the unifying presence of finalities is one with a process of naming. To say that something is a unity, a being, a substance, has a nature, or is existent or quantitative, would be one with engaging in a process of naming an actuality or set of them, and would never end with a characterization of them. And, conversely, to say that the finalities are distinct or multiple, or to speak of them in other terms derived from actualities, would be to approach them from the position of actualities, functioning as so many one's, and therefore would result in a naming and never in a name.

I said that I was 'somewhat' inclined to accept this view because I sense but have not yet focussed on a difficulty. Does this view require one to say that the referent to a unity contained in a proper name has to do with the naming process and not with what is named? Or must we not, instead, distinguish between the names of transcendentals and the naming by transcendents, the one referring to what is intruded and specified in particular cases, and the other to the conditions which are applicable to all particular cases?

Where a Kantian would be inclined to say that the naming of conditions might never get to the length of producing a name, I am maintaining that   A] this is the result of our starting with actualities, and   B] that there is a reciprocal naming achieved when one starts with finalities and seeks to reach actualities from that position. A Kantian would perhaps allow for B, and take the attempt to get to actualities to be an attempt to realize an ideal, or to speak of a thing in itself.

If it be possible on my view to start with finalities and make use of names by having those finalities specified and delimited in the actualities, it should also be possible to start with actualities and provides names for the finalities as ultimate realities which are affected by those actualities. But now it seems to be true that there is no need to speak of a naming which never comes to an end.

There is a naming, apparently, and nothing more so far as one remains within one domain and tries to deal with another. To get to the other domain one must move beyond a naming by giving oneself to the items in that other domain. To name, consequently, is to be possessed, adopted, accepted, by that which is in another domain from the names. Does this conclusion apply to ordinary names or only to those referring to actualities and finalities, and then as contrasting with one another? To allow it to apply to ordinary names is in effect to say that every name awaits the concluding of a naming by that which is named, because the naming starts in a domain alien to the object named. The conclusion must be reflected on; for the moment it seems too odd to be true.

I have stated a variant on the above position in the current draft of "First Considerations." I there set the cosmos, as involving the actual copresence of finalities and actualities, in contrast with an ideal unity of finalities and actualities, and maintain that there can be only a naming of the latter from the position of the former, and never the having of a name for the entire set of the actual and ideal cosmos. The question that still remains is whether or not the principles underlying that contention do not apply to the use of names for the actualities and for the finalities as they now are, not as together in an actual cosmos or as confronting an ideal, but by themselves.

August 7

Conceivably it might not be possible to name   A] actualities,   B] finalities,   C] the cosmic factual unity of the actualities and finalities,   D] the totality of the actualities and the finalities as they independently exist,   E] the ideal harmony of the actualities and finalities, measuring the excellence of the cosmic factual unity of them,   F] the totality of the ideal unity and the cosmic factual unity of them,   G] the totality of the actualities and the finalities, as existing together with the actualities,   H] the totality of the actualities and finalities as constituting an ideal cosmos, or   I] various combinations of the above.

The denial in all these cases would be rooted in the acknowledgment of realities which cannot be reached from the position from where a name would be used. Naming in all cases involves a movement from one domain to another. If this is so, then since we can in fact name actualities and finalities, we must be able to move from one domain to another. And this we do in symbolization. The names we use are all caught in a process of naming which is always moving beyond the reach of those names.

We can name actualities and finalities; we can also name the factual unity of them—the cosmos. We must therefore be able not only to penetrate to each of them from a position made possible by the other, but be able to reach to them as factually unified. This is possible because of man's ability to take himself to be a unity for the very world in which he is a part. He can take himself to be the focal point in terms of which the entire cosmos, himself included, is approached and finally named.

It is questionable, though, whether it is possible to forge a name for the totality of actualities and finalities as they independently exist, and therefore for any of the subsequent cases (E–I) mentioned, since there seems to be no position from which one could envisage them. But if so, in what sense can we even acknowledge that there is a totality? When speaking of a 'totality' of independently existing actualities and finalities, we must start with one of these realities and approach the other in terms of it. We then seem to imitate the act of turning an apple around to see it on every side, while never being able to see the apple all around at one time. Such an imitation, though, is not exact, for we already have some grasp of the apple as a unit which makes it possible to have all its profiles connected, whereas in the case of the totality of the independent actualities and finalities, there is no connecting entity which can be fastened on, beneath the different distinguished items.

There are a number of difficulties that immediately surface: *1*] To refer to something as 'totality' is already to use a name.   *2*]   No trouble was found in using 'totality' to refer to all the actualities as together under the aegis of a finality; there should be no trouble in using the term to refer to a totality of actualities and finalities under the aegis of some other unity.   3] It has already been allowed that a man can speak of the whole of which he is a member; why does not this allowance extend to the totality of actualities and finalities?   4] Any whole of which a man is a part can be imaginatively added to, so that the actual world and finalities, or these together and supplemented by the ideal, could be named by him.

1] It is an old paradox that the 'unspeakable' is being spoken of, and that the 'unnameable' is being named. The paradox is overcome when it is recognized that 'unspeakable' and 'unnameable' are signs, and not proper names; they do not share in a penetration into the reality of that which is thereby acknowledged. A totality of independent actualities and finalities, or of these together with an ideal, is not a summed totality, not a totality which is governed by a unity and thereby actually named.

2] This objection has now been anticipated: the totality of actualities is dealt with from the position of a finality or an expression of it, which effectively unites the items in that totality and thereby enables that totality to be one, actually reached by means of a name.

3] A man is not part of the whole made up of independent finalities and independent actualities. He does, to be sure, forge a concept of unity and uses this to refer to all the actualities and finalities, but that unity has no power to unite these; he faces them as an aggregate of items which, so far, has no unity other than that which he provides.

4] Any whole of which a man is a part can be added to in imagination. But it does not follow that a man then becomes a part of me; when I am together with you my hand does not become a part of the two of us, but continues to remain a part of me alone.

These are swift answers, and may not be able to withstand long scrutiny, but they do seem to take care of the more obvious objections, and to be on the right track. Still not clear are the answers to the questions: A] Does the name of an actuality have its roots in the realm of finalities or in man's replacement of this, or does it instead begin on the side of actualities?   B] Does the name of a finality have its roots in the realm of actualities or in man's replacement of this, or does it instead begin on the side of the finalities?

If names take their start in some other domain than that in

which their objects are, all use of names must involve a leap into an
alien domain where the names are taken over by the objects. But
does it make sense to say that we start somewhere with finalities
before we in fact have names that can be used properly of actualities, even though it is conventional to say that we start with actualities
before we in fact have names that are used of finalities. Honorific
names of actualities are derived from finalities, but adherent, ad-
dressive names of actualities seem to involve no such derivation.
And if it be possible to have such derivates, and to leap from one
domain to another, why must we stop with a process of naming and
not go on to a name which becomes part of and is accepted by the
object named? Is it not that the proper name of an actuality starts at
a finality as already involved with and affected by that actuality, so
that when we use a proper name of an actuality we are already
involved with it, even though we begin with what is part of another
domain? Is it also true that the proper name of a finality starts at an
actuality as already involved with and affected by that finality, so
that when we use a proper name of a finality we are already involved
with it? If so, there are no names which do not originate with a
naming starting in some other domain. The name itself would be
the result of a leap into a domain where the object of the name takes
over. But then why should it not be possible for a naming of a
totality of actualities and finalities, or of the actual and the ideal
cosmos together, to end with a name for these? Is it not because
there is nothing there able to take over and accept the name?

*   *   *

Bellow's *Mr. Sammler's Planet* is not as good as his *Herzog* in good
part because his main character is not rounded out. There is a strong
emphasis in the book on the distinctive nature of women—slightly
mad, with eyes, smells, and movements which mark them off from
all men. Bellow is most attentive to smells everywhere, but particularly of women. This unusual specificity is balanced by continuing
philosophic reflections of considerable breadth, validity, and originality, mainly with reference to the import of life and basic human
responses. But he seems unable to sustain a long, intricate plot and
a multiplicity of characters interlocked and making a difference to
one another.

   I have been reading Robert Fitzgerald's translation of the *Iliad*.
It is a splendid work. But so was Lattimore's. Yet the two are

radically different in concept and execution. Lattimore tries to recapture the very rhythm of the Homeric verse; Fitzgerald tries to recapture its verve and spirit. The two occupy the extremes emphasized in the debate about the nature of a translation. Should it let one know what the poem or other work was like for those who then heard it; should it instead let one know what is being said, by getting it into the form that allows for its full appreciation in another civilization and at another time? Lattimore gives more weight to the need to know, Fitzgerald to the right to enjoy, though neither ignores the other factor, and in fact attends to it. Perhaps the right answer is that we need both types, for we want and ought to know the work as it is in its context, and we want and ought to enjoy the work in our own.

August 8

A word uttered or written down is not yet a name, and most surely, not a proper name. At the very minimum, a name must become part of an appearance, providing it with A] a boundary, and B] an infusion of emotional energy which either remains within the confines of that boundary, and thus allows for the naming of an actuality, or which overflows the boundary and thereby enables one to make contact with a finality.

An adherent proper name is used penetratively of an actuality. By means of an emotion, such as sympathy, it is made integral to an appearance which it helps bound. This requires it to move beyond the condition, which is a constituent of that appearance, toward the actuality. The name can be said to begin in a different domain from the actuality, since it begins at a sympathetic but private individual who operates in terms of his own internalizations of the finalities. But the name becomes a proper adherent name only by moving beyond the finality's contribution to the appearance, thereby becoming integral to the actuality's contribution to that appearance. The more appreciative one is of another, the more does one move toward him as a particular source of a contribution to an appearance; a proper name refers to the actual individual, but as one who has manifested himself and been encountered by an attentive man who bounds him in thought and by means of the name. Not until the named man takes the name into himself do we have the name properly functioning.

The name of a finality also begins its career with an emotional man and is brought to bear on an appearance. But the accompanying emotion does not permit of a penetration to the actuality; instead it spreads beyond the borders of the acknowledged appearance to become one with the condition which is a constituent of that appearance and, via that condition, is made to move toward a finality. The name of a finality becomes a proper name only through the help of the finality itself, when it accepts the name as an integral part of an emotionally intensified condition.

The foregoing account does some justice to the use of such expressions as 'Thomas Jones' or 'Being'. It does not seem to be appropriate to the use of such expressions as 'this-green-leaf', 'this-small-bird', 'this-heavy-rock', which could be given proper names. Such names are necessarily ambiguous. We cannot tell from them whether we are to move toward actualities or toward finalities, since we cannot tell from them just what kinds of emotions are to accompany them. They seem in fact to be accompanied by emotions which are diffuse mixtures of those directed at actualities and those directed at finalities, since they neither remain within the boundaries of the appearances nor spread to the conditions which are constitutive of those and other appearances.

The cosmos, since it is the outcome of the interplay of actualities and finalities, is the product of distinct realities. But unlike an appearance, it characterizes actualities as constituting a single plurality governed by laws fitting within a single space, time, and dynamism, with each actuality standing apart from the others. To name it properly one must make a single name out of the different names of the different finalities, and then produce a derivative name for the totality of actualities, by confining the application of the name to that totality. What is then done is similar to what is done when one speaks of a particular actuality as a 'substance' or 'being'. These, too, were initially names of finalities, but are derivatively used in restricted ways with respect to actualities. The initial emotions, which were involved with the conditions, are subject to a constraint enabling them to be brought to bear on particular actualities. They are, then, not so much accepted by the actualities as thrust upon them. A converse set of operations is involved when one speaks of the finalities as 'many', 'diversified', and the like, since these are derivatives from proper names used with reference to actualities.

Not until a name is accommodated by an actuality or a finality, via the emotion which is conveying it, does it in fact function as a proper name. Until then it is an inseparable part of a process of naming. It is the acceptance by an actuality or a finality of the content of the naming which allows for the separation of the name, and for the identification of this with the actuality or finality.

There is no name for actualities and finalities as an aggregate of independent realities; there is no name for them as ideally together. In these two cases, there is nothing which is able to accept a name and therefore is able to have a name be apart from a naming. But if this is so, there seems to be a difficulty in treating 'cosmos' as a proper name, for this would seem to require that there be some way in which all the actualities be able to accommodate it when, as a matter of fact, they are independent entities which are together only for a common condition and presumably for a common name.

The cosmos is the result of the effective operation of finalities on all the actualities. The name 'cosmos' is inseparable from that operation; it is accommodated only in the sense that it compels the actualities to be together. The aggregate of independent actualities and finalities can not be named. A naming of them never comes to an end. Nor is there a name for them as ideally together; an ideal unity of all the actualities and finalities is a single entity, but it lacks the power to accommodate a name for it. An ideal unity of all actualities and finalities can not be named, then, for the opposite reason from that which precludes the naming of actualities and finalities as they now are, independent of one another. The one lacks interiority, a power to take a name into itself; for the other there is no name able to be part of a unity which can bring those independent realities together. The most that can be done in the latter case is to bring them together imaginatively as an aggregate.

August 11

The proper names of actualities are emotionally charged and accepted by those actualities. The acceptance does not mean that the individual is conscious of the name, but only that the entire complex of emotion, name, and bounded, symbolically used appearance must be used penetratively, and eventually be accommodated by the individual if it is to function as an adherent, properly addressed name. The proper name of a finality is also emotionally charged and accepted, but here the emotions spread beyond the borders of any actuality to become one with a condition which is intruded on an actuality and then continued into the finality, which eventually takes over.

Harder questions are raised with respect to the names of all the actualities together, all the finalities together, the totality of finalities and actualities, the ideal union of all the finalities and actualities, and the juncture of the latter two.

The name of the actualities together is 'the cosmos'. The name is to be identified with the cosmic pattern which is produced by the totality of finalities as affecting all the actualities. Identified with the pattern produced by all the finalities, the 'cosmos' cannot be understood without an understanding of all the finalities. But before that time, one can deal with the cosmic pattern in five distinct ways, emphasizing now this and then that aspect of it, reflecting the presence of this or that finality. This is done by deriving the name of all the actualities together from the name of a finality, but sustaining it by an emotion pertinent to the actualities.

The name of all the finalities together is 'the totality of finalities', or some equivalent. That name is a derivative from the name of an actuality but sustained by an emotion pertinent to the finalities. The totality of finalities can be understood from the standpoint of an actuality as their unity. A name for that totality will start from the actuality as a single entity and emotionally refer to the finalities.

A totality of actualities can not sustain or satisfy an emotion directed at them. There is a unity imposed on those actualities, but there is no object beyond that unity to which a name, united with that unity, applies. Similarly, a totality of finalities can not sustain or satisfy an emotion directed at them. Here, too, a unity is imposed on those finalities, but that does not have an object beyond that unity to which a name, united with that unity, applies. How then could one name a cosmos or the totality of finalities? And if one could name them, would one not also be able to name the totality of the finalities and actualities, the ideal union of the finalities and actualities, and the combination of these last two?

Each finality has power enough to intrude on the actualities together, and any name which can be joined with the condition that the finality provides will be able to function as the name of them together, not because it has been accepted by those actualities but because it is in control of those actualities. But it is not plausible to reverse this supposition and take each actuality to have power enough to intrude on all the finalities together so that any name joined with the unity that an actuality provides will be a proper name for them. And, in any case, no account is yet given of the naming of all the finalities together.

Is there any need to suppose that there is a single name to be assigned to all the finalities, either from the position of one or a number of actualities? We do refer to them as together, but that togetherness may be no more than a conceived togetherness of an aggregate, having only a blurred, ambiguous meaning. If this be accepted, then we can go on to say that the most comprehensive of names is that provided by the cosmos in one aspect, such as its rationale, or its extension, and that there is no proper name for A] the cosmos as governed by a fivefold condition or pattern, B] the set of finalities, C] the set of finalities and actualities, D] the ideal unity of finalities and actualities, and E] the combination of C and D. All of these will be subject to a naming which never gets the length of becoming or precipitating or terminating in a proper name.

*   *   *

Last night I saw *The Scarecrow* by Percy MacKaye, a revival of an old work. It was directed by Austin Pendleton who provided a box seat for me. (He'll be having breakfast with me tomorrow morning, when I hope I will be able to ask him about the specific problems of a director, and how his work compares with that of an actor and a film performer, in which Austin also has had experience.)

The play was not altogether satisfactory; the witch and the devil, confessedly hard parts to act, were overacted; they were not amusing nor ominous nor attractive. Is this the fault of the director or of the actors? It can not, I think, be the fault of one of them alone. The best of directors can not do anything with poor actors; the best of actors needs guidance and suggestion. The actors in this play have performed excellently elsewhere, though I think their reputation depends on what they have done in film and not on the stage. A most demanding, insistent director could surely have made them act differently no matter what their predilections, though he may not have been able to change the effect of the play as acted by just those actors.

A director should be able to convey to actors something of the overall effect that is being created by them, and require the modification of voice, gesture, and position so as to bring about that effect; each actor should be alert to the import of his part in itself, its bearing on the other parts, and the bearing of those other parts on it. In ignorance of just what went on in the rehearsals, I would hazard the guess that it is the director's fault that the play lags in the beginning and does not grip one at any time, for I am inclined to believe that were an actor to be told to be quieter here or there, to show more exuberance, sympathy, concern, and the like, he would know what to do.

August 12

The article on me in *The New Columbia Encyclopedia* summarizes my views inaccurately and with little perception. It takes me to be trying to combine the general outlooks of Peirce and James and some Europeans. What would I put instead? Trying to fit into the neutral, objective outlook of an encyclopedia I would sum it as: "His pluralistic metaphysical system attempts to show that all particulars, separately and together, are subject to a fivefold condition, originating with distinct, irreducible, insistent realities." If I were allocated more room, I would refer to *Modes of Being* and *Beyond All Appearances.* If I could elaborate on the one sentence, I would say something about the evidences for the conditions and their sources, and give some account of those sources.

I have at last begun to work on "You, I, and the Others." I am trying to write it with great care, and will not be troubled if I do not manage to finish more than a decent page a day, even if the whole comes out to be not much larger than an essay or a small book. It is a great pleasure to begin to work through something. "First Considerations" is now an object for revisions, and the present work is written episodically. Neither provides me with the kind of satisfaction, and the feeling that I am learning, as does my carefully working through a systematic account.

Instead of coming for breakfast, Austin Pendleton came by for dinner. In sharp contrast with what I have maintained in *Cinematics,* he thinks there is little difference between theatrical and film acting, and between theatrical and film directing. The major difference, in some accord with Russian film theorists, he holds, is that a film director has charge of cuts and oversees the montaging and, therefore, can give new weights to the performances of the film actors. He thinks that a play is mainly the work of the actors, and that a director provides an overall view, and not much more. He, with me, is impressed with the high native intelligence of actors, and the great devotion and sincere giving of themselves that is characteristic of great ones. He thinks, though, that a great stage actor will be a great film actor; I neglected to press the question as to whether he thought the reverse to be true as well. I find it hard to disagree with him, but I also find it hard to hold the positions he does, particularly since he does admit that a film actor may not have a good understanding of what the part means in relation to the whole. He did think that there were child actors who had a good perception of the meaning of their parts in relation to others and conversely. If he is right, I am wrong in maintaining that there can be no great child actors except those who act the part of spoiled children who have no awareness, interest, or appreciation of what concerns adults. Evidently, I must allow some of his views to simmer around the back of my mind for a while; they are too directly opposed to those I have long held that I will not be able to do justice to them until I have allowed them to become somewhat familiar.

August 13

A defect in this, and perhaps every other diary, is the fact that items which constantly recur are rarely remarked upon, with the consequence that they might be overlooked and the import of what is written exaggerated and distorted. Again and again, for example, I have remarked that I am tired; I have commented on my youth and antecedents; I have reflected on my possible death, and the like. When these observations are read in one or a few sittings, the impression is given that these are matters that come up frequently. Just the opposite is true. I am usually full of energy; I find thinking about my past to be quite boring; I hardly ever think about death. This diary would express what I am like and what I in fact am thinking only if I were to write almost every day that I am full of energy, and if I recorded all the thoughts which, at least negatively, have to do with my past and my eventual future. A diary contains pivotal entries; it gives little evidence of what occurs in between, though this is usually what is normal, the measure of the others.

August 30

For the past weeks I have done hardly anything but work on the chapter "You," in "You, I, and the Others." Writing and rewriting, I have now written some sixty typewritten pages, and have some more still to do. "First Considerations" is almost completely retyped; I will set it aside for awhile, to await comments by critics and to allow me to look at it afresh. I will try to reserve entries in this work to thoughts which do not fit in "You, I, and the Others."

*   *   *

I have long been dissatisfied with the account I gave in *The World of Art* about the difference between a product of nature which was indistinguishable from a created work of art, and a created work.

A possible view: a created work is a tensed, nuanced related set of items stretched over alien material. That fact is most conspicuous in connection with sculpture, where one so evidently may use material which has a nature of its own and is made subject to a new condition. The artistically determined meaning here is at once controlling of the matter and is subject, with that matter, to a unitary control by a particular, natural object. To know a work of art is to know it as controlled by the new condition. It is so controlled apart from the artist, but not apart from a world of art which orients all works toward an appreciation, which is able to ignore the unity that the object provides, to attend to the unity which is imposed on the material by the artist.

An object in nature might be altered by the forces of nature so that it is indistinguishable from what an artist might produce. That object in nature will not have had a meaning imposed on and controlling the material. When it is brought within the domain where artistic appreciation occurs, its unity will be dislocated and taken to be a function of the meaning then discerned. We might not know whether or not some one work which we are confronted with is the result of such a dislocation, and is not a created artistic product. But that is because we will have viewed the work in isolation from all other works.

An artistic product might be said to be governed by an artistically imposed unity, not merely from the position of the artist or those who are then appreciating it, but from that of a community of appreciative men. Each work would then be seen to be inseparable from a continued, persistent effort to attend to imposed, created meanings. A work of nature, which by itself we could not distinguish from a work of art, would then be identified with the work of some unknown artist whose artistic abilities we could not know since we had no other works in terms of which we were able to determine the manner in which he was able to make a meaning be in control. Not unless nature was able to produce work after work which we could not distinguish from the products of artists, or not until we could tell from a single product of a man that it was the work of an artist rather than an aberrational product of some activity on his part, would we be in a position to avoid this approach. But nature intersperses ugly things with beautiful ones and apparently haphazardly; and one must produce a number of works before one can be an artist.

In opposition to such a contention, it could be argued that we should be able to separate out all the beautiful works as the works of an 'artistic' nature, and set aside the others as having been brought about by nature operating under different conditions, somewhat as we now distinguish the work of an artist in his studio from what he does when he eats or plays a game or even when he ventures into a new field of art and there performs badly. And it could be even more strongly argued that anyone who produces a single splendid line of poetry is a poet. A Rimbaud, who stopped writing poetry at the age of nineteen, was surely a poet. If his poetry could be produced by accident through the random operation of a machine, or by the blowing of the wind across sheets with all the words in the dictionary on them, would we have anything different from what we now have? Must we not say that no matter where the discarded words were placed, the discarding and the displacing would be different from that which characterized Rimbaud's writing? Does the issue then come down to determining the type or rejected item or the kind of rejection of that which is not accepted as art? Does nature reject what men do not? Is it possible that nature can not hold the ugly away from the beautiful, whereas an artist can? How is it possible to determine from any number of works the type of rejection that is involved in their production?

I have taken the following from "First Considerations." It is not altogether relevant there, and it bears on the present issue, though it does not settle it: the unsatisfactory rides on the back of the satisfactory. It not only fails to measure up to a standard but does not refer to the world where its components are. It is unable to tell us that there is a realm, other than where it now is, where its terms are units governed by natural laws. Only what meets standard conditions refers to a domain where components of the unsatisfactory are on a footing with the components of the satisfactory.

The unwanted—the prejudicial, empty, bogus, mechanical or elitist, or the defective, erroneous, frustrative, or wrong—is a set of natural items which customary rules place in the same realm as the wanted—the appreciated, outstanding, disciplined, enhancing, classical, revelational, novel, or innovative—whether this be a sentence, a work of art, a name, or a document.

The fraudulent takes advantage of normal practices to lead one to the conclusion that it is genuine. It is parasitic on the genuine. Just as the genuine is, it is an object of intention. But where the genuine intends a truth, the fraudulent intends only to be accepted as a truth. It can confess itself to be fraudulent only by ceasing to be so—though, of course, someone might refuse to accept the admission. Though a lie takes place in the same domain that a truth does, and though we may be led to accept it as a truth, it does not, as the truth does, also refer to a world where its components are. Were one to lie about his lies, however, he would take the initial lies to constitute a basic set where, for the moment, they are identified as truths.

To know whether or not a word was produced in nature by animals or machines, or by an intending man (and then freed from all reference to his intent), one must see if it can be assimilated to *established items,* conform to a *paradigm,* be in consonance with accepted *principles,* exhibit a *creative power,* or be an instantiation of a *primary value.* Each of these defines a distinctive kind of desirable status—appropriateness, excellence, truth, success, or importance. Each also defines a distinctive kind of rejectable item—the alien, the defective, the erroneous, failure, or the worthless.

The spirit of a discipline provides a measure for what is to be adopted, just so far as this can be assimilated to established items. It provides a measure of what is appropriate and what is alien, the one to be accepted, the other to be rejected. In its acceptance of items not yet known to have been intended, it includes what satisfies an appreciation. But it will not yet be able to exclude what is merely prejudice, for this is also assimilable to the established items. Similarly, in its rejection of the alien, it will exclude what is disruptive, but this may well encompass the revolutionary—which is to say, the disruptive produced in opposition to the prevailing spirit—though it may well establish another, perhaps even better spirit.

A paradigm provides a measure for what is excellent and for what is defective. Its acceptance of the excellent permits it to allow for items not known to have been intended, provided that they are outstanding. This, however, makes it receptive of the bogus, since the bogus can conform to the paradigm. A paradigm enables one to avoid only the irrelevant. But its success here is inseparable from its rejection of all novelties, even those which conform to paradigms that may be superior to those now in use.

Principles measure validity and invalidity. They prompt the acceptance of whatever bears the marks of a requisite disciplining. This does not enable one to avoid accepting what is purely formal and empty, a mere exhibition of a principle. A principle requires the rejection of the irresponsible, as that which does not submit to the principle, but it does not enable one to avoid the rejection of what is produced by innovations; instead it prompts the labeling of them as irresponsibilities.

Effectiveness provides a measure of what is to be deemed successful or frustrative. Anything that is enhancing will be found to be acceptable—but so will the mechanical which maximizes efficiency. The effective also allows one to reject the frustrative as that which takes us downhill. But that very test leads to the dismissal of discoveries as well, for these too may fail to be effective in the way the enhancing or mechanical are.

A standard for assessment provides a measure for both the important and the wrong. It promotes the acceptance of classical works, at the same time that it endorses what is merely elitist. It dismisses what is worthless but also what could prove to be important had one begun with a different assessing standard.

Every measure promotes the acceptance of some undesirable items and the rejection of others, at least as desirable as those that were accepted. Nothing is altered when, in reaction against this fact, one accepts whatever these measures reject and rejects whatever they accept. One would then merely have allowed the unmeasured to provide a new standard of measurement. Use of that standard will end with the rejection of what the other accepted, and the acceptance of what it rejected. And that also is regrettable.

Least harm is done if one uses rules. These, though, will also allow for the acceptance of what is empty. But even the most creative work involves a good deal of empty formality; in any case the acceptance of the empty requires that it be the object of disciplined effort. Least harm would be done were one to allow a standard of assessment to dictate what is to be rejected as worthless. But this can lead to the dismissal of what in fact needs another category, and perhaps therefore what might be the beginning of a new direction or even of a new epoch. The best of policies is to balance the use of rules with standards of assessment; what each might dismiss may be supported by the other.

September 1

We speak of referring to the past in memory and in history. There is something which we did not create, something which will test what we now say. We can not confront it, but we know that it is determinate, that which allows for no further specification in itself, and is thus different from what is now in the future, and is able to exclude the present as surely as the present excludes it. Still, it makes no sense to say that there are concrete objects in the past. Not only would one then have to suppose that there is a different space for them to occupy from that which now exists, but one would have to suppose that they, like the present objects, are active and expend energy. As a consequence, we would have to maintain that energy, instead of being conserved, is multiplied, for at each moment there would be energy expended for ever and ever.

It will not do, with Whitehead and Hartshorne, to say—as I once did in the book on history—that the past is preserved by God. If he preserves it as a genuine present, the energy would still be expended; if he preserves it in some denuded form, we would be faced with the question as to what he might remember and to what he might refer were he concerned with what had happened in fact, and not merely with what he happens to extract from it.

Croce, Collingwood, and Mead hold that the past is reconstructed in the present. We make it. Not only does one then lose any check on what one is maintaining, but there would be no real distinction between fiction and fact, between what had been and what we are supposing to have been. If, in contrast with them, we recognize the existence of genuine structuralizations of time which were produced by the passage of entities from moment to moment, it is possible to utilize these structuralizations by starting with present features and tracing these back, along the lines of these structuralizations, to the past. The past at which one then arrives will be constructed, but since it is constructed in accord with the established structuralization of time, it will be a past which is known to be what it is, independently of us. We will arrive at it, but as that which is objective because it is the recovered origin of that with which we began our reference.

The structuralization of time, which is used in order to trace back present traits to others equally determinate, located at a previous time, is one we come to know in the course of experience. We now see that it takes time to go from one place to another, or that broken columns and doors follow on violence done to complete and functioning columns and doors. It is that kind of knowledge we use when we try to understand the structuralization of time that made possible the present features of things, and which we can use as the beginning of a transformative process that is to take us to other features. We can not take those features to be ingredient in or grounded in some real object in the past; whatever underpinning we take them to have we then and there suppose. The substances that possess features in the present are seen—to use Hegelian language—to be only subjects.

If this be correct, Hegel's dialectic was made by him to run in the opposite direction from that which it in fact does. He took it to move from substance to subject, but this occurs only when we seek to know the past from the vantage point of the present, for we then unify the transformations of the present to constitute a single 'phenomenological' determinate totality.

*　　*　　*

Last night I saw *The Apprenticeship of Duddy Kravitz*. The film has a very strong story line, and that is what is wrong with it. Pushed into prominence, a strong story line does not allow for a plurality of facets. In this picture there are some fine scenery shots, some very good interior dialogue, and interesting local scenes, but all are pulled into the story even when they could be considered in some independence of it because of their intrinsic merit—which in fact one can see. It is not that details, asides, enrichments, multidimensionality are ignored, but that the strong story line projected itself through and above all these so that one was not able to rest with them except in those few cases where there was an intended comic relief. A dramatic story must evidently buckle, rest, relax, fall into the background occasionally. Otherwise, like a detective story, the work becomes mainly plot, with characters and supporting events, but without maturation, subtilization, uncovering.

*   *   *

Is it possible for a philosopher to be too eccentric, too odd, too alien, too dissociated from established or current ways of thinking to be considered a philosopher, or taken seriously? This does occur as a matter of fact; I suppose Peirce would be one instance, and Alexander Bryan Johnson another. Perhaps Frege is a third. All were comparatively neglected in their day, only to be recognized much later. Undoubtedly, there are others who have not received this later recognition and who may never be recognized. Will this be because of some defect in them? But how could that be if a philosopher is one who is no respecter of accepted beliefs, even those of the community of philosophers? If he does not make contact with them, they will of course not know of him or read him, or attend to him. But if he is freely and honestly thinking about fundamentals with some originality and truth, perhaps let us say as much as characterizes others well-known and accepted, approved, discussed, or criticized, is he not doing all a philosopher should be doing? I think so.

September 8

I saw *Equus* in New York this weekend. I would not have known from the reviews I had read that the play was such good theatre, that it was so splendidly directed and acted, particularly by Thomas Hulce and by the publicized star, Anthony Perkins. The critics were disturbed by the psychoanalytic factor which ran throughout the play, but I think this motif was not as important as the ongoing of the play itself.

It made more evident to me than had been before the great difference there is between a film and a play. In the play, for example, six horses were represented by horse heads which men put on and took off, and by hooves which they constantly wore. The stage was almost bare, and all the actors were visible throughout. Were this play presented on film, live horses would have been used. Had there been a use of men acting the part of horses they would then illustrate someone's fancy and not the presumed horses that were involved in the activity being portrayed. This does not mean, as some students of the film maintain, that the film is necessarily 'realistic', for one could, through montaging and other devices, have the horses behaving fantastically. Were the scene bare on a film, that would mean that all was occurring in an austere setting, but on the stage one was being led to suppose that one was in a stable, on the street, in a movie house, in a hospital, and so on.

A film sets the conditions under which one is to see the transactions; in the play it is the transactions which carry whatever conditions there must be presupposed. Stage designing is suggestive; even when most realistic it is only representative, something to be vivified by what is going on. But in the film, the setting is a prop, a performer, an integral factor in the whole, having a role together with the actors and the more evident items in the foreground.

September 27

I have been holding two distinct views of God or Unity. The earlier followed the lead of Whitehead, and took God to be that power which encompassed all entities, but only by reorganizing them so that they were able to fit harmoniously within him. What was discordant was left behind; only so far as something was harmonious within itself was it preserved. But more lately I have been speaking of God as making all actualities fit in a hierarchy of better and worse.

In talking with Andrew Reck today about the former view, I became convinced that the latter is the better alternative. Reck remarked that if God does preserve he preserves everything; nothing is let slip, nothing is forgotten or dismissed into limbo. What ought to be said is that God, or Unity, on "reconciling the world to himself" orders all items in a hierarchy of better and worse. Instead, then, with the Neoplatonists maintaining that the initial state of affairs is a hierarchy resulting from the progressive manifestation or overflow of a primal One, it would be maintained that this is the outcome of God's or Unity's assessment of the world. The entire world would be said to be made up of items on a footing, whether as items created, or as items each of which possesses a being or a substantiality, and to be in a value hierarchy only so far as the items there were differentially evaluated by the primal Unity. If that Unity be taken to be a finality operative together with all the other finalities, there would of course not be a time or a state where the items were just together on a footing or in other ways, and then subsequently assessed and thereupon hierarchically ordered. They would be together in various ways at the same time, one of which was a hierarchically ordered totality under the governance of a unity which was empowered by a primal, final Unity.

*   *   *

I have now begun typing on my new IBM typewriter with its distinctive ribbon and erasure key. It is a skittish machine, and I think I will have much trouble with it, much more than I had with the other. But it is a pleasure to read the clear print, to be able to make erasures with some ease, and for the time being not to worry about a breakdown in parts, which became more and more the case with the ten-year-old machine that I replaced. I think, though, I have done something not altogether correct with this new machine for it does seem noisy and to move with less grace than the other.

September 30

Meaning accrues to an expression from what conditions it. The conditions are of many kinds. They can be idiosyncratic: "I believe in ghosts" where what is intended is to express a not well understood private supposition about the existence of departed spirits. They can be deceptive: "I am your friend," says the confidence man, within the context of a plan of deception which is unknown to others. They can be in guise of a conventional, partly common setting: "Don't call me, I'll call you" is understood by the speaker to be expressed within a context where the other is being told not to make further inquiries, and is to be extended at least a courteous expression of hope. Normally, the conditions are conventions productive of ordinary discourse, backed with a rough hewn set of grammatical rules: "This is a cat" is understood in the ordinary course of communication in roughly the same way by speaker and listener. Any one of these sets of meaning can be taken to be the primary or the sole permissible type, with the consequence that the others are taken to be derivatives or not to possess any meaning at all.

There are, however, other contexts besides these. The expressions of mathematics, logic, and the exact sciences are all embedded in distinctive domains ruled by distinctive sets of conditions, so that what is meant in these fields is quite different from what is meant in the others, for example, 'a variable'. But one can go on and also recognize distinctive meanings in religion, mysticism, art, and metaphysics. In these there is no necessary violation of the grammar or even the customary uses of the words. As a consequence, there is always a core of meaning which these have, expressive of the fact that their assertions are embedded within the context of a grammar where they are subject to conditions governing correct unit expressions.

Some conditions are purely formal, abstract, without any power beyond that which is given to them by the user; others, like mathematics and logic, seem to have some power, since they govern expressions apart from individual intentions to do so; still others have an objective power because they originate with realities which are intruding them on all that is. Metaphysical assertions have this third kind of meaning. They can be understood by anyone who knows the language of ordinary use; and yet, at the same time, they have a meaning which can not be grasped except so far as one is operating within the frame of the conditions. A metaphysician makes use of that kind of meaning when he speaks of ordinary things as 'appearances'. When he attends to the conditions and their sources (into which they continue and of which they are expressions intruded on actualities or other finite particulars), his expressions have to be understood to re-present their conditions. To say 'Unity' is to say something which is subordinated to the condition of Unity (and of course other conditions originating with other finalities). The discourse is objectively meaningful, meaningful not because there is someone who is speaking, but because the condition is rooted in an ultimate reality. In metaphysics we understand the primary terms to be conditioned by the very realities they name, and to be conditional for the other terms that are used in explicating them. Here alone we say what we mean, not in the sense of dealing with objective meanings, but in expressing in one way what the expressions are presupposing in another.

October 4

We are always somewhere between the one and the many, the interior and the exterior, but never exactly in the middle. Consequently, there is a stress on the one or the other. To get from the stressed to the unstressed, one must conform to the nature of the other. From the many to the one we move with the help of the one, and from the one to the many with the help of the many. The movements themselves can be external or internal to one another, and so on without end.

Whitehead's acceptance of the given external past (actually a set of desiccated substances shorn of all 'accidents') and future possibilities, natively inert but given emphasis by God, requires that there be a process of internalizing them and taking them toward a unity. But the reciprocal should also be recognized. The union of the two in the present involves an external process of separating them, terminating in them as distinct; otherwise there would be no externalized past and no prospective future. To accept process as ultimate is to minimize the plurality which is nevertheless presupposed; to emphasize substances is to minimize the process which is required for the connection between them.

Appearances have their own integrity and therefore have a being and intent. When these are taken as limited fringes of the appearances, the appearances are seen to be continuations of their realities. An appearance transforms the one into the other, taken either as prior to the integral and fringed appearances and thus having them as exterior, or as subsequent to them and thus as interior.

When we speak formally, we emphasize unity; when we speak dynamically, we emphasize diversity. Process does the second, translation the first. The two are connected by process or by translation, and so on without end. Here we have process in the opposite sense from what we had when we were contrasting it with substance, for then process unifies givens and is under the governance of the future which is undivided; when we contrast process with translation, process sets the intertranslated items outside one another. The issue though is far more complicated than these instances would indicate. A table makes that evident:

Let a B c represent any item B functioning as the locus for a and c, which therefore are so far external to it. Let a' B' c' represent any item B' functioning as a mediator for a' and c' at its limits. We have the following fourteen possible cases. We can go from:

1] a to c

2] c to a

3] a' to c'

4] c' to a'

5] a to c'

6] c' to a

7] c to a'

8] a' to c

9] a to a'

10] a' to a

11] c to c'

12] c' to c

13] B to B'

14] B' to B

Perhaps four more: B to a and c; a and c to B; B' to a' and c'; a' and c' to B'. And still four more: B' to a' and c'; B to a' and c; a' and c' to B; and a and c to B'.

The moves from a, B, or c to the others are moves from externally connected items to what is internally one, and are carried on by what is a translation of 'substance' to 'subject'—to speak with Hegel. But instead of supposing that this must have a progressive nature, because it goes in only one way, it seems more correct to say that there is a reciprocal movement going on, a movement of process in which what is unified, a' B' c', is diversified to leave one with a hard nucleal unit, an appearance having its own integrity, or a Whiteheadean completed actual occasion. Process instead of moving one toward the future would in effect be a way of making what was unified be diversified. (In Whitehead there seem to be two processes, one characteristic of God, which goes forward from unity to diversity, and another in the world, which goes backward, making what is multiple achieve a unity maintained apart. The process in God is a function of the fact that he has a consequent and a primordial nature; the process in the world is a function of the fact that an actual occasion pulls itself away from the factors available to it to constitute a one whose being consists in its vanishing.)

A word or other part of speech has its own integrity; it is a B; but it is a B only so far as it functions as a locus for an intent, the expression of an individual (not necessarily intended or intentional), and for a meaning, the outcome of the action of a controlling condition. The connecting of a and c, and a' and c', backward and forward (1–4) makes the locus and the mediator function as ways of converting the one into the other. The connecting of a and c', and of a' and c (5–8) introduces another agency which converts an external intent or meaning into an internal, or conversely. The passage from a to a' and c to c', and conversely (9–12) turns intent and meaning from internal or external into the other. The move from B' and B, backward and forward (13–14) is between mediator and locus, and requires that each in turn operate on the other. The move from B and B' to their own components and conversely (the next four) uses the B and B' to connect or separate the components. The move from B and B' to the components of the other, and conversely (the last four) also requires that each control the move from locus to the mediated fringes and conversely, and from a mediator to what is external, and conversely.

B and B' have roles between factors and also roles with respect to one another. As the former they can be said to transform the factors; as the latter to convert them. If B and B' are the same appearance, once as an integral item with its conditions beyond it, and the other as fringed, each has the other as a product and as a condition. This green has the green-of-the-x (and conversely) as that which was unifying (or reciprocally, diversifying) it. Green is internalized by the green-of-x at the same time that the green-of-x is externalized by the green. Neither vanishes, but each is to be understood in terms of the other. This is in addition to them in relation to the factors, and this, too, in a double way, by internalization and externalization.

October 5

Yesterday's formulation of the problem in terms of $a\ B\ c$ and $a'\ B'\ c'$ was incomplete, and as a consequence some of the explanations were inadequate. The diagram

$$a \; B \; c$$
$$A \qquad\qquad C$$
$$a' \; B' \; c'$$

allows one to remark that, once we ignore B and B'—locus and mediator of the factors a and c, and a' and c', respectively—we can explain the one in terms of the other by remarking that the term into which the other is being translated is continuous with an A or a C. We get to c from a, for example, through the action of C on a, while C continues to maintain a hold on c (*1–4*). Since a similar observation applies to the cases *5–9*, it is evident that A and C allow for the transformation of two distinct items—a and a', for example, into the same, c, a to c, and a' to c. This points up the fact that A and C operate in two ways, depending on whether they are transforming what has a locus or what is a limit.

We also have cases *9–12* where localizable items are transformed into fringed ones, and conversely, for example, a to a', a green into a green-for-space (where c' is a space involved with the object B') or into a green-of (where B' is an object which possesses the green-of). Evidently, account here will also have to be taken of A.

We are left with the cases *13–14*, where B, a locus, is converted into B', a mediator, and conversely. Here account would have to be taken of their factors as subject to A and C.

In all cases the transformation depends on some more basic reality which may stand in between the factors, as in cases *1–8*, or which is outside them, but is continuous with one of them for which it explains the transformative value of the other. We get from green to green-of through the agency of the object which possesses the green; and we get from green-of to green through the agency of the same object as a locus and, therefore, as distinguishing itself from the green. Green has a status in contradistinction from grass only so far as the grass distinguishes itself from it, which it does in the act of converting the green-of-grass into plain green.

Is the conversion a process, dynamic, or is it a translation, an interpretation? Is grass in the process of making green be a green-of-grass and conversely, or do these have some status which the grass serves to explain? At present it seems to me that if we start with the factors, then conversion is a process, but if we start with the B or B' it is a translation. But suppose we are dealing with a conversion from the factors in the locus to them as mediated, or conversely? Do we then have a process engaged in by A or C, or do these serve to translate only? I think we must say again, that if we start with them, they serve to translate; if we start with factors, A and C have to be understood to be processes. As translators they are not formal entities, but substantial.

October 12

Max I. Fisch spoke yesterday at the Washington Philosophical Club on the history and development of Peirce's proof of pragmatism. In my commentary I remarked on the fact that Fisch was the most knowledgeable and authoritative figure in Peircean studies, that the paper was carefully articulated, had a host of important references, and revealed the travail which accompanied the development of the doctrine. I said that his paper suffered from the double defect of excess and defect, the one because he brought his multitude of references together without in any way indicating that one was more important than any other, and the other because he omitted references to Kant, Scotus, critical commonsensism, and the stoics to whom Peirce again and again made reference as important figures in the development of his ideas. Fisch had trouble understanding why Peirce had allowed a long gap to separate early examinations of the pragmatist maxim from later ones, overlooking the fact that Peirce himself thought little of the view until it was forcefully brought to his attention by the prominence given to it and the accompanying distortions by James, Schiller, and others.

Fisch also overlooked the way in which Peirce understood a proof of pragmatism to be formulated. It had to do with the breaking the idea down into its primary components—Peirce's three categories—and the recognition that these were to be employed so as to promote a concrete reasonableness for a presumed unlimited community of scientifically minded men. Concrete reasonableness is the embodiment of a final truth in the body of a totality of particulars harmoniously together.

The pragmatic maxim is designed to provide a third grade of clearness, supplementing but not replacing the grade of definitions or clarity, and of analysis or distinctness, defended by the Cartesians. This third grade of clearness analyzed intellectual concepts in terms of their ability to promote a final concrete reasonableness. It did this by attending to the conceivable consequences of the idea for those concerned with attaining the final purpose of inquiry, which was the settlement of doubt in a final continuum in which truth was able to permeate the totality of distinguishable items. It therefore told us what ideas were admissible as hypotheses, to be used in the ongoing quest.

Once it is seen that definitions express a conformity to a formal condition, that analysis expresses a conformity to an equalizing one, and that pragmatism expresses a conformity to a spatio-temporal-causal condition in which the totality of inquiries over time brings about the final result, the way is open for the recognition of two more kinds of clearness, one expressing a conformity to a condition imposed by Substance, and the other by Unity or value.

Substance dictates that the 'meaning' of ideas is to be determined by the ways in which those ideas are able to fit together in a final affilative harmony. A limited form of that condition is met by those who turn to a conventionally used language, and appeal to the use of terms there. In effect, in some accord with the associational psychologists, they take the meaning of a word to be the kind of associations which the language permits.

From the standpoint of Unity, the determination of the 'meaning' of an idea depends on the kind of value or importance that it has in a world of ordered degrees of value. It is this aspect which appealed to James.

These five types are not ordered as better or worse. All, I think, are necessary if one is to get the full import of a word. And all five have a fixed, present, eternal aspect, and one which is caught up in history, inquiry, and alterable perspectives. As the first, they are to be understood imaginatively under the aegis of the five finalities or specialized forms of these, expressed in language, inquiry, and the like. One could deal with language as if it had to do only with one type of meaning, or as including all five, and so on with the others. I think the latter method is better, for language has its associative, coordinating, formal, historical, and evaluative dimensions, as has inquiry. One could still take language, with its five sides, to be a formal enterprise and, then take inquiry to be existential, ethics and religion to be evaluative, society to be associational, and law to be coordinative. Whether this be done or not, the meaning, or better, import of an idea would be found by attending to the way in which it fitted within the totality of items governed by a finality.

The enterprise would be speculative and imaginative, tending to provide a 'speculative grammar' which all are to use.

An alternative way of dealing with the five types in different enterprises, would be to envisage, with Peirce, some ideal state of affairs toward which the various items would be taken to contribute. But before a final state, which was in fact distinct from that which the speculative approach had focussed on, was dealt with, one should take into account the specific limited goals that are characteristic of a particular epoch. The accepted theories would then be used to define the kind of area within which all results were to be fitted. And when one came to an impasse one would (following Kuhn) abandon that set of theories for another which required another way of organizing facts. The abandonment would not, of course, involve a rejection of every theory or organization of facts that had been acceptable in the past, but only the acceptance of a new condition in terms of which the old theories and the old facts would be newly judged. It could then be argued that the envisaged totality, according to the first alternative, would enable one to know the direction and the most general permanent features which characterized the theories, ideas, and facts in every epoch.

*   *   *

"First Considerations" has now been retyped. I have still to receive criticisms and comments in detail from the various philosophers to whom I had sent the manuscript.

There is a long discussion in the chapter on Unity which I think is important, but which seems out of place in the work. I am therefore taking the liberty of inserting it here:

Men can create   A] different conditions,   B] different contents, and   C] the two together, each matching a similar creation by a finality. All deserve some examination.

A] Men envisage and produce wholes within which a plurality of distinct qualities supplement, contrast with, and sometimes clash with one another. New programs in the arts are primarily directed toward this end. Related activities involve the production of political considerations with their assignment of mutually involved rights, duties, and privileges. The formation of clubs and other combinations can be brought under this heading. When the organization is applied with control and knowledge, we speak of craftsmanship.

The exhibition of a context on the way to the production of a cosmic pattern is the counterpart of a human act of craftsmanship. A craftsman is aware of the affinities of items; he is sensitive to the ways in which they clash and support one another. He and Substance, the source of a power of affiliation which governs actualities and their exhibitions, are alike. A carpenter, attentive to the grain of the wood with which he is working, and Substance as well, take account of that on which they operate. They both force to the fore what is already present, and link each item to what is most in consonance with it.

Taxonomy subjects items to classification, and thereby brings to the fore functions and features that the items would not otherwise display alongside one another. An outstanding example is Mendeleeff's table of the periodic elements. The elements are there related, not as they had been previously on the basis of similarities in appearance or on other grounds, often occult, but on principles which have no regard for the appearances. Applied with control and knowledge, classification takes the form of a disciplined discovery.

The power of coordination revealed in taxonomy is traceable back to Being. In relation to that finality, items achieve a status alongside one another, none more or less real than any other. Apart from the coordination, the items would still remain; coordination does not produce them but only enables them to be together without loss to their independence, and regardless of the fact that they may differ from one another in nature, dignity, career, and value. The coordination, though not deliberate or consciously instituted, is nevertheless freely imposed; it is a creative addition to the actualities and their exhibitions, enabling them to be or help constitute units in a cosmos or a context.

Applied mathematics, and particularly the sciences, are occupied with the application of controlling, intelligible rules. Items are brought into relationship with others quite alien to them in function, quality, or status. This mode of creating conditions is most effectively promoted when it follows on a prior creation of the mathematics itself, without regard for its application. Mathematics is the only case where the creative imagination, exercised without a concern for its applicability, has made possible the promotion of intelligibility in content of concern to science.

Unlike dream and fantasy, which are equally without necessary bearing on what occurs, pure mathematics is disciplined and controlled by the knowledge of what had been achieved. It is creative, it could be said, of intelligible rules which are pertinent to imagined content of the same order as the imagined content that had been mathematically mastered before. But if it is dealt with in a constructionistic spirit, it will be taken not merely to yield organizing rules which are operative on material that is linked with what already exists, but to produce both the rules and the items on which it operates. It will then exhibit one way in which men might produce both what controls and is controlled—the third of our types of creation.

One of the familiar ways in which theologians try to ground a proof of a concerned, thoughtful God is by tracing back to a final mind the intelligibility of the world of appearances or of the cosmos. Granted that the intelligibility is intruded on actualities and their exhibitions, there is still no warrant for supposing that the presence of structures, rational connections, or meanings is due to a mind that understands them. Intruded intelligibles have a wider reach, a greater generality, and a greater governing power than any actuality or exhibition. But they need be attributed to no source other than a final Possibility.

Universally applicable conditions are ontological and empowered; they make a difference to that on which they operate. But they operate, not due to a decision to have them apply, but as a consequence of the expression of an all-inclusive finality, to which all items are subject, and thereby enabled to function as terms in a rational whole.

Ours is the age of the engineer. He is usually occupied with the use of well-established mathematical principles and scientific achievements. But in his programs, constructions, and the making of effective machines, he creates agencies by means of which space, time, and causal activities are reorganized and put at the service of men. There are some who are willing to attribute a mind to highly complicated, quasi-automatic machines, with their memory banks, feedbacks, and capacity to alter direction. By a reverse twist men are then said to be some kind of machine similar to these others. What is overlooked is that the machines have minds only so far as they embody the plans of engineers and carry out appropriate programs. The machines are already under the control of a created design.

All cosmologies contain a latent metaphysics, for all involve the recognition of encompassing extensions which enable entities to be spatially and temporally extended and located. These should be accounted for. Such an accounting involves the acceptance of an extensional dynamism as well, and the tracing of all three types of extension back to a finality. This expresses itself in the guise of threefold extensions where all appearances together, and all the actualities together, are located.

Standards, ideals, objectives are created by men and used as bases for assessing the various items that are then dealt with. Regardless of their affinities, their belonging together in groups, the ways in which they are intelligibly connected, or how they are brought within a design, items are ordered in hierarchies, and assessed for preservation, use, and interest.

Men creatively play a role in determining the importance of what they encounter. The fact does not warrant the supposition that there are no values apart from man or his evaluations. Though there are standards that individuals and groups of men forge and apply, men are also faced with values which items possess apart from men, and in terms of which human judgments are sometimes revealed to be incorrect.

Though nothing would have a value were it not subject to an evaluation by an operative condition applicable to all, each actuality still has a status, reflecting the way in which its parts are harmoniously united within it, and how it fits together with all other entities. The imposition of a value, originating with a final Unity, takes account of these harmonies; it adds to them by bringing the parts within the unity of their enclosing actuality, and by bringing the actuality within the unity of an enclosing cosmos, at the same time that the exhibitions of all the actualities are enabled to supplement one another maximally within a single aesthetic totality.

B] Men spontaneously, exuberantly express themselves. Without concern for any rules, without thought, they produce new words, engage in new acts, and sometimes make novel things. Innovators in the arts, aware that others are too often and too much in the grip of established principles, take this as a primary desideratum. But if there is no genuine art without a measure of control, and thus without involving craftsmanship, what the innovators produce are just aesthetic objects, not works of art.

From another side, it is sometimes said that men can not create; all they can do is reorganize what is already in existence. But this is also true of the finalities, even of Unity. The supposed creation of the universe from nothing may make religious sense, but not otherwise. Not only is the idea faced with the problem of a change in the creator from the state when he did not create to the state when he does, but he can not completely create something unless he makes it be, and therefore sets it over against himself as a distinct entity. But if there be anything which stands apart from God, it has a reality that God does not have, and therefore shows that God can not be perfect, all-inclusive, lacking nothing real. If God creates all else, he must at the same time diminish himself, make himself less than he had been. His would be an act of sacrifice, a giving up of his perfection in order to allow for the presence of other realities. In any case, the counterpart of a human innovator who produces, not new organizing principles, but new entities, is not God but Substance. Though Substance presupposes actualities and their exhibitions in order to have something to govern, it also creates them in the sense that it makes the actualities substantial, and counters their exhibitions with a context in which the exhibitions are affiliated and sustained.

Items can be empowered to function in ways they had not before. They can be freed from the restraints to which they are subject, and set into new situations, without prevision, or without any concern but to enable them to show themselves afresh. Part of the adventure of bringing up children is the determination of the degree of freedom they are to be allowed at different times in order to be able to become full individuals on their own. Carried out by rule, the result is wooden; creatively carried out, it is full of risk, but unavoidable if the children's distinctiveness and promises are to be preserved and enhanced. More generally stated: education is the creative enterprise of enabling individuals to achieve new levels of understanding and achievement and, so far, to be new.

From one standpoint, Being has no power to create; particulars achieve being by converging on it, while it continues to remain remote. But it is also true that they have beings which they owe to Being. Being evidences itself everywhere, and thereby endows different particulars with the status of being equally real in relation to it. More conspicuously here than in the case of the other finalities, creativity has no dependence on consciousness or intent; it is an ontological occurrence, expressing the fact that particulars are given a new status and role by a finality. Men add to that creativity by internalizing the beings which have been imposed on them, and then exhibit themselves as self-maintained beings with intrinsic rights. Other actualities are also affected by the very Being which qualifies men, thereby making possible the copresence of them and men in the very same world. The creative power of Being operates indifferently on all of them, humans and nonhumans, but it is only the humans who can make the result be an intrinsic part of themselves.

Discovering is not simply an uncovering, the making evident what is already there. But even an uncovering has an element of creativity to it, since it allows the bared items to have new neighbors and new roles. Discovery is more consequential; it brings items within a framework. The Vikings may have uncovered America, but it was Columbus who discovered it. Though he misconstrued the relationship America had to Europe, he did see it to have a relation to Europe and thereby made it an object for further exploration. This, and other lesser discoveries, attend to particulars; they are not primarily concerned with imposing an order on material already available and known. Instead, they creatively transform items, already present before the discovery, by placing them within another setting than that which the items had occupied. The creative act here is directed at bringing something existent into a setting provided by the discoverer. Though that setting, more often than not, is also altered, the emphasis is not on it or on the relating of the items to it, but on these as having been made available for the new governance. Related considerations have bearing on what is exposed in analysis, observation, and even ordinary acts of perception; in these cases, too, new roles accrue to items and thereby enable them to acquire new meanings.

Neither the cosmos nor the world of appearances waits on man for its rationale, intelligibility, or order. Indeed, one way of accounting for man and his thought is to see them as the outcome of the ordered movement of nonhuman beings. It is a man, to be sure, who frames the hypotheses and formulates the laws taken to govern all physical entities and all natural occurrences. Again and again, finding that the entities and the occurrences do not conform to his account of them, he tries to alter his views so that they reflect the rationale that had been found to proceed in a different way from what he had envisaged. Sometimes he is blocked by what seems irrational, absurd, brute, but again and again, by taking another perspective, he finds that they had a rationale he had not suspected. That the new perspective is not the source of the new rationale becomes evident the more precisely and correctly one predicts what will ensue; successful predictions are in accord with a rationale already present. But since the rationale governs the items severally and together, it evidently is not intrinsic to those items, but imposed on them. A final meaning gives all particulars a new standing by imposing meanings which have rational connections with one another.

Men work on things and work over them; they transform them, thereby giving them a new status and career. They make use of material already there, but what they then bring about is not always a variation on the old. Practical men are constantly creating new things; their alterations in the old make possible new outcomes, many of which none could foresee. The course of a nation is in the hands of such practical men; its destiny precariously depends on their ability to avoid creating what destroys and, instead, create what improves.

There is a kind of creativity to be credited to artists and even to craftsmen which is not utilized by the practical. The first is a creator of a form in something, the second is a creator of controlling designs. Though they both have their practical moments and persistent styles, their creativity is at the service of excellent prospects beyond the concern of practical men.

A practical man may think of the distant future and plan accordingly. He may exhibit artistic gifts and be the master of a number of crafts. Everything, though, is made subject to an effort to alter particulars creatively so as to enable them to have new positions and powers. While the artist seeks to create what is sensuously excellent, and the craftsman what has grace and utility, the practical man is satisfied if he can create what is most effective.

The best of practical men are men of practical wisdom; they guide themselves by rules which have been learned in the course of experience. Their practice is not blind; it is disciplined, controlled, guided. But their wisdom is a habituated summary of what had been done. The artist, surely, and the craftsman, most likely, give more weight than the practical man does to controlling unities creatively used.

Actualities and their exhibitions are stretched out, distended; that is why they are able to fit in and be located in space, time, and causal chains. But they can not fit in and be located until they are brought within all-encompassing extensions. A distension is enjoyed from within; an extension is related extensionally to other extensions beyond. By acquiring an extension and therefore a position in relation to other extended items, actualities and their exhibitions are caught up in larger domains which have their own pace, geometry, and causal power.

The transformation of actualities and their exhibitions from unrelated items into extensionally connected positioned ones is the outcome of the creative insistence of Existence. It makes itself felt in the way in which it gives particulars distanced connections with one another. Film, especially in its montages, exploits this fact.

Dialectical materialists take account of the power of Existence, but ignore its power to extensionalize particulars. They concentrate instead on the controls to which men are subject. These thinkers allow that men are altered by being caught up in cosmic extensions, but give insufficient weight to the fact that, apart from a place in larger extensions—or more particularly, for the dialectical materialists, in an economically qualified time—men are still independent irreducibles who achieve new import by being given an extensional guise. An Existence that takes men to be nothing but members of historic-economic classes skips over their individual transformation into distinctive occupants, with their own unit extensions, rights, and dignities. Existence also gives extensions to other actualities besides men, in the form of qualifications which can be internalized to make those actualities into existents in an environment.

Through the agency of appreciations and antagonisms, through reactions and attitudes, we attribute values to what we consider. Those values are not idle adjectives, simply expressing likes and dislikes; they involve the items, to which they are applied, in situations from which they would be excluded had they been credited with different values. They are to be contrasted, too, with the objective values which the items obtain by being subjected to a comprehensive impersonal evaluation.

Appreciations and attitudes have some generality to them, and can therefore be applied somewhat like principles which creatively govern items. Applied without deliberation, and reflecting individual biases, they function as agencies for the creation of values in particulars. The particulars are then taken to be so many different determinants of the ways in which the parts can become constituents absorbed within unitary wholes. The value ascribed to a leaf is the requirement that the parts of it have an importance proportionate to their capacity to be unaltered in being made into harmonized components of the leaf. The more they must be altered the less their value in relation to it; the less they must be altered the more are they not only parts within the leaf but integral constituents of it.

The creation of values by a primal Unity gives the parts of every actuality the status of constituents in a unity. The degree to which the parts must be altered in order to have that status is identical with the degree of value that they have in an actuality.

C] It is possible to create both organizing unities and the items to be organized. But the one must apply to the other, making the second relatively objective for the first. If nothing is done to sustain the second, the outcome is a controlled self-expression, in which both the unities and the items governed vanish as produced.

When men speak, they create both the grammar and the words grammatically used. The grammar may have its roots in a latent, native grammar, or in the community's or individual's practices; the words may have been heard before, and be part of a common vocabulary. But each speech is fresh, and the grammatical connections and the words themselves are freshly forged. There is genuine language and communication when the words with the grammar are externally lodged in listeners, in practices, and in writing. A language spoken in private must, at the very least, be sustained by memory.

Whether or not content and organization are produced at the same time, or by the same reality, so far as the organization is dominant, the outcome is a nuanced unity maintained without reference to anything else—even without reference to the content as it exists apart from the organization. This is the state of affairs that prevails both when actualities are qualified and when their exhibitions are subject to a context. A similar situation is found when men bring evidence and evidenced together under a governing principle which is intended to be instanced both by the evidence and evidenced. Since a principle is a special case of a structure permitting one to reason from premiss to conclusion, evidently a similar situation occurs every time a rule of inference is formulated.

Men alone forge rules of inference; men alone deal with

metaphysical evidence; men alone submit the evidenced to a finality which transforms it until it becomes a nuanced facet of the finality; and men alone make works of art, nuanced unities with constituents but no parts.

Parts are distinct entities, opposing one another and the whole which comprises them; constituents are delimited portions of nuanced unities. Constituents can be distinguished but are not distinct from one another; nor do they stand or function apart from the unity. Between any two constituents there is always another; this may be an emptiness, silent, vacant, bleak, but it will still be just as much an integral part of the unity as any of the more vivid constituents.

A poet need not violate conventional grammar; he may use words in common currency. Yet he creates both the words and their connections. In a poem, the weights and resonances of words are created by being forced to the fore together. Their connections are also created; the poem intimately joins words in distant places while separating and contrasting those which are close together, and conversely, all in fresh ways. The resultant poem is given an objective status in listeners, memory, and writing.

Similar observations are pertinent to paintings and dances. The painter's canvas gives an objective status to created colors, with their different powers and demands, and to the connections to which he subjects them. What is spatially distant he may bring quite close, and what is close he may forcefully hold apart.

A dancer's bodily moves are somewhat like the words a poet uses; the choreography is somewhat like the structure of a poem, though the latter is normally not envisaged before the poem is produced. In any case, the moves and the choreography are exhibited creatively together, and achieve objective status when seen or remembered.

Substance creatively produces substantialized actualities and governs them and their appearances within grounding totalities. Did the actualities not have a status of their own apart from it, it would simply fulgurate. There can be creativity by Substance of the substantializing ground of different actualities in which all the actualities are interrelated, only so far as the actualities remain apart, resistant, insistent, sustaining the evidence that Substance intrudes on them.

Sculpture, stories, and theatre give more credit to the independent status and nature of the particulars with which they work than painting, poetry, and dance do. Their accommodation of the stabilized natures of that of which they make use enables them to give a clear exhibit of the fact that what they create is objectively maintained by actualities outside the creator's control. Still, like painting, poetry, and dance, these other arts can also be said to create both the particulars and the organization to which those particulars are subjected, since they make those particulars have roles and meanings, additional to those which they had apart from the created works of art.

In some consonance with Neoplatonism, a final Being can be credited with the power to express itself in a diminished form of itself. If that result is taken to be produced together with the particulars that it governs, Being will be taken to be a source of a domain within which particulars are so many distinct, equalized entities. Being will not be a creator of both of them, however, unless the result also finds lodgment outside Being itself—and this requires that the particulars be sustained by actualities having a status not dependent on Being or the domain it imposes on them.

Being's functioning, and the sustaining by actualities of the domain which Being makes possible, would be too narrowly restricted were they confined to man and what concerns him. Like all the other finalities, Being is neither empowered by nor enabled to function by man. Apart from him, other actualities have beings on a footing with one another within a cosmos, itself dependent for its presence on the persistent expression of Being.

Architecture, musical composition, and music, no less than the other arts, can be taken to create both governing forms and the particulars that are governed by these. Even more conspicuously, however, than is the case with sculpture, stories, and theatre, they give overwhelming importance to the overall structure, allowing the particulars to remain comparatively unaltered.

The point will be readily granted, perhaps, in connection with architecture, but emphatically denied by many to hold of music. Hegel went so far as to take architecture to be the lowest of arts since its forms were so clearly alien to the brute stone on which they were imposed. In contrast, there is a common tendency to think of music as so evidently creating beautiful sounds through the use of special instruments that it seems even more fresh and creative than poetry. But music has room for every sound; the ones that are produced by special instruments need not be included, and where they are, need not be taken to be essentially 'musical'. In any case, music, like architecture, seeks to give full value to the particulars it uses; the structure it imposes on these, thereby transforming them, is one in which their distinctive tonalities are enriched.

Despite the strong Platonic strand which has persisted in Western thought over the centuries, there is a disinclination to accept a final form, or Possibility, as a reality capable of producing intelligible domains and the particulars which they encompass. Meanings seem to be derivative from the more robust realities we encounter every day, or from the interchange of men.

Armed with a theory of internal relations, idealistic rationalists drive themselves from limited situations to an absolute all-inclusive meaning. This, though, is so complete and self-enclosed that there is no way of accounting for the starting points from which they began a movement to it. But once account is taken of the independent presence of actualities and their ability to specialize and sustain the meanings that impinge on all of them, it is possible to acknowledge Possibility as the most inclusive of meanings, without affirming that it alone is real.

A strict constructionist takes mathematics to be wholly a human achievement, the outcome of man's creative effort to produce both the terms and the principles which govern the terms. But constructions need an area in which they are made. Whether one takes this to be the pure forms of space and time, or something quite different, it produces the limitations under which men create both structures and what these govern.

In a community, men accept a space, time, and a dynamics which are already contoured. Within their confines the men creatively forge new connections while they give a new import to what is connected. The accepted extensions, though themselves sustained by still greater and more basic extensions, serve as loci for what the men produce. Human inter-involvement in daily life and over history thereby achieves an objectivity in which communications and other transient interchanges are embedded.

Existence expresses itself in a threefold diversification, delimited and specialized by the actualities and exhibitions on which Existence impinges. It makes particulars be contemporaries, all concordantly moving into the next moment together, despite their difference in rhythm and their indifference to one another's presence and nature; it gives them locations within a single space, despite their differences in strength and variations in the extent of their self-expressions; and it confines them within a single dynamism despite their relative degrees of passivity and effectiveness, and their apparent indifference to most of what occurs before, after, or at the same time with them.

Existence is somewhat allied to what materialists take to be the primary reality. Its acknowledgment, though, does not require the acceptance of a historic dialectical process, or the denial of the reality of particulars. Indeed, these are presupposed by Existence as the agents of delimitation and the supports for what it brings about.

Not until we come to the creation of values by men, together with the unifying condition which gives them a status in relation to one another as more or less like it, do we arrive at a view which has a significance approximating that which has been traditionally accorded the idea of a divine creation. When men face the world about, they do so with attitudes and emotions that entrain standards and measures of the worth of that which they confront. They deal with particulars primarily as occasions for the imposition of common conditions which ascribe relative importance to different items, in accord with the degree to which these, separately and together, must be altered in order to be turned into constituents of a final value.

God, as reached philosophically, is most properly identified with Unity, one among a number of finalities. But even if all the finalities were solidified into one, or taken to have their source in some more basic, single reality, it still would not be true that God could ever be or have been the only reality, or that a creation out of nothing was possible. A perfect being lacks nothing; if it made anything to be in addition to itself, it would add to the realities in the universe and, by that very fact, make itself be less than perfect. The very demand that a God or perfect Unity create something out of nothing requires that nothing real be produced, for he then will not make anything distinct from himself and therefore will not in fact have created. God's creativity does not enable anything to maintain itself apart from him. His creation, like the creations of other finalities and the creations of men, presupposes independent particulars or an independent domain able to sustain the conditions he produces and the items organized and governed by those conditions.

Granted independent particulars or an independent domain, God can be said to create both evaluations and values. Each actuality is then given a new import by being encompassed within a created, evaluating unity. The result is different from that which is produced by the creative activity of the other finalities, though they, too, can be taken to have produced actualities and what conditions them, if at the same time the actualities are granted to have the status of independent realities, able both to sustain the conditions and to be transformed by them.

An organism has parts that are also constituents. A heart is at once a part clearly distinct from the liver, and also a constituent of a living body, from which it can not be separated in thought or in fact without ceasing to be the heart it was. In a transplant, the heart is reduced to the status of a part, and then set in another organism where it is to achieve the status of a constituent as well.

The created portion of a work of art contains no parts, but only constituents. It may be a collage, making use of distinct entities; it may be created over a long period, with one segment completed early and never altered. But encompassed within a work of art, they are just constituents. The work does not allow them an opporuntity to function as parts as well; if they do have independent natures and careers, this will be a fact about them as not caught up in the artistic creation.

The works of an artist are themselves constituents of a creative life, yet even here, more evidently than is the case with a single work, single items are made which are distinct from all others. They can be separately bought and sold, and can be set in different stages of an artist's career. Nevertheless, they bear a single 'signature' or personal style which makes them all his artistic work.

A style is a set of accents—stresses, pacings, ornaments—which mark off one set of works from another, in abstraction from subject matter, message, or referent. There is a Western style of painting, a Dutch style of painting, an early Vermeer style of painting. The style of the first contrasts with the style exhibited by Eastern painters; the second's contrasts with the style exhibited by Italian painters; the third's with the style exhibited by other Dutch painters, and with the style which Vermeer exhibited later in life. In all these cases, a style is a symbol which can take one to a root that is characteristic of producers of a number of works which are distinguishable from others by their emphases, spacings, patterns, devices, and usages—usually inadvertently exhibited and repeated by creative men, and deliberately duplicated by both copyists and imitators.

A copyist builds up larger structures, themes, and events out of parts, where the original had only unities with distinguishable constituents inseparable from a personal style. A copy has parts which are separated by gaps over which the copyist moved but which he did not work through; the original, instead, contains not gaps but less saturated regions, with emptiness as a limit. Those regions, in the course of the exhibition of a style, are creatively made as integral to the work as are other constituents.

Imitations, the works of a disciple, and forgeries may be works of art. Unlike a copy they then have no parts but only constituents, integrated with the duplicated style of the original artist. The various works produced by imitators, disciples, and forgers have the status of parts within the lives of these men. The original artist, in contrast, produces his different works as so many constituents of his life. The others reuse the established style of the original artist; he, in unpredictable ways, reestablishes his own style again and again in the course of the production of new works.

Copying is not imitating. The one duplicates an extant work; the other creates within the compass of a duplicated, extant style. Both are parasitical on the original artist, coming after his creative effort has realized a stylized unity carried out in a work or over a life. Forgetting this, men are sometimes inclined to say that what an artist has done, a machine, an animal, or a child can also do. But at best, all one could plausibly claim is that a machine, animal, or child could be a fine imitator. But even that claim goes much too far. An imitator fills out the gap between the known works of a creative artist in accord with what the imitator learned about those works. But since the original creator vitalized a region in a distinctive way, either by works not now known or by the way he readied himself for the works he later produced, any work an imitator inserts in the gap must be different from what the creator might have produced. The greater the artist, the more surely he can not be imitated. A child or a machine presumably lacks the flexibility and imagination of a great imitator. Since he can not make a work which fills out a gap in the way the artist did by works as yet undiscovered, or by the way the artist creatively used the intervening time when he produced no works, neither can the child nor the machine.

It is true, to be sure, that the greatest of critics has been taken in by forgeries—imitations produced with malicious or criminal intent—and that the forgeries were discovered by attending not to the character of the works but to the material in which the forgeries were embedded. But it is also true that after the discovery of forgeries, it is sometimes possible to show that the imitation could not have been produced by the artist. The imitator had to stay close to the known and attested expressions of the artist's style in order to win creditability. The deviance which the imitator does not dare to exhibit is precisely what is found in the different known works that the artist produced; it should also be found in any of his works later discovered.

An artist, of course, may imitate himself. Like other imitators he will then do creative work, but the style exhibited will no longer be integral to his work, or the work itself will fail to be a fresh, new creation.

Confronted with an original and a splendid copy, without any further information, we may not, despite the lack of creativity involved in producing the copy, be able to tell which is which. Still, it should be possible to detect an incapacity for imitations to fill the gaps that the artist lived through in going from work to work. Were we faced with a set of imitations mixed up with the originals, and had no other knowledge, it should therefore in principle be possible to separate out the imitations from the original set.

Nature might so act on some material that the outcome is an exact duplicate of a sculpture by a great artist. Without anything but the two works before us, we would not be able to tell which was which. Might it not be possible then for nature to produce sculpture after sculpture duplicating artistic productions? To make this conceivable, nature would have to be credited with operations which are cosmic counterparts of an individual's artistic activities. The operations of the counterparts, on the hypothesis, would have to match the kinds of works and gaps between them which the artist creatively produced. Our present understanding of nature would then have to be changed, so that it became an artist writ large, imposing unities and producing constituents creatively.

A good part of the difficulty in understanding how a work of art differs from a copy (or a product of nature) is that attention is not paid to the transformations to which both the original and copy (or natural product) are subjected in the course of getting them where they can be compared. We can not get the copy (or the product of nature) to be in the very same world in which a work of art is, without giving it the status of a work of art; we can not get the original to be in the very same world in which a copy (or product of nature) is, without making it into a disjunct item like the copy (or into a localized occasion for the operation of cosmic laws like the product). But neither of these results is possible.

Nothing becomes or ceases to be art without implicating an indefinite multiplicity of relevant items, past, present, and future, not all of which we are in a position to control or to specify. All that one can do is to subject the work of art to new conditions and thereby make it an item in a new domain, as a collector does; to work artistically on the copy or natural product to make it into a work of art as a collagist does; or to approximate a neutral position where the work of art and the others are on a footing, and one can no longer discern the kind of domain to which each belongs.

So far as different kinds of product retain their characteristic natures, they can be inserted into other settings only in the way a lie can be inserted into the world of truths—by being given supplementation without end in order to mesh fully with the other items in that world.

When a work of art is made or destroyed, the material in the one case and the created contribution in the other is transformed at the same time that it is made to function in a new domain. But, though the material in a work of art still continues to function within nature, the created contribution can continue to be, when the work of art is destroyed, only in the guise of a constituent of an artistic domain. If a work of art is burned, smashed, broken into scattered fragments, the physical side of it is all that is observably left over, though in an altered form. While the work was in existence, that physical side was subject to the same conditions which operate on what remains when the work of art is destroyed. This does not mean that the work of art does not have the physical side as an integrated factor, but only that it gives this neighbors and roles it otherwise would not have.

Just as a man, by taking a walk, makes the particles within his confines move along paths and over distances they of themselves could not cover, at the same time that he is limited by the invariant behavior of those particles in the physical cosmos (as his need to use counteracting energy and his free fall from a height reveals), so a work of art gives its material new functions in a world of art, without abrogating the fact that the material continues to function just as it functioned before it had been used in art.

Concerned with a knowledge of that to which he attends, a man must involve himself in one or more sub-domains from which effective, consonant approaches to actualities can subsequently be made. When he slips, cries out, and is afraid, he is involved with a number of them at the same time; he is similarly involved when he states something, for he then forges a sentence in his particular language, makes noises, and expels air. If he exaggerates the importance of one domain or sub-domain and thereby obscures or distorts the roles of others, he misconstrues himself and what he ought to do. Inauthenticity results both when a man fails to make adequate provision for everyday occurrences and physical events, and when he fails to concern himself with what is universal and forever.

Domains and sub-domains are unities governing different kinds of entities in distinctive ways. Each has its own kind of spacing, to be gone through at a distinctive pace. Each is traversed by engaging in a distinctive way of excluding what is not allowed to be part of it. What an artist *dismisses* in an evaluative act lived through in the course of making his next move, a copyist will merely *refuse* when, after attending to the original, he sees that it is not suitable. A machine, instead, will simply *reject* or *omit* it, as that which the machine is not programmed to include, while nature will not produce it at all or will just *set* it *elsewhere*. A man can engage in all types of exclusion at the same time.

Artist, copyist, programmed machine, and a fixated law-abiding nature can all be identified as bounded sub-domains within a single all-encompassing domain which includes all that occurs in the civilized world and the knowable cosmos. A good name for it would be The Domain of the Conceivable.

The present view seems now quite close to an idealism which internally relates everything within a single rational whole. There are, though, signal differences sharply distinguishing what is here maintained from an idealism. Idealism overlooks the fact that bounded domains are distinct; that the boundaries in a domain are placed around material which originates elsewhere; that what is taken from one limited domain to another is subjected to transformative conditions; that practice, indeed all acts and work, fills out a gap between bounded domains and can not be entirely assimilated to either terminus; that a move from one domain to another need not take place creatively or inside a freely acting mind, but can occur bodily or mechanically; that there can be fillings for domains only so far as there are actualities apart from them; that a domain enables only items of a certain nature to become constituents of it; that the most comprehensive domain is never more than an expression of a final Unity and is not to be identified with it; that there is more than one domain in which all items can be encompassed; and that all names and therefore all domains are overarched by a naming, reaching beyond the limits of any and all names. But now it is necessary to avoid the opposite error which takes naming to be a primordial process out of which all else is precipitated. The error builds on the truth that a primary naming stretches from an actual to an ideal cosmos, while overlooking the fact that each of these has an integrity of its own, and can be independently named.

A machine could be constructed to imitate a style, or to duplicate something created. It could be made to start, rest, and, with the help of random numbers, operate in unexpected and unpredictable ways. Since it has only parts, not constituents, its products lack an essential characteristic of a work of art. It can be programmed. Sometimes it is said that men are already programmed. Both contentions presuppose that there is a program and that there is a power which can apply it. The blueprint of a machine and the physiology of a man could be identified with a program. The utilization of such a program depends on the imposition of some power which enables distinct items to become identified with and to intensify the nuances in an initial unity, the program itself expressing such a unity conceived by some man whose parts are so arranged that a particular sequence of operations will take place and thereby yield a set of distinct occurrences. In action the program, with constituents ascribed to it, is converted into a programmed set of parts.

A concept, a hypothesis, a rule, or a program are beyond the capacity of any machine to produce, for these are nuanced unities. The best that a machine can do is to provide distinct units which break up its programmed unity into an ordered sequence of items. It can, of course, bind a number of items together; it can be made to start and stop, and after an interval start and stop again. But the ability to raise the parts to the level of constituents is beyond it. This is possible to a man, because he can approach the world as one who instances omnipresent finalities in universally applicable ways. His life-style is a personalized, temporally expressed form of such a universally applicable unity or combinations of unities; his creative style is a specialized version of this. Though an imitator also has a life and a creative style, he foregoes the use of the latter so that the former can be at the service of the creative style of another.

A machine can order the parts of another machine and set it tasks. It could conceivably be made to lay out and to state the elements of a program before that program is imposed on the other machine. It still would not be doing exactly what a man does when he considers a program, makes a machine, or sets it to work, for a machine can get no further than to place a number of items within the confines of an order where it may start and stop, but which it can neither begin nor end, because it is not a unity and has no way of using a unity. Nor can it give itself or give to another inseparable constituents which merge into one another and the intervals that distance them.

It is not surprising that empirically minded philosophers are inclined to speak of man as though he were a complicated machine, for without the ability to recognize final unities, and the intellectual counterparts and instances of them that men provide, it is hard to distinguish the two. Nevertheless, the difference is not between two opposed views of looking at things, but between one that does so with an awareness of what it presupposes and another that does so without such an awareness.

Empiricists, like everyone else, take account of metaphysical unities. But they do so uncritically. That is why they can suppose that their data are ultimates known without error, that their accounts hold for all time, and that any other view is necessarily false or commonsensical. Their views are somewhat like the machines they admire, for these too presuppose acknowledged unities.

October 13

Why should one be concerned only with the clarification of ideas? Ought there not be at least four more goals, each having five distinct grades? It seems reasonable to suppose so.

1] There is the goal of happiness, pleasure, harmony, of fitting in with whatever there be, the finding of one's proper place within the totality of men and other things. It is this which the Stoics had in mind. It requires the subordination of the immediacies of experience and life to a single substantial affiliating power. Its achievement will be promoted when the various items are each given their full distinct import, are formally interrelated, are set in extensional contexts, and are dealt with in terms of their importance.

2] The goal of justice, equality, cooperation, of being together in a society or state, so much in the forefront of the thought of democratic thinkers, requires the acknowledgment of the equality of each item as having its own integrity and rights. This state of affairs depends on a grasp of substantial realities as irreducible individuals, of the ways in which these, legalistically and in other ways, can be brought intelligibly together, of their relations to one another in space, time, and causal operations, and of their ability to constitute a single unity together.

3] The pragmatic maxim with its five (if I am right) degrees of clearness will be occupied primarily with the clarification of concepts and the understanding of that clarification as dictating just which ones are acceptable—and this because and so far as they contribute to the achievement of a final, universally acceptable truth.

4] The goal of effective action has to do primarily with the utilization of material in space, over time, and by making use of causal agencies. It must take account of the ways in which different things support and counter one another, of their distinctive dignities, of the rationale by means of which they can be related, and of the goods that are to be attained and how these attain them.

5] Finally, there is the goal of excellence or perfection in which each item finds its proper place in relation to all the others within an all-encompassing Unity. The items will cluster and disperse according to their affiliative capacities, will have their own integrities, will have a rational connection with one another, and will be capable of being altered and related in different ways in space and time.

All five goals are independent, and can be independently pursued, though in each case the pursuit will involve a consideration of the factors which are of primary importance in the pursuit of the other goals. The end result would be a mere aggregate were it not that any four can be dealt with as subject to a fifth. This, of course, still leaves an aggregate of sets of four. The final reconciliation will be in individual men; each provides that unifying base in terms of which all five goals, while remaining distinct, are together. The unity that a man provides for these does not preclude his being subordinated to each of the five. Each finality is a one for all men, and each man is a one for all the finalities.

October 19

In the thirties I came to see that everything was incomplete, and that there was an omnipresent need to be completed. An actuality engaged in such an act—an inquiry too—was grounded in the attempt to answer questions and thereby complete what was already known. In the fifties I began to see that entities are intruded upon by factors which are completed by being brought back to their sources. It is now becoming more and more evident that these fundamental positions are part of a single thesis, for an actuality is incomplete just so far as it has been combined with alien factors, and these factors are themselves incomplete just so long as they have not been brought back to their sources.

When one arrives at the finalities or actualities, the one by tracing intruded factors back from the actualities (or from appearances together), the other by tracing the factors back from single appearances, one never reaches a still point where the finalities or actualities are pure; instead one finds other intruded factors. A finality arrived at is where we can find effects of the actualities which we thought we had left behind in tracing the intrusions of the finalities back to those finalities. An actuality arrived at, also, is where we can find the effects of finalities which we thought we had left behind in tracing the intrusions in a complex actuality back to the actuality itself.

The pragmatic quest for meaning is a quest for what completes a word or concept, so far as this is united with its meaning, or completes the meaning that had been accreted. This is done by tracing the meaning back to a primal, all-inclusive meaning. The complete truth is not simply something which is in the distant future, but what had already given the word or concept its limited meaning. If, as was suggested the other day, the pragmatic theory be expanded to include other goals, and if it be supplemented by other efforts occupied with items other than meaning, related considerations would be relevant. Each enterprise would begin with an intruded factor and trace this back to its source, where it awaits acceptance by the source. A new enterprise would start with that source as intruded upon—perhaps but not necessarily by the very item on which the source had intruded—and arrive at what had intruded on that source.

A pragmatist in trying to make his ideas clear should ask himself how there was something which had to be clarified. Related questions are pertinent to the other five types of effort distinguished the other day. The attainment of the source of an intruded factor does not yield the source as intruding the factor; as a consequence, something is learned by getting to the source by tracing the factor back to it. The source arrived at from the factor must be adopted by the source; as productive of the factor, the source is countered by that in which the factor is intruded, and is thereby diversified.

The attainment of the goals of different enterprises yields unities which need grounding. The origin of the effort is with dispersed fragments of the reality which could provide that grounding. We know that a word, for example, has a meaning because it is subject to a meaning context; we get the full meaning of the word only when we complete it as that which must be congruent with the original source of the meaning with which we began. If, for example, we accept Peirce's view that the final goal is the truth as known to an unlimited community of scientific inquirers, that truth would have to be supported by a reality. That reality could be a meaning, as idealists claim and which perhaps Peirce was ready to hold, but it would be a meaning which had a different status from the meaning arrived at, for at the very least it would not be arrived at but be that which makes it possible for what was arrived at to have a status apart from the arriving. The reality is the source of the meaning with which we begin so as to arrive at the meaning which will be accommodated by that reality.

*   *   *

Only ex-colonials—Americans, Australians, Indians—consider all English philosophizing to be serious and important; the English philosophers don't.

Many thinkers have good aims but bad aim.

Political aspirants have high aims. Why then do they aim so low?

Philosophical method: trace back intruded factors to their sources, and use the results as guides in classifications, descriptions, and inquiries in limited fields.

October 24

There is a common core to the forms of the various ontological arguments which, so far as I know, has not been remarked upon either by its defenders or its opponents:

1] I have an idea—or alternatively, a proper name or a description—distinguishable from all others.

2] It is an idea which alone is attached to an essence, that is, a nature which might be possessed by some reality.

3] That essence is fecund; its very presence requires that it be insistent.

4] The insistence of the essence is an existence inseparable from it.

5] As I attend to the essence I find that my idea, in order to be the idea of the essence as it in fact is, must be the idea—or name or description—of an existent essence.

The uniqueness of the argument makes it questionable for logicians. But it is possible to treat it as one of an endless number of possible cases, by following Spinoza's lead and holding that every idea is involved with something other than itself, so that it is affirmed, denied, doubted, and so forth, depending on what its content is, and at the same time (going beyond Spinoza) that it matches what occurs in the world of objects. When one attends to the nature of an object by means of an idea one notes that the nature necessarily has such and such experiential relations to other objects and, as a consequence, one can recognize that the idea must be that of an object in such and such a relation to others.

The essence in the ontological argument and the nature in the other cases have in common the fact that they are constitutive, since they provide the grounds for the additional factor—existence or relations—which the idea must then take account of. The idea in both cases is made to expand its range by virtue of the discovery that the essence or nature to which it is attached is unavoidably involved with some other element—existence or relationship.

I am not persuaded that the argument is sound, for I am not persuaded that all the five steps are justified. But the opponents of the argument should recognize its strength, since they make use of its form when they speak of metalogics, metalanguages, governing rules, language, forms of life, and the like, since these are like the fecund essence, or are, through the agency of the thinker, given an effectiveness which leads to their becoming involved with particular meanings, occurrences, acts, sentences, and so on. They in effect have an idea of the rules, metalanguage, forms of life, and so forth, which they are forced to expand when they discover that the use of these makes them be involved with particulars that otherwise would be independent of those rules. If the forms of life, and so forth, of themselves govern what occurs, they become miniature exemplars of the divine essence, so that any idea we may have of the forms of life will have to expand if we are to understand what such forms are in fact.

If an idea of a logical or mathematical formula is to be distinct from it, the idea must be given an extra feature, or the formula must be enabled to stand away from the idea. If the former, the idea is subjectified, personalized, and it becomes questionable whether it can be just to the formula; if the formula is enabled to stand away from the idea, the idea, to do justice to the formula, must then be expanded to become an idea of that which is involved in a domain other than itself.

October 25

According to Spinoza, an adequate idea has all the internal marks of a true idea. One need not refer outside it in order to know that it is true. But if this is the case, it is possible that there might be nothing outside, or what is outside could be changed without the idea being affected, so that it would then become a false idea. Of course, for Spinoza, this is not possible since the occurrence outside is already determined in the same way as the idea, each within its own attribute. But, then, strictly speaking, the adequate idea is true only because it is oriented in God, who also makes provision for the presence of that which makes the adequate idea be true.

For Spinoza, too, every idea has a status accreted to it in accord with its internal nature. An adequate idea is a true idea for which there is an actual occurrence in extension; a dubious idea, instead, is one which has answering to it some confusion of elements in the realm of extension; a negative idea is one which matches some lack or privation. An idea of God presumably would be one which matches a *causa sui;* it would, by the nature of its content, be that which requires it to refer to an existent. The ontological argument discussed yesterday will here bypass a reference to essence, and will concern itself solely with ideas, distinguishing them according to their contents and then recognizing that these contents not only have different statuses, such as being dubious, true, and so forth, but that they have exactly matching items elsewhere. God is known to exist because the idea we have of him is a distinctive idea which requires affirmation, and therefore the acknowledgment of an existence appropriate to it. The idea we have of God would be like the adequate ideas we have of other entities, differing from them only in the kind of existence that it has—the other true ideas answering to existents in the attributes, or pertaining to the attributes, or to what is common to the modes of an attribute. Every idea has the internal marks of a certain kind of occurrence, and every true idea the marks of a certain kind of existence.

Taken this way, Spinoza can be said to have provided a single ontological argument with many applications. Since he holds that any adequate or true idea is an idea of what exists, but in a way which is in consonance with the kind of nature it has, his ontological argument would be one which holds that every true idea is the idea of an existent, but that the existence is different in kind from case to case, in accordance with the nature of the idea.

Every true idea, for Spinoza, is the idea of an existent, and that existent has an existence proportionate to its nature. Every idea has its own internal marks of whatever kind it is—true, false, doubtful, and so forth, and answers to a different type of existence—the idea of God answering to an internally produced existence, and the idea of a cat answering to an externally produced existence.

For Spinoza, then:

1] Every idea bears the internal marks of its reliability.

2] True ideas express the essence of what in fact exists.

3] True ideas are clear and distinct; others are confused and, so far, dubious, false, ambiguous, and so forth.

4] Confused ideas could be said to be reliable in that they express what exists only as involved with other items from which they have not been properly distinguished. (Spinoza does not mention this possibility, since the standard of reliability for him is that of the true, and what falls short of the true is so far treated as unreliable.)

5] A reliable idea has an existent object.

6] Ideas differ in their power, depending on the excellence of their topic.

7] Each true idea has an existent object which has power proportionate to the power of the idea.

8] The idea of God is a true idea of that which has maximum power; the idea of a present cat is a true idea of a mode and thus of what has less power; the idea of a present man is a true idea of a mode which has more power than any other.

9] The ideas of individual men or of individual cats are true only so far as these are understood in terms of common rational components—the universal laws which are instanced by their physiology, for example.

10] The idea of God is the idea of what necessarily exists, for it is a true idea of that which has maximum power, and what has maximum power is that which is self-existent, *causa sui*.

I don't think any of these, with the exception of 2, is true, justified, or useful.

October 26

It is possible to view what I have maintained as Hegelian, filtered through Peirce, and qualified by Aristotle, Bonaventure, and Kant, tinctured by Whitehead. But there are some very important differences:

1] Hegel would like to start with something known, or with some category, and proceed from there to his final goal. I think it desirable to attend to experience and find there whatever clues I can to allow for a movement beyond what is found. There are at least three distinct kinds of beginnings:

A] With what fringes appearances; the pursuit of these takes us to two different types of forces which together make those appearances be. The closest that Hegel comes to the acknowledgment of such fringes is in his taking what is known to be fringed by what is yet to be found out; he overlooks the other side, that which sustains the first—an actuality or a knower.

B] With each of the sources of the fringes: Hegel, because he allows only one kind of source, makes it perform multiple functions. It provides for him the domain in which his dialectic is carried out, the factor in each finite item which brings it and us to what it needs, and that which terminates all efforts. Had Hegel recognized a plurality of beginnings, it would have been apparent to him that there are a number of distinct endings, all equally final.

C] With each finite entity seen to be incomplete, and also with each finality seen to be incomplete in the opposite direction. Each finite and final entity is incomplete because it is limited in being by the presence of others of the same kind—by other actualities or by other finalities. Hegel recognizes the latter limitation in connection with actualities but does not make it the ground for an investigation. The only completeness in which he is interested is that which involves what has been intruded on, and then by the absolute.

2] That which completes is for Hegel either equal or better than what he starts with—equal when, as in the case of Being and non-Being, he goes backward and forward, and unequal in most of the other cases where the antithesis seems to be on a higher level. But there are cases where the missing factor is less than that with which one begins—when, for example, one starts with a finality and tries to move to actualities in terms of what had been intruded there. The intruded factor is always less than its source.

3] Hegel's absolute idea is seen in its working, but not seen to be itself engaged in the working; we watch it go from one position to another, but do not see it leave its self-contained being to involve itself elsewhere. The diverse cases where something is constituted by universal conditions is also neglected.

It is remarkable how pure a Hegelian Wittgenstein is: Hegel would have applauded his insistence that there is no private language. Wittgenstein, too, accepts an absolute position in a Hegelian spirit—logic in the *Tractatus* and the common language later—which is not to be examined but to be used as the standpoint in terms of which all else is to be understood and, despite the appearance of atomism, even interlinked within that domain. Wiggenstein, to be sure, adds to the absolute idea an absolute Substance when he turns to ethical questions and treats them in a Schopenhauerian fashion.

Whitehead represents a genuine opposition to Hegel, since he allows for no encompassing domain or power and, as a consequence, has a world broken up into disjunct items. The plurality of actualities is held together for him, along Aristotelian lines, by having God function as the confining place in which the actualities occur. But that God is not constitutive of what occurs; he merely presents something at the boundary of each actuality.

4] Hegel takes the synthesis not only to be dynamic but to have a fixity, allowing it to be treated as a thesis for a subsequent synthesis.

But the dynamic and the fixed sides are distinct; there is no warrant for passing from one to the other. In any case, there is no reason to suppose that a synthesis in either form is itself incomplete in the ways in which the items synthesized are. The thrust of an incomplete entity is not a separate topic; nor is an intruded item. Only when isolated do they require actualities and finalities as grounds or sources.

5] Actualities, just like finalities, have the power to receive what they had intruded. Hegel does not allow that the actualities could be anything other than items instancing and governed by the undivided absolute.

6] That which completes also needs completion. To see this, one must not only arrive at the terminus of a thrust or at the source of an intruder, but must sink within it. A finality is then found to be both intruded upon by and to thrust itself toward actualities—the one diversifying it, the other expressing its fecundity. Hegel's absolute absorbs all. The absorption (he seems to hold) leads to their being united properly with all else, and nothing more.

7] A completion of one task such as, for example, the tracing of an intruded factor back to the intruder, can be completed without requiring a further move. If one attends to the intruder as a source of that intruded factor, one sees it itself to have factors intruded on it, perhaps from that on which the intruder had intruded. If this circle is completed, that is the end of the matter. It may be completed within the orbit of the totality of actualities and the finalities, but it is not a function of this. A language, for example, could be said to be the juncture of a universal meaning stemming from a final Possibility as met by intents from individuals. If one starts with the language, goes to these sources, and then back to the language again so as to see them functioning together in their purity, one does not have to take account of the way in which the Possibility and the actualities also are directly involved with one another to constitute appearances, or complexes in which there are intruded factors. We can understand a world of appearances without having also to consider how the realities, which make it possible, are involved with one another in other and even more basic ways.

8] The speculative adventure for Hegel is identical with the ontological course of a dialectic. But actualities and finalities thrust toward other actualities and finalities; toward one another; and intrude upon all else, regardless of thought. When we start with appearances and intruders and trace the factors of the one and the termini of the others back to their realities, we do not affect those realities.

November 9

Spinoza says that one will tend to pity those in adversity—or more precisely, that "the nature of man is generally constituted so as to pity those who are in adversity." Would this apply to a Nazi? Yes, if he pitied a crippled Jewish child, if only within the limited compass of an accepted view that the child, like all other Jews, was properly destined to die in a concentration camp. We should be able to say to such a Nazi that the pity he showed thrusts itself beyond that particular case to any cripple, because the crippling was not caught within the compass of the Jewishness. Presumably the Nazi would not have pity on one who was terrified because of fear of the concentration camp, who was unable to say his prayers as he had before, and so on.

The illustration points up a way of looking at ethics in some consonance with Aristotle and Confucius. (The suggestion I owe to Tony Cua.) Both of these start with a particular domain—a civilized world of men. We could extend their accounts not by a generalization, which would lose the concreteness so characteristic of their views, but by showing how the acts which were primary in such a domain thrust themselves toward all men. The fundamental fact would be a specific involvement with other men, a way of being allied with them as individuals in the particular domain, and the following out of the thrust as that which ended only by including all men. We would move from situation to situation only under the guidance of the initial alliance, extending this by concretely carrying it out in the next domain in which we found men whom we had not considered before. A domain, it might be said, has limited value and loose constraints; the more far-reaching any particular mode of activity is, the more surely is it more deeply rooted and forceful than any other.

An ethical theory, having a concrete application in the world as it now is, attends to the particular ways in which men in particular situations and groups ally themselves with others. Were someone to be found who refused to ally himself with anyone else, or who refused to give any role to himself as that unique individual, we would have to suppose him to be deficient, and would have to act as his surrogate. There would not be anyone who refused both to ally himself with any and who allowed no value to himself as an individual, without ceasing to be a man among men. He might be included among men, but only if one then provided a constitutive alliance of individuals and made him one instance of this, regardless of what he himself supposed or did. Apart from him, in every situation we would be able to distinguish the better and worse by attending to intentions and actions in terms of their promoting the alliance of individual humans with one another in each situation.

An alliance of men is what a social contract theory presupposes. But the foregoing shows that such an alliance is an ideal outcome of human activity and not a presupposition of their moving from a primitive to a political stage. A state, on such an account, instead of being built on the agreement of men who have allied themselves would, instead, be an instrument which promotes such alliances; it would carry out in another way the various relations men have to one another when they in fact are engaged in increasing the degree and extent of their alliances.

There should be no objection to isolating the general principle: ally oneself with all other individual men. But such a general principle is without practical force. By starting with a limited situation in which the efforts at alliance are in fact expressed and then in various discoverable ways, one already is involved in a practical ethics. The thrusting beyond the effort to ally oneself with just these individuals in this particular group will sometimes require argument in order to be made evident to others; but it can also be counted on to have some momentum of its own, and require not admonition but practice in order to be carried out in the new situation with something like the efficacy shown in the old. One who did not act sufficiently well in a particular situation to promote his alliance with other individuals would so far be condemnable; and so would he when looked at from another domain which he had, perhaps unknown to himself, occupied through the thrust of the alliance that he had initially instituted. Each situation would be morally judged, but the moral judgment would illustrate in a specific place and time the effort to be allied with all. The principle would allow one to provide an abstract formulation having a role with respect to the particular acts, somewhat like what a law of logic has to particular inferences—it will provide a check and allow for the determination of what to do in hard cases, but it can be ignored by one actually engaged in acting or thinking in a particular situation.

November 10

The successors of Kant saw him as having been caught in the problem of the one and the many. He had four sets of categories and a unity of apperception. The latter had only a logical import; it lacked the constitutive power of the categories. We could go from there in one of two directions: we could emphasize a One, and eventually make the categories themselves so many different expressions or variants of it. This is the alternative that Hegel took. But we could also stop with a plurality of ultimates; whatever defects were found with Kant's categories would be corrected not by reducing them to a One or by making them creatures of it, but by finding a better, more ultimate plurality. Without attending to Kant, this is the alternative which I have adopted. It is not alien to the position that Peirce intially, apparently, wanted to hold; but he quite soon came to the point of viewing one of his primary manys, Thirdness, as superior to the others. In that act, though, he pointed up an alternative that Kant had neglected. It is possible, while allowing that there is a plurality of ultimates, to recognize that each could have subordinate functions under the aegis of the others. Once again, without thinking of Peirce, this also is a line I have followed.

All the finalities—which are not just categories, as Kant, Hegel, and Peirce thought—but powers producing distinctive kinds of unifications in actualities severally, and in actualities as well as in appearances together, are equally ultimate and equally capable of expressing themselves through the subordinated use of the others. Each, too, meets resistance by that which is never reducible to them, and is thereby multiply exhibited but in restricted, qualified, attenuated forms. We can come to understand limited areas of the world and various disciplines by attending to specialized forms of those finalities, limited resistances to them, and the distinctive kind of outcome that results. It is this which I am in part doing in the course of the writing of "You, I, and the Others." (At the present moment I have written a little more than half of the first draft of it; I am toward the end of the chapter on the I and the Self, and have yet to write one on the We, and another on the Others.)

1976

January 10

I have just completed a draft of "You, I, and the Others." I call it a first draft, though every page of it was gone over a number of times on the day it was written, and then corrected again at a later time. But as a whole, it has not been reread. It is my plan now to set it aside for a little while, perhaps a month or so, and then to read it as a single work, correcting and rewriting it. I hope I can get it ready by the beginning of the summer, have it finally typed and multilithed, and then use it in a graduate course next September. Perhaps I may have it ready for the publisher by the end of the year.

I have sent out "First Considerations" to about a dozen thinkers who have expressed interest in criticizing it, but I have received only three critiques. I will reread that manuscript in the next weeks and tackle the criticisms when I finish rereading it and perhaps rewriting some passages. During that interval I plan to complete this volume of *Philosophy in Process*.

I have concentrated on the writing of "You, I, and the Others" to such an extent that I have hardly gone out and have given up painting and drawing. It remains to be seen whether I will soon have the urge to engage in the multiple activities which interested me last August, particularly since a new term begins on Monday. But before doing anything else, I will try to write the paper I had promised to read at the Metaphysical Society of America on the mind-body problem. I will retype while I correct the very last twenty pages or so of the book which deals with that problem.

January 13

At least five distinct meanings of 'unity' are worth distinguishing: 1] The unity of each of the finalities. Each is not only undivided, but provides a one for all the actualities and for the remaining finalities. 2] There is a finality which is primarily a unity, whose role is to enhance and ultimately absorb whatever diversity there be. 3] Each finite actuality provides a one for all the finalities. 4] The actualities and the finalities are in constant interplay to constitute a single actual totality. 5] The finalities and actualities together constitute an ideal togetherness of them which is forever different from them as actually together, more or less harmonious.

The obvious and hard question that now arises is the sense in which all of these are unities, and whether or not there is an overriding unity of them all. If there is no such overriding unity it is hard to see how one can speak of them all together; and if there is, it is hard to see how one will avoid introducing still another unity which will have to be reconciled with the original set, and so on without end.

Once again, I return to the perennial problem of the one and the many. The answer that now seems most promising holds that the question of how all the unities are together, or what their unity is, starts with them as aggregated. But that is the position which they have for an actuality; it is the unity of all of them as distinct from one another. Whatever we set down as an aggregate will be a special case of an actuality confronting a sheer plurality of ultimates as their one.

Granted this answer, there is then a question as to whether it is possible ever to get beyond it. How is it possible to escape from the one which has the finalities as its many, so that it can be said that "each finality is a unity," "there is a finality which is a unity," "there is a single interplay of all the finalities and actualities," or "there is an ideal unity of finalities and actualities"? If the finalities, on being acknowledged, are encountered as powers able to take over what is referring to them, inevitably all else is dealt with from a position determined by them. The center of a finality is never arrived at, but it is possible to get to the position where an abstract version of what it envisages and does can be obtained, in the way in which it is possible to take a position at an actuality and there grasp the fact that there are a number of distinct finalities. When we refer to some one of the unities, we may be taking a stand at any one of the unities and therefore seeing the chosen unity in a special guise. The position of an actuality allows us to be neutral to them all; in that neutrality we are also most distant from them.

Why should it not be possible for us to have just one unity for a plurality, say the plurality of actualities, and then abstract from that unity to envisage other subordinate unities governing other limited situations? I think the answer is that once we have arrived at such a unity we become involved with pluralities in a new way. An abstraction can be made, but it will be imitating the original unity; this leaves it exposed to the control of the items for which it provides a unity. But then it seems we must say that the unity in terms of which there are a number of unities is possessed by them. If so, in what sense could it be a unity for them? How is it possible to speak of a number of real unities without in that very act becoming caught up in some one or all of them? Must it not be the case that the abstraction, though itself powerless and immediately rendered impotent, unable to even face an aggregate, must either face an abstract aggregate, or be maintained by the actuality?

January 15

A persistent viewpoint throughout civilization has stressed dichotomies. Truth and falsehood, virtue and vice, inner and outer, mind and body, time and eternity, here and there, right and wrong, and the law of contradiction, are just some examples. The result has been that the solutions offered have either brought inquiry to an end or have led to the acceptance of the result as a term in a new dichotomy. Overlooked has been the question as to whether or not the dichotomy is produced from a position in which not only the dichotomous elements but others are involved, all on the same footing.

When logicians, in the attempt to justify a trichotomous logic, introduce the third 'truth-value' 'doubtful', they set it alongside the others. But such an attempt to have a trichotomous system, precisely because it is built on the idea of finding a third element for a given dichotomy, in effect sets the third not in equal opposition to the other two in the very way in which they are in opposition to one another, but as a kind of equilibrium point between them. From that equilibrium point it is possible to see that other dichotomies are also sustained by it. The doubtful is not only between truth and falsehood but between belief and unbelief. We now have four terms—truth, falsehood, belief, and unbelief—which themselves could be paired: truth, falsehood; truth, belief; truth, unbelief;

falsehood, belief; falsehood, unbelief; belief, unbelief. The same doubt is at the center of all, though it may have to be understood with different emphases if we consider it only with respect to this or that pair. The doubt which is set between truth and falsehood is qualitatively different from that which is set, let us say, between truth and unbelief. Once this is allowed, one can go on to deal with trichotomies in a new way. In the present illustration, truth, false-hood, and belief could be set in contrast with unbelief; truth, belief, and unbelief set in contrast with falsehood; and belief, unbelief, and falsehood set in contrast with truth. We would then have a dichotomy, but would have it function between a trichotomy and a single item. And, of course, we could take all four of the items as terminal points for a single central doubt.

If the last position is adopted, one begins with doubt as a central pivot for truth, falsehood, belief, and unbelief, all on a level. In a purely formal system one could replace the doubt with any one of these four. One would then, of course, lose the difference that sets the doubt apart from the other four. The four have a purity to them, without any admixture of the others, which is, of course, one of the reasons that they have been dealt with dichotomously. Doubt, instead, has them all suffused, interpenetrating one another. It has its own integrity, but the others can be derived from it by a purga-tion. Truth is doubt freed from all tinge of possible falsehood, belief, and unbelief; unbelief is doubt freed from all tinge of possi-ble truth, falsehood, and belief, and so on with the others. Each of the four is an extreme. If this be tenable, doubt would not properly be made into a third value of a three-valued logic, but would instead be the common ground for some such triad as belief, falsehood, and unbelief; truth, falsehood, and belief, and so forth.

Carrying over such observations to the traditional mind-body problem, it becomes evident that the Aristotelians and Cartesians are not as sharply opposed as one had been taught to take them. Both approach the question as though it were one of connecting dichotomous units. Aristotle's human nature or substantial form and his essential definition in terms of genus and differentia, give us a midpoint between a final but indefinite rationale and an ultimate matter or flux of which mind and body are special delimited re-gions. The Cartesian emotion, which Descartes thought was where the two were together, though in an undesirable confused state, was for him really a kind of midpoint in which a rationale was muddled by being involved with what was extended. Both philosophers combined the two extremes, the one doing it in a definition, the other in an experience. But the Cartesian midpoint is not a genuine emotion; it is rationality confused, and thus is but an alternative way of stating the unified nature of intelligible units. Aristotle took them to be joined in a superior, more definite intelligible human nature; Descartes took them to be joined in an inferior, confused, interfused manner. Descartes could be held to point to the fact that the central reality was experiential and not formal, and therefore unable to tell one what was central to mind and body, but rather what was central to a fourfold set—mind, body, involvement, and concern. The latter two are delimited portions of an ultimate process or ongoing, and a final fixity or being. From this point of view, the central fact would be an I or self or ego which was exhibited in all four directions, which could be taken two at a time in every possible way, or three at a time, or in all four, each placing a different emphasis on the I. The traditional mind-body problem emphasizes the Aristotelian substantial form or nature, without necessarily requiring one to accept his definition of definition or the allied supposition that a man is a rational animal. One could take such an answer to require nothing more than a formal connection between the mind and the body. If this is done, then the Cartesian emotion would yield an answer to the problem, not by discarding the emotion, or better, confusion which he found to be at the heart of their juncture, but by refining this to leave one with a purged, purely rational connection.

Had Aristotle or Descartes considered the dichotomy of involvement in an ongoing world through work and deed on the one hand, and concern with obligation, responsibility, attention to an eternal undifferentiated being on the other, they would have had to think of a different kind of midpoint from what was rational through definition or (as is implicit in Descartes) was rational through an overcoming of a confusion. Such a midpoint would be more properly called emotional, though I think this introduces a bias toward an involvement with the world, rather than a midpoint between mind and body, even when that midpoint is taken to be a muddled form of both. (I have long supposed that emotion was the way in which mind and body were united, because I, too, accepted the usual presentation of the problem.) The midpoint is what a medieval would call an 'act', though unlike him one need make no reference to potentialities except so far as these are themselves the act as oriented in one direction or the other. From this point of view, an act has in equipoise tendencies toward involvement and concern.

The acknowledgment of involvement and concern allows us now to make the combination: body and mind, concern and mind, concern and body, involvement and body, involvement and mind, and involvement and concern. Each requires an emphasis on an aspect of the I—human nature, consciousness, presence, will, or freedom. The I is all together, or alternatively, it is human nature in act, consciously free with an insistent presented will. If the I is understood to be never entirely sundered from its diverse manifestations, there will be no need to rigidify any of these aspects. Nor need it be in equilibrium with respect to all; it is biased now in this direction and then in that, always involved with the body to some extent, enlivening it, making it 'my body'. The mind-body problem arises because of the prominence of a bias in one of these directions, and a swallowing up of involvement and concern within them; but involvement and concern are opposed to one another and to the body and mind in the same way that these are opposed to one another.

The primary fact is the I centering four distinct extremes, each as basic as the others. The I is all four inter-involved, compressed; it is no more rational than it is emotional. When an aspect is isolated, it should be taken to be a function of what it relates.

An entirely new line of inquiry is now being opened. I do not see my way clearly, but I do sense that previous formulations of basic ideas, my own included, will have to be modified, supplemented, and subtilized. One issue stands out at once. If, as I have maintained, that there are five finalities all equally ultimate, does this not conflict with the supposition that there is an I or center for four basic realities? It does not, because the I is not centered at the finalities but at them as mediated by the body, mind, involvement, and concern; because these are being viewed as extremes, purged cases of something empirical; because the I is the condensed version of all five finalities. It should also be the case that each one of the finalities should have a finite representative for whom the other four are purified extremes. Or is it just adventitious that there is an I which is the compressed presence of all? Is there, or could there be something like the I, but which is to be understood as a kind of pivotal being, substance, process, or fixity? Or does the fact that I am trying to understand mind, body, and so forth, force into the fore what is an exemplification of possibility or meaning? If we did not try to understand but simply wanted to participate would we then not have to ignore the I and attend to man as creator, believer, aware, and historical? If so, then the having of an I as a center is only one of a number of possible alternatives; each of the terminal items, precisely because it is pure is also to be understood as having a pivotal form in some finite center. What was said earlier today about doubt must then be changed to allow it also to be an extreme for some form of truth, falsehood, belief, or unbelief treated as central.

The best thing to say I think is that an I is neutral with respect to all five specialized forms of the finalities, that it has these inter- fused, and that if it be contrasted with this interfusion it can be said to be just unique, the juncture of a distinction from all five plus a difference from all other particulars. Taking it to be central is not to favor it as a nature; that occurs only if it is biased toward meaning more than toward some other finality. None of the extremes is to be made a center for the other four, but one can see the I as giving a preferential status at some moment to this or that extreme; when an extreme is given preferential status it functions as a center for the others, all the while that it is interfused with them. To bring this result to bear on doubt, and so forth, one starts with some such complex as attitude, which has doubt, truth, falsehood, belief and unbelief all intertwined. Any one of these could be emphasized; when it is, it has the others as extremes, making pairs and triplets and one quadruplet set of oppositional items.

January 16

When we set mind and body in opposition, we can also consider any pair of the three, meaning, concern, and involvement. Whatever pair we take, the remaining one functions as a center. Human nature is at the center of mind, body, concern, and in- volvement. If concern is put at the center, then human nature and involvement are coordinated with mind and body; if, involvement is at the center, concern and human nature are coordinated with mind and body. Were one to give up a concentration on mind and body, the mind or the body could have its own representative center—that is, a consciousness or a will.

If this approach could be carried over to truth, falsehood, belief, and unbelief, we would have to take attitude as being able to be made coordinate with any three of the others, with the fourth functioning as the base in terms of which one could envisage them all. Thus, truth could be said to be expressed in different ways in falsehood, belief, unbelief, or attitude.

January 17

The I can be said to be the individualized juncture of a presence, consciousness, willing, freedom, and human nature. Since these are the epitomizings of a primary substance, unity, existence, being, and possibility, the I is then the juncture of epitomizings of what is ultimate. That I does not form a self-enclosed unit; it is inseparable from expressions. It manifests itself as the living of the body, the activity of the mind, an involvement in what is going on, a concern with what is fixed, and an intentionality with what is possible. Each of these manifestations is a segment of a finality. The finality treated from the position of such manifestations has the guise of a world, reason, process, totality, or language.

The lived body, the world, and so forth, are explicable as the I made manifest in specialized ways. Conversely, the I is explicable as the life, and so forth, interlocked, and made central to, that is, as the unity for the finalities. This unity, though ontologically neutral to all of the finalities, is biased now toward this and then toward that, with the consequence that the I is known primarily as a located I, a thinking I, an involved I, a concerned I, or an intentional I. Or, to stay closer to the I itself, as present, conscious, willing, free, or a nature.

These remarks amount to more than a map or a set of labels; they have important consequences. They lead one, at the very least, to dissect the I in two ways—horizontally and vertically. The horizontal exposes the I at the center of all the finalities, and as a source or ground of segmented finite cases of these. The vertical, instead, takes it to be the unity of all the epitomizings of the finalities. It is because one of these epitomizings is dominant at a particular moment that the I is to be characterized as present, conscious, will, free, or a nature, and why it is that it therefore is attentive to this or that finality or segment of it. One can also take the distinguishing of the layers of the I to be due to the dominant presence of this or that finality. A man could then be said to emphasize his will, for example, and thereupon make conspicuous his involvement in existence.

But there could be an insistence by Existence which so conquers the individual that the will is forced to the fore. The latter in fact is what should be said since it does more justice to the power of the finalities.

An alternative and, I think, more correct view would maintain that the more surely we make a vertical slice and therefore emphasize some particular aspect of the interfused epitomizings of the finalities, the more surely do we hold it away from all the finalities. A particular finality will make evident a distinctive aspect, and have this related to it as an instance. The very distinguishing of that aspect will make it be the primary note of the I, compelling other aspects to be expressed in finite forms and to terminate in their respective finalities. A human nature will be congenial to the possibility it instances, but will not be expressed; instead, it will release expressions of the other dominated aspects of the I. The dominant will be metaphysically keyed to its proper object, and the others will be empirically spelled out in the form of finite expressions.

January 18

The observations of the last few days require subtilization of what I have said about the emotions both in *The World of Art* and *Cinematics*. I followed Descartes and took the emotions to be the correct and adequate locus of the occurrence of what was at once mental and physical. As a result I overlooked the possibility that there might be other factors also involved. Once that possibility is opened up, it becomes fairly easy to see that the mind or the body, or both, might themselves be set aside or recognized to have subordinate roles from other perspectives which require something analogous to the emotions.

When the will dominates over four other aspects of the I—human nature, freedom, consciousness, and presence—it is directly involved with Existence, and with a finitely relevant version of this, process. As directed toward Existence, the will is the basic emotion of awe; as dominating over and being expressed through the other aspects of the I, it is emotion as it is normally understood. In the latter guise it changes the way in which the nature, freedom, consciousness, and presence of the I will be exhibited, as intention, concern, mind, and the life of the body.

The will, as dominant over other aspects of the I, and inseparable from Existence, affects intention (what human nature is like as faced with possibility), and concern (a freedom directed toward a fixed totality). The mind as directed toward reason and the life of the body as directed toward the world then exhibit the tonality and turbulence normally associated with the emotions. If one attends only to these two, one must read into them the way in which human nature, the substantial form of Aristotle, has a willed intentional thrust toward Existence—its primary concern with what is external—modified.

If, instead of emphasizing the will, one had emphasized human nature, there would have been a basic thrust of interest or duty toward Possibility, with a consequent affect on the way in which the will, together with the others, was being exercised. If, instead, the emphasis was on freedom with its thrust toward Being, concern would be dominant and make a difference to the others. Replacing freedom by consciousness or presence, with their respective thrusts toward Unity and Substance, or reason and world, makes the other expressions of the I be colored by a kind of faith or belief, and an appreciation or humility.

I am, evidently, still filling out, and then only with little more than verbal distinctions, a schematic view of the aspects of the I, its finite expressions, the ways in which one of its expressions is involved with some finality, and the affect that its dominance has on all the others, as finitely exhibited. It is time, I think, to free myself from the scheme and look more directly at the phenomena, though not in complete indifference to what the scheme takes to be pivotal.

There is a primary emphasis on the emotions when one is concerned with art, particularly if art, as I have held, has an emotional connection with the Existence. We do, though, also speak of emotions in connection with religion, in our communications with others, and sometimes in connection with intentions. If, as the existentialists claim, man has a fundamental concern with what is ultimate, this too will be emotionally toned. But if we keep the reference of the emotions to Existence, we will have to say that it is only when this reference occurs that the other aspects of the I are altered in their functioning in finite situations. When, instead of an emphasis on Existence, there is a thrust toward the fixed object of religion, for example, though one could then speak of an emotion inseparable from reverence or worship (or of these themselves being emotions), it might be better just to characterize the thrust as worship or reverence.

There is difficulty here with terms, because it is not uncommon to use 'emotion' to cover everything other than that which was either in the mind or body. The use of the idea of emotion to include concern and intention as finite expressions on a par with the mind and body, all under the influence of a will which was directed toward Existence, allows one to use 'emotion' in the usual way, but to supplement it with a consideration for other types of expression besides the mental and the bodily. A second expanded use takes account of the fact that emotion has its own subject matter, Existence, and that this is the objective of the will. The recognition that other aspects of the I and their expressions are affected in various ways occurs when the will sharply thrusts forward toward its own final objective. The use of 'emotion' to refer to situations where, instead of will and process (or Existence) being primary, other aspects—presence, Substance (or world); consciousness and Unity (or reason); freedom and Being (or totality); and human nature and Possibility (or language)—are taken to be so. A dominant will, with its thrust toward Existence, also reconciles intention and concern—and these two with mind and body. The most satisfactory way of making contact with Existence in its roots requires the emotional union of mind, body, intention, and concern.

When mind and body are reconciled with intention and involvement, or concern and involvement, what is primary is not will, but either a concern with an ultimate fixity, or a human nature inseparable from what is possible. The mind and body, evidently, are reconcilable in three basic ways, each of which requires that they be subject to aspects of the I which have their own subject matter—process, fixity, or language.

This discussion is not entirely free from the table I have made covering these distinctions. That table ought to be set down:

Finite Exhibitions and Cosmic Divisions	Finality as relevant to the finite	Finality	Dominant Aspect	Instance of Wonder
1] body	world	Substance	presence	appreciation
2] mind	reason	Unity	consciousness	worship
3] involvement	process	Existence	will	awe
4] concern	totality	Being	freedom	openess
5] intention	language	Possibility	human nature	interest

I have taken the third row to be where emotion is to be studied, primarily because it is the emotions aroused in art which lead us to Existence, and because the will can be understood to be at the root of creativity. The philosophic tradition, though, is most concerned with the intelligibility of the I. When this is to the fore, we are occupied with the fifth row, and particularly human nature. Such a nature, when dominant over the other aspects of the I, affects them with its interest. The more that interest is caught up with Possibility, the steadier is the human nature and the more effectively it makes a difference to the functioning of the other aspects of the I. Its intentionality is then manifest in the body, mind, involvement, and concern. The way it is present, the nature of consciousness, and the exercise of the will and freedom will then be affected; they will be subject to what the human nature requires and, so far, will be unable to express themselves as independent, pure presences, conscious, willing, or free.

All, or even most, of what occurs when one thinks, is involved, concerned, or intends, has a bodily counterpart or accompaniment. This means that the presence of the I, with its appreciation and expression in the body and through this on the world, is dominant over the others, while geared to a final Substance in a direct way, at the same time that the body is the medium through which a dominant consciousness, will, freedom, or nature is expressed.

A human body is among all the bodies in the universe, where it is subject to the same laws governing the rest. In this setting it is but a complicated instance of the same conditions which govern all the other bodies. At the same time, a human body is one of four channels connected with cosmic realities, inseparable from the finalities into which it enables us to penetrate. The finite, human, separated body, when allied with any three of the others will, with them, be affected by the dominance of consciousness, will, freedom, or human nature. As a consequence, the body will have to be understood in one of four ways: A] It will belong to a larger world and, as so belonging, make a difference to the functioning of other dimensions of the I; it will do this, though, not as the palpable, familiar body of everyday, but as the living presence of the I, the life of the body concentrated and interfused with but dominant over other aspects of the I.   B] It will be inseparable from a dominant mind which is directly interlocked with a final Unity.   C] It will be inseparable from a dominant involvement in Existence, with its creative will;   D] it will be inseparable from a dominant concern with a final Being, expressed in the I as a freedom. And   E] it will be inseparable from a dominant intention, directed to Possibility via language, and expressed as a human nature.

In the last three cases, the body is somewhat like what the existentialists have taken it to be—charged with various powers which are to be understood from within and which can not be equated with what could be understood by attending to a part of a larger whole of bodies. The body is finitized by parts of larger wholes, or finitizes what itself is part of a larger whole. As part of a world of bodies a human body is as real as mind, involvement, concern, and intention, each itself a segment of some larger cosmic reality. But it is also affected by these. It is then not a part of a world of bodies, but only a finite channel for those other aspects of the I.

The failure to recognize a human body to be part of a larger world is one with the failure to see how it is able to make a difference to the finite functioning of mind, and so forth. The body, that makes a difference to mind, involvement, concern, and intention, is cosmically conditioned, not the body of the existentialists. That cosmically conditioned body is a precondition for the body on which the existentialists concentrate. Mind and the others finitize and enrich that cosmic body, turning it into a living humanized body, while they continue to be cosmological in their thrusts.

In order to give an existentialist account of the body, one must take it in the guise it is understood to have by scientists (or what is built on their knowledge), for it is this which carries out in a finite way what a dominant mind, involvement, concern, and intention demand. Similarly, in order to give a materialistic interpretation of the mind as essentially a brain, one must start with the mind as a segment of a reason, and then see it to be subject to bodily conditions, and thereby cut off from the reason. Attempts to treat involvement, concern, and intention as though they were just finite occurrences, and there affected by one another and mentality, similarly require that one first understand these in their cosmic positions, and then account for their finite forms as the result of a finitizing of them through the dominant operation of some other one of them, or of the body, functioning within a cosmic setting. All finite situations are to be understood to be the outcome of a finitizing of something cosmic, due to the dominance of some other cosmic occurrence whose epitomized form in the I gives the I its significance, and is expressed through and affects the original cosmic entity. We start with the acknowledgment of something cosmic, and look for a dominant factor in the I having a cosmic reach, which makes the original cosmic item have a finite and qualified status.

January 19

All the aspects of the I are interfused. As so interfused they are attached to the finalities and the finitely relevant forms these have. The attachment is not well focussed; we are dimly aware of the termini but have as yet no way of making their natures evident or getting closer to them. When some aspect of the I becomes dominant, due to the fact that the I is never in perfect equilibrium, and is always thrusting outward in a biased insistent way, the other aspects are cut away from their cosmic setting. Consequently, their finite expressions are forced to the fore. The fact that some bodily expression always occurs—if fact it be—means that one's body has been finitized. This requires that the mind, involvement, concern, or intention be dominant, and be sharply directed toward reason or Unity, process or Existence, totality or Being, or language and Possibility, at the same time that they affect the body's finite functioning. Depending on which of them is dominant, other finite functionings will also occur. Thus if the dominance is mind, then not only body but involvement, concern, and intention will have finite forms affected by mentality; if, instead, involvement is dominant, then not only body but mind, concern, and intention will have finite forms affected by the will.

It is awkward to be speaking of a body as though it were coordinate with mind, involvement, concern, and intention, for it seems so palpable, so different from all the others in a way they do not seem to be different from one another. The awkwardness is partly overcome with the understanding that it is not body as extended in a particular locality which is being referred to—for that is a finite body governed by mind, involvement, concern, or intention—but the body as instancing cosmic laws, and contrasting with the humanized living body. The one is part of a world, just as mind is part of reason, involvement of process, concern of totality, and intention of language; the other is a finitized version of this, but filled out by expressions of other aspects of the I.

Instead, as I have been doing, of taking the finite body to be a living body in and of itself, its living might more properly be identified with the conjoint presence of a dominant mind, involvement, concern, and intention. These, of course, are all dominant relative to the body, only so far as they are also dominant over one another. It is only when one focusses on the finite body that one is forced to see it as providing for the presence of all the others as dominating it.

A dominant aspect of the I has four finite channels. When mind, involvement, concern, or intention is dominant, one of those channels is the body which is thereupon finitized and filled out by it. When we isolate the finite body, what we evidently do is to blur together all the aspects. Had we sought to focus on one truly dominant item, we would have to consider the body together with three other channels, all expressing in finite ways what they are as affected by that dominant. If it be involvement which is dominant, the body will be affected by the will with its thrust toward Existence, at the same time that the mind, concern, and intention are also affected by that will.

If there is a thrust toward Substance with the presence of the I dominant, it would seem that the finitizings are mind, involvement, concern, and intention, but not bodily at all. Either it is possible that the I has no finite bodily expression in this case, or presence can never be wholly dominant. The former would seem to be the correct alternative, since there would seem to be no reason why the presence of the I should not be as effectively insisted on as the other aspects of it. There is no difficulty with this alternative once it is remembered that by a finite bodily expression is not meant the having of a part of a cosmos of bodies, but only a body which has been cut away from the cosmos and is inwardly determined. The dominant presence of the I means that there is a cosmically determined body; there is a human, personal, living body only when the presence of the I does not dominate over all other aspects.

Does this mean that when the presence of the I dominates, the body is depersonalized? If so, it would seem to be like a corpse. How then could the presence of an I be dominant? One would expect, instead, that it would be recessive. The presence of the I, though, does not mean that there is a consciousness, but only that the body is part of a cosmos. When the I becomes conspicuously present, it dominates over and affects other aspects, forcing mind, involvement, concern, and intention to have finite forms in a cosmologized body.

What could be meant by finite forms of mind, involvement, concern, and intention, in the absence of a finite body? Must one say that these are just localized within the cosmologized body, that is, the body as belonging in a world? If so, there will be cases where mind, involvement, concern, and intention will be exhibited in a cosmologized body and in a decosmologized one, the first occurring when the presence of the I is dominant, and the others when other aspects of the I are.

A dominant aspect of the I   A] thrusts sharply toward a specific finality,   B] is expressed as a detached part of a distinctive cosmological situation,   C] affects the other aspects, changing their rhythms and directions, and   D] finitizes them within its own cosmological unit. The body is consequently either finitized within the cosmological units of the other manifested aspects, or finitizes the other manifestations within its own cosmological reality. The finite living body channels the thrusts which relate finite activities in those channels to ultimate realities with which the body has nothing to do; the cosmological body thrusts toward a world at the same time that the presence of the I dominates over other aspects and finitizes them. The finite living body is the localized ground for thrusts far outside its reach; the finite forms of intention, and so forth, are the localized grounds for a bodily thrust, and thus for an appreciative reaching into the world and Substance.

A finite mind, occupied with daily matters, is under the dominance of the presence of an I (or some other aspect of that I such as consciousness, will, freedom, or human nature) and therefore within the body (or involvement, and so forth) which is part of the cosmos. A cosmological mind, which thrusts toward reason and a final unity, and comes into focus with the dominance of consciousness, finitizes the body, making it mentally tinged, a body which is distinguished from all others by virtue of the effectiveness of that mind in it.

When the finite mind, (or the finite involvement, concern, and intention) is under the dominance of the presence of the I, it is in the body known to science. When, instead, the body is finitized, it is the body known to existentialists, but with the mind, and so forth, all having a transcendent reach.

A cosmological body is finitized by a dominant will, freedom, human nature, or consciousness. When any of these occurs, one is occupied with what thrusts toward process or Existence, totality or

Being, language or Possibility, or reason or Unity at the same time that the body is humanized in a special way. When presence dominates, the body is not finitized at all but remains cosmological. Then, due to the presence of the I, there is exhibited within the cosmological body finitized forms of consciousness, will, freedom, and human nature. When the body is finitized (together with other finitizings), it is to be located within a cosmological, nonbodily unit. The body will, therefore, be found either within the cosmological whole of bodies, of which it is a part, or within some other cosmological whole—reason, process, totality, or language. A finitizing of a body presupposes a cosmology of bodies and ends with a setting of it within a division of some other type of cosmological whole.

Finitized forms of nonbodily, expressed aspects of the I are all locatable within the confines of the cosmologically defined body. Must not the finitized body, therefore, be located within the confines of cosmologically defined units of a nonbodily sort? Can this be done? One is inclined to put the limits of cosmological nonbodily units at the limits of the finitized body. But this is not necessary. Indeed, we know that we are caught up in situations outside the finitized body. Can existentialism explain this? I doubt it. In any case, one must say, I think, that there are finite reaches of the mind, involvement, concern, and intention, which are independent of the body's limits, and provide the finitized body with settings inside nonphysical wholes.

A finitized body is located within a portion of reason, process, totality, or language. (I am not satisfied with the last two terms, the one trying to express the meaning of Being as it is pertinent to willed involvement, and the other trying to express the meaning of Possibility as it is pertinent to an intentional expression of human nature. Even 'intentional' is not altogether right, since it leads one to suppose that reference is being made to the intentionality views of Brentano and Husserl). And, of course, within those portions of reason, process, totality, or language, not only the finitized body, but finitizings of involvement, concern, intention, and mind are also to be found. If we have consciousness dominant, a region of reason, which is to say a purified mind like Aristotle's active reason, will be a cosmological unit finitized, say, by a free concern with Being. We now have no bodily referent. Either we must be able to speak of cosmological units which are nonbodily and which can be finitized or which can provide loci for finitizings of other kinds of units, or we will have to deny that any cosmological unit can occur without a body.

The present procedure reverses the usual way of looking at these matters, since it starts with cosmological units. Usually one starts with the lived body, a finite mind, some limited fixity, or with a unique individual. However, an approach by way of a definition of human nature is along the lines I am following, for human nature is a dominant facet of the I, inseparable from a cosmological intention, a division of an all-encompassing language, or a realm of meaning. Such a dominant human nature, individualized in the I, makes body, mind, involvement, and concern have finitized forms within the limits of an intention. The intention here is the source of the referential and separational features of a language which otherwise would be a single, undivided, syntactical whole, or divided according to grammar and not by living discourse.

I am far from clear on most of this, but I do think that I see the mind-body problem to be part of a much larger complex; that the emotions can serve to ground a finitized body, mind, concern, and intention; and that the emotions can also be finitized when any one of these others provides the emotions with a place in a cosmological unit.

January 20

If one were to substitute 'emotions' for 'involvement', the emotions would be understood to be primarily directed toward Existence, but to be finitized and thereby made to be involved with purely human matters when they are subjected to a dominating presence, will, freedom, or human nature. The emotions will then be, with other finitized items, subjected to a cosmologically determined body, mind, concern, or intention. I am now close to one of the Cartesian ways of understanding the emotions as exhibiting the outcome of a cosmological body's union with a mind. (Though the mind, in the *cogito,* is taken to be individual, since it is occupied with mathematical and other clear and distinct ideas it is evidently a detached part of reason.) But I am also acknowledging a concern with Being, and an intention directed at Possibility.

The emotions are capable of remaining attached to Existence when the will becomes dominant over other aspects of the I, and is thereby able to finitize body, mind, concern, and intention. These are then charged with the emotions and made to function, not as cosmologically detached units, but as requiring for their understanding the dominant presence of the emotions. This approach takes us close to another Cartesian way of viewing the emotions; as confusing what is in the body and in the mind, the emotions (he thinks) dominate over and give a special Aristotelian twist to the nature of the mind and the body. Since the emotions also finitize a concern with Being and an intention directed toward Possibility, something like a Cartesian reference to God will be understood to be muddled by the dominant emotions and their presumed confusing finitizing. A reference to a finitized intention directed at Possibility, though perhaps derivable from Descartes's concern with what is right or proper, seems to be additional to the items which he acknowledged.

The emotions, on this account, are cosmologically detached from process, at the same time that they are directly connected with, inseparable from, and governed with other portions of process. They are limited in range and, indeed, affected in nature and functioning by body, mind, concern, and intention when these are cosmologically detached at the same time that some aspect of the I, other than will, is dominant. The emotions humanize the mind and body, as well as the concern and intention, when the (creative) will is dominant, awe at Existence is the primary mood, and the emotions consequently understood, not as occurring due to the mind, body, concern, or intention, but as part of a primary thrust toward Existence. The thrust toward Existence will then be taken to be as primary as a cosmologically defined body (one subject to the laws of nature), a cosmologically defined mind (one occupied with eternal truths), a cosmologically defined concern (one occupied with what is forever remote and fixed), and a cosmologically defined intention (one occupied with what is able to be). The cosmological definitions of these items show them to be units within what is under fixed conditions; but none of the items is just such a unit, for while it is detached, it both thrusts toward what is final, and at the same time has within the I the status of an aspect dominating over other aspects.

I have been long aware of the thrust of the emotions toward what is final, but I took their presence within the body and mind, or as unifying and permeating the body and mind, to be a beginning or limiting case of the emotions as thrusting beyond these points. But now it becomes evident that the emotions, when confined within the body and mind (to concentrate on these), are the emotions which have been finitized and thereby given a bodily and mental import. When they are directed at Existence they are of a different type, with their limited expressions reflecting not a limitation in them but the fact that they are being understood within the finite limits of the mind and body. The fact was in a way recognized in the distinguishing of the state of awe from the state of being a juncture of mind and body, for not only is awe emotion directed at Existence, while both mind and body are emotion finitized and thereby confused and turbulent, but awe is present in the form of the finitizing power of these two, even while it is directed beyond them. A finitizing power is evidently directed at what is ultimate in two ways, one in a more or less sharpened manner, and the other rooted in, locatable at, dominating over, and through their mediation thrusting far beyond the reach of the mind and body which the emotions finitize and thereby make function in humanized ways. If a mind be contrasted with a body in the way emotions have just been contrasted with both mind and body, the mind will have to be understood as not only a limited activity explicable as subject to a cosmological body but will be limited in its operation within a mentally conditioned body, at the same time that it thrusts directly with its consciousness toward a final reason or Unity.

Evidently, there are two finite forms of body, mind, and so forth, and two transcendent forms. Each is finite because it has been made so by a dominant aspect of the I which is pertinent to the others, and each is finite because its own pertinent aspect of the I makes it affect various finitized items and thereby become involved with them. Each is transcendent because it is directly involved with what is ultimate, and each is transcendent because it is directed at what is ultimate from the base of what is finitized.

The mind is finite because will, freedom, and so forth, affect consciousness, and force the mind to be detached from reason; it is finite, too, when consciousness has a dominant role, and as such is affected by the will, and so forth, operating in finitized emotions, and so forth. The mind is transcendent because it is directly related to Unity, and it is transcendent, too, because other items, when finitized, merely provide it with a ground. The body is finite because, through the dominant activity of consciousness, and so forth, it has been detached from the world; it is finite, too, when finitized versions of mind, and so forth, are expressed in it, for it then is so far involved with them. The body is transcendent because it is subject to the same cosmological laws that govern all other bodies, and thrusts beyond the common cosmos to a final, affiliating Substance; it is transcendent, too, because when finitized versions of the mind, and so forth, humanize it, it continues to be related to the world and Substance.

One finite form is due to the dominance of some aspect of the I that is pertinent to other items, and another finite form is due to the fact that what is finitized affects it. One transcendent form is cosmological even when it is taken as just a unit; the other transcendent form is humanized and therefore distinctive, to be understood from within, still a part of a cosmos, but grounded in what is affecting it from within.

Each of the finite segments of the cosmos is impersonal, a segment of that cosmos inseparable from a finality; each is also humanized and turned into a distinct finite unit, by being made the locus of finitized forms of other cosmological units. The latter, while quickening the locus, may extend and usually do extend beyond its confines. Each of the finite segments of the cosmos is finitized while being set in other cosmological segments, and each offers finitized items a cosmological unit with its continued thrust. Finitized items humanize the body and ground its thrust; the body is impersonally cosmological and also finitized. A humanized body, which is quickened by finitized forms, is cosmological at the same time, thrusting beyond itself, but it does so from a ground which is outside the reach of any cosmological consideration. The finitized forms within the cosmological unit ground its thrust as well as humanize the unit. The cosmological unit is impersonal, because expressive of a dominant aspect of the I, at the same time that it is humanized because that aspect dominates over other aspects. A cosmological unit functions independently in an impersonal way, at the same time that it is humanized by and grounded in other dimensions. Each cosmological unit has a purely finitized form which humanizes other cosmological units. Each, too, is humanized by finitized items.

I have been stating the matter in various forms again and again in good part because I do not have it wholly clear. It is quite possible that I have confused various cases some of the time. What seems clear is that there is a cosmological, impersonal status enjoyed by the body and the others, and that each has a finitized form due to the fact that its appropriate aspect of the I is dominated by some other aspect. Evidently, too, each finitized item is set within a cosmological setting. What is not altogether clear is the relation between a finitized item and the cosmological unit in which it is set. The former, the finitized item, is said again and again to humanize the latter. It is also said that the item provides the unit with a ground. Are these the same thing, the one telling us that the cosmological unit has behaviors which require a reference to finitized units, while the other tells us that the cosmological unit has a distinctive localized intensity while it continues to be involved with what is transcendent? Are these but two ways of referring to the cosmological unit, the one revealing its separate internally explicable functioning, and the other that it has a distinctive starting point? It seems so.

There is an independent cosmological status and an independent status of being finitized; and there is a single state of affairs where an entity is at once humanized and thus finite and cosmological in the sense that it continues to thrust forward, though now as grounded in its humanized form and, therefore, finitized factors.

January 21

Keeping to the emotions, mind, and body, there are two primary cases. In one, the will is dominant over other aspects of the I, and sets the body and mind within the context of a thrust toward process and Existence. In the other, presence or consciousness is dominant, and the emotions are set within the context of a body which is a part of the world or within the context of a mind which is a fragment of reason.

When the will is dominant, and body and mind are set within transcendentalizing emotions, we have a finite local body and an emipirical mind providing a base for those emotions. The body and mind are governed by the will and so far humanized and finitized. If we had been dealing with the body in cosmological terms, we would find that it is sustaining a thrust toward Existence at the same time that there was a willed determination of its direction and activity. An analogous observation is pertinent to the mind. When, instead of the will being dominant, either presence or consciousness is, the emotions will be finitized. They will then either make the mind confused or the body turbulent. The mind that is being confused will not be the empirical, but the transcendent mind; the body that is turbulent will be the body which is part of a world.

The first of the cases, where will is dominant, has a bearing on art and its illumination of Existence via the thrust of the emotions. It leads one to say that the mind and body are not confused and made turbulent by the emotions but rather that in the course of an emotional thrust, the body and mind are subject to a willed activity, which presumably is the creativity of the artist.

When I made out a table some time ago, I put the mind in relation to Unity. This was due to my initial understanding of the mind-body problem as one between the unified and the diverse. But I think it would be more correct to remain with an earlier understanding of the various finalities and take mind and reason, consciousness and interest to be related to Possibility. A new table would be required:

Finite Exhibitions and Cosmic Divisions	*Finality as relevant to the finite*	*Finality*	*Dominant Aspect*	*Instance of Wonder*
1] body	world	Substance	presence	appreciation
2] mind	reason	Possibility	consciousness	interest
3] emotion	process	Existence	will	awe
4] concern	totality	Being	freedom	openness
5] intention	language	Unity	human nature	worship

I am not altogether satisfied with this. Concern, totality, and freedom have not yet been explicated; the alliance of language with Unity and this with human nature seems odd. Nor is it clear that will should be connected with emotion, and freedom with concern, rather than the reverse.

The emotions, when set within the body or mind, affect the cosmological performances of these. When, instead, these are set within the context of the emotions, the emotions acquire mental and physical colorings, intensities, at the same time that the emotions have their cosmological performances affected.

January 22

There is something amiss in the account I have given of the nature of the present in the book of history and in other places. I there say that the present is a single stretch and that it nevertheless may embrace a number of smaller presents which succeed one another, outside the provenance of that one present which encompasses them all. This seems right, and yet it also seems to have the implication that there could be a present as long as history itself which is undivided. I attached this view, too, to the idea that there was some final cause or possibility which governed the ways in which the various presents that passed away were related and achieved significance, but this seems too easy a solution, and leaves one with the idea of a history indefinitely long.

A battle is fought as that which is to be decisive, and therefore to terminate the war—or perhaps as crucial, essential, or unavoidable and, therefore, which provides the war with a possible closure of a certain kind that is to be realized subsequently. In either way, the battle seems to be governed by the possibility of a war being terminated either by that battle or by what follows on that battle. There is a war which is relevant to that battle and which that battle is in the process of realizing in the form of a determinate battle inseparable from a partial determination of the character of the war. If one had been involved in the war in order to make the world safe for democracy, to establish the thousand-year Reich, or to assure the triumph of the proletariat or of a classless society, there would seem to be a possibility which stretches far beyond the war and which the war could help make determinate in the way in which the battle makes the war determinate. Must one suppose the possibility of these highly abstract remotely realizable presents? The thousand-year Reich, to be sure, was never realized. Does not this mean that there was a more encompassing possibility, one of whose conceivable realizations might be the thousand-year Reich, and one of whose conceivable realizations was in fact realized? What is the nature of that encompassing possibility? Is it something remote? Is it a present?

We can not, I think, string out possibilities in the future as having successive dates of occurrence; the possibilities might be linked, and the realization of one may be a precondition for the realization of others, but one is no more remote than any other. But then we must say that they are related as the more to the less general, the realization of the less providing a precondition for the realization of the more. As encompassing its precondition and the alternative that would preclude it from being realized, does not the encompassing possibility stretch over smaller presents? Or would it be enough to say that the possibility continues to be a possibility for any number of realized smaller possibilities, without ever being the present of any occurrence? Yet, if after one has realized all these smaller possibilities and finally brought the highly general possibility about as that which encompasses all these smaller realized possibilities, has not one realized the encompassing possibility in a single stretch of present time? If one were just to say that the possibility is realized sequentially through the realization of the smaller presents, there would seem to be no time when the larger possibility ever did occur. That larger possibility could be conceived to be as small as one pleased; and yet there could still be other, smaller possibilities that one might suppose had to be realized as the precondition for its realization.

A realized present moment seems to be part of an as yet incompleted present moment; the realized present moment passes away and is followed by another, also tied to that incompleted present moment or, in the limiting case, to the completion of that encompassing present moment. And the latter seems to be part of a still larger incompleted present moment, and so on. That larger incompleted present must be occurring now, for otherwise it will be that which had been brought about, but will never in fact be taking place.

Is there a hierarchy of presents, and are the contents of the different members of the hierarchy different, somewhat like classes of classes of classes, and so forth? The present of the war, is this only the present of the battles? Is a history of dynasties or civilizations concerned with what is less concrete than is a history of a negotiation or an assassination? Is there not a limitation imposed on the realizations of the smaller presents by the nature of the larger which, after all, dictates at least in part, which battles are to be fought and why?

The prospect of the thousand-year Reich dictated just what battles were to be fought and how, just as surely as the way the particular battles were fought determined the nature of the Reich and the kind of realization that was given to the possibility of which the thousand-year Reich was a supposed specification. If we attribute the thousand-year Reich solely to the minds of the Nazis, it will still be the case that there was a Nazi regime and that it had a single historic status extending over many battles. And if the course of such a regime be taken to be somewhat abstract, it becomes a question as to just what in fact is most concrete. Is a battle less concrete than a skirmish, and this than a shooting, and this than the aiming of a gun, and this than a touching and a lifting, and this than a muscle contraction, and this than the movement of electrons, and so forth? It does not seem plausible to suppose so.

There seem to be three dimensions to distinguish: A] the whole of time as a single undivided present, B] the smallest possible or actual changes or movements, c] the interlocking of A and B. The items in B must be overriden by a single act which is the unit act of an identifiable object, such as a man, and this act must at the same time be part of the whole of time or some division of it, which functions as the act does both with respect to what is smaller and what is larger.

A historic event is always two-faced and doubly characterizable. It faces toward external items which follow in sequence, but it absorbs these within itself in a series, that is, as merely before and after. It also determines and continues into an indeterminate more encompassing possibility, and is characterizable as one of a series of determinations within that more encompassing possibility.

History is not only the product of the interplay of men and nature, but of finite human acts, the topics perhaps of a biography, and of long-ranged presents, the topic perhaps of differently scaled events—or at the limit, of a cosmology or metaphysics. Such an account, while it allows one to see how there could be a history of a nation, or a war, or a presidency, also allows for a history of civilization and eventually of all mankind, and thus brings us back to the original perplexities. It also raises new ones, or at least ones that were not initially stated. Does a particular historical occurrence realize the whole hierarchy of possibilities with different degrees of determination, so that a battle for example, is realizing the possibility of that battle, the possibility of a war of such and such a character, the possibility of new human prospects, the possibility of civilization of such and such a kind, and so on? Do we have two dimensions of a historic occurrence, one in which it is an unbroken present, and the other in which it is concretized in the form of a series of smaller events which, outside it, are in an order of earlier and later? Is the war the battles arranged sequentially only so far as those battles are taken one by one, and is the war the battles in a single series? Is the latter state nontemporal, merely an extended unidirectional nonpassing time? If one accepted a cyclic theory of history, or one of fixed stages, it is possible to suppose that there are presents of quite definite extents, to be followed by quantum jumps of other cyclical histories. But if there be no definite end of time or history, the matter is not so easy to get into focus.

Does history here raise a problem which is in principle or even in significant detail different from that which characterizes an utterance in discourse? We say one word after another in the attempt to present a single claim or assertion. The words are all within the frame of a possibility which they determine sequentially and serially. It is only as serial that they constitute the single assertion, but they are not available serially except as occurring sequentially, one after the other, the one allowing for no real divisions in time and the other requiring them and so far not allowing for the presence of the single assertion. In the hierarchy suggested by discourse we come to an end with language—or where this is given an historic import, with logic or mathematics—but we do not seem to have such a final scheme available for history.

Does a historic event give determinations to two kinds of constituents and make them, even as distinct from it, have new roles? Do the unit occurrence and the largest present become finitized within an historic occurrence, which denaturalizes the one and de-eternalizes the other, while it itself thrusts forward into the future in its own distinctive way? These last two questions apply to history the kind of solutions I have been trying to forge in connection with the emotions, mind, and body. Since the solution there is not altogether clear, I can not expect to find a satisfactory answer by applying the same distinctions in a new area, unless perchance the one happened to make a solution easier and throw light on the way to deal with the question as it is raised by the other.

A truth claim or belief which was coldly dissected would have all its divisions carved out of it; but a truth claim or belief that was being forged would have as part of it the very travail by which it was being forged. One would not know that claim or belief except so far as one in fact went through something like that travail. The travail is made up of distinct moments at the same time that it is a set of pacings, hindrances, inside the having or being of the claim or belief. But now it seems nothing is being said but what had been said before. An actual temporalized occurrence requires the absorption within it of what occurs outside it in an indifferent, sequential way. The present of the claim or belief has multiple layers, depending on how many of the sequential items are part of it. It becomes constitutive to the degree that it is progressively inclusive. But then it does not become a concrete present until it is over. Perhaps this is all right? Only when it is all over is anything completely determinate; the present itself is always partly indeterminate just so long as it is present. Does this not require us to say that the sequential items pass away as determinates, but as included within the ongoing present they pass away only so far as they are and continue to be indeterminates, awaiting the completion of the encompassing present before they can be fully determinate? If so, the items have two determinations, one of which characterizes them as distinct present items, and the other of which characterizes them as within a constitutive present. The second characterization allows one to adopt a Collingwoodean view of the constant reproduction of the past as having a constitutive nature as well, at the same time that one holds to an objective sequence of historic units, or at least of units which occurred in time. It is possible to avoid this alternative by denying that one could control the determination of an item once it had been part of the historic encompassing present. But surely as part of a larger present, the determination of one of the preceding items in the series would have its nature modified (it would be the first or the second or the misbegotten beginning or turning point, and so forth) by what else there is inside that single present.

The first part of a symphony is the first part only because there are other parts; the first part of a German verb awaits the completion by the rest before there is an assertion or even a verb in fact used. Perhaps one can, and should, as with the mind-body problem, distinguish between a cosmological body and a humanized single one? If one did achieve a parallel, then one would have to say that there is a way of having temporal events which are cosmological or historical, but which are subject to unspecifiable aberrations and a way of having other thrusts—toward the future?—which are limited by the historical. Once again, I am evidently moving further and further into an abysmal darkness.

January 23

Each part of a larger present, a phrase in music, a part of a symphony, a battle in a war is endowed by the whole with thrusts toward other items to come. These thrusts can be understood as instancing the different finalities and thus as associations, diversifications, implications, extensions, or unifications. When the item passes away it becomes a point attached to those implications. The item still remains outside the whole and there functions to separate out the interinvolved connections which characterize the whole.

The whole occurs when each part occurs. The whole remains a constant as encompassing all the connections. It also occurs, becomes a stretched out present, by having the interconnections separated out and sustained by the different parts which pass away. The entire whole occurs with all its connections sorted out when all the successive parts are completed. The existence of the present is dependent on there being that which sustains and makes possible the sorting out of the connections.

The most comprehensive of all wholes has within or subordinate to it smaller wholes, and so on, until we come to the limit in the form of a physical pulsation. The most comprehensive of wholes, and a number subordinate to this, are outside history; and so are the physical pulsations and various clusters of items with their distinctive activity. A historic world is in-between these extremes. What is more inclusive than it is a time in which the entire course of history is implicated in what is not history at all—say the deadly monotonous vibrations that occur in a final state of thermal equilibrium. As the events in history occur, the whole of history is partially separated off from what is not history within the whole which is to be understood as relating the history to the rest of time.

The identification of history and its characteristic unit occurrences requires emphasis on a social or humanistic man. This is one who has a commonsense outlook, is involved with others in public, and is occupied with some of the traditionalized goods of civilization. When that man is dominant over other types—the private I, the artistic individual, the man of practice or work, and the man of religion—the connected smaller units of the historic present (units which thrust forward as separated one from the other, and which as within the present and thus before and apart from their occurrence are interinvolved with one another) become loci for manifestations of these subordinated types of men. The historic event then has the characteristic of being dependent on the I, art, and so forth. When, instead, the reverse process takes place and the historic occurrence, due to the subordination of the humanistic man to some one of the others, is located within some larger nonhistoric setting, the historic occurrence provides a distinctive kind of base in terms of which the units appropriate to other disciplines are to be understood, while they are being envisaged within the constant cosmological frames of those other disciplines.

January 24

For history, the primary present is that of history itself. Outside it there are now well-determined occurrences with determinate relations to others. The occurrences are directly related to those which succeed them and sometimes to those that come much later. Those that come much later are also related to much earlier ones through the mediation of what comes between these. The well-determined occurrences sustain the sorted-out factors in the whole of present history. Those sorted-out factors are inseparable from unsorted-out ones which constitute the unfinished part of history itself.

Taking one's stand within the present of history at some particular sorted-out part, one faces further and further general ranges of implications, associations, and so forth. These become specified, limited, and ordered in the progress of the present's continuous coming to be and as sustained from without. The sorting cannot be stopped until all of history is over, without destroying the whole of history. The coming to the end of history is its concretizing in the present. This is to say that the present becomes past when all its components are externally sustained, and that they continue to be inseparable from one another with indeterminate consequences and unspecified implications until that time.

Unless history itself contains sharp epochal breaks, the fastening on any limited history will either involve an arbitrary cut in the whole of history, and make it therefore distortive just so far as the rest of the history makes a difference to the nature of what has been accomplished, or it will require the construction of a history on the basis of the determinate occurrences of the past. Historians will not be concerned with those occurrences, since this will require the historians to be within the presents of those occurrences. But in their narratives the historians will have to produce accounts in which the past events, though in fact followed by other past events, all determinate, are shown to be distinguished within an ongoing history while sustained outside it. Historians, in other words, must envisage a history or whole in which a set of occurrences is not yet determinate, and take the writing of the history to capture the way in which they did unfold. The narrative will break the whole of history at an arbitrary point, unless history itself has well-defined divisions of its own. There does not seem to be any justification for supposing that there are any such breaks. If there are none, historians must mimic the whole of history in a limited period by accepting a sequence of distinct past occurrences, which are not and never had in fact been in history but only sustained the distinctions that are made in the single coming to be of the one present of history itself. They will then have to conceive of a narrative present in which all those past occurrences are indeterminately together. Their exposition will consist in making the envisaged present of their narratives be divided in accord with the determinate occurrences they discovered through their use of historic evidence.

Starting with the present, a historian uses evidence there to discover a set of determinate past items. Having found these, he envisages a single historic present in which they were initially. Ideally, that single present is a segment of the whole of history. His narrative provides determinations by means of the discovered determinate items for the present that the historian accepted, and thereby exhibits that present as it is coming to be. He writes about the Enlightenment or the Hapsburg dynasty as though his narrative were an actual historic present being unfolded through the presence of determinate occurrences outside the history; but unlike what happens in fact, he already is in possession of the determinate items.

I have said that the sorted-out portions of an ongoing present are sustained by the determinate items outside that present. But the determinate items are past. How could what is no longer sustain anything? Don't we instead have a problem of understanding how the past could itself be?

The distinguished portions of an ongoing present are being distinguished together with the coming to be of particular determinate occurrences. It is the coming to be of those occurrences that provides a sustaining for the distinguishing of the portions of the ongoing present. When the particular occurrences are over they do not sustain those distinctions. The reverse is the case. The past determinate items are sustained by the distinguished portions of the ongoing present and thereby are able to have relations to a future. But now it would seem that some mysterious reversal of sustainings takes place, since I say, first that the exterior events sustain the distinguished portions of an ongoing present and then that the distinguished portions sustain those exterior events. Do both kinds of sustaining occur at the same time?

When a present is unfolding there is a present occurrence of shorter duration which is specifying a portion of the present. The specified portion of the present is that occurrence as part of a single ongoing present. As such a part it sustains the particular occurrence by giving this a place within a single ongoing present, since the part is sorted out. An exterior occurrence thus makes possible the sorting out of inseparable indistinguishable portions of an ongoing present, but in that act the particular occurrence is sustained by the entire present via the portion of that present which the exterior occurrence specified and thereby enabled to be a sorted-out component within the ongoing present.

If such a view is accepted one must give the whole of history a kind of substantiality that is denied to the actual events in history, for the whole of history will give the events a ground not only when and as they are taking place outside the history but after they are over. Its present will remain the present of the past as well as of the future particular occurrences which take place independently of it, so far as they are finished, discrete unit occurrences. And one will also have to consider a present which has the historic present as only one factor, as well as such shorter presents as the life of a man or a state, and credit these with some kind of substantiality. One could conceivably root all in one ultimate substantial present, or could suppose a hierarchy of such presents, larger and larger in scope. In the first way one seems to lose the integrity of spans shorter than that which includes all time and of which history is but a part; in the second way one seems to multiply metaphysical entities to a suspicious degree.

Should one say, in some consonance with those who take the embryo or fetus to have within it all the potentialities of a human—and thus risk losing all contingency, novelty, and the production of new potentialities rooted in the new actualities—that there is a present man unfolding through the agency of specific acts which are of limited duration and are exterior to him but which the man sustains and also exhibits in the form of sorted-out precedent occurrences within his single life-span? And, using him as a unit, should one also say that the completion of his life is the distinguishing of a unit occurrence in another ultimate present within which his life and all other lives are somehow intertwined, and which, when distinguished, will sustain all the lives as past?

A man's life seems at least as concrete or substantial as the whole of history. To speak of it is not to make an arbitrary cut in something larger. Yet it is also true that in the history of a people it is only one distinguished unit in a single ongoing. Might there not be just one substantial ground, but this have a depth to it which the different shorter spanned occurrences occupy? Time would then have to be taken to be not only linear but to have a thickness to it. The thick ongoing time would be exhibited in the dependency of the less on the more recessive and longer-ranging stretch. A future moment would have the interlinkages of the various levels indistinguished; the distinguishing of one level from another would be one with the determinate occurrence of short-span items sustained by longer-ranged ones.

The more a present progresses toward its completion, the more does it become constitutive of the entire range of particular, determinate entities to which its distinguished components owe their separation from one another within that present. The distinguished components sustain the external items, and the externally occurring items are overarched by the continuing present. Does the overarching become more and more intimate to the externally produced items as it is progressively completed, or is there a constant degree of intimacy but for shorter portions of the present? I think we must say, both. The present, though it is not yet completed, has distinguished portions within it just so far as there have been distinct occurrences. They are appropriate to those distinct occurrences when those distinct occurrences take place, and thus before the present is completed. It is correct to say that such and such a well-defined present encompasses such and such a set of past items. But it is also true that the present does not break up into portions which are well-defined and another in which a whole set of intermingled possibilities and their interconnections occurs. The separation has to be made from the position of the discrete past items. From the standpoint of the ongoing present there is no full embodiment, no full constituting of the past discrete items as belonging together, until that entire present is over. Past discrete items make portions of the ongoing present be involved with them, at the same time that the entire ongoing present is gradually made more and more integral to what is past. A limited set of past items has its own limited encompassing present, but only at the price of being torn away, as within that present, from the whole of history with its ongoing present. Even then, if it is the present that gives being to the past, the past items, and the segment of the present that is germane to them, will have to be sustained by the entire ongoing present.

January 25

Yesterday I saw Bergman's film of *The Magic Flute.* I had never seen this opera before. Indeed, I have seen very few, three or four at most. The plot is idiotic; the overture is accompanied by photographs of the audience, with particular emphasis on a girl I would guess of about twelve. After a while these photographs become tiresome, and it is particularly tiresome to see the girl again and again. But the actors in the opera are almost all attractive; the little boys and the maids of the night queen are exceptionally appealing. Yet I found that the more I attended to what they were doing or saying or singing the less I was aware of the music. It is not only difficult to marry music, acting, and drama, but when it is done, someone like myself will nevertheless not be able to attend equally to all. The presentation nevertheless was, I think, unusually successful. One shared in the adventure even though, if one were like me, only a single dimension at a time could be attended to.

There were some oddities in the film. Bergman tried to show it as something which was being presented on a rather old-fashioned stage. Why, after taking liberties in other ways in order to make a film, he thought it necessary to preserve what was part of another type of presentation I do not know. He could have given us not a filmed version of an actual opera performance but a film of the opera. Also, the film I saw gave no indication of who the actors were; nor was there any mention of the orchestra. There were pictures of Mozart shown again and again. Apparently it was thought that Mozart was the sole begetter of the entire work. This is not only to overlook the librettist, but the performers. A composed work is one art, a performed another. It is the performance that is seen and heard. It adds dimensions, relations, timings, emphases, and a time not includable in any composition. There are no speeches or silences in a musical composition—only indications when they are to occur in fact.

Bringing in reflections on history, I think we must say that the score as not yet written has the various notes as possibilities in unsorted interrelationships, and that the writing of the composition sorts these out. The result is an articulated present score. That score, when taken as the score for an actual performance, has the notes interlocked in a new set of interrelationships which take account of actual pitches, rhythms, and sounds, as well as of some acting and speaking. The ongoing present of the performance involves the sorting out of the interlocked involvements of the composition as a present for the performance.

I, who did not know the plot beforehand, or anything about the music, lived through it, part after part. But I would not be seeing a single performance did I not have some single present which I was making progressively determinate through my living through of the parts. The present I made use of is one in which there is little differentiation beyond what was required for me to know that I was attending to an opera. More knowledgeable spectators come with fuller, richer presents, and in the ideal case with the very one which the musicians and players have; that is, the very composition which Mozart and his librettist provided, together with the stage and circumstances in which it was to be presented.

The problem of the intermission was not solved by Bergman. He seemed to believe both that it was and that it was not part of the opera. As a consequence, instead of showing the audience during the intermission, he showed the actors and singers. But this is still to avoid the problem. Is the intermission part of the performance? I think it is not. The work continues where it had left off before the intermission. The intermission is not even a resting place between the beginning and end of it, but something outside the entire opera, allowing the audience to do something other than attend to it, and allowing the performers to rest and also do something having nothing to do with the performance. The intermission is no more a part of the presented work than is the buying of tickets, or the sweeping out of the aisles.

Does not every occurrence provide a way of separating out and making determinate some one of the multiple interlocked connections characteristic of the ongoing present? But then in what sense could one occurrence be more significant than another? In what sense could one set of adventures in history be better, more successful, fruitful, progressive than another? An easy answer, of course, is to say that we will know this after the fact; we can then decide whether or not some successful, desirable, valuable state of affairs ensued. But if we shift attention to the consideration of a work of art, say a symphony, taken as a mere possibility not yet worked out in time, and thus with many connections unseparated, must we not say that any tone or sound that we might elect would be a way of making the symphony begin? And what would require that such and such a sound be next?

Put another way: may not the present be specifiable in an endless number of equally justifiable ways? Would all of these ways be equally good or satisfactory, apart from some exterior evaluation of them in terms of their constituting an excellence? Must we not say that any number of realizations are possible of the same given matrix, the symphony to be, to the same extent, but that only one or a few are excellent in that they constitute an actual excellence? A symphony in idea or as a mere possible three-part single musical work with such and such essential features, and nothing more, could be realized well or badly, but nevertheless completely in that it could be unfolded progressively; but only this or that actual production of sounds which that present sustains, is one which has the character of excellence. Excellence, or some degree of value less than this, would supervene over the sequence of past occurrences; the concretization of the entire present of the symphony would be one with its acquiring a value from the very items it sustains and which allows that present to unfold progressively.

January 26

1] A present has its interlocked indeterminate components sorted out by the unit occurrences which take place outside it. The sorting out of one item requires the completion of an external unit occurrence.

2] The nature of the present is relative to the unit occurrence. If there be smaller stretches of occurrences than the historical, they require a reference to a present which is as long as time itself.

3] A present, on being realized, sorts out items in a larger present, and this in a larger, and so on, until we come to the whole of time.

4] The whole of time can be realized only if the whole of history has occurred, and then it will take the nonhistoric occurrences to enable it to be realized. The time itself becomes a sequence only relative to its occurrences.

5] Since time itself can include the whole of history as one moment followed by another in which there is no history but simply a time for physical occurrences, and since time apart from history is the time of such physical occurrences, it is being sorted out in two ways, moment by moment by physical occurrences, and slowly as divided into a historic to be followed by a nonhistoric present, which may then be the present for just physical occurrences.

6] While a historic present is being sorted out by historically pertinent occurrences, the whole of time is being sorted out by smaller unit occurrences. At the same time, a segment of that whole of time, stretching over the smaller unit occurrences, will be realized as undivided, a present for a history.

7] Each particular occurrence is sustained by the present for which it isolates a component. Since both history and physical occurrences isolate components in the whole of time, there must be components there of different magnitudes.

8] When a present has been spelled out, it is also in the process of spelling out a larger present.

9] In being spelled out, a present is successively made part of external occurrences. When the entire set of occurrences is over, the historic present for those occurrences is integral to that set. It is as determinate as they are. The past is made up of determinate items which are nested within a determinate encompassing unit, a present which they successively realized.

10] Particular occurrences are sustained by a present unfolding. When the present occurrence is completed, it continues to sustain the items within its compass, but only so far as it is in turn sustained by a larger present which is still in the process of unfolding.

11] A present that is being spelled out remains undivided while sustaining items. As a consequence, those items are indirectly sustained by a larger present.

12] As realized, made determinate, a present provides a unity for the past items that are within its compass.

13] A present, which has been realized, still contains the alternatives which had not been realized. But the past is wholly determinate. The integration of the determinate present, with the particular occurrences which had followed one after the other as that present unfolded, has an overall character. Let us call it the significance, the import, the meaning of a historic episode or epoch. The integration has a single import, which permits of the distinguishing of abstract unrealized phases.

14] A realization has maximum significance if all abstract unrealized factors are measurable as incomplete in terms of it.

15] In a minor event in history, conceivable abstractable dimensions define a present which is not integral to particular occurrences. Where a major event allows for an abstraction from the unity of the particular items and the present which encompasses them, the minor allows for that abstraction from the determinate relationship as that which is distinct from, not integral to those items.

16] A major occurrence in art is beautiful. It is the outcome of the union of an encompassing project with particular actualized, step-by-step, produced units. The beautiful allows for, measures, and controls what else is suggested, because it is in fact contained there. A minor work of art has items together in such a way that alternatives take one away from the work itself.

17] A man lives a good life when the occurrences he has gone through are together with his entire span in such a way that all other occurrences or connections among them are derivative. His life is defective so far as the occurrences and their connections allow for the abstraction of an indeterminate, encompassing life; the particular occurrences do not combine with that life to make a single integrated unitary past in which the life is encompassing and determinate.

January 27

If it be true that some type of expression and thrust toward a finality becomes prominent because of the dominance of some aspect of the self or I, and if, in addition, there can be another set of expressions traceable not to the I but to the me or the individual in society, state, the world of art, history, or religious rituals, we are faced with the question as to just what a man is, and what he ought to be. Unless we give priority to the I, and therefore take history and social existence to be in some sense derivative from a private mental life and a living through of the body, a man will have to be understood to be an I and a me at the same time.

If the I epitomizes all the finalities in an intensive interfusion, and if the me is subject to the conditions which govern all public entities, the problem of the unity of a man reduces to the problem of reconciling an epitomizing of all the finalities with one item which is governed by all of the finalities. If the I can control the me in the way the me is controlled by the conditions, it will be from within; it will govern the me as that me is conditioned apart from the I. Since the conditions control the me as having a reality apart from them, if the I is to reproduce that state of affairs the me can not be understood to be just an expression of the I; instead, it must be an object with respect to which the I operates. The reconciliation will then be of an I with a me which it conditions, but which continues to have a status apart from the conditioning. The reconciliation does not reduce the me to the I, but it does account for the union of the two as the result of the operation of the expressions of the I on a me externally presented for such operation. When the I is dominant it ignores the obstinate independently determined nature of the me; when the me is dominant it ignores the conditioning to which the I subjects it.

The I is the individual in his privacy, a privacy which could include both the mind and the lived body; the me is that individual as affected from without; a man is a private being who is being externally determined and limited. Equally, a man is a unit in the world, a unit which is conditioned from within in the same manner that it is being conditioned impersonally by conditions operating on all other units in the world.

Does it make sense to speak of the union or juncture of the I and the me? If it did, this would be an epitomizing of the two, maintained perhaps not only against these but also against the finalities as epitomized in the I and as operative directly on the me. Is this not the 'reasonable man', the locus of viable rights (in contrast with native rights and endowed rights)? The primary fact about man would then be that he is reasonable, at once expressing himself as a private I and a publicly determined me. The private I would have its own mode of operation and terminate in the me which is being determined from without. The me, though, would already be determined from without and be accommodated by the reasonableness.

There is no need to suppose that the I and me are in equilibrium. At one moment one of these might be dominant and at another moment it might be recessive. The mature man is always more or less reasonable because he always gives some play to both sides. Always being private and public, he could not, as just reasonable, be said to be just one or the other. He will unify the finalities as an epitomizing I, unify them as a me at which they converged or qualified, and unify these unifications. A reasonable man is an I solidified with a me, both of which were inseparable from the finalities.

The me is easily locatable; the I can be understood to be at the center, the dense terminus of a withdrawal. Which is the reasonable man? Is it the I as readied, the me as internally experienced? Is the lived body as externally limited simply the externally conditioned and localized which is being undergone from within? Is the body that is publicly known, but which is being insistently expressed from within, identical with the I as expressive but blocked and qualified by what comes from without? These questions, I think, must all be answered affirmatively.

In himself a man has native rights, in the world he has endowed or allowable ones as spelled out in practice. In himself a man is an individual, in the world he is accountable. In himself a man is identical, in the world he is identified. In himself a man has worth, in the world he is more or less worthy. A mature man has native rights which are viable; he also has an accountable individuality, an identifiable identity, and virtue and vices. Each of these is specialized in the I and in the me.

But surely the I is not an expression of the mature man? How could his viable rights be specialized as native rights? Must one not proceed in just the opposite way and show how the native rights become viable? There would be a difficulty here did not the I have a status and functioning of its own. Though its native rights are intrinsic to the I, and can even be said to increase in number and be modified in kind as the I makes its different aspects more and more distinguishable, they are there only so far as the I is distinguished from the reasonable man.

Does not the reasonable man follow late, much after the I has been distinguished? This surely is the case. We must, therefore, contrast the matured man whose nature is definitely expressed privately and socially, with that man as not yet able to express himself. The two are extremes; we begin at one and hopefully end at the other, though we never seem to get to the other completely, and never seem to have been at a state where one is cut off from the other. Even a fetus is involved with another being, its mother; though it does not know an external world when it is just born, it nevertheless functions with some regard for what is there. Even if this is not allowed, we still have the fact that initially there is a state of affairs in between a mature reasonableness and an inchoate juncture of I and me. We can not take one who is in the latter state to be private or social, and we cannot say that it is reasonable or mature. Yet it is a person.

A person is an I and a me together. According to the Supreme Court, an embryo is not a person. Either then we must say that it does not have a well-defined I or a me, or that it is a person in a sense that the Supreme Court does not recognize—or both together. The last is the case, I think. The embryo can be said to have an I. Though this is not yet clearly and independently functioning, it nevertheless allows the embryo to be individual, identical, have a nature, an identity, and a worth. The embryo does not inwardly control its externally reached being and is not allowed by the Supreme Court to have the viable rights of humans; nevertheless, the embryo is both externally and internally conditioned. It is a person but not a matured one. We do not have to suppose, with some of the Thomists, that it has all that it will actually be and do within it as potentialities; it is sufficient that it allows for an eventual clear distinguishing of the I and the me, which can then adventure in unpredictable ways.

From the beginning, there will be viable rights, but there will be no well-defined native rights. Distinct native rights are aboriginal claims made on behalf of distinguishable expressions of the I or self, and these will come later. When they come they will provide articulations for the viable rights. Before then, the viable rights are all together in the form of a native right to have a public status. This outcome brings me on the side of the anti-abortionists, particularly when the right to have a public status is equated with the right to life.

January 28

I have held that the I epitomizes the mind and body, and is consequently a centered interfused consciousness and living. But I have also held that a person is the union of the I and the me, and thus apparently an epitomizing of consciousness, living, and an external conditioning. Is the difference between these two simply that the expressed I stops short of the me as that which is externally conditioned, while the person includes this? It does not seem so.

Firstly, the person is always voluminous, and this apart from expression, whereas the I is voluminous only as expressed. Secondly, the I is incipiently just conscious, able to be conscious apart from its living involvement with the body, while the person is not incipiently conscious but incipiently just unique, with native rights, an individualized nature, self-identity, and worth, all characteristics of the I. A person has rights articulating what he is privately, and taking the form of public claims expressing what he is in the world.

A person, if this is correct, is able to achieve an I, but is not, strictly speaking, able to attain a consciousness, since that depends on the I expressing itself in contradistinction from the person. That consciousness, as brought to bear on the body, is exhibited as feeling and a sustaining of the me. But then it would seem that a person does not necessarily feel, and of course does not necessarily have a distinguishable I, with its distinctive individuality, worth, and so on.

If a desensitized man, or one in a stupor, is a person, then it makes sense to say that a person has neither a distinguishable I nor a consciousness, nor therefore feeling. And he will not continue into the me as determined from without. He will include the me just as surely as he includes the I, but will not give a place to the conditions which relate that me to other public items, and therefore to the me as approachable from without. How does such a me differ from the me as sustained from within by the I? It will not be consciously, feelingly sustained, but it will be interfused with the I, and therefore with feeling of some kind. What would such an interfusion of an I and a me, not yet expressed as a distinguishable I and me, be like? There will be a maintenance of the me in the face of conditions at the same time that the conditions are exhibited in the form of an insistence.

There is perhaps no time when either the person or the I is entirely unexpressed, or expressed in one direction and not in the other. A person, unlike an I, does not merely match a me, but encompasses it, reaches to it as it were from the outside, not by taking a stand or pivoting about some outside occurrence, as a self-conscious being does, but by having it as a conditioned item. This means that if I approach my person from within, it will have a me only so far as it makes use of the conditions that constitute the I. What is still wanting is an account of the me of the person apart from the I. Evidently, a person presents his body for determination from without in the way it is determined by his I. But then what is the contribution of the me in the being of the person? Is it the submission to a bounding, externally imposed? If so, this would be together with a distinguishable I which is free of such bounding, an I which has within it the very conditions which are qualifying the me, once this is distinguished from the unity of the person and contrasted with the I.

When we come to another and face his you as that which is being internally sustained, do we know him as a person or as one who has an I? A sustained you is one in which an I is united; it is therefore the person met with at the surface. But now it seems as if the person is being understood in terms of the I. Must it not be said, instead, that what is encountered is a person, and that only when we distinguish the me of him, that is, the you which he is for another, do we have an opportunity to distinguish his I, and the mind, and so forth, which that I has as its expressions?

On such an account a person is not only primary in fact but primary for others. The others will meet the person at the surface of the body, but the individual himself will be a person throughout that body. But it still seems to be allowed, on this account, for there to be a person who is not yet externally conditioned. And if the person is externally conditioned, there would be nothing like a mere person, a person who has simply submitted to a bounding. Or, more sharply, since there is a bounding to which it must submit or accept as an entity which is not yet divided into an I and a me, it would seem to be the case that a person is a derivative, and not that out of which an I and a me can be distinguished, except after it has been achieved through the solidification of these. Must it be the case that a person is primary only so far as it is also expressed, so that there is no person except within a physical setting, even though it may then not distinguish an I?

On the last supposition, it must be said that though a person has its own integrity and exists in independence of the rest of the world, it also is expressed and is so far involved with an external world, with the conditions governing this, and with an I which is internally those very conditions in an epitomized form. Maturation would consist in the person becoming more focussed as a distinct item, with a consequent distinguishing of an I and a me, each expressing that person more and more. A personality will be the I and the me as exhibiting the person above the degree that they necessarily have from the beginning.

Animals feel, have some rights, and yet are not persons. Must we not say that they do not distinguish the components in the interlocked private and publicly determined sides of themselves, and thus do not have incipient I's and me's? If this is correct, and if the embryo is a human person from the very beginning, we should say that from the very beginning there is a distinguishing of the I and the me, though these are not held apart, or enabled to function in some independence of one another. Such a view allows one to take men and animals to be on a continuum, but it leaves undetermined whether or not the newly made embryo has a distinguishable, even if not distinct, I and me. Must we be content with saying that, at the very least, the I and me of the human embryo are to be distinguished and are even distinct, and that no device from the outside could enable an animal or any being which did not have the two already distinguishable could ever get them to be so? If so, what is to be done with the apparent consciousness and even thinking of some chimpanzees and porpoises? Must it be held that a consciousness and thinking might be possible even when the I was not distinguished from the unity of the animal, but that in the case of the human the I is always distinguished from the person?

What is able to have an I and a me separately functioning, even if they are not so functioning, or even if they cannot at that time do so, is different from what is not so able. If so, there must be something like a demarcation or crease within the person, allowing for the I and the me to be distinguished and to function separately eventually, but nothing of that kind within the single, feelingly, lived-through body of an animal. Let this be granted. How can it be accounted for? On an evolutionary theory, it would have to be the result of a sport which is forever after preserved.

How could such a difference come about through conception?

Is it possible to discern it? One would have to claim that a human sperm and egg combine at the same time that a single person is being produced. And we must not forget that the union of an animal's egg and sperm will also require the production of a single, lived-through bodily reality, replacing the lived-through bodily realities of sperm and egg.

It is difficult to see how any lived-through reality could ever be merged with another, or give way to some more inclusive one. But if it could be understood, there should be no difficulty in principle in understanding how the unity of an embryo will be different in man from the unity of an embryo in an animal, particularly since all that is required is that creases be in the human case, allowing for a distinguishing of an I and me, and then for their distinctness later on. We do not discern such creases, but when we come to the mature individual man, we seem able to attend to the me as sustained by the I in contradistinction from just having the two of them together. The latter is what we get when we attend to a person, provided that there is some grasp of the former.

To know that one is facing a person, one must know that there is in him a distinguishable I and a distinguishable (you) me, and not merely the juncture of the two. We seem to have such knowledge when we attend to his speech, address him by name, sympathize, and see him function independently of the single unity he is making with the (you) me that is being externally encountered. When we encounter another person we come to him as sustaining the you at which we arrive and at the same time functioning apart from such sustaining; he is not only in pain but knows its injustice, resents it, judges it, dislikes it, associates it with what had been and what will be. Might such achievements not come about in the course of growth, so that the fetus or embryo might have no more rights than an animal, but in the course of growth attain the position where it had creases in its lived-through reality which enabled it to achieve a genuine distinctness of its I and me? So long as that remains a possibility there can be no guarantee that the combination of human sperm and egg yields a person. If it is claimed that the subsequent differentiation of I and me would not be possible unless they were in principle already distinguished, one would then be beset with the problem of how the evolutionary coming to be of man was possible. If man with his person could come from what was not a person, why should it not be possible in each individual case for a person to originate from the living reality of a fetus which was not a person? Yet if, as the Supreme Court allows, there comes a time when a person does originate, how is it that such a quantum jump occurs and then apparently only as a consequence of complication in growth?

If man differs solely in degree from an animal, he should be said to have merely more rights or more insistent rights than an animal. But if he is a person and it is not, he can be said to have rights which are also expressed as native on the one side and as claims on the other. Since the most radical occurrence is that in which sperm and egg are united, it would seem most plausible to suppose that the quantum leap occurs then. This will not be due to the physiological character of the sperm and egg, though these may be contributing factors, but to the manner in which their lived-through beings as at once inward and acceptive of what is outwardly conditioned, are combined.

Do not mature men also merge with one another as beings who are living through distinctive careers? They seem to, at least to some extent. But also, they seem always to preserve their individualities, their unreachable privacies. Do the sperm and egg continue to preserve theirs? How could they, if their bodies are no longer? Do the bodies just function as units within a newly lived whole which is able to supersede theirs because it assimilates theirs, has them as analytic components? The union of sperm and egg in both the human and animal case would seem to require the absorption of their minor, lived-through states within another where they are preserved while ennobled, by being made into aspects of a new inwardness. The kind of new inwardness that is brought about in the case of the human is different from that of an animal immediately; the mere fact of growth does not seem to be sufficient to make for the radical change which marks out a human person.

The conclusion I am coming to is that a person is not achieveable through mere growth but requires a radical change in the composition of an entity, and that this is achieved at conception. Does this occur always and necessarily at conception? Is this an evolutionary result? If so, it would seem to be an achievement which, not only in the individual case, but for mankind, cannot be undone. Once human beings are produced, only human beings are produced. But we are still left with the question as to just how a human could ever have originated given that there were once only non-humans.

Does it perhaps require a multitude of circumstances for the initial jump to be made from animal to man, and only a peculiar egg and sperm to have it occur in the individual case? Does the former occur sometime after birth (which is the way the anthropologists see the situation, with the acquisition of tools or speech, or a living on the ground) or in the meeting of some animal sperm and egg—which would seem to require that a human is being gestated by an animal? Perhaps both conditions are needed. Perhaps only in some unusual state of the world can the new kind of unity appear, be carried to term, and then live somewhat like a public man?

The condition for being a person is general, requiring only that there be an acceptance of what is being conditioned together with others. A person is not affected by the different ways in which he is subject to influences by others, or by the kind of career he has in public. But his personality will be different, depending on how and what he makes manifest. Differences in sex, color, and even in stablized practices, diets, and rituals entrain differences in personality. A friendly woman is different in personality from a friendly man; so is a friendly black from a friendly white.

January 29

The position I am developing is readily confused with two others: A] a traditional, where a person is taken to be an individual substance of a rational nature, and B] a sociological, where a person is taken to be primary, and the self or I a mere derivative. A] The traditional view holds that a person is a composite and, therefore, in some sense a derivative. In addition, it takes self or soul to have a capacity to be maintained for an indefinite time apart from the person or the bodily part of the person. This, at least, is the way I understand Aquinas's version of Boethius's definition of a person. It is hard to know on this view whether it is the self or the person which is the locus of rights, identity, individuality, worth, and definition. Apparently it is the person. But that person, if a derivative, will presuppose the individuality, and so forth, of the self, or produce a new item out of what is without individuality or the other dimensions. We do have to allow that a person is a derivative if it has a biological origin in the juncture of egg and sperm, but on the traditional view one would have to hold, in addition to this, that it was a derivative from the rational and living bodily component, and not, as I have been maintaining, a source of

these. On the traditional view, the person would arise as the outcome of two junctures, one involving egg and sperm, and the other
a rational and a bodily principle, and these two junctures would
have to be united. There would be a pure, inextinguishable rationality which would somehow have been captured, subdued, not
available until much later. The view I am developing, instead, does
not allow for a prior existence of a rationality, unless it be in the
shape of a final reason or Possibility in which an I can share and to
which I am subject together with others.

B] If the self or I is a mere derivative, it would seem unable to
possess or act on its own. It would be one of the offshoots of the life
of the person, and allow merely for a centering but no actual center.
Some such view seems to be held by Strawson in his account of
the person. He remarks that 'person' is a neutral predicate, applicable alike to you and to me. I think, putting aside the idea of
predicate, that this is only partially correct. It does seem, at first
glance, that when another says "You are a person," and when I say
"I am a person," we are talking of the very same being, having
expressible rights, an identifiable identity, a lived-through body,
and so forth. Neither seems to be making any reference to a reality
apart from what is being lived through. When I say "I am a person" I
seem to be saying that I have rights, just like every other human.
But there is, I think, a difference in a reference by another and one
by me to myself as a person. The import of the other's remark is to
give primacy to the person, using the 'you' as a locating term. To say
"you are a person" is like saying "you are here." It would be best
conveyed by saying, "a person (is what) you are," paralleling a more
familiar usage "here you are," that is, "here (is where) you are." But
when I say "I am a person," though the emphasis may be on the very
person to which another is attending, there is a note of possession
and acceptance by the I.

The view I am developing, with the traditional, gives an independence and a dignity to the I; in addition, it accords the I other
properties besides rationality, and takes it from the start to be
continuous with and never entirely separable from the person. In
contrast with the sociological view, it allows for the separate functioning of the I, its possessiveness, and its independent rationality,
enabling it to be self-conscious and to attend to what is not bodily.
With the traditional, it sees the person and the I to explain and not
be explained by the body and its adventures; with the sociological,

it sees the person to be inseparable from an objectively conditioned factor.

The present view suggests that there are two kinds of feeling, one a sense of bodily presence and the other a product of an I making itself manifest in and through the body. The one kind of feeling is like that of an animal's and has undergone pain and pleasure as its primary modes; the other is directional, emotional, never entirely separate from a thrust outward. The consciousness involved with the first is peripheral, and varies in accord with the kind of determinations its externally approachable factor undergoes; the consciousness of the second occurs apart from the body, can be occupied with what is transcendent, and permits of a self-consciousness. An animal undergoes and suffers, but is not self-aware; a man can be in that state and, at the same time, consciously attend to something having nothing to do with what he is undergoing. When one is given an anaesthetic, consciousness in the second sense is lost, but not in the first.

The consciousness or I which is faintly distinguishable in the person from the beginning is not identifiable with the id or other subterranean aspects of the acknowledged I of maturity, for it is part of the person, without distinct functionings. Suppressions of what otherwise would be clearly faced and understood, if they are displaced to an unconscious, presumably remain within the I. But it is possible to envisage a theory which would take such suppressions to be content for the person or for the I which is not yet functioning in contradistinction to this.

It is not clear whether or not, on the traditional view, a person changes over time. The reference to it as a "substance" would seem to indicate that it does not change. But then it is not really involved with the body's adventures, as it is on my view. Since it does incorporate what is subject to those adventures it is, on my view, also selfsame. The continuity of the person to which we can attend is converted into an identity through the help of the I. Nor is it clear on the traditional view just what is the locus of native rights. On my view native rights are characteristic of the I or of a person, but they do not have clear and distinct, well-defined natures from the start.

I am not sure what the traditional view would say about this. Why don't I ask my colleagues who are experts in this area? I do at times raise such questions with them. I find that they usually disagree in their interpretations of Thomas, and that they have recourse to other writers, often obscure, to defend a particular interpretation. Nevertheless, I will try to make a point of getting clear about this issue by talking with them. In any case, it does not make much difference whether I get their position straight as long as I get straight what I think must be the case. On the view I have been developing, the I has an identity, rights, individuality, nature, and worth; it epitomizes all the finalities; it expresses itself both as consciousness and thought, and as living; it thrusts itself outward in and through the body, and can also occupy itself with transcendents; it is never separable from the person; it is possessive; it can initiate a self-consciousness act; it can give a mental tonality to the process of living and thereby make this be emotional; it may never get to the stage where it exercises a pure rationality unaffected by living, nor have this living unaffected by the person as voluminously occupying the entire body which is being determined from without; it has an identity as an epitomized unity, not as a form, or as a consciousness, but as an existent; it is human nature epitomized and interlocked with other epitomizings; the human nature is individualized by it, and is expressed as mental activities and bodily living; it comes into focus and is able to function in a distinctive way on maturation; it does not have its future acts within it as potentialities, but only in the form of a single power which is diversified through what it expresses and by what it encounters.

January 31

An I is both an expression of a person, and an independent functioning part of it. As the latter, it possesses what it terminates in. It can also meet and sustain the you at which another arrives, and the me at which it itself arrives when it pivots about something external. Since it traverses the person on its way to meeting the me, it is partly cross-grained by that person (so far as this is expressing itself in the direction of the I) and partly enriched by this. As cross-grained, it encounters the me, and this without having to pivot in something external. In facing the me, the I thus is self-conscious of itself via the person. There are, then, two possible kinds of self-consciousness: one is the self-consciousness which pivots about something, usually external; the other returns toward the I from the base of the resistance of the person. So far as the latter occurs, there is no reaching to the me. Of course, if there is an encounter with the me, it can be accompanied with a self-consciousness involving an encounter with the person. The two encounters are independent and involve independent references and acts.

The I as traversing the person on its way to meeting the me, or on its way to making itself effective external to the body in alien objects, adds to the feeling of the person which has expressed itself as that I and as that which is voluminously occupying the body. A mature person is conscious of, even partly conceptualizes, the feeling of being a person while living through a body. His I expressing itself in this way is primarily a living tinged with mentality, and thus emotional.

Emotionality, on this view, is dependent on the bodily manifestation of the I, never entirely freed from the mental expression, but making it follow along the lines of the bodily. That emotionality, since it is dependent on the distinctive functioning of the I, is not within the power of an animal, an embryo, a fetus, or the newborn infant. All of these can feel pleasure and pain, for all of these have states which are lived through. One should not, therefore, say that an animal is angry or even terrified, if more than outward manifestations are intended.

I have seen pictures of cats so conditioned that they seemed to be acting with terror when confronted with a mouse. I would have to say, if I follow the present line, that the cats are feeling intensely, and that does not seem to be correct. The cats seem to have a kind of consciousness or awareness, even though they have nothing which is identifiable as an I. Are we not forced to say that there is an expression of the inward state of cats in the form of a consciousness or awareness which traverses that state and comes out into the open as an expression of terror? If so, the difference between a cat and a human would lie only in the ability of a man to give an opposite emphasis to the conscious component, and make this primarily mental, and eventually to be able to act as a mind in which the other component is forced along the track of the mind's functioning. Since a cat can have a memory, and can direct its body in terms of what it remembers, it seems that a subordination of the bodily factor is also possible to it. All then that would be denied to the cat would be the ability to engage in a primarily mental activity. What I am saying is not too far from Jude Dougherty's understanding of Thomas Aquinas's view of the person. He takes the person to be involved in three conjunctions: A] that of a rationality, which unites a form and a (intelligible?) locus of potentiality, matter, B] which union is united with the existence of an individual, C] which union is united with properties and accidents. A person here has rationality as a distinguishable factor, and that rationality is capable of some activity of its own, such as discursive understanding.

Is a person in this traditional sense equatable with the inward state of a body? Does it have an externally affected component which is as basic as the rationality? Does that person change over time? It would seem that the answer to the first is negative, since the person is viewed as a supposit or substance. The second answer would be only partially negative, for the bodily presence would be an expression of that supposit, not equal in value to the rationality. The third question would be answered in the negative also, since the person would be selfsame from conception to death. The view I have been developing would require me to say, instead, that the inward state of the body is an unavoidable component of the person either as a unit or as expressing itself; that this bodily dimension is as basic as the rational, and may even be more conspicuous and effective; and that it does change over time, since it does have an externally determined component, but that it overcomes the external determination by taking the component within itself. There is, of course, no reference to composites, and the substantiality of the individual is seen by me to be subject to the determination, not only of a final Substance, but of other finalities as well. However, I do not yet have either my own view or this other in clear focus.

The view that personality expresses a person in public is compatible with both my account and what I understand to be the traditional. It seems correct to say that a woman is kindly in a way a man is not, that a black is friendly in a way a white is not. But these small truths entrain a multitude of questions. Is every public expression filtered through such traits? Is every expression modified by such traits? Are some of these traits more basic than others?

Have we any right to say that a black, a woman, an Israeli, or a handsome man is intelligent in a distinctive way? Suppose a woman who is black and an Israeli: does she express her blackness through the other, or conversely? Evidently, we must distinguish between more and less basic traits, and between those expressions which are affected by the traits and those which are not. As a first approximation, I think we can distinguish those traits that are permanent from those that are not, even when it be allowed that the latter also make a difference. A strong or successful man is perhaps kind or friendly in a way that a weak or an unsuccessful man is not; the two, though, reflect a more basic and effective determination by sex. It seems to be the wisdom of the world that sex differentiation, and those stages of life marked by rites of passage, are basic to all others. But as a rule these are results which hold for homogeneous societies. And fundamental social conditions, except comparatively recently, have been ignored in that wisdom; they were not recognized to make a great difference to what people are and do. What principles are justified in helping one to distinguish more basic from less basic traits, and to know their effectiveness on other expressions?

*   *   *

I have just seen a devastating review of my *Cinematics* in the *American Film* for January/February. I had a devastating review of *Sport* in the *Journal of Philosophy,* and quite a while ago a strongly negative review of *History: Written and Lived* in the periodical called, I think, *History and Theory.* All three find me entirely off the track, impenetrable, dogmatic, caught within my own web. At the same time, the book on sport has been received with enthusiasm by physical educationists, and continues to sell better than anything I have written; it has been anthologized a number of times, and has been referred to in article after article. The book on history, though very well received by Page Smith, a historian, has made hardly any headway; *Cinematics* has not yet had another review, though a few notices have appeared. How are these facts to be understood?

It is evident that what I write and the perspective I assume are not readily approachable by some students of the subject. It is also evident that my books on sport and history have considerable importance for certain people who are knowledgeable in the field. Am I to hope that the others will catch up, or am I to infer that I am dealing with matters outside my competence in ways that are of little value to a good number of concerned people? I should also add that some philosophers say that I am eccentric, that I make no contact with other philosophers, and that these do not and will not take me seriously. I have been inclined to dismiss such criticisms on the ground that there is no given 'philosophic' center from which a philosopher must not deviate, that it is not his task to conform to any set of 'professional' rules beyond those of being honest, not incompetent, not careless, not stupid. But if I add these criticisms to the foregoing, and add the fact that when I criticize others they take me to have missed the point, it does begin to look as if I am failing in an alarming way.

I write and rewrite, I make some effort to have a style, to be clear, to argue, to defend, to deal with objections which I formulate to myself in as strenuous a way as I can. I suppose at this late stage of my life I can not do much to change my ways. It would be easy to take myself to be like Peirce, Kierkegaard, or Spinoza, and hold myself to be ahead of my time, but this escape could too readily become an occasion for self-deception. I could take such a view in order to shore up my confidence—but it has not been shaken by these criticisms. The criticisms perplex me and I can not honestly say that I am confident about their import. Perhaps some light will be thrown on the entire matter as I now turn away from this book to attend to the final writing of "First Considerations," and to the criticisms that I have solicited and to which I will attempt to reply after I have gone over the whole.

February 6

What are the differences among "the battle took place," "I remember that the battle took place," and "it is a historic fact that the battle took place"? Evidently I am making reference in the latter two cases to the evidence I am bringing to bear. What is the difference between "the battle took place" when it is asserted without any knowledge, when it is asserted because I remember it, and when it is asserted because I have historic evidence for it? Is it not that the bare assertion is indeterminate, and that the others are determinate? It is their determinateness that makes me wish to deal with them as in the past, where there is only the determinate. That past is now resident within the present as a determinate dimension of it. The separateness of the past from the present depends on a (conceived?) separation of the layer of determinateness from the present occurrence as it is now in its process of coming to be.

Determinateness requires a reference to a reality which would disconnect what we have in mind and place it in a determinate setting. Earlier occurrences than some given one are logically related to it. A historical narrative gives us the link between the items which otherwise would be parts of distinct domains.

We must find either the particular substantial ground for an isolate, determinate appearance or relate that appearance to others. The world of the past is one of determinate appearances. Only in the present do we have an actual concrete reality. Though we can not find that reality as it is in fact making some item determinate, we can find it as that which is determinate enough to allow us to fill it out with all the determinate appearances. In the case of historic occurrences we must look at entities other than ourselves for the determinateness in which we are to embed the determinate content that we now are taking to belong to the past. The past is here and now functioning as a domain interrelating determinate appearances.

Do I sustain my shape, for example, and all the appearances that are antecedent to this? Am I the channel through which filter all the appearances that are determinately together with some past one? Is it the same thing to say that I sustain a present appearance and that I provide a medium through which or in which all determinate appearances are together, with one or a few of them having a primary value for the present?

Historic items are in the determinate aspects of various objects. The objectivity of the past might be due to its presence in a determinate layer in the present. Are there such layers?

We must avoid complete contextualizing, for this ends with a relativity of contexts—the position at which Kuhn ends with his view that scientific theories are all interlocked and upset together; with which Quine ends with his incapacity to translate; and at which Wittgenstein ends with his natural language of a particular society. Yet we must grant that   A] a child has the proposition, p, in a context of its vagrant thoughts,   B] the logician has it in a context of implications, and   C] the historian has it as having a determinate fringe requiring it to be within a single determinate whole of appearances, all embedded within the determinate dimension of something present. What is common to all of these? Is it not the p taken as alone, not as an atom, not as a unit, but as all there is? If so, the movement to one domain or the other is the making it one item among others. Historic reference is to an item as one among others within a fully determinate whole.

February 7

1] A single item which is not part of any domain is itself an immediacy within which nothing is contained. It is lived with, lived through, enjoyed. It could conceivably be known as a residuum of an abstraction, separated from the factors which it accretes by virtue of the place it had in some domain. But then it will accrete new determinations as one among a number of abstractions, as having been involved in the process of abstraction, and so forth. We either enjoy it, free from all additions, or we know it and thereby have it with additions. But while we have it with additions we can distinguish that portion of it which is being added to. Our domain will then be the item, with the addition of being something to which determinations are added.

2] The closest we can come to having a single item as an object of knowledge is as that which is determined to be capable of having this or that set of determinations. It will be that which could be in some domain or other. This in turn will require that actual domains be abstracted from to yield a single item, "some domain or other." As able to be in some domain or other, the item is capable of having this or that set of determinations. It would then be known as that which can be made determinate.

3] Knowledge of a single item, in contrast with its enjoyment, is the facing it as that which is had as indeterminate but able to be made determinate. The having it as something merely lived through is an extreme which is never fully attained; at every moment we are more or less involved in some particular domain.

4] As in a particular domain, there is a portion of an item which is made determinate there; that portion is free of all domains. Our act of attending to it, of course, occurs within the domain where abstracting, and so forth, take place, but if we can reach what remains unchanged, no matter what the domain, we will have moved to the position of just living with it. While not living with it, we know it as that which could be lived with it. Also, while not living with it, we also live with it as a factor there. Since knowing is also a part of living, we can also say that what is determinately present is also lived. This is one with saying that the domain (of knowledge) with all its content, is itself lived with and capable of being made part of some domain or other.

5] There are two dimensions to everything—what it is as determinate with respect to others, and what it is as indeterminate because inclusive, functioning as something to be made determinate.

6] It is just as true to say that what is in a domain is always a final item and that the domain and the determinations, too, are final as well. In moving toward it as final, as not being made determinate by anything, one also moves to the stage where what had made it determinate, and the domain in which the determinations occur, are themselves made final. The supposed single entity would then be indistinguishable from all else with which it had been connected.

7] The use of an item distinguishes it from others and introduces it into some specific domain where it is subject to determinations. Or, not to set item and domain in opposition to one another, use of an item is one with the use of a domain and other items, enabling the chosen one to acquire determinations within the one and by the others.

8] The content of memory has more determinations than can be accommodated in the present, confronted world of appearances. So is anything which is the terminus of the use of evidence, for example, some historic occurrence known to a historian. The terminus here is a claim, not the historic fact. But the claim is referred to the historic fact. That fact is not available except in the form of the determinateness which characterizes some particular object or set of them, and it is to this that the claim is referred and of which it is made a part.

9] Each present item stands away from others by virtue of its ability to act from within and express itself. At the same time, it has a determinate nature. That determinate nature in it is apart from the rest of it and is continuous with the determinateness of others. Any part of the determinateness is in a world with other determinate entities.

10] We can take the determinate dimension of an item to be its past only so far as it constitutes a layer which is in contradistinction with what is now occurring. The past is a layer which is distinguishable from what is now occurring, but the entity itself has the two dimensions—the determinate and what is now being made determinate—as one.

11] An individual occurrence is to be understood in two ways: as present, distinctively expressing itself apart from others, and as past, determinate and together with others. The former is prospective, ongoing, involving changes, novelties; the latter is retrospective, dividing the entity into dimensions each contrasting with the others. Its expressiveness involves both; it makes itself manifest only by distinguishing the expressed from itself as providing a new content for determination. The expression is continuously making itself be discontinuous, by setting its own beginning in opposition to its own ending.

12] There is no longer any need to speak, with Whitehead and Hartshorne, as though there were a past that was preserved by God, or one that persisted and was being sustained somehow, for the present items, in their coming to expression at that very moment, distinguish the determinateness of themselves from what they are presenting for determination in the present. The new determinate content becomes one with previous ones, differing from them only in the way in which it is to be subdivided.

13] There is just one determinate dimension, but this is the locus of a multiplicity of ordered ways of being subdivided into components. The multiplicity constitutes the historic past. The divisions of it are in a sequential relation of predecessor to successor; this the historian tries to know.

14] In symbolizing an actuality, one moves from surface to depth. The depth is the individual expressing himself. In the process of expressing himself, he distinguishes his determinate dimension from the rest. Reference to that determinate dimension also requires a symbolic movement in depth. If one takes that route, one traces the appearance, not to the individual as expressing itself, but to itself as having distinguished its determinateness from its activity, and made it thereby be that which precedes the present exhibited appearance. This symbolization has a temporal stretch to it, requiring a reference to its terminus as that which had been earlier than the beginning of the symbolization.

February 8

The various historical developments in the special disciplines need make no reference to an immediate datum serving as the entire field of experience. The transition from one period to another is with reference to limited data. All one need provide is the item as the transition between one determinate to another. One could anticipate other revolutions, but this will require one to free the item on which one has focussed from a number of determinations without ever getting it into the position where it is free of all. A freed item is approached when we speak of "Western scientific thought from the Greeks to the present," or "philosophic thought from Locke to Hume."

In these cases, as well as when one translates, and when an individual is living through a period of time, there is a determinateness which is retained at the same time that it serves as the beginning of a temporalized exhibition of the item, departing from that determinateness to acquire another. At home a man breakfasts; he then walks to work. He arrives at work as a breakfasted man, and therefore as one who is less tired than he might have been. At his arrival he is part of a larger determinate scheme. To know him as in that determinate scheme is to know him as one who incorporated determinations within him as "a breakfasted man" and altered this into "a man attentive to his work." The walk transforms the one into the other. At the same time, it is true that he breakfasts, walks, and works, in successive presents. At each moment he expresses himself as an individual. When he breakfasts or works at the office he himself, as a substantial being, is expressing himself in these ways. Evidently, an act has a double status: it is that which has been arrived at through a transformation of an item which has incorporated determinations within it, in separation from the items which in fact provide it with the determinations in a context; and it is that which is now freely being made manifest. The double fact can be accounted for by taking the man to be one who, while moving from one determinate state to another (the one settled, the other being produced), also expresses himself.

The man working at the office is expressing himself at the same time that he is the outcome of one who had breakfasted and walked. As the former, he is a constant individual; as the latter, he is one who has a determinate antecedent. This outcome is close to that which Kant presented in the third antinomy, where he tried to reconcile determinism and freedom. I differ from him in allowing the transition from one determinate state to a succeeding one to be free in its development, consistent with the structure which expresses the difference between the antecedent and subsequent state. In expressing himself now, the individual at the same time distinguishes his determinate past and incipient future, and provides the transition from one to the other. The structural difference between beginning and ending of the sequential occurrence is filled out by the individual expressing himself then and there. The intermediation between determinates is by an indeterminate, mediating the others by virtue of its difference from and continuity with both. This is vitally filled out every moment by the individual as a constant. What occurs at a particular moment is thus the product of a transitional structure and a constant individual expressing himself. Every expression could be taken to be a beginning or an ending of a structural transition, but all—what lies between the extremes of that structure, no less than the extremes—will express the individual.

A translation, a revolution in scientific theory, a pivotal historic occurrence are to be understood as vitalized, comparatively indeterminate structures providing a transition from a determination credited to some item to a new determination which a new item achieves by becoming embedded in a new domain and thereby becoming determinate. In the very act of expressing himself, a man distinguishes a determinate base in himself as the antecedent of what he is expressing. The distinguishing allows him to be in the present as an expressive being, a constant, and to provide a specific transitional connection between that expression and a determinate antecedent. The latter, since it is also due to him, could be taken to be an expression of him. If so, he expresses himself   A] in this manifest act,   B] as having separated out such and such a determinate base in himself,   C] as providing a structure connecting the determinate base to the expression, and   D] as providing the dynamism for moving from the base to the expression in the role of its consequent. The expression as part of a domain will be accounted for by the antecedent, the structure, and the dynamic filling out of the structure with its inevitable termination in the expression; but the expression will still have its singularity, its being now sustained by the individual—as will the separating out, the structure, and the dynamism.

Starting with the expression, one can proceed toward a man, the constant source of it; or one can move to its antecedent in an item wholly determinate from which one had moved to the consequent along the lines of the structure. The latter is an externalized whole in which antecedent, structure, and consequent are related; in it the individual has also manifested himself in the form of a dynamism not entirely sunderable from these. At one and the same time, he is now expressing himself in his work, and is making his having breakfasted to be structurally and dynamically antecedent to his work. Starting with his working now, we can trace this back to him as real, active, substantial, a constant over time capable of many expressions, or to him as having issued from the past in such a way as to end with his working now. His working now is at once the man now expressed, and an aspect of him terminating a past expression and exhibiting itself in a present structured transition.

This is not yet right. A present expression can be read in two ways: it is a manifestation of a substantial being and it is a transition from one end of itself to the other (or from what is bordering it on both sides). The identification of the extremes forces a distinction between the structure and the vitality of the expression. As just an expression it is now; as having a temporal stretch it is present, bounded by a past and a future. If the past be taken to be within the individual who is expressing himself, the expression will be part of a larger, in which the past determinateness is distinguished as the antecedent at the limit of the expression.

Apparently, an individual expresses himself within the compass of an expression and also as having that expression part of a larger. If the entire expression be taken to be an outcome, its antecedent will be outside it; if we include that antecedent in the expression, there will be another expression, and so on, just as when we probe into the actuality from the vantage point of the expression wherever we stop is a position beyond which we can still go. Taking the expression as a single unit, it is to be read either in depth or temporally as present.

February 9

Every moment of the time in which one is exhibiting oneself can be broken down to make the whole a continuum of sequentially ordered items. The expression of an individual is a single unit related to him as surface to depth, product to source. It is not, as Kant supposed, introduced at a point in a causal sequence, but throughout. A machine differs from a living being in not having the occurrence as a single unit. Though the machine can be made to go through a number of steps and, on completion of the last, be made to engage in another kind of sequence, and though any combination of steps can be given a number which precedes the next set, there will not be a single unitary occurrence which is to be attributed to the machine. The machine goes through a sequence which is capable of being dealt with as a temporal continuum, but it itself does not possess the continuum as a single exhibition. A machine begins and ends, but has neither a beginning nor an ending to its activity.

An organic individual expresses itself in unit items which are capable of being temporalized in the ways in which the different moves and steps of a process can be temporalized in a machine. But a machine is unable to have a stretch as a single item, either in the form of an observable feature or as an exhibition of itself. (I am using 'expression' and 'exhibition' interchangeably.) A man would, on this account, differ from an animal in the kind of acts (with their unitary natures) which he alone is able to produce—speech, artistic works, systematic inquiries, references to and enjoyments of finalities. He also is alone able to lay claim to them, take them to be his responsibility, possess them, make them part of a reference to himself as a me, and thereby use them not merely as intermediates, as an animal might, but as part of a single unity. An animal might act in terms of the action of another which followed on its own; a man can go further and take the entire set of action-intermediary-action to constitute a single unitary meaning, himself in communication with another.

Any given expression can have many nuances; it may vary in coloration throughout, and we may be able to mark off where it is red from where it is green, and so forth, but it will still be a part of a single unitary expression. Qualitative expressions are only some of all there are—or more accurately, they are dominant in only some outcomes and are present in dominated forms in others, where the contexts provided by finalities dictate the nature of the unitary wholes.

Must not the activity of a machine be sustained by the different parts of it? Do not things have qualitative characters? Surely a rock is gray, round, heavy, in somewhat the sense in which a man is white, well built, fat? Or are the limits of machines and things arbitrary, whereas in the case of the living being there is a self-bounded unity to it?

How do we account for the fact that some of the lower living beings are so interlocked with one another that it is not possible for them to live apart? It seems that we here have the features of

particular items and also features which characterize them as together, more or less persistent.

The exhibitions of a thing are sustained throughout as continua,
but not as being completed, as unities, with termini which belong to
them. Living beings also exhibit themselves throughout as continua, but at the same time hold on to the whole by virtue of
possessing both the beginning and the end. If the end is taken to be
present, the beginning is retained as a determinate base; a machine
has every portion of a continuum antecedent to others, but never a
region of the continuum antecedent to another region. An entire
continuum can be a unit serving as a base for another continuum, so
far as an organic being is concerned, but this is not possible to a
machine. Unlike a machine, a man is able to freeze time in his
expressions, perceptions, enjoyment of the arts, programs, and
plans, and in his involvement with transcendents. He is also able to
take any portion of these single items as an antecedent for what
comes after, and so far be like a machine.

As sustained, an item needs further determination from others.
Because there is no sustaining of any unified factor by a machine,
there is no determination for which it can be present. What is made
determinate is every portion of the continuum as it is being made to
be. But in the case of living beings the singleness of the expressed
item requires a determination from within or by others, in which
guise it becomes a component in the determinate past.

Is it not true that the color of copper, even though it may not be
an expression of it in the sense in which organic beings have
expressions, is in a determinate world with other colors, even those
of organic beings? I think we must say so. Does that not mean that
men, animals, or the colors which are sustained by these are in the
same universe with the color of copper? Do these others make the
color of copper be a single color of determinate magnitude instead
of a continuum of occurrences in sequence no member of which is
the color or has that color? Yes. In a world of inanimate things there
would then be no colors—as the traditional rationalists suppose—
but these would arise as soon as there were organic beings. Those
organic beings do not have to know inanimate beings or perceive
them; their presence in the world with their single well bounded
colors gives the inanimate items colors too, making the physical
continua into discrete extended units. And what was true of color
would be true of other qualities and of other features, such as

transcendents as resident in organic things. Does that not require one to say that the finalities do not operate on things as units, but only on the particles there, or on continua, or on 'points' distinguishable in the continua? But then, strictly speaking, there would be no particular things.

Is this piece of copper not one thing and that piece another? If we said that they were one copper, we would have to overlook their separation in space. And in any case, we would have to distinguish kinds of things, for copper is not lead or water. And if we allowed that there could be different pieces of copper would we not have to allow that they are governed in common ways, and that, with those common ways, they constitute appearances of which the color of copper is one? Or does a context merely take up the continuum provided by a piece of copper and allow this to be fixated in relation to the particular kinds of appearances which organic beings produce? What is the state of affairs then when there are no organic beings?

The old poser, "if a tree falls in the forest with no one about does it make a sound?" is answered by saying that a single sound must be bounded by other sounds. If this be correct, it would be right to say that copper has a color, but only so far as there are organically produced colors in the world sustained by organic beings. The copper, too, would be located, affiliated, real, intelligible, and have value only in relation to other, organically produced items which were located, and so forth, because they had in fact been effectively interlocked with finalities or their contextual expressions.

Apart from all organic beings, would the copper not be located where it is now in a particular space, at some time, be intelligible, and so forth? Or must we say that the copper would not occupy the place but merely be there, that it would not enter into the time but merely be caught up in it, and so forth? If so, it would lose its integrity, and it would not be true that some exhibitions of it were functioning when there were no organic beings. Or must we say that the particles (or a continuum) of copper were present, occupying a region, and so forth, but not until there were organic beings could the copper be a unit occupying space, and so forth, as a single entity? If organic beings were different from what they now are would that mean that copper might have different dimensions and qualities from what it is now made to have by virtue of the determinations that have been imposed on it? Organic beings might perceive copper differently, but would copper be different just by virtue of their existence? And if so, why should copper now not be different for the different kinds of organic beings that there are? Granted that all organic beings have similar expressed colors, they differ at least in that men have intelligence. Does the presence or expression of human beings require that appearances of copper be different from what they had been in the absence of men? It looks as if I am driven to that conclusion. Would those appearances be sustained by the copper, if the copper itself did not take as its own what the others made possible? That does not seem to be right, for copper exists independently of those others and what they do. Accordingly, it will have to be said that there are appearances credited to the copper which do not belong but are ascribed to it. We would not be able to read back from the appearances into the copper, not because it had manifested itself poorly or blocked our attempts, but because there are no symbols for it.

Must we not go on to say that some features attributed to subhuman living beings are not expressions of these, but are due to the fact that the beings are in the same world with what men have intelligently expressed? And if the intelligent expression is identified with the linguistic, would it not be true that they would have to be credited with appearances—though in fact they were nothing more than organizations of particles and points on continua—which owe their presence to the fact that they are in the same world with what men say? The appearances which things and animals had would then all be due to man, at least in the sense that they were there only because of the appearances he provided and which made the others determinate.

Men, of course, express themselves in other than linguistic ways, and this distinctively; and animals, apart from man and speech, express themselves in their own ways. To the degree that men brought in something new in the realm of appearances they apparently would allow for appearances elsewhere which were not internally produced and sustained by those others, except as sequential continua. Is this not to deny the integrity only of the volume of items? No, because time is also broken up into endless subdivisions no less than the space is. But then do we not deny the integrity of a spatial and temporal region appropriate to a thing? I think the answer must be that we do.

In contrast with those who hold that man's mind is the source of all qualities, and with those who hold that man's being makes a radical difference to all else, I am here coming to the conclusion that it is the presence of appearances in him and in animals which provide determinations making appearances out of the continuous manifestations of physical particles together. The things are themselves not unities, but just so far as the appearances belong to them, they will either be constituted at the very same time that the appearances are, or the appearances will be nonrevelatory of the things. Since things have some integrity and the activities they exhibit are appearances of them, we must say, I think, other appearances make appearances be coextensive with things, without thereby making those appearances revelatory of the things.

February 10

Since a thing sustains the ongoing continuum that is discernible on its surface and, since as located apart from others a thing also has a continuum of limited extension, it is correct to say that a thing does exhibit itself, and that the exhibition permits one to penetrate a little toward its substantial reality. This conclusion is compatible with the view that the presence of that continuum, in a determinate world where it is together with others, and to which one refers when concerned with the past, provides an occasion for the other appearances, under the aegis of a context, to give the physical entity additional, nonrevelatory qualities.

A physicalist who seeks to identify mind and brain would have to hold that the brain or portions of it function as single units with qualitative features which make it possible to perceive qualities in things, maintained as single units throughout a continuum of antecedents and consequents. He would also have to cosmologize the continuum, making it an illustration of a cosmic passage, and not permit it to be used as a symbol. The brain would then be seen to have a fixated unitary nature of some kind which, by being brought into the same world where things are, would provide determinations for these and thereby enable them to be decorated with observed qualities.

Is it possible to identify the determinate, settled dimensions of the brain with a fixated unitary character of it? If so, it would be the brain as having already gone through an activity which would be responsible for the presence of nonrevelatory qualities in things observed in the present. Might not one also say that it is the past of the thing in the form of its determinate base which enables it to have a revelatory quality, or which enables a perceiver to face a quality as that which is made determinate by the past of the thing? There seems to be nothing repugnant to the facts in these ideas. But if the last be accepted, the determinate nature of a thing would have to have a double effect, making the perceiver entertain a determinate quality and also enabling the thing to exhibit a determinate quality which may be similar to that which the perceiver entertained. In all these cases, where a determinate occurrence in the past is taken to be the source of a determinate occurrence in the present, we have the past acting on the present, and not functioning simply as an antecedent for it. It seems to be more correct, therefore, to say that what is now occurring is being made determinate by what is now determinate and alongside, under the governance of a context, rather than by what is a determinate base for what is observable.

February 11

The fact that this rock is located at a particular place does not suffice to show that it is a distinct entity. Distinct entities occupy, command, are in possession of the region they fill out. It is more correct to say, I think, that there are no particular things in nature, but only a single cosmic totality in which the different items are interlocked and function together under cosmic laws. The modern scientific way of speaking of space as that which contracts and expands and thereby exhibits the 'influences' of objects on one another is in accord with that idea. Even ultimate particles would not be units, but merely distinguishable points within a field of cosmic dimensions. So far, it is possible to be in accord with the seventeenth-century view that there are no colors, smells, and other 'secondary' characters in nature. But it is also true, as the existentialists maintain, that man's presence makes a difference to the world.

In contrast with the first view, I am saying that there are no individual things as well as no individual qualities or demarcated bounding characters. There are neither rocks nor particles, no things at all, but only a cosmic field within which delimited regions can be discriminated. In contrast with the existentialists I am also saying that the presence of organic beings makes a difference to what is cosmic, giving portions of the field boundaries and features they otherwise would not have, and that this is done without consciousness. Each organic being stands away from the rest of the world as an individual substance and, as such, makes the cosmic field break up into smaller regions, each of which, in accord with its physical constitution, thereby acquires a unitary nature.

A rock is distinguished from the rest of the cosmos because of the presence of organic beings; and in that distinguishing it is given determinate features. These do not ride on the surface of the rock, but instead are integral to it as a distinct item; they are symbolic of the rock in the way in which the displays of living beings are symbolic of them. But if we continue to insist on the field as the reality, the demarcated—gray, heavy, and even the rock itself—will merely be accredited to a location and not reveal anything of what is there.

One consequence of such an approach is that, apart from the existence of organic beings, the ocean is not wet, and indeed is not an ocean, or even water. There would still be molecules and other ultimate physical particles which interplay with the particles in what we now call land or sky or atmosphere. Another consequence is that wet will be integral to water. The water that is wet is a cosmically conditioned H_2O which has been delimited by the presence of organic beings. The coming of organic beings is the coming to be of distinguished individual units; these by their presence transform the rest of the cosmos into things with unitary characters. Starting from such an organically conditioned set of items one arrives at the scientifically known cosmos by freeing oneself of restrictive boundaries.

An application of this idea to the problem of natural beauty permits one to say that this requires one to detach some portion of nature from the rest as a kind of aesthetic object, which permits it to have the status of a beautiful entity. Where an artist in producing something beautiful makes it self-contained and therefore an aesthetic object standing in contrast with others, nature must be helped to have some segment of it be an aesthetic object before this segment can have the status of something beautiful. The beauty is present in nature, but only on the condition that some agent made a portion of nature stand away from the rest. If an iceberg created a duplicate of Michelangelo's *Moses,* or some other sculptured object which seems to be as excellent as this, there would not only be something which had been produced by the wind and ice within a cosmos, but also an assimilation of the item within the frame of aesthetic objects, where it then acquires a character in the form of beauty.

It is correct to say that a rock is gray and water is wet, apart from man and apart from any animal. But there is no rock or water until they have been bounded off from the world by organisms already bounded off. These manifest themselves and thereby provide determinations for portions of the rest of the universe. As soon as the rock and water are distinguished they are gray and wet, relative to the organic beings, and apart from any reference those beings may make to the rock and water. Within the limits of the wet water one will be able to locate H_2O, but those molecules are interlocked with others in the cosmos just as surely as they are with one another. It will be wet water which dictates just how many molecules are to be distinguished in a place. Apart from the water, there are no boundaries for those molecules; apart from organic beings there is no water.

If this is true, then were there no other organism but a single amoeba, the entire cosmos would be affected and subdivided into distinct unit entities. Only those distinctions would be made which were pertinent to the amoeba; other types of organic beings would introduce further divisions, with man making the maximum. It would be due to the presence of man that there are the kinds of things there are. There would, for example, be rocks none of which is possible in the world of the amoeba, and rocks some of which would not be possible in the world of other animals, particularly if we think of the rocks as having faults, grains, and histories. Just as grass becomes food only when there are beings which can eat it—as Dewey observed—so a portion of the cosmos becomes rocks for beings which can be bruised by them or for which they are obstacles.

Grass becomes food for the organisms which can eat it; it remains a living item apart from those organisms. Evidently, even the living acquire features from others. The presence of man will not only make for the existence of all the things that any other living beings can distinguish, and more, but will affect those living beings themselves. And when men, in addition to their presence, and their biological needs and appetites, their acts and functionings, engage in thought, formulating hypotheses and theories, classifying and ordering what they face and may face, further distinctions are made. But these are not of the same type as those which result without thought. The distinctions, demarcations, and unitary qualitative features that men introduce by their presence and activities apart from their thoughts are caught within the contexts that finalities provide. It is as within a context that a man makes a difference to the single domain that is nature.

Each expression by itself is inert and unrelated to the others; but as caught in a context it is brought to bear on what others are exhibiting, and thereby makes these determinate. Doesn't the context operate directly on whatever is manifested? Why say that this organic being or its manifestations make something be determinate? Must not the answer be that there are no bounded manifestations to be subject to the context until there are other bounded manifestations—those which organisms provide—which, via the context, are related to other portions of the cosmos?

Each distinguished entity faces the rest of the cosmos, breaking it up into smaller regions according to its needs and nature. When it does this, it provides content for the context to encompass, and thereby place in relation to the distinguished entity. This adds, to its original generic demarcation of portions of the cosmos, special ways of referring to those portions, thereby enabling the demarcated physical entities to provide occasions for the production of finite, qualitative, expressive things. These, while relative to the original entity, are objective, distinct units, since they are in the context with natures that depend for their differences from others on the physical constitution that they have in fact.

The cosmos is variegated. When some portion is isolated, its distinctive nuance comes into play as that which is to provide the material that is made determinate by others. A rock is hard because of the physical constitution of the rock. It is a rock and hard both because it has been demarcated and made determinate by something else with which it is related in a context, and because it has such and such a molecular constitution.

February 12

If it is due to the presence of organic beings that the cosmos is broken up into distinct things, each of which has or even is an appearance in determinate relation to the organic beings, it still is a question why the cosmos is so divided. Why does one distinguish or separate out a rock, sand, and boulder when they are together? No appeal can be made to their independent status if they are supposed not to be independent until organic beings make them determinate. How explain the fact that once distinguished they function and act on their own as independent realities?

Account must be taken of the fact that in the cosmos we are dealing with actualities as subject to the finalities. So far, there are no objective appearances. If the cosmos contains physical particles only, they will be governed as making up a single unit, a cosmos encompassing a multiplicity, no one of which is wholly separate in being or function from the others.

An organic being bounds off a portion of the cosmos within which are such and such physical particles. It thereby enables those particles to have a new status, that of being within it. Without losing their connection with the rest of the cosmos, the particles will then be caught within the volume which the organic being provides. Evidently, the space of the particles in an organic being has a double import. It is a fragment of a larger space in which all the particles are together but in which no one of them functions independently of the rest, and it is a space of an organic being which closes them off from the rest of the cosmos.

When an organic being expresses itself, its exhibitions are subject to conditioning by contexts which express the finalities. The result is a set of appearances. These provide symbolic agents for a penetration into the organic being. They also affect a separation of a portion of the cosmos. It is about that separation that the present questions are raised. No separate particles are there separated out, for they are not relevant to the organic being. What is separated out is a region which can be affiliated, coordinated, intelligibly connected with, extensionally distinguished from, and evaluated in relation to the organic being. The region is turned into an object of attention, interest, need, or obstacles to these.

The expression of an organic being is brought to bear on a portion of the cosmos, via an expression of a finality, to produce that which has a substantiality relevant to the organic being. A region of the cosmos is thereby turned, not into wetness, but into wet water, a water for which the wet is an essential feature, a water within whose confines there will be a set of physical entities cut off from those with which they are in fact interlocked in the cosmos, and which preclude the water from being nothing more than a function of the needs of organic beings. It is not the mere appearances (as I think I was maintaining a little while back) of an organic being which dictate the separation of a set of particles from the rest within the confines of some thing, but those appearances as expressing the organic being. As mere appearances these are subject to contexts; as continuations of the organic beings they are subject to cosmic conditions.

The cosmos has to be understood in two ways—as a single set of interlocked particles, and as a multiplicity of complex actualities (some of which are organic) which function in considerable independence of one another. The actualities are qualified by the finalities; their appearances, at the same time, are set in contexts where, like the particles, they are inseparably together. The organic beings, by being subject to qualifying finalities, thrust beyond themselves, demanding demarcations in an undivided cosmos, and have those demands countered by unseparated particles. The latter are broken off from the totality of unseparated particles in the very act of being subject, under the pressure of the organic being's presence and the finalities which qualify this, to the demands which the organic being makes because pertinent to its continuance.

But, surely, the gull has no concern with the ocean but only with this little segment of it where it spies the fish. Is there no ocean for the gull? Must we not say that the segment in which it concentrates its attention is continuous with an indefinite region beyond, where it is subject to wind, clouds, sun, other gulls, and so forth? No. It does not exist in a universe with an ocean but with a constantly expanding and contracting region somewhat larger than that where its present need is satisfied. It will demarcate and have as separate one set of items pertinent to it as a gull, and another set pertinent to it as a gull now hungry, and so on. It makes a region be pertinent to it as an environment, and within that environment distinguishes relevant items in somewhat the way in which it separates the environment from the rest of the cosmos. Does the distinguishing proceed by the imposition of a single qualitative unifying factor—as I have been supposing—or is it achieved by the organic being as an expressive reality? I think we must say that the gull and its expressions give determination to a region of the cosmos, making it be a thing or usable content or an environment which has its own status, expressions, and functioning, and is capable of being further determined depending on the distinctive ways in which that organic being expresses itself. The expressions of an organic being make a portion of the cosmos stand out as singular items having expressions of their own, and related via cosmic conditions to the organic being.

The primary conditions are evidently affiliative, making items relevant. The affiliative power of a primary Substance connects an organic being with a region and thereby produces distinct entities, with their own expressions, related in relevant ways to that organic being. That result is consistent with the contention that the primary fact about things is that they are substances.

Is not the entire cosmos of particles, even when taken to be interlocked, subject to Substance, apart from an organic being? It must, if finalities are conditions which make it possible for a cosmos to be. But the cosmos of particles as affiliated is distinct from the world of organic beings and the complex unities which are relevant to it. Consequently, we must say that Substance operates directly on all the particles together and then, as interplaying with organic beings which issue from some cluster, operates on other clusters to make them into things relevant to the organic beings.

Ultimate particles have sufficient independence of the cosmic pattern to be able to make their individual contributions to it, and to be able to cluster together in various ways so as to constitute molecular combinations, and eventually to be able to make a distinctive set within the confines of an organic being. One might, with the emergent evolutionists of some decades back, suppose that the molecules themselves constituted a new dimension, go on to hold that they were subject to cosmic conditioning, and then proceed upward by stages until one arrived at man. If this path is followed, one would have to think of the molecules as forming a layer above the particles where they would be in a single cosmic field, and so on. There could then be things with their own separations from one another, but yet all together in a single cosmos or layer of the cosmos. But the molecular world seems to be just the world of ultimate particles with an emphasis on various clusters.

Not until we come to the organic do we have complex items with integrities of their own, due to nothing outside them. Those organic beings are the product of clusters of particles or molecules subject to Substance. This, because of the proximity of some particles, or some aberrational fact about them, was able to be specialized and fragmented there in the form of a unity. This made the cluster be organic. Organic beings are members of a cosmos on a different level from the clustered particles, but there is no need to interpose other levels of cosmic import between these two.

A limited set of clustered particles is not only governed by a cosmic condition but interacts with this to constitute an organic actuality. This is subject to the source of that cosmic condition and, through its agency, makes a difference to the particles that exist outside the confines of that organic actuality, turning sets of those particles into things.

February 13

The power of affiliation exhibited by Substance sweeps over the cosmos, making the different ultimate particles part of a single field, and allowing them the status of only self-maintained units. Some of those units are clustered in such a way that the Substance is able to unite them in a steady, intimate way at the same time that the Substance continues to operate on all the other units as before. The result of the clustered units and the portion of the Substance as uniting them is a vortex, pulling both of these factors toward a center. The outcome is a complex actuality. That complex actuality is subject to Substance, at the same time that it enables the Substance to operate with it as a base. As a consequence, the centered unit is a part of the cosmos (since it is an item which with everything else is being imposed on by the Substance) at the same time that it limits the operation of the Substance to the provision of a connection for units which are relevant to that complex actuality.

A complex actuality makes use of Substance as a medium through which to express its unitary nature. The expression requires certain units on the same level with itself, in order for it to survive and prosper. The complex actuality, by means of Substance, adds a controlling unitary factor to the regions it incipiently marks out of the cosmos of particles. As a result, the complex actuality becomes part of a world in which it is together with other complexities.

An organic entity is the product of an initial clustering and a cosmic condition which are united in a detached, unified, centered, complex actuality. That actuality expresses itself in attitudes which terminate in groups of particles. But unless the complex actuality is mediated by Substance there are no unities imposed on those groups. By means of Substance a unity is imposed which, because that Substance is operative on the complex actuality, is relevant to what the actuality is and needs. The outcome is a plurality of complexes, one of which at least is organic, and the others of which are relevant to it, exhibiting in their unities something of the nature of their clusters. Unlike the cluster of the original, complex, organic actuality, theirs do not dictate to other clusters that they have some unitary nature.

February 14

Some logicians take "Columbus discovers American in 1492" to be a tenseless, timeless truth. Nothing, they think, is altered if it be stated by itself, be held together with other statements, be affirmed by a child, a historian, and so on. Their contention can be maintained only if there is some truth which is common to all these, or which can be abstracted from, or is indifferent to them all.

When a child makes this statement, the child has no evidence for it, does not relate it to a historical event, nor have it as a part of a body of historical knowledge. Instead, it is only a part of a set of assertions the child learned by rote, some of which may be false; it makes no reference to a particular time and has therefore something of the tenseless character of the logician's unit; and it may or may not be divorced from all relation to fact. A historian who makes the assertion does so on the basis of evidence; it is a conclusion not an isolated item; the truth it has is an inherited one, derived from evidence, through the help of a historical inferential act. The historian also has it together with other historically certified truths, which conceivably could be joined together on the basis of their degree of certitude in comparison with some other set. The historian, too, refers the assertion to the past, thereby making the truth no longer one which is oriented toward the evidence but, instead, is in the form of a claim about a settled fact.

To be in the historical world is to be cut off from the world of nature by being subject to a distinctive kind of causality in which antecedents must be relevant to and not merely be preconditions for the consequents. The individuals in that historical world are also part of the cosmos.

A man is part of the cosmos in many ways, at the same time: A] as confining whatever particles there be within his unified actuality,   B] as together with the unitary things which he makes possible by virtue of his very presence,   C] as together with other men within a society having a world of nature outside,   D] as together with other living beings having a world of nature outside, and   E] as together in history but related there to what is outside. To this list we must add man as religious, artistic, inquiring, and so on. Individually, and together with some other complex actualities, men stand apart from the rest of the universe at the same time that they are in it, subject to the same conditions governing the rest.

February 15

1] The finalities govern all the ultimate particles.

2] The finalities govern limited sets of particles.

3] The limited combinations have an integrity of their own.

4] As having integrity, the limited combinations have distinctive natures.

5] The governance of the particles within the limits of the unitary natures varies in degree, from the organic to the merely aggregated.

6] The particles set limits to the activities of the unities within which they are.

7] The action of an entity, its act or exhibition in the world, is a function of the ways in which the functioning of the unity and the functioning of the particles cohere, at the same time that the unity and particles continue to have the natures they do.

8] As having their own natures, the unity and the particles act, but do so in different ways, the unity functioning as a disjunct item and the particles as part of a cosmos.

9] The understanding of the unity as together with its particles is in terms of its acts; this requires an approach to it from an outside position.

10] A unity as embracing a limited set of components, and that unity as having its own integrity, both have cosmological roles. The same cosmological conditions rule them; those conditions also rule the particles.

11] The particles, when cosmologically governed, react to their common condition according to the ways in which they are clustered. The resultant singular union of them is subject once again to those conditions. The result—multiple unities each with its confined particles—is subject to those conditions once more. The conditions are always present and are presented with new occasions to operate; some of those new occasions are the product of the conditions with what they had already encountered.

The two sentences "This is a cat," and "Here are two dogs" contain four words each. We can therefore say there are A] two sentences, B] two sentences of four words each, C] eight words. The case C is like that of a cosmology of ultimate particles, B is like that of a cosmology of unities; A is like that of a combination of the first two cases, also viewed cosmologically. But B is also to be understood as having the unities with their words disjunctive, each, for example, sustaining a truth claim independently of the other.

Sentences lack a dynamism; the distinctive nature of a unity as embracing a set of subordinate elements and standing disjunctively apart from all the rest is brought out best by considering an organic being, for this can pull the subordinated elements away from other subordinated elements with which they are in fact connected in the cosmos. The particles within me are now closer to those in the chair; later, they will be closer to those in my friend. It is as if the four words in one sentence were forced to have new relations to the four words in the other sentence. One could not make them count to eight without overlooking the jump that has to be made from the fourth in one set to the fifth of another, a jump which is not necessary so long as one deals with purely formal, numerical entities.

A unity with its particles, which is expressed in an act and is thereby able to be understood to be a single entity—the source of the act—is the object of social sciences. But it also has a cosmological status, so far as it is taken as continuous with its act. The complex entity, of unity and particles (or combinations of these), is given integrity by its act; it becomes a cosmological entity together with its act in the same way that, as a unity, it had been made into a cosmological entity.

The same conditions operate on the particles, the unity, and combinations of these. The second presupposes the first, and the third the second, but the second and the first are incorporated in part in the third to constitute a new entity definable in terms of the act. The third does not have an integrity of its own as a kind of object. There is no water which is combined with molecules of H₂O. There is only A] the molecules, B] the water, and C] the molecules within the limits of the water and even confined and controlled by the water, but D] no entity which is molecules plus water except so far as A and B are dynamically interrelated in the course of an action. As having passed away, the active entity is one with its act within a single, determinate totality.

In four cases—the particles, the unity, the unity confining the particles, and the particles limiting the functioning of the unity—we have entities with natures governed by cosmic laws. In the fifth case, where the particles and the unity function independently but come together to constitute a single action, we have no nature but only an action which, with its source, could be taken to be a single entity governed by cosmic laws. If we transfer this idea over to man, almost everyone would be inclined to suppose that in the fifth case we do have a real entity—a person. Using classical terminology we would then have five cases: the animal or bodily nature of man, the mind or the rational; the animal nature unified and controlled by the mind; the body limiting or conditioning the mind, and the person as the source of an activity in which both mind and body are interlocked.

If this be allowed, why should one not take water and molecules together to constitute a single entity? Would this be the water with which persons are concerned, a water which is owned, needed, satisfying? Suppose there were no persons, would not there be a water satisfying to animals and plants? Must we then not say, in contrast with what was said earlier today, that in the fifth case, we do have a single entity but that this is relative, because relevant, to the organic? If so, the organic not only makes possible the water as a unity—and perhaps also the water as constraining, the water as limited by the molecules—but the water as a unity interlocked with the molecules to constitute a single relevant entity. Might there not be such a single entity even in the absence of organic beings? Not unless water itself could be in the absence of such beings.

The presence of organic beings in the world is the basis for there being water or any other unities other than particles, and water and particles functioning together, each constrained and qualified by the other. The water and the particles as together would have natures of their own, though only so far as they were in a world with organic beings. The organic beings would have a unity and particles united, but still be unities. Intention and desire, one might then say, are concerned with just water, while satisfaction, drinking, washing, drowning are concerned with water interlocked with particles. These are relevant to organic beings which are themselves unities interlocked with their own sets of particles and combinations of these.

'Thing' must be understood in two senses—as a unitary nature, and as the unity of that nature with particles. Do these come to be at the same time? If the latter is due to appetite or incipient action, the former would either be a part of it or a later achievement due to the ability to entertain or want a prospect. But is it possible for a unity to come after the having of a unity together with particles? Do we live first in a world where there is a desired or desirable water with particles and then in a world where there is a water which satisfies a thirst that is felt? It seems so. But then must we not say that a cluster of items is not merely given a nature by a cosmic condition, but that the nature is interlocked with the items to constitute a new entity? Only subsequently will one have the unity apart from the cluster, and then only if some being, such as an animal or a man, was able to feel, or in some similar way be able to confront a mere unity without regard for the ways in which it might be involved with particles.

February 16

I have distinguished in the world of actualities A] a unity, B] a unity confining particles, and C] a unity and contained items united to constitute a complex, such as a person, a living being, and what these might make relevant to themselves. In Scholastic or Aristotelian terms I have been saying that there is an essence, that this functions as a substantial form, and that the substantial form and what it governs constitute a more complex substance. In *The World of Art,* I took account of Thomas Aquinas's observation that there was a kind of matter involved with even thoughts about existents. If I remain with that suggestion (and I think I ought), a mere unity will have to be treated as an abstraction. There would then not be something correlate with the particles; every unity will be involved with something beyond it. The coming to be of an organic being would involve a clustering which had the ability to cling to the common field in which its elements were. This field would be separated off from the cosmos, and confine the clustered items. Then, in response to the finalities, the combination of unity with confined particles would be pulled toward a center, thereby giving the unity a distinctive role and providing a new unity for the confining centered unity and the centered particles. The result will exhibit unitary thrusts of some magnitude expressive of its needs and appetites. Those thrusts, on alighting on various clusters, make these have a unitary nature which confines the clustered items. If the clustered, confined items, with their confining unity, constitute a thing rather than a living being, the result will be a single complex actuality, in which both the particles and a unity play a role within the confines of a unity. The whole will be relevant to organic beings.

Every living being faces enmattered forms, that is, unities within whose limits particles are confined. It has them at a distance, finds them resistant, functioning as items within a cosmos. But every living being also has appetites and needs; the termini of these are not the confining unities, but single entities within which one can distinguish the confining unities and what they confine. Those single entities have a field character as the result of the ways in which the confined particles are encompassed together with the confining unity. The field character is qualified by the finalities; as so qualified, it is pulled inward to a center. That center has one of various grades of excellence, depending on what qualifications it can make integral to itself. We have, then, a field character produced by the clustering of particles, and another which is produced by the result of the former clustering as confined by a unitary nature. That unitary nature was achieved when the initial field character was subjected to conditioning by organic beings and finalities.

February 17

The members of a cluster of particles or of some more complicated set of physical entities are   A] subject to the same finalities and in the same way that distinct items are,   B] together constitute a single unitary tone having no power,   C] are, as together with the unitary tone, subject to conditioning by the finalities, as already grounded and affecting organic beings,   D] together with the conditioning are, with the tone, subject to the finalities as grounded in organic beings which are expressing needs, and   E] are abstracted from when the organic beings attend to the outcome of D through the agency of desire, intention, concepts, and so on.

The unity of a thing is given in C and D. In C a thing internalizes the affect of the finality, Substance. Things are not substances except in a world where there are organic beings; they then maintain themselves by holding on to the unitary tone as together with the particles (C). In D the qualification which is internalized is modified by virtue of its relevance to the needs of organic beings.

March 13

There are rests in music. They could come anywhere. There could be a rest at the beginning. Rests have no prescribed length. Rests are lived through with tension. There are no absolute noises or absolute silences, for the one would require an absolutely sealed room and the other an extinction of heartbeats and pulsebeats. Some parts of a musical piece could conceivably constitute a single work. A performance with one kind of instrument is different in nature from that involved in the use of another. The acceptance of all these considerations makes it possible to face the question, somewhat better than I have before, as to whether or not John Cage's piece *4' 11"* (I think that is what he called it) is music.

1] A distinction must be made between silence or emptiness and a determinate silence having distinctive borders; also between a definitive length, which is appropriate to those borders and the kind of artistic domain it is pacing. A merely empty page is not equatable with the pause of a poem; it could be the emptiness of a drawing or story; there is no way to know where to begin or end. Cage sat before a piano. Had he used a harp or a cello, presumably the piece would have had a different length. His sitting before the piano had to be a sitting appropriate to playing the piano; otherwise it would be just a sitting on a piano stool before a piano.

2] The piece, if neither preceded by nor succeeded by what were relevant musical notes, would still be parasitical on actual heard music. We take it to be the silence of a piano piece only because we had in imagination or in fact environed it with music. An imaginary environing allows it to be a silent piece, with our knowledge of what music is like enabling it to be bounded as a silence of music.

3] The ascription of a time length to the piece measures it not in terms of a musical time, internally constituted, but by a watch calibrated to something else. We can take it to be the time of the piece only if we view it as a kind of musical, internally used measure, at the limit of which, like a stripe in a Barnett Newman painting, a climax occurs. It will be a *4' 11"* lived through and with, moment after moment. Cage, to be sure, attended to his watch; but this means only that the *4' 11"* arrived at by the watch was to coincide with the tensional passage of the single silence.

4] A mere silence is generic, a mere possibility to be specialized into a number of relatively indeterminate silences appropriate to different arts and different instruments. An even more generic possibility would be sheer emptiness or nonbeing, a nothingness which is to be specialized into silences, the standings of a dancer, the pauses in plays, the openings in sculptures, the open spaces of architecture, and the like. Each of these specializations will require preparation in the sense of requiring one to set them within the bounds of a contrasting fullness, imagined or actual.

For a dancer a standing is danced through. It is a different standing from that which an actor would exhibit, for his has to be understood in terms of where he had come from and where he is going. A dancer is tensed in the standing, attentive to the position and placing of his neck, arms, hands, back, and head; if account is taken of what lies beyond its borders, his standing does not require movement any more than the movement requires it. Lived through as originating with an actual or imagined movement, and ending with the beginning of another, the standing is still different from an actor's, for an actor's movement, like the actor's standing, has an origin and an ending outside it. All constituents of an actor's movement or standing are expressions of a character, whereas a dancer's standing or movement depicts nothing.

If a dancer and an actor were side by side and asked to stand erect for a minute, let us say, not only would their standings be quite different, but their minutes would have different tensions, and perhaps would be too long or too short for one of them. It would be an interesting experiment in an acting class to have an accomplished dancer stand erect alongside an accomplished actor. The dancer's attention, I think, would be entirely on the problem of standing; the actor's on what it meant in some larger context.

Would there be a difference between an actor standing; an actor acting the part of a dancer standing; a dancer standing; a dancer acting the part of an actor standing; a film performer standing; a film performer exhibiting an actor's standing; a film performer exhibiting a dancer's standing; an actor acting a film performer's standing; a dancer dancing a film performer's standing? There are higher order questions than these, but these suffice to enable one to focus on the difference amongst participants in these different arts. I think the engaging in all these standings would be different, but it is hard to express the difference exactly. A film performer, in contrast with the other two, would (with the dancer) exhibit the standing as a unit; with the actor he would have it bounded by a position from which and a position to which he was to go; unlike the actor he would not have definite positions to consider, the definiteness being provided by the director, cameraman, montagist, and editor. Clarification of these issues should make it comparatively easy to understand the 'positive', 'full' activities of the participants in these different arts.

If, as I have been contending for many years, art takes us to the deeper recesses of Existence, we would have to say, if the foregoing is correct, that emptiness, in whatever form it takes in the different arts, is also revelatory. This at first seems to be what a Zen Buddhist would maintain; for him quiet calls to quiet, the undifferentiated to the undifferentiated. But if the silence is genuinely lived through and is just as solid a part of the music as sound, it will not be the silence of which the Zen Buddhist speaks. His silence is the silence of a religious man, not that of an artist. The revelatory character of an artistic silence is emotionally sustained, and reaches to the very same point, and even together with that at which the sound does—or more precisely, it is the piece itself which enables one to reach what is ultimately real, and the silence would be doing this only if it were the entire piece. But it would then do it in a way which was not radically different from that made possible by sound.

March 14

If a dancer were to walk, he would concentrate on the nature of the walk. An actor, instead, would make the walk be in consonance with the character that was being developed. A film performer would concentrate on making a determined, a casual, or some other kind of walk which was to be fitted into a larger scene. If a dancer were to show how an actor walked, the dancer would give indications of where he had been or was going, or the kind of individual who was walking; if he were to show how a performer walked, he would distinguish walking from other acts, and interrelate the walking with other parts of a dance. If an actor were to show

how a dancer walked, he would have to give indications that it was a dancer who was being portrayed and then show the dancer engaged in dancing in the form of a walk; if he were to show how a performer walked, he would act the performer as engaged in the task of producing a certain kind of walk. If a performer were to show how a dancer walked, he would set himself in a position where it would be seen that he was a dancer trying to dance a walk; if he tried to show how an actor walked, he would show the actor assuming a part which requires a certain kind of walk.

*   *   *

Last week I sent off the manuscript for "First Considerations." I must have rewritten it about ten times. In the end only six people finally sent me criticisms. After some very flattering remarks the verdicts seem to be that I am unclear and unconvincing.

The critics did not seem to think there was much of a problem in the ways in which conditions function. But in that work I distinguish between the conditions functioning as expressions of finalities interacting with the expressions of actualities to produce appearances; the action of the finalities directly on individual actualities with internalizations of the qualifications determined by the grade of the actualities; and the interplay of the actualities with the conditions as governing them all together and thereby constituting a cosmos. In addition to these different and not always easy to distinguish ways in which the conditions operate, the conditions are subject to a number of limitations:

A] There are a number of independently operating conditions grounded in the different finalities. The conditions do not, therefore, have simple units on which to operate, but units which are affected by other conditions.

B] There is always a degree of spontaneity reflecting the independence and oppositional nature of actualities, a fact that is overlooked as a rule because the units supposed to be subject to conditions are treated as mere values of the variables in terms of which the conditions are stated, as if they added nothing but the innocuous fact of instantiation.

C] The entities which are subject to conditions are also subject to limitations provided by the presence of other entities which are together with them in situations, or to limitations due to the totalities in which those entities are together with others.

D] Actualities have a density to them, but laws apply to aspects of those actualities as well as to the actualities in their full concreteness, exhibiting more and more resistance or transformative power in the face of the presence of the conditions.

A physical particle, even in a mechanically governed situation, A] is subject to affiliations, coordinations, extensional wholes, evaluations, as well as intelligible laws; B] each is an independent entity and exhibits this in the way in which it expresses itself and possesses the termini at which conditions end; C] each is subject to the limitations and activities of the complex in which it is, and perhaps also to limitations by the molecules, cells, and so forth, which are also present in the same complex; and D] each particle, in its full concreteness, is subject to conditions.

The last is a rather new idea. Unless one assumes that more attenuated, more publicly expressed aspects of a concrete particle are only incidentally affected, so that whatever is true of the entity in its full concreteness will be derivatively true of the aspects of it, one must allow that the aspects are themselves affected by conditions but in ways which are distinct from those characteristic of the entity in its full concreteness. This does not require that the entity be viewed as made up of layers, each independently subject to the same conditions as all the others, but simply that the conditions operate in depth, and with different results. A concrete entity's law-abiding ways would be an average, or a summation, or a limit of a set of functionings which a condition makes possible.

This view is not yet clearly in focus. I see it most clearly when I think of the affiliations of an entity. Superficially having such and such expressions, it may be affiliated in one way; as having steady habits in another way; and as having a certain nature in a third way. Its affiliations, as a single concrete entity, will be multiple with respect to multiple items, and yet all could be understood to be the product of the same conditions operating on diverse material. Does the view imply that mass, for example, is an average, a summation, or limit of quantifiable characterizations of physical bodies dealt with as subject to forces in different degrees, depending on the level at which the units for such forces are identified? Apparently so. For the moment I am not clear as to just what the implications of such a supposition are.

March 15

'Objectivity' has a number of distinct senses worth distinguishing: A] It refers to what is acknowledged by the members of
a community, even though this may not be what those in other
communities might acknowledge.   B] It refers to what all men
acknowledge. This, though, may not be anything more than what
answers to the special interests and apprehensions of man, a matter
which could be known by comparing what they acknowledge with
what is reported by a machine, or which one might be able to come
to know after analysis.   C] What is judged unites what is contemplated with what is indicated in a unity where they are presumably united in fact. Such judged contents may be personalized,
socialized, or humanized. But all involve a note of self-maintenance
of the entity as present for the perceptions. If account is taken of
the different kinds of contents and locations which are to be solidified, one can make further subdivisions within this particular type
of objectivity.   D] It refers to what is made to function in accord
with externally operating conditions. These conditions may have
limited scopes or may be all-encompassing; in either case there are
many of them.   E] Each entity by itself is subject to conditions
functioning there as transcendents, qualifiers, and the like, making
the entity be objective in the sense of being characterized without
regard for any individual or any particular's relation to it.   F] One
of the conditions stems from Being and makes that to which it
applies be coordinate with others; the entities are then related, but
as entities which are self-contained.   G] Each entity maintains
itself apart from all relations, as that which is beyond all perceiving
and even beyond all penetrations, though not cut off from
these.   H] Each entity expresses itself in interplay with the conditions and thus reveals itself to have an objective status or power.

It is sometimes said that what one sees in the sky at night is what
happened years ago in some other place. If so, what is either
confronted or perceived is a transformation of something presumably objective in the sense of being knowable to all men were they
at that other time and place. But this is not the occurrence which is
supposed to be the source of photons or other physical entities that
are supposed to start from the occurrence, impinge on a man, and
make him take something to be a star in the sky, either because he

externalizes what is in his mind, or because he has been enabled to produce or attend to the transformation of the original observable occurrence.

In any case, why should one believe that were one in the vicinity of the occurrence one would see it in its full objectivity? It is also a question as to which of the above senses of objectivity is pertinent here: if observable, we have something which is subject to the conditions of perception; if we have what is outside those conditions we cannot rightly speak of being able to observe it, without adding personal or social notes to it.

March 21

I have previously remarked that a philosopher must face the question "Where shall we begin?" I have also maintained that the proper answer to that question is "Here." I have gone on to say that "Here" refers to where we now are, in a room, at a typewriter, looking at this and that, with such and such beliefs, memories, and so forth. That reply is not altogether satisfactory; it involves moves from other positions, and therefore can represent a beginning for a certain kind of activity but not the absolute beginning from which all other special beginnings must take their start.

The asking of a question is already the outcome of a move toward oneself as putting the question to oneself or to another. One moved to that position from another in which it was indeterminate whether or not one was going to ask a question (or perhaps just be in a position where some thought was to occur), engage in some practical activity, lose oneself in experiencing, or be awaiting something. These alternatives are intermixed in what is found by moving away from other points in which one was involved. Initially, it is not clear whether or not one is going to engage in intellectual activities—make use of his I; experiencing—find himself within a we; be involved in practice—be caught up with others; or merely await for something to happen—be a you from the perspective of others.

The forging of a question involves an antecedent move into oneself as apart from others. That move takes one into another indeterminacy, that of the kind of adventure in which the I is to engage—explication, completion, distinguishing or analysis, rooting or grounding, or synthesis (answering to the finalities, Possibility, Existence, Being, Substance, and Unity). It is only because, on having escaped the first indetermination, one has moved into the indetermination characteristic of the I which has not yet begun a special kind of activity, that one is in a position to move to the determinate attitude of questioning (which is a form of completing, and therefore shows a bias toward the finality, Existence, as now being exemplified by the I). Once I am at that position, I have to make it determinate still further by the actual questions and the actual using of these in an inquiry which ends in answers. To arrive, then, at the position where I have the question "Where shall I begin" is to have made a move from my not fully determinate involvement with others, to my not fully determinate assumption of a position in myself, to the not fully determinate stage where I am asking a particular question.

How can I know about these indeterminates? They are surely the result of inquiry and reflection, and are to be known only as a result of what they themselves make possible. We learn about ourselves as having indeterminate positions or states or ideas only after we have in fact made ourselves determinate successively in a number of ways. The so-called 'pre-thematic' is a conclusion achieved by reflecting on the thematic. This reflection on the thematic, on what is in fact attained after some inquiry and determination, is never altogether cut off from areas of indetermination. In making the withdrawn self, for example, determinate as a questioner with one particular question, or as involved in some particular form of inquiry, we never cut it off entirely from the indeterminate whole in which it had been. We sharpen one part of that indeterminate whole at the same time that we leave the rest of it still continuous with the factor we make the determinate.

The conclusion to which we come in the course of our reflecting on the work in which we are engaged, on ourselves as engaged in it, or on the results, is a conclusion which we find sustained by encountered content. We conclude to the existence of an indeterminacy and find ourselves faced with an indeterminacy which is inseparable from the conclusion. The conclusion that there is an indeterminacy is an intellectual determination of the indeterminacy. To say that there is an indeterminacy is a specific conclusion whose referent is an actual indeterminacy.

The statement that there is an indeterminacy is not itself indetermate, but a determinate conclusion whose truth depends on its being sustained by an indeterminacy in fact. This, at first, seems to express an impossibility.

A determinate conclusion about indeterminacy is determinate by virtue of its connection with a determinate premiss. When we refer that conclusion to an actual indeterminacy, we separate it from the premiss, and allow it to be sustained by the actual indeterminacy. This sustaining has degrees, running all the way from our retention of the conclusion to a maximum degree so that it is on the surface of the actual indeterminacy, to our abandoning ourselves to the indeterminacy in which the conclusion is absorbed. If we do the second, we approach the state which we had originally occupied. As a result, we first come to know, and then come close to occupying the position we had before we began to ask about the 'pre-thematic' state.

The decision to ask a question about a beginning shows that we have come to the state where we seek completion, something which will answer the question. We come there only after living for a considerable while. It is a position for sophisticated thinkers; indeed, it is one which requires so much sophistication that it has been overlooked by many thinkers, or has been misconstrued by those who have taken it seriously. Hume just supposed that he could start with impressions. Hegel did take the question seriously, but he also limited it to one which was put and answered by a reason. He did not ask himself whether or how he could get to such a position; whether or not there had been an antecedent beginning, in which he was just as surely involved in practice, with what was immediate, or final, or the two together, as he was in experiencing or knowing.

We know the nature of the beginning which is made determinate by particular types of activity only after we have developed a philosophic account, for it is only then that we are able to recognize its full complexity and the multiple directions in which it could be made determinate. When Merleau-Ponty tries to turn away from metaphysical ideas to face the world directly as a kind of wilderness of ultimate realities he is trying to get back to a true beginning. And it is a true beginning for a speculative system, since in such a beginning one can find evidence for a movement to finalities, as well as faint adumbrations (or lucidations) of those finalities. But it is a beginning which evidently was achieved after he had moved from another beginning where it was indeterminate whether he was going to act or to think (or feel, or observe, or assess). He had to decide, in other words, whether he was moving toward Existence, Possiblity, Substance, Being, or Unity. Such a decision is not something planned, nor is it willful or mysterious. One is indeterminate to some degree always. An absolute beginning is where it is indeterminate whether one is in oneself, involved with finalities, somewhere between these two, has the two in opposition, or is entertaining them both as prospects. (These are specialized results reflecting the dominant presence of Substance, Unity, Existence, Being, and Possibility.)

What is evidently unclear is just who we are. The movement into ourselves from the indeterminate situation where we are with other entities is a way of providing a determination for ourselves. The achievement of a position in one direction rather than some other yields a distinctive nature and role for oneself. From there, the movement into oneself as engaged in clarifications, practical acts, and the like is the achievement of still further distinctiveness in nature and role. At every stage there is a finite locus of all else.

If we can make the other factors in the indeterminate stand out from one another, we can sharpen our formulation of the nature of an individual. In all cases, an individual is a focal point. Initially, that focal point imperceptibly merges into the other items, so that one could just as well say that there is only one indeterminacy. We can say that there is an undistinguished focal point there, only afterward when we recognize that the initial situation did not permit of a focussing on any factor.

When we isolate the self as that which marks itself out from all else, we contrast it with what it had been as imperceptibly merged with all else. This could indifferently be oneself indefinitely spread out, or all else coming together. It is an individual only when made determinate as a finite locus for what is clearly set in contradistinction to all else. An individual is primarily a kind of me, you, part of a we, others, or an I, none entirely separated from the others.

When questions are asked and efforts are made to answer them, one has already moved into the I, and has done so by emphasizing one or the other of a number of possible ways in which the withdrawn self could make a basic indeterminacy more determinate. The more sharply we distinguish the finalities from the individual with which they are initially intertwined in a single indeterminate whole, the more surely we make the individual their single unity, a focal point at which they can be together, while they continue to enjoy the status of distinct finalities to be reached from the position of that unitary focal point.

The foregoing account does not make clear whether an epistemological, an ontological, or a twofold epistemological-ontological point is being made. Is there an actual indeterminacy or is it one relative to our knowing? Is the achievement of determinacy a coming to know what is already there, or is it the production of determinate items? Or is coming to know also a way in which something is made to be? All the alternatives seem plausible. The epistemic stays close to the act of discovery; the ontological attends to the fact that something objective is being learned about, and tests what we are claiming; the double-edged approach allows one to see that knowing is not without its implications for what is.

I am now inclined to take the last of these alternatives, for it does seem to be the case that an individual achieves a certain kind of reality when he engages in a particular kind of adventure. We need not suppose, though, that he has no ontological status apart from that which he has either as a determinate or as an indeterminate object of knowledge. He does merge with others within an indeterminate whole; the attainment of some determination there is not the outcome of an epistemic inquiry or activity, any more than it is the outcome of the outcome of a practical act, an experiencing, and so forth.

Each way of engaging in determinate activity produces a different set of determinations, but these determinations are all claimed of the same indeterminate. My engaging in an inquiry allows me to formulate a cognitive account of the indeterminate with which I begin; the indeterminate with which I begin, however, is not the indeterminate only for inquiry, but an indeterminate for other types of effort as well. While I engage in an epistemic inquiry, I continue to have the other dimensions in their original indeterminate union with it, but as approached from the position of the relatively determinate inquiry in which I now engage. It is just as true to say that the inquiry is giving a meaning to an objective, residual indeterminacy as it is to say that a known indeterminacy has a focus in an objective, relatively determinate, actual inquiring.

March 22

The absolute, most primitive beginning is a singular juncture of indeterminacies—the *ungrounded,* the *undiscriminated,* the *general,* the *incomplete,* and the *vague.* This juncture leans toward one or the other of these indeterminacies at different times; it never is marked off from them nor alters them. It is distinguishable from them and permeates them at the same time, but with varying emphases.

If we take account of the singular juncture as contrasted with what is being joined, we get the individual as the indeterminate union of all the indeterminacies—but that is a position at which one arrives. Similarly, if we take account of the different indeterminacies, each needing clarification in different ways and with different results, we get separate items each of which could be the indeterminate center for another type of investigation—but this, too, is a position arrived at.

In the beginning, an individual is not separable from indeterminacies. Nor is it separable from what else is found to be part of it when it is separated from those indeterminacies. Also, those indeterminacies, while not separable from the individual at the beginning, are not separable from themselves as having depths. The individual and the indeterminacies it has joined together are all grounded, distinctive, unduplicable, complete, and unified, the individual juncture having them in a self-maintained, the final indeterminacies having them in an eternal form.

The beginning is moved away from in a clarifying passage toward the individual or toward the indeterminacies. If we go in one direction we have the indeterminacies solidified and at the service of the individual; if we go in the other direction we get the finalities all together, with the individual serving as an area spreading to and into them all. The passage in either direction proceeds primarily in depth, as a diversification, as a directionalized structured move, as that which is being undergone, or as being governed by its terminus. There is no choosing of the passage; one is always stressing one or the other type of passage toward the individual or the finalities, to end at a position which is relatively determinate with respect to the original beginning. That relatively determinate result is an indeterminacy with respect to what else is to be done; it is a beginning of a more specialized and controllable activity.

A passage is one of a number of possible types, whether it is moving toward the individual or the finalities, and whether it is doing this in depth, diversifying, directed, experienced, or controlled by the terminus. It could be a way in which a self-maintenance, a conditioning, a thinking, an undergoing, or an evaluation was taking place. Initially, then, we have an absolute beginning which is moved away from toward any one of a number of entities so as to achieve a certain type of result and in such a way that the result is concrete, that in which others participate, meaningful, lived through, or assessive. The passage ends with the individual functioning as the juncture of the others.

In *Beyond All Appearances* I moved intellectually in depth to a withdrawn individual; in *Modes of Being* I moved intellectually to a diversification of the original indeterminacy to reach determinate finalities; in "First Considerations," with its stress on a rational process of evidencing, I moved intellectually to engage in inquiry; and in *The God We Seek* I moved intellectually to take account of what was being experienced of all the finalities together. In the present discussion I am moving intellectually to the original beginning where all the items are together as at a point beyond which I can not go further. None of these efforts is deliberately engaged in, in contradistinction with the others. I now at last see, as a result of the present consideration of the nature of an absolute beginning, what I had been doing before.

Arriving at the individual by thinking in depth, I see him to be indeterminate with respect to what is next to be done. He must occupy himself with possession, discrimination, proof, completion, or synthesis. If he asks a question, he is occupied with completion, and I, in assuming the burden of the question, make myself be one occupied intellectually with the act of completion.

The progress from an absolute beginning is the outcome of stresses and moves begun without thought; it might take any number of directions and have any one of a number of characteristics. The movement ends with the individual in a state of indeterminacy involved with other indeterminate items. Once again, there are unprepared moves out of this state until one finds oneself in fact at some distinct position which is indeterminate in itself but held away from other factors, thereby setting the stage for a systematic, controlled way of arriving at those other factors. If we are concerned with a philosophical account, this position will be our official beginning. This will be contrastable with other possible official beginnings which, starting with the same withdrawn individual and even occupied with the same entities, deals with them not as topics for thought but as that which is to be experienced, diversified, and so forth. I suppose it is proper to say that every individual engages in short moves in all the different ways at different times in the course of even a day's living, but it is not until one of them is focussed on and kept at steadily that we have thinking, practice, and the like. We do not have a thinking, and so forth, which is systematic and characteristic of a particular type of inquiry or work until we have some degree of self-consciousness, or at least a persistent continuation in the face of temptations to go in other directions.

March 23

Indeterminacy is only one type of inchoateness. It is oriented toward an individual who, by withdrawing or advancing and then in a certain direction and manner, makes himself relatively determinate, preparatory to other acts of determination. The other types are:

A] *Disorder.* I have elsewhere remarked on the fact that disorder is an excess of intermixed orders. Each of these orders has a definiteness to it, and maintains itself apart from the others; but they are encountered as not yet separated out from one another, and we have no clear understanding as to just which items belong with which items. The disorder is a reflection, I think, of the fecundity of Substance. Indeterminacy is a feature of it, an expression of an epistemic state of affairs, for apart from us, the orders are distinct.

B] *Emptiness.* Phenomenologically speaking, there are as many kinds of emptinesses as there are situations in which they can be located. There are the empty spaces in sculpture, the entrances and exits of architecture, the intervening spaces between buildings and sculptures, the spaces and untouched areas in painting, the silences in music and theatre, the standing stills of dancing, the pauses and stops in poetry and in prose. There is also the waiting of the baseball player at bat, the hockey player in the penalty box, the tensed getting ready for a race, and so on. One lives through these emptinesses; each is what it is because of what it is environed by in fact or in imagination. It can be contrasted with disorder as silence to noise. But, as we shall see, there are other types of inchoateness, precluding a comparison with disorder as the only possible.

C] *Unintelligibility.* Students of logic put great emphasis on the conditions for well-formed expressions. Paradoxes both in logic and elsewhere are often characterized as nonsensical, meaningless, unintelligble. I will use these terms equivalently, though they obviously intend items which are different from one another. Unintelligibility reflects an emphasis on possibility, the ideal, meaning. Disorder and emptiness could be held to be unintelligible, and unintelligibility could be dealt with as allowing for an excess of interpretations or Meaning (as is the case with a contradiction) or as an emptiness in which nothing is in fact being said.

D] *Incompleteness.* This is the inchoateness of what is in the process of sorting itself out; it is the state which Whitehead has focussed on when speaking of the impossibility of subdividing a single moment of coming to be. But a process can also be of indefinite length; all the while there will be a falling short of a settlement of what is. We can say that it exhibits disorder until it comes to a close, an emptiness in that nothing is as yet accomplished, or an unintelligibility since there is nothing fixed or capable of being articulated. It is also possible to speak of disorder, emptiness, and unintelligibility as types of incompleteness, the first failing to complete a distinguishing of the orders, the second failing to have content which would fill it up, merely having environing content spill over into it, and the third not yet living up to the prescriptions and conditions which govern intelligibility. The emphasis on incompleteness is toward Existence with its extensionality.

E] *Vagueness.* Here we have various items together in such a way that what otherwise would be a contradiction does not arise; the items merge into one another, as twilight merges into day and night. The borders between items are blurred and there is no clear distinguishing of any of them. Disorder is vague in the sense that we do not yet see which are the orders to be marked out; emptiness is vague since it unites what is environing it on various sides; unintelligibility is vague in that it allows for alternative distinct interpretations; and incompleteness is vague because its beginning and ending are not yet sorted out. It is also true that the vague is disordered, since it does not allow distinct items to be distinct; empty in that it has no room for the distinct; unintelligible since it violates the law of contradiction, or allows it no play; and incomplete in that it itself will be given a definiteness as the vague or will be dissolved into distinct components.

Is it true of these five, as it is of indeterminacy, that there are five varieties to each, and that in fact they are the loci of five special cases of themselves? Does disorder, for example, contain five types of disorder all somehow together? I see no reason to suppose so. Do emptiness, unintelligibility, incompleteness, and vagueness have five varieties each, somehow together in a primary form of emptiness, and so forth? It does not seem so. Yet it surely is true that disorder and the others can be disorders, and so forth, of or in individuals, Substance, Being, and so forth.

There can, of course, be disorders within a larger disorder, an emptiness within which other emptinesses can be distinguished, an unintelligibility containing unintelligibilities, an incompleteness containing incompletenesses, and a vagueness which has components which are themselves vague. And the contained items in these various cases could conceivably be together in disorderly, and so forth, ways. But unlike the indeterminacy of the individual, all five reflect the dominant presence of a finality, not as it in fact is but as an object of inquiry, action, and so forth. The finalities, apparently, are self-contained, even when they act on or are acted on by actualities; any blurrings they are found to have are due to the actualities. There can be many varieties of these types of inchoateness, as we saw in relation with emptiness.

But is it not true that the different finalities can function as conditions for the rest? Does that not mean that each may provide a kind of inchoateness for them without making a difference to them? If an individual is a one for the finalities and can be in various stages of indeterminacy with respect to them, should this not be possible to the finalities? I think not. The action of the finalities on one another is a way of uniting them in one move and in a definite way, in contrast with the actualities which stand away from and approach the finalities with various degrees of success.

When an actuality is in some inchoate situation with the finalities, do those finalities themselves exercise their characteristic ways of being ones for one another? If an actuality is indeterminately in a mental state, for example, about to attend to Being, is Being then being subject to an ordering, made intelligible, completed, and clarified? It seems so, but only in a derivative sense, for they are all together via the unity of the actuality, and only within that togetherness are able to provide conditions for one another.

March 24

Determinations specialize something indeterminate which could have been specialized in another way. Wherever we have determinations we can in principle therefore always envisage an antecedent indeterminacy. This need not have existed prior to the determinations, but nevertheless can be said to constitute an absolute beginning in that it does not presuppose some prior act which could have gone in a different direction with different results. It is, of course, arrived at from a determinate position and in a determinate way. The 'pre-thematic' is a 'thematic' outcome. Let it be the outcome of an intellectual inquiry. Then we would have to say that an absolute beginning is the outcome of an intellectual inquiry. This will not place us at the absolute beginning but will let us know it. Our knowledge will be determinate knowledge of what is not determinate. This means that we will reach the indeterminate, not in its full concreteness, but as envisaged from a special angle. There is no reason to believe that the absolute beginning exists in any other form but that of a determinate outcome of a determinate intellectual inquiry. Still, it is good to know, particularly since the indeterminate is encountered beyond the determinate agency by which we arrive at it.

We can recognize that there is an indeterminacy out of which our intellectual inquiry issued by noting that the inquiry is not altogether separable from experiencing, withdrawal, submission, self-assertiveness (reflecting the involvement in Existence, Substance, Unity, Being), and also that there is an indeterminacy which is fringing the determinate inquiry in which we are engaged. In the one way we are alert to alternative accompaniments, in the other to a generic feature we are specializing. The indeterminacy, even if one in which we had previously been, need not have been perfect. While immersed in it and, therefore, not altogether in ourselves or involved with others, we may have some bias in one direction or the other. It need not be supposed, therefore, that we were ever in a stage where there was absolute indeterminacy, without any biases or strains in any direction. We need not even suppose that we were ever in anything but some particular state of determinacy. But whether we were in such a state or not, we can understand it as constituting an absolute beginning in terms of which we can understand the limitations and the alternatives to the position from which we consciously start out.

If we were to start with some primal indeterminacy, we would have the problem of accounting for the determinacies. It is only because we already know that there are actualities and finalities in the indeterminacy, and that we can advance or withdraw, that we are in a position to say that the determinations are to be understood as achievements.

March 25

One might maintain that the indeterminate state, an absolute beginning, is the only true reality, and that every determination of it is arbitrary, a kind of interpretation which falsifies precisely because it moves away. One will then end as a sceptic unless somehow one is able to get back to the beginning. One way of doing this might be by trying to throw oneself into the state of indeterminacy, perhaps by refusing to engage in any thought, and by withdrawing into oneself to such a radical extent that one merges with what is the supposedly ultimate indeterminacy. Are these not acts of determination? Is not the losing of oneself in a final indeterminate something achieved, an outcome? One who held that the ultimate reality or 'truth' was indeterminacy presumably would have to arrive at the truth by a process of determination, but find that this was taken over, possessed, converted by the indeterminacy to become one with it. The determinate truth of indeterminacy would be made to lose its determinateness by being absorbed in that of which it was true. Not only is there no reason for supposing that there is an aboriginal indeterminacy, but the absorption by it of the truth claimed of it would free that truth from its determinateness. If it did free it, how could one say that it was a truth of the indeterminate?

One must distinguish a beginning *of, for, from,* and *in.* A beginning *of* makes reference to what is to follow as part of itself; a beginning *for,* instead, refers to what is to follow as something apart from it; a beginning *from* takes account of the fact that the beginning is arrived at or at least bounded by what has some definiteness and antecedent nature; a beginning *in,* finally, already is away from the starting point and involved with what is to be. It seems to me now that the absolute beginning is a beginning *for,* since it awaits determinations which are to be introduced to produce something else. A beginning *of* seems to presuppose a determination in some direction. A beginning *from* obviously takes account of something determinate. A beginning *in*, like a beginning *of*, though not separable from an enterprise, is already on its way; it is the beginning *of* carried further, without ceasing to be a beginning. It is what the absolute beginning is in fact, since that absolute beginning is always biased in some direction.

Does a beginning remain throughout? Does it become refined, a kind of determinate indeterminacy, the more surely we are engaged in making it determinate, not because we in fact transform it but because the determination which moves away from it affects it, backward as it were?

Another series of questions is raised by Hegel: Is an absolute beginning abstract? Does it become a beginning only when one arrives at the determinate end it makes possible? Is it always present in the background of the determinations? It would be abstract, only if it could not have a status apart from our consideration of it. It does not become a beginning only at the end of a quest or become such a beginning in a more basic or definite a way, except so far as the subsequent determinations affect it. But the determinations which we engage in may be creative, bringing us to something else. The determinations will then be not determinations of or in it, but determinations which are achieved by adding to it. We can say that indeterminacy is always present until we arrive at a position where we have pure determinateness and nothing else. But this seems possible only in the absolute past or in the abstract world of logical symbols.

March 26

When in the course of a historic investigation I get back to the beginning of some great event, I do so from the perspective of what has since occurred. But what I may want to learn about is the beginning as that which had occurred at that time, and thus as that which had not been specialized as the beginning of this which I now know as an end. My return would have to be to the beginning *for*, and not to the beginning *of* what occurred afterward. But if I get to the beginning *for*, and thus to what is cut off from what is to follow, I still am not where I had been earlier, for that earlier position was one which did give way to an activity that ended in the answer or in that with which I began my investigation. The beginning *for,* which I arrive at in history and presumably also when I try to find an absolute beginning, must be that which gives way to the beginning *for* what in fact ensues. One way of seeing how this is possible is to acknowledge that once we arrive at a beginning *for,* we relax the attitude we had assumed in our arrival at it, so that it is taken up by the beginning *for* which thereby becomes converted into a beginning *of.* Is this an epistemological answer, one which needs to be supplemented by an ontological? Martin De Nys suggests to me that this is the case. But does not the process of getting back to the beginning, whether this be a conceived or present indeterminacy or something in the past, have to be epistemological, since I cannot recover the actual past or the radically indeterminate?

Why should my relaxation of the conditions governing my arrival at a beginning *for* be conditions which convert this into a beginning *of,* even a beginning *of,* viewed epistemologically only? And why should the conditions which terminate at the beginning *for* be turned around to become the conditions which transform this in to a later beginning *of?*

When we move back toward a beginning as a root indeterminacy or as an antecedent, we do so from a base in what we have now. As starting from that base we arrive at a beginning *for.* Relaxing our efforts allows for the attaching of the entire structure to the beginning *for,* thereby enabling that beginning to be a beginning *of.* The relaxing allows the structure to become ontologized. It is to be noted that the beginning *of,* which then results, is not the beginning *of* which in fact brought one to the determinate present from which the inquiry was started; if it did, we would be doing the entire past over again. The beginning *of,* which we make possible, is a product and not the actual beginning *of* what had occurred.

The beginning *for,* that we isolate as a result of reflection, was initially continuous with the beginning *of,* since it is a beginning *for* only as fixated at some moment. When we attend to it as a beginning *for,* we concentrate on it as separated from a beginning *of.* When we relax and enable ourselves to have a beginning *of,* we obtain a formal or abstract version of the actual beginning that took place in the actual transition from a beginning *for* into a beginning *of.*

If one takes literally "In the beginning was the Word" one must say that the 'Word' is approached from the vantage point of a present finite moment, and arrived at as an eternal beginning *for*. But if it be a genuine beginning, that eternity must give way to a beginning *of* whatever ensues in the course of time. To know the beginning which in fact took place we must convert the beginning *for* the 'Word' (or logos) as a state in eternity, into a beginning *of* an actual temporal world.

March 2 7

Everyone has some streak of meanness, smallness, pettiness. Nixon gave us a public exhibition of these traits, epitomizing them and exhibiting their consequences both on himself and on others. Most of us despise him for it. Is this not in part because he makes most evident a despicable side of ourselves? The hatred of him would then be a form of self-hatred, at least in part. If this is correct, must we not say something similar about Hitler, sex molesters, vicious murderers, and the like? I think so. This does not mean that these men are not to be despised, for while the rest of us keep the traits suppressed, give them at best little opportunity to be expressed and to produce their consequences, and are ashamed of what we then exhibit, these men seem to exploit these weaknesses and sometimes to enjoy their consequences. It is not, then, that they have traits that the rest of us do not have, but that they do not control and limit them, do not regret them, do not try to avoid expressing them.

*   *   *

There are silences in the talking films. Those silences are like the pauses in poetry or on the stage, and the rests in music. Is the silent film, a sound film lacking sound, so that its silence is like the silence that occurs inside the sound film at various places, marking pauses and intervals? Or is it, instead, like the silence of a painting, not an absence of something which should be there but an absence of what is irrelevant?

Walter Kerr, in the *Silent Clowns* quotes Mary Pickford as saying that "It would have been more logical if silent pictures had grown out of the talkie instead of the other way round." Kerr understands this to mean that art progresses by omissions, deletions, by leaving more to the imagination. He also remarks that there was sound accompanying both the producing and the presentation of the film, and that the silent film was most successfully developed when it was the vehicle of the great clowns. These observations do not help answer our question, for even if the silent film were developed from the base of a talking film, it would still be possible for it to be a new art. The accompaniments of the silent film, too, might be merely aids, and perhaps should have been dispensed with, particularly if the silent film was successful. And the clowns, instead of making the silent films in a better way than most, or even having a medium which was most suited to them (which is what Kerr suggests), might be the very reason why the silent and the talking films are distinctive types.

A clown, like a king's fool, is any man, every man, no man, one who is not to be identified with except so far as he is exposing what we have kept hidden. He exhibits man without inhibitions. He can be hit and he can adventure, dare, move, and act in ways which are not only outside the physical powers of others, but which reveal him not to be limited and conditioned in the way in which ordinary men are. If we start with him, we can say that he uses the film to exhibit his universality, and for that it is necessary to escape the limitations which language or even music involves.

But is it really the case that there are two distinct arts, the silent film and the talking film? I think we need not go so far. Just as we can take a clown or fool to be an actor in a play, with a special role, analogous to a deus ex machina, so we can take a clown in a silent film to be representing every man, and find that he is most effective in a silent film. The difference between such a film and a talking one of today would lie in the pacing and in the amount of montaging that the former involves, particularly in order to exaggerate the nature of the acts in which the clown engages. We need not, however, go on to maintain that a silent film is a sound film lacking sound, or that it is one for which sound is irrelevant. Rather, we should say that it is a sound film which is so made as to turn sound into an irrelevancy.

If this suggestion is accepted, it seems reasonable to look for similar cases in the other arts. Can we, for example, speak of the standing of a dancer, not merely as that which is environed by movement, but as being performed in such a way as to make the movement irrelevant? To do this, the standing of the dancer must have a completeness to it, not by virtue of the movements that environ it before and after, but by virtue of the kind of standing it is. Similarly, there would similarly be pauses in drama which are 'pregnant', rests in music which had their own vitality, beginning, and ending, and so on. It would still be possible to maintain that there is an environing fullness on which the emptiness is parasitical. The present contention adds to this only the consideration that the environed emptiness could have its own beginning and ending within the limits that the sound provides. Pickford's observation should be taken to refer to the limits which silence has of itself; the view that sound is an essential part of film could still be maintained, though the sound would in these cases be external accompaniments or externally defined borders within which the silence occurred.

The reference to a clown as being any man, and so far no man in particular, ties the observations about the film to the observations about Nixon, Hitler, and others who exploit the vices we keep hidden or repressed, more or less. A clown, too, lets us see ourselves, but instead of letting us see something vicious, allows us to see something foolish, ridiculous in fact, or what we conceive as the antithesis to the determinations which we have imposed on what might be called 'man in general'.

A silent film, unlike a rest in music, has a development. Something occurs over the course of its existence, a fact which points up the collaborative nature of the art. This, perhaps, is too easy an answer. Might not a musician go through the movement of blowing on a horn, using a bow, playing a piano over a developed silence? It seems reasonable to maintain this. Can something analogous be done in connection with sculpture, painting, and other arts? Yes. A sculpture could conceivably have its indentations and holes and other emptinesses, such as the space between the fingers or hand, and shoulder, or head, or feet, given a distinctive background, requiring one to live through them in a distinctive way. A painting's empty space has a color, if only the color of the canvas and, as a consequence, has its own internal rhythm, tensions, and resolutions.

March 28

A beginning *of* is indeterminate because it merges in an indeterminate continuation of itself. It is inseparable from a process of becoming determinate in one of a number of alternative ways. A becoming *for,* though an indeterminate in itself, is a determinate entity, cut off from the beginning *of,* and what this merges into. When we, by relaxation, allow our approach to the beginning *for* to become attached to, and thereby make it possible for us to have a grasp of a beginning *of* which in fact took place, we no longer have a beginning *for.* Yet, within the beginning *of,* one can always isolate a more indeterminate core, from which position the beginning could have been a beginning *of* in a new direction.

Though there never was a beginning *for* at the beginning, and though there is a beginning *for* only in an isolated determinate past moment, or as the counterpart of some claim, there could be a genuine indeterminate beginning *of,* if there were alternative ways of proceeding. Without such alternatives, a beginning *of* would be indeterminate in the sense of awaiting the provision of determinate units to be added to it; it would be an indeterminate beginning *of* in not having the supplements that are to be provided. In effect, it would be just a beginning *for,* isolated within a larger complex in which it was just the first of a number of determinates.

A beginning *for* which could have been made determinate in the form of any number of beginnings *of* (each with its own progressive determination of an indetermination inseparable from the beginning *of*) though internally indeterminate, is a determinate unit which is externally related to an indeterminacy which the beginning *of,* that had occurred, had made determinate in one way. The transformation of a beginning *for* into a beginning *of* is one with the obtaining of a more restricted indeterminacy out of the indeterminacy which was externally related to the beginning *for.* From the position of the beginning *for,* there are many possible beginnings *of* into which it could be merged; one of these is achieved by tracing back to the beginning from the position of the end attained; others are obtained by imaginatively determining the beginning *for.* The acknowledgment of a mere beginning *for* allows for any one of an indefinite set of alternative partial determinations of the indeterminacy which follows on the beginning *for.*

In order to translate an expression from one language to another we must arrive at a position analogous to a beginning *for* as it stands away from the means for arriving at it. But, evidently, we are at an indeterminate position before we translate; there is an indeterminacy appropriate to the very language with which we begin just so far as we have retreated from it toward a position from which we might be able to translate it. It is a position which is close to that which we occupy when we initiate a new set of expressions in our language. Both when we do this and when we translate, we introduce a process of determination in one direction.

March 30

To get to color from red we can proceed in one of seven ways:

A] We can move to an individual as indeterminate, and thus to it as having some color or other, which it will be able to determine in other ways besides red. Such a movement, as was previously indicated, has a number of subdivisions, depending on whether we wish to move to the individual by itself, to it as not yet clearly distinguished from the finalities, from others, and so forth.

B] We can move to an inchoateness, as providing many possible groundings for the red. As deprived of those grounds the red is just a color as part of a localized Substance. (A little while back I spoke of inchoateness as though it were the mark of all the different lacks, and referred to Substance as a kind of disorder. But this would be to speak of Substance as it functions to relate actualities, whereas I am now considering it as operative on individual actualities. Perhaps it is better to use 'disorder' to refer to all the kinds of lacks together, so that when Substance is dealt with even in its relational, affiliative guise, it will still be taken to be a kind of inchoateness so long as the different possible ways in which items could be affiliated are not sorted out.)

C] The emptiness of Being will be the result of a movement away from the differentiations which different actualities enable it to have. Being in itself will be empty of every kind of determination, and will allow red to be reduced to a color that has no actual locus in a particular individual.

D] What is usually thought of as abstraction, the losing of the specificity of the red so as to end with just color, is only one way in which color can be obtained. It involves a movement toward Possibility itself, as beyond all specifications. Since color is one kind of limited domain, the movement will stop far short of Possibility itself.

E] The incompleteness of Existence is moved toward by moving away from the particular beginnings and endings which individual entities provide. If one of these be red, or a reddening, or a perceived red—the one in space, the other in time, and the third in both together, or in a third, dynamic setting—the move toward Existence will go toward color as that which has not been completed in the sense of not yet having a foothold in what has a beginning or an ending.

F] The vagueness of Unity is due to the fact that it does not allow of exclusive disjuncts of whatever might be distinguished within it. Color would be a special case of Unity, a subdivision of it which we have conceived but which, like Unity itself, does not allow for the separation of the different colors from one another.

G] Red as a color is the outcome of the interplay of the expressions of actualities and the different finalities. If those expressions be made less intensive, not allowed to be as determinate and particularized as they in fact are, we get 'color somehow' or 'related color' as a consequence. It is to take the actuality, not in its full indeterminacy, where we could not distinguish what it is by itself from what it is as involved with the finalities, but only as indeterminate in such an involvement; and it is to take the finalities all together, since it is as together that they initially interplay with the actuality's expressions.

Do actualities and finalities come together solely in their determinate expressions, or do they at the same time come together in more and more fainter ways? The question takes us in a new direction. Conceivably, we could move closer to each as ultimately real, even though our characterizations left us with what was one form of a disorder. The question, too, leads to a consideration of richer appearances, of which qualities are only aspects or special forms. It forces us to face the fact that though the expressions of realities are attenuations of those realities, those very attenuations might have stronger and weaker forms, more intensive and less intensive ways of being, apparently at the same time, since we have no warrant for supposing that there is first a juncture of the weaker and then of the stronger forms, or conversely.

A whole new line of inquiry is now opened up. It ought eventually be brought into relationship with the fact that a determinate item in the cosmos could be conceived of as indeterminate, and thus as 'a unit in the cosmos'; and that the qualifications which are due to the action of the finalities on actualities could be taken to be indefinite by having the action of the finalities minimized at the actualities.

April 2

It is not possible to get to a beginning which we are sure is absolute, and this for a double reason. We will approach that beginning from the position of particular determinate situations, and our approach will itself be determinate. Since the determinate approach is one of relaxing or rejecting the determinations with which we begin, the outcome, one might say, is simply freed of those initial determinations. But the relaxing or rejecting will be a rejecting of these determinations and not of some others, and may be affected by that fact. And even if it were not, it would still be true that we were approaching the indeterminate from one direction. If this one direction is simply identical with the getting rid of the determinations, it should be possible to say that we do get to the indeterminate free of all the limitations which are due to the fact that we started with such and such determinations and therefore proceeded with such and such relaxations or rejections. But there is still a difficulty:

Whatever we may arrive at as indeterminate—even if it be no longer affected by the fact that we had started at some determinate and then proceeded in a determinate manner to free ourselves of the initial limitation—will not be known to be without determinations of its own, for all we could do was to get rid of the determinations with which we started. Though we can arrive at the acknowledgment of an actuality as diffusely interlinked with whatever else there be by considering weaker forms of the ways in which these are interlinked, or can arrive at a diffusion of the expressions of an actuality which contrast with specific expressions of it, we do not yet arrive at the actuality as anything more than a source of strong and weak interlinked expressions, or of expressions as diffusely together. If we acknowledge the fact that diffused linkages and diffused expressions are themselves determinate modes of expression, contrasting with stronger forms of the expressions and with specific expressions, we will have to move one further step to arrive at an indeterminate actuality. That actuality will be a source of weak and strong expressions, and of diffuse and separate expressions. Though indeterminate with respect to which of these will be exhibited, that actuality may still have determinations of its own.

If we attend to an actuality in itself, we are not forced to consider what is radically indeterminate, but only what is without the determinations which require a selection to be made or a creation to be instituted so that some one particular determination, if only in the guise of a diffusion of a number of expressions, be exhibited. In itself it might well have determinations which are constitutive, or even inwardly produced, and from which a start must be made. Making those inward determinations into indeterminacies would be tantamount to making an actuality into some actuality or other. Similar observations could be made with repect to the inchoateness of the different finalities. Each one of these could be recognized to be indeterminate relative to the determinate expressions it produces or the kind of oppositions with which it is involved, without being denied all determination. The being of each could conceivably be involved with some definiteness, making it the kind of entity it is. The supposition that there is some primal One out of which the finalities issue or to which they are subject is in effect an outcome of the attempt to free ourselves from the various determinations characteristic of the different finalities, particularly if those finalities are viewed, in a Neoplatonic fashion, as issuing out of that One.

Spinoza did not suppose that the primal One was without determination, though he did affirm that determination and negation were the same. His God or nature had an infinite number of attributes (to take the objective interpretation of those attributes) and this precludes it from being without determination. Spinoza was evidently thinking of determinations as conditions imposed from without, and thereby limiting the range of an entity. But determinations can be unities maintained in contrast with anything else—in Spinoza, in contrast with the modes.

Must we not characterize every thing from without, and therefore give it alien determinations? How can we speak of what it is in itself, even if we grant that it is then determinate and not radically inchoate? The difficulty is insuperable if the determinations remain external. But if inward determinations are external determinations unified, with the unity dominating them, a thing in itself could be characterized in terms of predicates which reflect other entities, but itself understood as being determinate by virtue of the way in which it brings two sets of determinations together.

An actuality is an individual because and so far as its difference from all other actualities is united with its distinctness from the finalities. As different from the other actualities, it is the various finalities epitomized, while as distinct from the finalities it is the effects of the other actualities epitomized. As a consequence, it could be said to be determinate in itself as different from all actualities because it is a locus of the finalities, and as determinately distinct from all the finalities because it is a locus for the other actualities. The finalities in turn can be said to be determinate with respect to one another and with respect to actualities; as the one they are merely different and as the other merely distinct. But now I am beginning to lose my way again.

April 3

An actuality in itself has relativized features, due to the action and presence of other actualities. It possesses those features internally within the position of a unit distinct from the finalities. At the same time, it is also affected by the finalities; as such it stands away from other actualities as different from them, a difference which is controlled by the finalities as affecting it. The actuality is constantly producing its own unity in two ways. It is engaged in the process of uniting difference and distinctness, and it is engaged in the process of having the difference controlled by the absorbed finalities and the distinctness controlling the features due to other actualities. When the actuality expresses itself with reference to others, it is engaged in a process of self-diversification; when it is expressed with reference to the finalities it functions as a unit.

A finality in itself is a singular, not a derivative as an actuality's unity is. It, too, though, is approachable from the outside in two ways. It is qualified by the other finalities, and gives a role to the expressions of the actualities, subjecting them to its characteristic inchoateness. A finality, too, expresses itself with reference to the other finalities, modifying their import, at the same time that it expresses itself in relation to actualities, determining itself so as to give them a context. So far, it is self-diversifying. An actuality is self-diversifying with respect to other actualities; a finality is self-diversifying with respect to all the actualities. An actuality functions as a unit with respect to each of the finalities; a finality acts as such a unit with respect to the other finalities.

Using red and color as illustrations, we can say that in the case of an actuality   A] the actuality is red in a world where there is light and other conditions which enable it to possess red in relation to others conditioning it,   B] the red is intelligible, extended, and so forth, because of the way in which the finalities operate on the actuality,   C] in itself the actuality is color as not yet sorted out into components, and thus is indeterminate in different ways, D] it expresses itself as a dense color in the form of a red,   E] it presents itself to the finalities as color, and   F] it will be given a particular determination as red by the finalities, which relate it in characteristic ways.

A finality is inchoate. Beginning from there, we can see that it is qualified by other finalities so that its inchoateness has a limited role, and in turn modifies their import, delimiting their characteristic inchoateness. At the same time, it finds a place within its inchoateness for the specific expressions of actualities, and provides a context for the expressions of the actualities so that the red can be exhibited in a context. In the latter act it overcomes its inchoateness by providing a context.

Unlike actualities, which could have expressed themselves in other ways, a finality has no alternative expressions. When it modifies the others it does so in a single act; when it provides a context it allows its own inchoateness to be exhibited in the form of just one context. In compensation, though, the context has depth to it and becomes more and more inchoate as it becomes more and more merged with the finality itself.

An actuality in itself is in disequilibrium, a finality is not. An actuality is always verging toward others or toward the finalities, but never succeeding in being oriented exclusively toward one or the other. A finality in itself is self-contained but inchoate, and sorts out its multiple dimensions only with the help of the actualities, at the same time that it is able to be subjected, as a special kind of inchoateness, to the other finalities.

An actuality in itself is indeterminate relative to what it could express. Its individuality is a single, undivided condensation of difference and distinctness, each sustaining the other. Its density is subject to various types of inchoateness at the same time that it expresses that density through the different types of inchoateness and thereby shows itself to have individuality, rights, and other marks of the presence of localized, epitomized finalities.

As at the equilibrium point between other actualities and the finalities, an actuality is not indeterminate; it is such only as a relativized result of the relaxation of the determinations it received from others, or which had been expressed by itself. It is lush, fecund, rich, and thus more rather than less intensive and concrete than what it is in relation to other actualities or the finalities. We can, though, refer to its indeterminacy when we refer to the way in which its epitomized use of the finalities governs and is also subject to the difference it has from other actualities. Finalities, too, are fecund, but not as outcomes. Each is inchoate, and gives itself inwardly a multiplicity of determinations by the way in which it absorbs the affects of the different actualities in itself.

God, some theologians have said, is superabundant. This is an idea similar to what I have been calling inchoateness, but it is restricted to only one finality. And no provision is made for the fact that the different components are there sorted out by virtue of his accommodation of the actualities. We, too, are superabundant, but this is a derivative result, and can be subject to limitation when, instead of expressing ourselves under epitomized forms of the different finalities, we express ourselves through them in the guise of beings with rights, identity, and the like.

April 4

If we take the finalities one by one we distinguish them as different kinds of inchoate persistent realities: disorder, emptiness, unintelligibility, incompleteness, and vagueness. But just what these mean and how these are to be articulated awaits the understanding of them as set in contrast with intrusive actualities. They are then to be seen as accommodating those actualities in different ways. Substance allows them to be in multiple relations to one another within its own inchoate disorder; Being, instead, keeps itself empty by maintaining the actualities at different distances from itself, depending on the degree to which they would make it filled out in a particular way; Possibility generalizes them to make them be variables of different ranges; Existence brings them within a complex extensionality where they provide distinctions but no divisions; and Unity transforms them to the degree that is needed for them to be reduced to a nuanced factor in it at the same time that they continue to be in some position in an objective value hierarchy.

If it be allowed that actualities have a double role in relation to Unity, being both reduced in it as nuances and standing outside it in an hierarchy, must we not say something similar for the actualities with reference to the other finalities? Or must we instead say that the double role is the result of a shift from a consideration of Unity in itself to a consideration of its effect on the actualities as they are apart from it? The latter seems to be the case. If so, the last way of speaking, in the above paragraph, about Unity, should be altered so that Unity is said merely to accommodate the different actualities by reducing them to mere nuances.

The consideration of Unity brings to mind the controversy in Catholic circles about the so-called economic Trinity, which is the Trinity as it is expressed in the world, in contrast with the immanent Trinity which is what God is supposed to be in himself. Some thinkers hold that there is only an economic Trinity; but the established view is that this Trinity depends on the presence of an immanent Trinity, though the latter does not allow for the divisions that the former does. The point I have been making, carried over into this controversy, would require one to say that the immanent Trinity is to be understood in terms of the economic, and then only because that economic was made possible by a world. The return to God from the position of an economic Trinity, and thus one which was not cut off from the world as making for the primary divisions in that Trinity, would be a return to a reality which accommodated that Trinity in the guise of a vague and therefore inseparable plurality of items that were together as nuances there. Starting with such an immanent Trinity one could then go on to try to understand it as expressing itself and therefore as being diversified in the shape of an economic Trinity involved with the world in a threefold way.

An actuality contrasts with the finalities in having its inchoateness in the form of an indeterminacy which requires an expression of epitomized finalities through features relating to the presence of the actuality with other actualities—or the converse, the expression of references to the finalities under the limitations provided by the actuality's differences from other actualities. In the first way, an actuality expresses its individuality, rights, meaning, identity, and value, each of which is indeterminate as a kind of disorder, emptiness, unintelligibility, incompleteness, and vagueness. In the second way, an actuality attends to conditions and thus to the finalities but with a limited biased emphasis on itself as standing apart from all the other actualities. As the locus of the finalities, the actuality is just distinct from all of them; as a focus for the other actualities it is just different from them. As able to be the locus of the finalities, the actuality is a unit different from all others; and as able to be a focus for other actualities, it is a unit distinct from all the finalities. As both locus and focus it could be said to be an individual, but then this individuality should be set in contrast with its substantiality (which I have sometimes spoken of as 'individuality').

An actuality is red as a unit standing in contrast with other actualities. To arrive at the actuality as merely colored, and thus as able to have some other color than the red it now has as a result of its own expressions and interplay with other actualities, one moves into it as indeterminate, not as being less intensive than it had been as red, but as more, and thus as fecund. The actuality in its indeterminacy is colored; its being colored comes to expression in the guise of this color or other. It is a disordered individual making itself manifest in the form of one particular color so as to be in a distinct order with reference to other actualities; an empty bearer of rights making itself manifest in the form of one particular color so as to be copresent with others; an unintelligible source of meanings whose particular color expression will enable it to be intelligibly understood in relation to others; an incomplete identical being which expresses itself as this or that colored reality in the course of becoming a single determinate reality over the course of its career; or a vague, undiversified unity which expresses itself with such and such a color and thereby is able to use its unity as a mode of evaluating that and other expressions of itself. Such expressions occur always. Emphasis is constantly on our expressing the indeterminacy which is exhibited in epitomizings of all the finalities so as to allow those epitomizings to be clarified by means of those expressions.

A man is always ready to express himself as a unit, different from all others, directed toward the finalities. He expresses himself in the world of actualities as an instance of the finalities. He also expresses himself with respect to the finalities as a unit who is not yet expressed in relation to the other actualities, but stands away from them as intensive, indeterminate, relative to them. He expresses himself with reference to other actualities on behalf of epitomized finalities. He also expresses himself with reference to the finalities as a unit with indeterminate capacities for being related to other actualities.

An actuality is doubly indeterminate—indeterminate with reference to other actualities and with reference to the finalities. However, it is never in fact at a midpoint, but always biased in one direction or another, so that it is not only fecund in a twofold way but is always determinately directed in one direction or the other, primarily toward other actualities and secondarily toward the finalities. Concern with the finalities requires withdrawal from most of the involvements with the other actualities and a selection of some mode of dealing with the finalities such as thought, (answering to Possibility), emotion (answering to Existence), intuition (Substance), submission (Unity), and self-maintenance (Being). Any one of these modes, though most suited to one or the other of the finalities, can be followed in dealing with them all.

The finalities, like the actualities, are all fecund in themselves. This means that the emptiness of Being must be understood to be an emptiness of distinctions with a richness of content; and that the generality of Possibility must be understood to be not without meaning but overrun with it, with each variable having all the content of the different values. They will then be seen to be on a footing with the God of tradition, the Substance of a Schopenhauer, and the Existence of a Bergsonian *élan vital*.

(These paragraphs were written after I had my orange juice and coffee and had gone out to buy the Sunday papers. I have now returned from a two-hour walk and finished lunch. On the walk I reflected time and again on what I have here written, and now see the need for some changes.)

An actuality expresses itself in relation to other actualities by a double differentiation of all the epitomized finalities in it. One differentiation consists in having the finalities separately exhibited; the other in having each finality diversified in the form of a plurality of expressions. It is not then correct to say that it manifests a color in all the forms that the finalities make possible; rather, it expresses color as a red or green or whatever in the course of its giving determinacy to Existence as epitomized within it, and thus in the form of an incompletness which needs to be expressed in order to become completed. At the same time that it expresses color, it provides expressions of an epitomized Substance in its individual way of affiliating with others; of Being, in making itself rightfully present in public; of Possibility in its understanding and judging; and of Unity in its evaluations. Its red is not, as was suggested earlier, a way of exhibiting all the epitomized finalities. All of the finalities are exhibited at the same time but in different ways, only one of which is the color. The exhibitions separate out some part of the finalities and diversify this; color, for example, is but one way in which Existence is given determination, and when it is exhibited it is diversified in the form of an extended stretch.

It would be better to speak of Being, not as empty but as full; I had used 'empty' merely to emphasize the fact that there was no diversification within it. But 'full' points up its superabundance. It is better, too, to speak of Possibility as being incomprehensible rather than unintelligible, since this allows for the fact that Possibility, too, is superabundant. The fullness of Being lies in the fact that it takes different positions with reference to the particular realities which it equates, making itself a point of orientation for them in different ways. Nothing can enter into Being. But also, nothing leaves it. It is not to be added to or subtracted from. The richness of Possibility is somewhat more difficult to pin down. Following the lead of Peirce, I have thought of it as the domain of the general, and with him have taken the general to be less determinate than the specific, as though this involved a lack. But if we think of the general on the analogue of white having all the colors of the spectrum within it undifferentiated, Possibility—despite the variables in terms of which the possibilities are to be expressed, and despite the fact that possibilities facing one in the future are lacking in concreteness—will be all the subordinate possibilities preserved, but not yet subject to the law of the excluded middle and thus not permitting of the disjunct separation of the subordinate possibilities. 'Man', to take Peirce's example, will not be either male or female. However, this is not because it is outside all specifications but because it is its specifications together as available for an eventual disjunction, first in the form which does not permit the male and female to be separated, and then in a form which does. The latter is due to the presence of some act or entity outside the possibility; the former is due to the fact that the factors, male and female, are below the level of a disjunction.

A related observation pertains to the Trinity—or more generally to the attributes of God. In him in himself there are no divisions; but he can be taken to encompass all possible limited unities below the level of a conjunction of them, and then to express the conjunction by diverse specifications of the conjoined factors. In the case of Spinoza, one should say (with those who give a subjective interpretation of the attributes) that there is no distinction of any kind in God or nature in itself, at his innermost depth, but that (with those who take an objective interpretation) the attributes are distinguishable from a position, still within God, which is nearer the surface, and that they become distinct only when there are modes, distinct particulars standing away from one another and the different attributes.

Actualities express all their epitomized finalities at the same time, and do so by publicizing limited, separated aspects of them, which are then and there diversified. Finalities, instead, express themselves with reference to all the other finalities and all the actualities at the same time.

Psychoanalysis is built on the acknowledgment that behavior does express an indeterminacy in the individual, an indeterminacy which was initially, as Freud put it, 'polymorphously perverse', (thereby revealing a bias with respect to that polymorphousness, or fecundity). It also attends only to what occurs within the area of actual or possible consciousness. Keeping to that restriction, we can say that when an individual expresses himself as a locus of an epitomized Possibility or Meaning, he does so only in part, and then within the established patterns of articulation. But he never succeeds in making a sharp division and, as a consequence accompanies this with undistinguished products of other layers. It is the discovery of the latter that leads one to 'analyze' out what is contributed by an unconscious. But if it be true that a man also expresses other indeterminate, epitomized finalities, there should also be 'unconscious' forms of these. One's individuality, rights, vitality, and values also have an express, stabilized, public expression, accompanied by 'aberrational' expressions which do not fit within this, and lead one to probe into the individual to learn their source. All the while there will be depths which will not be exhibited at all.

April 5

Men exhibit themselves in steady and in variable ways. They have features such as the color of their eyes, the composition of their bones, the color of their skin, and the shape of their noses, without making an effort to have them; and they speak and act in ways which vary in accord with circumstance and intent. At the same time, they tend to be religious, intellectual, practical, intuitive, or egocentric, sometimes giving little indication that they have any other interests, and when they concentrate in one of these areas, they express themselves with more or less diligence, persistence, effort, and concern.

If it be true that each individual expresses and articulates inchoate finalities epitomized in himself in the course of directing himself at other actualities, and that he expresses and articulates his own individuality when he concerns himself with this or that finality, how can one account for his steady expressions? Does it make sense to say, for example, that since a man exhibits himself as black, he must in root be indeterminate, and could conceivably be white or brown or yellow, or even some as yet unrealized color in humans such as purple? We have no warrant for supposing that in root a man is some color or other in an indeterminate form and that he makes himself be black when he could in principle be some other color. In any case, we could not stop with an indeterminate color, for black, like gender and many other steadily exhibited traits, is associated with many others. One would, therefore, have to suppose, at the very least, that a man was indeterminate, not with respect to color but with respect to being a black or a woman, and so forth, where these are understood to refer to a set of features. But does it make sense to speak of this or that black woman as being in root a possible white man as well as a possible black woman, the latter being a realization expressive of the fact that the individual exhibited an epitomized Existence in one of a number of possible ways? Once again there seems to be no warrant for the supposition. The indeterminacy of a man does not cut behind all the steady traits he has, allowing us to define him as able to be expressed in some alternative way. And yet we do want to refer to him as not identifiable with such traits; we want to say that he has rights, a mind, a reality, just like any other.

One way of providing a satisfaction for the double condition that he be recognized to be black, and that he be recognized to be a man, equal to every other and this without being taken to be an indeterminate who might have had a different color, is to view these traits, not as expressive of what could have been specified in an alternative way, but as conditions to which he is forced to submit on becoming public. But now it seems as if we are back to the old idea of a self-enclosed soul which is led to take account of external conditions, or which is overlaid with adventitious accidents. One must instead, I think, maintain that an individual in himself is expressive always, expanding outward toward whatever else there be—an idea which I accepted when I was trying to understand space and time in *Reality*—and that he receives determination by the resistance he encounters in the body and beyond. What is externally determined will be possessed by him from within, making the determinations part of his possessions, but in himself he will be indeterminate as not yet bodily determined and will, so far, lack something. Only what he transiently does will express his fecundity, for only the transient could conceivably be otherwise and therefore express in a limited way what has other possible ways of being exhibited. As free from the determinations which are due to his body and the steady conditions of the world, a man will be less than he otherwise would be; but as free from the determinations exhibited by his own initiated acts he will be richer than any of these determinations could be. What is true of an individual in relation to others, though, will not be true of him in relation to the finalities unless his steady ways of dealing with them are due to conditions over which he has no control.

Men face all the finalities at the same time in an attitude of wonder; when they attend to one of those finalities in a steady way, or with different emphases, or by alternating the attention given to one with attention given to others, it is they who break up that wonder into specific modes of being occupied with the finalities. As a consequence, we must say that it is not because their individuality is being expressed through the avenue of different epitomized finalities that they reveal themselves to be fecund individuals, but that, because the finalities that they have epitomized are exhibited through limited channels where they are met by specific resistances, their exhibitions of those finalities are determined in ways those individuals can not control. Since such an account does not as yet make provision for the determinations that the individual himself produces, one must, in addition, affirm that the individualized exhibition of the various finalities is never fully determined by the resistances an actuality encounters, and indeed is not fully expressed, since it is initially expressed only as capable of receiving determinations.

An actuality makes evident its indeterminate reality, as the unity of epitomized finalities, by expressing these through a steady individuality which is made determinate by what is resisting it; further expressions of it will require that it use its epitomized finalities under the restrictions of the determinations already suffered and possessed, and also as themselves being made determinate by the individual in the guise of this or that way of making the epitomized finalities effectively present. Such a view will take every individual to be indeterminate in itself as a set of epitomized finalities, so that everything that is exhibited, steadily or otherwise, will articulate and diversify a substantiality, rights, a nature, a distention, and a sense of value. An individual will express himself as one who stands apart from all others only in the way in which he attends to the finalities.

In these references to the finalities I am close to the practices of those who solve their problems by making an appeal to God. God, being all powerful, is taken to solve the problem of induction, the mind-body question, and so on. But the view I am offering does not, as these views do, appeal to the deliberate action of a being whose actions are beyond the knowing; nor is an appeal made to the finalities in order to solve a problem which has nothing to do with them. The finalities operate without consciousness or deliberation; they provide conditions and not specific acts; and they are arrived at as continuous with the very factors they explain, being nothing more than the constant unitary sources of the alien elements we find present in daily experienced objects.

April 6

If a being is so fecund that its expressions are ways of diversifying itself, it is a free, self-determining reality. If, instead, it is indeterminate in the sense of not only lacking specifications but density, and therefore unable to make itself determinate in this or that form, it is not free. Men are not free with respect to their steady traits, but are free with respect to their 'accidental' or transient ones. The finalities, instead, are entirely free, since they exhibit themselves in attenuated forms on their own. They could be said to be externally determined only so far as the detailed resistant determinations which are provided by actualities are in fact possessed by those finalities as their own properties. A finality will be free as self-expressive, but will be determined in the sense that it has no alternative ways of being attenuated.

The freedom of men involves decisions because there are alternative ways in which it can make itself determinate; the freedom of the finalities involves expressiveness, an overflowing, which is not controlled. Men, it can be said, are free to be transient causes; the finalities are free to be constitutive ones. If, as I have been maintaining recently, the finalities accommodate the actualities in various ways, the finalities will also be free in their ability to preserve themselves through their own adjustment to what is made available to themselves, and in that way will be somewhat like the actualities' possession of the determinations which are externally introduced by other actualities.

Plotinus's One was understood by him to be fecund, and to express itself inevitably in more and more attenuated and diversified stadia. But he could not provide a way in which those stadia could remain distinct from one another; this demands the presence of independent actualities on which one stadium at least would have to be imposed. Whitehead (whom I have heard remark that the Neoplatonic philosophy was the most absurd he had ever heard of), has a God who is without any fecundity at all; his role is primarily that of a mediator, assessor, and lure. Whitehead has a principle of creativity which is forever productive, but it is not clear whether this productivity is an outpouring and diversification, or just a kind of unpredictable thrust forward into the future.

April 9

If every discipline—science, history, economics, sociology, art—attends to distinctive types of space, time, and other universal conditions, one is faced with the double question as to whether or not metaphysics is not given a special dispensation in being held to avoid these limitations, and whether or not there is something more fundamental than any one of these limited forms. If one were instead to take some one of these disciplines and its fundamental categories or areas as primary, the others would be metaphorizing derivatives from it. Whichever one we chose to make fundamental in this sense would be matched by another urged by some other thinker. Against Descartes there is Vico, and against both is Bonaventura with his emphasis on religion, and against them is Merton with his emphasis on sociology, and so on.

One can allow that there is a more basic reality beyond all the special forms that the different disciplines use, exploit, and know, and which is known both emotionally and by speculation, without supposing that either of these will yield superior knowledge. We will know or come to what is more real, but will know or come to it only at the price of losing the empirical controls, the specific knowledge, the important details, the verifications and practical consequences that the special enterprises alone allow and promote.

Beyond what is known by special agencies there is either something empty or full. Both could be understood in the radical sense of not allowing for any self-determination, but the latter also allows for a determination internally produced. One could conceive of the empty as a dimension of something which is richer than it, and thus have the determination produced by this richer being. In effect, this reduces to the other view, merely indicating how the full will be exhibited. Such a position is sometimes entertained by those who think of a creative artist as having an empty canvas or an open mind, and using his imagination to give it content. He is thought to be free but, in contrast with the free expression of the full, to engage in a free specification within the limits of the empty, or general.

The full may express itself as a source of what fills out the general; as that which inescapably overflows and thereby diversifies and attenuates itself; or as that which produces the diversification as the outcome of an act which in effect adds to what it is in itself. In the first way, the full is faced with a condition; in the second, it itself is the source of all; in the third, it engages in two acts, one of which involves something like what the second does, but adds to this further power, with the result that the diversification is not an attenuation at all, but a specialized way of exhibiting the full.

Sometimes we think of creative men as overflowing, with large reservoirs of untapped power, and therefore look at them with awe; but sometimes we take their creativity to consist in the production of something new out of a disordered totality. The first create in a frenzy; they are necessitated not free, though their products are not predictable and depend on the way in which the overflow occurred. They could be said to be unbounded, spontaneous, but not free in the sense in which the other kind of creative person is, who actually, by deliberate effort, makes something. The former ends with what is less than himself; the latter, because of the additional effort that is being made, ends with what, despite its diversification and limited forms, is more than that with which he began. The results the latter produces are like those which result when external objects provide determinations for what is exhibited; in both cases there is an ending with something which is more than what is exhibited spontaneously.

There seems to be a paradox in the conception of the second

kind of creativity. That which is creative is being understood to diversify itself in some way which has conceivable alternatives, and yet this is taken to be richer than the beginning. But if this is paradoxical, it should also be paradoxical that what one says achieves an enriching determination by the reply to it. One way of minimizing the effect of the paradox is to take the specific form that results from a determination to be an epitomizing of the undifferentiated unity with which one began. It will be enriched either by the individual himself making determinate something which was inseparably merged in the unity, or by the action of others adding a public dimension and value to what the individual had merely externalized but had not yet succeeded in separating from himself.

The determinations which others provide allow what one does to stand apart. But the determinations which are provided from within do not produce a separation of the result from the source. This can not occur unless the determinations produced in the course of an action which is outward thrusting terminate in what is remote from the origin.

The finalities are all fecund, superabundant, and express themselves necessarily in attenuated forms. These attenuations are not made determinate by them, but by the particulars on which they impinge. A man, in contrast, because he can face the finalities and therefore take them to be areas which he is to make determinate, can be taken to express himself freely or necessarily in the shape of that area as something which he is to fill out, and then fill it out in subsequent, free acts. The result, like the other things he does, can itself receive externally produced determinations.

Both actualities and finalities are superabundant. This is in effect denied by nominalists who take the only ultimate realities to be individuals. The theory of family resemblances, which supposes that each entity has features that may be similar to those of some other entity, and this with some third, without the first necessarily having its features similar to the third, is nominalistic. It denies that there is a superabundance that the items diversely instance, or even some common character to which they add their own individual specifications. But, of course, nominalism is a general theory about all cases and is either empty, needing specifications, or about a superabundance which the individuals in fact diversely exhibit in a limited form.

Zen Buddhism and other adventures in the achievement of an

enlightenment are occupied primarily not with a finality—apparently either Being or Unity—in itself, but with the abstracting of evidence for this. All the efforts of the teaching are in isolating the evidence (which I think can also be done by analyzing and noting what is a transcendent, intrusive factor governing a multiplicity). After this is achieved, apparently, the sage spends his life trying to get deeper and deeper into the finality. But he tells us little about that venture. (What I have read in this area is apparently written for the novice and is devoted to telling him how, by withdrawal and discipline, he can free himself from an involvement with particulars.) A philosopher who achieves this result by analysis is, of course, still involved with particulars. He, with Aristotle, is engaged in a leisurely occupation. Not concerned with practice, he can maintain that attitude and occupy himself with the intellectual apprehension of what is experienced by the mystic and similar intuitive apprehendors of the detached evidence. He can then go on to recognize that he is already in the domain of the finality, and proceed by inference to arrive at an understanding of its denser, ultimate reality. That understanding, of course, is less than the finality; its content awaits acceptance by the finality before it can serve as a means for allowing one to get deeper into the finality. But a speculative thinker can still understand, via the outcome of the process of evidencing, what the nature of the finality is.

Santayana, in his *Scepticism and Animal Faith,* shares with the Eastern mystic the view that there is one finality (a realm of essence, for him, which is supplemented by other realms) enjoyed in its purity apart from all particulars. He does not tell us how we get to it; it apparently is where we had been from the beginning. I think there is a truth in this; no matter how much we are involved in particulars, we always have some acquaintance with finalities. Santayana does not think that the individual expresses himself in attending to the realm of essence. Here, I think, he errs. But in supposing that the essences are brought to bear on particulars through the exigencies of living, he rightly takes them to have particularized meanings or roles.

April 10

'Mine' has at least a dozen different applications: A] what is constituted by me, such as dreams and memories; B] what is or has been vitalized by me—nails, blood, hair;   C] what may not be vitalized by me but which had been, and for which I am now a representative—my corpse-to-be;   D] that to which I submit, which conditions me—my country, my ruler;   E] what is had by right but which I do not in fact have—money in the bank;   F] what is in the control of others—my reputation and the assessment of my appearance and deeds or virtues;   G] what I claim in my assertions—even when I am wrong;   H] what has a special relation to me which may also have special relations to others—my teacher, my family, my state;   I] what is no longer present but to which I refer for grounding—my ancestors, the founding fathers, the people of antecedent civilizations to whom I am in debt;   J] those who depend on me—my children, my posterity;   K] what is lent to me but which I alone use—my uniform, my office;   L] what is alien to what I now am—the not-mine which is a not-mine in relation to me and is thus my not-mine;   M] what no one can deprive me of—my I, my self. (I can, of course, be killed, but then I lose not only what is 'mine' but the reality which is able to make something be mine.)

What is most surely mine, perhaps what is most authentically mine, is what I myself freely produce. This has one of three forms: A] it is a domain selected, to be subsequently specified in one of a number of alternative ways;   B] an alternative selected within a selected domain;   C] the precipitation of myself in the form of some limited epitomizing. Both A and B can be taken to be specific forms of C, so that a man is most himself when he expresses himself by attending to some one kind of general area which needs specification, by providing the specification, or by producing a delimited version of what he is in himself. The last we usually identify as creativity, but the other two will also be creative acts, just so far as they are the product of the individual's free activity. When, for example, there is a production of a general area to be specified, the producing will be creative in the third sense but will not necessarily end with something epitomizing the fecund individual. It will, instead, set before oneself any one of a number of possible generals. But it is possible for an individual to select a domain to be further specified and to do this in such a way that his total being is epitomized there. A man, thus, may emphasize an interest in Possibility as the domain in which he will occupy himself. Though the domain is, with respect to subsequent specifications, something general and so far empty, that very emptiness, as still to be filled, may epitomize the individual. It can never do this completely, since the very power which produced that selection is what makes the specification possible. Consequently, a man who chooses to be a mathematician or to be involved in practice, and does nothing further, remains unsatisfied in a way that one who in fact fully epitomizes himself in an actual making does not.

How are we to distinguish a merely general, relatively empty domain, to be specified in any one of a number of possible ways, from a creative epitomizing of oneself in the form of some limited occurrence? How are we to distinguish a red which is the specification of an empty color or general from a red which is a delimited portion of a white in which all colors are interlocked and not yet distinct? One way, of course, is to see if there are specifications, alternative to the red, made without losing the domain. If, in order to get green, one must go back into the source and not, as is the case of green as a specific color alternative to red, remain within the domain, we will have green as that which is epitomizing white, and not merely specifying color in general.

Men are dissatisfied, unhappy, at odds with themselves just so far as they are involved in a domain which is not being specified. They may specify it in ways that do not satisfy them, even though those specifications are expressive of their rich unitary beings—just as a creative epitomizing act does not fully exhaust the domain. A proper specification, if it is to satisfy fully, must not only exhibit one's creativity and in that sense partially epitomize oneself, but must epitomize the domain. But then it seems that what must be done when one specifies color in general is to produce the color white. If so, we must either begin with white (as epitomizing ourselves) and epitomize it in delimited forms, such as red or green, or we must epitomize ourselves both in the form of color and in white, a specification of this. In the one case, white will be a precondition for and be fully expressed in the red or green; in the other, it will be a product, and be set alongside red or green.

If we shift the illustration from sight to sound, this outcome seems to leave us with an intolerable paradox. The analogue of white is noise. But it does not make sense to say that a man does most justice to himself when he chooses the domain of sound and then specifies it as noise—though one could well argue that he could start with something like noise as an excessively rich way of exhibiting himself, and proceeed to delimit it in the form of particular sounds. The noise which is the outcome of a specification and serves to epitomize sound will have to be thought of as the beginning of a process of composition. It will be noise as relative to the domain of sound, but also that which is being exhibited in the course of a musical production.

Is the difference then between a white or noise which can be epitomized in a single delimited red or middle C, and a domain-specified white or noise which must be spelled out over a whole series of colors or sounds? Yes.

Specifications provided from without are different from those issuing from within in that they introduce alien factors, making one aware of something other than the generic form that had been provided. The specifications we bring about from within, though involving perhaps a different act from that which brought forth the domain, are rooted in the same source; they tell us that the individual who produced the domain is richer than that, able to specify it in any one of a number of ways. But the specifications will always fall short of the specifications which others introduce, unless supported by actions which set them in an external world.

April 11

In order to arrive at oneself in oneself it is necessary A] to free one's expressions from determinations by other actualities, B] free them from determinations by the finalities, C] free them from the outcome of the application of one kind of expression or internalized finality on another, D] free them from efforts of expansion and diffusion so as to have them in a concentrated form. All the freeings occur at places withdrawn from those where the various determinations occur.

Once we arrive at the self—which is most completely done only on reflection, for a withdrawal is never complete—one can recognize various degrees and kinds of freedom: A] The self spreads itself without division; this is done in waves of which there are at least two, one remaining within the individual, the other impinging on what is outside him. B] Through the help of the body and through the help of what is outside, there is a concentration or emphasis on different parts of the spread-out, attenuated area. C] One of the concentrated areas can be applied to others.

Possibilities can be entertained and decisions made privately; spatial regions can be faced and attention concentrated within them; in both cases we apply one distinguished expression of the expanded individual to another.   D] It is possible to apply an inside, concentrated distinguished factor on what is distinguished outside. This is what happens when we impose an interpretation on what is being confronted.   E] The reverse application also occurs; some external distinguished expression, say something attended to, can be used to dictate what we are to think or plan, guiding ourselves by it.   F] We can direct one of the distinguished internal factors to its final counterpart.   G] We can direct evidence, in one of the distinguished external items, toward a finality.

These are all free acts. We begin to expand, to express and to apply freely, and we also freely withdraw from the result of a free encounter with external limiting conditions. The withdrawal is necessary if we engage only in reflection; but an attempt to reach the self by itself also requires further effort. It can not, I think, be accomplished except for a fleeting moment, for as soon as we arrive at it from one angle we are already involved with what is beyond it in a different direction.

One rejects these withdrawals if one supposes that only determinate particulars are real, and what is thought to be obtained from a free creative expression of the self is in fact only an abstraction from what is encountered. This is the strictly nominalistic position. Hume does not go that far, for he allows for the use of a mind with respect to what is received from without. Associative activities of the mind presumably are free for him, even though their outcomes conceivably might be known in advance.

April 12

Phenomenology, in Husserl's sense, moves from subjective appearances into the individual and arrives at the conscious intensional being who is then said to be constituting a world in the way others do. But unless the constituting is done by what is in fact common to them all, there is no warrant for supposing that what one individual constitutes is also constituted by another. And unless some provision is made for getting to what is beyond consciousness, one will fall short of the individual as a locus of rights, individuality, practice, and religious or speculative interests.

What is left over, once one has separated off the individual or the human conscious, intensional contribution? For one who accepts the phenomenological starting point, there can be only the irrational or the unreachable into which one might plunge, or toward which one might orient himself, but which he could not know—alternatives taken by Sartre and Heidegger.

What is left, I have claimed, are objective appearances, appearances which are constituted by particular entities as interlocked with finalities, freed from subjective notes introduced by human knowers. How could such objective appearances be known? How could one come to know what a man actually is as a reality outside the world of objective appearances?

I have held that what a man introduces are boundaries and that what is objective defies those boundaries. It is necessary to go further: he adds specifications, interpretations, and possibly distortions into the content that is being bounded. If he can note that an object is escaping the boundaries that he introduces, he should be able to discern that it is doing so with what is relatively indeterminate in relation to what is being added by him when he makes a subjective appearance out of the content. The knowledge will be symbolic so far as it is governed by the object, so that what a man then knows, while he knows subjectively, is something indeterminate in control of something more determinate than it. His knowledge involves a moving from the determinations he provides to determinations which have careers he does not control. Once he recognizes those objective appearances, of which his own body or actions or accomplishments might well be cases, he can by analysis, guided by the fringes of the objective appearances, note the components of those appearances. As the objective appearances come into focus, they evidently become more and more under the control of conditions intruded on them. It is with the recognition of the conditions that one comes to know what belongs to a particular actuality, which might in fact be oneself.

It is not necessary to go all the way to the final reduction of Husserl in order to be able to attend to objective appearances. These are not merely passive residues but effective factors, pulled away as they are by their constitutive realities and therefore requiring us to attend to them as standing away. It is as if one were to turn at once, after one had bracketed Husserl's naturally and naïvely faced world (of subjective appearances, which we had individually adjusted to one another's understanding in the course of daily living) to what remained over, and there at once began to break it down either into a factor originating with a particular, or with one or more finalities. If an objective appearance is an appearance of ourselves, we find, by attending to what is being withheld and withdrawn from us, that the appearance is under the control of an alien power. We then become aware that we contribute the other component of the objective appearance. We know this, the more surely we are aware of the alien power, and therefore the more surely that we see it in contrast with what we contribute. We come to that component by continued intensification and penetration, or through a reflection on what this must result in. If the latter, we will be making use of the conditions in the form of categories and then for the purpose, not of categorizing what we encounter, but of discovering how those categories are in fact diversified by the actual components with which they mesh.

April 13

I am involved in five sets of determinations: A] After I have expanded into a stretch in which there are nuances of myself in an attenuated form of myself, I am able to engage in a self-determination which results from the application of one component of the stretch on another. We are most familiar with an emphasis on rules, plans, programs which are applied to control oneself, to dictate how one is to face others, to think, to prepare to act, or to evaluate. But one might conceivably take the rules to be subject to the others. Indeed, each seems capable of being applied to any of the rest. B] In addition, I am determined to be in a world with other things as present there in the same way that I am; I am then one who maintains himself together with others maintaining themselves. C] I also have a nature which, though general and shared with others, is still determinate in the sense that, unlike myself in myself, there are only certain things that are possible for it. D] I am determined, at the same time, in interaction with others, adjusting myself to what they do to me and how they reply to my actions. E] Finally, I am subject to the kind of determinate governance that the finalities provide, according to their different types of unitary power.

The totality of these determinations of the attenuated expression of myself in the form of a nuanced expanded stretch should equal what I am in myself, when I am withdrawn from the determinations in fact or through thought. What I lose by expansion, I recover through the various determinations, once these are accepted as part of myself—which they are, so far as I belong to a world of self-determining entities. To know who I am, I must read into myself those very determinations and reduce them to a single undifferentiated density. If I am made to be coordinate with a cat, I must in myself be 'cat coordinative'; or if I live by rule, in myself I should be one in whom the rule is.

I have held—I am not sure, all the time—that things are able to internalize and therefore be just substances, that plants, in addition, internalize Possibility and therefore have individualized natures; that the lower living beings have made themselves coordinate with others by internalizing the qualification due to Being; and that the higher animals internalize Existence as well, and thus have an environmental status. Only man has all these together unified. If this is maintained, evidently none of the others can be determined to the degree that man is.

It seems to make sense to say that a thing needs to be perfected by being known, by the action of others, and by the finalities, that it makes itself present, and that it has some possessive control over its own externalized expressions. What it must be determined to be by knowledge, action, and so on is a publicized substance. Plants, in addition, have to be made to be publicized substances and natures. Animals and men are richer publicized actualities.

The finalities are evidently superabundant. Spinoza made the point in connection with Substance, claiming that it had infinite attributes; Plotinus took Being to be overflowing; Plato placed the 'good' beyond all knowledge and Being; Marx took Existence to have a historically unfolding richness; and Bonaventure held that God was fecund. Since all of these finalities expand and impinge not only on actualities but on one another, must we not also say that they are determined in ways that compensate for their expanded attenuations? Do they not benefit from their expressions being sustained by individual actualities, by being grasped by one another, by being caught up in this world's adventures (at least so far as they evidence themselves), and by pivoting about particular actualities?

None of these thinkers seem to hold that their chosen finalities benefit from anything. I think they must. Like actualities, they too benefit from having what they are as manifest in attenuated ways be articulated and therefore made determinate. Am I saying anything more than what Hegel called the conversion of substance into what is also subject, the making the unarticulate articulate? Yes. He had self-determinations that were internally produced but did not take account of diversities. Even the self-determination of an actuality, which makes use of concentrations in the single expanded attenuation of itself, depends, for its carrying out, on the sustaining presence of what is able to make the concentration stand away from the attenuated field. Is this too neat? Where is contingency? Suppose something is not known?

The contingency evidently lies in the production of independently produced determinations. The completion is ideal, and depends on the provision of those determinations and their possession by the actuality or finality. Each of these makes itself available for the determinations, because its attenuated expanded form needs the determinations in order to be an adequate expression of the actuality or finality, though in another domain. Each has a need to accept the determinations, while keeping them as the determinations of its expanded attenuated form, in order that what it is being externally determined should be its own, somewhat in the way in which I accept the spatial boundaries of my body as my own boundaries, even though they are boundaries which relate me to and have determinations due to a larger space.

There are, to be sure, determinations which injure. These can be understood as being beyond the capacity of the individual to internalize except by radically altering them or himself. But this is not possible to things, and is possible to the subhuman only in limited ways. It does seem, though, that all other actualities and the finalities always make a difference to all determinations; no totality of particular determinations at any one time could be adequate without making unnecessary later determinations.

There is a nest of problems here. And evidently, if what is said is correct, one must give up the Aristotelian actuality-potentiality division, since individuals and finalities in themselves will be potential only relative to their externally conditioned determinate guises.

April 14

It seems evident to me now that things are self-determined, determined to be coordinated and so on in only one way, as substances; that plants, lower and higher animals add to these, but that it is only man who is determined in five ways in all five modes. The hard problem is to understand the determinations which the finalities need. Are they not due to the resistance of individual actualities, to the joint presence of them all, to the presence of the attenuated forms of these so as to provide appearances, and to the other finalities, severally and together?

Do the finalities need to be known in order that their attenuated forms be given their proper determinations? Yes. The presentation of a claim for acceptance by a finality is a determination of it through knowing. In what sense, though, does a finality exhibit itself so as to be made available for that knowing? I have taken this to be the finality itself in the guise of evidence. In addition to merely expanding in an attenuated way, it makes itself available for the actualities separately and together, and for the appearances together. But it evidently is their copresence in a man, able to internalize them all, that makes possible the use of the evidence. Only he can know the finalities and thereby provide determinations for each in the form of claims.

A thing is known. What addition does the knowledge of it make to its mere intelligibility or nature? And how does a thing's being known add to its determinateness and match what is incomplete in it? We must say, I think, that what is known of it is its substance, and this knowing is a way of making its expanded presence determinate, matching its self-groundedness. Must we then say that a plant is known as substantial and as having a nature, in a somewhat similar way? It seems so. A thing's possession of its own attenuated presence is not sufficient and needs supplementation by knowing; similarly, a plant's possession and sensitive apprehension of water and what else it needs are not sufficient and also need to be supplemented by being made determinate by knowing. In knowing a thing I know its unity as adumbratively substantial, present, self-maintained. In knowing a plant I know also that its adumbratively recognized unity is one of a class with which it is interinvolved. In knowing a higher animal, I know, in addition, that it is with others in an environment. When I know a man I know him to have a unifying value as well.

If a man is determinate in all the ways possible to him—by himself imposing one attenuated portion on another, by being subject to limitations and conditioning by other entities or by the finalities, and by having his knowledge faced with the adumbrated unity of what he knows—there is still the question of what he gains by being known. Since by being known he is brought into intelligible relations with other known items, being known gives him a determination as a nature. When he is known he provides a unity which is adumbratively as rich as it can be, since he is one who has all the finalities in an individualized form. If he knows himself, he brings himself, as a unity of all the finalities, into intelligible relations with similar individuals or other kinds of entities. Knowing, he achieves the determination of being in contrast with his unity; being known, he achieves the determination of having intelligible relations to others; knowing himself, he is determinate as a me in intelligible relations to other items known.

Every actuality benefits from being known because it is then able to have its attenuated presence given intelligible roles. And in being known, it gives determinations to what knows it, because it gives that knower a unitary presence of a certain kind which allows him to bring into prominence what this is as present in his own unity. A thing can express itself only partially; by being known, that attenuation gets determinations which make up for that partiality. A man can possess his attenuation only partially; by knowing anything he is able to possess it better.

Finalities gain from being attenuated, for the actualities and their expressions then punctuate them, give them an articulation, make them into 'subjects' where before they were only 'substances'. Do they gain from one another? Do they gain from being known? Each gains new roles from the others. These should compensate for the attenuated form each has as impinging on or as being impinged on by others. From its impingement it gains new types of properties which should compensate for the fact that it is a distinctive kind of finality. From their impingement on it, it gains by having its own attenuation given a determinate form as a single whole. In being known, finally, it gains the status of having intelligible relations to everything, including particulars.

The Spinozistic Substance, the Plotinian Being, the Platonic

Good or the Hegelian Idea, the Marxian extended matter, and the God of the West or the ultimate of the Buddhists are all fecund, overflowing, needing particulars in order to be able to have that overflowing be held away and thereby become determinate. All must take into themselves the determinate result, and thereby make themselves completed by having all diversification interfused and, at the same time, having it differentiated by the determinate presence and action of what is external to it. To be self-articulate, to be determinate as attenuated, is to offer each of its own interfused components a status of its own, with the help of what is alien to it.

April 15

Realities attenuate in order to be able to give full value to the factors which are interfused in them. As merely attenuated, they continue to be single. The attenuation does not have any divisions; it is just the reality in a lesser form. But, through the aid of external realities, the attentuation acquires determinations and division. The determinations provided by the other entities enable a reality, whether it be a finality or an actuality, to exhibit its richness. Each of the interfused components in it is thereby enabled to be exhibited without losing its status as interfused.

There is a gain for each reality in being known, for knowledge gives it the determinate status of a bounded entity related intelligibly to others. If the known entity is a finality, it is reached by means of a claim; the claim gives the finality the status of that which is rationally present in the world of actualities (in the form of evidence). If the known entity is an actuality, it is reached by a judgment which pivots about a unity having an adumbrative base reaching into the entity, with the consequence that the known actuality acquires a unitary status in the attenuation of itself, like that which it has in itself. Without our knowledge, a finality's attenuated form (where it initially accepts the claim) would not have the role of a term in relation to actualities, but would merely function with respect to those actualities, while, without our knowledge, an actuality's unity would not have a role in a public world.

The knowing of actualities or finalities by a man makes him determinate in that it sets before him the unity at the root of his judgment of them; the resistance of this, and the fact that it serves as the measure of the truth of the judgment made, forces into the fore his inward reality as that which is different from the known actualities or distinct from the known finalities. In knowing himself, the two determinations are united, with the consequence that a man is made determinate in an exhibited unity and still has the unity beyond all the knowing.

From the position of the determinations that are provided, what is available is indeterminate, and could be said to be 'potential'. But that indeterminate in itself is full, with the determinations articulating its public guise. The ideal would be to have the determinations exhaustively match the components which are interfused in the reality in itself, and have the totality of the determinations be adopted by the reality. But so long as the determinations are due to finite transient entities, one set will never be enough. We need the totality of all determinations over the whole of time before we can have an adequate determination of what any actuality is in itself.

One's primary involvement is with appearances oriented either toward actualities or finalities. The judgment that is made, though, is initially not of the actualities or finalities as they are by themselves, or even with their objective appearances, but with their 'subjective' or socialized, humanized appearances. This does not make a difference in principle so far as the adumbrative unity at the root of the judgment is concerned, for the difference between a judgment of subjectivized or humanized appearances and objective ones is a difference in the depth of the unity to which we refer in our judgments, and about which we orient the distinctions acknowledged to be pertinent there.

The knowledge I have of others gives me a base for knowing my contrasting unity. Non-cognitively, the determinations which others provide articulate my attenuated guise, and permit me to take them into myself as inwardly belonging to me, transformed. When I withdraw from them, I must give up any attempt to face the determinations as apart from me. But my absorption of them is never perfect; it leaves me with a referential note to them.

Every actuality, no matter what its grade, is a substance. What is the difference between the determination given by any actuality and that by Substance itself? An individual substance makes evident that it is self-maintained and possessive; we, as faced with it, become aware that this is true of us too. Substance, instead, is encountered as a power which makes us aware that we instance it, epitomizing it in a limited form. The one gives us a particular determination, the other gives us an enveloping one, encompassing the whole of our attenuated reality. The cognition of the one faces us with a limited substantiality which allows us to become aware of our limited substantiality; the cognition of the other faces us with an absorptive power which allows us to become aware of our congeniality with it.

April 16

An abstraction or variable such as color is   A] an outcome of an act, and   B] is imposed and thereby made determinate by something else. That which makes it determinate has a status apart from it, and is also involved with it. The value of a variable is no exterior item, having nothing to do with the variable; the variable is made determinate by the value, and the value is so far involved with the variable, not something altogether apart from it.

A variable (or abstraction) differs from a plenitude which an individual might be said to be in himself. He has a color which is to be understood as the intensified unified meaning of all the diverse determinations he can receive; those determinations are to be distinguished from the determinations which other actualities receive from the same external determining entities. A color in its plenitude receives a plurality of externally produced determinations which are to add up to its import; in contrast, a variable receives alternative specifications.

Every actual present entity could be considered to be the outcome of five 'becauses'. Aristotle noted two of these as having a plenitude to them—the formal and the final; he minimized the nature and role of two others, the efficient and material and, because of his interest in scientific knowledge, overlooked a fifth, the individual substantial entity which is manifest only in part at that moment and is, as an individual, richer than what it is being known to be. All five have a role in history.

The use of present evidence leads one back into the past to that which is its cause. That cause is just an occasion for the occurrence in the present as following over a series of distinct intermediaries: it is what one fastens on if one is a reporter or is checking the facts. In order to understand the present from which one began a historic investigation, one must give an explanatory context to what otherwise would be just an occasion. It must be set within A] an epoch or other segment of the whole of history which will persist until one arrives from the past occasion to the present occurrence which is being used as evidence; B] it will take account of the actual energies and activities which men engage in within the frame of that segment; C] it will be understood as terminating in something future that is explanatory of it and which now must be viewed as effectively controlling the way in which the history unfolds; D] it will allow that the occasion itself is the outcome of a past; if it be used as a beginning, it will, therefore, be used as that which summarizes a past and is not merely a single incident; and E] it will itself be possessed of a dense depth which is being exhibited at that moment in only one of its aspects.

A historian sees an acknowledged past occasion to be a determinate reality which fits within a historic fivefold plenitude whose functioning explains the presence of that occasion and all that relevantly follows on and precedes it. He knows himself to be on the right track when the normal activity of the fivefold 'becauses' also accounts for all the items that occur between the initial occasion and the present evidential one.

That historic occurrences are due to the activity of a richer reality explanatory of it and others is seen by different thinkers. Marx sees the fruitfulness of the matter or energy of the world, particularly when it has an economic role; the 'God' of history is taken to be in charge of a final goal toward which everything will eventually be brought. A Hegelian philosophic history puts its emphasis on a fecund formality. Whitehead's accumulative theory of causation, and theories of an earlier golden age, put their stress on an efficient 'eminent' cause in the past whose effects are less than it. (Strictly speaking, the doctrine of eminent cause should be used of the constitutive 'form' and 'matter' and not of the exterior final or material cause, since this would require one to allow that there is a possible falling away from the reality of the cause, despite the fact that an effect might be a cause of what comes later in the same sense and to the same degree that its antecedent was a cause. Still, the second law of thermodynamics apparently does allow for such a falling away.) Finally, Carlyle's great man theory of history takes an individual substance to be fruitful of the lesser outcomes which make up the course of history.

An appearance is constituted, not caused, being the product of the interlocking of actualities and finalities—or more precisely, their expressions. Unlike a present actuality, as at that moment, the appearance itself has nothing in reserve. What is in reserve in the actuality are not 'potentialities', unless these be taken to be active, and separated and made determinate by what is external.

Must we not give a similar fivefold account of any occurrence in any domain—art, science, technology, education? Are they not all present entities characterizable as the outcome of the interplay of the expressions of rich realities? If so, my account of what the cosmos is like (in "First Considerations") must be added to, for it speaks as though the cosmos were the outcome solely of the governance of actualities by the five finalities. According to the present account, each domain is a segment of each of the five finalities, with the fifth, Substance, alone being present in an individual guise. The five finalities all operate in each domain in limited forms, with one of them alone, Substance, being manifested through individuals and therefore (as was not said above) also involving some inter-involvement with other individuals as affiliated with it in various ways.

My previous discussions of the cosmos took individual entities for granted, instead of seeing that the outcome of the operation of the finalities on actualities yields a product which, though not an appearance, is still not the actuality in its full concreteness. An actuality in its full concreteness is an individual contributing to itself in the role of a cosmological entity, countering Being, Possibility, Existence and Unity in limited segments. No actuality is exhaustively present in the cosmos; it always has reality beyond this—just as the historic epoch, the total energy, the goal to be reached, and the past that is being accumulated have.

Am I saying anything more than that a historic occurrence, an art object, or a law-abiding physical entity is just an objective appearance with an added reference to a domain, energies, and a final goal? Or conversely, that an objective appearance is a truncated part of an object in a domain of entities vitally connected with one another? I think I am, for I am saying that the object in a domain is not a mere product of the fruitful sources, but is those sources conjoined. An appearance is a product, something with a distinctive nature in which its constituents cannot be found, whereas the historic and other entities in domains, including the cosmological particles of physics, are junctures of realities, exerting different degrees and kinds of control over one another. But now it seems as if an appearance is being said to have an integrity of its own, while this is denied to the art object, the historic entity, the physical cosmological particle, and so on. The conclusion is avoided when these entities are recognized to be at the limits of each fecund power. The five limits are to be added together, and this identified with an occasion. An occasion is identical with the historic object, and so forth, but held in abstraction from the powers at whose fivefold limit it stops.

The killing of an archduke was the occasion for the First World War. In turning it into a historic event one sees its various components to be limits of segments of more basic realities. The killing, of course, occurs in a domain of social events. Even if we take it to be a merely natural event, it limits five powers. Having been located, in addition to having a fivefold explanation as an occasion, it will have a fivefold explanation as a historic event, as at the limit of five constituent powers. The appearance of the killing has the expressions of actualities and the finalities intermixed; the occasion and the historic event or art object or whatever, face five limits.

April 17

Every entity is at the center of a fivefold determination. It is an occasion, something treated as though it were just a unit, when the determinations are by segments of limited aspects of the powers producing those determinations. The placing of an isolated entity of this type in a world of physics, history, art, or some other large-scaled area is the having it governed by more powerful agents and brought into relationship with other entities by means of those relationships.

If one attends to the finalities and actualities as constituting appearances, one attends to them as having expressions which are there exhaustively, to constitute entities with natures of their own. If, instead, one attends to the finalities and actualities as sources of power, occasions (and these as transformed into historic, scientific, artistic, and so forth, objects) will be those very appearances vitalized, made part of larger schemes in which they are not merely related, as are the appearances, but are in a course of being produced, thereby making a difference to other entities.

An appearance has rational connections with other appearances, enabling one to transform one into the other according to rule. But an actuality as subject to a domain of a formal kind expresses itself via its appearance, to make the connection that this had to other appearances not simply one between appearances but between actualities. Each actuality expresses itself in and through appearances, to connect with others expressing themselves in and through other appearances.

Since even physical entities are the outcome of the expressions of five powers—one of which is Substance as expressing itself in the entities as well as in their affiliative relations—they cannot be said to be just units of energy, mere existent centers, but must be understood to be themselves involved in five areas. (Fr. William Wallace has pointed up something like this fact, stopping with the Aristotelian four causes—which is perhaps what should be done in view of science's concern with what is cosmic rather than individual.)

If one emphasizes one area, whether formal, material, final, efficient, or substantial, an actual entity will be seen to be a merely contingent concentration in one part of it. When we attend to unit entities, as we normally do, we will have to see the expressions of those entities to be not merely interlinked with the finalities, but vitalized, and as such caught up within the attenuated but forceful presence of conditioning finalities.

An actual entity, when viewed in contradistinction to all else, is a source of expressions. Its expressions are effectively vitalized by it. Since it cannot be entirely cut off from the influence of the various finalities, it must be seen to be a reality with a diffused presence in all the domains, at the same time that it has a fecund center in itself. A man in particular has to be seen to be a me involved in all areas, at the same time that he is an I inseparable from these, and indeed vitalizing the me from his own side.

April 18

Too great a concern with the fact that every actuality is a substance, has led me to minimize the role of Substance in the discussions of the last day or so. An actuality contrasts with Substance no less than it does with the other finalities. What it is as an occasion, consequently, is the product of six overflowing powers, one of which is the actuality itself. If one adds that the actuality could be known, and that the actualities alongside it also provide it with determinations, the number of kinds of determinations to which any actuality is subject is increased by two more kinds. And if we remember that a man expresses himself cognitively well as in ways which reflect the presence in him of instances of the other finalities, and that his cognitions and other activities determine him both in the sense that they involve delimited expressions and selections from him as a seminal center and make him involved with other centers, we must take account of five more types of determination. Within the confines of these, we will have determinations imposed by other actualities, and by a man's awareness that he is standing in contrast with them. To all these we must add the self-determinations which result when one of the types of expression of men is imposed on some one or more of the others. To get to man as in himself, one will have to free him from every one of these determinations.

An individual as an occasion is often recognized to be of considerable interest, and to be weighed down with affiliations, rights, meanings, activities, and values. It is also true that when such an individual is placed within some domain, such as history, it is often treated as a denuded form of some other. But this need not be done. An occasion can be preserved in all its complexity while it is given a place within a domain. If we preserve it as it is, and thus as within conventional, limited settings, it will serve as a nucleus for what it is in all larger domains. It is the acknowledgment of such a nucleus which allows one to make a connection among the various domains. It is because there is such a nucleus that we can say that it is the same man who is in nature, society, civilization, the world of art, history, religion, and so on.

If, instead of referring to these various ontological conditions which an occasion localizes in limited ways, one were to consider formal conditions, for example, one would enter the region of current controversies regarding the role of interpretation, language, possibility of translation from language to language, and revolutions in the development of scientific thought. It is possible to relate various conceptualizations, if we attend to the nucleal occasion which is at the center of all of them. The conventional daily object of experience provides a connection between the scientific objects and views of different epochs, just as surely as it provides a connection between the entities dealt with in history and those in art.

If history be taken as a guide, there will be no gaps allowed in any domain. History takes all insignificant events to provide transitional, transformational connections between the major occurrences in which it is interested. A history of philosophy, strictly speaking, takes all the lesser figures to connect the major. The point is partly made in Hegel's dialectical treatment of the history of philosophy, but Hegel neglects the multiplicity of figures involved in that transition. Those who do not help explain the change from one major figure to another do not belong in the one history of philosophy. They may, of course, be great philosophers, and may say what is true, but they will not help constitute the ongoing history. We will have to take them to belong to another domain, where they may be alone, or where the figures in the accepted historic domain function as intermediaries between them and other 'eccentrics'.

April 19

An occasion, a nucleus, a cosmological entity, and an ontological product should be distinguished:

1] An occasion is a complex within the normally accepted, uncriticized domain of daily life or practice.

2] A nucleus is what is common to all the roles which an entity has in different domains. We usually take the occasion to be the nucleus, since we usually are content to rest with what commonsense maintains when we have to decide what is common to a number of different domains. But a nucleus is not in any domain at all. It is a determinate—as the occasion is—but without a determinate role.

3] A cosmological entity, such as a physical particle, is sometimes taken to be a fixed reality, objective, fully determinate in nature and in role. It is within the domain of nature. Strictly speaking, it is there together with more complex entities such as men and animals as governed by the same conditions that govern the particles. The men and the animals do not then function in their full concreteness, with all their power.

4] The most comprehensive domain covers the whole of time, where the totality of beings makes itself maximally manifest—each individual in principle and the totality in fact—and for which there is an accumulation of the entire past, a governance by an all-comprehensive ideal future, an all-embracing affiliation, a rational connection amongst them all, and the time supplemented by space and dynamism, or 'creativity' as Whitehead calls it. A physical particle in such a final domain will have its affiliations, accumulations, meaning, energy, and directionality exhausted over the entire run of it.

In contradistinction to the present acceptance of time as definitory of what the other expressions of the finalities and actualities should do, one might, with Christians, take account of a final goal or day of last judgment; with Peirce take the view, which all scientists will eventually formulate, to provide a rational connection of all; or with Whitehead take creativity to be the primal power.

When we consider some such item as the pen with which a treaty is signed, we are confronted with the question as to whether or not it belongs to the history in which the treaty is. It evidently accompanies the treaty and is in the same domain with it. But it is not constitutive of the realities in that domain as they are actually interrelated with one another over a period of time, involving an extended use of energy, making use of an accumulated past, belonging to some rational whole characteristic of the history epoch, affiliated with certain items in ways which are relevant for that domain, or occupied with and subject to the goal, say of peace, which governs the treaty. It will be an entity whose nature as a pen is not to be understood, except as a tool within the limited domain of men engaged in communicating with one another. As connected with the signing of the treaty, the pen will be identifiable with some of the conditions, or parts of these, which enable the treaty to be an occurrence in that limited history. Though it has a unit reality within its own domain, it will function only as a demarcated part of one of the conditions, the physical, enabling the treaty to be signed. Such an accompaniment should be distinguished from the previous four different types of entity involved in domains.

April 21

Over the last weeks in the back of my mind has been the thought of stating the principles that were governing the methods that I was using or ought to be using. At present, I would say:
1] We begin in the world of what Plato called the 'mixed' and separate out factors that are alien to one another. As in that world we ourselves are diffused, neither wholly in ourselves nor wholly involved with actualities or finalities.

2] We move to actualities or the finalities progressively, stopping at certain nodal points where we thrust forward at the same time.

3] Or we take the points to be limits which force us back beyond where we had been before, only to make us stop once again at other limits and thereupon proceed back toward where we had been, but at a deeper level. The progressive movement goes on in a loop, but we ignore the limits which are sustained by others to attend only the points where the loops begin.

The Hegelian dialectic method moves toward a limit but identifies it as a stopping place, since it takes itself always to remain on the same progressive path. The Hegelian move has its counterpart in Plato who moves straight to an ideal; in a move to Aristotle's God who is a fertile, final, and formal cause, to be arrived at by freeing such causes from the material and efficient causes with which they are interlocked; in Thomas Aquinas's five ways; in Descartes's move to a creative constitutive God; and in Locke's acknowledgment that actualities have a substantial being apart from subjective appearances.

In the *Phenomenology,* progress for Hegel seems to be by wider and more inclusive loops; in the *Logic* it is by more intensive ones, and in that sense smaller than the initial 'being-becoming-nothing'. The one takes us to a finality, the other takes us within the world which the finality constitutes by stopping at what would be limits, were there in fact something external which could sustain what happened there. Plotinus, Saint Bernard, and Scotus all seem primarily concerned with the move from a finality to the world of particulars, but they do not take sufficient account of the 'mixed' nature of the world at which the move terminates.

There is no way of checking the stopping points which Hegel acknowledges. They could be checked, if one were to allow for a plurality of finalities, since what one arrived at requires for its completion the presence of others equally rich. Those stopping points, if we are moving to the Hegelian absolute, must be taken in an order which reverses that followed when we move from the absolute to the particulars—a move which Hegel fails to make, but which his beginning (in the *Phenomenology*) presupposes. Husserl's move into the ego is the counterpart of the Hegelian move to the absolute. Husserl could know that he has arrived at the greatest possible depth if he could grasp the ego as capable of being involved in the richest possible domain. Hegel knows that the objects he confronts have a depth to them, but takes this to be relative to some position.

We must move to the finalities, to actualities other than ourselves, and into ourselves. Having arrived at one of these positions we must recognize other factors to have a richness which is expressed both extensively and intensively. At one extreme are expressions pertinent to ultimate particles; one of these is the whole of time. At the other extreme are the expressions of men; these not only require intensifications in the form of segments of time, yielding limited temporal occurrences, but large-scale intensifications characteristic of history.

Machines are never in history except as accompaniments. Animals have no participative role in history; they do, however, help constitute limited situations. Animals can form groups but cannot be intimate; they may know their parents but have no traditions; they may communicate but have no conventions agreed upon. But do not the vast majority of people go about their daily tasks without having any affect on history? Or is it not, rather, that they do belong to history as part of a people, which can never include animals and machines, even though these may accompany the men and even enable the men to make a considerable difference to the course of the history? I think so. The stress on history, here, requires counter-stresses from other intensifications of space, causality, affiliation, coordination, formalization, and evaluation—and actual men. When one speaks of machines or animals in the attempt to 'reduce' man to them, one tacitly makes considerable use of man's mind, body, emotions, and so forth, within situations which are not possible without man. It is only a theory that a brain works in such and such a way. That theory needs to be countered by energies, a past and future, a space of observation, a time of inquiry, an acceptance of data, a sense of relevance, and an assessment of what is available.

April 24

No art, and perhaps no enterprise of any kind, is undergoing such radical changes as the dance. It should be almost unrecognizable in a decade or so. Last night I saw the Pilobolus Dance Theatre group. (Pilobolus, I see from the *Century Dictionary,* is a kind of fungus; the titles of some of the dances seem just as willful and esoteric.) It was an exceptionally splendid performance, marred a little by an attempt to be cute and funny. What was made evident is the extraordinary range of possibilities that still are to be explored in the dance. The company made exciting combinations of bodies intertwined with one another, played variations on walking, moving about on the floor, body postures, suspensions, and sizes (by having the women lifted at various heights by men whose legs alone, for a while, were visible beneath long skirts). The discoveries of this group will undoubtedly be adapted by others; they will also undoubtedly change the rather constant pace that this company carried out in all its different pieces. Combined with other more established and other novel ways of using the body, a new set of prospects opens up at once. But one need not take the company to be purely preliminary to some other. The dances themselves were splendid ways of making use of the arms and legs of individuals as intertwined, interactive, and in various positions. There was more coherence than in a Cunningham performance, and it was at least as novel.

*   *   *

Thinkers over the course of time have urged various positions and data as alone providing the inescapable preconditions and beginnings for any systematic study of what is. Favorites have been feeling, interpretation, situation, privacy, science, logic, history, religion, understanding, language, work, the individual alone, the I and me together, me and you, the problematic, judgment, substance, being, reason, existence, God, particulars—the last six sometimes being given the restricted form of sensations—a sheer emptiness, necessary truth, a lived-through intuited presence, revelation, and simples. Almost every one of these has provided the inspiration of some school which has then gone on to criticize other views as presupposing theirs. But the justification of the choice for one of these rather than for any of the others still has to be made out. We can not communicate if we have no thoughts, let us say; it is also true that we must speak, write, or gesture, that there must be someone to talk to, that thinking is an action, and involves interpretation, private intents, work, a reference to others, reasons, consciousness, and values.

What is needed is a systematic presentation of all the possible inescapable beginnings that could be offered. A first attempt:

1] Commonsense items and distinctions.

2] A diffused whole in which separations involve some abstraction.

3] An established discipline with its characteristic method.

4] Action, private and public.

5] A community or other setting.

6] Determinate items.

7] A man as having at least a mind and a body.

Each of these has its own subdivisions, some of which have been emphasized by thinkers in the past:

1] A commonsense outlook may emphasize the privacy of the individual, his acquaintanceship with certain other entities, a world in which he and others are, the fact of their difference, or the society in which they are.

2] A diffusion can be understood to be the product of a fecundity, to be just feeling or an implicit interpretation; to exhibit the problematic or an involvement with something transcendent.

3] The primary disciplines that have been acknowledged are aesthetics, science, logic/mathematics, history, and religion; to these one might add what is known of man as distinct from others—anxious, reflective, a locus of virtues and vices.

4] Action can be acknowledged to involve one with others who are relevant and who maintain themselves in opposition, or to be necessary to understanding, to having effects, or to being accepted.

5] In a community one might emphasize discourse, the equality of its members, their language, their work, or the spirit that pervades them all.

6] The determinate items on which one might fixate are the I, the I and the me, the me and you, limited conditions, and absolute conditions.

7] A man, viewed as a mind and body, allows for a beginning with freedom, personality, judgment, will, or responsibility.

The above, sixth division, itself allows for subdivisions:

I: Individuality, rights, consciousness, insistence, and value.

I and me: expression, limit, nature, the here, the focal.

Me and you: opposition, coordination, intention, copresence, we.

Limited conditions: relevance, facts, reasons, situations, and ends.

Absolute conditions: Substance, Being, Reason, Existence, God—and actualities.

These multiple headings reflect the use of the five finalities and the actualities as guides to the divisions that are being made. It is the advantage of a systematic view that it allows for the laying out of such a schema. However, it does not suffice to justify that schema—nor does the discovery of other supposed indubitables or necessary beginnings show that the schema is incorrect, for some of those indubitables or beginnings may be subdivisions of some of the above. Thus, the doctrine of clear and distinct ideas can be said to be the outcome of the acceptance of logic or mathematics as a basic discipline, or as due to the sharpening of the difference between body and mind.

The entire topic is worth a treatise. What is to be remarked on at once is the fact that if there are a number of equally justifiable irreducible beginnings, one evidently must arrive at some chosen one from a position which allows for an arrival at others, or take them all to be disjunct items which never were together, one of which somehow happened to come into focus. Today there are a good number who take their stand with language, on the ground that what we know can be checked and understood only so far as it is framed within a language common to a number. But that language is found within a larger setting, is approached in terms of some chosen discipline, involves action, presupposes an ongoing community, and makes use of a speaker and a listener as distinct, determinate, oppositional beings. And once a distinction is made between deception and openness, one will have to distinguish between language as a public object and as expressing the intent or mind of an individual.

Evidently, when such a comment is made about language, or any other supposed primary beginning, one is looking at it in a setting, identifying it, knowing it, and therefore already finding it within a different beginning. Does one inevitably begin within the largest possible setting established by the finalities, and focus on what is explained by all of them together? Yes. One does not initially know these finalities, of course, though they could be said to be present diffusedly, and then the more surely we fasten on man. He is daily involved in commonsensical limited forms of these. The fact seems to require giving up a beginning with a particular discipline and, instead, concerning oneself with the problem of how to separate out the men and their limited conditions from one another, and then tracing those conditions back to their grounds in the presupposed final conditions within which we are in fact operating.

April 25

A better approach than that made yesterday is exhibited in a schema which acknowledges an individual man in one of seven guises, and then characterizes him by himself and as characterizable from six positions:

We can distinguish the individual as fecund; as a private I; as dispositional and thus an I passing into and sustaining a me; as public, and thus as a me in relation to a you; as qualified by limited conditions; as absorbed in limited situations; and as absorbed in the finalities. Each of these is to be characterized from the six positions, emphasizing the individual, or any one of the five finalities. This yields the table:

According to this table, there are forty-two inescapable positions which one can assume as basic, and from which one can deal with all else. Each position has an individual making a contribution envisaged from five external standpoints. For example, the fecund freedom of an individual is a creativity from the position of Substance, a personality from the position of Being, a consciousness from the position of Possibility, a will from the position of Existence, and a responsibility from the position of Unity.

When we refer to creativity we are referring to a primary freedom envisaged from the position of Substance. When, instead, we attend to freedom, we refer to the contribution that the individual is making when faced with a more inclusive substantial creativity which transcends that individual in scope and power. Alternatively, one could take creativity, personality, consciousness, will, and responsibility to be the constituents of a domain in which the fecundity of an individual can have the status of freedom. Common sense combines the position of the private I and that of the individual as absorbed in limited situations. But the defenders of common sense usually attend only to the second.

Though it would be hard to justify on systematic grounds, one might take a position in one column or row and combine it with some other in another column or row. And any one of the positions can be specialized. Certitude for example could be taken to be the result of judgment, a topic of logic, or a matter of clear and distinct

	A Individual	B Substance	C Being	D Possibility	E Existence	F Unity
1] Fecund	Freedom	Creativity	Personality	Consciousness	Will	Responsibility
2] Private I	Individuality	Satisfaction	Rights	Certitude (intentionality, judgment)	Identity	Value
3] Dispositional I and Me	Feeling	Insistence	Claims	Interpretation	Insistence (occupancy)	Assessment
4] As Public (I) Me and You	Independent	Relative	Opposition (difference)	Intention	Copresence (here)	We
5] Qualified Particular Reality	Finitude	Aesthetic	Cosmic	Intelligible nature	Historical	Religious
6] Absorbed in Situations	Limited	Discourse	Complex We	Language	Effective	Spirit of a people
7] Absorbed in Finalities	Punctuate	Sensation	Simples	Necessary Truth—Clear and distinct. Logic	Intuited Real Events	Emptiness

ideas. Inquiry could be placed under the historical, perhaps with the restriction that it conform to the conditions of intelligibility, or do justice to the finite.

When one begins an examination of some such limited item as you, one starts on the fourth row and second column with what is relative to oneself. Such a beginning has no prior claim over all others. Indeed, it is to be taken to be a limited case within the frame of the entire fourth row, requiring one to acknowledge oneself as an independent being, who is not only in a relative position with respect to the you, but who opposes it as different, semantically intends it, is copresent with it in extensional domains, and with it constitutes a we. If this be true, there would seem to be seven primary positions, presented on the seven rows. Is there no choice to be made amongst these? Since the last two rows make no provision for the independent functioning of the individual, the alternatives could be reduced to five. The first and second evidently must be arrived at, the one by getting rid of all determinations, the other by ignoring the presence of other entities. There are then only three cases to consider: the dispositional, the public, and the qualified. The dispositional holds one away from all else, while the qualified sets the finite individual in sharp contrast with the domain in which it is to be explicated. The public seems to be prior to these others in experience.

Is it correct then to say that we begin in experience with a public me and you which are taken to be independent of one another within a domain where they are also relative to one another, opposed, the object of semantic intentions, copresent, and constitute a single, simple we? If so, the initial situation would be where oneself and another are together, but as independent, relative, opposed, referential, copresent, and under the aegis of a we. But surely nonhuman things are also faced. And, precisely because we know ourselves to be independent realities, we know something of our freedom, individuality, feeling, and finitude.

The priority of the situation in which one faces a you is not due to the supposed impossibility of having an I without first being together with others, or to a supposed need to have a public criterion, but to the double fact that a you is richer than other types of entity, and therefore allows us to see just what else is involved in the confrontation of something by oneself, and that one can move from it to the other rows by following out the consequences of the fact that the me and the you both need sustaining from beyond themselves, not merely in a fivefold domain, but in individuals, with fecundities, privacies, dispositions, and qualifications.

April 26

All inquiry begins in a not-well-defined commonsense world where objects are connected with one another, at least through our sense of relevance; are conditioned by the past, at least through our memories; are structured, at least through our attitudes and expectations; are vitalized, at least through an existence independent of us; are guided, at least by the object of our determinations and anticipations; and counter us, at least in the sense of being termini of our attention. We are aware of ourselves as in that commonsense world but, just so far as we emphasize the others, are forced back into ourselves as more than merely copresent with those others in a public scheme.

We can attend to various types of entities, depending on accident, what intrudes, or on what we might alight upon. But we remain with things because of their familiarity and impersonality; animals because of their oddity and danger, or similarity and lack of challenge to us; on another because of his richness in comparison with all others; on me and the I because they are basic and inescapable; and on conditions because of their power and range.

Whatever objects we attend to have determinations expressive of the relationship others have to them, of one's occupation with them, and of the conditions which are in control. To get to an object as it truly is we must free it from these determinations. The result is that it becomes an available indeterminate, backed by a powerful inwardness which sustains that indeterminateness. Other objects, oneself, and the conditions, at the same time, are acknowledged to be effective and determining, ready to impose the determinations from which the object has been freed. Had one instead sought to free oneself from determinations, one would have left oneself indeterminately available but powerful, with other entities and conditions effective and determining. The Husserlian move to an ego is possible only so far as it is carried out with a correlative move to other entities and conditions as still productive of those determinations. One's freedom from determination by others does not cancel their power; it involves instead a retreat into ourselves to a position where we can take the determined part of ourselves to be at the limit of the others. To retreat into an ego is to leave one's body and indeed every expression of the ego subject to the others; at the same time, it is to move into oneself as not yet determining those others and therefore leaving them as indeterminately available but powerful.

Descartes could not really begin with "I doubt" or "I think." Not only did he have to arrive at the position by raising difficulties for himself with respect to what he confronted in daily life and then eventually with respect to what he entertained when considering mathematical propositions, but there is no doubting or thinking without something doubted or thought about. This may be something external, independent of the individual, or something which he is then constituting. So far as he is able to separate off the doubting or thinking, he leaves the external entity indeterminate, no longer qualified by the doubting or thinking. Were the thinking or doubting constitutive, there would be no way in which he could separate them from the objects they were constituting; at best the holding off of the thinking or doubting would involve a facing of a bare manifold (to use Kant's term) which not only will be deprived of the determinations due to the thinking or doubting but would be powerful enough to present itself for determination.

May 2

I have received a raise in pay, the second since I came here seven years ago. I suppose this is most unusual, for when one has a post after retiring, there is a tendency either to reduce the salary; give one a part-time job usually at half-pay—though the work rarely is less than two-thirds of what one had been called upon to do, since only the teaching load is cut in half, and the theses and other obligations continue; or, at best, to keep one at the same pay. The situation, though, is not yet all it should be, for I still do not have tenure and am denied a sabbatical. I have no complaint to make, except one in principle. I have enough money to retire now and to live fairly well for the rest of my days, and I do like and profit from teaching. There is no place I would want to go on a sabbatical. All a sabbatical would do would be to free me from classes and preparations, and I would lose the stimulus that I do get in trying to meet the difficulties and questions of students. Still, ideally, I ought to have tenure, with a clause perhaps which said that I was to have the contract terminated if I were ill, say for a few months or something like that. I think The Catholic University of America would in fact be very generous to me were I to become ill, and I think my contract will be renewed as long as I am in good health, and continue to teach and perhaps publish as I have. But the very excellence of its treatment of me underscores the fact that age is still a factor where it should not be. I see no reason why I should not have tenure and all the perquisities that go with being a full professor.

*   *   *

I have now begun to work on "You, I, and the Others." I have rewritten about half, and am having it multilithed for use next term. I am dissatisfied with what I now read in the chapter on the 'we'; it is written within too rigid a frame, making use of the same principles again and again with minor variations. I will have to rewrite it radically, and then go on to the last chapter in the light of what is done. For the moment, though, I am occupied with writing the introduction, which I conceive of as laying out an all-comprehensive schema within which I will locate the discussion. As I now see it, it is occupied with showing that there are eight conditions—the five finalities, an actuality, an actuality as separated off from others, and an actuality as part of a continuum, all of which environ what we daily confront, stand in contrast with one another, interplay with one another, and constitute appearances. I should deal with all thirty-two cases. Each has a subjective, objective, and a mixed form. These I think are to be treated at the same time, since they raise the same problems though, of course, in different areas.

The triads I have now distinguished are:
1] The agreeable, the attractive, and experience.
2] Certitude, claims, and the many.
3] Concepts, judgment, language—or assertions, statements, and sentences.
4] Distinctness, interest, and field.
5] Desirable, fitting, importance.
6] Maintained, bounded, determinate.
7] Ignorance, effort, completion.
8] Insistence, controlling possession, expression.

This set has to do with environing conditions; the next has to do with an opposition between the actuality in itself and the finalities by themselves, and their merged juncture:

9] Ego, events, intuited reality.

10] Self, emotions, horizon.

11] Mind, forms, reason.

12] Consciousness, will, energy.

13] Evaluation, awe, revealed God.

14] Self-bounded, inquiry, finitude.

15] Freedom, contingency, chance.

16] Power, challenge, fecundity.

The next set has to do with the way the finalities affect the actualities:

17] Individuality, affiliation, clusters—scientific cosmology.

18] Rights, feeling, ultimate particles—realities/Being.

19] Essence, theory, simples—logic of necessary truths.

20] Identity, work, events—history and the historical.

21] Singularity, wonder, values—evaluation of objective order.

22] Incompletion, self-boundedness, distinctness—qualified by others.

23] Unit, potentiality, difference—qualified by finalities.

24] Control, interaction, conditions.

The final set has to do with appearances:

25] The relative, the associated, the aesthetic.

26] The coordinated, affirmation, data.

27] The rational, classes, classification.

28] The located, the distinguished, the positioned.

29] The harmonized, assessment, the unified.

30] The incomplete, attention, determination.

31] The dependent, predication, adumbration.

32] The fragmentary, the referential, the presented.

Many of these are just headings, and some duplicate others or are close to doing this. I set them down as a mere guide, knowing that I will change many of the terms, and make distinctions and introduce changes as I begin to think through the cases, and articulate what I now sense in a vague way.

May 23

I have put this work aside for almost a month now, in order to concentrate on "You, I, and the Others." This is now in draft form running to some 700 typed pages, of which I have corrected some 400 or so. I have decided to write an introduction to the whole. The proposed introduction is now growing in size, and I think it will end up as the first part of the book, though one which is capable of standing alone and also able to introduce the examination of the you, I, you and I, you and me, we, and the others. I will continue to work on that book, but will break into this occasionally, in the hope of having it ready around July, since that is when an editor is supposed to be free to deal with it.

I have recently passed my seventy-fifth birthday. A former student, Peter Colasante, in cooperation with the department, gave me a party, and displayed some of my drawings and painting. The paintings and drawings were entitled and given prices without consultation with me. At the opening, two of the drawings were sold for $75.00 each. I had mixed feeling about the transactions. I have no real need of the money, and like to have the drawings for myself; yet it seems silly to hold on to them, particularly since I have been willing to sell some in the past and have given away many others.

In my concentration on the writing of the book I have cut myself off from almost every other activity. I now do not paint or draw, I rarely go to any parties, I have not been to a film or dance or a show in weeks. I do not miss them; I am so absorbed in what I am thinking and writing that almost everything else seems to be an intrusion. After I take my walk in the morning—sometimes after I have spent an hour or so writing—I spend almost all the rest of the time writing and rewriting, thinking and rethinking.

I go over some of the old ground, but from different angles. It is hard to know whether or not this is wise. Was Monet wrong to paint Chartres in the sunlight again and again? If not, is it wrong to compare my many traversals over one large terrain with what he did? I do not think I am repeating myself; in any case, I find that I am forced to think through the issues in new ways. The result should be able to provide a check on what I have done, and conversely. The great risk is in becoming mechanical, following a path and dealing with problems according to a set scheme which is based on the acknowledgment of five finalities and the irreducible nature of actualities.

May 28

It is well known that some of the most distinguished singers, musicians, poets, painters, chess-players, and athletes are men who otherwise would not be admired. There is ample evidence that some of great distinction were inhibited, inconsiderate, cruel, foolish, stupid, mean, and apparently somewhat mad. We recognize that they nevertheless did do great work. Perhaps, we suppose, the oddity of their behavior is but a special dimension of the kind of unusual personality that enabled them to make great contributions to their particular fields.

A philosopher, we are inclined to think, must be all of a piece; his work is supposedly the outcome of sober, careful, self-critical hard thinking, and we suppose that this must be rooted in something deep in him. Kierkegaard, Schopenhauer, and Rousseau seem to provide exceptions. But these could be taken to be romantic philosophers, philosophers whose own views are tinged with emotionality. Heidegger, who has just died, presents a harder case. He was not a romantic. Yet he became a Nazi, and never seemed to have objected to the incredible outrages they perpetrated; if he did not know of them when the Nazis were in power, he certainly learned of them later. How account for him?

In replying to Richard Rorty's criticisms, to appear in "First Considerations," I said that Heidegger always exhibited a failure of nerve—not completing his one great book, accepting the dominant political view, substituting philology and historical studies for basic inquiries, boasting, and an ignoring of all criticism. The truth or falsehood of what he says and the value of his insights are not affected, but I think that the nature of the overall view is and has to be, for at every moment the virtues of self-control, patience, self-criticism, honesty, sensitivity, and thoughtfulness must be shown by the philosopher in the course of his writing and rewriting.

Was not David Hume somewhat prissy? Yes, and it shows. Again and again in the willful and arbitrary distinctions he makes, and the way he carries out his inquiry.

*   *   *

I have just returned from the first half of my yearly checkup. I am apparently as I had been last year; my blood pressure is 105/70, and all other signs seem to be as before. My weight, 135.5 clothed, without jacket, is about what it was last year, too. Next Friday I take the final part of the examination and get the results of the cardiogram and chest X-rays.

* * *

Last night I saw *Face-to-Face* by Ingmar Bergman. Ullman gives a brilliant performance of a person undergoing an emotional upset; the photography of this is almost all in close-ups, an effective carrying out of a tendency more and more manifest in Bergman over the years. He dwells a little too much on faces, particularly when music is being played; he has no way of conveying motive; there is little dramatic sense displayed, hardly any sense of plot. He is primarily a photographer's director, with a splendid awareness of the depths of individuals and a sensitivity to the emotions of women, but beyond that he lacks some of the main requirements of a film director—a sense of the whole, timed throughout, with episodes subordinate to the entire story, with some awareness of background and multiple characters, a use of distance as well as of close-ups, and a sense of action. I like seeing good pictures more than once, but I have no interest in seeing his twice, for I think I will not find anything in the background which is worth looking at and watching for.

June 21

I have just returned from a four-day visit to Southern Illinois University. I gave a talk to various members of the media department and some of the students. I spoke on the nature of art and particularly on the film. There were about forty or fifty in the audience, and the discussion was good. Plans are now under way to get $5,000 from the National Endowment for the Arts to have me be there for four weeks next June.

Southern Illinois University, which was, I think, a teacher's college around the early fifties and before, has grown enormously. The campus is very large and attractive, and the student body is now made up of many from upper Illinois, a good number of them blacks. I think the university brings out an aspect of higher education in America hardly known to the established, prestigious places such as Harvard, Yale, and Princeton. These are heavily invested in traditional disciplines and have made little or no effort to accommodate new developments—film departments, mass media, such as television and radio and periodicals—dance, design, the more technological aspects of architecture, and space exploration. The students in these established places are accepted mainly on the basis of entrance examinations which emphasize literary abilities and knowledge. The other places accept equally able students who, though not as much at home in literary fields, are excellent in music, drama, or engineering. Without belittling the need for a liberal arts core, I think it would be good for the long-established prestigious places to consider these other fields more seriously than they have, and to admit students whose aptitudes in these areas are equal to the aptitudes of the current students' in mathematics, conventional science, and literature. If this is not done, the center of gravity of education in this country will be determined by the large state universities such as Southern Illinois, Minnesota, Wisconsin, and Texas. Higher education need not minimize the liberal arts in order to make ample provision for the now neglected enterprises which the large state universities are supporting with great vigor. As a matter of fact, Harvard, Yale, and the others in the so-called Ivy League in recent years, have recognized the importance of theatre, film, architecture, education, and laboratory studies to a degree they did not at the beginning of the century. But their faculty and facilities are such as to make their moves slower and more restricted than is possible in the rapidly expanding, heavily supported state universities.

I spent an entire day at the press, answering the questions raised by Mrs. Beatrice Moore, the manuscript editor. Mrs. Moore has an uncanny eye for errors, oversights, confusions, bad grammar, and the other associated sins involved in writing a book. Most of my difficulties seem to be with commas; I put them in very often to express my own speaking pauses. She rightly remarks that others do not speak the way I do and do not know how I speak. For the most part I just endorse her changes. Perhaps four out of a few hundred are questioned by me, or even obstinately insisted on. The manuscript was of "First Considerations." Vernon Sternberg, the director of the Press and now a good and old friend, thinks the time has come to make the larger world aware of the kind of things I have been writing, and plans to elicit attention to it and other works when "First Considerations" is published somewhere around April of next year. It is quite possible that there is some slight shift needed in the direction of the attention of the philosophic and the larger literary public before what I have written receives the full consideration that he and I think it deserves. He says that my books sell better than the other philosophical works he is publishing, and that his own record in publishing philosophical writings is as good as those of the long-established university presses. (My best seller is the book on sport—almost 9,000 copies.)

He thinks that it is time, though, to put a stop to this series of volumes. He made a similar suggestion before, and I thought and wrote that the sixth volume would be the last. Later he said that I could go ahead with the seventh, but he has now decided that perhaps there is not a sufficiently large public for any more. This, therefore, is the last of the volumes of the volumes of *Philosophy in Process* that I am now planning to publish. I have not yet decided whether or not to continue with the writing of this kind of entry; if I do, I will simply add it to my *Nachlass* or await a new decision by Sternberg. In the meantime I will continue with the completion of the writing of the first part of "You, I, and the Others," and will then go on to complete the revision of the last two chapters of that book. I have no plans for anything to be written after that, though I have been toying with the idea of doing something in political thought, and something in the area of mental health.

The ostensible main reason for my going to Illinois was to attend a number of meetings in honor of Henry Weiman, a quasi-naturalistic theologian who had a great effect on students in the University of Chicago, and then, on his retirement from there, on the students at Southern Illinois University. He died around ninety-two, having lived a full life of teaching and writing that extended almost until he was ninety.

It was to be expected, I suppose, that most of the papers would be filled with sweetness and light, and had hardly anything much to say about Weiman except that he had influenced the writer in some such area as education, religion, or psychiatry. One conspicuous exception was Charles Hartshorne who emphasized the differences between his own view and Weiman's. He made a number of very shrewd criticisms, but also was inclined to suppose that this meant that the only alternative was Hartshorne's own view. I criticized him—I was the critic for the section where he spoke—and we had some lively exchanges. Speaking to him afterward, we both modified our oppositions somewhat.

I think that Hartshorne is convinced that my views are unduly complicated and therefore are not finally viable, that they do not show the same concern for logical structure or rigor that his do, and that, though my writings are highly original, they are not sufficiently free of tradition to make them able to take philosophers in the new directions they ought to go. I, in contrast, take Hartshorne to make many dogmatic statements, for which he provides no other justification but that given in arguments by analogy, or questionable interpretations of Whitehead and Buddhism. Our relations continue to be amiable and gentle, even though in public we vigorously oppose what the other says on crucial issues.

Hartshorne is almost eighty years old, but looks almost as he did when I first met him almost fifty years ago—with the exception of his goatee. He has a most beguiling smile and laugh. His readiness to accept suggestions (which he somehow converts into variations on his main view), are backed up with sharp and sometimes severely stated objections. The full force and true bite of these is sometimes missed by his listeners because they are stated in an apparently diffident and friendly fashion.

I think Hartshorne has not read much—perhaps not anything—of mine, since *Modes of Being,* to judge from what he takes to be my view. But perhaps I reciprocate in a way, since I take him to be offering in the main just a variation on Whitehead's position in *Process and Reality.* These differences are, I think, overshadowed by the continued friendship and respect that we have maintained and which we show in our greetings and private conversations.

INDEX OF NAMES

INDEX OF SUBJECTS